THE MULTIPLY HANDICAPPED CHILD

The Multiply Handicapped Child

Second Printing

Compiled and Edited by

JAMES M. WOLF, Ed.D.

Coordinator of Special Education
Director, Educational Achievement Center
Division of Schools
Canal Zone Government
Balboa Heights, Canal Zone

and

ROBERT M. ANDERSON, Ed.D.

Associate Professor of Special Education
Illinois State University
Normal, Illinois

CHARLES C THOMAS · PUBLISHER

Springfield · Illinois · U.S.A.

Published and Distributed Throughout the World by
CHARLES C THOMAS • PUBLISHER
Bannerstone House
301-327 East Lawrence Avenue, Springfield, Illinois, U.S.A.

© *1969, by* CHARLES C THOMAS • PUBLISHER

ISBN 0-398-02105-8

Library of Congress Catalog Card Number: 69-12070

First Printing, 1969
Second Printing, 1973

*With THOMAS BOOKS careful attention is given to all details of
manufacturing and design. It is the Publisher's desire to present books that are
satisfactory as to their physical qualities and artistic possibilities and
appropriate for their particular use. THOMAS BOOKS will be true to those
laws of quality that assure a good name and good will.*

Printed in the United States of America
R-1

Contributors

Robert M. Anderson, Ed.D.

Associate Professor of Special Education
Illinois State University
Normal, Illinois

Barbara Bateman, Ph.D.

Associate Professor
School of Education
University of Oregon
Eugene, Oregon

William M. Cruickshank, Ph.D.

Director, Institute for Study of Mental Retardation
Professor of Psychology and Education
School of Education
University of Michigan
Ann Arbor, Michigan

Powrie V. Doctor, Ph.D.

Editor, American Annals of the Deaf
Gallaudet College
Washington, D. C.

Anna S. Elonen, Ph.D.

Professor of Psychology
Department of Psychology, Pediatrics and Psychiatry
Children's Psychiatric Hospital
University of Michigan
Ann Arbor, Michigan

The Lady Jessie Francis-Williams, M.A.

Research Psychologist
Centre for Handicapped Children
Guy's Hospital
London, England

Robert Frisina, Ph.D.

Vice-President, Rochester Institute of Technology
Director, National Technical Institute for the Deaf
Rochester, New York

Marianne Frostig, Ph.D.

Director, Marianne Frostig Center of Educational Therapy
Los Angeles, California

Else Haeussermann

Formerly, Educational Consultant
Division of Psychiatry
Jewish Hospital of Brooklyn
Brooklyn, New York

Robert A. Henderson, Ph.D.

Professor of Special Education
Institute for Research on Exceptional Children
University of Illinois
Urbana, Illinois

A. C. Higgins, Ph.D.

Field Director
North Carolina Study of Handicapped Children
Chapel Hill, North Carolina

Kenneth S. Holt, M.D.

Director, Wolfson Centre of Developmental Pediatrics
London, England

R. S. Illingworth, M.D.

Professor of Child Health
The University of Sheffield
Sheffield, England

Theodore H. Ingalls, M.D.

Professor, Preventive Medicine and Epidemiology
Boston University School of Medicine
Boston, Massachusetts

Harold Jacobziner, M.D.

Formerly, Assistant Commissioner for Health
City Health Department
New York, New York

Thomas Jordan, Ph.D.

Professor and Chairman
Department of Guidance and Educational Psychology
Southern Illinois University
Carbondale, Illinois

Samuel A. Kirk, Ph.D.

Director, Institute for Research on Exceptional Children
University of Illinois
Urbana, Illinois

Marcus A. Klingberg, M.D.

Israel Institute for Biological Research
Ness-Ziona, Israel

Hilda Knobloch, M.D.

Illinois Pediatric Institute
Chicago, Illinois

Samuel Levine, Ph.D.

Professor of Educational Psychology
San Francisco State College
San Francisco, California

Steven Mattis, Ph.D.

Director, Day Treatment Program
Jewish Guild for the Blind
New York, New York

Arden C. Miller, M.D.

Vice-Chancellor, Health Sciences
University of North Carolina
Chapel Hill, North Carolina

Benjamin Pasamanick, M.D.

Associate Division Director
Division of Mental Health
State of Illinois
Chicago, Illinois

Margaret Polzien

Principal, Michigan School for the Blind
Lansing, Michigan

Maynard C. Reynolds, Ph.D.

Director and Professor
Department of Special Education
University of Minnesota
Minneapolis, Minnesota

William P. Richardson, M.D.

Professor of Preventive Medicine
School of Medicine
University of North Carolina
Chapel Hill, North Carolina

Mary D. Sheridan, M.D.

Research Fellow, Newcomen Centre
Guy's Hospital
London, England

G. Kinsey Stewart, Ph.D.

Kennedy Child Study Center
Santa Monica, California

Jean Rose Stifler, M.D.

Director, Bureau of Preventive Medical Services
Maryland State Department of Health
Baltimore, Maryland

McCay Vernon, Ph.D.

Research Psychologist
Institute for Psychosomatic and Psychiatric Research and Training
Michael Reese Hospital and Medical Center
Chicago, Illinois

Bluma B. Weiner, Ed.D.

Associate Professor of Special Education
Ferkauf Graduate School of Education
Yeshiva University
New York, New York

Samuel M. Wishik, M.D., M.P.H.

Associate Dean, Academic Affairs
Graduate School of Public Health
University of Pittsburgh
Pittsburgh, Pennsylvania

James M. Wolf, Ed.D.

Coordinator of Special Education
Director, Educational Achievement Center
Division of Schools
Canal Zone Government
Balboa Heights, Canal Zone

*To the many children with more than
one handicapping condition who represent
a crucial challenge to special educators*

Preface

IN the past decade, few developments in the education of exceptional children have had greater impact upon special education programs than the burgeoning prevalence of children with multiple handicaps. Increasing concern about the quality of services for children who are afflicted with more than one disabling or handicapping condition has been expressed in professional and scientific publications. These children present complex management problems to those responsible for their treatment, education, training, and rehabilitation.

In recent years, there has been a growing awareness of the problems involved in the differential diagnosis, classification, education, and rehabilitation of children with multiple disabilities. From time to time, articles relative to multiple disability have appeared in the literature of the behavioral sciences and professions. While these widely scattered publications have called attention to the magnitude of the problems pertinent to the education and rehabilitation of children with multiple disabilities, no single comprehensive treatment of this problem area currently exists.

This book is about those children who must learn to cope with concomitant impairments, disabilities, or handicaps. This volume combines the knowledge and skills of a number of outstanding authors from divergent fields. The editors are of the opinion that no single authority or discipline could adequately treat an area as complex or multidisciplinary in scope as multiple disability.

The material in this book has been developed to meet the needs of individuals who serve exceptional children in almost any capacity. Psychologists, social workers, rehabilitation counselors, physical therapists, physicians, as well as educators and other professional personnel, should find this book to be a valuable reference.

It is also hoped that this volume will prove useful as a book of readings for senior college undergraduates and beginning graduate students who are majoring in special education. In addition, since the majority of exceptional children have multiple handicaps, it is imperative that all special classroom teachers have some understanding and knowledge of multiple exceptionalities. We hope classroom teachers will find this book informative and helpful. Many state departments of education now require teachers to have a course on multiple handicaps to meet certification standards, and many universities are offering a specific course on this subject. It is hoped that the book will prove useful as a general textbook for courses on the multiply handicapped. The organization of the book should lend itself to the teaching of a survey course on multiple handicaps, and the extensive bibliography with cross-references to principal topics should provide a ready resource of related literature.

This book has been organized into five parts, and each part has one or more chapters related to the specific topic under discussion. The purpose of Part One is to acquaint the reader with the increased challenge presented to medicine, education, and psychology by multiply handicapped children. The first chapter provides an overview of the subject and also serves as a general review of the literature. Articles taken primarily from medicine provide the reasons for the increased number of multiple handicaps among children and also describe the effects of these handicapping conditions. Implications are suggested for the preventive health procedures needed to reduce the number and effects of multiple disabilities.

Part Two makes available in one book the most extensive and significant incidence and prevalence studies completed in the United States on handicapped children. Persons planning studies of this aspect of epidemiology should find this part along with additional references most helpful.

Part Three is a collection of articles illustrating modifications of special educational procedures utilized in providing services to multiply handicapped children. Several of the chapters describe experimental programs for the blind child with multiple handicaps. Apparently, educators of the blind have shown more interest in multiple handicaps than practitioners in other disability categories and have been more productive in writing on the subject.

Part Four is concerned with the psychological evaluation of the multiply handicapped child. The articles included deal primarily with testing the cerebral palsied child and the blind child; however, these testing pro cedures have implications for evaluating the exceptional child with other concomitant handicaps. Psychological evaluations must be practical, useful, and must facilitate the translation of psychological data to educational prescriptions. An article is also included in this part on learning disorders. Its inclusion is justified on the basis that one of the major problems presented by multiply handicapped children is related to difficulties in learning. The nature of the learning disorder must dictate the nature of the instructional program. Therefore, psychological evaluations must not only facilitate decision-making but must primarily provide the direction for corrective and remedial instruction.

The need for more precise definitions, terminology, and nomenclature and the need for an educationally conceived classification scheme for exceptional children are becoming more apparent to special educators. A comprehensive taxonomy is needed. The multiply handicapped child is challenging the present system of classifying exceptional children since he does not fit neatly into one of the "pigeonholes." A taxonomy may provide a theoretical framework for viewing the multiply handicapped child and will lead to more appropriate pedagogy for these children. Part Five includes theoretical articles that have significance for developing a taxonomy in special education. The last chapter is entitled "Compendium and Comments" and serves as a summary for the book. Stevens' theoretical construct is presented in the last chapter since it offers considerable potential for formulating a concept for teaching the multiply handicapped child. This concept represents a significant contribution to special education.

We wish to express our gratitude to the many people who at one stage or another have assisted in the preparation of this book. Our principal obligation is to Dr. Godfrey Stevens, Professor of Special Education, University of Pittsburgh, who was most influential and helpful during the "incubation" stage. Dr. Stevens was one of the first special educators to propose that the dilemma involved in classifications of multiple handicaps could be resolved by standardizing classification language. He has been far in advance of the times in proposing a tentative taxonomy in special education for children with body disorder. We have drawn heavily on his ideas in this area and we acknowledge our gratitude and indebtedness to him.

We are, indeed, indebted to the many outstanding authorities in education, medicine, and psychology who have consented to the use of their articles which have appeared in leading professional journals. We are also thankful to the publishers of these journals for generously granting reprint permission.

Very special thanks are due to the following individuals who assisted the editors, under the direction of Dr. G. D. Stevens, with two related studies that preceded the publication of this book: Reverend Thomas Bartley, Mrs. Genevieve Barnes, Dr. Jack W. Birch, Dr. Guinevere Chambers, Dr. Sam B. Graig, Dr. Alton G. Kloss, Dr. Ralph Peabody, Dr. George H. Shames, Mrs. Ada Smith, Dr. Robert M. Smith, Dr. E. Ross Struckless, Dr. L. Leon Reid, Dr. William Tisdall, Mr. Roger W. Walker, and administrators and teachers in the residential schools for the blind and for the deaf. Of course, none of these persons should be held responsible for any of the shortcomings of this book. Thanks are also extended to Mrs. Janet Service, Miss Elba Diaz, Mrs. Bonnie Culbreth, Miss Margaret Jackson, and Mrs. Penny Young who have shared the responsibility for typing the manuscript. Miss Paula Sullivan, School Psychologist, Division of Schools, Balboa

Heights, Canal Zone, also has been of great assistance with many aspects of the book.

Our warmest thanks go to LaVerne B. Wolf and Janet L. Anderson for their assistance, patience, and understanding—especially during the 1967 summer session at the University of North Carolina.

JMW
RMA

Contents

PART THREE
THE MULTIPLY HANDICAPPED CHILD IN
SPECIAL EDUCATION

PART FOUR
EVALUATING THE MULTIPLY
HANDICAPPED CHILD

PART FIVE
A THEORETICAL FRAMEWORK FOR THE MULTIPLY HANDICAPPED CHILD

THE MULTIPLY HANDICAPPED CHILD

PART ONE

The Multiply Handicapped Child:
A Medical and Educational Challenge

Introduction

THE initial chapter in Part One offers an introduction to the multiply handicapped child, with a review of incidence and prevalence studies and a discussion of multiple disabilities associated with cerebral palsy, impaired hearing, visual impairments, and mental retardation. Many of the points stressed in this overview are presented in more detail by other authors in later chapters. The educational problems presented by the multiply handicapped child in a wide variety of educational and training centers are also emphasized in this lead chapter.

Illingworth, in Chapter 2, describes the causes and results of the increased number of handicapped children and recognizes that attention must not only be given to the care for handicapped children but to the prevention of handicaps.

Ingalls and Klingberg, in the chapter on "Congenital Malformations: Clinical and Community Considerations," stress the need and potential import of recording and classifying congenital malformations in a standardized form. Community surveillance systems are essential in collecting accurate data which may lead to the development of preventive measures which will in turn reduce the number of congenital malformations.

Recently we have become aware of an increasing number of infants who are severely disabled as a result of epidemics of rubella (German measles) among expectant mothers. The epidemic of rubella which occurred in 1964 was the largest that the United States has experienced in more than twenty years. Children handicapped as a result of the rubella epidemic are now enrolling in preschool programs for handicapped children and will represent a future challenge to special educators comparable to the challenge presented by children disabled by retrolental fibroplasia. England experienced a rubella epidemic in 1950 through 1952. Sheridan, in Chapter 4, summarizes the effects of rubella as studied in infancy and later when the children were between the ages of three and six years. Sheridan reports the results of her investigation when these same children were between the ages of eight and eleven years. This article indicates the significance of rubella on expectant mothers and will be useful for comparative purposes as long-term follow-up studies are completed in the United States.

In addition to congenital malformations and rubella virus, prematurity represents another significant cause for increased numbers of multiply handicapped children. In Chapter 5, Vernon reports on his investigation of the relationship of premature birth to deafness.

In Chapter 6, Pasamanick and Knobloch summarize their extensive research on prematurity and complications of pregnancy. These distinguished researchers coined the term "reproductive casualty" which is conceived as a continuum from death through varying degrees of disability. Reproductive casualty is used to describe those harmful events which occur during pregnancy and parturition that cause damage primarily to the central nervous system of the fetus or new born infant.

Dr. Pasamanick and his co-workers have studied a dozen conditions among the many factors that make up the continuum of reproductive casualty. Cerebral palsy, epilepsy, mental retardation, behavior disorders, and reading disabilities have been found to be significantly associated with both complications of pregnancy and prematurity. Tics were found to be associated with complications of pregnancy but not with prematurity.

Research conducted at Columbus, Ohio, by Dr. Pasamanick has also shown a significant relationship between complications of pregnancy and prematurity to strabismus, hearing defects, school accidents, infantile autism, and juvenile delinquency. A number of preventive implications are drawn by Pasamanick and Knoblock from these epidemiologic investigations.

A number of disciplines are required for the effective management and education of the multiply handicapped child. The disciplines of education and medicine share the challenges presented by these children. In the final chapter of Part One, Miller points out that medical schools should train their students in the long-term treatment of handicapped children and emphasizes the need for the coordination of services in the care of handicapped children.

Chapter 1

The Multiply Handicapped Child: An Overview

JAMES M. WOLF and ROBERT M. ANDERSON

THERE is a growing demand for expanded services for multiply handicapped children. Concurrently, the problems presented by the multiply handicapped are of increasing concern to educators, psychologists, rehabilitationists, pediatricians, neurologists, and other specialists. Medical clinics and special education programs have been charged with the responsibility and the task of diagnosis, educational management, and modification of the learning problems and behavior of multiply handicapped children.

A number of different terms have been used to describe children with two or more handicapping conditions. Historically, these children have been referred to as *doubly afflicted, doubly defective, dual handicapped, multiply handicapped, additionally handicapped,* and *multiply disabled.* Authors have also referred to this diverse group of handicapping conditions as *multiple exceptionalities, concomitant disabilities, manifold disorders, the multiplex child,* and simply, *the exceptional child with other handicaps.*

Who are multiply handicapped children? What can be done for them? How can they be classified? How can they be taught? What are the most prevalent combinations of handicapping conditions? What are the reasons for increased numbers of these children in the child population? How can multiple handicaps be prevented? These are but a few of the many questions being raised by special educators and their colleagues in allied professions. At the present time there appear to be more questions than answers to the special problems posed by multiply handicapped children. Although there are many unanswered questions, there does exist a body of information that provides the professional worker with a few answers and some direction for future investigations. A review and synthesis of available data on this topic may make it possible to formulate questions that will lead to new ways of viewing the exceptional child with additional handicaps.

REASONS FOR INCREASED NUMBER OF CHILDREN WITH MULTIPLE DISABILITIES

Current interest in multiple handicaps is stimulated by the increased number of children with multiple disabilities. The expanding birth rate only partially accounts for the increased number of such children in the child population.

There are several other important reasons for this increase. Research relative to the etiology and treatment of communicable and infectious disease, the establishment of improved public health services, advances in prenatal care and reduction of infant mortality, improved nutrition, increased education, and better housing have contributed to the higher incidence and prevalence of children with multiple disability.

There is presently, for example, a much higher survival rate among premature infants, but unfortunately the incidence of disabilities is high among these infants. Drillien found that 22 per cent of 92 babies weighing three pounds or less at birth had major physical handicaps.[284] Lubchenco and his co-investigators studied 63 premature babies and found that 69 per cent had visual and neurological disabilities. Thirty-seven per cent were spastic, and 42 per cent obtained an I.Q. score below 90.[684]

De Hirsch and her colleagues completed a study of prematurely and maturely born children of average intelligence. Her clinical findings indicate that the central nervous system functioning of the prematurely born children seemed more primitive, the behavior controls less established, and the level of neurological integration lower than maturely born children. These children "have to be regarded as an academic high risk group. In view of the fact that at the very least 4 per cent of our school children are prematurely born, these findings would seem to have more than theoretical relevance."[243 (p. 626)]

Perfected surgical treatment of hydrocephalus meningomyelocele by use of the Spitz-Holter value has saved the lives of large numbers of children. Approximately 33 per cent of these children need special education services following surgical correction.[508]

Benda showed that in New York State 19 children per 1,000 who in 1920 would have died from congenital debility and malformation survived in 1949.[81] Exposure of mothers to irradiation during pregnancy and improper use of certain drugs was thought to have also increased the number of children with multiple birth defects.[350]

Richardson and Higgins have pointed out "that the greater the medical significance of the primary condition [disability] the greater the likelihood of some other condition [disability] being present."[920 (p. 1828)] As discussed above, medical science has reduced the infant mortality rate and has also extended life by more effective control of acute infection and disease. However, a large number of these children who are saved today because of advances in medical science often must live out their remaining years under the handicap of one or more disability.

Finally, changing social and educational philosophies of the past century which reflect a concern for the handicapped have created increased interest in educating handicapped children today, with the result that more children with multiple disabilities are being reported by school administrators. In addition, greater numbers of these children are currently being identified through the use of improved diagnostic procedures.

INCIDENCE AND PREVALENCE OF MULTIPLE DISABILITIES

Although no studies of incidence and prevalence of children with mutiple disability have been conducted on a nationwide basis, a number of studies have been executed at the state or local level. While it is recognized that the number of children with multiple disabilities is increasing, studies on incidence and prevalence of such children are characterized by certain inconsistencies. Classification schemes based on disability, confusion in terminology, diverse criteria for defining disability categories, difficulties involved in differential diagnosis, and the unreliability of tests all make it difficult to compile statistics and to estimate the number of children in specific disability groups. However, the following studies present evidence of the extent of multiple disability in a variety of geographic locations in the United States.

Wishik, in a study of prevalence, disability, needs, and resources of handicapped children in the state of Georgia, found that handicapped children had an average of 2.2 disabilities each. Only 29 per cent of the handicapped children had one disability; 39 per cent had two disabilities; 17 per cent had three; and 10 per cent had four.[1126, 1127]

In an extensive census of exceptional children in Illinois, Farber found a total multiple disability prevalence rate of 11 per 1,000 children between the ages of 7 and 17. He also found that 18 per cent of the exceptional children, aged 7 to 16, who were not attending school had multiple disabilities.[513]

An investigation of ten school districts of Westchester County, New York, revealed a high incidence of children with multiple disabilities in an economically and culturally favored population. In excess of one thousand children were listed as having two or more disabilities.[217(p.6-8)]

In a study of 412 handicapped children, Stifler *et al.* found that only 8 per cent of these children had one disability, while 70 per cent had three to six additional disabilities.[1026] Quibell *et al.*, in a study of crippled children, noted that 90 per cent of these children had two or more disabilities.[899] Fouracre found that 80 per cent of 171 crippled children had multiple disabilities.[342]

Richardson, in a survey of handicapping conditions and handicapped children in Alamance County, North Carolina, found an average of 1.63 disabilities per handicapped child. Richardson concludes that there is a distressing deficiency of services and facilities for children with multiple severe disabilities.

> In North Carolina, and doubtless in many other states, the excellent facilities being provided for single specific conditions [disabilities] just do not have available services needed by those with two or more serious handicaps. Here is a deficiency which urgently needs to be remedied.[920](p. 1830)

There are numerous possible combinations of multiple disabilities; in fact, the number of such combinations could be listed *ad infinitum*. The seven traditional categories of exceptionality which are frequently cited in the literature provide forty-two different diads of disabilities. (A diad is a pair or two disabilities in one individual.) In the remainder of this chapter, additional epidemiological data and related information will be presented relative to (1) multiple disabilities with cerebral palsy; (2) multiple disabilities with hearing impairment; (3) multiple disabilities with visual impairment; and (4) multiple disabilities with mental retardaton. Only two specific diads of disabilities will be reported in considerable detail, the deaf–mentally retarded and the blind–mentally retarded. Inferences may be drawn from these specific diads that have significance for other combinations of disabilities.

Multiple Disabilities With Cerebral Palsy

A national agency estimates that every fifty-three minutes a cerebral palsied child is born. The incidence rate is determined at about three cerebral palsied children per thousand population. Most cerebral palsied children are multiply handicapped, and prior to the last quarter of a century, this undoubtedly was the reason cerebral palsy was considered a hopeless problem. Twenty-five years ago brain injury was thought to be irreversible and intellectual potential fixed. Our view of the child and of brain injury has changed as recognition has been given to the fact that development is modifiable and the effects of trauma to the central nervous system can be, in many cases, ameliorated or overcome.

Although William Little, an English surgeon, provided the first clinical description of cerebral spastic diplegia, Temple Fay believed that a debt was owed to Dr. Bronson Crothers who gave the first impetus for special consideration of the spastic problem.[1133] Crothers also included a chapter on cerebral palsy in his book which was published in 1926.[213]

Phelps, although he did not coin the term *cerebral palsy*, is given credit for popularizing it. The term itself was used before 1900. Dodge and Adams have stated that "the name [cerebral palsy] is not altogether appropriate, nor is such a crude classification of nervous disorders particularly useful from the viewpoint of the physician, because it results in a collocation of diseases of widely differing etiologic and anatomic types. . . . Nevertheless, the term has been adopted as a slogan for fund-raising societies and for a major rehabilitation movement throughout the United States, and it will not soon disappear from medical terminology."[265(p.1547)]

Definition and Classification

The term *cerebral palsy* literally means "paralysis of the cerebrum." The cerebrum is that portion of the brain comprising the two large hemispheres, in contradistinction to the crus, the midbrain, the cerebellum, the pons, and the medulla. Paralysis of the hemispheres, therefore, would include many additional losses of function besides movement; it would also include sensation, sight, memory, hearing of words, speech, etc.[326]

Fay was one of the first leaders in the field to recognize and attempt to classify the various types of cerebral palsy. In a letter to Meyer Perlstein in 1947, Fay wrote: "The time is fast approaching when we must reorganize our present classification of cerebral palsy and place the boundaries more distinctly than they have been accepted in the past, if we are to have intelligent and progressive consideration of this problem." Fay and Phelps collaborated on the formation of a classification scheme that includes six major types: (1) spastic paralysis, (2) athetosis, (3) tremors and rigidities, (4) ataxia, (5) high spinal spastic, and (6) mixed type.[325]

Over the years others have proposed different classification schemes. A sevenfold classification of cerebral palsy is used currently that is generally acceptable to members of the American Academy for Cerebral Palsy. It includes (1) spasticity, (2) athetosis, (3) rigidity, (4) ataxia, (5) tremor, (6) atonia, and (7) mixed.[769] The four major types in this classification are spasticity, athetosis, rigidity, and ataxia. The Little Club provides clinical features on which differentiation of cases might be made. Hemiplegia accounts for about one third of all cerebral palsy cases; bilateral spasticity comprises about two fifths; cases with involuntary movement about one seventh; and the remainder are cases difficult to classify. These difficult to classify cases which usually are of a mixed type account for one seventh of the cases.[661]

Phelps implied that the word *cerebral* referred to the brain, and the word *palsy* described a lack of muscle control. Because of this interpretation, the term *cerebral palsy* became used to designate "any paralysis, weakness, uncoordination, or functional aberration of the motor system resulting from brain pathology." Several other definitions have been formulated for cerebral palsy, but most of them include reference to an abnormal, orthopedic, or neurological condition due to brain damage before, during, or after birth that results in a particular sensorimotor disability.[325, 661, 769]

Denhoff and Robinault have proposed a broadened concept of cerebral palsy that differs somewhat from the traditional one currently held. Cerebral palsy is seen as a varied rather than a specific entity.[249](p.25) These authors use the term *syndromes of cerebral dysfunction* to represent various syndromes which include cerebral palsy, mental deficiency, epilepsy, the hyperkinetic behavior disorders, and visual and auditory perception problems of a central origin. These syndromes are related by similar causes and none have a specific characteristic pathologic entity. The same neuropathologic findings are common to all categories. "Since it seems senseless to isolate by semantics such closely allied neurologic disabilities, syndromes of cerebral dysfunction is suggested as the term to help unify our thinking about cerebral palsy and related disorders."[249](p.1) Organic types of childhood psychoses, such as autism, are also included within this spectrum of disabilities.

In the concept of syndromes of cerebral dysfunction, one component is generally predominant and upon this one the diagnosis depends. A diagnosis of cerebral palsy is made when the neuromotor disability is outstanding. Intellectual subnormality will lead to a clinical designation of mental deficiency. "A practical definition implies that the mentally deficient person is one who at maturity is permanently incompetent because of intellectual inadequacies due to maldevelopment or damage to the brain."[249](p.39) The epileptic child shows distortions of consciousness. Behavioral variances of a special type are labeled as the hyperkinetic behavior disorder. Impairments of vision, hearing, speech, or tactile discrimination of central origin are called respectively the blind, deaf, aphasic, or clumsy child syndrome. Children may demonstrate neuromotor, intellectual, sensory, and behavioral findings singly or in combinations and in different degrees. The cerebral palsied children frequently have associated problems and, as a result, are multiply handicapped.

Mental Retardation

Many studies have been completed to determine the disabilities associated with cerebral palsy. The problem of intellectual functioning was one of the first associated disabilities to be investigated. Many cerebral palsied children were denied admission to special education classes for crippled children during the early history of these special services. A large number of children with arm and leg involvements were enrolled in special classes as a result of disabilities associated with poliomyelitis; however, their intellectual abilities were intact. There were a limited number of spaces available in these special classes to cerebral palsied children. Therefore, interest developed in establishing a technique for deciding which cerebral palsied children were educable and would profit from school. The cerebral palsied child became the subject of numerous psychological studies.

McIntire[706] and Phelps[883] found that 70 per cent of all cerebral palsied children were of normal intelligence. These findings are inconsistent with later studies. Asher and Schonnel,[47] Holloran,[493] and Heilman[472] conducted epidemiological studies of the extent of mental retardation among cerebral palsied children and concurred that approximately 75 per cent of these children were below average in intelligence and at least 50 per cent were seriously retarded or mentally defective.

Bice,[99] Burgemeister and Blum,[153] Hohman,[490] Holden,[492] Jewell and Wursten,[547] Richardson and Kobler,[917] Katz,[568, 569] and Sievers and Norman[994] have also investigated the intelligence of cerebral palsied children. All of these empirical studies show a greater proportion of mental retardation in cerebral palsied children than in the normal population.

In 1952 Dunsdon stated, "Available evidence suggests that an I.Q. of about 85 may be taken as a fairly reliable guide to the minimum level of mental ability required to allow cerebral palsied children to profit from special education."[288(p.115)] This generalization justified the continued exclusion of many cerebral palsied children from public school programs for crippled children.

The formation of the American Academy for Cerebral Palsy in 1947 and United Cerebral Palsy, Inc., in 1949 stimulated both professional and lay interest in the welfare, medical treatment, and education of those afflicted with cerebral palsy. However, it was the advent of polio vaccines that was indirectly responsible for providing increased educational opportunities to severely involved cerebral palsied children. The use of polio vaccines has significantly reduced the number of postpolio disabilities. The vaccines have been conservatively estimated to be effective in preventing paralysis of 70 per cent of the cases.[895] Following the administration of polio vaccines, additional vacancies became available in special schools and special classes for crippled children. Many cerebral palsied children with I.Q.s below that proposed by Dunsdon have benefited from a special class placement.

Strother[1040] and Michal-Smith[763] have indicated the importance psychologists should give to sensory and motor disabilities in testing the cerebral palsied child.

Haeussermann[428] has recognized the importance of multiple handicaps in cerebral palsied children and has devised a procedure for assessing the developmental potential of young children. She refers to her own assessment procedure as an educational evaluation. United Cerebral Palsy, Inc., has produced a film in which this assessment technique is demonstrated.[1058]

Klapper and Birch conducted a follow-up study on cerebral palsied adults fourteen years after their I.Q.s had been assessed in childhood. In both initial test and at retest individual I.Q. scores below 90 were preponderant. The retest group, however, showed a higher proportion of normal I.Q. scores than were obtained at initial testing.[595]

The predictive value of intelligence tests is questioned today by many educators and psychologists, especially in measuring the potential of the multiply disabled cerebral palsied child. Phillips and White compared children with motor handicaps from early infancy to other physically handicapped children of the same age range. When allowances were made for the uncontrolled variables of age and intelligence, there was a significant difference between the two groups in the acquisition of reading and arithmetic skills. It was hypothesized that prediction of response to educational opportunity by such tests as the Stanford-Binet may be invalidated by perceptual deficiencies in cerebral palsied children.[888]

Hearing Impairments

Cardwell reports that multiple disabilities are common in cerebral palsy; 50 per cent of these children have visual defects; 25 per cent have hearing impairments; 50 to 75 per cent speech defects; and 50 per cent have convulsive disorders.[160]

Other investigators have also studied the associated sensory- and perceptual-motor dysfunctions in cerebral palsied children. Estimated hearing losses range from as low as 10 per cent to over 41 per cent. The much cited New Jersey study reported hearing impairment in 22.6 per cent of the athetoids; 18.4 per cent of the ataxics; 13.7 per cent of those with rigidity; and 7.2 per cent of the spastics in the population under study.[496(p.11)]

Fisch, in a survey conducted in England, found a hearing loss incidence of 20 per cent among cerebral palsied children.[333]

Gerber attempted to distinguish the incidence of hearing deficiencies among subgroups of cerebral palsied children. His results indicated that "the hearing of erythroblastotics was significantly poorer than hearing of athetoids with other etiologies, whose hearing in turn was poorer than that of the noncerebral palsied children."[383] The incidence of hearing loss in per cent for each subgroup was as follows: spastics, 50 per cent; non-Rh athetoid, 100 per cent; combined athetoids, 75 per cent; and total for the cerebral palsied groups studied, 59 per cent.

Myklebust[806] and Rosen[936] have indicated that athetosis due to kernicterus may cause a child to demonstrate an inability to listen rather than an inability to hear. Such children need placement in special classes for the brain injured rather than the deaf.

Speech Defects

Since speech is basically a neurophysiological activity, it is not surprising to find a high incidence of speech defects among cerebral palsied children as a result of neuromuscular involvement. A significant number of cerebral palsied children exhibit abnormal tongue movements and breathing, abnormal sucking, chewing, and swallowing patterns. Denhoff and Holden have shown that spastics, as a group, have fewer speech problems than athetoids.[250] The results of the New Jersey study show the following percentage of speech defects among 1,224 cerebral palsy cases: spasticity, 52 per cent; athetosis, 88.7 per cent; rigidity, 72.2 per cent; and ataxia, 85.3 per cent. The total for the four major classifications of cerebral palsy was 68 per cent.[496]

Visual Impairments

It must be remembered that cerebral palsied children might have any kind of a health condition that noncerebral palsied children might have. Visual problems that occur in the normal population also occur in cerebral palsy. However, there are some visual problems which occur more commonly in cerebral palsy. The most frequently associated ocular defect is strabismus or squint.[960] Hemianopsia, a visual field defect, was found in about 25 per cent of spastic hemiplegics.[1064] Nystagmus, congenital cataracts, and optic atrophy are associated with cerebral palsy but in smaller percentages of the cases.

Guibor[425] and Breakley[131] report that over 50 per cent of cerebral palsied children have oculomotor defects and 25 per cent subnormal vision. Illingworth[511] also estimates that about 25 per cent to 50 per cent of all cerebral palsied children have significant visual defects.

Seizures

Hopkins and his co-workers found that almost one third of the cerebral palsied children included in their study had seizures. The percentages of seizures reported for the four major classifications of cerebral palsy were as follows: spastics, 28.2 per cent; athetoids, 20.8 per cent; rigidity, 41.9 per cent; and ataxics, 36.3 per cent.[496] Illingworth also estimates that one third of all cerebral palsied cases have convulsions at some time.[511] Findings by other investigators support this view.[11, 877]

Perception: Tactile, Kinesthetic, and Visual-Motor

In recent years there has been a growing interest in (1) the effects of sensory stimulation on motor development, (2) the effects of sensory deprivation on intellectual and perceptual development, and (3) the nature of sensory disturbances in cerebral palsied children. McDonald and Chance have aptly expressed this concern for sensory stimulation when they write, "In fact, a current quip has it that everyone is now talking 'sense.' Earlier researchers and therapists were preoccupied with the nature of the motor output, but now they recognize that to a large degree what comes out depends on what goes in."[701(p.49)]

Abercrombie,[5] Ayres,[54, 55] Bexton,[97] Hohman,[491] Tizard,[1064] Wiedenbaker,[1115] Wedell,[1103] and Zubek[1156] emphasize the importance of tactile sensitivity and tactile perception in cerebral palsied children. Increasing evidence seems to be developing that suggests that defective sensory functioning may be responsible, in part, for defective motor functioning and may also have a detrimental influence on intelligence and perception. Denhoff and Robinault report the result of two studies of perceptual dysfunction. These studies "reasonably indicated that previously unrecognized perceptual and conceptual discriminatory disturbances in physically disabled as well as nonphysically disabled brain-damaged children were responsible at least in part for school failures."[249]* Williams[1119] has described the special learning problems presented by cerebral palsied children with associated perceptual disorder.

Cerebral palsy, more than any other disability component, illustrates the problems presented by exceptional children with multiple handicaps. Since most cerebral palsied children have one or more associated disabilities, it is apparent that a number of specialists are required in the evaluation, treatment, management, and education of children with this condition. Shepherd has said,

> I suppose we all feel at times that nothing short of a god-like combination of knowledge—medical, neurological, psychiatric, psychological, social, and educational—could be adequate to these children's needs. But we have to face the fact that no one of us can hope to have more than a small part of this knowledge.
>
> It is for this reason that a "multidisciplinary approach" is a phrase increasingly heard nowadays.[986]

Multiple Disabilities With Hearing Impairments

Mentally Retarded–Deaf Diad

Efforts to provide educational services for the deaf have reflected attempts to modify the misconception that all deaf people are mentally deficient. This misconception has had deleterious effects upon research on the education of deaf children and adults.

---

* The reader is also referred to the Denhoff-Robinault book which is destined to be a classic in cerebral palsy for more detailed information on associated disabilities with cerebral palsy.

The notion that the deaf were not educable was first questioned during the sixteenth century.[359] In the United States, a distinction between the deaf and the mentally deficient was made concomitantly with the movement to establish educational programs for the deaf. With the establishment of the first permanent school for the deaf in this country in 1817, the American School for the Deaf, a clear distinction was made between mental deficiency and deafness.

Since the sixteenth century, the lay public has become cognizant of a number of the misconceptions erroneously attributed to deaf individuals. While it is now generally recognized that a diagnosis of deafness does not imply mental deficiency, it is obvious that a percentage of the deaf function at levels of measured intelligence and social adaptation which tend to result in approximating mental retardation.

Incidence and Prevalence

Evidence of the magnitude of the prevalence of deaf children with low intelligence and other concomitant handicapping conditions is presented by Doctor, who lists the following statistics pertaining to children enrolled in schools and classes for the deaf in the United States.[259] Doctor reports 537 pupils diagnosed as aphasic and deaf, 108 blind and deaf, 640 cerebral palsied and deaf, 405 brain injured and deaf, 186 orthopedically handicapped and deaf, and 1,274 mentally retarded and deaf. According to these figures, 40 per cent of the deaf with multiple disability in the United States are mentally retarded.

Weir observes that data compiled by Doctor do not represent a complete census of all the deaf with additional handicaps.[1108] However, Doctor's data show that in 1954 the number of children with multiple disabilities was approximately 4.5 per cent of the total number of deaf students, but by 1961 this number had increased to approximately 11 per cent. Leenhouts cites further evidence from a study conducted by the Bureau of Special Education of the State of California.[635] In this study, 15 per cent of the entire group of deaf children of school age in the state were classified as mentally retarded. In addition, "it was found that there was approximately 700 'multiply' handicapped deaf children in California, and of this number, a large proportion were being denied any kind of public school training."

Frisina studied the populations of three midwestern residential schools for the deaf. Using an I.Q. criterion of 79 on the Grace Arthur Point Scale of Performance, Form II, Frisina found that 9.2 per cent of the schools' populations were mentally retarded. Children who were aphasic, psychotic, cerebral palsied, or who showed gross motor disturbances were not included in the 9.2 per cent figure. If these children are included,

Frisina concludes that "it seems reasonable to hypothesize that approximately 10 to 12 per cent of children in residential schools for the deaf are in need of special help on the basis of mental retardation."[359]

Anderson reported a total of 1,345 pupils below 83 I.Q. enrolled in forty-three residential schools for the deaf. Readers were cautioned to interpret this prevalence data as a gross estimate.[35]

A number of investigations have shown a high incidence of hearing impairment in populations of the retarded. Using puretone audiometry, Birch and Matthews,[102] Schlanger,[969] Johnston and Farrell,[557] Foale and Patterson,[338] Schlanger and Gottsleben,[972] Kodman *et al.*,[610] and Siegenthaler and Kryzywicki[993] have called attention to the prevalence of impaired puretone sensitivity in the mentally retarded. The results of these studies have been summarized and suggest that incidence and prevalence of impaired hearing is considerably higher than that found in nonretarded populations.[613, 743] Estimates range from 13 to 49 per cent depending upon the hearing loss criteria used. In public school children, the estimates range from 3 to 10 per cent.

The Concept of Deafness

The Office of Education of the United States Department of Health, Education, and Welfare has collected data on the number of exceptional children in the United States for almost one hundred years. In order to obtain accurate data, the various areas of exceptionality must be reasonably well defined. However, a single definition of *deafness* suitable to all of the professions which provide services for deaf people does not exist. Consequently, estimates of the prevalence of deafness in the United States range from ninety thousand to sixteen million individuals.[962]

Connor indicates that terms used to report the extent of hearing impairments lack unity, and he lists fourteen such terms.[202] Doctor reports that there are at least five definitions of deafness from as many different professional areas.

> The audiologist probably expresses his definition in decibels. . . . The social worker has a definition that is contingent upon the place of the individual in the community and whether or not he fits in with the hearing people or the deaf people. . . . The definition of the otologist is couched in medical terminology. . . . The rehabilitation worker is concerned with whether or not a worker can use the telephone or receive directions orally. . . . The psychologist has still another definition fitted more directly to his professional needs.[263(p.24)]

Educators use a definition of deafness which attempts to differentiate between the deaf and hard of hearing for educational purposes.[263] A number of educational definitions of deafness have appeared in the literature.[199, 1114, 1142] Streng's Classification of Deafness has been widely used by educators and incorporates the behavioral consequences of deafness.[53] In a recent conference designed to explore the possibilities of developing uniform statistics on incidence and prevalence of hearing impairment, Schein states that it may be more practical to describe deafness than to attempt to define it for epidemiological purposes and suggests that a description of auditorially limited children now in schools and classes for the impaired hearing may lead to an empirically derived classification system.[962] Silverman concurs that a suitable classification scheme for severe hearing impairment does not presently exist, and he discusses the need for standard classification.[997]

The Concept of Mental Retardation

To complicate further the problems of identifying the mentally retarded deaf, a definition of mental retardation mutually acceptable to the numerous practitioners involved in the education and care of the deaf has not been formulated. Several factors may account for the lack of a clear-cut definition or classification scheme.

During the early development and use of intelligence tests, it was thought that the intelligence quotient obtained on such tests would be immutable throughout the life of the individual. Since then, the immutability of the I.Q. has been questioned and considerable evidence suggests that the I.Q. should be regarded as a phenotype, like height or weight, for which the genes set limits of potential development but which is finally developed through encounters with the environment.[463, 504]

The utility of the I.Q. concept has also been questioned. Osler states,

> If our main object were to make long-range predictions of ultimate intelligence at the time of infancy, the I.Q. is not of much use. If on the other hand we confine ourselves to less remote prediction or to the solution of problems current in the child's life, we can rely on the intelligence test result as a reliable and valid measure of intellectual function.[830]

As with definitions of intelligence, past definitions of mental retardation referred to intellectual capacity, constitutional origin, or incurability. The concept of intellectual capacity was used to refer to some genetically determined maximum level of potential performance or to maldeveloped or malfunctioning cerebral structures which had diminished the capacity for intelligent behavior.[465]

The Mentally Retarded Deaf

Operating within the conceptual framework mentioned above, educators of the deaf have been reluctant to use the term *mentally retarded* to designate deaf children with low intelligence. The phrase *slow learning deaf child* appears to have gained some acceptance. In dealing with parents, the term is sometimes used because it is viewed as a kinder term than *mentally retarded,* not because it has greater scientific meaning. In a discussion of the term *slow learner,* Kirk and Johnson state,

> From the point of view of educational organization, the term *slow learner* should be applied to the child who seems to have some difficulty in adjusting to the curriculum ot the academic school because of slightly inferior intelligence or learning ability. He will require some modification of school offerings within the regular classroom for his maximum growth and development. . . . For educational purposes the slow learner does not belong in the special class for mentally handicapped. He is the child for whom the regular class should so differentiate its instruction as to adjust to the wider concept of the average. Slow learners should remain in the regular classes of the public schools, and teachers should adapt instruction to fit the wide variation which will include the slow learner, the average, and the superior. The reason for the organization of a special class for the mentally handicapped is that the mentally handicapped child presents too marked a deviation from the broad average. His retardation in school is so significant that he requires a different curriculum from that presented to the slow learner or the average child.[587](p.12)

Cruickshank reports that

> The term *slow learner* usually refers to children whose measured intelligence quotient is somewhere between 80 and 95. Sometimes the term is applied to all levels of mental retardation, at other times, only to the educable group of retarded children. The general tendency at the present time, however, is to face reality with parents and educators, and thus the term *slow learner* is rapidly becoming restricted to the higher group referred to previously in this paragraph.[217](pp.4-8)

The term *slow learning deaf child,* as used to refer to deaf children with low intelligence, has been used loosely to apply to all grades of deaf children with low intelligence. The literature thus reflects contradictory and ambiguous usage of the term *slow learning deaf child.*

For example, in a discussion on counseling and vocational planning for slow learning deaf students, it was stated that sheltered workshops may be terminal for some slow learning deaf children and that partial custody of the slow learning deaf or personal management is sometimes necessary.[412] This prognosis seems to correspond to a prognostic description of a trainable mentally retarded child. Kennedy defined the slow learning deaf child as one who is a slow learner because of below average mentality or one who learns at a slower rate than his peers for reasons other than low mentality.[576] In writing about the slow learning deaf child, Leshin defined such children as "those with average or above potential intelligence who do not learn well, or forget quickly, and for whom there is no obvious physical or mental reason for academic failure.[646](pp.197-202) In presenting an example of a slow learning deaf child, a child who had obtained a performance I.Q. of 115 on the Wechsler Intelligence Scale for Children was used.

In a subsequent article, the slow learning deaf child was defined by Leshin and Stahlecker as falling between I.Q.s 80 and 90, and mental retardation was defined, in terms of I.Q., as 90 or below.[645] Warren and Kraus criticize this definition of mental retardation and point out that, according to surveys of the intelligence of deaf children, about half of all deaf children would be considered mentally retarded if the Leshin–Stahlecker definition were used and if verbal intelligence tests alone were administered.[1093] To use the Leshin and Stahlecker definition of "below 90 I.Q." one would include one fourth of the total general population of the United States.

Warren and Kraus suggest the utilization of the terminology adopted by the American Association on Mental Deficiency in classifying deaf children. Although the AAMD classification, with respect to measured intelligence, considers as mentally retarded those individuals who fall more than one standard deviation below the mean of the standardization sample on a general test of intelligence, Warren and Kraus recommended that the I.Q. criterion for mental retardation be placed at two standard deviations below the mean. This would place the upper I.Q. limit of mental retardation at about 67 or 70.[465 (p. 3)]

However, if the upper limit of mental retardation were placed at 67 or 70, children in residential schools for the deaf between I.Q. 67 and 80, or better, who actually function as mentally retarded, would not be included. That many deaf children above 67 I.Q. do, in fact, function in the school setting as mentally retarded, is attested to by Leenhouts.[636]

Leenhouts makes the assumption, based on clinical and educational experience, that in considering the I.Q. of deaf children, the performance potential is depressed by approximately 15 to 20 points. Therefore, under this assumption, a deaf child who has obtained an I.Q. of 83 probably compares in achievement potential with the hearing child with an I.Q. of about 63 to 68. Leenhouts asserts that a number of deaf children who obtain an I.Q. of 70 or 80 cannot cope with nor benefit from the school program and social routine of a residential school for the deaf.

> Careful staffing results in the conviction that these children's retention is more harmful than helpful to themselves, and so dismissal is recommended. From our viewpoint these children's best interests would be met in a program such as that offered at our State Hospitals for the Mentally Retarded. However, here we meet the problem head on. The child's 70 or 80 I.Q. is "too high" for eligibility there, and so his application must be rejected or acceptance must be postponed for a long time. The child is suspended in NO MAN'S LAND. He is unable to function in a regular school or class for the deaf, yet his "apparent" potential excludes him from the state hospital program.

Vernon and Fishler[1082] observe that the overwhelming majority of deaf high school age students in the 90 or below I.Q. range will not achieve more than a third or fourth grade level. This level of achievement is typical of the educable mentally retarded child who does not have a hearing loss.

Based on the review of the literature relative to terminology and definition, the conclusion must be drawn that no definitions of hearing impairment or low intelligence are acceptable to all professions which provide services for deaf children with limited intellectual functioning.

Problems in the Education of the Mentally Retarded Deaf

In view of the problems inherent in definition, terminology, and classification it is not surprising that little research on the education of deaf children with low intelligence has been conducted. Indeed, a survey of the literature in 1963 indicated that research pertaining to the education of auditorially impaired mentally retarded children was practically nonexistent.[395] The research issue of *The Volta Review* lists only eight publications on the auditory impairment-mental retardation diad.[203] Only four articles in this disability category are summarized in the *Review of Educational Research: Education of Exceptional Children.*[629] Despite the lack of research, administrators, psychologists, and teachers have expressed concern in professional and scientific publications with respect to the quality of services for deaf children with low intelligence. These children present complex management problems to staff members responsible for educational planning in schools for the deaf.

In discussing the impact of the "multiply handicapped" deaf child on special education, Weir states,

> The second area in need of research concerns new or improved methods and materials to be used in teaching the "multiply-handicapped" deaf. One can find little research to aid the teacher in knowing how to approach these children or in knowing what materials to present to them. How is speech and language taught to a retarded deaf child.[1108]

Brutten and Stevens emphasize that the schools have been approaching the educational needs of handicapped children in terms of disability.[147, 1021] The educator is often called upon to revise the curriculum of the school to meet the needs of the child with multiple disabilities. However, due to the problems which current diagnostic classification schemes seem to incur, the educator is usually uncertain as to how to proceed. Terms such as *neurological deficit, aphasia, cerebral dysfunctions,* and *experiential deprivation* tell a classroom teacher little about the ways in which appropriate educational plans can be derived.

Diagnostic tools and methods are often inadequate and placement is sometimes based on expedience rather than on the child's educational needs. Not infrequently, the curriculum of schools for the deaf has not been adapted to the needs of the deaf child with additional disabilities. There are inadequate educational methods and instructional materials well suited for teaching mentally retarded deaf children. Many teachers of the deaf are not qualified by virtue of training, experience, or temperament to teach deaf children with additional disabilities.

Whether the child should be primarily considered a mentally retarded child and educated as such, or whether deafness should be given priority, has been an issue. While the practice has been to assign priority to one or the other of the disabilities, no adequate rationale for the assignment of priority of one disability over another presently exists. There does not appear to be a sound theoretical basis for establishing the primacy of one disability over another disability.

Conflicting viewpoints have been expressed concerning the facilities in which the mentally retarded deaf might best be housed and educated. It is Cruickshank's opinion that the children with multiple disabilities should be handled by the residential school due to the research potential of such centers.[220] Sellin proposes that "residential schools for the deaf should be expected to provide for the educable but not the trainable retarded child. The trainable child should be placed in an institution for the mentally retarded."[982]

Leenhouts questions having mentally retarded deaf children enrolled in a residential school for the deaf and states the need for a separate facility for mentally retarded deaf children.[635] This facility would be on the campus of a residential school for the deaf but would be a separate unit. MacPherson has listed the problems of the education of mentally retarded deaf children and recommends that facilities should be established and staffed by teachers who are trained to teach the deaf and the mentally retarded.[722]

Leshin and Stahlecker have postulated that mental retardation, or limited potential to learn results, is a greater "education handicap" than deafness and that when deaf children are severely mentally retarded, they should be housed and educated in institutions for the mentally retarded.[645] Warren and Kraus, however, disagree with Leshin and Stahlecker and contend that

> Since all teachers, whatever their specialty, are trained in problems of learning, one might better plan to have the communication and language problem given primary consideration; the degree of learning difficulty could be taken into account in training. The problem of trying to develop techniques of communication with deaf children is a highly specialized one. Few, if any, teachers of the mentally retarded have been given instructions in techniques of

communication with the deaf. One would assume that all teachers of the deaf have been given instructions in how to help children learn.[1093]

James summarized the results of a recent panel on deafness and mental retardation, concluding that

1. No child who is deaf and mentally retarded should ever be restricted to the pure oral method alone. The simultaneous method, a combination of manual and oral communication, is used in the programs in California, Tennessee, Minnesota, and Michigan.
2. Education and training of mentally retarded deaf children should be extended beyond the regular school day schedule to include twenty-four-hour services.
3. Commitment of a deaf retarded child to a state hospital where no special program is designed to meet his needs is tantamount to a life sentence.[543]

It has been common practice in some residential schools for the deaf to assign deaf teachers to classes for retarded deaf children. However, Leenhouts emphasizes that being deaf is not, in itself, a professional qualification, and that many deaf teachers do not possess the qualities necessary for teaching deaf children with low intelligence.[636] The same may be said for teachers who have no hearing impairment.

The point has been made that the education of the deaf has not kept pace with the development in the education of the mentally retarded.[477] Many schools for the deaf provide a "watered down curriculum" for educable retarded deaf children until they can be placed in some other agency. It was observed that if these same children had the benefit of a differential curriculum, many of them would have a greater opportunity to develop skills which would enable them to do unskilled or semi-skilled work and to partially support themselves in adulthood.

Anderson *et al.* studied provisions for the education of mentally retarded deaf children in residential schools for the deaf.[35]

The mentally retarded deaf were operationally defined as "those individuals who attend residential schools for the deaf, as listed by the American Annals of the Deaf, and who fall more than one standard deviation below the mean on any standardized individually administered performance test of intelligence."[22] This definition places the upper I.Q. limit of mental retardation at about 83.[465]

Inquiry schedules, based on questions raised in published professional literature, were directed to administrators of residential schools for the deaf and to classroom teachers of mentally retarded deaf children. The responding schools, sixty-four in number, included in their enrollment a total of 14,534 pupils, or 79.4 per cent of the total number of pupils enrolled in residential schools for the deaf in the United States. A total of 150 teachers of mentally retarded deaf children completed the inquiry form for teachers.

The objectives of this investigation were as follows:

1. To describe policies and procedures for admission of mentally retarded deaf children to residential schools for the deaf;
2. To describe special academic and vocational provisions for mentally retarded deaf children in residential schools for the deaf;
3. To describe the qualifications of classroom teachers of mentally retarded deaf children in residential schools for the deaf;
4. To estimate the prevalence of mental retardation among deaf children in residential schools for the deaf;
5. To report judgments of administrators of residential schools for the deaf relative to the most effective organization for instruction of mentally retarded deaf children.

The results of this study seem to justify the concern about the adequacy of services for deaf children with low intelligence currently being expressed in the literature. The following conclusions were derived from this study:

1. There is a wide variation of admittance practices among residential schools for the deaf in the United States.
2. In a majority of instances local administrators of residential schools for the deaf have the prerogative to establish admission criteria.
3. In general, an intelligence test score is not a criterion for admittance to residential schools for the deaf.
4. Intelligence tests designed specifically for use with deaf children or standardized on deaf populations are not always the most preferred instruments to test deaf children.
5. The administrators of most residential schools prefer not to admit children with multiple disabilities.
6. There is an increasing demand for administrators of residential schools for the deaf to provide services for pupils with low intelligence.
7. A definition or classification of mental retardation mutually acceptable to residential school administrators does not exist.
8. It will be difficult to obtain accurate prevalence data on mentally retarded deaf children until standard definitions, terminology, and nomenclature are adopted by educators of the deaf.
9. There are considerable differences in extent of special educational and vocational services for deaf children with low intelligence provided by various residential schools.

10. In most residential schools for the deaf, mentally retarded deaf children follow essentially the same curriculum as deaf children within the normal range of intelligence.
11. Special training of teachers is not perceived by most administrators as an important factor in assignment to teach mentally retarded deaf children.
12. A large number of teachers with hearing loss are presently teaching mentally retarded deaf children in residential schools.
13. Considerably more than half of the teachers of mentally retarded deaf children in special classes would prefer not to teach mentally retarded deaf children.
14. Most teachers of mentally rearded deaf children do not feel adequately prepared to teach such children and feel the need for additional training.
15. There is a striking similarity in the characteristics of mentally retarded deaf children and educable mentally retarded children.
16. Almost half of the administrators were of the opinion that deaf children below 83 I.Q. could best be housed and educated in separate facilities for the mentally retarded deaf.

A relatively large number of mentally retarded deaf children are enrolled in schools and classes for the deaf and in various facilities for the mentally retarded in the United States. Without extensive changes in the present character of educational services, many of these children will not achieve social competence.

Deaf-Blind Diad

Concern for the management of the deaf-blind in the United States emerged early in the history of special education and had its origin with the tutoring of Laura Bridgman by Samuel Gridley Howe.[309] The most instrumental force in developing interest in the deaf-blind was the successful education of Helen Keller by Ann Sullivan Macy.[129] Helen Keller undoubtedly has had great influence on calling attention to multiple disabilities. Miss Keller has described the deaf-blind disability as "a comparatively few people surrounded by a multitude of cruel problems."[574]

The register of the American Foundation for the Blind shows 372 deaf-blind children in the United States as of January 1, 1960. There are relatively few children in the deaf-blind group compared to other multiple disability groups. The National Study Committee on the Education of deaf-blind children provides the following definition which has educational implications:

> A deaf-blind child is one whose combination of handicaps prevents him from profiting satisfactorily from educational programs provided for the blind child or the deaf child.[812]

This definition implies that children with two or more disabilities so severe as to make it impossible for them to profit from a program established for any one of the disabilities are in need of special facilities and services.

Multiple Disabilities with Visual Impairments

Blind–Speech Defective Diad

The little information available regarding the incidence of speech problems of the blind is inconsistent. Stinchfield found that 49 per cent of the blind children tested at the Overbrook School for the Blind in Philadelphia and the Perkins School for the Blind in Watertown had some form of speech problem.[1028] Rowe surveyed the blind children in the Northern California area and found that 6.7 per cent of the blind children would benefit from speech correction.[943] Miner attempted to investigate the incidence of speech deviations among children at the Michigan School for the Blind and the Illinois Braille and Sight Saving School. Two hundred and ninety-three children were tested, and 33.8 per cent were found to have some sort of speech deviation.[770] Wolf, in a study of presumptively diagnosed disabilities, found that 30 per cent of the blind and partially seeing children enrolled in special classes for the mentally retarded in residential schools for the visually impaired had speech defects.[1129] Different populations used, different admission standards to the schools included in the survey, and differences in testing procedures may account for the variations in findings.

Mentally Retarded–Blind Diad

From almost the inception of residential schools for the blind, educators have debated whether children with additional disabilities, especially mental retardation, should be accepted. A paper read at the International Conference on the Blind in 1905 concluded that feeble-minded blind children, when admitted to schools for the blind, "not only absorb undue energy from caretakers and teachers but also exert a deteriorating influence on the rest; hence they should not be received into a school for the blind."[552]

Early proceedings of the American Association of Instructors of the Blind record serious questions of "what to do with the feeble-minded blind child."[25] Farrell, after analyzing the problem of the feeble-minded blind child in America, concluded that these children should be put in special classes in institutions for the feeble-minded.[322] By the 1940's a change in attitude toward the mentally retarded blind child was noticeable. This change was reflected in an article by Lowenfeld and Spar[681] in which the authors suggested that the most desirable way to provide for these children may be the establishment of special units within schools for the blind.

Even today, educators of the blind and of the mentally retarded are concerned about the adequacy of services available to children with multiple disabilities and the appropriateness of instructional methodology. The problem of the blind child with additional disabilities is becoming more critical today with the increased number of blind children. There was spectacular growth in enrollments of blind children in local public school programs between 1948 and 1958. Mackie and her co-workers report a 448 per cent increase in this period. The gain did not result from a loss of enrollments in residential schools, for these enrollments also increased during the period by 34 per cent.[715]

Fraenkel states, "with few exceptions, blind-retarded persons live in a socialized 'no-man's land.' Too often they are shunted between agencies or persons who can provide little or no assistance."[344] Long, concerned over the lack of resources available to blind children with multiple disabilities attempted to study the problem through a questionnaire returned from fifty-nine institutions for the blind and fifty-five institutions for the crippled. She reported that slightly more than half of the cerebral palsied blind children applying for admission to institutions for the blind and/or institutions for the crippled were accepted for placement between the years 1942 and 1952. Long strongly recommended coordinated services for the multiply disabled blind child.[675]

A report from the American Printing House for the Blind gives the results of a survey of multiple disabilities among 6,009 children in residential schools and day classes for the visually impaired. The study revealed that 19.6 per cent of visually impaired children included in the study had one or more disabilities in addition to blindness. Residential school programs had fewer (18.5%) multiply handicapped children than did day school programs (24.4%). Mental retardation was found in 7.9 per cent of the blind children. One of the major limitations of this study was the nonspecific criteria used for identifying multiply disabled children. Administrators of residential schools and public school classes were asked for brief descriptions of children meeting the criteria of the following definition: "A multiple handicapped individual may be defined (educationally) as a person with more than one handicap, each of which in and of itself makes special educational provision or therapy necessary."[31] It was thought that more objective judgments could be made in classifying children as to extent and type of multiple disabilities from the description of the children than from labels. Therefore, definitions were not given for the nine types of disabilities reported with blindness. Returned descriptive statements varied from detailed, technical descriptions to oversimplified and barren descriptions. In some instances, the lack of more precise definitions resulted in ambiguous responses making interpretation and tabulation difficult. The value of the study "lies less in broad generalizations that may be made from them than in revealing the possible extent and nature of the problem, and sensitizing us to the need for serious consideration of many aspects of it."[31 (p. ii)]

Cohen *et al.* completed a longitudinal interdisciplinary study of forty-three children with retrolental fibroplasia born in the Chicago area between 1945 and 1954. Eighty-two per cent of the children were either totally blind or had only light perception. The intellectual level of 42 per cent of the cases ranged from mildly retarded to profoundly retarded. Thirty-five per cent of these forty-three children showed some evidence of pediatric disorder. The most common finding in the pediatric examination was muscle hypotonicity. Other abnormalities included hearing deficit, heart disorder, poor appetite, poor teeth, and nutritional disorders. Neurologic disorders included spastic diplegia, hemiplegia, quadriplegia, and convulsive states, and extrapyramidal manifestations.[188]

In a survey of twenty-nine residential schools for the blind, Paraskeva found that approximately 15 per cent of the blind students in his sample were also mentally retarded. A trend was noted that more residential schools for the blind were willing to accept mentally retarded blind children into residential schools. In the past most of these schools excluded blind children with multiple disabilities.[834] Long and Perry surveyed forty-three residential schools for the blind and found a total of one thousand mentally retarded blind children. The report emphasized the need for research on the methodology for teaching mentally retarded blind children.[676]

Norris *et al.*, in a five-year study of approximately three hundred blind preschool children in the Chicago area, noted that some blind children committed to institutions received psychological ratings which were average or above. The fact that 84 per cent of these children had other disabilities in addition to blindness was thought to be a major factor in the placement.[824] DiMichael indicates that 10 to 14 per cent of blind children in the age range 5 to 17 are retarded. However, he questions the validity of the intelligence score in his statement, "The basic question is whether the I.Q. and M.A. guide given for the educable and trainable apply without change to the retarded-blind. We would expect that they would not because the individuals have two disabilities; in fact, it would be more correct to say that most of them have multiple disabilities."[254 (p. 15)]

Dry and Cooper many years ago raised the question as to whether or not the large incidence of retardation in schools for the blind was truly congenital feeble-mindedness or pseudo-feeble-mindedness which may be curable.[285]

Additional disorders such as cleft palate or certain crippling conditions in blind children are easily detected. Many blind children have additional disabilities of an intangible behavioral nature, such as autism, mental retardation, psychosis, aphasia, emotional disturbance, and brain injury. Moor, discussing this type of blind child, writes that "Many of them have been denied admission to or have been dismissed from educational programs as being too immature, not fitting into the school, uneducable, unable to talk, or in need of more individual attention."[784]

Berkson and Davenport[93] and Guess[423] have investigated stereotyped movements also referred to as blind mannerisms and autoerotic behavior. Included in stereotyped movements are head banging, eye poking, rocking, twirling, head shaking and complex hand movements, and posturing. Although these characteristics are common to normal blind children, they are more frequently observed and persist for longer periods of time in mentally retarded blind children. Guess suggests that stereotyped movements provide stimulation and motor tension release.[424]

A variety of complex and interrelated factors are associated with multiple disabilities. Assessment instruments and methods are many times inadequate with this group of children.[239, 478, 618]

Several reports indicated that mentally retarded blind children are frequently committed to institutions where very limited educational and training programs are provided for them.[28, 31, 824] Boly and DeLeo conducted a survey of educational provisions for the mentally retarded blind in 52 of the 104 state institutions for the mentally retarded and found great variations between institutions in terms of the number of blind and educational provisions for them. The median number of blind persons in residence at each institution was 23 and limitation of educational programs for the retarded blind was noted.[120]

Walsh, in a study completed at the Rosewood Training School, found 4 per cent of the patients to be blind or nearly blind.[1091] In another study, Cawley and Spotts found 1,458 blind and partially seeing children between 3 and 15 years of age in a survey of 30,000 children in sixty-one state and private schools for the mentally retarded. About 5 per cent of the population in residential schools for the mentally retarded were also visually impaired. However, only twenty-five teachers, five of whom were qualified, were working with 714 mentally retarded blind patients; none of the sixty-one institutions was actively engaged in research related to mentally retarded children with concomitant sensory deficit.[169]

Winschel, utilizing a subjective approach through personal correspondence, attempted to summarize services available for the mentally retarded blind within each state. A respondent in each state described the services available. Winschel found that the main facilities providing service to this disability group were: classes within institutions for the mentally retarded, public school classes, private schools, educable classes within schools for the blind, and foster homes. Although the results of this study cannot be considered definitive, they do present a broad outline of the services on a nationwide basis.[1125]

The National Association for Retarded Children attempted to discern the degree to which member units were aware of the need for services to the mentally retarded blind. One hundred and fifty questionnaires were returned by NARC units representing thirty-seven states. Ten states estimated the number of mentally retarded residents, but the reported figures showed little relationship to the population of the state. Fifty-one units included a statement regarding the need for increased specialized services; 113 replies indicated an awareness of the problem in varying degrees, while 41 units reported that there were no retarded blind persons in their communities. Although this study has many limitations, it does indicate that there are unmet needs in reference to the education of mentally retarded blind children.[171, 809]

Because of an unexpected increase in the number of blind children in New York State and the lack of resources to handle them, a comprehensive study was completed by Cruickshank and Trippe. It was revealed that approximately one third of all blind persons studied had additional disabilities. Local schools reported 23.3 per cent of their blind children as having multiple disabilities; residential schools reported 35.8 per cent of their enrollees having multiple disabilities. The residential schools for mentally retarded indicated that 75 per cent of the mentally retarded blind children had additional complicating disabilities.[224]

A survey completed by the United States Office of Education, Division of Handicapped Children and Youth, indicates that there has been a substantial increase in recent years in special school services for visually impaired children with multiple disabilities. Almost 80 per cent of the programs in the United States served visually impaired children who also had one or more additional disabilities. The report states that research exploration is clearly warranted on almost every aspect of special education programs for visually impaired children who also have other major disabilities. According to the study the particular process of classification and placement needs much investigation.[560]

Wolf completed a study to determine the number of mentally retarded blind children in residential schools for the visually impaired and the extent and nature of educational services provided for these children with concomitant disabilities.[1129] Data, collected from a national survey of residential schools for the visually impaired, were related to the following specific objectives:

1. To determine the prevalence of mental retardation among blind children in residential schools for the visually impaired;
2. To determine the prevalence of additional disabilities among mentally retarded blind children in these schools;
3. To identify criteria used for admissions of mentally retarded blind children to these schools;
4. To describe modifications of organization and instruction for mentally retarded blind children in these schools;
5. To obtain and report judgments and recommendations from administrators and teachers in residential schools as to (a) appropriate organization for instruction, (b) professional training and skills needed by the teacher in conducting classes for mentally retarded blind children, and (c) instructional methods and techniques utilized.

Data were obtained from inquiry schedules mailed to the chief administrators of forty-eight residential schools and to classroom teachers in schools that conducted special classes for mentally retarded blind children. All the chief administrators and more than half (56%) of the special class teachers responded. The residential school population participating in the study included 6,696 visually limited children. Thirty-five schools, representing 70 per cent of the residential school population, reported an enrollment of 1,170 mentally retarded blind children. Fifty-three special class teachers from twenty-nine residential schools provided data concerning 453 children.

Standard methods of descriptive analysis were applied to the collected data which were reported in tabular and anecdotal forms.

The principal results of the study indicated that

1. An increased number of residential schools for the visually impaired were accepting mentally retarded blind children.
2. A noticeable increase was reported in the incidence of mental retardation among blind children in residential schools.
3. Over two thirds of the schools conducted special classes for mentally retarded blind children.
4. Mental retardation rather than blindness was considered the primary disability in the special classes.
5. Mentally retarded blind children and mentally retarded partially seeing children were grouped together for instructional purposes in three fourths of the special classes.
6. Curriculum for the mentally retarded blind were primarily eclectic, drawing from content in mental retardation and blindness. Educational objectives did not appear to be clearly defined for these classes.

7. The average number of presumptive diagnoses for children in special classes was 3.2 disabilities per child.

8. There were more partially seeing children with severe concomitant disabilities than there were mentally retarded blind children with severe concomitant disabilities in special classes.

9. Special class teachers in residential schools tended to be reasonably well trained, although they reflected a concern for more precise professional training.

10. Various definitions of mental retardation were used in the residential schools. A definition did not exist that was mutually acceptable to all residential school administrators.

11. Educators in residential schools registered some reservations about classifying blind children as mentally retarded. Most frequently mentioned reasons for the reservations were insufficient knowledge concerning the impact of sensory deprivation on the learner and the lack of reliable measurement instruments.

12. Special classes for the mentally retarded blind were in reality classes for the multiply disabled rather than classes for a particular diad of disability.

13. Although the needs of children with multiple disabilities were not being completely met, educators in some residential schools were exercising leadership in providing reasonable exploratory attempts to improve the quantity and quality of educational services for such children.

14. School administrators recognized that there was an increasing demand for residential schools to provide more specialized services for multiply disabled children. Educators of residential schools recognized the changing character of their pupil population and as a group appeared willing to accept the challenge of providing specialized services to multiply disabled blind children.

15. Residential school administrators recognized that the development of optimum provisions for multiply disabled blind children was a cooperative process involving special programs in public schools and programs in residential schools for the mentally retarded.*

One of the significant results of Wolf's study shows that 35 per cent of the mentally retarded blind children in special classes had only two disabilities and 65 per cent had three or more disabilities. Thirty-one per cent had three disabilities, 20 per cent had four disabilities, 6 per cent had five disabilities, and 5 per cent had six or more disabilities (Table 1).

Table 2 shows that blind, mentally retarded children and partially seeing

---

* Reprinted by permission from American Foundation for the Blind, 1967.

TABLE 1

FREQUENCY OF CONCOMITANT PRESUMPTIVELY DIAGNOSED DISABILITIES
AMONG MENTALLY RETARDED BLIND CHILDREN

Number of Disabilities Per Child	Number of Children with Disabilities	Per Cent of Children
2	160	35.2
3	144	31.6
4	93	20.4
5	31	6.8
6	13	2.8
7	9	1.9
8	2	0.4
9	1	0.2

mentally retarded children had approximately the same average number of additional disabilities: 3.12 presumptively diagnosed disabilities per blind child, and 3.32 presumptively diagnosed disabilities per partially-seeing child. The average for all children was 3.17 different presumptively diagnosed disabilities per child.

Personality defects and speech defects were the most frequently occurring disabilities. Other conditions such as brain injury, asthma, kidney dis-

TABLE 2

FREQUENCY OF CONCOMITANT CONDITIONS AMONG BLIND AND PARTIALLY
SEEING CHILDREN IN CLASSES FOR THE MENTALLY RETARDED
BLIND IN RESIDENTIAL SCHOOLS

Disabilities	Blind Children (N = 310)		Partially Seeing Children (N = 143)		Total (N = 453)	
	Number	Per Cent	Number	Per Cent	Number	Per Cent
Blind	310	100.0	0	0.0	310	68.4
Partially seeing	0	0.0	143	100.0	143	31.6
Mentally retarded	310	100.0	143	100.0	453	100.0
Cerebral palsy	13	4.1	13	9.0	26	5.7
Cleft palate-lip	4	1.0	0	0.0	4	0.2
Epilepsy	27	8.7	16	11.1	43	9.4
Hearing defect	27	8.7	13	9.0	40	8.8
Orthodontic defect	21	6.7	18	12.5	39	8.6
Orthopedic defect	26	8.3	13	9.0	39	8.6
Personality defect	94	30.3	44	30.7	138	30.4
Speech defect	83	26.7	48	33.5	131	28.9
Cosmetic defect	21	6.7	8	5.5	29	6.4
Other defect	32	10.3	17	11.8	49	10.8
Total	968		476		1,444	

Average number of presumptively diagnosed conditions: 3.18
Per blind child: 3.12
Per partially seeing child: 3.32

orders, heart conditions, bone cancer, and diabetes were reported for 11 per cent of the children. Approximately the same percentage of mentally retarded blind children were reported to have epilepsy, hearing defects, orthodontic defects, and orthopedic defects. The 453 children had 104 different combinations of concomitant disabilities.[1129] [(p.34)]

Wolf's results indicate that it is not practical to refer to a specific diad as "the mentally retarded blind." In reality, we are talking about a blind child with several concomitant or coincidental disabilities. Educators of residential schools for the visually impaired recognize the changing character of their pupil population and as a group appear willing to accept the challenge of providing specialized services to multiply disabled blind children.

The results of Dauwalder's study emphasize the changing demands that are being made on residential schools for the visually impaired and the adaptations that will be necessary in the near future. Dauwalder found that the majority of state departments of education anticipated that total enrollments in programs for the blind will continue to increase slightly.

> However, the percentage increase will be material in the multihandicapped group while an actual decrease will probably occur in the enrollment of blind and visually impaired students who do not have other physical or mental disabilities. This will probably result in a further increase in the percentage of enrollment in residential schools, which are more able to handle the student population of the future and increasingly multihandicapped individuals.[234] [(p.11)]

Frampton and Kerney in an analysis of the history, contributions, and future of the residential schools for the blind apply the following measures as a standard of social utility to institutions for the blind: (1) time and endurance, (2) social adaptation, (3) demand, and (4) product. The authors make the following point in regards to social adaptation:

> As an organization it has changed with the changing demands of the whole social structure. . . . Few social investigations can point to any item of social importance in the long history of the residential school for the blind which has remained static long enough seriously to affect the continuing high-quality service to the blind child through the passing decades. As in all social organizations, necessary changes are sometimes delayed, sometimes not as completely realized in action as their proponents would have wished. But the end-result has been a steady, continuously vital, living social organization, alert and sensitive to the specific needs of its clients in its generation, a social organism destined to continue as long as this fundamental law of survival is observed in theory and practice.[346] [(p.36)]

The future of residential schools for the visually impaired is closely related to program development for blind children with additional handicaps. Unquestionably, expanded services and research for multiply disabled blind children is indicated and desperately needed.

Multiple Disabilities with Mental Retardation

Mental retardation is one of the most prevalent handicapping conditions found in children with multiple disabilities. Studies cited in this chapter indicate that mental retardation occurs in approximately three fourths of cerebral palsy children, one fourth of blind children, and one fourth of deaf children. The review of the literature also reveals a lack of clarity in definitions and confusion in criteria of mental retardation. Undoubtedly, this confusion contributes to problems of diagnoses of mental retardation and the establishment of reliable incidence and prevalence figures. The diversity of definitions of *mental retardation* provides substances to Cantor's observation that "Mental retardation, like any other abstract concept in science, has as many meanings as there are people willing to give it different meanings."[158(p.954)]

Mentally retarded children present a heterogeneous group of symptoms, and it is difficult to include mild to severe cases under the same rubric. In a school setting, the mild cases are usually a statistical deviation from a psychometric norm while many of the moderate and most of the severe cases represent a clinical, behavioral symptom-complex. Although both groups are considered mentally retarded at the present time, they require distinctly different curricula and management modifications. There appears to be some need to again include in the concept of mental retardation the present status, previous status, and prospective status of the individual.[270]

Kuhlmann has written that "Many attempts have been made to define mental deficiency. Scientific literature offers but few instances, if any, in which a given field or object has been so frequently or so variously described."[623(p.206)]

Through the joint sponsorship of the United States Department of Health, Education, and Welfare and the American Association of Mental Deficiency (AAMD), a desperately needed terminology and classification manual on mental retardation was formulated. The manual was published in 1959.

As stated in the manual,

> Mental retardation refers to subaverage general intellectual functioning which originates during the developmental period and is associated with impairment in adaptive behavior.[465(p.111)]

This definition places complete emphasis on the present level of functioning of the individual and in no way implies incurability. In this concept of mental retardation, the individual must meet the dual criteria of reduced intellectual functioning and impaired social adaptation.

Subaverage general intellectual functioning is defined as "performance greater than one standard deviation below the mean of the standardization sample on a general test of intelligence." On the Arthur Point Scale of Performance Tests (Form I), for example, minus one standard deviation to minus two standard deviations is referred to as "Borderline Retardation of Measured Intelligence." This is a purely arbitrary criterion. Therefore, subaverage psychometric scores are inadequate as the sole criterion of mental retardation since we would find individuals below the cut-off score whose social adaptation is adequate and individuals above the cut-off score whose social adaptation is inadequate. This would be true regardless of what test score is selected as the cut-off point.

Heber defines impairment in adaptive behavior as "the effectiveness of the individual in adopting to the natural and social demands of his environment." Impaired adaptive behavior may be reflected in reduced maturation, learning, and/or social adjustment. These three aspects of adaptation are of different importance as qualifying conditions of mental retardation for different age groups. Impairment in learning, for example, is usually most manifest at school age and in the school situation.

The Measured Intelligence Dimension is intended for the classification of the *current* intellectual functioning of the individual and *in no way* reflects any inference of potential or absolute level of intelligence. In some instances, a person may meet the criteria of mental retardation at one age and not at another, particularly at the borderline level. This definition indicates that mental retardation is now viewed as a reversible condition, as opposed to the classical and historical concept of "once mentally retarded, always mentally retarded."

Although the AAMD definition of *mental retardation* has been widely adopted, there has been growing dissatisfaction with it; and questions have been raised concerning its adequacy. Garfield and Wittson challenged certain sections of the manual following its publication.[375] These authors believe that the *Manual on Terminology and Classification in Mental Retardation* is not sufficiently clear or detailed. Garfield and Wittson object to the extension of the development period to sixteen years of age and think that there are some dangers in the concept of subaverage intelligence as used in the definition. Defining *mental retardation* as beginning at just one standard deviation below the mean seems to extend the concept much further than has been the case traditionally. "While the manual indicates that such subaverage functioning must be manifested in some maladaptive behavior, it still offers potentially too wide a range for error."[375 (p.953)]

Cantor in defending the AAMD definition may have inadvertently provided a possible explanation as to why one standard deviation below the mean was used in the AAMD definition instead of the more traditional two standard deviations. In discussing the concept of incurability, Cantor states,

> I direct their [Garfield and Wittson] attention to inferences made by the layman—particularly the layman as taxpayer and legislator. If such individuals are given to understand that mental retardation is "incurable," by definition, what will their inference be? The answer can be found by examining the starkly inadequate programs of institutions for retarded in all but a few of the more progressive states.[159]

Level V in the manual is designated as borderline retardation but is included as a specific category of mental retardation. Level V which includes those individuals who exceed one standard deviation below the mean to two standard deviations below the mean usually include about four times as many individuals in the general population as would be found in the other four levels combined. Thus, the AAMD definition offers the possibility of greatly increasing the number of mentally retarded individuals in the population. There is some speculation that as I.Q. level increases so does the number of mentally retarded workers in skilled occupations. Using one standard deviation below the mean includes more individuals who might be successfully "cured" of mental retardation than would be possible if two standard deviations below the mean were used.

Dunn has recognized the potential in the AAMD definition and has indicated that as far as the schools are concerned, a pupil is identified as mentally retarded when he is both low in measured intelligence and impaired in learning ability. If I.Q. scores were used as the single criterion, about 16 per cent of the population would be more than one standard deviation below the mean and would have to be classified as mentally retarded. "While only 2 to 3 per cent have been considered educable mentally retarded for school purposes to date, this number may need to include nearly all of the 16 per cent in the future."[290 (p. 56)]

Yepsen completed a study of more than a hundred criteria and descriptions of mental retardation which had appeared in the literature and concluded that none actually defined mental retardation. All the definitions were descriptive of the results of mental retardation. Yepsen stated the following:

> A satisfactory definition of *mental deficiency* sponsored by the American Association of Mental Deficiency would do much toward cleaning up many of the problems from the social, educational, legal, and research points of view and, in the end, benefit the individual and society.[1154 (p. 200)]

With the confusion that still exists concerning the definition of mental retardation, the search for an acceptable definition continues to be a fertile field for study. Only through the standardization of nomenclature will it be possible to accurately determine the extent of mental retardation in multiply handicapped children.

Even with the limitations imposed by varying definitions and criteria of mental retardation, a number of investigators have found that mentally retarded children frequently have associated handicaps. For example, as early as 1937, Goldwasser found in a study of 900 mentally retarded school children that 756 had one or more physical defects. An investigation by Lapage, also reported in the Goldwasser study, indicated that 90 per cent of mentally retarded children had physical defects of some kind and that 25 per cent had three defects in addition to mental retardation.[402]

A census conducted in Onondaga County, New York of children referred because of a presumptive diagnosis of mental retardation found accompanying disabilities in one third of the mentally retarded children enumerated.[823]

Beck studied the incidence of brain injury among educable mentally retarded children in public school classes and found 60 to 70 per cent of these students had some neurological damage.[79]

Blatt compared mentally retarded pupils in a special class with mentally retarded children in regular classes and found that the number of disabilities in special class children average 1.55, while those in regular classes averaged 1.08.[109]

It seems reasonable to assume that approximately one fourth to one half of all mentally retarded children can also be considered multiply handicapped.

SUMMARY

The educational problem presented by children who have multiple disabilities is as old as man's attempt to provide services for exceptional children. Current interest in multiple disabilities is stimulated by the increased number of such children in the population. These children present complex management problems to staff members responsible for educational planning in a wide variety of educational and training centers. A review of related research from epidemiological surveys and other sources on multiple disabilities reveal the following:

1. Lack of a theoretical concept concerning multiple disabilities;
2. Confusion and lack of agreement on definitions, classifications, and terminology;
3. Inadequacy of a rationale by investigators in assigning priority to a disability;
4. Conflicting viewpoints concerning which facilities are most appropriate and the extent and availability of such facilities;

5. Inconsistencies in reported incidence and prevalence.
6. Lack of a precise methodology for teaching children with multiple disabilities;
7. The need for additional research on any or all of these findings.[1132]

Chapter 2

The Increasing Challenge of Handicapped Children

R. S. ILLINGWORTH

NOW that the United States is showing a welcome interest in the problem of mental retardation, as evidenced by the Report of the President's Panel,[894] the President's statement to Congress, and the "Five Years of Progress" of the Collaborative Perinatal Research Project, it is important to direct attention to the fact that the number of handicapped children is ever increasing. Very little has been written about this.

One obvious reason for the mounting number of handicapped children is the phenomenon of the *Bulge,* to use a British term, denoting the increase of the birth rate after the war. In the United States, there were approximately one million more births in 1962 than in 1952. It is usually estimated that about 2 per cent of children are found at birth to be handicapped, and that the figure rises to about 4 per cent by the age of five. If the figure were 2 per cent, this would represent an increase of at least 20,000 handicapped children, if the proportion of handicapped children were static. In the United States, with slightly over four million births per year, the number of handicapped children born will be approximately 80,000. In England and Wales, with about 850,000 births per year, the corresponding figure will be 17,000.

But, apart altogether from the increased birth rate, the relative number of handicapped children has increased considerably as well. The reasons are several.

In the first place, the care of premature babies has improved greatly, with a much higher survival rate. Far more of the smaller premature babies are being saved now than was the case twenty years ago. But unfortunately the incidence of abnormalities in small premature babies is high. Drillien[284] found that 22 per cent of 92 babies weighing 3 lb. or less at birth had major physical handicaps. Lubchenco *et al.*[684] studied 63 children who had weighed 1,500 gm. (3 lb. 4) or less at birth, and found that 68 per cent had visual or neurologic handicaps. Twenty-five out of 60 had an I.Q. score of less than 90. Twenty-two out of 63 were spastic. And, as our methods of treating the respiratory distress syndrome improve, the number of small premature babies saved will rise still more.

Irradiation of mothers during pregnancy is thought to have increased the number of handicapped children born. The effect of gross irradiation at Hiroshima and Nagasaki is now well known.

It is hoped that as a consequence of the thalidomide tragedy, drugs will no longer cause children to be handicapped.

The use of antibiotics, and advances in modern surgery, have been responsible for the survival of many children with other forms of handicaps. Carter[166] pointed out that in 1929 one in 4,000 ten-year-old children in the United Kingdom was a mongol, whereas in 1949 the figure was one in 2,000, and in 1960, one in 1,000. This increase in the survival rate of mongols is probably related largely to the use of antibiotics for their respiratory infections, and of surgery for their duodenal atresia and other anatomic abnormalities. Benda[81] showed that in New York State 19 children per 1,000 who in 1920 would have died from "congenital debility and malformations" survived in 1949.

There is no doubt that the life span of mental defectives is increasing considerably. The death rate of mentally defective children when admitted to institutions was extremely high some twenty years ago. The standards of institutional care have now improved, and there is an increasing tendency to look after mentally defective children at home. This has the inevitable effect of improving their chance of survival.

Modern treatment of hydrocephalus and meningomyelocele by means of the Spitz Holter valve and other technics has resulted in the salvage of large numbers of these children, for whom death was previously almost certain. Whereas formerly about 95 per cent died in the first two or three years, the mortality rate now of cases at the Children's Hospital, Sheffield, is only 30 to 35 per cent.[677] At this hospital, where we treat about 120 new cases each year, we forecast that of 265 surviving affected children seen in 1959 or since, 34 (13 per cent) will be ineducable, 53 (20 per cent) will have to be placed in schools for educationally subnormal children, and 171 (66 per cent) will need places in schools for children of normal intelligence —ordinary, residential, or special schools.

Apart from the effect of the increased birth rate, it is uncertain whether the frequency of children with hydrocephalus or meningomyeocele is increasing but it is known that there are remarkable geographic and seasonal variations in its incidence. For instance, the incidence of anencephaly is fifty times greater in Belfast than in Lyons.

Improved medical and surgical care of many other conditions has led to the survival of children with many other handicaps. These include children with congenital heart disease, cystic fibrosis of the pancreas, phenylketonuria and other metabolic defects (such as galactosemia, nephrogenic diabetes

Reprinted from *Clinical Pediatrics*, 3:189-191, April, 1964. Copyright 1964 by J. P. Lippincott Company.

insipidus, leucinosis, and hypercalcemia), and infants of diabetic mothers or children with diabetes. Heart surgery saves children with congenital heart disease who would otherwise certainly die: antibiotics and other treatment of cystic fibrosis of the pancreas prolongs life in many; surgical treatment of meconeum ileus saves infants who otherwise would die in the newborn period. Medical treatment of the metabolic conditions, apart from preventing mental subnormality, prolongs life, but the basic handicap usually persists. Improved pediatric diagnosis has led to more prompt diagnosis and treatment of pyogenic meningitis in infancy; this disease used to be almost invariably fatal, but now most affected infants survive. Regrettably, the incidence of mental and psychologic sequelae is fairly high.

It should be noted that the salvaging of children with the above conditions not only leads to an increased number of handicapped children of school age. These conditions are mostly of genetic origin, and in many instances their survival means that in adulthood when they reach the childbearing age, they will be more likely than others to have children affected with the same disorders that they themselves have.

It is also true that the incidence of some handicaps has decreased. Kernicterus is now preventable by the use of replacement transfusion for hemolytic disease and for the hyperbilirubinemia of prematurity. Some of the causes of hyperbilirubinemia have been removed with advances in knowledge; such causes include the excessive dose of vitamin K in the newborn, and the use of drugs such as sulfonamides which interfere with the proteinbinding of bilirubin. Certain forms of mental subnormality secondary to metabolic defects can now be prevented: they include phenylketonuria, hypercalcemia, hypoparathyroidism, hypoglycemia, galactosemia, and nephrogenic diabetes insipidus. Improved social conditions, antibiotics, and preventive measures have greatly reduced the incidence of rheumatic fever, tuberculosis, and nephritis. For instance, a survey of the incidence of five handicapping conditions in the Children's Hospital, Sheffield, over a period of years gives these figures:

		New Outpatients Total
Rheumatic fever	1910	234
	1948	137
	1960	1
Nephritis	1948	38
	1960	2
Syphilis	1924	130
	1959-60	0
Bronchiectasis	1947	74
	1948	52
	1960	6
		All Admissions
Tuberculosis	1909	44.8%
	1948	4.6%
	1960	0.10%

In contradistinction to the above figures, there was an enormous increase in the total number of new out-patients attending during this period. Unfortunately the increase in the number of handicaps is far greater than the decrease in certain other types of handicap.[506]

The challenge of the increasing number of physically handicapped children is not merely one of numbers. There is the problem of the time which they take and the expense of treating them. Every child with cerebral palsy at the Cerebral Palsy Centre, Sheffield, is examined and assessed by two physicians, an orthopedic surgeon, an ophthalmologist, an otologist, physiotherapists, occupational therapists, speech therapists, a psychologist, and a social worker. Treatment is prolonged and unless there is a health service, as in England, the costs to the parents are extremely high.

Every child with hydrocephalus and meningomyelocele requires extensive investigation, including air encephalography and numerous surgical procedures. In the so-called developing countries, the pressure of urgent work is such that time and money cannot be devoted to such handicapped children. Elsewhere, the care of the handicapped child, ever increasing, has become a major part of the work of pediatricians and their associates.

It need hardly be added that it is our responsibility not only to care for handicapped children but to apply our thoughts to the prevention of handicaps. It would be far more profitable to prevent them than to treat them.

Chapter 3

Congenital Malformations
Clinical and Community Considerations

THEODORE H. INGALLS and MARCUS A. KLINGBERG

TWO of the most significant medical events of the century, the epidemic of post-rubella anomalies in Australia during 1940 and 1941 and the pandemic of thalidomide embryopathies in Europe and elsewhere during 1960 and 1961, have demonstrated clearly the importance of monitoring programs to record the occurrence of congenital malformations at group (for example, hospital) and community (especially city) levels. The principle of reporting malformations and utilizing the data for service programs or, better still, for prevention, is not new, but the methodical use of vital statistics in a scientifically constructed surveillance system is new. So also is the joint endeavor on the part of clinicians, public health workers and basic scientists to reconstruct an epidemiology of deformity on the basis of time, place, person distributions of malformations. A primary need has been for standardized methods of classifying and reporting congenital malformations. The purpose of this communication is to review some of the background of contemporary knowledge in the field, to examine principles governing a standardized classification and to reappraise some of the important clinical and epidemiologic contributions of the last two decades.

Two main sources exist for the reporting of deformities present at birth, the clinical protocols available through hospital record rooms and the vital records to be found in modern health departments. The two kinds of data are often treated as though they furnished the same statistical information, but they do not do so. On the contrary, each activity has both potentialities and limitations that make them distinct from each other and supplementary to each other as sources of information. In principle, the basic facts are straightforward enough, but in practice the distinctions between the two kinds of data have been neither clear nor simple and the data themselves have been fragmentary or altogether wanting. Nor is it warranted to separate the two methodologies sharply.

For example, the outlines of the outbreaks of post-rubella defects during 1939 and 1940 in Australia[420, 1048] and the thalidomide embryopathies in Germany in 1960 and 1961[643, 882, 1116] are nebulous for lack of good com-

---

Reprinted from *American Journal of Medical Science*, 249:316-344, March, 1965.

munity statistics. But this is not to gainsay the reality of those epidemics as implied by clinical observations made in those years. Initial information was necessarily derived in retrospect, for it was the first time the cause-and-effect observations had ever been made. In Australia during the early years of World War II, neither the community incidence of rubella-induced anomalies nor the clinical risks of maternal rubella could be established. Similarly, with thalidomide embryopathy in 1960, neither the community prevalence nor clinical risks could be appraised for lack of the needed parameters of measurement. Indeed, even today, prospective clinical studies of thalidomide ingestion in early pregnancy, except for the series of Mc-Bride,[693, 695] are virtually unknown. If the incidence of phocomelia had been a matter of record in the hospitals and city populations of Sydney, Australia or Hamburg, Germany in 1960 and 1961, the evidence that the deformity was occurring in epidemic proportions in those years would have been unmistakable within six months or a year of the time when the "epidemic" started and long before 5,000 deformed babies were born. With such considerations in mind, an attempt is made to point up differences between the monitoring of data on vital records of liveborn or stillborn babies, and the prospectively accumulated data recorded in the clinical protocols of children examined in both infancy and childhood, before proceeding to compare published results of different investigations.

The information to be gained from a monitoring program of birth certificates is altogether different from the kind of information that results when a series of suspect infants is examined on several occasions as the months go by or at necropsy if death intervenes. Among survivors, repeatedly examined, it is possible to establish functional status with respect to vision, hearing, locomotion, cerebral palsy, and mental retardation, epilepsy, and the like. When an infant dies, direct examination for visceral anomalies of the heart and kidneys is readily accomplished if necropsy is permitted. This is not possible in life.

Time and experience have demonstrated the inadequacy of reporting malformations as though they were manifestations of a single disease. Today we know that maternal rubella causes only a fraction of all cases of congenital heart disease, thalidomide ingestion only a fraction of all cases of phocomelia. Moreover, the facts emphasize the importance of recording and analyzing incidence by specific kinds of deformity: cataract, cleft palate, phocomelia, spina bifida, mongolism and so on.

METHODS OF STUDY
Definition and Classification

Gross defects and "monstrous" deformities have been recognized and described from ancient times. However, the evident need for a standardized classification of congenital malformations as the basis of a surveillance activity is of comparatively recent origin. Most definitions of *congenital malformations* do not differ materially from what is to be expected after consultation of Webster's Dictionary; *congenital* is defined as "existing at birth," "malformation" as "anomalous, abnormal, or wrong formation or structure." Thus, Stevenson described them for statistical purposes as macroscopic, anatomical developmental anomalies, recognized at birth or later or at postmortem examination, but before the child leaves the hospital.[1022] Similarly, McKeown and Record[710] interpret a *congenital abnormality* to be any microscopic or macroscopic structural abnormality attributable to faulty development present at birth. There would appear to be little opportunity for semantic confusion were it not for the insertion into this category of "inborn errors of metabolism" by some, and for the fact that by no means all gross congenital malformations and hardly any microscopic malformations are diagnosed by the time the birth certificate is filled out. Warkany and Kalter[1092] advocate that the term *congenital malformations* be used for gross structural defects present at birth and recommend that microscopic malformations, inborn errors of metabolism, or physiologic disturbances present at birth be covered by the wider term *congenital anomalies* and be listed to avoid confusion under special categories.

In principle, congenital malformations include visceral and hidden malformations. In practice, only the anomalies that are grossly visible at birth or identifiable in photographs and roentgenograms at that time are reported on birth certificates with anything approaching completeness. The number of reportable conditions is thus found to be limited to some fifty[518] to seventy-five.[813] The diagnosis of mongolism, for example, is manifest even in a photograph at birth although the clinical diagnosis is frequently deferred for months. The indications are that between 20 and 50 per cent of cases may be recorded on birth certificates and that the routine taking of photographs at birth (Figs. 3-1 and 3-2)

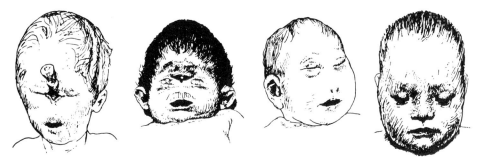

FIGURE 3-1. *Left to right:* Anophthalmia bordering on cyclopia; cyclopia bordering on cebocephaly; cebocephaly bordering on mongolism; mongolism.

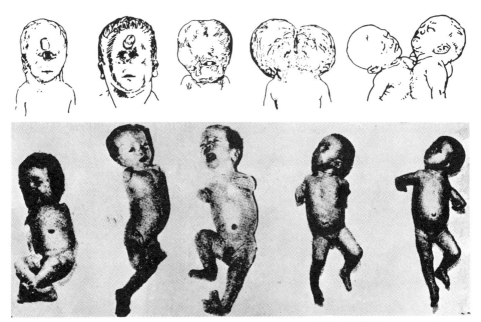

Figure 3-2. Gradations of deformity. *Top:* Cyclopia, cebocephaly and conjoined twins. *Bottom:* Ectromelia and phocomelia. From Pfeiffer, R.A.; Weicker, H., and Bachmann, H.D.: *Deutsch Med Wschr*, 88:1, 1963, by permission of the publisher.

would aid appreciably in both the areas of clinical diagnosis and reporting. On the other hand the accurate diagnosis and reporting on a large scale of visceral defects is not possible in liveborn infants.

An etiological classification of malformations, as is done for most infections of clinical importance, is seldom possible in the same sense that the rash of measles is synonymous with the infection of measles. The same developmental deformities can be produced by diverse agents and conversely, a single teratogenic agent may produce multiple defects when acting at a specific stage of embryonic or fetal development.[517] Even gross anatomical classification, however, presents some obstacles, since many variations and combinations and degrees of deformity may occur (Fig. 3-2); and the designated defect may refer to only one striking feature or a complex syndrome or association of "Synchronisms."[526] On the other hand, the occasional designation of etiology by the obstetrical attendant may be of use. Thus, the only case of thalidomide embryopathy encountered in Philadelphia from 1961 to 1963 was so designated on a birth certificate. Under the heading, "Complications of Pregnancy," the physician had noted "thalidomide ingestion in first trimester." Investigation, as will be brought out later, confirmed the notation.

No classification is wholly suitable for diagnostic, therapeutic, embryologic, metabolic, etiologic, and epidemiologic purposes. For example, relative to a proposed embryologic classification of limb deficiencies by somites of origin,[351] Smithells[1012] comments, "common sense suggests that it is better to call an absent fibula an absent fibula than 'complete intercalary fibular hemimelia.'" The common sense point of view is incontestable for reporting purposes. And yet in the interests of embryological understanding of a clinically manifest gradation of limb deficiencies varying all the way from partial to complete limb deficiencies,[430] Smithells' modification of the embryologic diagram (Fig. 3-3) of Frantz and O'Rahilly is very useful.

The inability to recognize and make satisfactory functional classifications at birth must be recognized. Mental retardation, epilepsy, cerebral palsy, blindness, and deafness take time to manifest themselves and take time for evaluation. Thus Jackson and Fisch[538] deferred final diagnosis of congenital deafness for as long as four years, during which time periodic examinations of hearing were made, before they were willing to give an empiric risk figure (30.4%) for congenital deafness following first trimester maternal rubella. Gross deformities on the other hand, anencephaly, a missing

		TRANSVERSE (-) Deficiency involves entire width of limb			LONGITUDINAL (/) Deficiency involves part of width of limb		
	Symbol	Name	Anatomy	Symbol	Name	Anatomy
TERMINAL (T) (No normal part distal to defect)	T-1	Amelia		T/1	Complete paraxial hemimelia	
	T-2	Hemimelia		T/2	Incomplete paraxial hemimelia	
	T-3	Partial hemimelia				
	T-4	Acheiria/Apodia		T/3	Partial adactylia	
	T-5	Complete adactylia		T/4	Partial aphalangia	
	T-6	Complete aphalangia				
INTERCALARY (I) (Normal part distal to defect)	I-1	Complete phocomelia		I/1	Complete paraxial hemimelia	
	I-2	Proximal phocomelia		I/2	Incomplete paraxial hemimelia	
				I/3	Partial adactylia	
	I-3	Distal phocomelia		I/4	Partial aphalangia	

FIGURE 3-3. Classification of Congenital Limb Deficiencies. From Smithells, R.W.[1012] (after Frantz, C.H. and O'Rahilly, R.). Reprinted by permission of *Developmental Medicine and Child Neurology.*

arm or finger, duplication of a hand, or fused fingers, or a cleft lip, such deformities can be identified promptly by the attendant, the nurse, the mother herself.

The basis of a standardized classification of these conditions at birth is a limitation of concern to rapidly diagnosed, readily named conditions which (at least one of them for each malformed infant) can be recorded and reported with relative completeness in the neonatal period. Anencephalus, spina bifida, cleft lip, and phocomelia are representative of such conditions. Tracheoesophageal fistula and mongolism may not be diagnosed at birth but they are always congenital and when confirmed the diagnosis can be restored to appropriate documents. Finally, it is hardly realistic to expect to obtain accurate information about congenital heart disease or obscure renal anomalies in the neonatal period.

Once classified, both primary and associated defects can be punched, coded, and processed by conventional statistical methods as has been done for some years by many groups of investigators.* A technical measure that that increases effective liaison with a city's system of reporting births and saves much time in the processing of data is to use photostats of birth and death certificates for case-finding and to convert them directly into code sheets by stamping them on their margins with a rubber code stamp.

Clinical Reports and Registries

In many countries, particularly in the Scandinavian countries, registries recording congenital malformations have had a long and honorable place in clinical practice and in community research. In Denmark, for example, the University Institute for Human Genetics has for many years maintained a registry of congenital defects and many of the resulting studies have been submitted as doctoral theses and then published as comprehensive, beautifully documented and illustrated monographs, usually two hundred to four hundred pages in length, and written in English. To cite in order of publication but four of these studies that have been published since 1940 and which still provide excellent factual background for specified kinds of congenital malformations, there are: in 1941 "Chondrodystrophic Dwarfs in Denmark" by Mørch,[793] in 1942 Fogh-Andersen's classical study of "Inheritance of Harelip and Cleft Palate";[340] the 1949 prethalidomide publication "Congenital Deformities of the Upper Extremities"[104] and the 1953 "pretrisomy" monograph, "Mongolism" by Øster.[831] Many other such works could be cited but, in a review article such as this, one can do no more than list a few by way of illustration.

---

* References 8, 58, 122, 314, 352, 393, 518, 634, 728, 700, 813, 889, 905, 907, 1003, 1017, 1022.

The most significant advance in understanding congenital malformations during the whole decade in which three of these four studies were
done is that the rubella episode had introduced a new "environmental"
dimension to studies of this kind. The impact of the new discovery was
not immediately noticeable, but slowly during the decade a new interest
in the relation of maternal health in pregnancy to fetal defects, first discernible at birth, manifested itself in an increasingly quantitative and objective approach to congenital malformations. Increasing attention was
given to determining the natural occurrence of deformity in groups and in
populations, and increased attention was given to the pregnancy preceding
the birth of an abnormal child.

In 1950, Stevenson, Worcester and Rice[1024, 1148] reviewed the obstetrical
and pediatric records of all mothers who gave birth to (677) congenitally
malformed infants, live or stillborn in the Boston Lying-in-Hospital during
the years 1930 to 1941. Malformed infants accounted for 15.9 per cent of
the total stillbirths and 13.2 per cent of neonatal deaths. Thirty-two per
cent of the latter group had defects referable to the cardiovascular system.
Twinning occurred among malformed infants with twice the expected
frequency in this series of hospital births and hydramnios occurred in 15
per cent of these pregnancies. Nearly 15 per cent of mothers vomited with
sufficient frequency to merit note of it in their records; 17 per cent of
mothers bearing infants with congenital heart disease were classified as
toxemic, and 25 per cent of mothers of infants with multiple malformations
gave a history of threatened abortions. Thirty-nine per cent of the mothers had hemoglobin levels below 75 per cent. No attempt was made to
follow the malformed babies as a cohort after they were discharged from
the hospital.

In 1950, McIntosh and his coworkers[708] undertook to compile and maintain a registry of all newborn infants delivered on the obstetrical service
of a large New York City hospital. They reported 433 (7.5%) deformed
infants among 6,053 total deliveries. Among 5,530 liveborn babies (neonatal deaths were included) they had 386 malformed babies (7.0%).
They derived their estimate of incidence from repeated physical examinations carried out at birth, at 6 and 12 months of age. Diagnostic procedures
included head and chest radiography and ophthalmoscopy of all surviving
babies. The percentage of necropsies performed on stillborn and neonatal
deaths was over 85 per cent. The series of McIntosh and his colleagues also
includes anomalies of function, such as mental deficiency and nystagmus.
When malformations diagnosed at birth were compared with those revealed by follow-up studies, the incidence rose: 43.2 per cent were detected
at birth, 38.7 per cent after 6 months, and the rest at one year of age.

In another cohort study performed by Kleinman *et al.*,[598] the incidence of

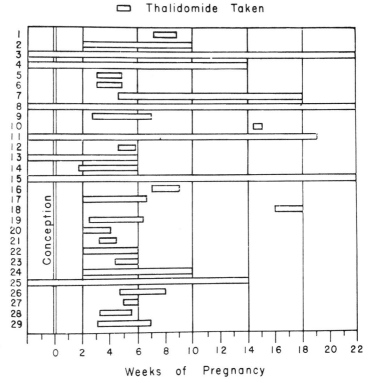

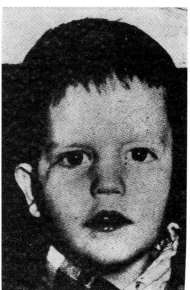

FIGURE 3-4. *Top:* Thalidomide ingestion by week of pregnancy—29 mothers of deformed babies, Netherlands, 1962.[417] *Bottom:* Anotia following ingestion of thalidomide by mother in the fourth week of pregnancy.

deformities also rose steeply with repeated examinations performed at one year of age: 40 per cent of anomalies were diagnosed at birth and 60 per cent within one year. Total incidence rate was 41.4 per 1,000 livebirths (419 malformations found in 10,109 live births). McKeown and Record[710] in Birmingham, England, followed a series of babies for five years after birth, but in their series the follow-up increase was smaller: 17.3 malformed infants per 1,000 births were identified within two weeks after delivery, as compared with an estimated 23.1 after five years. They included only those defects which are grossly visible.

Although such studies have not as yet furnished the lightning flashes of insight that come out of a naturally occurring rubella or thalidomide epidemic, they are useful parts of the background against which the meaning of dramatic advances is to be appraised and doubtless extended. Moreover, the potentiality of the clinical registry is as much for the clarification of environmental causes of congenital malformations as it is for the clarification of genetic and maternal environmental factors acting adversely on the conceptus to induce congenital malformation. The great potentiality of the registry is in the maintenance of continuity of gynecologic, obstetric, and pediatric protocols between maternal and child health. This dual role is inherent in the original Australian rubella observations[420, 1048] and is demonstrable by reference to the observations on the action of thalidomide of Lenz and Knapp,[643] Pfeiffer and Kosenow[882] and Bekker and Van Duyne[80] (Fig. 3-4). Nor is there necessarily any clear-cut dichotomy between the registry and the surveillance system, especially if the registry is based on the majority of births within the community.[632, 633]

Community Surveillance

Since 1950, McKeown and his colleagues have developed a surveillance program as indicated earlier in this review based on the natural occurrence of congenital malformations in the vicinity of Birmingham, England. This kind of activity at community levels has come into special prominence since 1960 with the impetus provided by the thalidomide episode. In the United States, such monitoring programs have their basis in vital documents. In the Birmingham program, a special public health record card for notification of congenital malformations observed soon after birth (live and stillbirths) is completed by hospitals, district midwives, or health visitors. Recently Leck[632] has summarized data on malformations relating to 147,500 Birmingham children born in the period 1957 to 1963. The contribution is especially useful as one by which to measure observed increases, of thalidomide embryopathies, for example, against background expectancies. No type of malformation showed significant increase extending over the whole

period, although anencephalus became less common and the incidence of
amelia and phocomelia rose and fell in 1961 and 1962.[633] An influenza epidemic in 1961-1962 was followed by an increase, comparable to those observed previously, in the combined incidence of cleft lip, esophageal atresia, anal atresia and exomphalos.

The "Liverpool Congenital Abnormalities Registry" is another model
community surveillance system in England started in 1960.[1012] Notification
of congenital malformations detected within a week after birth is voluntary and the information regarding congenital anomalies comes from and
depends upon cooperation of various sources: maternity units, pathological
departments (for postmortem studies of stillbirths and neonatal deaths),
special and hospital clinics, infant welfare clinics, midwives (for babies
born at home) and pediatricians. The population and annual births covered
represent about 2 per cent of the total for England and Wales. One of the
most interesting accomplishments of surveillance in the Liverpool area was
the quantitation of congenital limb and ear defects of the types often caused
by thalidomide in babies born to mothers residing in that area in 1960 and

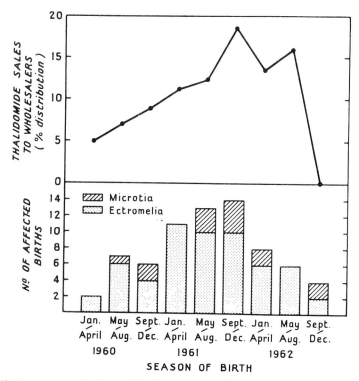

FIGURE 3-5. Frequency of affected births in Birmingham, Liverpool, and Bootle, compared with the output of thalidomide to local wholesalers nine months earlier. From
Smithells, R.W., and Leck, I.[1010]

1962.[1010] The frequency of these malformations rose to a peak in late 1961 and rapidly subsided (Fig. 3-5) to rare sporadic cases after thalidomide sales ceased in 1962.

Surveillance involves, in addition to those considerations of classification described in the preceding pages, relatively prompt (that is, monthly, or at least, quarterly) processing of reported data and community-wide coverage. Also, if a large hospital is engaged in the clinical trial of an untried drug, the hospital itself becomes the universe at risk for the appraisal of that drug's teratogenicity[41, 419] or lack of it. Indeed, this is the significance of the therapeutic trial of thalidomide for morning sickness at the Women's Hospital of Sydney, Australia, in 1959.[693] Again, it is not rewarding to draw too fine a line between the clinical group and the community itself, especially when the surveillance system is based on a previously operating registry. Only a few selected programs are mentioned here, those already cited in the cities of Birmingham and Liverpool in England, New York,[314] and Philadelphia[518] in this country. Reference is also made to the reporting systems in larger areas, New York State,[766] South Sweden,[121] West Germany[764] and the Netherlands.[80] The surveillance systems of the state of New York and the city of Philadelphia, Pennsylvania, are singled out in order to exemplify patterns that already have developed or doubtless will develop at state and city levels in this country where such activities are mainly based upon the reporting of congenital malformations on birth or infant death certificates.

Birth and stillbirth certificates filed at the New York State Department of Health have contained an entry for reporting congenital malformations since 1940. Analysis of the data, however, was sporadic and no routine or continuous appraisal had been made until May, 1962, when the department established a surveillance system for monitoring of malformations by monthly periods (Fig. 3-6). No less than eighty-four malformations are reportable, including six specified congenital heart and four genitourinary defects. Only two of these ten conditions (hypospadias and extrophy of the bladder) are easily detected by gross inspection of a liveborn baby at birth.[766] Some 99.4 per cent of births in upstate New York take place in hospitals and more than 90 per cent of the birth certificates are completed with a positive or negative response. Since the number of births show only minor fluctuations by month, a numerator without a denominator is accepted for surveillance purposes, thus sidestepping the almost insuperable task of having to determine rates each month. As of 1963, no malformations had been found to show a sustained increase beyond expectancy and the total malformation rate had fluctuated mildly between one and two per 1,000 live births for years.

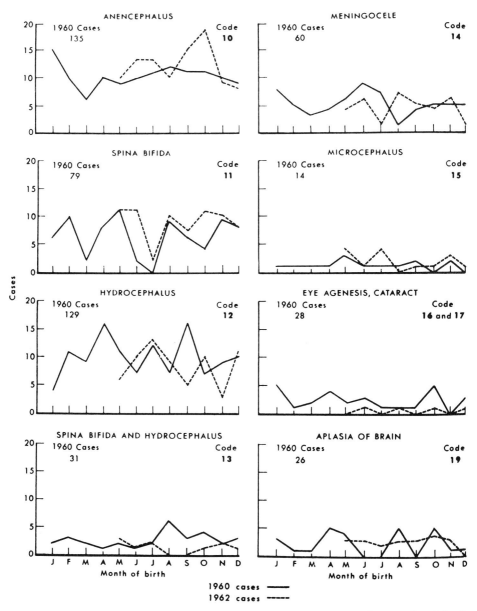

FIGURE 3-6. Congenital malformations of the central nervous system by months of birth in New York State, 1960 to 1962.[766]

Regional data from other states and abroad show comparable rates. In the Commonwealth of Pennsylvania, Murphy,[794] using observations recorded on death certificates, estimated that the frequency of gross congenital malformations in the Philadelphia area during the years 1929 to 1933 was 4.7 per 1,000 live births, or about one in 213. Ivy[536] in a more recent study over a five year period (1951 to 1955) of congenital anomalies recorded on live birth certificates in the Commonwealth of Pennsylvania, found a frequency of about 8.5 deformities per 1,000 live births. In Victoria, Australia, 15 per 1,000 of all infants born have a gross congenital malformation;[889] Böök in Sweden[121] and Neel[814] in Japan estimate the incidence of deformities recognizable soon after birth as 13.5 per 1,000. No attempt is made here to discuss differences or ascribe great meaning to such overall figures. Both the rubella and the thalidomide episode indicate that epidemiologic analysis is likely to be more fruitful when restricted to particular deformities made in well-defined regions with the data processed at quarterly, monthly, or even weekly intervals.

In Philadelphia, city-wide surveillance of the occurrence of congenital abnormalities since January 1, 1961, has been undertaken in cooperation with Dr. F. Herbert Colwell, Director of the Division of Statistics and Research of the Department of Public Health. Emphasis was placed on the limitation and objective classification of data, on processing methods, and on standardization of results. The Division provided us with photostatic copies of records needed for study and analysis. Coding of recorded malformations is made, as previously mentioned, upon the same sheet using a rubber stamp. The original photostat thus assumes the place of notification, work sheet, and code card. Another rubber stamp should be designed to present an abbreviated clinical protocol describing maternal health at the beginning and during the first two months of pregnancy. It is hardly possible in city clinics to initiate needed analyses of early pregnancy in women most of whom will not even report to an obstetrical clinic until they are more than halfway through pregnancy. The challenge is one for obstetricians who will be following selected patients, almost from conception.

Our own grouping and classification of congenital malformations has been described elsewhere.[518] The classification is much the same as that proposed for the Eighth Revision of the International Classification of Diseases and approximates those used by the New York State Department of Health[766] and the Liverpool Registry in England.[1011] The list of malformations, however, is sharply limited to gross deformities that can be diagnosed at birth by external inspection or at death by necropsy. Most can be seen at a glance or can be instantaneously recorded in a photograph (Figs. 3-1 and 3-2). Some, such as mongolism, may go undiagnosed for some weeks but they are potentially recognizable and can be photo-

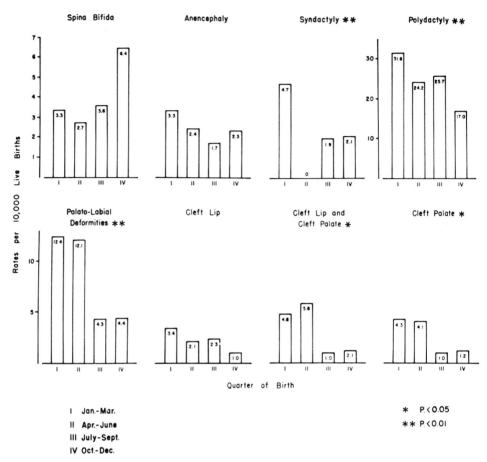

FIGURE 3-7. Selected malformations per 10,000 live births by quartile of birth, Philadelphia, Pennsylvania, 1961 to 1963.

graphed. Routine photography could play a much needed role in documenting the nature of the primary and associated defects. It would have the added advantage of standardizing nomenclature in different countries and languages, permitting, for example, direct comparisons of data obtained in Philadelphia, Pennsylvania, with observations made in foreign cities; for example, in Tel Aviv, Israel, Lima, Peru, or Nagoya, Japan.

From the processed data we are able to determine such features as the background frequency of selected deformities and associated malformations in the community, their seasonal fluctuation, their epidemic occurrence, their geographical distribution (health district) within the city, sex and plurality of birth, correlation between deformities and race, and other parameters (Figs. 3-7 and 3-8).

During the three-year period 1961-1963, 1,183 malformed infants were reported among 131,000 live births, a prevalence of about 9 malformed babies per 1,000 live births. There is little doubt that the low rate reflects gross under-reporting. Indeed, in comparing the recording of selected anomalies on birth certificates with those described in hospital records, Babbott and Ingalls[58] found that only 63 per cent of infants born with anencephalus, spina bifida, mongolism, cleft lip and palate and tracheoesophageal fistula were so recorded on birth certificates. Nearly half of these malformations (4.05 per 1,000 live births) were for bone and joint deformities and of these more than half (1.91 per 1,000 live births) were cases of polydactyly. In Ivy's report the incidence of malformations of the extremities on a statewide basis was only 2.9 per 1,000 live births; this difference is doubtless due, in part at least, to the higher percentage of nonwhites among Philadelphia residents, than in the state as a whole.

Among the more striking findings were significant racial differences for selected malformations as shown in Fig. 3-8. Mongolism, cleft lip and palate were reported far more frequently in white populations, whereas omphalocele and polydactyly occurred with greater frequency among nonwhites. The graph seems to present true racial differences. One such factor could be the difference known to exist between the races as regards frequency of sickle cell anemia. Harris and his colleagues have recorded the association of three cases of congenital heart disease among seventy patients with homozygous S disease. The finding warrants further study as a maternal factor.[443]

In any region as small as a city the identification of an outbreak poses a difficulty. The recognition of thalidomide embryopathy in Liverpool, England, or Hamburg, Germany, is not difficult in retrospect. However, the identification of a small cluster as of environmental, genetic or chance origin is indeed difficult. For example, spina bifida is seen in about 5 per 10,000 live births in Philadelphia; and yet five patients with the malformation were born within four days of each other in October, 1962. The circumstance could be meaningful as a point epidemic involving five people, or it could be as fortuitous as the chances of five persons at a cocktail party discovering that they had been born within four days of each other. In general the numbers, which are inconsequential from a statistical point of view, approximate a base line of expectancy. When it has been possible to demonstrate significance in relation to a teratogenic agent, this has involved the clustering of rarely seen specific deformities rather than the occurrence of "congenital anomalies" of all sorts in epidemic proportions. For example, experience with post rubella cataract and post thalidomide phocomelia illustrates conclusively the rationale of grouping different kinds of anomalies into appropriate gradations, categories and constellations. Before proceeding to examine some of these categories, a short consideration

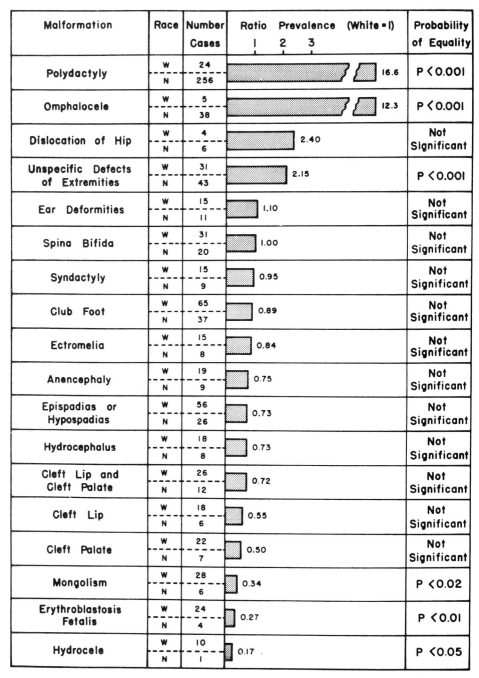

Malformation	Race	Number Cases	Ratio Prevalence (White = 1)	Probability of Equality
Polydactyly	W	24	16.6	P < 0.001
	N	256		
Omphalocele	W	5	12.3	P < 0.001
	N	38		
Dislocation of Hip	W	4	2.40	Not Significant
	N	6		
Unspecific Defects of Extremities	W	31	2.15	P < 0.001
	N	43		
Ear Deformities	W	15	1.10	Not Significant
	N	11		
Spina Bifida	W	31	1.00	Not Significant
	N	20		
Syndactyly	W	15	0.95	Not Significant
	N	9		
Club Foot	W	65	0.89	Not Significant
	N	37		
Ectromelia	W	15	0.84	Not Significant
	N	8		
Anencephaly	W	19	0.75	Not Significant
	N	9		
Epispadias or Hypospadias	W	56	0.73	Not Significant
	N	26		
Hydrocephalus	W	18	0.73	Not Significant
	N	8		
Cleft Lip and Cleft Palate	W	26	0.72	Not Significant
	N	12		
Cleft Lip	W	18	0.55	Not Significant
	N	6		
Cleft Palate	W	22	0.50	Not Significant
	N	7		
Mongolism	W	28	0.34	P < 0.02
	N	6		
Erythroblastosis Fetalis	W	24	0.27	P < 0.01
	N	4		
Hydrocele	W	10	0.17	P < 0.05
	N	1		

Figure 3-8. Selected malformations by race, Philadelphia, Pennsylvania, 1961 to 1963.

is given to both the rubella and thalidomide episodes in order to highlight a few facts about these two known teratogens.

Congenital Cataract and Rubella

The discovery in Australia of the teratogenic impact of maternal rubella in the first trimester of pregnancy and the potentiality of the virus to cause irreparable damage to the conceptus while causing no more than discomfort and mild symptoms in the mother was one of the important, scientific "breakthroughs" of the present century. The story is too well known to be repeated here. Moreover, the advances of two decades were reviewed in these columns five years ago,[520] before definitive virological techniques had been brought to bear against rubella.

Although congenital cataract was the central manifestation of fetal disease first associated with maternal rubella, it was soon realized that it was only one of a larger "constellation" of defects, most of them not apparent at birth. Congenital heart disease, deafness, mental retardation, and dental defects were not to be diagnosed for months or years after birth.[1048] Moreover, cause-and-effect significance of the maternal infection was not derived from vital statistics but from clinical cohort studies. Even in retrospect it could be demonstrated that the timing of the maternal infection in the first trimester of pregnancy, usually between the sixth and seventh week of pregnancy, was then a critical epidemiologic feature that could only be explained on the assumption that the association was one of cause-and-effect. The point is worth stressing, for this also was to become the method of demonstrating the cause-and-effect relation between thalidomide and phocomelia.[643]

With the introduction of an interference test for infection[835] the way was open to cope directly with problems of immunity, virus identification, and a succession of methodological improvements, one of the more important being the demonstration of a cytopathogenic test for identification of the virus by McCarthy *et al.*[698] Using direct testing methods, Green, Krugman and their colleagues,[417] Alford, Neva and Weller,[14] Plotkin,[890] and others have been able to show that the fetus may become a veritable tissue culture itself for the virus of rubella over a period of months following maternal infection. With the introduction by Brown *et al.*[137] of a promising fluorescent antibody test for immunity, the principles of control became discernible. Immunity of the population will expectedly follow naturally occurring infection in childhood. If necessary, during adolescence or before childbearing, rubella will probably be artificially induced. The main obstacle still in sight to the satisfactory control of rubella in pregnancy is the possibility of inducing unwanted infection in a few women who might be both susceptible and pregnant. However, these are the very women who are at risk of contracting the disease naturally and the solution of the problem would seem to be the production of a solid population immunity as is done against smallpox. Perhaps a better analogy is with measles where the disease occurs both naturally and after administration of an attenuated virus.

Until the realization of a vaccination program and the establishment of population immunity becomes a reality, the effectiveness of gamma globulin as a prophylactic measure against rubella is increasingly dubious.[622] It has been shown to fail frequently as a preventive measure against viremia.[14, 417] The following case-history of ectromelia after maternal exposure to rubella was picked up through the surveillance of birth certificates, traced back and reconstructed through the obstetrical and pediatric records of Woman's Medical College Hospital of Philadelphia.[358] Relevant maternal events included: Last menstrual period: March 1, 1963, with probable onset of pregnancy after intercourse on March 9. Exposure to rubella occurred with a neighborly visit of a friend and her two small grandchildren around May 21, 1963, shortly before both children were diagnosed as having rubella. On May 27, 7 ml. of gamma globulin were given to the exposed mother in each buttock. At birth of a baby girl on December 5, 1963, the right arm was found to be missing below the elbow (Fig. 3-9). The possibility of a cause-and-effect relationship is raised by today's knowledge that a pregnant woman may have rubella subclinically and that gamma globulin cannot be counted on to prevent infection or long continued viremia of the conceptus. This may manifest itself as a thrombocytopenic purpura in the newborn.[622] It seems permissible to speculate that if a virus-caused purpura can be present at birth (Fig. 3-9) months after the original infection, a purpura-like disturbance could be present also in the prenatal period and play a role in the pathogenesis of some anomalies.

Phocomelia, Ectromelia and Thalidomide

Even the discovery of the teratogenic impact of rubella on the fetus did not supply the impetus to establish modern surveillance systems. Perhaps the reason is simple: we could recognize the risk but not do very much about the disease. With thalidomide embryopathy the task was first to identify the unknown agent, chemical, physical or microbiological, which was quite evidently at work in many cities of Germany in 1960.[643, 882, 1116] Once the drug had been identified, offending medications merely needed to be withdrawn from public sale. This was the effective public health measure but it also meant the end, unlike the enlarging investigation of rubella embryopathy, of scientific study of thalidomide embryopathy in human beings. Secondly, an effective monitoring system now was clearly needed to insure that this kind of event did not happen again. For lack of monitoring systems some 5,000 to 10,000 cases had developed insidiously in many parts of the world, with gradual clinical appreciation of the terrifying fact to be sure but with little objective evidence of the shape and extent of the community problem. The possibility of intrauterine injury to the conceptus by a hundred milligrams or so of a drug had never been seriously considered as part of ordinary everyday medical practice. It seemed almost unthinkable, but proved true.[643, 695, 882]

The most striking characteristics of the epidemic embryopathies were hypo- and aplastic anomalies of the limb, specifically phocomelia and ectromelia of both upper and lower extremities (Fig. 3-2). Anotia, microtia (Fig. 3-4), congenital heart defects, anophthalmia and microphthalmia, stenosis or atresia of duodenum and imperforate anus are other parts of the constellation of associated malformations that go to make up the complete syndrome.

A little known part of the thalidomide story points up the need for both community and clinical study and the documentation of small outbreaks both in registries and surveillance systems. Early in 1960 a batch of thalidomide, with the trade name of Distaval, had been furnished the Women's Hospital of Sydney, Australia, in order to evaluate the place of the drug in the control of morning sickness in early pregnancy. After the experiment was underway, Dr. W. G. McBride of the hospital staff encountered three cases of congenital absence of the radius in babies born within a period of six weeks to mothers who had been given Distaval early in pregnancy. In the middle of July, 1961, the Women's Hospital terminated its clinical trial but neither community nor clinical data were available to confirm McBride's expressed suspicion.[696] Confirmation came as three more malformed babies were born in the late summer and early fall of 1961, but this is the confirmation of hindsight rather than contemporary recognition and public announcement of thalidomide embryopathy and its solution. It remained for Lenz of Hamburg, Germany, to demonstrate a causal connection between maternal consumption of the Germany preparation called Contergan at about one month of pregnancy. The evidence was mostly of a clinical nature of the kind demonstrated in Fig. 3-4. An important biological correction needing to be introduced for the interpretation of much reported data is the simple fact that pregnancy does not date from the first day of the last menstrual period but from about two weeks later. A two weeks' correction places the sensitive period for thalidomide embryopathy close to one month of pregnancy.

Of fifty women who had received thalidomide during the first trimester of pregnancy, 10 (20%) had nonviable babies; 15 (30%) gave birth to infants with major deformities, and 25 (50%) escaped teratogenic impact of

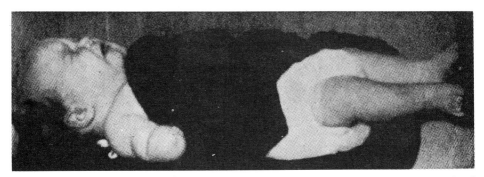

Figure 3-9. Ectromelia of right hand after exposure to rubella about the 9th week of pregnancy; gamma globulin given about 10 weeks after conception.

the drug, as far as could be determined in infancy. However, before these children, ostensibly free of congenital malformations are pronounced normal, they should be followed periodically for years in order to appraise the possibility that not a few may be yet found to have kidney malformations, congenital heart disease, or other visceral defects. This critical series remains the only well-documented cohort study which records all the basic data needed for an estimation of thalidomide risks when the drug is taken in early pregnancy.

Today, it is apparent that this epidemic in Sydney should have received the same kind of meticulous scientific publicity and scrutiny that was given so fruitfully to nine cases of poliomyelitis in Idaho during the 1957 clinical trials of the Salk vaccine. Only in retrospect, however, can it be recognized that to conduct a clinical trial of thalidomide for morning sickness in pregnancy is to hit accidentally upon the most critical of all human experiments that could possibly have been devised to expose, test and define the true nature and extent of the hazard.

Until the thalidomide disaster, ectromelia and particularly phocomelia were seldom encountered. The background incidence of reduction deformities, constructed in retrospect, is given by Mildenstein and his colleagues[764] for Finland, Norway, East and West Germany as shown in Table 3. The

TABLE 3

REDUCTION DEFORMITIES OF THE LIMBS—GERMANY, NORWAY AND FINLAND

Rates per 1,000 Births—1950-1961 inclusive

	1950	1951	1952	1953	1954	1955	1956	1957	1958	1959	1960	1961
West Germany	0.28	0.64	0.43	0.58	0.30	0.59	0.45	0.51	0.58	0.61	1.24	2.52
East Germany	0.00	0.26	0.27	0.56	0.66	0.31	0.32	0.97	0.93	0.36	0.43	0.58
Finland	0.57	0.58	1.70	2.22	1.31	0.45	1.04	1.37	0.88	0.88	0.96	0.49
Norway	0.00	0.41	0.00	0.25	0.00	0.37	0.12	0.12	0.23	0.36	0.36	0.69

drug was sold, of course, only in West Germany and until the 1960-1961 outbreak the idea of an epidemic of these deformities would hardly have been entertained seriously anywhere.

These data present statistical evidence of the epidemic occurrence of reduction deformities of the limbs at the beginning of the present decade in West Germany. The data shown in Table 3 are based upon 447,530 births. As can be seen from this Table, hypoplastic and aplastic anomalies of the extremities in West Germany occurred in the years 1950 to 1959 at a rate of 0.28 to 0.64 per thousand births. A marked increase of those deformities was found in the years 1960 and 1961 with a peak of 2.52 per thousand in 1961. Between January and July, 1962, the incidence was 2.29 and for the latter part of 1962, after thalidomide was withdrawn from sale, the incidence rate fell dramatically to 0.49, a rate prevailing in prethalidomide years.

Although scientifically illuminating in retrospect, this kind of reporting at a national level played no part and plays little part in the actual detection and solution of an outbreak of congenital malformations. Of greater potential value have been studies undertaken on clinical and city-wide bases. Thus, besides clinical observations already described, Leck and Millar were able to show that the number of cases of phocomelia and ectromelia occurring in the Birmingham area rose as the amount of thalidomide sold to Birmingham wholesalers rose.[634] Similarly, Smithells and Leck present the abrupt disappearance of cases after the withdrawal of the drug from sale in 1962 (Fig. 3-5).[1010]

In this country, thalidomide was never approved for dispensing and use. Nonetheless, twenty-three infants were born in Philadelphia with missing extremities in whole or in part, an incidence of only 18 per 1,000 births. The only case of thalidomide deformity uncovered in the three-year surveillance of Philadelphia has been mentioned earlier; it did not involve limb deformities. On the birth certificate of a baby born on August 24, 1962, with agenesis of the right external ear appeared the notation "anotia" and the defect was attributed to "thalidomide in first trimester." Conversation with the mother, who was herself a physician from Canada residing in Philadelphia, revealed that the LMP had started on November 17, 1961; and that she had taken "Kevadon" as follows: 50 mg on December 15; 25 mg on the nights of December 19, 23, and 26. It may be pertinent to note that the mother had had some vaginal bleeding on December 27 and 28 when she would have been nearly one month pregnant. When the baby was about a year old, the diagnosis of noncyanotic heart disease also had been made.

So revolutionary was the idea of drug teratogenesis that it was probably necessary for society to pay the price of many thousands of grossly deformed babies to find out how to detect and measure this kind of an episode. From now on animal experiments will no doubt play a significant role in testing drugs for teratogenic properties, but as was so ably stated by Wilson.[1124] "Society must depend upon actual human experiments to detect teratogenic effects of new agents in women. If prompt reporting of the appearance of congenital malformations," he added, "with careful records by physicians of the medications given, had been made, the extent of the thalidomide disaster in Europe could have been enormously reduced. Difficult as it is," continues Wilson, "this public health procedure of constant surveillance of the incidence of disease must be, in the last analysis, the final protection against a similar great disaster."

In this task of constant surveillance of human populations many health departments have already turned to vital documents in order to measure the incidence with which different malformations occur at different periods. These "different malformations" present as a continuum, the prototype of which includes multiple variations.

BIOLOGICAL CONTINUUM OF DEFORMITIES

Anencephalus, Spina Bifida and Hydrocephalus

A word may be in order to explain why anencephalus, spina bifida and congenital hydrocephalus are logically grouped together. There is no certain evidence that they have the same etiology or epidemiology, but, like cleft palate and harelip, they have manifest interrelationships and they are grouped together if only as an expedient practice.

In the first place, these conditions are usually identified together and in the words of Böök[121] constitute deformities with a high "observational value." Böök explains this phrase: "Some conditions . . . can not reasonably have been missed, like anencephaly, harelip and cleft palate . . . or like atresia of the oesophagus, rectum or duodenum . . . giving alarming clinical symptoms." Another reason for the high observational value of anencephalus is its frequent, about 50 per cent,[711, 896] association with hydramnios, the frequent, 10 per cent, association of anencephalus with spina bifida or meningocele, and the frequent, 30 per cent, association of spina bifida with congenital hydrocephalus.[711] Such features warrant further clinical and population studies especially, in our opinion, the meaning of the very high association with hydramnios and the meaning of the usual two to one prevalence in females over males in anencephalus. There is some evidence that this sex ratio in stillborn anencephalic fetuses may be more pronounced than in the liveborn.[896]

Anencephalus and spina bifida are among the commonest and most distressing of all major deformities of the newborn infant. Indeed, anencephalus results in death and the condition is ordinarily seen only in stillborn babies. Extensive surveys of anencephalus have been made in recent years at national levels, in Scotland,[905] in France,[357] on a regional basis in Sweden[121] and the United States,[393, 719] and in large cities such as Birmingham, England,[906] and Philadelphia, Pennsylvania.[518] No attempt is made to review all of the available data gained in such surveys. Suffice it to point out here that anencephalus is a link between the congenital malformations of liveborn babies and those that result in prenatal death and the unsuccessful termination of pregnancy. In this regard, it is pertinent to recall that the distinctions between abortion, miscarriage, and stillbirths are necessarily arbitrary. These names designate outcomes of pregnancy and how long the conceptus lived, rather than what it had.

As to the frequency with which anencephalus occurs, it is variously set at between one and five per 1,000 stillborn infants depending on whether rates are based upon the stillborn population only, upon the liveborn only or upon the total population of newborn infants. Record's study of anencephalus in Scotland, for example, is based on records of stillbirths classified according to cause and distinguishing between anencephalus, hydrocephalus, and spina bifida. Using these records, Record found an incidence of 2.46 per 1,000 stillbirths from 1939 to 1948 and 2.72 in the decade 1949 to 1958. Incidence was highest in the period November to January. Slater, Watson, and McDonald,[1003] in a survey conducted for the College of General Practitioners in the United Kingdom and Eire, also found a winter excess of anencephalus and spina bifida. The implication of these and other researches is that there is real need to follow seasonal and secular trends in greater detail than can be gained from quarterly examinations. Probably community rates for anencephalus are best calculated on the basis of total births and upon "numerators" even without "denominators" if the data are examined at monthly intervals, as has been done in New York since January 1, 1960 (Fig. 3-6).

Gittelsohn and Milham, in their study of anomalies of the central nervous system occurring in New York State between 1945 and 1959, found a steady decline of over 50 per cent in the annual incidence of anencephalus, spina bifida, and hydrocephalus during the 15-year period examined (Fig. 3-10). They were unable to attribute this to the operation of specific genetic or environmental factors. However, they did feel that the rapidity of the change was consistent with the operation of varying environmental influences. They found it difficult to reconcile a genetic explanation with such dramatic, short-term changes in incidence.

In recent years, two communications have been published describing

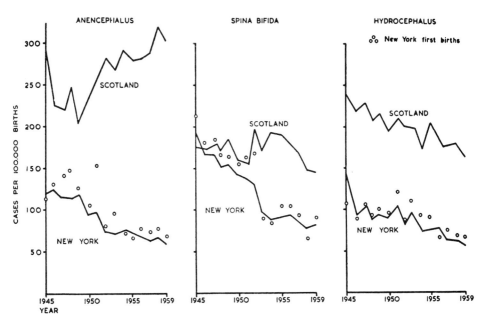

FIGURE 3-10. Congenital malformations of the central nervous system, New York State, 1945 to 1959.[393]

local "epidemics" of spina bifida occurring in 1962, in each of two cities in the eastern United States. Boris and his colleagues in Atlanta, Georgia,[124] alerted by the birth of three infants with meningomyeloceles among white babies born in a single hospital within a three-week period in the fall of 1962, undertook to search for other cases in four other hospitals in Atlanta. During the three-month period August through October, 1962, sixteen cases occurred among 3,630 white live born babies, an incidence of 4.4 cases per 1,000 live births. The incidence of these anomalies in the white newborn population of the city during the preceding ten-year period (1952 to 1961) was 0.76 per 1,000, and for the first six months of 1962 was 1.00 per 1,000 white live births. Among the nonwhite infants of the same city the incidence of spina bifida for the ten-year period was 0.33 per 1,000 live births and during January to June, 1962, 0.26 per 1,000. No cases of spina bifida occurred in the nonwhites during the "epidemic" August to October, 1962. The authors felt this clustering could not be explained as a chance occurrence. "Some teratogenic factor at work briefly in the community may account for the outbreak."

A similar "outbreak" or clustering of spina bifida was reported by Lucey *et al.*[686] from a city in central Vermont. During the year 1962, twenty-one cases among 9,039 live births were found, an incidence of 2.3 per 1,000 live births, whereas the average incidence for this anomaly during the preceding ten-year period (1952 through 1961) in this community was 0.99 per 1,000 live births. The increase in the frequency of spina bifida was highly significant statistically.

Perhaps it is worthwhile to recall that the small cluster of babies with spina bifida born in Philadelphia and mentioned earlier in this article also occurred during October, 1962. Within a one month period, six cases of this anomaly were reported on birth certificates as follows: October 10, one case; October 24, two cases; October 25, one case; October 26, one case; October 28, one case. Of the six infants, five were born between October 24 and October 28; three came from the same health district. Such findings point to directions of needed monitoring and investigation rather than to solutions of the problem they raise.

Achondroplasia

The predilection of this defect for particular families is demonstrable. As a familial defect the condition has a "high observational value" for it can be identified in family members at a glance and would be remembered in relatives even by those who are not medically trained. Achondroplasia is widely seen throughout nature in dogs, in Dexter cattle, in Ancon sheep and in Creeper fowls. Moreover, the familial transmission of the defect is easily documented merely by photographs[893] (Fig. 3-11). Achondroplasia is a superb "tracer" malformation with which to probe the pedigree of affected human beings.[718] In order to appreciate the value of the pedigree approach to achondroplasia one need only consult Mørch's masterful thesis[793] with its 442 references and its documented account of achondroplasia in history, in art, and in families.

The deformity is readily recognizable as the counterpart in human beings of achondroplasia in animals and here man's knowledge of the condition in dogs in particular, and of Stockard's years of breeding experiments with basset hounds and bulldogs, provide a priceless fund of knowledge against which to interpret observations in human beings. The new dimension that has been added to understanding of the human condition comes with improved reporting systems, modern data processing techniques, and computer analysis. It is possible to determine easily the background prevalence of achondroplasia in different populations, races, and small groups in order to compare variable rates in other populations, races and specified groups. Neel and Schull,[813] for example, report the birth of one achondroplastic baby among births of 14,768 infants in Hiroshima and two such babies among births of 12,324 newborn infants at Nagasaki. This compares with the four cases reported in Philadelphia among 131,002 births during the three-year period 1961 to 1963, inclusive.

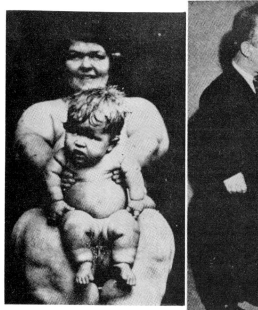

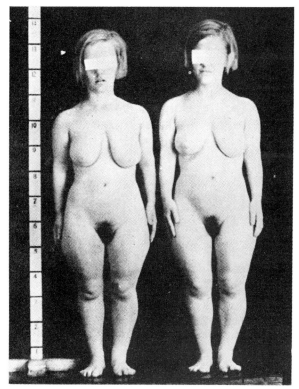

FIGURE 3-11. Achondroplasia. *Left:* Mother and child. *Right:* Husband, wife and child.[893] *Bottom:* Identical twins.

Polydactyly

Polydactyly is another useful "tracer" defect, although it seems likely that its marked predilection for the Negro race must be ascribed to an influence over and beyond the genes that govern limb formation. Thus there is a well-marked seasonal variation (Fig. 3-7) in the occurrence of polydactyly, a finding which surely speaks for an association with environmental influences. Presumably associations exist with both a seasonal factor and a racial attribute such as the sickling trait that characterizes Negroes to a much greater extent than Japanese or Caucasian peoples.

In Nagasaki and Hiroshima, Neel and Schull found only one case among 27,092 newborn Japanese infants, whereas in Philadelphia the rate was about 0.2 per 1,000 live births with the prevalence ratio about 10 to 1 in the Negro over the white population (Fig. 3-8). The rate for the whole state of Pennsylvania was about four times lower, 0.58 per 1,000 live births.[536] Similarly, the incidence of this abnormality, polydactyly and adactyly combined, was 0.61 per 1,000 total births in New York State during the period 1950 through 1960,[766] but much higher, 5.42 per 1,000, in a series of live births in New York City.[708] Evidently the racial constitution of the city or state population will determine, to a large extent, its rates of polydactyly.

Cyclopia, Cebocephaly and Mongolism

There are no good figures on the first two of these essentially lethal conditions. Cyclopia is ordinarily incompatible with extrauterine life to any extent whatsoever, cebocephaly incompatible with life beyond the neonatal period and mongolism is incompatible with economic independence and the ability to mate and reproduce. On the other hand, we are familiar with the case of a cyclopian child who survived two months. Moreover, scattered case reports indicate that cebocephalic children occasionally survive for several months, if not years,[141] and that mongoloid females may rarely become pregnant and bear children.[1061]

Biologically, a most provocative feature of cebocephaly is that like mongolism, but to a more marked degree, it is characterized by a flattened facies, slanted eyes, and grossly defective or absent nasal bones. Both conditions are also characterized by associations with chromosomal trisomy, albeit of different groups of chromosomes. Also suggestive of a biologic relationship was the finding by Hecht *et al.*[467] of three cases of trisomy 21 (mongolism) among the siblings of 60 proband patients with trisomy 18. Another extremely challenging circumstance is the observation that cyclopia and cebocephaly occur naturally in sheep[100] (Fig. 3-12) as does also a third condition, "snub nose," characterized by a brachycephaly which is quite compatible with life. In sheep, cyclopia and cebocephaly are manifestly parts of the same continuum of deformity and the question has been raised previously whether the cyclopia–cebocephaly–snub-nose gradient in sheep corresponds with a cyclopia-cebocephaly-monogolism in human beings[516] (Fig. 3-1).

Among human malformations, mongolism is of particular interest as a key deformity, the full meaning of which and correct placement in the biological continuum of deformity is certain to further the understanding of pregnancy wastage at clinical levels in obstetrics, pediatrics, and preventive medicine at basic science levels in embryology and genetics and at community levels in maternal and child health. The problem itself is of capital importance and involves the understanding of the whole area of intraspecies variation and perhaps even of interspecies variation and evolution itself. Fittingly enough, this state of affairs comes about a century after Down's first description of an "ethnic classification of idiots."

During that hundred years, clinical and statistical definition has been

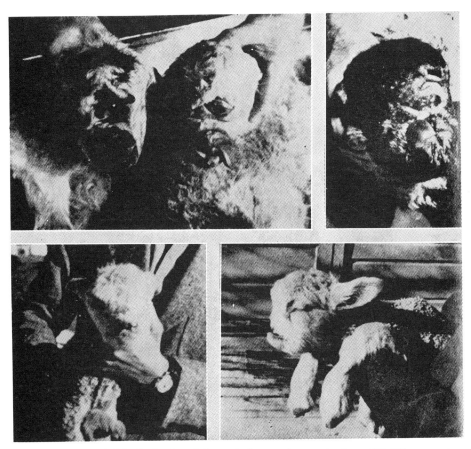

FIGURE 3-12. Cyclopia—Cebocephaly—snub nose in sheep.[100, 516]

made of the multiple nature of the somatic defects that are clustered about the central stigmas of mongolism. The characteristic defects are at the base of the brain and involve the face and skull. They are pathognomonic of the condition just as a defect of the palate is always to be found in the condition we call so simply, "cleft palate"; but there are also associated "constellations" of malformations about the central stigmas of any deformity, whether it be cleft palate, mongolism, or phocomelia. Even today a naturally occurring counterpart of mongolism, unless it be "snub nose" in sheep, has not been observed in animals.

The identification of chromosomal trisomy by Lejeune and his colleagues[638] as a characteristic defect at a cell level in more than 90 per cent of patients strongly suggests an inherited etiology; but annual, seasonal, and geographical variation,[193, 799] racial differences,[314, 518] the well-documented history of first trimester maternal disorders[82, 519] and the correlation between advanced maternal age and the frequency of mongolism[112, 545, 991] can be interpreted to argue as strongly for the hypothesis that environmental factors may influence the occurrence of this abnormality. From studies to date it is impossible to draw final conclusion in our opinion as to etiology, epidemiology, and indeed the placement of mongolism in the biological continuum of congenital deformity in human beings. Perhaps there are both genotypic and phenotypic forms of this deformity. The evidence is interpreted to indicate that at times the condition is inherited and that at other times it has its origin in the early weeks of prenatal life in environmental adversity, like snub nose in the sheep during embryonic life.

Whatever ultimate judgment be made of the origin of mongolism, the proposed solution needs to give a harmonious explanation of the following epidemiologic characteristics: the frequent association of mongolism with advanced maternal age and with disturbances of early pregnancy; the more recently established association with chromosomal trisomy in many, but not all cases; and the evidence that mongoloid females may reproduce mongoloid infants.[436, 640, 910, 1061] The whole area needs objective reappraisal, for the findings to date appear to offer a clue to the origin of some of man's most puzzling malformations and possibly even to species variation.

Cleft Palate and Lip

These deformities have major observational value. They can hardly be missed. Furthermore, and in contrast to completely hopeless conditions like anencephaly and cebocephaly, they can be repaired and hence occupy a place of prominence in inquiries and registries recording family and racial susceptibilities. Occurrence in several generations can often be determined with a high degree of accuracy merely by questioning suitable informants.

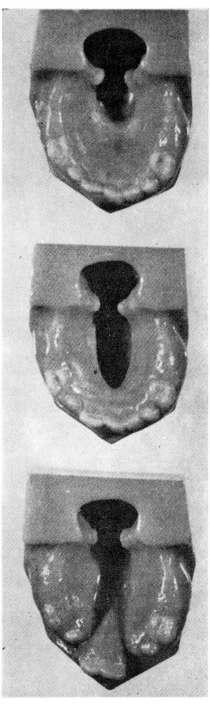

FIGURE 3-13. Three variations of the palatal deformity in "cleft palate."

Thus the unmeasured impressions of Taylor of a significantly high frequency of palato-labial defects of high altitude in Nepal[1054] and those of Marticorena in La Oroya, Peru, which is above 14,000 feet in altitude,[738] could be quantitated merely by methodical census taking and questioning of physicians, midwives, and key members of the populations at risk.

Many studies have been undertaken on epidemiologic features of palato-labial defects, two of the more important being those of Fogh-Andersen published in 1942[340] and a second study on prevalence and incidence twenty years later.[339] Another notable contribution is that of Fraser and Calnan on parental age, season of birth, birth weight, rank, sex, site, and associated defects of children with palato-labial defects.[353]

These and other epidemiologic investigations show highly significant racial and familial factors which determine prevalence. This frequency of occurrence is between one and two cases per 1,000 live births in general, whereas the frequency among relatives of affected babies is almost ten times higher.[514] Of considerable interest also is the greater involvement of white rather than nonwhite populations. The incidence of cleft lip and palate in Philadelphia among newborn infants[418, 537, 679] was 1.24 per 1,000 live births for the white and 0.59 per 1,000 live births for the nonwhite population.[521] This was about one half of the expectancy for Negroes and the difference was highly significant statistically. That the further study of the classification and family distributions of palato-labial defects will be rewarding is implicit in variations of the palatal le-sions (Fig. 3-13), and their associations with cleft lip and with other anomalies, particularly of the skeleton. These defects, being both accessible and compatible with a long life, provide a natural proving ground for theory and for an improved control. The findings to date indicate the epidemiologic distinctiveness of children with cleft lip with or without cleft palate from those with cleft palate only; yet there are also evident interre-lations, an improved understanding of which can only mean an improved understanding of causes of congenital malformations.

Congenital Heart Disease

Unlike palato-labial defects, accurate determination of congenital heart disease can seldom be made in a live born baby at birth. The task of as-certainment is so difficult that the Atomic Bomb Casualty Commission, in their survey of 456 malformations among 49,645 births in Nagasaki and Hiroshima, did not include congenital heart disease among the list of sev-enty-five malformations "occurring alone or in combination. . . ."[813] Other investigators approaching the problem at a community level through the ascertainment of defects noted at birth have had to record manifestly in-complete data. For example, Shapiro *et al.*[984] reported a rate of only 1.02 per 1,000 live births, and Record and McKeown,[908] 2.11 per 1,000 births in the vicinity of Birmingham, England. This was similar to the incidence given by Pitt from lying-in hospital statistics in Australia.[889] Such statistics, based upon community surveys or birth certificates, are manifestly inaccu-rate from underreporting. From published reports and his own hospital ex-perience Anderson[33] has estimated the incidence of congenital heart disease in the general population as three to six per 1,000. Similarly, Mustacchi *et al.*[797] in a three-year study in San Francisco, estimated the incidence of cardiovascular defects at birth to be 5.9 per 1,000 live births.

It is in the area of congenital heart disease that the cohort study emerges as the more satisfactory method of ascertainment of incidence and preva-lence. By this method, whole cohorts of infants are followed for a year or more, as in the fetal life study reported by McIntosh and his colleagues.[708] Thus, Kleinman *et al.*[598] observed forty-eight cases of cardiovascular anom-alies among 10,109 live births; twenty-five of them were detected at birth and the remainder within one year after birth. Davis and Potter[240] in their study of 5,000 consecutive births listed cardiac anomalies in the second place and found them to comprise about 16 per cent of total malformations. McDonald[700] found the incidence for definite congenital heart disease to be 4.7 per 1,000 births, with an association demonstrable between advanced maternal age and births of babies with congenital heart disease.

The highest rates of all, and perhaps the ones more closely approximating the fact, are those of Richards *et al.*[916] and McIntosh and his colleagues. The former investigators observed a rate of 8.3 cases of congenital heart disease per 1,000 total births and 15.5 per 1,000 live births. Their results are not unlike those of McIntosh *et al.* who found defects of the cardiovascular system in 6 per 1,000 live born surviving infants, in 102 per 1,000 neonatal deaths and in 54 per 1,000 stillbirths. In their series, 35.7 per cent of the cases were diagnosed at birth, 47.6 per cent at six months, 11.9 per cent at twelve months and 4.8 per cent when the infant was more than one year of age. In their opinion, also, the overall rate of 8.3 is certainly low because of the failure of some children to develop symptoms and signs before the age of one year.

CONCLUSIONS

Ecologic events of the past twenty-five years show that birth certificates, infant death, and fetal death certificates can provide accurate data with which to construct community surveillance systems for congenital malformations and with which to initiate clinical registries of malformed babies. The fragmentary data given on certificates could be augmented with photographs taken at birth and factual observations emerging from postnatal medical care and study. Such surveillance systems operating in representative large cities of the world would enable the early detection of the kind of epidemic episodes that developed after German measles in Australia in 1939 and 1940 and after the marketing of thalidomide in Germany in 1959 and 1960. The discovery of these two community-wide epidemics presumably marks the beginning of an enlarged understanding of an ecology of prenatal disease in general, and of congenital malformations in particular. The clinical registry serves the purposes of providing counsel, service, prosthetics and training, and cohort material for further analysis of malformations as they are influenced by both genetic and environmental factors.

The successful functioning of combined surveillance and clinical registry units would require some years more to plan, to staff, and to operate. The limitations of knowledge and methodology are still very real. For example, contemporary studies and research accomplishments give great promise of controlling maternal rubella in the foreseeable future. Nevertheless it has taken twenty-five years to reach this point of potential control. As of today this objective has not been realized in fact.

The basis of a standardized classification that satisfies both clinical and epidemiologic criteria is the need to limit, to diagnose rapidly, to name, to

record, and to report at least one (and by custom this is the defect consti-
tuting the greatest handicap) of the many malformations that may be present and recognizable at birth. Vital statistics so founded form the basis of
meaningful comparisons and the points of departure for compilation of
clinical registries.

In the future, it would hardly seem wise to separate sharply surveillance
systems from clinical registries or from appropriate laboratory facilities
which to date have contributed more to research activities than to the
practice of either medicine or public health. Today the efforts of many
workers at all three levels (laboratory, clinical, and community) of approach are needed to interpret chemical, chromosomal, embryological,
obstetrical, pediatric, epidemiological, and statistical aspects of a multi-
factorial, multidisciplinary problem.

Chapter 4

Final Report of a Prospective Study of Children Whose Mothers Had Rubella in Early Pregnancy

MARY D. SHERIDAN

A CONTROLLED prospective inquiry regarding the effects of rubella and other virus infections in pregnancy, beginning early in 1950 and ending in December 1952, and sponsored by the Ministry of Health, was fully reported by Manson, Logan, and Loy.[732] The total number of pregnancies complicated by rubella available for analysis was 578. The controls numbered 5,717. Follow-up of the infants showed that when rubella occurred during the first sixteen weeks of pregnancy the incidence of congenital abnormalities in the children was significantly raised. When the infection occurred after the sixteenth week, the incidence of abnormalities in the children of the rubella mothers was no higher than in the controls.

The number of pregnancies complicated by rubella in the first sixteen weeks was 279. Of these, eleven ended in abortion and eleven in stillbirth, and sixteen children died before two years of age, leaving 241 in the original group. A number of medical officers of health continued to send in records of children born in 1953 whose mothers had been notified for rubella before the end of 1952. Since these cases fulfilled the criteria laid down by Logan,[674] a further eighteen infants whose mothers had rubella in the first sixteen weeks of pregnancy were added to the original group. This gave a final total of 259 children available for assessment at two years, by which age it had been anticipated that all major abnormalities would have been diagnosed. This examination is designated No. 1 in Table 4-1.

In order to check the possibility of hitherto unidentified defects, however, full pediatric and otological examination of fifty-seven "early rubella" children and fifty-seven controls living in the London and Middlesex areas was undertaken in 1956-7 by Jackson and Fisch,[538] the children concerned being then between the ages of three and six years. The results of their inquiry indicated that the proportion of children suffering from significant hearing loss had been underestimated at the original examination. It was therefore considered advisable to extend the inquiry to "early rubella" children living in the rest of the country. Reports for 237 children were

78

received and the results were included in the report of Manson *et al.*[732] This examination is designated No. 2 in Table 4-1.

Finally, in order to discover how they developed in later childhood a third inquiry was carried out in 1962, when the children were between the ages of eight and eleven years. The present paper reports the results of this examination, which is designated No. 3 in Table 4-1, in relation to findings of the previous examinations.

THE REPORT FORM

The medical officers of health were requested to provide the following particulars: (1) any abnormality of the eyes—visual acuity right and left, distant and near, without and with spectacles if worn; (2) any abnormality of the ears—hearing right and left for quiet conversational voice without lip-reading at 3 and 10 ft. (0.9 and 3 m); also a full puretone audiogram; (3) condition of the heart as reported by a cardiologist or pediatrician; (4) intelligence quotient, naming testing scale used; (5) assessment of the child's emotional development and social behavior; (6) any other pathological condition present; (7) type of school attended.

A total of 227 completed reports were received. Of the remaining thirty-two, one child had emigrated, the parents of five children refused to participate, and twenty-six were untraced.

Owing to the wide geographical distribution of cases and the large number of medical examiners concerned, it was inevitable that the reports received were not equally informative, but the general standard of recording was high. Assessment of an abnormality as major or minor on the evidence available sometimes required much thought, and final classification is necessarily the result of my personal judgment. For this reason, and because there were no controls, it proved difficult to submit the very varied information collected to any sophisticated statistical analysis. It has therefore been decided to present it in tabulated form.

The final outcome of this prospective study has confirmed the findings of previous, mainly retrospective, inquiries regarding the special vulnerability to rubella infection of the eyes, ears, and heart of the developing foetus during the first sixteen weeks of pregnancy. It does not, however, bear out the very pessimistic evaluations of attendant risks which have sometimes been offered on the basis of retrospective studies. *Major* abnormalities were present in thirty-three (15%) children, twenty of whom had more than one abnormality. *Minor* abnormalities were noted in thirty-seven (16%) children, of whom nine had another abnormality. In both groups,

Reprinted from *British Medical Journal*, 2:536-539, August, 1964, by permission of author, editor and publisher.

TABLE 4-1

Week	No. of Children		No. with Abnormalities	No. of Abnormalities Per Child	Nature of Abnormalities and When First Noted
1	11	Major	1	5	Cataracts 1; deafness 2; C. heart 1; subnormality 1; motor handicap 3
		Minor	1	2	Malformed right ear 1, with unilateral deafness 3; undescended testicles 3
2	6	Major	0	–	—
		Minor	1	1	Defective vision 3
3	8	Major	1	1	Congenital heart 1
		Minor	2	1 1	Mild deafness right and left 2. Heart murmur 3
4	16	Major	2	2 1	Cataract left and right squint 1. Severe deafness 2
		Minor	4	2 1 1 1	Mild deafness right and left and heart murmur 3. Deafness right and left 3. Heart murmur 3
5	14	Major	4	3 2 2 1	Cataracts 1; C. heart 3; maladjusted 3. Squint 3; deafness 2. Deafness 2; C. heart 2. Deafness 1
		Minor	1	2	Deafness right and left 3; heart murmur 3
6	5	Major	1	3	D. vision 3; deafness 2; heart murmur 3
		Minor	3	2 2 1	Squint 3; heart murmur 3. Deafness right and left 3. Squint 3
7	11	Major	3	4 1 1	Squint with d. vision 1; deafness 3; C. heart 1; undescended testicle 3. C. heart 1. Deafness 1
		Minor	2	1 1	Minor C. heart 1. Heart murmur 3
8	22	Major	5	3 3 2 2 1	Cataract R. 1; deafness 2; C. heart 1. D. vision 3; deafness 1; spasticity 1. Deafness 1; C. heart 1. Pyloric stenosis 1; asthma 1. Deafness 2
		Minor	3	2 2 1	D. vision 3; deafness right and left 3. Deafness 3; squint 3. Unilateral deafness 3

80

No.						Findings
9	Major	4	4	4	2	1	Cataract right and left 1; deafness 1; C. heart 1; spastic 1. Cataract left 1; Cataract right and left; 3 C. heart 1; E.S.N. 3. Cataract left 1; C. heart 1. Duodenal stenosis 1
	Minor	–					—
10	Major	4	1	1	1	1	Deafness 1. Deafness 1. Deafness 1. Pyloric stenosis 1
	Minor	2	1	1			Heart murmur 3. Deafness right and left 3
11	Major	1	3				Deafness 3; heart murmur 3; asthma 3
	Minor	0					
12	Major	3	3	2	2	1	1	Deafness 2; C. heart 3; aphasia 2. Squint with d. vision 3; deafness 1. Deafness 1; migraine 2. Deafness 2. C. heart 3
	Minor	7	1	1	1	1	1	1	1	Unilateral amblyopia L. 3. Unilateral deafness 2. Unilateral deafness 2. Unilateral deafness 3. Deafness 3. Heart murmur 3. Heart murmur 3
13	Major	–	–				Unilateral deafness 3
	Minor	1	1				
14	Major	0	–				
	Minor	3	2	1	1		Unilateral deafness 3; undescended testicles 3. D. vision 3. Deafness 3
15	Major	2	4	2			D. vision 3; deafness 1; E.S.N. 1; undescended testicles 3. Unilateral amblyopia 3; asthma 3
	Minor	6	2	1	1	1	1	1	Deafness 3; heart murmur 3. Unilateral amblyopia 3. Deafness 2. Deafness 2. Heart murmur 3. Heart murmur 3
16	Major	–	–				
	Minor	1	1				Heart murmur 3
Totals	Major	33					Major 15%
227	Minor	37					Minor 16%

The figures 1, 2 and 3 in the last column refer to the number of the examination (see text).

81

particularly the latter, it is probable that some of the children included were suffering from conditions unrelated to the rubella infection, although in compiling the tables only those children whose abnormalities were considered from the information available to be certainly or possibly due to rubella have been included. Hence eleven children showing single abnormalities which were either known or thought unlikely to be connected with the maternal rubella infection have been omitted from the tables— that is, two cases of myopia developing in middle childhood, two cases of hearing loss associated with active otitis media, six cases of uncomplicated educational subnormality, and one case of paralytic poliomyelitis.

Table 4-1 summarizes according to the pregnancy week of rubella infection the number of children at risk, the number showing abnormalities, and the number and nature of the abnormalities occurring in each affected child.

Major Abnormalities.—The number and associations according to week of infection are shown in Table 4-2.

Minor Abnormalities.—The associations and number of cases are shown in Table 4-3.

TABLE 4-2

No. of Abnormalities	Nature	Week
5	Bilateral cataract, deafness, congenital heart, spasticity, mental defect	1
4	Squint, deafness, congenital heart, undescended testicle	7
	Bilateral cataract, deafness, congenital heart, spasticity	9
	Unilateral cataract, deafness, congenital heart E.S.N.	9
	Defective vision, deafness, E.S.N., undescended testicles	15
3	Bilateral cataract, congenital heart, emotional maladjustment	5
	Defective vision, deafness, heart murmur	6
	Unilateral cataract, deafness, congenital heart	8
	Defective vision, deafness, spasticity	8
	Deafness, heart murmur, asthma	11
	Deafness, congenital heart, aphasia	12
2	Unilateral cataract, paralytic squint	4
	Pyloric stenosis, asthma	8
	Deafness, congenital heart (2 cases)	5, 8
	Squint, deafness (2 cases)	5, 12
	Unilateral cataract, heart murmur	9
	Deafness, migraine	12
	Unilateral amblyopia, asthma	15
Single	Deafness (8 cases)	4, 5, 7, 8, 10, 10, 10, 12
	Congenital heart (3 cases)	3, 7, 12
	Duodenal stenosis	9
	Pyloric stenosis	10

TABLE 4-3

No. of Abnormalities	Nature	No. of Cases
2	Malformation of right ear with unilateral deafness, undescended testicles	1
	Bilateral deafness, heart murmur	4
	Squint, heart murmur	1
	Squint, bilateral deafness	1
	Defective vision, bilateral deafness	1
	Unilateral deafness, undescended testicle	1
Single	Squint	1
	Unilateral amblyopia	2
	Defective vision	2
	Bilateral deafness	7
	Unilateral deafness	5
	Congenital heart	1
	Heart murmur	10

Cataract was noted in seven cases and never as a single abnormality: six of these children had congenital lesions of the heart and five of them were also deaf; the remaining child had a paralytic squint. The cataract was bilateral in three cases and unilateral in four. All seven were associated with infection in the first to ninth week. Visual acuity was recorded for all but four of the 227 children: two of these were blind and two were noted as having been successfully operated upon—one for cataract and the other for squint. Squint was noted in seven cases, five of them for the first time at the third examination. Defective vision was noted in eight cases for the first time at the third examination, and unilateral amblyopia was noted three times—one in association with another disability. Some of these visual defects may have been due to causes other than maternal rubella. In the absence of any note to the contrary, it is not possible to differentiate. Nevertheless, the need for continual reassessment before and after school entrance is clearly indicated.

EAR DEFECTS

The inquiry has shown up very clearly the importance of rubella in early pregnancy as a cause of congenital deafness.

The cases were associated with infection from the first to the fifteenth week. Puretone audiograms as well as the results of clinical voice tests—that is, quiet conversational voice without lip-reading at 3 and 10 ft. (0.9 and 3 m) right and left were available for 179 (79%) children and the results of clinical tests alone were available for forty-six. The remaining two were attending schools for the deaf and were incapable of responding to either test. In assessing the audiograms for summary in the tables it was necessary to adopt some standard of classification. It was finally decided that hearing loss over 20 decibels must be shown for at least two adjacent frequencies and the degree of deafness was evaluated as follows: Mild deafness = loss of 25-45 db.; moderate deafness = loss of 45-70 db.; and severe deafness = loss of 70+ db. On these standards, forty-three (19%) children had a significant hearing loss: twenty-three (10%) had severe or moderate bilateral deafness necessitating some form of special education; fourteen had mild bilateral loss; and six had unilateral deafness which was moderate or severe. These last twenty (9%) children were able to attend ordinary school, some of them wearing hearing-aids, and others receiving speech therapy or other forms of special help.

No fewer than seventeen cases with significant degrees of deafness were noted for the first time at the third examination and in ten of these the hearing loss was bilateral. Five of the ten showed a serious loss, three of these five children had additional abnormalities, which had been duly recorded at previous examinations. The need for thorough periodic investigation of the hearing in all children at risk, whether or not there is another presenting abnormality, is obvious. It is, of course, possible that some of these late discoveries were children whose deafness was not due to rubella, but there was no suggestion of other causation in the reports.

Of the forty-three children with significant hearing loss, thirty-six audiograms were available. Of the other seven, two were in schools for the deaf, four were in ordinary schools wearing hearing-aids, and one was the multi-handicapped child in hospital. Of the the thirty-six available audiograms, twenty-six showed a flat loss over the whole speech range and ten showed curves sloping from left to right—that is, high-tone deafness—thus confirming the original observations of Fisch[332] regarding the audiometric patterns commonly associated with rubella deafness.

HEART DEFECTS

The amount of information available regarding cardiac abnormalities was particularly satisfactory. The report of a cardiologist or consultant paediatrician was available for all except about a dozen children whose attendance at hospital or special clinic had been too difficult to arrange. In these cases the school medical officer had examined the child. Fourteen cases were definitely diagnosed as congenital lesions, the weeks of infection being from one to twelve. In ten cases the cardiac lesion was associated with another abnormality; in four it was the sole abnormality noted. Eighteen heart murmurs described as "innocent" or "of no significance" were recorded (16 of them for the first time at the third examination), but it is noteworthy that nine of these (7 of the 16) were associated with another abnormality.

OTHER CONDITIONS

Asthma was noted three times and migraine once, all in association with another abnormality. Four cases of undescended testicles were noted, also in association with another abnormality. Spasticity of the limbs was noted in three cases, and all three children had other handicaps. Two cases of pyloric stenosis and one of duodenal stenosis, which were reported at previous examinations as having been successfully operated upon during infancy, were noted to be doing well.

SOCIAL ADJUSTMENT

It has been suggested that rubella children often show emotional instability and difficult behaviour, but although the information was specifically requested there was little supportive evidence in the reports. Twelve children were variously noted as "shy," "immature," "lacking in concentration," or "liable to outbursts of temper," but only one, a blind child, was reported as "psychologically difficult."

INTELLIGENCE

Intelligence quotients were available for 191 (84%) children and teachers' assessments for the remaining thirty-six. The testing scales were Terman-Merrill (174), WISC (14), and other standard scales (3). In the

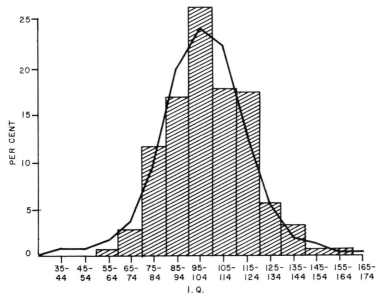

Figure 4-1. Distribution of I.Q.s of rubella group with superimposed curve of T.M. standardization group.

TABLE 4-4

INTELLIGENCE. DISTRIBUTION ACCORDING TO TIME OF RUBELLA INFECTION

Week	No. of Cases	Given	I.Q. Mean	Range	Additional Assessments
1	11	9	102	88-141	1 below average, 1 severely subnormal
2	6	4	116	83-131	2 average
3	8	8	110	96-139	
4	16	11	103	80-128	5 average
5	14	13	101	71-150	1 average
6	5	5	112	80-130	
7	11	10	103	80-142	1 average
8	22	19	108	84-134	2 average, 1 borderline
9	14	13	95	63-110	1 average
10	16	11	107	82-160	4 average, 1 below average
11	17	17	107	83-140	
12	20	15	107	70-143	2 average, 3 below average
13	16	14	110	80-133	1 above average, 1 average
14	15	14	103	83-134	1 average
15	24	18	109	70-145	5 average, 1 below average
16	12	10	116	93-143	2 average

I.Q. mean for 191 cases = 106.8.

circumstances it was thought permissible to combine these to plot a curve of distribution, which is shown in Figure 4-1. It proved to be strikingly normal.

The mean I.Q. was 106.8, with a range of 63 to 160. The teachers' estimates for the remaining thirty-six were as follows: twenty-seven average, one above average, six below average, one borderline, and one mentally handicappd. The number of children concerned, range of I.Q., and teachers' assessment according to the week of maternal rubella are given in Table 4-4. It is worthy of note that of the thirty-seven children with I.Q.s under 85, or designated "below average," thirteen had a significant hearing loss, which raises the question to what extent their lowered performance on tests was due to their sensory disability. Although it is convenient for statistical purposes to record the results of intelligence tests in terms of a numerical I.Q., it needs to be kept in mind that the results of testing (British) handicapped children with intelligence scales standardized on a normal (North American) child population can only be justified clinically by using some such form of words as "the I.Q. is not less than. . . ." It can safely be said that this inquiry has produced no evidence that mental subnormality is a common sequel of early maternal rubella.

EDUCATION

The educational placement of the 227 children is shown in Table 4-5. Thus 206 (92%) of the children were attending ordinary schools. Of these

TABLE 4-5

Ordinary school	199
Ordinary school with special help	7
Special schools or classes, etc.:	
For deaf or partially deaf	15
For partially sighted	1
For speech defectives	1
For E.S.N.	1
Home tuition	1
Hospital for mentally subnormal	1
(P.H. school—paralytic polio [not rubella])	1

seven (3%) are noted as having special provision such as hearing-aids, speech therapy, and remedial teaching. Twenty children were attending special schools or classes, including the child whose handicap was the result of paralytic poliomyelitis. The majority of those in special schools were severely deaf. The child receiving home tuition was blind and maladjusted. He had also been operated upon for a congenital heart lesion, a residual murmur being present. The child who was in a hospital for the mentally subnormal had multiple handicaps.

BIRTH WEIGHTS

Birth rates were available for 226 of the 227 children. The missing record referred to a (fifth week) child with multiple major abnormalities. The figures (Table 4-6) show a suggestive trend.

TABLE 4-6

BIRTH WEIGHT OF 226 CHILDREN

Children	Mean		Range		
	lb. oz.	*g.*	*lb. oz. lb. oz.*		*g.*
Normal (157)	7 2	3,230	4 10-10 2		2,100-4,590
With minor abnormalities (37)	6 10	3,005	3 13-10 6		1,730-4,705
With major abnormalities (32*)	6 4½	2,850	3 13- 8 8		1,730-3,855
With multiple major abnormalities (19)	5 14	2,665	4 6- 8 4		1,985-3,740

* These 32 cases include the 19 with multiple major abnormalities.

MISSING CASES

In order to complete this record the previous reports of the missing thirty-two children were scrutinized. Four of them had abnormalities associated with maternal rubella in the first, eighth and eleventh weeks of pregnancy as follows:

Week 1: Severe unilateral deafness noted at second examination.

Week 8: Congenital heart noted at first examination; and at the second examination reported as having had a successful operation at 2½ years.

Week 8: Unilateral deafness noted at second examination.

Week 11: Squint, severe deafness, talipes, and mental subnormality noted at first examination; no record of any second examination.

SEASONAL DISTRIBUTION

It has often been suggested that a larger proportion of handicapped children are born in the months of winter and early spring than in the summer. The months of birth of the 259 early rubella children, with and without abnormalities, are given in Table 4-7.

TABLE 4-7

MONTHS OF BIRTH FOR WHOLE SERIES OF 259 EARLY RUBELLA
CHILDREN WITH AND WITHOUT DEFECTS

Month	Normal	Abnormal	Total
January	21	15	36
February	18	3	21
March	6	4	10
April	5	1	6
May	1	1	2
June	2	1	3
July	4	2	6
August	6	5	11
September	21	6	27
October	34	6	40
November	35	18	53
December	32	12	44
Total	185	74	259

Although the larger number of "early rubella" children were born in the months October to February inclusive, reflecting the usual springtime incidence of rubella epidemics, there was no significant difference in the proportion of handicapped and nonhandicapped children born at any season of the year.

SUMMARY

A controlled prospective inquiry regarding mothers who had rubella during the first sixteen weeks of pregnancy was begun during 1950-2.

Three follow-up medical examinations of the children resulting from these pregnancies were carried out, the first at two years (259 children), the second between three and six years (237 children), and the third between eight and eleven years (227 children).

The results of the first two examinations were published by Manson, Logan, and Loy.[732]

This paper reports the final outcome of the inquiry, with special reference to the findings of the three examinations.

Major abnormalities, mainly of the eye, ear, and heart, occurred in 15 per cent of the children, 8 per cent having more than one abnormality. Minor abnormalities were present in a further 16 per cent, 4 per cent having more than one abnormality. These are outside estimates, as it is possible that some of the abnormalities discovered were due to causes other than maternal rubella.

The distribution of intelligence among the children was normal.

The need for long-term follow-up and periodic full reassessment of children known to be at risk from maternal rubella during the first sixteen weeks of pregnancy was clearly demonstrated.

This inquiry would not have been possible without the generous help of medical officers of health throughout Britain. Dr. M. A. Heasman, of the Ministry of Health's Medical Statistics Section, kindly prepared the graph for the Chart.

Chapter 5

Prematurity and Deafness:
The Magnitude and Nature of the
Problem Among Deaf Children

McCay Vernon

I N recent years medical advances have greatly increased the survival rate among prematurely born infants. In the period from 1933 to 1955 alone, the mortality rate was reduced 55 per cent.[438, 819] Although many infants now live through the catastrophic events of the perinatal stage, the prevalence of severe multiple handicaps among them has increased. Communicative disorders are one of the major types of these disabilities.[123, 296, 438, 684, 1080]

The full significance of prematurity and its possible ramifications in the area of deafness are further illustrated by the fact that the condition takes a higher toll of infant life than any other single factor. It also ranks as one of the leading causes of death among the general population, accounting for 10 per cent of the total mortality.[105, 605, 819, 798] A condition of this type and of this pathological magnitude, often involving the central nervous system, could logically be expected to cause sensorineural hearing loss.

PROBLEM

Aside from a few studies which indicate that premature birth may be a significant etiology of profound hearing loss, the relationship of prematurity to deafness has been largely ignored.[236, 296, 699, 818, 874, 946] The paradoxical nature of this lack of research becomes even clearer with the awareness that such major etiologies of deafness as maternal rubella, complications of Rh factor, anoxia, and meningitis are also either major causes of prematurity or conditions which are especially likely to attack infants of low birth weight.[575, 818, 992, 1080]

It is the purpose of this research to survey the extent to which prematurity is associated with deafness and to examine the characteristics of these deaf children of low birth weight.

Reprinted from *Exceptional Children*, 33:289-298, 1967.

METHOD

All 1468 deaf or profoundly hard of hearing children (loss in better ear of 65 dB or better between 500-2000 cps by ASA 1951 standards) who attended or were given preadmission evaluations at the California School for the Deaf in Riverside from its opening in 1953 until 1964 constituted the sample studied in this research. The age range at the time of evaluation was three to twenty-one years. The criterion used for prematurity was that established by the World Health Organization: a viable fetus weighing 5 pounds 8 ounces or less. Children meeting this criterion and with no other known cause of deafness were operationally defined as premature for the purposes of this research. The characteristics studied were (1) intelligence, (2) educational achievement, (3) psychological adjustment, (4) psychometric evidence of brain damage, (5) audiometric findings, and (6) multiple handicaps.

RESULTS

Prevalence of Prematurity

Of the 1468 deaf children in the sample, 257 had been premature. This represents a prevalence rate of 17.4 per cent, which is in sharp contrast to the 7.6 per cent incidence in the general population,[105, 279, 998] an incidence which results in a 4 per cent prevalence by school age.[243] Thus, there are proportionately more than four times as many deaf school children as normally hearing children who were born prematurely. Not only are there more, but within the very low birth weight categories (3 pounds 4 ounces or less) this disproportion is even greater.[1080]

In view of the fact that emotional, physical, and learning problems have been found to be much more common among premature children, especially those below 3 pounds 4 ounces,[205, 280, 605, 1106] it follows that among school age deaf children there are probably significantly more of these problems than among the normally hearing.

Of the 257 premature cases in this sample, fifty-six were postrubella children, six were cases with complications of Rh factor, eleven had probable genetic deafness, six were postmeningitic, and three were cases in which premature birth was not clearly established.[1080] This means that in 175 cases (11.9%) prematurity was the only known factor that could have caused the deafness. The other 5.5 per cent were not only premature, but had a history of other pathologies known to be associated with prematurity, deafness, and damage to the central nervous system. In other words, approximately one third of deaf children who were born prematurely face both the residua of early birth and that of rubella, erythroblastosis, or some other known secondary condition.

Other than to point out the existence of this 5.5 per cent of the deaf school age population and to state the potential significance of their problem, this research will restrict itself to the remaining two thirds of premature deaf children for whom there is no other known cause of deafness. It is thought that this is a meaningful categorization which identifies a large group of deaf children who have many problems in common and about whom much needs to be known.

Intelligence

An extensive review of comparative studies of the intelligence of deaf and normally hearing children indicates that the two groups are essentially the same in terms of intelligence.[1079] However, in this sample the premature deaf have a mean I.Q. of 89.4 and a 16.3 per cent prevalence of mental retardation (I.Q. below 70). Only 58 per cent of these children have I.Q.'s of 90 or above (Table 5-1). Many educational programs for deaf children will not include youngsters scoring below 70 in I.Q. In fact, Brill[134] found that an I.Q. of at least 90 was required to achieve minimal standards for graduation in an educational program for deaf children. This means that many of these premature youngsters (16.3%) could not be accepted into a pro-

TABLE 5-1

I.Q. DISTRIBUTION FOR 115 PREMATURE DEAF CHILDREN

| | | | | I.Q. Categories | | | | |
	0-69	70-79	80-89	90-99	100-109	110-119	120-129	130 up
Premature	16.3	9.5	15.6	25.2	24.3	5.2	2.6	.8
Normal Distribution	2.2	6.7	16.1	25.0	25.0	16.1	6.7	2.2

Note: Mean I.Q. = 89.4; standard deviation, 19.0. Mean I.Q. of 89.4 has a .0001 (one tailed) probability of being significantly different from the population mean I.Q. of 100.

TABLE 5-2

I.Q. DATA ON PREMATURE DEAF SAMPLE

Birth Weight	Cases	Mean I.Q.	Standard Deviation	Per Cent Mentally Retarded	Mean Difference from Population Norms Probability[b]
4 lb. 7 oz.-5 lb. 8 oz.	49	95.28	16.67	8.1	.0239
3 lb. 5 oz.-4 lb. 6 oz.	34	90.05	20.39	17.6	.0022
2 lb. 4 oz.-3 lb. 4 oz.[a]	23	79.04	18.85	30.4	.001
1 lb. 2 oz.-2 lb. 3 oz.[a]	6	76.16	15.67	16.6	.05

[a] Student's *t*'s were used because sample size was below 25. Probabilities in the *t* table are given at confidence levels, not absolute probabilities.
[b] One tailed test.

gram for the deaf and that approximately 42 per cent would never graduate.

Table 5-2 shows that as the birth weight of a premature deaf child drops, the average I.Q. diminishes appreciably. For example, the mean I.Q. for those below 3 pounds 4 ounces is below 80. With medical science saving more and more of the fetuses within the extremely low birth weight classifications, these findings assume major significance.[1080]

Educational Achievement

In view of the depressed I.Q. scores of the premature, it would be logical to expect a limited overall academic achievement for these youngsters. The data indicate this to be the case. Of the 175 who applied for admission to the California School, 10.3, per cent were judged to have too little academic potential or achievement to be admitted even on a trial basis. Another 9.7 per cent were dismissed from school for inability to achieve at the minimal standards. Thus, one out of five of these premature children was regarded as essentially unable to be educated.

The academic achievement of those who were accepted into the California School and remained until they were nine and a half years of age or older was measured by the Stanford Achievement Tests. Based on these data, the premature were found to achieve at less than half the rate of normally hearing children and at two thirds the rate of deaf children of deaf parents. Relatively few premature children earned academic diplomas, none passed the Gallaudet College examinations, and many were vocational graduates, which at the California School indicates the minimal educational attainment required for graduation.

The written language of the premature children, as rated by their classroom teachers, was appreciably below that of average deaf children of their ages. Only 10 per cent were judged to have good language relative to the general population of deaf children. Thirty per cent were rated average and 60 per cent were judged poor. In speech and speech reading, the premature group were rated lower than the five other etiological groups studied, although these differences were not interpreted as statistically significant.

To further examine the critical factor of communication, an attempt was made to determine the prevalence of aphasia among the premature. Authorities such as Hardy and Pauls[438] have suggested aphasia (or an aphasoid disorder) might be common among premature children. Because a diagnosis of aphasia in a deaf child is difficult, the classroom teachers and the supervising teachers were asked to list the children they thought to be aphasic, based upon the operational definition: "The child has abnormal difficulty with language relative to other deaf children of his age and I.Q."

(both age and I.Q. were provided for the teachers). Only students regarded as aphasic by both their classroom and their supervising teachers on this criterion were classified aphasic. Thirty-six per cent of the premature children were diagnosed aphasic, using this definition.

In sum, educational data based on achievement tests, records of academic success and failure, written language, oral communication, and the prevalence of language disorder indicate premature deaf children as a group have profound educational problems relative to most other deaf youths.[1080]

Psychodiagnostic Evidence of Central Nervous System Dysfunction

Prematurity is frequently associated with conditions such as intracranial hemorrhage and anoxia.[132, 992] Anoxia is an especially important factor to consider because the brain needs an ample and continuous provision of oxygen, more than any other part of the body. The gray matter, the center for higher thought processes, is particularly dependent upon a full oxygen supply. For example, a deficit for as little as 90 seconds can result in lasting and irreversible consequences.[783]

In view of both this medical basis for expecting premature children to have a high prevalence of brain damage and the already existent central nervous system involvement of sensorineural deafness in the children of this research, the Bender Gestalt and the Diagnostic Screening Form for the Detection of Neurological Impairment in Deaf Children[1076] were administered to assess neurological dysfunction.

Three clinical psychologists evaluated the Bender Gestalt responses independently, classifying them as pathological, suspicious, or normal relative to organicity. The raters were given the child's age and I.Q. score. Only children of eleven years of age or above were included, in order to reduce the confusion between the variables of maturation, retardation, and organicity. Two thirds of the premature children's Bender Gestalts were judged pathological, meaning the psychologists felt that they clearly indicated brain damage. Of the remaining one third, approximately half were classified normal and half suspicious.

The Diagnostic Screening Forms for the Detection of Neurological Impairment in Deaf Children is a rating scale which lists twenty academic, emotional, and physical traits which the literature on brain-damaged children indicates to be most characteristic of these children. Although it is a published scale used in audiological clinics here, in Canada, and in Great Britain, data on reliability, empirical validity, and normative values are lacking.

Results of the administration of the Diagnostic Form essentially substantiate the Bender Gestalt findings in that they indicate a high prevalence of brain damage to be associated with prematurity in deaf children. The picture of behavior yielded is that of difficulties most directly related to academics. Two critical symptoms, abnormal difficulty with language and a large discrepancy between I.Q. scores and school achievement, characterize the children. Poor abstract ability and distractibility complete this unfavorable academic syndrome. On traits indicating emotional and physical symptoms associated with brain damage, the premature cases had scores indicating pathology; but the difficulties were not centered on specific clinical patterns.

In sum, the data from both the Bender Gestalt and the Diagnostic Form indicate a high prevalence of brain damage among premature deaf children. This evidence is consistent with medical knowledge of the neurophysiological concomitants present in infants of low birth weight.[1080]

Psychological Adjustment

The communication handicap resulting from deafness makes the assessment of psychological adjustment of deaf children extremely difficult because most conventional psychodiagnostic tests are inappropriate.[1078] In order to overcome this difficulty, three separate approaches to assessment were used: psychological evaluations based on both interviews and individual testing, teachers' ratings, and school records.

Of the 117 premature deaf children who were given psychological evaluations, thirty-four were diagnosed maladjusted, based on the criterion that they had severe emotional problems which profoundly jeopardized their ability to function adequately in a school setting. A majority of these disturbed cases fell into one of three broad pathological syndromes. The first was a schizoid pattern, which in some cases consisted of passive homosexual behavior and hallucinations (the seven diagnosed psychotic were all schizophrenic). The second syndrome was one of immaturity, hyperactivity, explosiveness, and an anxiety ridden impulsiveness. Many of the children with this syndrome were obviously brain damaged, having abnormal EEG's, positive neurological signs, and gross perceptual disabilities. The final syndrome involved a combination of an above average performance scale I.Q. and an almost total aphasia. The frustration to which a school setting exposed these youngsters, their awareness of their ability to reason but not to remember, and the many other realities of life with the double handicap of severe aphasia and profound deafness were shattering to the ego structure of these youths.

Table 5-3 shows the relationship between birth weight and the psychological diagnosis of emotional disturbance. The general trend is for a greater prevalence of disturbance to be associated with a lower birth weight. For example, in this sample 17 per cent of the children having a birth weight of less than 3 pounds 4 ounces were diagnosed psychotic. However, the numbers of cases per weight category are too few and the differences too small for these data to be conclusive.

The second approach to assessing emotional adjustment was teachers' ratings, a technique especially appropriate in this particular investigation, because there were only six to ten children in a class, making it possible for the teachers to know their students well. They were asked to rate them in terms of a five point scale of adjustment having the categories good, above average, average, below average, and poor.

Slightly more than 26 per cent of the premature children were rated poor in adjustment in contrast to only 4 per cent who were rated good. In general the distribution reflected a far greater prevalence of unsatisfactory adjustment with the premature than would be expected among the general population of deaf children or among other etiological groups such as the genetic or postmeningitic deaf. Only the postrubella group

TABLE 5-3

PREVALENCE OF SEVERE EMOTIONAL DISTURBANCE RELATIVE TO
BIRTH WEIGHTS OF PREMATURE DEAF CHILDREN

Birth Weight	Cases	Per Cent Diagnosed Emotionally Disturbed	Number Diagnosed Emotionally Disturbed
4 lbs. 7 oz.-5 lbs. 8 oz.	50	26	13 (1 psychotic)
3 lbs. 5 oz.-4 lbs. 6 oz.	33	27	9 (1 psychotic)
2 lbs. 4 oz.-3 lbs. 4 oz.	23	39	9 (4 psychotic)
1 lb. 2 oz.-2 lbs. 3 oz.	6	50	3 (1 psychotic)

TABLE 5-4

TEACHERS' RATINGS OF EMOTIONAL ADJUSTMENT

| | | | Ratings of Emotional Adjustment | | | | | | |
| Etiology | Superior | | Above Average | | Average | | Below Average | | Poor | |
	N	Per Cent	N	Per Cent	N	Per Cent	N	Per Cent	N	Per Cent
Heredity 59 Cases	7	11.8	19	32.2	22	37.2	5	8.4	6	10.1
Rh Factor 33 Cases	1	3.0	12	36.3	7	21.2	8	24.2	5	15.1
Prematurity 94 Cases	4	4.2	21	22.3	30	31.9	14	14.8	25	26.5
Meningitis 81 Cases	12	14.8	14	17.2	27	33.3	18	22.2	10	12.3
Rubella 91 Cases	4	4.3	20	21.9	18	19.7	21	23.0	28	30.7

$x^2 = 41.01$—significant at .001 level indicating significant differences between the five groups in Table 5-4.

yielded evidence of more adjustment difficulty (Table 5-4). As indicated earlier, 43 per cent of the rubella children were also premature, which further emphasizes the relationship between prematurity and maladjustment.

The final approach to the assessment of adjustment was to determine the percentage of premature children who had been dropped from school because of emotional disturbance. The figure was 6.2 per cent, a high figure for behavior representing this degree of pathology.

In sum, psychological evaluations and teachers' ratings are in remarkable agreement in indicating that one fourth to one third of prematurely born deaf children have severe emotional problems. Although in some cases these were Strauss syndrome type children, the majority were not acting out problems that lead to disciplinary difficulties. Passivity, schizoid patterns, and reaction to aphasoid involvement predominated.[1080]

Multiple Handicaps

Deaf children who have other handicaps in addition to their hearing loss are a major concern in education and in pediatrics.[262, 803, 1076] For this reason the problem of multiple handicaps was carefully examined in several aspects. The first question asked was, What is the prevalence of various handicaps among premature deaf children?

Table 5-5 reports these data, comparing the premature with other etiological groups. The 17.6 per cent rate of cerebral palsy (including hemiplegia) is far above the 0.1 to 0.6 prevalence found in the general population.[818] The findings of orthopedic problems and visual defects (all cases with glasses or with medical diagnosis of serious visual pathology) also exceed expectancies for the general population.

Among the visual pathologies were four legally blind children, six who

TABLE 5-5

PREVALENCE OF PHYSICAL ANOMALIES IN FIVE MAJOR ETIOLOGIES OF DEAFNESS

Etiology	Cerebral Palsy and/or Hemiplegia		Mental Retardation (I.Q. below 70)		Aphasoid Disorder		Visual Defects		Orthopedic (Excluding CP's)		Seizures	
	N[a]	Per Cent	N	Per Cent	N	Per Cent	N	Per Cent	N	Per Cent	N	Per Cent
Heredity	79	None	62	None	63	1.5	63	20.6	63	1.5	63	None
Meningitis ...	92	9.7	92	14.1	92	16.3	87	5.7	92	5.4	92	3.2
Prematurity ..	113	17.6	115	16.5	113	36.2	113	28.3	101	8.9	113	1.7
Rubella	104	3.8	98	8.1	105	21.9	104	29.8	104	4.8	104	None
Rh	45	51.1	39	5.1	35	22.8	45	24.4	45	2.2	45	6.6

[a] The total number of cases in each group on whom the needed information was available, not the number having the pathology. The latter data may be computed by multiplying the percentage having the pathology by the sample size (number of cases).

TABLE 5-6

MAJOR PHYSICAL DEFECTS ASSOCIATED WITH VARIOUS BIRTH WEIGHTS AMONG PREMATURE CHILDREN

Birth Weight	Total No. of Cases	Cerebral Palsy		Mental Retardation (I.Q. below 70)		Aphasoid Disorder		Visual Defect		
		N	Per Cent	N	Per Cent	N	Per Cent	N	Per Cent	Type of Anomalies Reported
4 lb. 7 oz.-5 lb. 8 oz.	49	5	10.2	5	10.2	16	32.6	8	16.3	1 Crossed Eye 1 Blind (Cataract)
3 lb. 5 oz.-4 lb. 6 oz.	34	4	11.7	6	17.6	10	29.4	8	23.5	2 Strabismus
2 lb. 4 oz.-3 lb. 4 oz.	23	5	21.7	7	30.4	9	39.1	10	43.4	1 Strabismus 2 Blind 1 Wandering Eye 1 No Upper Gaze
1 lb. 2 oz.-2 lb. 3 oz.	6	3	50.0	1	16.6	3	50.0	4	66.6	1 Blind 1 Crossed Eye
Premature but Exact Birth Weight Unknown	3	3	100.0	None	None	3	100.0	1	33.3	

had crossed eyes or strabismus, and one who lacked an upper gaze (visual field). Orthopedic problems included congenital defects such as one case of two toes on each foot; one bilateral dislocation of the hips; one defective rib cage; and one child who had a hand joined at the elbow, several fingers missing, and a misalignment of the outer, middle, and inner ears. Other conditions found, but not listed in Table 5-5, were cryptic orchidism (two cases), dwarfism (one case), and congenital exposed intestines (two cases).

Table 5-6 shows the prevalence of physical anomalies among the premature deaf children within different birth weight categories. As expected, the lower the birth weight the greater is the probability there will be other pathologies. This increase in probability becomes particularly pronounced with children weighing less than 3 pounds 4 ounces. These trends with deaf prematures are in keeping with the findings of studies on premature samples not restricted by the criterion of deafness.[601, 607, 992]

TABLE 5-7

TYPE AND PREVALENCE OF MULTIPLE HANDICAPS AMONG
115 PREMATURE DEAF CHILDREN[a]

Multiple Handicaps	Number of Cases	Per Cent of Cases
Deafness and One Other Major Handicap		
Cerebral Palsy	4	3.5
Aphasia	16	13.9
Mental Retardation	4	3.5
Deafness and Two Other Major Handicaps		
Major Visual Pathology	3	2.6
Emotional Disturbance	11	9.6
Orthopedic	—	—
Totals	38	33.0
Cerebral Palsy and Aphasia	5	4.3
Cerebral Palsy and Mental Retardation	4	3.5
Cerebral Palsy and Visual Pathology	1	0.9
Cerebral Palsy and Emotional Disturbance	2	1.7
Aphasia and Mental Retardation	2	1.7
Aphasia and Visual Pathology	1	0.9
Aphasia and Emotional Disturbance	9	7.8
Aphasia and Orthopedic Anomaly	—	—
Mental Retardation and Visual Pathology	2	1.7
Mental Retardation and Emotional Disturbance	1	0.9
Mental Retardation and Orthopedic Anomaly	2	1.7
Other	2	1.7
Totals	31	27.0
Deafness and Three Other Major Handicaps	9	7.9
Deafness and Four Other Major Handicaps	—	—
Grand Total	78	67.8

[a] In order to present this data in a two dimensional table it was necessary to use an *N* of 115 as a constant divisor in computing percentages. As noted from Table 5-5, data with regard to some disabilities were not available on all 115 cases. Consequently, certain prevalences, stated in percentages, are actually slightly higher than Table 5-7 shows.

TABLE 5-8

PREVALENCE OF MULTIPLE HANDICAPS ASSOCIATED WITH
VARIOUS BIRTH WEIGHTS IN PREMATURE DEAF CHILDREN

| | Major Disabilities | | | | | | |
| | Two Only | | Three Only | | Four Only | | Total | |
Birth Weight	Number	Per Cent	Number	Per Cent	Number	Per Cent	Number	Per Cent
4 lb. 7 oz.-5 lb. 8 oz.								
49 Cases	9	18.4	14	28.6	2	4.1	25	51.0
3 lb. 5 oz.-4lb. 6 oz.								
34 Cases	16	47.1	3	8.8	3	8.8	22	64.7
2 lb. 4 oz.-3 lb. 4 oz.								
23 Cases	11	47.8	10	43.5	1	4.3	22	95.7
1 lb. 2 oz.-2 lb. 3 oz.								
6 Cases	2	33.3	2	33.3	2	33.3	6	100
Premature (Exact Weight Unknown)								
3 Cases	—	—	2	66.7	1	33.3	3	100
Totals	38	33.0	31	27.0	9	7.9	78	

In addition to knowing the prevalence of various physical anomalies among these children, it is important to know how they are distributed. This is shown in Table 5-7. The most striking finding here is that slightly over two thirds of premature children are multiply handicapped. The disabilities other than deafness cover the full spectrum, including cerebral palsy, mental retardation, aphasia, visual pathology, and emotional disturbance. Thirty-three per cent had one disability other than hearing loss, 27 per cent had two additional handicaps, and 7.9 per cent had three disabilities in addition to deafness. The syndromes most frequently found were aphasia with emotional disturbance and aphasia with cerebral palsy. In cases where four or more major handicaps were present (7.9%) cerebral palsy and/or mental retardation were almost always involved.

Table 5-8 shows that as the birth weight of the premature child decreases, the probability of multiple handicaps rises sharply. This is particularly true of the more disabling conditions—mental retardation, cerebral palsy, and emotional disturbance.

It is obvious from these data on multiple handicaps that premature deaf children are characterized by having one or more additional disabilities. Furthermore, these secondary involvements are critical conditions in the lives of these children, conditions which demand intensive psychological, educational, and medical attention if the children are to be adequately prepared to meet the demands of today's society.[1080]

Audiometric Findings

The mean puretone hearing loss (ASA 1951) in the speech range (500 to 2000 cps) for the premature was 82.7 decibels. Although a profound loss, it represents somewhat more residual hearing than should be expected in a residential school for the deaf population. In addition, many of the applicants found to have too much hearing for admission to the school were born prematurely, indicating that the low birth weight represents a prominent etiology of defective hearing at all gradations of loss.

The patterns of the audiograms of the premature did not yield the configuration of the typical nerve loss, i.e., hearing did not decline linearly as frequencies increased. Instead, the audiograms were typically relatively flat, having a slight asymmetric curving with the thresholds at the extremes of the audiogram a little higher than those in the middle.[1080]

CONCLUSIONS

Premature birth is associated with deafness and with milder hearing loss to a far greater extent than has been previously known. This prevalence of children of low birth weight is of critical importance to the area of deafness. It accounts for much of the increase in multiply handicapped deaf children that is currently of primary concern to professionals of all disciplines working with the deaf and hard of hearing. Furthermore, it is probable that, with medical science saving more and more viable fetuses of low birth weight, yet not preventing serious residua from the trauma of prematurity, the prevalence of premature deaf children will increase.

A corollary conclusion from these research data is that there are major behavioral differences characteristic of premature deaf children in contrast to other groups of deaf children and in contrast to the limited normative data on deaf populations. Much of this behavioral variance is in critical areas of psychological adjustment and ability to learn. It has as its principal etiology the neurophysiological sequelae of prematurity. Just as these sequelae account for significant behavioral variance, they also explain many of the physical disabilities among premature deaf children. Audiometric patterns may also be the result of anoxic neurological lesions.

In view of the fact that approximately 17 per cent of deaf school age children are premature and that more than two thirds are multiply handicapped, it is essential there be an awareness of this heretofore overlooked problem. Such awareness makes it apparent that much of the behavior of some deaf children previously explained as a result of hearing impairment is actually an interaction effect of this loss and the psychoneurological residua of prematurity.

A final conclusion derived from these data is that the lower the birth weight of a premature child, the greater is the probability of deafness. Along with this relationship between prematurity and profound hearing loss, it was found that the lower the birth weight of the premature deaf child, the more other disabilities of a serious nature he is likely to have.

Chapter 6

Retrospective Studies on the Epidemiology of Reproductive Casualty: Old and New

Benjamin Pasamanick and Hilda Knobloch

R EPRODUCTIVE CASUALTY is a term coined some twelve years ago for the sequelae of harmful events during pregnancy and parturition resulting in damage to the fetus or new born infant, and primarily localized to the central nervous system.[850]

The hypothesis basic to the series of studies to be described stems from a number of propositions: (1) Since prematurity and complications of pregnancy are associated with fetal and neonatal death, usually on the basis of injury to the brain, there must remain a fraction so injured who do not die. (2) Depending upon the degree and location of the damage, the survivors may develop a series of disorders. These extend from cerebral palsy, epilepsy, and mental deficiency through all types of behavioral and learning disabilities which are a result of lesser degrees of damage sufficient to disorganize behavioral development and lower thresholds to stress.[837] (3) Further, these abnormalities of pregnancy are associated with certain life experiences, usually socioeconomically determined, and consequently (4) they themselves and their resulting neuropsychiatric disorders are found in greater aggregation in the lower strata of our society.[861] The term *reproductive casualty*, which was conceived as a continuum from death through varying degrees of disability, we used to replace a somewhat older term, *reproductive wastage*, applied chiefly to fetal and neonatal deaths. It was felt that wastage was an invidious term when applied to children at any time and, in any event, incorrect when used for a host of minor motor, perceptual, intellectual, learning and behavioral disabilities.[602-604]

The concept of a continuum of reproductive casualty is not really new. It has existed in various forms in the thinking of physicians for many decades, if not centuries. It was, for instance, implicit in the writings of Arnold Gesell. In the last half century, with the gradual assumption of con-

Reprinted from *Merrill-Palmer Quarterly of Behavior and Development*, 12:7-26, 1966.

trol over the acute infectious diseases and the uncovering of the enormous problems of the chronic disorders, of which the neuropsychiatric are by far most numerous, costly and disabling, the importance of pregnancy, its abnormalities and their sequelae has taken a commanding position in public health efforts and research.[854] Since literally many millions each year are affected, it is not surprising that the literature on the epidemiology of reproductive casualty and its precursors is enormous. From the concepts and writings of Ballantyne,[61] the father of modern scientific thinking in this area, up to the recent massive review by Montagu,[783] tens of thousands of papers have been published touching upon the subject. It is obvious, therefore, that in the short time available only some items can be mentioned and even fewer discussed.

To pick a few variables at random is to indicate how all-pervasive and common they are: maternal-fetal blood type incompatibilities, Rh, ABO, Duffy, and so on; maternal endocrine disorders such as hypo- and hyperthyroidism, diabetes, and others; radiation, both natural background and man-produced, with good or evil motivation, during radiography or the detonation of nuclear devices. All have been implicated in the production of damage to the developing brain.[851]

Maternal age has been shown to be a potent factor, both the very young and the older mothers more often producing impaired children. These are important data to bear in mind these days when the average age of marriage, particularly in the United States, has fallen precipitously and at the same time older women in the lowest economic strata, coming from various ethnic and religious groups, continue to have children in their forties. The entire field of reproductive readiness and efficiency is one just barely indicated by these data. By the same token heavy maternal work, and indeed all severe chronic stress upon the mother during pregnancy, would appear to have potentially injurious effects upon the fetus.

The recent reports of the production of phocomelia following ingestion of thalidomide in the first trimester of pregnancy dramatically highlight both the period of greatest sensitivity of the rapidly developing organism to exogenous sources of damage and the large numbers at risk of being damaged during a time of life previously largely disregarded. Without control, this era of enormous proliferation of profitably manufactured pharmaceuticals may produce effects which, although perhaps not as dramatic in nature as the congenital deformities mentioned, may be much more numerous because of the inherent difficulty of detection. When we remember that many of the modern drugs, biologicals, and antibiotics have very specific inhibiting effects upon one or more enzyme systems, some of which may be essential for the normal growth and development of the fetus, we must consider the possibility that the new therapeutic media, of which we are so justly proud, may turn out to be two-edged swords, cutting the more sharply in an unfortunate direction as they are sharpened for the good.

The effect on the fetal brain of the directly invasive action of the luetic spirochete and the resulting juvenile paresis has been known for a long time. More recently rubella and toxoplasmosis have been demonstrated to be damaging invaders of the central nervous system. Most recently cytomegalic inclusion body disease has been described as a fetal infection. However, other than these, and of course smallpox, maternal infections have not been demonstrated to cause fetal brain damage by direct invasion. We did find more tuberculosis and urinary tract infections in the mothers of children who were reproductive casualties. Some time ago the collaborative study on cerebral palsy in the United States reported an association between maternal urinary tract infection and prematurity in the offspring. Other infections such as influenza have been described as producing small increases in reproductive casualty. The most likely mechanism for the effects of these infections is a nonspecific toxic or physiologic stress, either by itself or, more probably, upon an already abnormal pregnancy. One must recall that infections are much more common in lower-class mothers who are at greater risk of having other complications of pregnancy as well. If these are valid observations, what must be the implications of the enormous burdens of malaria, schistosomiasis, and other chronic and acute infections in grossly malnourished and sick populations in the underdeveloped countries?

A good deal of debate has recently appeared about whether anoxia during or immediately after delivery, so long assumed to be the major pathologic factor, is in itself damaging. Significant damage in humans has been described by some but not by others. The newly delivered but not the fetal animal has been demonstrated to have marked resistance to anoxic damage. Most of those described as subjected to anoxia failed to secure oxygen because of a failure to assume respiration. It may very well be that many of these children who do not breathe spontaneously after delivery and require resuscitation have already sustained brain damage during fetal life and thus have impaired respiratory centers; this explains why only relatively few children subjected to prolonged anoxia are brain damaged.[600]

At least five reports have now appeared indicating that cigarette smoking by the mother increases the risk of producing a premature infant, as defined by birth weight. The most favored mechanism in the literature is that of the vascular effect of nicotine in contracting uterine and placental vessels and thus reducing the oxygen and nutritional supply to the fetus.

Interestingly enough, the most recent paper indicated that the effects increased as the social class fell and that, indeed, there was no detectable effect of smoking in the highest classes. It is difficult to conceive that the uterine vasculature in upper-class women differs so radically from that in the lower-class that it does not react to nicotine. It is much more likely that smoking exerts its effect by some other means or combination of pathways. It is quite possible that the well-known effect of smoking upon appetite may so reduce protein intake in the lower-class mothers, whose protein intake is already notoriously low, as to produce prematurity, either directly or by increasing the risk of complications of pregnancy. In the upper class, well nourished at the outset, protein intake is not likely to fall too precipitously because there are sufficient funds for both protein foods and cigarettes, whereas the lower-class woman probably substitutes carbohydrates.

We would like to turn now to a description of a dozen conditions we have studied retrospectively with the hypothesis that they might be included as constituents of the continuum of reproductive casualty. It should be explicitly noted at this point that retrospective epidemiologic research and clinical investigation of the individual patient rely upon data gathered, and possibly interpreted, in a manner that may introduce biases. In clinical work, unselected information secured from the patient or the parent of a patient cannot be compared to that secured from even a well-matched, healthy control. Such information, particularly in early childhood and before, is therefore not a very good source from which to draw diagnoses.[863]

Even cause and effect are frequently confounded in our psychodynamic formulations. In a study to be described in the paper on prospective studies,* we found a high positive correlation between the irritability and tension displayed by a mother during her interview with a nurse and the degree of neurological damage found in her infant by a physician. Since we know clinically that most of the neurological signs discernible during infancy disappear with maturation, it is possible to conceive that had this infant been presented as a behavior-disordered child ten or fifteen years later, its difficulties could have been attributed to the mother's behavior. The person who works with children must keep his head above the multiplicity of variables operating through time upon his patients and not be drowned, grasping at a single straw of causation.[840] In the strictest sense of the term, the studies to be reported are not truly retrospective since the data used were recorded contemporaneously with the event, rather than secured from the memory of an informant whose recall and reporting might

---

* See "Prospective Studies on the Epidemiology of Reproductive Casualty: Methods, Findings, and Some Implications" by Hilda Knobloch and Benjamin Pasamanick, pp. 27-43 of same. *Merrill-Palmer Quarterly of Behavior and Development, Vol. 12.*

have been biased by the fact that the independent variable, i.e., the clinical condition investigated, is present in the experimental group and not known to exist in the controls.

In naturalistic epidemiologic investigations an attempt is made to isolate the independent variable through parceling it out in the experimental sample. This is done by selecting a control sample similar in all aspects except for the variable under scrutiny and then determining how both samples differ in the dependent variables. Contrasted with this is the experimental study in which both samples are drawn from the same population and the independent variable is intentionally altered. While the latter type of study is much more likely to offer definitive conclusions, the naturalistic study is frequently the only method available for research on human populations, particularly in the chronic disorders. It is possible, however, to demonstrate that the results of such a study, interwoven with additional factors, present so weighty an argument for a given chain of causality that no other conclusion seems valid under the circumstances.[849]

Following upon some earlier studies leading us to the hypothesis of a continuum we began a series of retrospective studies[656] of the relationship between prenatal experience and certain neuropsychiatric disorders (Table 6-1). More than 9,000 children were involved in these studies. For each study a large population of children diagnosed as having the particular clinical condition under scrutiny was selected from the case files of hospital outpatient clinics, institutions, and public schools. The clinical data from the case histories were abstracted and coded for internal comparison studies. We then searched the birth certificate register to single out for further examination those children who had been born in Baltimore where the first seven studies were conducted, and for whom birth records were available.[842]

A series of controls to whom the cases could be compared was also selected. In all but one of the studies, the control was the next surviving infant in the birth certificate register of the same race, sex, and socioeconomic status as the case, who was born in the same hospital to a mother of the same age. In the behavior disorder study, the control was the next child alphabetically of the same sex in the same school class as the case. This controlled for teacher bias in reporting and automatically controlled for race since the study was done prior to integration.

Information about the parents and their socioeconomic status was derived from the children's birth certificates. For those children born in hospitals, information was gathered from hospital records on such items as number of previous pregnancies, abortions, stillbirths, premature and neonatal deaths, complications of pregnancy, labor, and delivery, operative delivery procedures, birth weight, and neonatal course.

TABLE 6-1

MATERNAL AND FETAL FACTORS IN NEUROPSYCHIATRIC DISORDERS[a]

Disorder	Number of Children in Study Group		One or More Complications in Pregnancy (%)				Prematurity[b] (%)				Neonatal Abnormalities[c] (%)			
	White	Non-White	Study Group W	N	Control Group W	N	Study Group W	N	Control Group W	N	Study Group W	N	Control Group W	N
Cerebral Palsy	561	—	38.0		21.0		22.0		5.0		—		—	
Epilepsy	274	122	27.7	50.8	18.8	43.4	12.9	15.3	3.8	12.3	17.2	13.6	5.7	3.3
Mental Deficiency	404	235	34.4	60.0	25.2	55.0	16.3	18.4	7.0	11.6	18.0	7.7	7.5	6.1
Behavioral Disorders	625	215	33.0	64.0	25.0	51.0	6.0	17.0	2.0	5.0	5.0	4.0	3.0	2.0
Reading Disorders	205	—	37.6		21.5		11.5		4.6		7.8		3.9	
Tics	51		33.3		17.6		4.0		6.0		37.3		25.5	
Speech Disorders	272		25		19		5		8		9		11	
Strabismus	398		22.9		16.1		13.6		7.8		22.4		13.8	
Hearing Disorders	124		24.0		11.5		16.1		7.3		17.1		13.3	
Accidents in School Children	725		17.8		16.3		8.0		5.2		15.0		12.8	
Autism	50		51.0		17.0		21.0		12.0		64.0		28.0	
Juvenile Delinquency	300		8.5		11.1		3.6		3.8		—		—	

[a] In last 5 studies only complications of pregnancy or those related to pregnancy were included; abnormalities of labor and delivery and diseases associated with pregnancy were excluded.
[b] Birth weights 2,500 gm (5.5 lb.) or less.
[c] Convulsions, cyanosis, and asphyxia.

In retrospective studies of this type, direct comparisons of current behavior between cases and controls are not made, but information that has been recorded in the past is examined. By this method, associations between prior conditions and current clinical entities can be demonstrated by showing significant differences between cases and controls in the incidence of various prior abnormalities under consideration. If those cases selected as controls from the birth certificate files had any of the clinical neuropsychiatric entities under investigation, any difference in the histories between the cases and the controls would be more significant in the face of the possibility that the control patient group was contaminated by clinical cases. The point has been raised repeatedly that studies of this nature are inherently flawed by the poor quality and almost universal underreporting of complications or abnormalities. This fact presents a bias against the hypothesis being tested. While relationships might be obscured or missed, the finding of significant differences is evidence for true associations.[648]

Thus far, five of the first seven clinical entities studied in the Baltimore children have been found to be significantly associated both with complications of pregnancy and prematurity. These are cerebral palsy,[655] epilepsy,[653] mental deficiency,[838] behavior disorders,[858] and reading disabilities.[571] A sixth condition, tics,[869] was found to be significantly associated with complications of pregnancy but not with prematurity. The seventh entity, childhood speech disorder,[859] when not associated with cerebral palsy or mental deficiency, showed no significant relation to abnormalities of pregnancy or prematurity, although slight differences in the predicted direction were found for pregnancy abnormality.

No difference was found between the cases and controls in the incidence of prolonged and difficult labor and of operative procedures during delivery, such as mid- or high-forceps, Caesarean section, breech extraction, or internal version and extraction, the types of situation that have previously been hypothesized as responsible for birth trauma. Rather, the associations occurred with the prolonged and probably anoxia-producing complications of pregnancy such as the toxemias and maternal bleeding.[841]

Two other general observations can be made. First, the incidence of abnormalities of pregnancy was much higher in the nonwhites than in the whites. Second, the differences between cases and controls tended to be greater in the more severe clinical conditions, e.g., cerebral palsy and epilepsy, and to decrease as the handicap became milder.

It should also be noted that in all the conditions studied, except speech disorders, there was a much higher prevalence of the clincial entities in males, perhaps a further lead as to the etiologic role of brain injury as a precursor of these disorders.

As in most epidemiologic studies there were a number of by-products that permitted us to examine other possible etiologic factors and to seek for the internal consistency necessary to help support the major tests of the hypothesis.

In the investigation of epilepsy we found that although differences between cases and controls were in the expected direction among Negroes, they were not statistically significant. This is probably at least partially attributable to the fact that the rate of pregnancy abnormality among Negro mothers and their offspring, both cases and controls, was so high that the number of cases available did not constitute a sample large enough to yield significant results.

In addition to direct evidence from morbidity statistics that postnatal insult following such conditions as lead intoxication, head injury, and infection is probably more common among Negroes than among whites, there is indirect evidence also for this in the findings of this study.[845] The younger the patient at the onset of convulsive seizures, the more likely is the condition to be due to brain damage sustained early in the development of the individual. In the white patients, there was a positive association between prenatal and paranatal complications and the onset of seizures in the first year of life. In the Negro epileptics, however, this relationship between age and onset of seizures and abnormalities of pregnancy was not observed.[857]

Since we had data available on the occurrence of epilepsy in the families of our cases we thought it might be fruitful to see what light our results cast on the genetic hypothesis. It is reasonable to assume that if prenatal and paranatal factors play a significant role in the causation of some forms of epilepsy and genetic factors in others, our cases in which the pregnancy factors were absent should have had more epileptic parents than those cases in which these factors were present. This was not found to be true, and makes it necessary to re-examine the genetic hypothesis in epilepsy. May not the familial aggregation of epilepsy be a reflection of the occurrence of familial aggregation of the prenatal and paranatal factors under discussion in this report? Prematurity, stillbirth, and neonatal death have been so described, and the socioeconomic factors with which these and other abnormalities are associated are usually a lifelong experience.

In the study of mental deficiency, although there was significantly more prematurity among the retarded Negro children, there was no significant difference between cases and controls as far as complications of pregnancy were concerned. However, when we examined the relationship between the degree of mental deficiency and these pregnancy abnormalities, a most revealing association was discovered.[654] Almost every one of the Negro children in the group with I.Q.s under 50 had been exposed to one or more abnormalities of pregnancy. For those above I.Q. 50 no such difference existed between cases and controls. This in contrast to the white cases where differences existed at all levels of deficiency. The most likely explanation for these results is that the Negro group with I.Q.s from 50 to 80 must have been diluted by the inclusion of cases who had no real brain disease but who merely reflected the widespread sociocultural retardation known to exist among Negro children.[843] We also found that very young mothers and older women had a significantly higher risk of producing mentally defective children. Increasing birth order also increased the risk of mental deficiency.

Among the behavior disorders investigated, the highest association with the complications under consideration was found for both racial groups in those children called hyperactive, confused, and disorganized.[933] These accounted for 40 per cent of the school referrals in Baltimore. When this diagnostic category was removed there were no longer any significant differences between white cases and controls. In the Negroes, however, differences were still present for the remainder of the cases. It may be that in nonwhites cerebral injury is so pervasive that it infiltrates all types of behavior disorder.

A number of socioeconomic and familial variables were examined in this study. Items previously incriminated by other writers such as family composition, parental age and education, employment, and housing were not found to be different among the cases and controls.[852]

The reading disorder investigation was confined to white children, since any sample of Negro children would have been heavily contaminated by cases whose disorders were a result of sociocultural retardation.[572] As a test of internal consistency we looked at association with degree of reading disability. The greater the disability, the more abnormalities of pregnancy were found in the background.

In the study of speech disorders, from which no significant association was found with complications of pregnancy, we did encounter a finding that helped confirm previous impressions. Contrary to our expectation, there was no greater incidence of speech disorders among males, which was in marked contrast to the other neuropsychiatric disorders studied. We also found a significantly higher proportion of multiple pregnancies among the speech disorder cases as well as an increased risk of disorder in the higher birth orders, both associations explainable on psychologic grounds.

Recently, in Columbus, we have examined five more conditions to make the dozen referred to. These five studied in the same manner as the previous seven are strabismus, hearing defects, school accidents, infantile autism and juvenile delinquency.[853] Strabismus, largely due to muscle paralysis or imbalance, we had previously found to be common, particularly in infants, as one of the symptoms of a syndrome of minimal brain damage; it has been described in cerebral palsy and other known sequelae of brain damage. We were therefore not too surprised to find quite a strong and significant association of complications of pregnancy and prematurity with this condition in children who had no other apparent sequelae of brain damage.

Hearing defect in young children, in these days of modern treatment of middle-ear infections, is largely nerve deafness with varying and unknown amounts of central nervous system damage producing aphasia. That this peripheral or central damage might be due in part to prematurity and complications of pregnancy might have been anticipated in view of the apparent relationship of almost any condition involving neural damage with these abnormalities. We did, indeed, find a very strong and significant relationship.

Accidents in children were hypothesized as being related to the brain-damaging effects of prematurity and complications, on the basis that muscular coordination, impulsivity and judgment might be impaired in children brain-damaged as a result of these prenatal and paranatal events. We took into account the site of accident, since it was quite possible that some children might be at greater risk of sustaining accidents because of the location and nature of their homes and families, by selecting as a control the next child alphabetically of the same race and sex in the same class. Our hypothesis was strongly supported as far as prematurity was concerned. Unfortunately, these were older children than in the two preceding studies and hospital recording of complications in Columbus was quite poor at that time. But the association with prematurity would indicate that some accidents might now also be considered one of the constituents of the continuum and be the basis for accident-proneness in some individuals.

The fourth condition, infantile autism, was studied in some seventy children, a small fraction of the large population available for study at the Clinic of Child Development in Columbus. When phenylketonuria was removed, the remainder, approximately fifty children, were found to have exceedingly high rates of both complications of pregnancy and prematurity. These children also had, with only one or two exceptions, neurologic signs of brain damage. These findings support those of Bender, Zitrin and Goldfarb who, in three separate samples of childhood schizophrenics, have found significantly increased rates of prematurity and/or neurologic signs of brain damage. It would seem advisable at this time to reconsider both the etiology and diagnosis of much of childhood schizophrenia and possibly assign those cases to the chronic organic brain syndromes.[847]

We believe the psychopathology in the autistic children to be somewhat analogous to that in the aphasics. It can be hypothesized that because of impaired perceptual and cognitive reception and integration consequent to certain types or continuations of cerebral damage, social stimulation and response because of their complexity and variation, may become far too difficult for the damaged child to manage efficiently. As a consequence, the child pushes people and social interaction out of his behavioral repertoire. Infantile autism in this framework might then be considered a form of "social aphasia."

On follow-up later in childhood most of the children have lost the autistic behavior, having apparently compensated with time and exposure to social stimulation at whatever level of functioning their cerebral damage permitted. Those too severely damaged remain mentally deficient, although no longer autistic in most cases. Similar findings were noted in the phenylketonurics on treatment with phenylalanine deficient diets—autistic behavior disappearing on treatment. Even in those cases where the diet was begun too late in life to affect the intellectual deficit, autistic behavior present for years yielded in a few months of treatment.

At least one report was published within the past year indicating that juvenile delinquency is associated with brain injury in some of the delinquents. Delinquency in the United States has been described by the sociologists as a phenomenon characteristic of a large fraction, if not the majority, of adolescent males in the lowest socioeconomic strata of large cities. It has become institutionalized over many generations in these deprived slum areas and is conducted typically as an activity of small groups or gangs.[860] In our previous investigations of behavior disorders as reproductive casualties, we had found that it was largely those children described as hyperactive, confused, and disorganized, who had histories of being premature or who were products of complicated pregnancies. These children were the least likely to be acceptable members of gangs and to be delinquents in the classical sociological tradition. Nevertheless, since attribution of brain damage had been made for these children, it was deemed advisable to test the hypothesis empirically. In a large group of adolescents from the Franklin County Juvenile Court in Columbus, it was found that no differences existed in rates of prematurity or complications of pregnancy between the experimental subjects and their birth certificate controls. It may very well be true that in European countries, where delinquency is much less common that in the United States, true antisocial psychopathic behavior would not be so heavily diluted by the garden variety of group delinquency so that the association with prenatal abnormalities would become evident on epidemiologic investigation. Thus the suggestions from England and Czechoslovakia that some psychopathic personality clinical pictures also be considered constituents of the continuum may be quite justified.

In any event, it would seem that at least two conclusions might be drawn from the negative findings of this last study. First, it would appear that the design of this type of retrospective investigation is adequate, since, even when drawn from the lowest possible socioeconomic stratum, the experimental subjects did not present increased rates in the dependent variable (despite general demonstration that such are found in these strata). Apparently the type of control selected is sufficient to control for this possible source of bias. Secondly, it would tend to support the sociological as contrasted to the psychiatric explanation for juvenile delinquency in the overwhelming majority of these children in the United States and to indicate where preventive efforts must be exerted.

We have most recently had occasion to examine in a preliminary fashion some data on what may turn out to be a thirteenth condition within the continuum of reproductive casualty, viz., left-handedness. It had been our clinical impression that we encountered significantly more left-handedness in preschool age children on whom a diagnosis of brain injury had been made. We felt that it was possible that if the injury was confined largely to the left motor cortex and its efferent system, or with greater injury there, the child would as a consequence during the maturation of the motor behavior tend to prefer the left hand because of the greater precision it would afford him. Further, since it is our belief that hand-preference is almost wholly a product of social learning in human cultures—as witness the almost equal distribution of handedness in other primates—difficulty in learning or integration accompanying brain injury might create difficulty in the assumption of right-handedness, obviously the socially preferred side. This, when added to some greater degree of difficulty in the motor system of the right hand, might conceivably result in a clumsy type of ambidexterity which would continue far into the age period when handedness had already been firmly established in the normal child.

We tested this possibility in a fashion different from the other retrospective studies. In the sample of children examined at three years of age, who were followed in the longitudinal study of prematures discussed in the succeeding paper, we examined the relationship of ambidexterity (nonestablishment of handedness) at three years to that of a diagnosis of brain injury made at forty weeks. A statistically significant association being found, we now intend to test this further in two ways. First we would like

to confirm our clinical impression by examining the relationship of ambidexterity and left-handedness to diagnosis of brain injury in the large cohort of neurologic cases available to us. Secondly we intend to follow the
pattern of investigation we have used before, i.e., to secure an experimental group of left-handed individuals from a school system with a control
group of right-handed children from the same classrooms and compare prenatal events in both.

It has been known for some time that the neuropsychiatric disorders
under discussion are more common among the lower socioeconomic strata
of our population, including Negroes and other disadvantaged minority
groups.[856, 868, 844] We suspected that this discrepancy extended to the
complications associated with these disorders. Of particular interest to us
were prematurity and abnormalities of the prenatal and paranatal periods.

An examination of the distribution of prematurity in Baltimore in relation to socioeconomic status, as defined by census tract, demonstrated a
significant negative correlation with socioeconomic status in the white
groups.[922] The incidence was 5 per cent in the highest economic tenth
compared to 7.6 per cent in the lowest. In the nonwhites, it was 11.4
per cent. In examining the distribution of complications of pregnancy and
birth in the white population only the lower and upper economic fifth were
compared. The findings were striking.[867] The incidence of complications in
the white upper economic fifth was 5 per cent and in the white lower fifth
14.6 per cent. In the nonwhites, it was 50.6 per cent.

These higher rates of prematurity and complications of pregnancy among
Negroes over even the lowest white socioeconomic group are so marked
that some workers in this field maintain that they must be attributable to
some innate racial characteristic. Since average Negro socioeconomic status
is generally lower than that in the lowest white groups, it seems more
parsimonious to eliminate the postulated racial factor and to hypothesize
that prematurity and pregnancy complication rates increase exponentially
below certain socioeconomic thresholds.

It should be noted that the differences in rates of prenatal maternal
abnormalities and/or prematurity between the experimental and control
groups do not furnish us with a true indication of the weight those variables contribute to the production of neuropsychiatric disorders in children.
When these differences are statistically significant all it indicates is that
there is a significant association which may be etiological. The true contribution of prenatal factors to the production of these disorders cannot be
fully ascertained from these studies because of the nature and origin of
the data and their analysis. In the retrospective studies (and in studies
where all events cannot or indeed, are not, fully recorded from the outset),

we have good reason to believe that the rates derived are minimal rates in both experimental and control groups. If we make the reasonable assumption that the amount of under-reporting is similar in both groups, the true differences would be much larger.

Secondly, the severity of the prenatal abnormality has usually not been recorded or utilized in comparisons, and it may very well be that while present in the control group it might be to a less severe degree. This helps to explain why even though the control group still had a certain rate of prenatal abnormalities, it might not exhibit the neuropsychiatric disorder. The possible factors for protection of the fetus from the potential damaging consequences of the maternal abnormality are not known and, in any event, have not been examined. In the same way that factors for protection are unknown, little is known about predisposing factors which might lead one mother to produce a damaged child while another exposed to the same complications, and even of the same severity, might have a normal offspring. There are some data to indicate that mothers who are themselves of lower-class origin and were exposed to lifelong deprivation from conception to adulthood, as indicated by their poorer physical growth, are the ones who are predisposed to produce the children who will exhibit the neuropsychiatric disorders we are discussing. This predisposition is frequently on a *post hoc* basis, given a hereditary explanation by some writers.

Thirdly, it might be wondered why a large number of children who have the neuropsychiatric disorder under consideration were not reportedly exposed to the prenatal abnormality. There are at least two possibilities to consider: (1) as indicated previously, it simply was not recorded; (2) not all types of prenatal events or abnormalities were examined largely because they go unrecorded. Such variables as maternal infections and nonspecific acute or chronic stress usually go unrecorded in maternal charts, and so their contributions remain unweighted.

We would like now to turn to a second group of studies which adds to our chain of evidence and at the same time strengthens the links already forged. These last studies concern the effects of summer heat on conception and the fetus.

It is known that children born in the winter months run a greater risk of developing mental deficiency, and a number of hypotheses have been advanced to account for this. Feeling that whatever damage is incurred in most cases of mental deficiency happens during the third fetal month, since cellular differentiation is at its height during this period, we examined the month of birth of all the children admitted to the Columbus State School from 1913 to 1949. We found a significant peak in the births of mental defectives in the first three months of the year, corresponding to a summer occurrence of the third month of pregnancy.[606] We then hypothesized an association with summer heat which, either by reducing protein intake or by direct stress effect through the hypothalamico-pituitary-adreno-cortical axis, produced fetal damage. If this were true, hotter summers should have produced more mental defectives than cooler summers. This was precisely what was discovered. Indeed, cooler summers were not associated with an increased risk of mental defect at all.

Since our studies showed that the incidence of mental deficiency is associated with complications of pregnancy and seems to vary with season of birth, we thought it possible that complications of pregnancy also vary seasonally. By examining a systematic sample of New York City birth certificates, we found that there was indeed a statistically significant higher rate of complications of pregnancy in the mothers who delivered in winter months. Interestingly enough, they were precisely the same complications we had previously found to be associated with brain damage, that is, toxemias and bleeding.[865] Differences in most of the other complications did not even approach significance.

Because of the relationship of low socioeconomic status to both mental deficiency and complications of pregnancy, there existed the possibility that we were dealing primarily with an increased rate of lower socioeconomic births in the same winter months. We were able to rule this out by examining the variation in birth rates for a five-year period in Baltimore, using census tract of residence as the criterion of socioeconomic status.[855] As a matter of fact, the lower socioeconomic strata, both white and Negro, had somewhat fewer deliveries in the winter months. There was marked variation in the seasonal birth rates by socioeconomic status with a large dip coinciding with summer conceptions for the lower socioeconomic strata. There was little or no variation in birth rates throughout the year for the upper economic group. A variety of socioeconomically determined factors may be operating to create these disparities, including the ability of the higher status groups to modify significantly the deleterious effects of climate, which may operate to a much stronger degree on the lower groups, either by way of disinclination to coitus, heat amenorrhea, maternal dietary deficiency, or direct effect on the viability of sperm or fetus.

Having found this socioeconomic association of birth rates with season of conception, we thought there might also exist a geographic variation associated with seasonal climatic differences. We therefore examined all the 1955 births in this country by month and geographic distribution and our expectations were completely fulfilled.[855] The southern states showed a marked decline in births during the spring months. The midwestern and northeastern states showed only a very slight trough in spring births. The northwestern states of Washington and Oregon exhibited no spring trough at all and were slightly higher in spring births than expected. In Ohio we have found that approximately one-quarter of the variance in spring birth rates is directly attributable to the height of the temperature in the preceding July and August.[848] The data also indicate, but not at all conclusively, that male births are fewer just prior to and during the descending curve of the spring depression. Since it has been demonstrated that males apparently run much more risk of prenatal brain injury than do females, the factor of increased pregnancy complications associated with summer conception may be operating here. We have also found that the peak neonatal death rate occurs in the spring, again coinciding with a summer conception.

Through the kindness of the National Office of Vital Statistics, we secured the seasonal distribution by birth weight for all the children born in the United States in one year. We thought that if maternal diet showed any effect upon birth weight this should appear in the children born during the summer since it has been demonstrated repeatedly that dietary intake, particularly of protein, decreases during summer weather and that the weight of the fetus is largely accumulated during the last trimester of pregnancy. Again, the predicted association was found. Children born in the summer are significantly lighter in weight.[870]

In a previous study in Baltimore, we had found that monozygotic twin births were less frequent in the lower socioeconomic white segments of the population.[657] If this lower incidence could be due to the greater risks of abortion in multiple pregnancy, we thought it might also appear as a seasonal variation. Using the same Baltimore data, we did find that the lowest rate of twinning occurred in the first quarter of the year and was confined to the lower socioeconomic strata. The peak rates of twinning occurred in the spring quarter coinciding with summer conception, with the possibility that this might be due to the teratogenic effect of heat stress upon the embryo.[866] We would like to remind the reader that multiple births are associated not only with a significantly higher incidence of prematurity but also with a significantly higher infant mortality, and that twinning was much more common among our cases of neuropsychiatric disorder.

We have just completed analysis of data from our Columbus study on seasonal variation in the births of schizophrenics. Although we were not able to confirm previous findings of an increased rate of schizophrenia in winterborn individuals, we did find a significant rise in the rate of schizophrenia in individuals born following hot summers, as contrasted to cool summers, similar to the picture discovered for mental deficiency.[839] We do not feel that schizophrenia is due to brain injury but rather that this may be an indication of a lowered threshold to stress serving as an additional organic precursor to breakdown in the individual who is already genetically predisposed.[864]

It would seem apparent by this time that a number of preventive implications could be drawn from these epidemiologic investigations. For some precursors of damage, prevention is specific and obvious. For radiation, smoking, toxic substances, some infections such as syphilis and rubella, the direction of preventive efforts is apparent, although for social reasons frequently difficult to institute. For other precursors such as maternal endocrine disorders and maternal fetal incompatibilities, early vigorous treatment of mother and/or the child may prevent much of the disability. For still other precursors such as the complications of pregnancy and prematurity, the epidemiologic data strongly indicate the direction of the efforts needed. The toxemias of pregnancy, placental disorders, and prematurity as well as maternal fatigue and most nonspecific acute and chronic infections, are all heavily aggregated in the lowest socioeconomic strata of our populations. These variables almost certainly operate multifactorially, each tending to aggravate the effects of the others. They operate by diverse physiologic paths and require preventive efforts on various levels.

Fortunately, improvement in one area can be expected to result in improvement in another. It has already been demonstrated experimentally that high levels of protein intake, when supplemented by vitamins, can significantly lower rates of toxemia, bleeding, and prematurity. Maternal fatigue consequent to heavy labor would undoubtedly require another type of social effort for alleviation and it would not be surprising that with control of this factor, as well as provision of good nutrition and other constituents of good prenatal care, and general social and welfare measures, infections would be treated early, if not prevented entirely. It would seem apparent from examination of the data and this discussion that a good deal of reproductive casualty is immediately preventible and that much of the remainder could in time be prevented if we begin to plan and institute our preventive measures as soon as possible.

Chapter 7

New Education for Old Problems

C. Arden Miller

O NE of the major handicaps of children with mental retardation, deafness, neuromuscular disorders, and other permanent handicaps may
well be deprivation—the deprivation of receiving less than what we know
to be good and complete medical services. The gap results, I believe, less
from lack of information about these services than from professional in-
difference toward them. This attitude may well have its beginnings in our
medical schools and other centers of professional education.

The education of a physician is heavily oriented to the diagnosis and
care of acutely ill patients. With few exceptions medical education takes
place in a general hospital where the length of stay may average ten days
or less. There may be little opportunity to evaluate a patient and his illness
against the background of family, job, and community, and little chance
for follow-up evaluations. Teaching hospitals are used extensively as referral centers for patients requiring procedures of diagnosis or treatment so
complicated that they are not available in the usual community. A student's
experience with chronic disorders is exceedingly limited except for diagnosis and care of acute complications. He has little opportunity for the
kind of diagnosis that results from systematic observations of the same patient over a prolonged period of time. Even though our hospital clinics are
filled with patients having chronic disturbances, students ordinarily are
assigned to those clinics for a span of time so brief as to allow for only a
few visits with the same patient. Experience with institutions providing
long-term care—state training schools, convalescent homes—ordinarily is
confined to a brief visit for observation.

Some medical schools have instituted family health plans which require
a student to follow the same family for four years of medical school. Such
a scheme must surely help to emphasize that health and disease must be
studied and managed in the setting of family and community. They do not
ordinarily provide an opportunity for a student to gain experience with
the special problems attendant upon a diagnosis which requires repeated
observations over a long period, or to observe treatment which is not curative but which is designed to assist in meeting some drastically readjusted

Reprinted from *Southern Medical Journal*, 57:259-263, 1964.

goals for living, or to work effectively with many colleagues from other disciplines involved in comprehensive care of a handicapped person. Some educators with experience in long-range family health plans have reported that difficulties arise when students are expected to guide a comprehensive health plan for a family, but the available services are fragmented and highly specialized.

This introduction should not be construed as a traitorous assault on the teaching hospital. These institutions provide the best environment in the world today for the education of the physician in modern medical science. We would be foolish to accept the many educational advantages of these institutions as entirely complete and lacking in problems. One of the major problems to my mind is the enormous emphasis which is placed on rapid diagnosis, rapid therapy, rapid results, sometimes with transitory interest of the doctor in chronic disorders.

Some medical problems do not lend themselves to a touch-and-go system of medical care. Among these are handicapping conditions of children. Deafness, retardation, and various neuromuscular disorders of childhood are examples of medical problems which may not yield to the usual diagnostic work-up and the writing of a prescription.

In 1959, the staff of the Children's Rehabilitation Unit at the University of Kansas reported on a study of deafness in preschool children.[252] The purpose of the study was to determine if significant lags occurred between the time a family suspected deafness in a child, sought medical advice, and the time the diagnosis was actually established. In this study all of the children had been under routine medical care for health checks and immunization since infancy. Nearly always the parents became concerned about a disturbance of development and suspected deafness before the physician openly considered such a possibility. Even after parents took their child to the physician to inquire about the possibility of deafness, long delays occurred before the diagnosis was confirmed. In nearly half the children the deafness was not established until after the third birthday. Even medical conditions such as meningitis seemed not to alert the doctor to the possibility of deafness as a sequela.

A similar study was done by Letson[648] on retarded children. Frequently parents, knowing something was wrong with their retarded child in his first years of life, took him to a long succession of physicians before they found one who would describe the child's handicap, discuss his limitations, potential, and alternative plans for care.

Mental retardation and its causes are difficult to diagnose in preschool children and delays may be excused in a number of instances. In a great many others, such as mongolism, with the diagnosis apparent from the time of birth, there seems little reason to hide our knowledge of this disease from parents until the child is nearly of school age. A number of such cases were found by Letson.

These situations are described, not to carp about medical services but to emphasize several points:

1. Physicians have little experience during their training with some of the most prevalent and difficult problems of the pediatric age group. These are the problems of handicapped children.

2. Physicians, by their training, emphasize acute problems—diagnoses that are revealed by a "work-up" indicating procedures or medications that will produce results quickly in terms of cure or symptomatic relief.

3. As a result of this training many students and physicians appear uncomfortable in clinical situations involving permanent conditions which will not yield dramatically to medical care. The physician may take refuge in empty reassurances and excuses of being too busy to render any care at all. These attitudes are to my mind largely a result of our medical education, and they should be rectified.

Several years ago an opportunity was presented at the University of Kansas to develop a program which might alter these attitudes in medical students and house officers.

In the late 1940's at the University of Kansas School of Medicine, a hearing and speech program was established, primarily designed to lead to a Master's Degree in Audiology, Education of the Deaf, and Speech Correction. A nursery school for deaf children was established as a laboratory for this educational program. The nursery school ordinarily had an enrollment of twenty to thirty children between three and five years of age. The children were instructed in speech reading until they were of school age, at which time they were placed either in classes in the public schools or at the State Training School for Deaf Children.

This program was well-staffed with people trained in education for the deaf, audiology, and speech pathology. They were doing an outstanding job, though I think an incomplete one in terms of comprehensive services to children. Pediatricians, psychologists, and social workers were not consistently involved in the program.

At about the same time the Medical Center established a Cerebral Palsy Clinic. This was a referral center for the state's Crippled Children's Commission. It was staffed by an orthopedist, physical therapist, occupational therapist, and, from time to time, a psychologist, speech therapist, and pediatrician. The clinic was almost entirely diagnostic. Many children returned from long distances for only infrequent follow-up visits.

In the early 1950's a program developed at the Medical School for retarded children. Several members of the Pediatric Department became interested in the fact that in the outpatient clinic, where forty to fifty patients were seen each day, there was a large proportion of patients whose needs were poorly met. They were not children with respiratory infections, or otitis media, or pneumonia, or diarrhea or any of the acute disorders about which we were instructing our students. They were children with problems in school achievement or adjustment, or problems in development. They were referred to our clinic for a great many reasons with which we felt poorly prepared to cope, even after the usual diagnostic study.

As a result of concern for this circumstance a special clinic for exceptional children was started on Saturday mornings. The patients were predominantly preschool retarded children, a group we thought could be helped most by counseling and by interpretation to parents. At this age the situation was not yet complicated with school difficulties; we could follow the children for a longer period of time and perhaps prevent many of the problems deriving from inappropriate school placement.

We carefully followed ten or twelve preschool retarded children in the Saturday morning clinic. In talking with the parents we became convinced that they had received shabby care in our clinics and other agencies in the community. Parents had a poor understanding of their children and the problems of retarded children in general, even though their child's hospital chart was thick and full of information. The parents seemed to know none of it. What was even more appalling was that no doctor on the staff knew the chart because it had been accumulated by handing the child from one clinic or laboratory to another. No one person had taken responsibility, and the parents had few of the advantages of knowing what had been done for their child.

In time the clinic for exceptional children expanded to include a small nursery school for educable retarded children of preschool age. In this setting we hoped students and staff members could learn about the behavior of retarded children in a way that was not possible with one hour examinations in a clinic. The first ideas of functional diagnosis began to develop as necessary adjuncts to traditional physical diagnosis.

From this account it is obvious that the Medical Center's services for handicapped children were highly fragmented. Children with hearing and speech difficulties were seen in the appropriate clinic. Children with cerebral palsy were seen in a special clinic for them. Children with retardation were seen first in our general pediatric clinic and then referred to the exceptional children's clinic. We were, in fact, guilty of something for which we criticized many volunteer agencies—restriction of interest. Clearly we, as an educational institution, were responsible for the restrictive nature of many children's services. We were teaching our students disciplinary isolationism. Is it any wonder that students who had trained in such a situation should leave the University and set up programs in state and voluntary agencies just as isolated as the ones we were running? *Unfortunately, handicapped children have a way of combining their handicaps in such a way that they do not fit neatly into many of the pigeon holes designed for them.* [Editors' italics.]

There are many examples of the kind of isolationism in which psychologists, speech therapists, social workers, and physicians too often function. Physicians communicate infrequently with school personnel about health problems which may affect school performance. School teachers and nurses refer parents to a physician for a "medical check-up" without giving sufficient information about the problem as seen at school.

It seemed to us that if we were going to have an impact on changing services for handicapped children, *we should first change our educational program to allow for coordination of services at this level.* If our students were expected to render their services in the context of a comprehensive and long-term plan for care, then they needed experience with such a program during their student years. Only in this way could they learn to work with local agencies and with colleagues from other disciplines. *Professional attitudes which we believed detrimental to handicapped children needed revision at the student level.* [Editors' italics.]

We began to develop plans for a facility which would bring together all of the services and educational programs within the University dealing with the problems of handicapped children. Many discussions were held about the "team approach." Experts have said, I think with justification, that the "team approach" is a necessity; one person does not have all the resources necessary to deal with the problems of handicapped children. Other experts have countered with the rejoinders that six half brains are not as effective as one good one; and that children and their parents cannot relate to a committee; they need a person to whom they can take their problems. It is for this reason precisely that a handicapped child needs the continuing care of a physician.

Teams function quite effectively for the care of many problems; they are not strange to physicians. When a child comes to the hospital with appendicitis, the medical student learns that a team effort is required to give complete care. Radiologists, surgeons, nurses, and others all fulfill their roles in an effective and unselfconscious way. This is a lesson we have not quite learned effectively in relation to handicapped children. Too often the student and the physician see their roles only to rule out correctible disorders, and then to abrogate any continuing responsibility to teachers, special therapists, or other agencies. We believed that physicians would work more comfortably in a continuing fashion, if their work as students brought them into contact with a team that functioned just as smoothly on behalf of the child with retardation, as for the child with appendicitis.

We conceived that a new facility was required for the demonstration of comprehensive care for handicapped children. There was considerable discussion as to the advisability of establishing a diagnostic clinic which would see large numbers of children, and having diagnosed them, send them on to various state agencies or community services for assistance. We decided against this course. Less is known about the pathogenesis of many handicapping conditions than we would like to know. But insofar as was know etiology and pathogenesis, the diagnosis is not difficult. The procedures are ones that can be carried out in any pediatric clinic. The personnel there ordinarily have the talents and skills necessary to plan and execute a good program of diagnosis and evaluation. The results are apt to be disappointing, but disappointing only in terms of incomplete medical knowledge.

We decided, therefore, that the pediatric clinic as it existed was a perfectly suitable facility for diagnosis and evaluation and that we did not need another. What we really needed was a facility where students and staff members could work in the long-term management of handicapped children in company with students from other disciplines. If physicians have a continuing responsibility for the care of handicapped children, and we believe they have, then they need an opportunity to participate in the management of these children over a long period of time during thirty years of training; and they should do this in a situation where every conceivable resource can be brought to bear. Only in this way can they see their own roles in providing the best possible care. We believed further that the program should not be restrictive in the sense that some children would be taken and some turned away as unsuitable. We would attempt to make the program sufficiently well staffed that any child coming to a student's attention could have designed for him an optimum program. We would bring together as comprehensive and as complete a facility as possible and take all comers, doing the best we could in their management, thinking that in this way our students would develop a sense of responsibility to every patient who came to them.

With this background of thinking we established the Children's Rehabilitation Unit. The Unit brought under a single roof and single administration the programs in hearing and speech, physical and occupational therapy for children, the care of cerebral palsied children who lived locally and who had been in attendance in our clinic, and the clinic for retarded children. These programs were expanded to include not only clinical facilities but complete educational programs. There were nursery schools for children with cerebral palsy and deafness, and special classes for retarded children from nursery school through high school. The Children's Rehabilitation Unit offers as comprehensive care as possible, including both medical and educational services. Initially about one hundred children, all of them outpatients, were accommodated. These were children who could be followed over a prolonged period of time.

From private funds and a Hill-Burton Grant we constructed a new building, part medical clinic and part school. The building is staffed with pediatricians, teachers, educational supervisors, psychologists, social workers, special therapists, and others. The facility is made available to every school and department of the University offering educational programs about handicapped children. Practice teachers from the School of Education work at the Unit, students in social work come for field placement, graduate students in psychology serve part of their internship at the Unit, and medical students from the pediatrics service participate in evaluations and case conferences and observe all aspects of the program. Residents on the pediatrics service spend a day each week at the Unit following their patients for an extended period.

The entire program may well be unrealistic in terms of community services. Few students will find themselves in a situation in future years where they have the richness of physical facilities and professional resources to supplement their work with handicapped children. *One can legitimately question whether educational programs for handicapped children belong in a medical center.* We expect, however, that our students will have a better appreciation than previously of all that can be done for handicapped children. We hope that they will see major contributions the physician can make in situations even where a cure cannot be effected. We hope that these students as physicians can work more effectively with schools, psychologists, social workers, and with whatever facilities may be present in a community where they find themselves. And they may be influential in expanding community services. [Editors' italics.]

A few other medical centers have instituted similar programs. Dr. Sylvia Richardson at the University of Oklahoma has described the excellent program developed there.

It should be emphasized that no attempt is made to have physicians step outside their role and to usurp the responsibilities of the teacher, the psychologists, or the social worker. *We hope only that the physician can more effectively fill his traditional role by knowing how to work effectively with*

colleagues from other disciplines on behalf of handicapped children.
[Editors' italics.]

There is no doubt that children with retardation, deafness, neuromuscular disorders and various other handicaps can be helped enormously. Some of these children are best cared for in institutions; most of them are best cared for at home. There is also no doubt that these children have been burdened in past years beyond their own limitations. They have been burdened by a degree of professional neglect which can no longer be tolerated. A great deal more needs to be known about early diagnosis, treatment, and management of handicapped children. There is tremendous interest in research in basic fields which will add to our knowledge on these matters. In the meantime, we already know far more than has been effectively practiced. We must do more than we have done in the past to close the gap between what is known to be good care and what is actually available.

As we face an impending shortage of physicians, we must face many medical problems not by ignoring those that take a great deal of time, but by learning how to work effectively with colleagues in other disciplines, and with many local agencies which share our responsibilities. In this way our talents can be applied more widely and more effectively than ever before.

We are not at all certain that our Children's Rehabilitation Unit is offering a reasonable solution to the better preparation of physicians to deal with handicapped children. Such an effort is difficult to evaluate. We are certain that the situation calls for some new educational approaches.

PART TWO
Incidence and Prevalence Studies

Introduction

WHILE it is generally recognized that the number of children with multiple disabilities is increasing, studies with respect to the incidence and prevalence of multiply handicapped children have been characterized by certain inconsistencies. Reliable census data on children with multiple disability in the United States are not available. Factors contributing to the increase in the prevalence of multiply handicapped children and the problems inherent in compiling statistics relative to the number of children in specific dyadic groups were discussed in an earlier chapter.

For the purpose of this brief introduction, it is redundant to discuss the factors which make it difficult to obtain accurate estimates of the number of handicapped children who have concomitant disabilities. Perhaps a factor which is often overlooked is the presumed large proportion of children in ostensibly "well" populations who may, in fact, have one or more adverse health problems. Indeed, the task of identification is compounded and a number of serious questions are raised by Dr. Jacobziner and his associates in their article entitled "How Well Are Well Children." Based on a major investigation of more than 20,000 children examined in 78 child health stations in New York City, this study presents data on the prevalence of health problems in the population under study. Thirty-nine per cent of all children examined had one or more adverse health conditions. Therefore, in at least one major study a significant proportion of infants and children receiving well-child supervision and presumed to be well are actually presenting evidence of some disorder requiring medical care. Failure to diagnose such children early and treat them promptly may often cause severe morbidity and serious lasting complications in later life.

Professor Wishik estimated the prevalence of handicapped children in one state, Georgia, and found that the handicapped children identified in the study had an average of 2.2 handicapping conditions per child. Wishik calls attention to the unpredictability of diagnoses of specific disabilities in children having multiple disabilities and observes that it is difficult to conceive of a service for any one of the diagnoses operating efficiently as a completely independent entity. Wishik recommends the utilization of a multidiagnostic rehabilitation service.

In recent years the effectiveness of services for exceptional children has frequently been questioned. Dr. Stifler and her associates report a study designed to determine the effectiveness of the Centers for Handicapped Children established in Maryland in 1959. The data indicated that the majority of children seen during the first year had multiple handicaps. Despite the complexity and severity of the disabilities of these children, the findings seemed to indicate that with adequate diagnosis and conscientious implementation of the recommendations improvements do occur.

Richardson and Higgins, in a survey similar to Wishik's study in Georgia, attempted to investigate several aspects of the problem which the Georgia study did not include. An attempt was made to estimate possible under-reporting which might have occurred in previous studies, through the examination of presumably normal children. Moreover, Richardson and Higgins attempted to determine the extent to which prevalence and disability rates of the various handicapping conditions might be found to vary from one community to another. Attention is drawn to the lack of services for children with multiple severe handicaps. The authors are of the opinion that the much needed facilities are a state responsibility rather than a local responsibility. The authors observe that the excellent facilities being provided for children with single specific conditions do not have available the services needed by those with two or more serious handicaps.

Professors Kirk and Weiner, in a discerning examination of the widely-quoted study of the prevalence of mental retardation in Onondaga County, New York, identify a problem that is generally inherent in most studies of the prevalence of handicapping conditions in children—the problem of adequately defining the condition. The authors seriously question the defensibility of the definition of mental retardation used in this study. The reader will find evidence and examples in Chapter 12 of some of the reasons for the inconsistency and unreliability of data on the incidence and prevalence of children with multiple disabilities.

Chapter 8

How Well Are Well Children?

Harold Jacobziner, Herbert Rich, Nina Bleiberg
and Roland Merchant

T HE Child Health Conference is devoted to the health supervision of "well" infants and preschool children with a view toward maintaining and promoting their physical, emotional, and social growth and development commensurate with the most recent available knowledge and with each child's maximum potential.[174, 462]

New dimensions based on most recent advances in medicine and public health are constantly added to the scope of the child health conference. A few added in recent years include the use of quadruple antigen, revaccination against smallpox at five years of age, routine PKU testing, vision testing, sweat test for cystic fibrosis and tuberculin testing in selected areas, use of live polio vaccine, treatment for "minor" illnesses, expansion of mental health services, i.e., individual and group-parent counseling, accident prevention, combined preventive and curative services, a pilot hearing testing program to determine whether it could be included as an integral part of the well child conference, extension of social and health services for the unwed mother, early identification and prompt referral of infants and children with handicapping conditions, new case-finding technics for the early detection of children with lead poisoning, and so on.[39]

While commendable progress has been made and the scope of the "conference" has been greatly expanded, changing times bring about changing needs and demands which pose new problems and challenges. Do the traditional services meet the aims and objectives? Are they meeting the needs of the community? Are modifications necessary and to what extent?

PURPOSE OF STUDY

The importance of early identification of the child with a health problem and prompt and adequate treatment is well known to medical practice and public health. Failing to diagnose early and treat promptly may often cause severe morbidity and serious lasting complications in later life. This study (to determine the extent and type of health conditions found in a "well" population in infants and children under supervision in child health sta-

Reprinted from *American Journal of Public Health*, 53:1937-1952, December, 1963.

tions) was therefore undertaken as an initial step in an evaluation of accuracy of diagnoses and adequacy of referral.

MATERIALS AND METHODS

Subjects

There were 22,873 children 0 to 6 years of age of a total 165,000 under supervision in child health stations.

Methods

Health examinations were made by 166 physicians assigned to the 78 child health stations. About 10 to 15 per cent of the physicians are qualified pediatricians and all have had some formal training in pediatrics. The subjects of the study are all residents of New York City. While no means test is required, the population served is in the lower socioeconomic group.

Planning for this study began in 1954; the field work began in September, 1956, and was terminated in May, 1957.

To insure greater accuracy in reporting, certain limitations and delineations were arbitrarily made on the latitude of diagnoses. These were embodied in a set of instructions which were sent out to all child health station physicians prior to the initiation of the study.

To rule out any seasonal bias, the survey was conducted in the various seasonal intervals. The data were collected on a special form which included identifying data and other pertinent medical information for each infant and preschool child examined.

ANALYSIS OF DATA

The original classification of the diagnostic data included 355 distinct diagnostic entities. There was further consolidation into twenty-three major categories or rubrics, based on the classifications in the "Manual of International Statistical Classification of Diseases, Injuries and Causes of Death."

RESULTS

The data in Table 8-1 indicate that of 22,873 infants and preschool children examined an adverse health condition was reported in nearly 39 per cent. This is a rate of 0.5 defect per child for the entire study group and 1.2 defects per child for the group in which adverse health conditions were found.

Children who were not classified as "healthy" are not necessarily ill and in urgent need of immediate comprehensive medical care. Many of the con-

---

° Copies of this form can be obtained from the New York City Health Department.

TABLE 8-1

SURVEY OF CHILDREN EXAMINED BY PHYSICIANS IN NEW YORK CITY CHILD
HEALTH STATIONS FOR WELL-CHILD CARE (NEW YORK CITY DEPARTMENT
OF HEALTH, OCTOBER, 1956-MAY, 1957)

PERCENTAGE OF CHILDREN, BY HEALTH STATUS, COLOR, AND SEX

			% of Total Children			
	Total No.	All	Color*		Sex	
Health Status	of Children	Children	White	Other	Male	Female
Healthy	14,008	61.2	65.3	59.8	58.3	64.2
One or more conditions ..	8,865	38.8	34.7	40.2	41.7	35.8
Number of children	22,873	100.0	27.6	72.4	50.8	49.2
Average No. of conditions per child		0.46	0.40	0.49	0.51	0.42

* 1,136 children, or 5 per cent of all children, were excluded from the color distribution because color was not stated.

TABLE 8-2

SURVEY OF CHILDREN EXAMINED BY PHYSICIANS IN NEW YORK CITY HEALTH
STATIONS FOR WELL-CHILD CARE (NEW YORK CITY DEPARTMENT OF HEALTH,
OCTOBER, 1956-MAY, 1957)

DISTRIBUTION OF CHILDREN BY NUMBER OF CONDITIONS BY "WEEK"

No. of Conditions	Total	%	Week I No.	%	Week II No.	%	Week III No.	%
No conditions	14,008	61.2	4,273	56.1	4,531	61.0	5,204	66.5
1 condition	7,169	31.2	2,610	34.3	2,407	32.4	2,152	27.5
2 conditions	1,343	5.9	582	7.6	390	5.2	371	4.8
3 conditions	227	1.0	112	1.5	64	0.8	51	0.7
4 conditions	16	0.1	8	0.1	5	0.1	3	*
5 conditions	3	*	3	*	—	—	—	—
Unknown	107	0.5	30	0.4	35	0.5	42	0.5
	22,873	100.0	7,618	100.0	7,432	100.0	7,823	100.0

* Less than 0.05.

ditions observed were of a temporary nature, an acute minor ailment, while others were of great medical import.

The distribution of children by number of conditions by "week" ("season") is shown in Table 8-2. "Week I," "Week II," and "Week III" represent the weeks of October 1-5, 1956; January 21-25; May 20-24, 1957, respectively. The number of children found "healthy" increases from 56 per cent in "Week I" to 67 per cent in "Week III."

While this pattern may be an actual reflection of the health status due to seasonal variation, it is also possible that inclement weather may have acted as a deterrent to bringing seriously ill children during the second and third weeks, thus resulting in an apparent relatively high proportion of "healthy" children.

Of the conditions found (regardless of the season), the three most frequent disease categories were respiratory, skin and allergy, hernia, and muscular. The rates per 1,000 children examined during each "week" of study are presented in Table 8-3. The high rates of respiratory infections recorded for Weeks I and II, as compared with a substantially lower rate for Week III, i.e., 161 to 116, is perhaps a reflection of seasonal variation. It is to be noted that the total rates refer to conditions not children (e.g., 546 per thousand for Week I means 546 conditions per 1,000 children and not 546 ill children of each 1,000 examined), since children may be included in more than one diagnostic group. In a few cases a child may appear twice in the same major diagnostic group because he had two different diagnoses in the same group.

TABLE 8-3

SURVEY OF CHILDREN EXAMINED BY PHYSICIANS IN NEW YORK CITY HEALTH STATIONS FOR WELL-CHILD CARE (NEW YORK CITY DEPARTMENT OF HEALTH, OCTOBER, 1956-MAY, 1957)

CONDITIONS DIAGNOSED AND RATE PER 1,000 CHILDREN EXAMINED DURING EACH WEEK OF STUDY

Condition	Total	Rate	Week I No.	Week I Rate	Week II No.	Week II Rate	Week III No.	Week III Rate
Respiratory	3,327	145	1,228	161	1,195	161	904	116
Skin, allergy	1,740	76	670	88	533	72	537	69
Hernia, muscular	1,068	47	431	57	319	43	318	41
Genitourinary	791	35	316	41	256	34	219	28
Infections	538	24	216	28	141	19	181	23
Orthopedic	504	22	200	26	152	20	152	19
Nutrition	456	20	195	26	148	20	113	14
Congenital malformations	426	19	195	26	120	16	111	14
Dental	357	16	137	18	111	15	109	14
Diseases of the blood	252	11	88	12	80	11	84	11
Emotional, behavior	187	8	89	12	54	7	44	6
CNS—eye	180	8	75	10	56	8	49	6
Gastrointestinal	180	8	91	12	45	6	44	6
Trauma, accidents	105	5	42	6	31	4	32	4
Neuromuscular, mental	104	5	38	5	31	4	35	4
Cardiovascular (nonorganic)	91	4	32	4	34	5	25	3
Cardiovascular (organic)	87	4	33	4	19	3	35	4
CNS—speech	43	2	14	2	16	2	13	2
Metabolic	35	2	11	1	12	2	12	2
Convulsive seizures	26	1	8	1	9	1	9	1
Cancer, leukemia, tumors	23	1	7	1	7	1	9	1
CNS—ear	3	0.1	2	0.3	1	0.1	—	—
Miscellaneous	92	4	39	5	29	4	24	3
Total	10,615	464	4,157	546	3,399	457	3,059	391
No. of children examined	22,873		7,618		7,432		7,823	

TABLE 8-4

SURVEY OF CHILDREN EXAMINED BY PHYSICIANS IN NEW YORK CITY HEALTH
STATIONS FOR WELL-CHILD CARE (NEW YORK CITY DEPARTMENT OF
HEALTH, OCTOBER, 1956-MAY, 1957)

CONDITIONS DIAGNOSED AND RATE PER 1,000 CHILDREN EXAMINED BY ETHNIC GROUP

Condition	White No.	White Rate	Nonwhite No.	Nonwhite Rate	Puerto Rican No.	Puerto Rican Rate	Unknown No.	Unknown Rate
Respiratory	812	135	1,334	137	1,054	176	127	112
Skin, allergy	424	71	886	91	337	56	93	82
Hernia, muscular	72	12	829	85	96	16	71	63
Genitourinary	65	11	364	37	313	52	49	43
Infections	156	26	193	20	162	27	27	24
Orthopedic	131	22	235	24	107	18	31	27
Nutrition	89	15	197	20	146	24	24	21
Congenital malformations	146	24	138	14	127	21	15	13
Dental	170	28	102	10	66	11	19	17
Diseases of the blood	61	10	57	6	119	20	15	13
Emotional, behavior	54	9	69	7	50	8	14	12
CNS—eye	49	8	77	8	48	8	6	5
Gastrointestinal	36	6	93	10	44	7	7	6
Trauma, accidents	22	4	45	5	31	5	7	6
Neuromuscular, mental	26	4	44	5	26	4	8	7
Cardiovascular (nonorganic)	24	4	42	4	19	3	6	5
Cardiovascular (organic)	18	3	33	3	28	5	8	7
CNS—speech	20	3	14	1	7	1	2	2
Metabolic	7	1	13	1	13	2	2	2
Convulsive seizures	9	1	7	1	8	1	2	2
Cancer, leukemia, tumors	7	1	6	1	10	2	—	—
CNS—ear	2	*	1	*	—	—	—	—
Miscellaneous	23	4	33	3	27	5	9	8
Total	2,423	403	4,812	494	2,838	474	542	477
No. of children examined	6,008		9,740		5,989		1,136	

* Less than 0.5 per 1,000.

Ethnic Variations

The rate of adverse health conditions by ethnic group per 1,000 children examined is shown in Table 8-4. While there were significant ethnic differences between white and nonwhite groups in the total rate for all conditions, significant ethnic differences are not observed in every specific condition. A significant increase in the incidence of congenital malformations was observed among the white, as compared with the nonwhite and Puerto Rican (24 per 1,000 in the white, 14 in the nonwhite, and 21 in the Puerto Rican). A much higher incidence of hernia and muscular conditions, however, was observed among the nonwhite, 85 per 1,000 Negro children examined compared with 12 for the white and 16 for the Puerto

Rican. A statistically significant difference was observed in the higher incidence of genitourinary conditions among the Puerto Rican, 52 compared with 11 for white, and 37 for the nonwhite. (An increased incidence of genitourinary conditions was also noted among adult Puerto Rican female patients in a large obstetrical service.*) No significant differences by ethnic group were observed for "emotional and behavioral conditions" or in the incidence of "trauma and accidents."

Sex

Table 8-5 shows the distribution of children by number of conditions by sex. A significantly higher number of males had adverse health conditions. Over 64 per cent of the females were classified as healthy compared with 58 per cent for the male.

The sex variation by major diagnostic grouping is shown in Table 8-6. No statistically significant sex differences were observed in the twenty-three major diagnostic groupings, except in diagnosis of genitourinary conditions (due in the main to phimosis).

The total rate of sex for all diagnostic groupings, however, shows a statistically significant difference between male and female, 508 per 1,000 males versus 419 per 1,000 females, which is a reflection of a condition (phimosis) which is found in the male.

Age

Variations by age are shown in Table 8-7. A significantly higher per cent of "healthy" was found above age 18 months.

---

* Personal communication from Dr. Louis Hellman.

TABLE 8-5

SURVEY OF CHILDREN EXAMINED BY PHYSICIANS IN NEW YORK HEALTH STATIONS FOR WELL-CHILD CARE (NEW YORK CITY DEPARTMENT OF HEALTH, OCTOBER, 1956-MAY, 1957)

No. of Conditions	Distribution of Children by Sex by Number of Conditions		Male		Female	
	Total	%	No.	%	No.	%
No condition	13,984	61.2	6,770	58.3	7,214	64.2
1 condition	7,157	31.3	3,824	33.0	3,333	29.7
2 conditions	1,341	5.9	801	6.9	540	4.8
3 conditions	227	1.0	140	1.2	87	0.8
4 conditions	16	0.1	10	0.1	6	*
5 conditions	3	*	2	*	1	*
Unknown	107	0.5	56		51	0.5
Total	22,835†	100.0	11,603	100.0	11,232	100.0

* Less than 0.05 per cent.
† Does not include 38 cases—sex not specified.

TABLE 8-6

SURVEY OF CHILDREN EXAMINED BY PHYSICIANS IN NEW YORK CITY
HEALTH STATIONS FOR WELL-CHILD CARE (NEW YORK CITY
DEPARTMENT OF HEALTH, OCTOBER, 1956-MAY, 1957)

| | | | | Male | | Female | |
Condition	Total	Rate	No.	Rate	No.	Rate
Respiratory	3,323	146	1,766	152	1,557	139
Skin, allergy	1,736	76	922	79	814	72
Hernia, muscular	1,067	47	525	45	542	48
Genitourinary	789	35	767	66	22	2
Infections	538	24	277	24	261	23
Orthopedic	503	22	282	24	221	20
Nutrition	456	20	214	18	242	22
Congenital malformations	425	19	209	18	216	19
Dental	356	16	174	15	182	16
Diseases of the blood	252	11	144	12	108	10
Emotional, behavior	187	8	96	8	91	8
CNS—eye	179	8	97	8	82	7
Gastrointestinal	180	8	84	7	96	9
Trauma, accidents	104	5	49	4	55	5
Neuromuscular, mental	104	5	57	5	47	4
Cardiovascular (nonorganic)	91	4	54	5	37	3
Cardiovascular (organic)	87	4	44	4	43	4
CNS—speech	43	2	30	3	13	1
Metabolic	35	2	27	2	8	1
Convulsive seizures	26	1	15	1	11	1
Cancer, leukemia, tumors	23	1	9	1	14	1
CNS—ear	3	0.1	1	*	2	*
Miscellaneous	92	4	53	5	39	3
Total	10,599	464	5,896	508	4,703	419
No. of children examined	22,835†		11,603		11,232	

* Less than 0.5 per 1,000.
† Does not include 38 cases—sex not specified.

Diagnosis in Order of Frequency by Age

Respiratory illness is the leading diagnosis at all age levels except in the under six-month-old group (Table 8-8). Skin and allergy is the leading diagnosis in this age category and the second in frequency in children between six months and three and one-half years. In each age group, the male had a higher incidence of adverse conditions, as has been observed by other investigators.[1042, 1074]

Newly Discovered Adverse Health Conditions

In a cross-sectional study of this nature, it is important to differentiate between newly discovered defects and those already known prior to the examination during the study period. Nearly 48 per cent of all adverse health conditions recorded were newly discovered during the three "weeks"

TABLE 8-7

SURVEY OF CHILDREN EXAMINED BY PHYSICIANS IN NEW YORK CITY HEALTH STATIONS FOR WELL-CHILD CARE (NEW YORK CITY DEPARTMENT OF HEALTH, OCTOBER, 1956-MAY, 1957)

DISTRIBUTION OF CHILDREN BY NO. OF CONDITIONS BY AGE IN MONTHS

No. of Conditions	Under 6 No.	%	6-11 No.	%	12-17 No.	%	18-23 No.	%	24-35 No.	%	36-47 No.	%	48 No.	%
No condition	3,946	60.2	2,567	60.4	1,406	60.7	1,219	63.8	1,847	63.4	1,353	62.5	1,501	61.8
1 condition	2,116	32.3	1,396	32.8	739	31.9	547	28.6	876	30.1	651	30.1	727	30.0
2 conditions	411	6.3	225	5.3	140	6.0	112	5.9	157	5.4	120	5.5	143	5.9
3 or more conditions	68	1.0	56	1.3	21	0.9	23	1.2	23	0.8	25	1.2	27	1.1
Unknown	17	0.2	10	0.2	11	0.5	10	0.5	9	0.3	15	0.7	29	1.2
Total	6,558	100.0	4,254	100.0	2,317	100.0	1,911	100.0	2,912	100.0	2,164	100.0	2,427	100.0

TABLE 8-8

SURVEY OF CHILDREN EXAMINED BY PHYSICIANS IN NEW YORK CITY HEALTH STATIONS FOR WELL-CHILD CARE (NEW YORK CITY DEPARTMENT OF HEALTH, OCTOBER, 1956-MAY, 1957, CHILD HEALTH STATION MEDICAL SURVEY)

FIVE LEADING DIAGNOSES IN THE ORDER OF THEIR FREQUENCY (PER 1,000 CHILDREN EXAMINED) IN EACH AGE GROUP

Age Group	First Diagnosis	Rate	Second Diagnosis	Rate	Third Diagnosis	Rate	Fourth Diagnosis	Rate	Fifth Diagnosis	Rate
Under 6 mo	skin, allergy	(113)	respiratory	(108)	hernia, muscular	(79)	genitourinary	(60)	infections	(30)
6-11 mo	respiratory	(166)	skin, allergy	(90)	hernia, muscular	(50)	genitourinary	(35)	nutrition	(21)
12-17 mo	respiratory	(157)	skin, allergy	(69)	hernia, muscular	(45)	orthopedic	(32)	genitourinary	(29)
18-23 mo	respiratory	(155)	skin, allergy	(6)	hernia, muscular	(37)	orthopedic	(31)	nutrition	(26)
24-35 mo	respiratory	(168)	skin, allergy	(50)	hernia, muscular	(27)	infections	(24)	orthopedic	(24)
36-47 mo	respiratory	(167)	dental	(34)	skin, allergy	(33)	infections	(24)	orthopedic	(24)
48-59 mo	respiratory	(151)	dental	(87)	nutrition	(36)	skin, allergy	(30)	infections	(23)
60+ mo	respiratory	(116)	dental	(114)	skin, allergy	(52)	nutrition	(29)	infections	(21)

TABLE 8-9

SURVEY OF CHILDREN EXAMINED BY PHYSICIANS IN NEW YORK CITY HEALTH
STATIONS FOR WELL-CHILD CARE (NEW YORK CITY DEPARTMENT OF HEALTH,
OCTOBER, 1956-MAY, 1957)

PER CENT "NEWLY DIAGNOSED" FOR SELECTED CONDITIONS

Condition	Total Cases	Per Cent New of* Total Known
Respiratory	3,327	61.3
Infections	538	59.0
Gastrointestinal	180	57.6
Trauma and accidents	105	51.1
Skin and allergy	1,740	50.2
Dental	357	48.2
Diseases of the blood	252	45.9
Emotional and behavior	187	40.5
Nutrition	456	35.3
Genitourinary	791	34.3
CNS—eye	180	31.0
Hernia, muscular	1,068	30.8
Orthopedic	504	30.1
Neuromuscular, mental	104	28.1
Congenital malformations	426	27.7

* Approximately 10 per cent of the cases in each condition were not designated as "old" or "new."

period. The distribution of newly discovered adverse health conditions by major diagnostic groupings is shown in Table 8-9. The per cent of newly discovered defects among total defects was highest in the diagnostic groupings for respiratory infections, gastrointestinal conditions, and trauma and accidents. A high percentage of newly discovered conditions was also noted in the skin and allergy, dental, diseases of the blood, and emotional and behavioral disorder categories.

Diagnostic Groupings

In the diagnostic group one, respiratory, over twenty different subgroupings are included, from hypertrophied tonsils to pneumonitis, but over 50 per cent of the total in this category includes non-specific upper respiratory infections, tonsillitis, and rhinopharyngitis (Table 8-10). The second major category, i.e., skin and allergy, includes over forty-five distinct diagnostic entities, but eczema, allergic dermatitis, and diaper rashes were responsible for over 50 per cent of the total diagnoses in this group. In the next most frequent major category, ten different diagnostic entities were included, but umbilical and inguinal hernia contributed over 50 per cent of the diagnoses in this group.

TABLE 8-10

SURVEY OF CHILDREN EXAMINED BY PHYSICIANS IN NEW YORK CITY HEALTH
STATIONS FOR WELL-CHILD CARE (NEW YORK CITY DEPARTMENT OF
HEALTH, OCTOBER, 1956-MAY, 1957)

THREE LEADING SPECIFIC DIAGNOSES FOR EACH RUBRIC*

Rubric (Major Diagnostic Category) Specific Diagnosis	No.	Rate/1,000 Children Examined
Respiratory		
Nonspecific upper respiratory infection	1,699	74
Hypertrophy of: tonsils, adenoids; tonsillitis	810	35
Rhinitis: rhinorrhea; nasal discharge, postnasal drip	381	17
Skin and Allergy		
Eczema; ichthyosis heat rash; sweat rash	435	19
Diaper rash; dermatitis; ammoniacal; meatitis; perineal rash	367	16
Allergic dermatitis, atopic dermatitis—allergc to woolens	116	5
Hernia, Muscular		
Umbilical hernia	998	44
Inguinal hernia	56	2
Flare (any part of body)	13	6
Genitourinary		
Phimosis; congenital; tight foreskin	710	31
Hydrocele	63	3
Ulceration-glans penis, vulva, enlarged clitoris, penile erosion	16	0.7
Infections		
Enlarged inguinal nodes; numerous inguinal glands	89	4
Granuloma; umbilical, navel, of cord; omphalitis	84	4
Enlarged glands; cervical, submaxillary	64	3
Orthopedic		
Club foot, talipes, equinovarus, deformity foot (feet)	164	7
Bowed legs and other leg pathology defects	89	4
Flat foot, pronation foot (feet) "congenital weak feet"	71	3
Nutrition		
Overnutrition: obesity, overhydrated, poor endocrine	196	9
Undernutrition: underweight	196	9
Malnutrition: poor nutrition	46	2
Congenital Malformations		
Hemangioma: birth moles or marks	209	9
Cryptorchidism	61	3
"History of enlarged thymus," enlarged thymus; NOS with laryngeal stridor	24	1
Emotional and Behavior		
Feeding problems; anorexia	48	2
Bladder-eneuresis, nocturnal, bedwetting; incontinence urine	27	1
Jealousy: sibling	18	0.8
Central Nervous System—Eye		
Strabismus	143	6
Nystagmus	16	0.7
Myopia	7	0.3
Gastrointestinal		
Diarrhea	69	3
Constipation	34	1
Gastroenteritis	34	1
Neuromuscular, Mental		
Retardation: mental, mental and physical	21	0.9
Ptosis of eyes: congenital, drooped eyelid(s)	16	0.7
Paralysis: partial, polio, paresis	13	0.6

TABLE 8-10 *(Continued)*

| Three Leading Specific Diagnoses for Each Rubric* | | |
Rubric (Major Diagnostic Category) Specific Diagnosis	No.	Rate/1,000 Children Examined
Dental		
Dental caries: Number filled	327	14
Malocclusion, dental overbite	16	0.7
Dentition: slow, poor, abnormal	5	0.2
Diseases of the Blood		
Anemia: secondary, hypochromic, microcystic, iron-deficiency	218	10
Anemia—nutritional	27	1
Sickle-cell anemia	3	0.1

* These leading rubrics in each category include over 50 per cent of the total for the respective category.

Genitourinary

This group, the fourth most frequently found condition, included 809 children.* Fifteen different diagnoses were made on the children in this group, ranging from phimosis to a cyst of the spermatic cord; 34/3 per cent of all diagnostic entities in this group were newly discovered.

Infective and Parasitic Diseases

The fifth most frequently found conditions included 558 children and over fifty diagnostic entities from "abscess" to "worms." Fifty-nine per cent of all conditions in this group were newly discovered.

Orthopedic Conditions

The sixth most frequent disorder was diagnosed in 525 children. It included forty distinct clinical entities ranging from club foot to rheumatoid arthritis. The most frequent diagnoses in this group were club foot (Talipes equinovarus) and flat foot.

Nutrition

Nutrition was the seventh most common disorder found. It includes both over- and undernutrition. It was diagnosed in 457 children and included more than fifteen different diagnoses. It is of interest that overnutrition was the most frequent diagnosis in this group. One hundred and ninety-six children or about 43 per cent of all children in this group were so classified.

Congenital Malformations

This group accounted for 4 per cent of all adverse health conditions. It included forty-five clinical entities from albinism to "thin enamel on teeth—

* A child is counted more than once if he had more than one condition.

dentine shows through." An impressive variety of congenital malformations was encountered. Twenty-eight per cent of all unfavorable health conditions found in this group were newly discovered.

Emotional and Behavior

It is of interest that the most frequent disorder found in this group was feeding problems. Twenty different clinical diagnoses were made on 189 children in this group.

Eye Disturbances

The largest single clinical diagnosis made was strabismus; next in frequency was nystagmus. The group included 185 children and ten different clinical entities such as amblyopia and congenital cataracts. Thirty-one per cent of the conditions in this group were newly discovered at the time of examination.

Gastrointestinal

This major category included 182 children and twelve specific conditions. The most frequent disorder found in this group was diarrhea. Next in frequency was gastroenteritis. It included such diagnostic entities as fissure of anus, pylorospasm, and colitis. A diagnosis of acute appendicitis was also made at the time of the examination and unknown to the parents when they brought the child to the well-child conference.

The remainder of the diagnostic groupings included about eighty distinct clinical entities, and while singly they represent too small a proportion of the total for critical statistical analysis, they included many interesting and rare clinical conditions of great medical import. The following is but a very few of the clinical entities observed in this group: double teeth and impacted teeth and dental fistula; anemias of all forms and blood dyscrasias such as Cooley's anemia, splenitis, and sickle-cell anemia; mongolism, Erb's palsy, cerebral palsy, parkinsonism, and mental retardation of various forms and severity; fractures, dislocations, concussions, accidents, and poisonings; tumors and neoplasms of various kinds from chalazion to teratoma and osteoma; several forms of congenital heart lesions, including dextrocardia and protrusion of the right auricle; various forms of contagious diseases, including tuberculosis, encephalitis and molluscum contagiosum, ascariasis, rickets, celiac disease; and many other conditions requiring great skill and acumen to diagnose.

COMMENT

Of the diagnostic groupings in order of frequency, respiratory, skin and allergy, hernia-muscular, and genitourinary conditions were the most frequently encountered. Together they were responsible for over 65 per cent of the unfavorable health conditions found in the children examined in this study. Our findings should not be interpreted as representing frequency of adverse health conditions in all infants and preschool children, since our study is limited to examining children under supervision in child health stations, i.e., a lower socioeconomic group with a preponderance of non-whites, and hence includes a biased population. We do not believe, how-ever, that they differ significantly from the general population in the same age group.

Our "selected" population does not, moreover, in any way detract from the purpose of the study which is to determine "How well are well chil-dren" who are seen in a public health child health conference.

In the course of routine periodic examinations of infants and preschool children in the child health stations, it soon becomes apparent that a con-siderable proportion of these "healthy" children have some adverse health conditions which require further diagnostic investigation and medical care. Since 35 per cent of all newborn infants and 22 per cent of the entire pre-school population are under supervision in the New York City Child Health Stations, it appeared important to investigate the extent and type of ad-verse health conditions seen in this presumed "well" group. The results of our investigation shed some light regarding the health status and med-ical needs of infants and children brought for well child supervision in a public health facility of an urban community.

A few pertinent observations emerge from this study:

1. Thirty-nine per cent of all children examined had one or more adverse health conditions at the time of the examination. Since a physician sees about fourteen children in a doctor session (three hours), about five to six children examined would be diagnosed as having one or more ad-verse health conditions.
2. The female and the white had fewer adverse health conditions than the male and nonwhite.
3. Children in the under 18-month age categories had a higher percentage of adverse health conditions than the 18 months and over group.
4. Gastrointestinal, hernia and muscular, nutritional disorders, and trauma and accidents were more prevalent in the female. Genitourinary con-ditions were strikingly higher in the male and the Puerto Rican. Con-genital malformations were much more prevalent among the white. Hernia and muscular conditions were much higher among the nonwhite. Respiratory conditions were higher in the Puerto Rican; orthopedic con-ditions were lowest in the Puerto Rican. Skin and allergic conditions were highest in the nonwhite and lowest in the Puerto Rican. Other ad-

verse conditions found did not show any statistically significant differences as to color or sex. Forty-eight per cent of the unsatisfactory health conditions were newly discovered during the study. Some disorders were commonly found, while others were uncommon, rare, and even bizarre, a few of them newly discovered at the time of the examination and presumably unknown to the family. Others, though known, were not under needed medical care. One hundred and sixty practicing physicians working in these child health stations detected these conditions during the course of routine examinations in the child health conference in about eighty child health stations throughout the city during the study period. Children register for "well" child supervision on the average from about two to four weeks of age. About seven routine examinations are provided during the first year of life, three to four during the second year, and two annually thereafter until entrance to school.[735]

A perusal of the adverse conditions found indicates clearly that the physician in charge of a well-child conference must be very alert, knowledgeable, well trained, possess diagnostic acumen, and above all have sufficient time to perform an adequate health examination and to treat or to refer promptly all children with health problems for indicated care.

The traditional well-child conference is designed primarily to provide preventive services, and it is an excellent device for providing health supervision to a large number of children who would otherwise not obtain it. For many years it has been obvious, however, that such a limited scope does not meet the actual needs, particularly of the great proportion of children in the lower socio-economic group who are in urgent need of comprehensive family-centered services.

In 1946 the first combined preventive and curative service to care for children in health and in disease was established at Bellevue Hospital and has been in operation ever since. This is a joint facility operated by the Health Department and the hospital. The physicians and nurses of the child health station and the pediatric clinic as well as the public health nurse and social worker, all function as a team in order to provide total medical care to the child and family in the same manner in which they would be cared for by a family physician. Every month in this one facility alone approximately seventy-five infants and children who report for "well care" present evidence on examination of an acute or chronic illness requiring treatment. Instead of referring these children elsewhere for medical care, which would result in a loss of time as well as inconvenience, they are treated promptly. The physicians working in this joint child health station are also members of the attending staff of the hospital. A unified record including both the child health station medical record as well as the pediatric clinic is utilized.

While the primary aim of the combined services is to provide continuity of care to the clientele, it is also profitably utilized for teaching of undergraduate medical students, interns, residents, and the attending staffs of the hospital. It also affords an excellent opportunity for clinical research.[111]

Attempts were and are being made to inaugurate similar services in most of the larger and all of the teaching hospitals. It has been, however, a very slow process because of a variety of reasons, i.e., administrative difficulties, space limitations, and so on. Four such joint facilities are now in operation.

To provide for at least limited continuity of care in the unaffiliated child health stations, physicians in the child health station were directed in 1955 to initiate treatment of acute respiratory conditions, diarrheal diseases, skin infections, and other ailments observed in children brought into a child health station for well child supervision. Physicians and nurses in the child health stations were also instructed to impress upon the parent the importance of seeking additional medical aid from a physician or clinic if the illness did not subside within forty-eight hours. Mothers were requested to report to the station about child's progress. A home visit by a public health nurse is made when indicated. A return visit to the station within one week is scheduled for all children who receive treatment.

It is felt that during periods of high incidence of upper respiratory infections prompt treatment provided in the child health stations avoided over-referrals to overcrowded hospital clinics, and the first aid therapeutic measures, advice, and guidance may have prevented many serious complications. Recently, the treatment facilities were expanded and medications were distributed in selected child health stations in the low socio-economic districts where high infant mortality rates prevail and where hospital pediatric clinics are inadequately staffed and overcrowded. An analysis of the results of the program clearly indicated that the program was instrumental in limiting referrals to overcrowded hospitals, was time-saving to parents, and allowed prompt treatment of many acute conditions which was apparently effective.[542]

Another mode of providing continuity of care to children attending well baby clinics is to affiliate such clinics with an approved hospital pediatric service in the area. This is now being tried in New York City. It is still in the experimental stage.

SUMMARY AND CONCLUSIONS

Data are presented on 22,873 children examined in New York City Well-Child Conferences in seventy-eight child health stations. Thirty-nine per cent of all children examined had one or more adverse health conditions. A total of 10,615 defects were found in 8,865 children or an average of 0.5

per child for the total group and 1.20 adverse health conditions per child for the group with medical disorders. Three hundred and fifty-five distinct entities were discovered during the study period. These were classified into twenty-three major groupings. Of all adverse health conditions found, 48 per cent were newly discovered during the survey. Variations were noted by age, color, and sex. The frequency of adverse health conditions is higher in the under 18-month-old, in the male, and the nonwhite. Respiratory illness was the most commonly diagnosed condition. Next in frequency was "skin and allergy." No significant differences by ethnic group were observed for emotional and behavioral conditions or in the incidence of "trauma and accidents."

"Feeding difficulties" was the leading diagnosis in the emotional and behavioral category and overnutrition, rather than undernutrition, in the nutritional category.

Congenital malformations were much higher in the white, and genitourinary conditions were strikingly higher in the Puerto Rican.

A significant proportion of infants and children receiving well child supervision and presumed to be well are actually presenting evidence of some disorder requiring medical care. In the low socioeconomic groups, it is important to provide preventive and curative services to avoid delay in treatment, unnecessary referral to overcrowded hospital clinics, and an inconvenience to patients and families. Several plans for initiating such services are outlined.

The child health conference is an excellent device for finding children with a health problem. An important and often overlooked aspect is the need for providing immediate necessary medical care and where indicated follow-up. There is little use in devoting a great effort to merely finding a child with a health problem unless something is done to insure that the infant and/or child receives needed medical care promptly. Thus, even if treatment is not provided as part of the well-child conference, the public health nurse has a duty and an obligation to motivate and advise the family in obtaining the indicated care. This may be done by home visits and conferences. In all cases, the medical treatment regimen and outcome should be reported in detail in the child's medical record.

The physician working in the child health conference must be well trained in pediatrics, a skillful diagnostician, and deeply concerned with the health and welfare of children.[175, 227] The well-child conference of the future must provide integrated, comprehensive, high-quality, family-centered services, both preventive and curative.

Chapter 9

Handicapped Children in Georgia: A Study of Prevalence, Disability, Needs, and Resources

THE Cerebral Palsy Society of Georgia decided that a survey was needed to determine the magnitude of the cerebral palsy problem in the state. The Crippled Children's Society of the State of Georgia agreed to cooperate in the study. From the outset two principles were followed. First, it was decided that the study should be done by professional workers and citizens in the state, so that the very process of doing the study would be more likely to have a continuing influence. Second, it was agreed that as many different childhood handicapping conditions as feasible should be included in the study so that there would result an overall and functional community approach to the problem rather than a focus on one or another specific diagnosis arbitrarily picked out of community context. A complete report of the entire study will be published shortly, so within the scope of this article only portions of certain aspects can be included.

The broad objectives of the study were twofold: to try to measure the magnitude of the needs of handicapped children and to assess the adequacy of existing resources to meet those needs. The first step in assessing the magnitude of the problem is to attempt to determine the prevalence of handicapping conditions among the childhood population. A mere count of the various diagnoses by noses or heads, however, would obviously be rather meaningless. The label of cerebral palsy, for example, could apply to a child who is mildly involved as well as to one so severely incapacitated that institutional care is the only possible solution. A second necessary step after a mere tally, therefore, must be to classify the children in terms of their functional disabilities. Regardless of medical diagnosis, what types of incapacitation and limitation exist in each child's life? The third step is the estimation of the types and amounts of services needed to help the children overcome their disabilities insofar as possible.

Reprinted from *American Journal of Public Health, 46*:195-203, February, 1956.
(For a more complete report on this study see WISHIK, S. M.: *Georgia Study of Handicapped Children*. Georgia Department of Public Health, 1964.)

Recognizing that such an intensive approach is the only one that can have meaning, an attempt at direct assessment of large numbers of children would be an overwhelming and prohibitively expensive task. In the Georgia study a 10 per cent sampling was attempted of the childhood population and two counties. The contiguous counties of Clarke and Oconee were selected because they are reasonably representative of the state in urban-rural distribution and in racial pattern. [They were also chosen because of the location there of the University of Georgia. Members of the faculty of the university carried heavy responsibilities in the planning and operation of the project.] It is recognized that no community can ever be identical with any other or broadly representative of the nation. So the findings of this study can be applied elsewhere only by adaptation. In such adaptation, approximations might be adjusted more profitably in terms of age distribution of the population than any other single factor of which we have knowledge. Population data for Clarke and Oconee Counties are here included for this reason (Table 9-1).

Just a word here about the other main objective of the study, which was to assess the adequacy of existing resources. This was done by setting up a "blueprint" of an ideal, comprehensive community program for each one of the twelve recorded abnormalities. Committees of persons who had professional experience with each one of the diagnostic conditions helped draw up the blueprints. After they were completed, a single composite blueprint was designed by combination of all. This was done so that the analysis of communities would be in functional terms of service to children rather than being compartmentalized by diagnostic categories. For example, speech therapy was regarded as a single community resource rather than necessarily separated for diagnostic groups. At the same time, the actual availability of speech therapy to children with cerebral palsy, cleft palate, or functional speech disturbances was also considered.

TABLE 9-1

POPULATION AND SAMPLE DATA

Item	Census Estimates Clarke-Oconee Counties	Sample Families	Per Cent of Total
No. of persons	54,291	4,840	8.9
No. of households	11,218	1,001	8.9
Per cent of nonwhite total population	27	31.3	
No. of persons under 21 years	16,082	1,373	8.5
0-4	4,094	375	9.1
5-9	3,738	359	9.6
10-14	3,069	327	10.6
15-20	5,181	308	5.9

TABLE 9-2

SOURCES OF VOLUNTARY REPORTS, 1,287 DIFFERENT
REPORTS (1,252 CHILDREN)

Schools	849
Physicians and nurses	176
Family	158
Other	104

In fourteen counties in the state, committees of citizens and professional persons compared the availability of resources in their community with the ideal composite blueprint. On the basis of the reports of these self-evaluation committees, an assessment was made of the adequacy of resources in terms of catagories of service. No attempt was made to do a critique of the quality of the services, but an estimate was made of adequacy in terms of quantity and distribution. The community evaluation portion of the study will be covered more fully in the Georgia report; the paper is limited to studies on the handicapped children and their needs, rather than the existing resources in Georgia.

For the quantification study in Clarke and Oconee Counties a process of community organization led up to a three week period during which all persons were asked to report to the local health department all children whom they suspected of being handicapped. Definitions of the handicapping conditions were drawn up as sets of questions in lay terms and were given broad publicity. Copies of the questions were distributed in churches, placed on counters of stores, printed in the newspapers and were otherwise readily available far and wide. Simple cards for making the reports were also widely distributed.*

Parents were urged to report any of their children who seemed to fit the description (Table 9-2). Physicians and nurses were asked to report any children they knew about. The schools reported children known to teachers or to the school health service and constituted the largest single reporting source. Because of the reporting campaign, the public schools instituted mass vision and hearing tests and reported large numbers of children who failed those tests. We did not wish to ask neighbors or friends to report children outside their own families but were overruled by the ardent local women's groups who felt, because of the possibility that parents might

---

* Example of case-finding questions used for orthopedics and cerebral palsy:
Does he have poor use of legs?
Does he have poor use of arms?
Does he have poor balance or coordination?
Does he have unusual jerking of arms, legs, face, or body?
Does he have deformed arms, legs, or trunk of body?

be neglectful, that all persons should be asked to report any children they might have seen in their neighborhood. We succumbed to this pressure and found that our fears of engendering hostility did not bear fruit. The reporting from this group, however, did not contribute appreciably to the end result.

At the end of the three-week period of widespread voluntary reporting an independent sample canvass of the community was made by selecting every tenth household by sampling technics. An example of the community spirit and cooperation that existed was the action of the mayor of one of the small communities who personally drew a detailed map of his town and put on it every residential structure in the town. Such an up-to-date map would not otherwise have been available. Fifty-three women from church groups were selected and briefed as volunteer interviewers. Interviewing continued over a period of two weeks.

The questions asked by the interviewers were identical with those that were used for the voluntary reporting, with the exception of an additional group of questions concerning one of the twelve diagnoses not included in the voluntary reporting—the diagnosis of personality disturbance.[†] When the list of diagnoses to be included in the study was first being considered by the planning committee, I resisted including personality disturbance because I was concerned about the difficulty of its definition and the possibility that it might overwhelm the rest of the study. Again, I was overruled. Under the leadership of the State Health Department the group felt that this was too important a diagnostic category to be omitted. It was agreed, however, that the focus would be upon obvious and gross aberrations in the behavior of children. It is extremely gratifying to have gone through this experience and to have learned how valuable a case-finding device such a technic can be. As will be shown later, 50 per cent of the reported personality disturbances were confirmed and in 83 per cent of the cases some handicapping condition was found to be present.

All the reports by both the voluntary and canvass technics were edited

---

[†] Example of case-finding questions used for certain types of personality disturbance (asked only for children over seven years of age):

Does he show very peculiar behavior, such as:

Twitching or other strange mannerisms which he does not seem able to control?

Often hurting other children without reason?

Destroying things so much that he has been put out of play or school group?

Extreme fear of anything new and always staying close to parents?

Complete lack of interest in anything, either people or surroundings?

Does he for long periods of time go back to a more childish manner of acting or speaking?

Does he repeatedly:

Run away from home?

Play hooky from school?

Have trouble with courts, school, or other authorities?

by a pediatrician and presumptive or working diagnoses were made on the basis of the reported symptoms. The children were then classified by presumptive diagnoses and a sample of each diagnosis was drawn for invitation to clinics. Data were kept separately for those reported by the voluntary method and those by the canvass method. Children who were reported by both methods were grouped in both groups for sampling purposes. Children who had more than one presumptive diagnosis were sampled for each presumptive diagnosis. Eighty-five per cent of the canvass report cases were invited to the clinics and 63.5 per cent were seen. Forty-one per cent of the voluntary report cases were invited and 33.1 per cent were seen at the clinics.

Ten different types of clinics were set up for the twelve diagnoses by combining speech and hearing into one clinic and combining orthopedics and cerebral palsy into another. Children reported to have mental retardation were seen either at clinics for mental retardation or together with those reported to have personality disturbance. Children with various neurological symptoms were seen together with children reported to have epilepsy.

Twenty-four all-day clinics were held over a one-month period under the supervision of the State Department of Public Health Crippled Children's division. Five hundred and eight children were seen. Eight hundred and forty-eight handicaps were found in 378 different children. Each clinic team consisted of from four to ten different professional disciplines, with as many of each as were deemed necessary to carry the clinic load.* It must be emphasized that all the professional services for the clinics were rendered without charge to families or payment to professional workers. Leading persons in each specialty in the state were invited and invariably responded to the invitation at a real personal sacrifice.

During the morning and part of the afternoon children and parents were seen in individual interviews by various professional persons on the clinic team. In the latter part of the afternoon the entire clinic team sat in conference and discussed each child.

The first responsibility of the clinic team was to confirm, deny, or correct the diagnosis. It is interesting to point out that even voluntary reporting, largely by nonmedical persons, can have real value for case-finding. Table 9-3 shows the degree of accuracy of the voluntary reporting—that is, the number of times that the different presumptive diagnoses were confirmed

---

* Example of a clinic team for mental retardation and personality disturbance:

1 Pediatrician	1 Neurologist
2 Psychiatrists	2 Public health nurses
2 Psychologists	1 Educator
3 Social workers	3 Volunteers

TABLE 9-3

DEGREE OF ACCURACY AMONG VOLUNTARY REPORTS

Presumptive Diagnosis	Diagnosis Confirmed Per Cent
Epilepsy	89
Mental retardation	79
Cosmetic	79
Personality disturbance	77
Orthopedic	77
Cleft palate and lip	75
Heart	67
Orthodontic	66
Cerebral palsy	60
Speech	53
Hearing	45
Eye and vision	40

at the clinic. Accuracy was quite high, with an overall 63.4 per cent confirmation. Speech, hearing, and vision, which are at the bottom of the list, are the educationally related diagnoses that were referred largely by the schools. The screening tests that were done in the schools were not repeated before referral. A certain amount of overreferral is, of course, inevitable when one aspires to reasonably complete case finding, but hopefully not as much as existed in this instance. The appearance of personality disturbance on this list, even though the set of questions on this diagnosis were not included in the voluntary reporting publicity, indicates that the reported symptoms led the editing pediatrician to establish this as a presumptive diagnosis.

It is important to look beyond the question of nonconfirmation of the presumptive diagnosis and to note the frequency with which reporting of a case uncovered other handicaps in the same child. When these other handicaps are added to the confirmed presumptive diagnoses Table 4 shows the frequency with which voluntary reporting constituted effective though not necessarily accurate case finding for some handicap. Seventy-seven per cent of the cases seen had some handicap and even the lowest presumptive diagnosis on the list was productive of information in well over half of the cases. We are convinced that voluntary reporting, even lay reporting, is an important case-finding device that should be given serious consideration, especially if the referral is strengthened by some kind of screening procedure.

In contrast, the canvass reporting which utilized practically the same questions as the voluntary reporting had both a higher yield and a higher proportion of overreferrals. One would expect that the interviewers' verbal recital of the questions item by item would result in detecting more cases and in more overreporting. Table 9-5 shows the per cent of canvass-report-ed diagnoses that were confirmed, 51.4 per cent for the total group, and for most diagnoses a lower percentage than resulted from the voluntary reporting. Again, when we look at the casefinding effectiveness of the canvass reporting in terms of uncovering any of the twelve handicap-ping conditions, rather than merely limiting ourselves to the confirma-tion of the presumptive diagnoses (Table 9-6), we see a much higher degree of effectiveness, an average of 64 per cent. Though the results are in most respects again lower than those of the voluntary reporting, the productiveness is still 50 per cent, or better, in each one of the diag-nostic groups.

By matching the voluntary reports against the canvass households it was

TABLE 9-4

CASE-FINDING EFFECTIVENESS OF VOLUNTARY REPORTING

Presumptive Diagnosis	*Showed Any Handicap Per Cent*
Cleft palate and lip	100
Orthopedic	94
Cerebral palsy	93
Mental retardation	92
Cosmetic	91
Personality disturbance	91
Epilepsy	89
Speech	86
Heart	78
Orthodontic	73
Hearing	65
Eye and vision	60

TABLE 9-5

DEGREE OF ACCURACY AMONG CANVASS REPORTS

Presumptive Diagnosis	*Diagnosis Confirmed Per Cent*
Cleft palate and lip	100
Mental retardation	90
Orthodontic	90
Heart	53
Personality disturbance	50
Speech	46
Orthopedic and cerebral palsy	42
Eye and vision	38
Cosmetic	37
Epilepsy	33
Hearing	31

found that the latter method was known to have missed 7.6 per cent of the cases in the sample. How many more may have been missed cannot be stated since children in the sample without reported handicaps were not invited to the clinics. Review of names of children living in institutions and other lists of handicapped children failed to disclose additional cases. The sample did seem low in the 15- to 20-year-old group and in certain diagnoses reported among Negroes.

On the other side of the coin, the total number of handicapped children discovered by the voluntary reporting alone would have been just about half that estimated from the canvass. Among the handicapped children actually found in the sampled households, only one fourth had been reported voluntarily. One can say then that the canvass technic is essential when, for one reason or another, approximately complete case-finding is sought. In the development of most health service programs, however, reliance is placed upon having a working case load through which the community may learn the value of the service and by increased demand may indicate the need for expansion of the program. For this purpose, voluntary reporting campaigns may be sufficient.

Voluntary reporting did better for certain diagnoses than for others. It did best for cleft palate, cerebral palsy, mental retardation, and orthopedic handicaps and did most poorly for orthodontic, hearing, heart, and cosmetic conditions. This confirms the existing impression that more community education is needed in respect to the handicapping significance of orthodontic and cosmetic conditions and that medical and audiometric examinations, respectively, rather than subjective impressions are necessary for case finding of cardiac and hearing impairments.

Furthermore, canvass reporting was better at uncovering milder cases than was the voluntary method. The case-finding method chosen in any

TABLE 9-6

CASE-FINDING EFFECTIVENESS OF CANVASS REPORTING

Presumptive Diagnosis	Showed Any Handicap Per Cent
Cleft palate and lip	100
Mental retardation	100
Orthodontic	100
Personality disturbance	83
Heart	80
Orthopedic and cerebral palsy	73
Speech	71
Epilepsy	67
Hearing	66
Eye and vision	52
Cosmetic	50

TABLE 9-7

PREVALENCE OF HANDICAPPED CHILDREN IN CLARKE-OCONEE COUNTIES

Diagnoses	Estimated No. per 1,000 Children Under 21
Cosmetic	43
Mental retardation	40
Personality disturbance	29
Speech	29
Eye and vision	24
Hearing	19
Orthopedic	17
Orthodontic	16
Heart	10
Cerebral palsy	5
Epilepsy	4
Cleft palate and lip	1
Any of above diagnoses	108

instance would therefore depend on the objectives of the program. It is aimed at the more advanced or the milder cases? Is the emphasis on preventative or palliative rehabilitation?

On the basis of the diagnoses made at the clinics, statistical calculations were made on the prevalence of the twelve handicapping conditions. The technic of calculating prevalence in the face of multiple presumptive diagnoses in the same children as well as varying completeness of attendance of the sampled cases invited to each clinic, is a subject for a separate presentation. We shall here merely give our calculated estimates of prevalence (Table 9-7). Ten per cent of all children under twenty-one years of age are estimated to have one or another of the twelve handicapping conditions. The mere presence of a condition was not sufficient to include a child. The clinic team had to decide whether the condition constituted a handicap to the child. Handicaps were classified as slight, moderate, and severe on the basis of agreed criteria.

It is of interest to note how often a handicapped child has more than one handicapping condition. A third of the handicapped children seen at the clinics had only one of the twelve handicaps.* Another third had two dif-

---

* Frequency of coexistent diagnoses among handicapped children:

No. of Diagnoses per Child	Per Cent of Handicapped Children
1	32
2	30
3	19
4	12
5	6

Average: 2.2 Diagnoses per child

ferent handicapping conditions and the remainder had three or more. The average for all the handicapped children was 2.2 different diagnoses per child. As would be expected, children with cleft palate and cerebral palsy have the highest number of different handicaps with virtually none of them having merely one diagnosis. Heart disease had the fewest number of handicaps per child, but even here the average was about 1.5.

The presence of multiple diagnoses in children was reflected in the unpredictability of diagnoses that were uncovered in each of the specialty clinics. Only 43.6 per cent of the diagnoses were the same as that on which the clinic placed primary focus. Another 37.6 per cent were reasonably related diagnoses and the remainder, 18.8 per cent, were completely unrelated.

This has important implications for program planning and operation. With few exceptions it is difficult to conceive of a service for any one of the diagnoses operating efficiently as a completely independent entity. If the service is sharply limited in breadth of specialties represented, the coexistence of other handicaps would require referral elsewhere in the majority of cases. If, on the other hand, the service aims ambitiously at attaining a comprehensive approach to the total needs of children in the single diagnostic group, it would necessarily deprive other children of these very same services. The only logical pattern and one that fortunately has been followed in different parts of the country is the multidiagnostic rehabilitation service. The full report of the Georgia study will dwell in greater detail on this question and will describe regionalization technics for bringing the metropolitan rehabilitation center and small peripheral communities closer together for effective care of handicapped children.

The second responsibility of the clinic teams after making the diagnosis was to assess the functional disability of the handicapped children, regardless of diagnosis or combination of diagnoses in each child.* Distinction was made between personal adjustment of the handicapped child and maladjustment and the rest of the family in respect to the presence of the handicapped child in the family. By "society's nonacceptance" was meant the extent to which social rejection of the individual occurred

---

* Categories of functional disability:

Physical	
Walking	Speech
Use of upper extremities	Mental retardation
Limitation of general activity	Educational limitation or need for special adjustment
Function of teeth	Vocational limitation or special need for preparation
Hearing	Personal maladjustment
Visual acuity	Maladjustment of rest of family
Cosmetic	Society's nonacceptance
Seizures	

TABLE 9-8

PREVALENCE OF FUNCTIONAL DISABILITIES IN CLARKE-OCONEE COUNTIES

Disabilities	1,000 Children Estimated No. per Under 21
Educational	62
Social nonacceptance	52
Cosmetic	49
Personal maladjustment	39
Mental retardation	36
Maladjustment of family	35
Speech	33
Vocational	24
Hearing	19
Dental	17
Vision	16
Walking	14
Upper extremities	7
Seizures	3
General activity	1

because of community attitudes, as nearly as the professional personnel were aware of them, rather than because of incapacitating factors inherent in the child's condition. Factors that might cause nonacceptance by the community, such as ugly appearance or strange sounding speech, were listed for each diagnostic condition and were then considered individually for each child.

Table 9-8 shows the estimated prevalence of the disabilities among the child population of the two counties. It can be seen that the physical disabilities are all at the lower end of the list in frequency of occurrence as compared with nonphysical limitations.

The conspicuous association of mental retardation with hearing, speech, cosmetic and orthopedic impairments and with epilepsy, personality disturbance, and cerebral palsy emphasizes the important role of psychology and psychometry in crippled children's programs. Personality disturbance was most frequently associated with cleft palate, speech impairment, and mental retardation. Speech disturbance occurred with cleft palate, hearing impairment, mental retardation, orthodontic defect, and personality disturbance.

Little correlation existed between the child's physical incapacitation, maladjustment, his family's reaction, society's rejection of him, and his vocational limitation. For example, the child with mild epilepsy had a much higher degree of social rejection than the child with mild hearing impairment. The child with mild degree of mental retardation was rather well accepted by his family but not so by society. All the physical and non-

TABLE 9-9

PREVALENCE OF CERTAIN SERVICE NEEDS AMONG HANDICAPPED CHILDREN

Services Needed	Per Cent of Handicapped Children
Rehabilitation appraisal and plan	100
Counseling, guidance, and parent education	70
Special education	34
Short-term hospital care	31
Vocational aid	18
Therapies (PT, OT, orthoptics)	15
Orthodontic	10
Institutional care	10

physical disabilities but one tended to have more children slightly handicapped than moderately, and more children moderately than severely. Vocational limitation, however, was most often severe despite milder degrees of other disability.

The third responsibility of the clinic team was to estimate what services were needed for the children. The estimate of type and amount of service needed by each child was made in reasonably immediate terms just as it is ordinarily done in the medical care of any patient. But it was done for each child at the staff conference, so that the final decision of the team was accepted rather than each member independently recommending his own respective type of treatment. The findings were then compiled for the entire group without regard to diagnosis. Table 9-9 shows the proportion of handicapped children who needed each one of the most commonly required services. All the children need a diagnostic appraisal and a plan of care. Almost three fourths need psychological or social service for child or parent. About one third need some type of special education. Although another third needed short-term medical or surgical hospital care, it must be clear that this high number constitutes to a certain extent a backlog of unmet needs built up in the years immediately prior to the time of the survey.

Need for each type of service was then calculated for the total child population in the community in terms of established units of service, such as number of hospital days, hours per week of physical therapy, number of children in special education, etc. These will be furnished in detail in the total report of the study.

It is worthwhile to give particular attention to the well-known great need for and universal inadequacy of family counseling. As long as this challenge remains unmet, the usual imperfect physical end result of the medical management of handicapped children will continue to be accompanied by disproportionate and unnecessary educational, vocational, and social disability. It is logical that guidance and support to the patient and the family should be offered as integral parts of medical or other services. In respect to handicapped children, however, certain factors often make such integration difficult. The rehabilitation center necessarily tends to give diagnosis and consultation for more patients than it can carry on a direct treatment basis. Responsibility for day-by-day supervision and care is scattered both in persons and in miles. Serious consideration must be given to setting up counseling services in newer administrative patterns, such as local field extensions of a rehabilitation center, direct patient focus by health departments rather than predominant limitation to social work consultation, major units in voluntary child and family agencies rather than begrudging acceptance of the exceptional case, and even specialized programs attached to a coordinating or referral agency. Close working relationship between counseling and other service programs is essential. Current explorations in the use of group methods should be intensified.

Chapter 10

Follow-up Study of Children Seen in the Diagnostic Centers for Handicapped Children

JEAN ROSE STIFLER, ESTHER WOLLIN, and ARTHUR KRAUS

D URING the past few years public and voluntary health agencies have shown increasing concern for neurologically handicapped children. Particular emphasis has been placed on providing services for the mentally retarded. Centers have been developed in many places, each devoted to children with a specific type of condition, such as cerebral palsy or mental retardation. A somewhat different approach, however, has been taken in Maryland.

In 1956, the Medical Care Committee of the Maryland State Planning Commission appointed a Subcommittee on Medical Services and Facilities for Handicapped Children. Its charge was fourfold. It was to obtain an estimate of the prevalence rates of physical, mental, and emotional handicaps in children; to provide an objective opinion of their special medical needs; to survey facilities and services in Maryland for case-finding, diagnosis, treatment, care, and rehabilitation of these children; and finally to recommend improvements in service.

The first major report of this committee recommended the establishment of Diagnostic and Evaluation Centers for children with complex or multiple handicaps.[197] In order to understand the reason for this recommendation a brief summary of pertinent facts about Maryland is indicated.

Maryland is a relatively small state with a land area of 9,880 square miles and in 1960 had a population of approximately 3,120,000 people, with about 41 per cent of the population under 21 years of age. The nonwhite population is about 17 per cent of the total. There are twenty-four local subdivisions—twenty-three counties, varying from very rural to metropolitan, and one centrally located independent city, Baltimore. Each subdivision has a full-time health department. There are two medical schools with large teaching hospitals in the state, both located in Baltimore. Responsibility for the Crippled Children's Program is vested in the State Health Department which is also located in Baltimore.

Reprinted from *American Journal of Public Health*, 53:1743-1750, November, 1953.

As was the case with most states, the official Crippled Children's Program began in Maryland in 1935 with the enactment of Part 2, Title V of the Social Security Act. At the outset, services were provided largely for orthopedically handicapped children. However, with the help of outstanding state legislation and excellent medical leadership, by the early 1950's the program had expanded to cover: orthopedic and plastic surgical conditions, cerebral palsy, hearing, speech, and visual problems, rheumatic fever, rheumatic and congenital heart disease, epilepsy, and other crippling conditions which included long-term illnesses and defects such as nephritis, nephrosis, cystic fibrosis, malocclusions, mental retardation, and others.

Specialty clinics jointly operated and financed by the state and local health departments are held throughout the state to provide for case-finding, diagnosis, some treatment services, and follow-up care. More definitive diagnostic and treatment services are arranged through outpatient and inpatient hospital facilities in Baltimore. Despite this network of clinics in the rural areas and the special facilities available in the hospitals in the city, the subcommittee reported that services "to handicapped children are more available in some parts of the state than in others and certain types of services are simply not available in some communities. This is most often true of children who live in rural areas of Maryland, and for those who have many handicaps regardless of where they live. . . . Some children need services of many specialists in many different clinics. A complete examination often takes more than a year for children who live in or near Baltimore and may never be completed for children who live in distant parts of the state and whose parents find it difficult or impossible to make all the necessary trips to city clinics. . . . Furthermore, when examinations are completed, there is frequently no single person or group responsible to weigh all the findings, to explain these to the parents, and to decide with parents on a plan of treatment."[197]

As a result of the committee findings and recommendations the State Legislature appropriated funds to the Crippled Children's Program to establish centers in conjunction with the two medical schools beginning in July, 1958.

The medical schools were responsible for staffing the centers and both selected eminently qualified pediatricians as center directors. Each center, which has quarters separate from the rest of the hospital, developed a full-time staff consisting of pediatricians, psychologists, social workers, and supporting staff. Arrangements were made for consultation services in the appropriate specialties utilizing the senior staff. Diagnostic procedures, such as x-rays, electroencephalographs, and the like, were made available by the associated teaching hospitals. It took the center directors several months to gather their staffs together, organize their facilities, and be able to see

The Multiply Handicapped Child

TABLE 10-1

NUMBER OF CHILDREN BY SOURCE OF REFERRAL, NUMBER AND PER CENT
(MARYLAND DIAGNOSTIC AND EVALUATION CENTERS FOR HANDICAPPED
CHILDREN: JULY 1, 1958-JUNE 30, 1959)

Source of Referral	Total 1958-1959		July-December, 1958		January-June, 1959	
	No.	%	No.	%	No.	%
Local health department	182	43.9	71	51.2	111	40.4
Division for Crippled Children, State Health Department	40	9.7	35	25.2	5	1.8
Facilities in parent hospitals	92	22.2	18	12.9	74	26.9
Educational authority	43	10.4	7	5.0	36	13.1
Family physician	45	10.9	7	5.0	38	13.8
Miscellaneous—other	12	2.9	1	0.7	11	4.0
Total—all sources	414	100.0	139	100.0	275	100.0

patients in any numbers. Even so, over four hundred patients were examined during the first year.

Private as well as medically indigent patients were referred to the local health department. All medical, social, educational, and financial information was collected by the health department. Referrals were then made to the state Crippled Children's Program and the patients were assigned to one or the other center for evaluation and recommendations. The follow-up services were to be in large part the responsibility of the local community utilizing the existing network of clinic and hospital services, mentioned previously, and other local facilities. Re-evaluations to determine progress were to be done by the centers as indicated for the individual children.

In order to determine the effectiveness of the centers, the Maryland State Department of Health has carried out an extensive study of the first year's experience. The first part of the study* was essentially concerned with the administrative aspects. It showed that the total cost for the 1958-1959 fiscal year for the complete evaluation varied between $250 and $280 per child according to the center. These costs included operating expenses, the salaries of the professional and supporting staff, consultation fees, investigative procedures, and the like.

Table 10-1 shows the source of referral of the children, comparing the first six-month period with the second six-month period. During the first six months, 76 per cent of the patients were referred by the local health departments and the Crippled Children's Program. Only 42 per cent were referred from these sources during the second six months. More than half the children had not previously been registered in the Crippled Children's

---

* Carried out by Bettie Rogerson, Sc.D., chief, Program Evaluation, Office of Planning and Research, Maryland State Department of Health.

Program. This suggests that as the centers became known the referrals from sources other than the health departments increased. This trend has continued to the present. Another encouraging trend that was noted was that at the beginning, 32 per cent of the children seen were under six years of age. Later on, it was found that 48 per cent of the children referred were under six years.

In the first part of the study an attempt was made to consider each child from the point of view of his major handicapping condition. This depended on the clinical judgment of the pediatrician in charge and also on the severity of the conditions, which might change from time to time. For example, at the initial evaluation of the child with uncontrolled seizures and mental retardation, the seizures might be considered the major handicapping condition. After proper medication the major condition would be mental retardation.

Regardless of how the children and their conditions were analyzed without actually detailing the individual records, little insight can be obtained into the difficulties in making definitive diagnoses, the complexity and sometimes the overwhelming seriousness of the handicaps, and the emotional, social, and educational problems involved. To illustrate, consider the child who was referred because he was a problem at home and failing at school. He had an I.Q. of 108, a specific arithmetical learning defect, conductive hearing loss, chronic otitis media, amblyopia and esotropia, ptosis, mild ataxic cerebral palsy, controlled seizures, and a behavior disorder. Two hundred and eighty-nine children had between three and six such diagnosed conditions. Only thirty-three children had a single diagnosis.

A further difficulty in concentrating on the major handicap was the fact that although the recommendations made considered the child as a whole, they were of necessity related to each diagnosis, not only to the major handicapping condition. For instance, the recommendation for a hearing aid for a child with cerebral palsy was because he was deaf not because he had cerebral palsy, no matter how closely the two might be connected.

For these reasons the second part of the study pertains to the children but takes into account the 1,326 separate diagnoses and 1,245 specific recommendations made by the centers. The primary purpose of this part of the study was to determine the extent to which the recommendations had been carried out and the effect of their implementation on any improvement shown by the children. This portion of the study consisted of a field survey carried out by a supervising public health nurse* two years following the initial evaluation.

---

* Mrs. Edna Troxell, supervising nurse, Division for Crippled Children, Maryland State Department of Health.

TABLE 10-2

NUMBER OF CHILDREN BY RACE AND SEX AND AGE GROUPS, NUMBER AND PER CENT (MARYLAND DIAGNOSTIC AND EVALUATION CENTERS FOLLOW-UP STUDY: 1960-1961)

| | | | Male | | | | | | Female | | | | | |
| | Total | | Total | | White | | Non-white | | Total | | White | | Non-white | |
Age Groups	No.	%	No.	%	No.	%	No.	%	No.	%	No.	%	No.	%
All ages	412	100.0	290	70.4	239	58.0	51	12.4	122	29.6	98	23.8	24	5.8
0-2	1	0.2	1		1		—		—		—		—	
3-4	46	11.2	36		28		8		10		9		1	
5-9	182	44.2	126		102		24		56		47		9	
10-14	134	32.5	91		73		18		43		32		11	
15-19	44	10.7	34		33		1		10		8		2	
20 and over	5	1.2	2		2		—		3		2		1	

A survey form was completed by the nurse after a home visit to each child supplemented by conferences with the local health officer, public health nurses, teachers, social workers, private physicians, and other personnel involved in the care of the child. An attempt was made to answer several questions. Had the recommendations been implemented and were services essential to the prescribed treatments available? What were the parental impressions of the services provided, and how well did they understand their child's problems? Finally, what was the child's current status, and to what degree was it influenced by certain demographic and sociologic factors?

Of the original 414 children, two died before the follow-up. Of the remaining 412 children, 76 per cent lived at the same address and 15 per cent had moved within the same political subdivision. Thus, for 91 per cent, the follow-up services were provided or arranged by the same health department which referred them for evaluation; fifteen had moved out of state, and four additional families could not be located.

Table 10-2 gives the age at follow-up by sex and race. Forty-four per cent of all children were between five and nine years at the time of follow-up, and about 70 per cent of the total group were males. Eighteen per cent were nonwhite, which follows closely the percentage of the nonwhite population in the state.

Table 10-3 groups the 1,326 diagnoses. Over two thirds of the diagnoses fall within the interrelated categories of mental deficiency, disorders of the brain, central nervous system or sensory organs, and emotional or personality disorders.

Analysis of the psychological tests of these children showed that 62 per cent had I.Q.s below 80 and 23 per cent were below 50. The median

I.Q. was 70. Many tests were used in order to determine the child's intelligence, but because of the intricacy of the problems, some of the scores were, of necessity, estimates. However, they were the best estimates of skilled psychologists trained in testing these severely handicapped children.

A careful look at the 1,245 recommendations made for the children indicated that they were essentially what would be expected from the diagnoses as seen in Table 10-3. The most frequent were for special educational facilities, speech therapy, appliances, mental health clinics, and follow-up in seizure clinic. Seventy-two per cent of the recommendations had been followed and there were plans to carry out another 6 per cent in the future. No information was available on 4 per cent. The parents were unwilling to carry out 9 per cent of the recommendations and were unable to comply with an additional 9 per cent.

This last group consisted of eighty-nine children who had 112 recommendations which were not carried out because of lack of available services. Of these, twenty-six were for speech therapy, twenty-two for day centers or schools for the retarded, nineteen for special educational services, nine for physical therapy, and six for vocational training. There were thirty other miscellaneous services not available.

For 323 children no unmet need was reported to the nurse doing the survey. This is hard to believe and may well reflect the fact that the parents and others involved in caring for the children were doing the best they

TABLE 10-3

DIAGNOSES REPORTED, NUMBER AND PER CENT
(MARYLAND DIAGNOSTIC AND EVALUATION CENTER FOLLOW-UP STUDY:
1960-1961)

	No.	%
All Diagnoses	1,326	100.0
Intellectual impairment	301	22.7
Cerebral palsy	112	8.4
Other locomotor disabilities	98	7.4
Epilepsy	57	4.3
Specific learning defects	42	3.2
Central communication disorders	86	6.5
Emotional disturbances	93	7.0
Hearing loss	46	3.5
Organic speech defect	16	1.2
Functional speech disorders	94	7.1
Blindness	7	0.5
Disorders of visual perception	6	0.5
Other visual disturbances	84	6.3
Congenital deformities	65	4.9
Cardiovascular diseases	21	1.6
Metabolic and endocrine disorders	27	2.0
Dental problems	84	6.3
All others	87	6.6

TABLE 10-4

NUMBER OF CHILDREN BY I.Q. BY SCHOOL PLACEMENT
(MARYLAND DIAGNOSTIC AND EVALUATION CENTERS FOLLOW-UP STUDY:
1960-1961)

School Placement	Total	I.Q.					
		0-19	20-49	50-64	65-79	80-89	90-up
Regular school, normal class for age	64	—	1	3	17	17	26
Regular class, special help	31	—	—	2	6	10	13
Special school or class for handicapped	134	1	23	28	44	18	20
Visiting teacher	17	—	2	4	4	3	4
Residential school for handicapped	17	2	2	—	4	3	6
Institutionalized	11	2	4	3	1	1	—
Not in school, not of school age	53	1	11	11	9	8	13
Not in school, school age (5-20 years)	75	9	33	12	11	6	4
Not stated	10	1	2	1	1	1	4
Total	412	16	78	64	97	67	90

could with the facilities available. Table 10-4 gives some indication of this fact. For example, twenty-one children with I.Q.s below 80 were in regular school and a normal class placement for their age, and seventy-five children of school age were not in school or in a day center for the retarded. This suggests that the unmet need is greater than the study actually showed, but in many instances remains unrecognized.

Table 10-5 gives the diagnoses by current status. Ninety-seven or 7.3 per cent of the conditions had improved to the point that they were no longer considered handicapping. Three hundred and four or 23.0 per cent of the conditions showed evidence of having made good progress, and 360 or 27.1 per cent showed some improvement. In other words, 57.4 per cent of the total conditions had improved to some degree. This is an encouraging picture when the extent and multiplicity of the handicaps are considered. Yet, scrutiny of the 565 or 42.6 per cent of the conditions which showed no improvement indicates that earlier case finding and increased facilities and supportive services would ameliorate many of these conditions in certain children.

Various demographic, sociological, and attitudinal factors were studied to determine any effect they might have on the current status of the children. Analysis of this material revealed several interesting facts.

1. *Age.* Children aged five to nine years at the time of follow-up showed a larger percentage of improved diagnoses than those in any other age group. The improvements seen could be explained partially by the expected growth and development for this age period.
2. *Legal Status of Family.* About 72 per cent of the children came from families of normal composition and legal status. This is approximately

the same percentage as is found in the United States population in 1960. The impression that a severely handicapped child might be a causative factor in a broken home was not confirmed.

Legal status of the family seemed to have little relationship to attitudes of family members to each other, to the child, to the center, or to the ability to carry out recommendations. The child from a family of normal composition and legal status did not, as might be expected, have any better chance for improvement than a child from less normal circumstances.

3. *Economic Status.* There was very inconclusive and weak evidence that the children from homes of higher economic status showed somewhat higher rates of progress and that more families from the low economic groups were unwilling to follow recommendations. However, economic status did not seem to be a major factor in the child's progress.

4. *Attitude.* Careful study of attitudes toward the child, the center, and toward the recommendations revealed that children from families that were cooperative and conscientious showed almost twice the percentage of improvement as the uncooperative, and 50 per cent more than the

TABLE 10-5

DIAGNOSES BY CURRENT STATUS (MARYLAND DIAGNOSTIC AND
EVALUATION CENTER FOLLOW-UP STUDY: 1960-1961)

			Current Status							
	Total		No Longer Handi- capping		Progress Good		Some Improve- ment		No Improve- ment	
Diagnosis	*No.*	*%*	*No.*	*%*	*No.*	*%*	*No.*	*%*	*No.*	*%*
All diagnoses	1,326	100.0	97	7.3	304	23.0	360	27.1	565	42.6
Intellectual impairment	301	100.0	—	—	69	22.9	105	34.9	127	42.2
Cerebral palsy	112	100.0	—	—	22	19.6	44	39.3	46	41.1
Other locomotor disabilities	98	100.0	5	5.1	12	12.2	27	27.6	54	55.1
Epilepsy	57	100.0	2	3.5	46	80.7	2	3.5	7	12.3
Specific learning defects	42	100.0	—	—	12	28.6	15	35.7	15	35.7
Central communication disorders	86	100.0	—	—	18	20.9	31	36.1	37	43.0
Emotional disturbances	93	100.0	2	2.2	35	37.6	25	26.9	31	33.3
Hearing loss	46	100.0	7	15.2	6	13.1	11	23.9	22	47.8
Organic speech defect	16	100.0	—	—	8	50.0	6	37.5	2	12.5
Functional speech disorders	94	100.0	7	7.5	24	25.5	47	50.0	16	17.0
Blindness	7	100.0	—	—	1	14.3	1	14.3	5	71.4
Disorders of visual perception	6	100.0	—	—	1	16.7	1	16.7	4	66.6
Other visual disturbances	84	100.0	8	9.5	25	29.8	4	4.8	47	55.9
Congenital deformities	65	100.0	7	10.8	7	10.8	10	15.4	41	63.0
Cardiovascular diseases	21	100.0	5	23.8	3	14.3	4	19.0	9	42.9
Metabolic and endocrine disorders	27	100.0	1	3.7	7	25.9	5	18.5	14	51.9
Dental problems	84	100.0	30	35.7	1	1.2	6	7.1	47	56.0
Others	87	100.0	23	26.4	7	8.1	16	18.4	41	47.1

partially cooperative group. This suggests that improved counseling and other supportive services to help families carry out recommendations would result in less severely handicapped children.

CONCLUSIONS

The diagnostic centers were established to integrate and supplement the existing facilities and services in Maryland for handicapped children and especially for those with multiple handicaps.

The study has shown that, as originally intended, the majority of children seen during the first year did have multiple handicaps. The large number of children with neurological conditions reflects the inadequacy of services for these children. Areas of the greatest unmet needs were identified.

Despite the complexity and severity of the disabilities of these children, the study showed that with adequate diagnosis and conscientious carrying out of the recommendations improvements do occur in a significant proportion of cases. Counseling, therapy, special educational, and other supportive services do alleviate the conditions and result in less severely handicapped children.

ACKNOWLEDGMENTS

The authors would like to express their appreciation to Dr. Bettie Rogerson, chief, Program Evaluation, Office of Planning and Research; Mrs. Edna Troxell, supervising public health nurse; and Mr. Robert Richter, research assistant, Maryland State Department of Health, for their invaluable parts in the study. They would also like to thank Dr. Frederick Richardson and his staff at the Johns Hopkins Center, Dr. Raymond Clemmens and his staff at the University of Maryland Center, and the staffs of the local health departments for their assistance and cooperation.

Chapter 11

A Survey of Handicapping Conditions and Handicapped Children in Alamance County, North Carolina

WILLIAM P. RICHARDSON and A. C. HIGGINS

THE North Carolina Study of Handicapped Children was begun in 1959 for the purpose of securing data on the prevalence and severity of handicapping conditions among the children of North Carolina and related social factors and service needs, on which effective community planning could be based. It is strange that in an area such as that of handicapped children, where there have been active programs over a great many years, there should have been so little effort at precise evaluation of the magnitude and many-faceted nature of the problem. The Hunterdon County[195] and Baltimore[179] studies of chronic illness and the reports of the National Health Survey[459] give glimpses of the total picture, but age breakdowns which are inappropriate for our purposes and the omission of categories significant among childhood handicapping conditions make these data inadequate for measuring the problem of handicapped children, save as a reminder that there is a substantial problem.

One previous community-wide survey, that of Wishik[1127] and his coworkers in Georgia, elicited for the counties they surveyed many of the kinds of data sought by the present study, but it did not include several aspects of the problem which we felt needed exploration, including the estimation of underreporting through the examination of presumably normal children. Moreover, there was the important question of the extent to which prevalence and disability rates of the various handicapping conditions might be found to vary from one community to another.

Specific objectives of this study were

1. To determine prevalence rates of various handicapping conditions among children and differences in prevalence, if such exist, among different segments of the population;

Reprinted from *American Journal of Public Health*, 54:1817-1830, November, 1964.

(For a more detailed report of this study see: Richardson, W. P., *et al.*: *The Handicapped Children of Alamance County, North Carolina*. Wilmington, Nemours Foundation, 1965.)

2. To evaluate the extent of disability caused by these conditions and the factors other than the conditions themselves which help determine the degree of disability;
3. To evaluate the adequacy of services and facilities available to handicapped children and additional services and facilities needed to provide optimum care and habilitation or rehabilitation;
4. To evaluate the effectiveness and efficiency of different data-gathering technics;
5. To explore factors other than availability of services which influence whether or not handicapped children receive the care they need.

The present report is primarily concerned with a description of methods and procedures and with findings related to objectives (1), (2), and (4).

The plan adopted was to carry out an intensive survey in one county, and for this purpose Alamance County, N. C., was selected. No single county can be truly representative of as large and diverse a state as North Carolina, but Alamance includes substantial representation of the major social, ethnic, and occupational groups which make up the state's population. It is located in the Piedmont, about sixty miles west of Raleigh. The center of the county, Burlington and its environs, is highly industrialized and growing rapidly. The rest of the county is rural with well-developed, diversified agriculture. Population in 1962 was 89,100. Negroes represented approximately 20 per cent, or 15,200, and persons under 21 years of age, 41 per cent of the total, or 36,500.

Three methods of morbidity data gathering are generally used in the United States: the examination of medical records which are maintained for various reasons by a variety of health agencies;[469] the use of health questionnaires;[457] and clinical examinations.[195, 179] These technics generate differing morbidity estimates because they measure different phenomena. Medical records report recognition and/or service by health agents; surveys get an individual or familial awareness of medical conditions and clinical examinations provide estimates of professional recognition of disabilities. Thus, these are three somewhat distinct and yet overlapping dimensions of the complex area of illness, disability, and health services.

The design of the present study included all three of these dimensions. The first step was the collection of all recorded information in the files of all health agencies dealing with persons under 21 years of age who were or had been residents of the county. Next, a questionnaire survey was carried out in a representative sample of the households of the county, and, finally, a sample of children reported as handicapped and not handicapped from steps one and two were given comprehensive examinations in a fully staffed health clinic. Each of these steps will be discussed in detail.

THE PROBLEM OF DEFINITION

The first problem a study of this kind must come to grips with is that of definition. Differences in definition doubtless account for many of the apparent inconsistencies between prevalence rates derived from different sources, and proper evaluation of the results of any specific study requires that the definitions used be stated as precisely as possible. Unfortunately, there is no one-dimensional definition of *handicap*. There are handicapping or potentially handicapping conditions, for which specific clinical definitions are available. Then there are handicapped children and their disabilities, which are a function of the clinical condition and its severity, plus a variety of social and psychological factors which have to be individually evaluated.

The concept of the handicapped child which forms the basis of this study is that set forth in the definition of the American Public Health Association:[196]

> A child is considered to be handicapped if he cannot within limits play, learn, work, or do the things other children of his age can do; if he is hindered in achieving his full physical, mental and social potentialities. The initial disability may be very mild and hardly noticeable, but potentially handicapping, or it may seriously involve several areas of function with the probability of life-long impairment. The problem may appear to be primarily physical, or perhaps emotional or social. Regardless of the nature of the chief mainifestation, physical, emotional and social components are all factors at one time or another and in varying degrees, in most handicapping conditions of childhood.

It was necessary, of course, to make use of various delimiting operational definitions for different phases of the study. During the agency review a child was considered handicapped if reported by a health agency as handicapped, and he was listed as suffering from a specific condition if the agency's files contained a specific diagnosis. For the household survey, a child was presumed to have a handicapping condition if his parents answered positively one or more questions on the questionnaire, and his condition was categorized by the question(s) so answered. Thus, a child would be orthopedically handicapped if his parent answered this question positively: "Has . . . ever had any paralysis of any kind, or had poor use of his legs, arms, feet, hands, or fingers?" In the clinical examinations children were categorized on the basis of diagnosis by the examining physicians of the presence of a condition falling into one of the thirteen areas of handicap being studied, without reference to presence or degree of actual handicap. Severity and degree of disability were a separate determination. Each child was rated for disability by the conference, held after each clinic session, of all participants in the examination, and the evaluation was based on physical, mental, emotional, social, and vocational factors.

THE AGENCY REVIEW

An attempt was made to examine every record on every child resident in the county known to a physician or agency to have a handicapping condition and from this, using population projections for June, 1962, to derive estimates of prevalence rates. There are obvious limitations to data secured from such sources, and, as will be explained later, there were gaps in the completeness of our coverage. Nevertheless, the prevalence rates derived were useful both as an indicator of the services, practices, and interests of the various agencies and, by comparison, with the rates estimated from the clinical examinations, as a measure of the completeness of recognition of handicapping conditions in the child population of the county.

In addition to practicing physicians and dentists, the following agencies were included in the record review: local Departments of Health and Public Welfare, city and county schools, and the two local hospitals, one of two nearby teaching hospitals, State Commission for the Blind, Board of Correction and Training, State Division of Vocational Rehabilitation, State Hospitals Board of Control, State Schools for the Blind and Deaf, State Cerebral Palsy Hospital, and the several voluntary health and charitable agencies which serve the county.

One teaching hospital which has many patients from Alamance County was not included because the volume and method of filing its patient records made it completely unfeasible to locate the records needed for the study. Since admission to this hopsital is usually made on the basis of a referral from a local source, we do not believe this omission constitutes a major limitation to the agency data.

A possibly more serious problem was the fact that it was necessary to rely on the memories of practicing physicians and dentists for recalling children whom they had treated with one or more of the designated conditions, since it was not feasible for them or for the study staff to go through all their medical records.

In approaching practitioners and agencies, the categories of handicapping conditions with which we were concerned were listed and the general concept of the handicapped child was discussed with them. Within this framework they were asked to list the children known by them to be handicapped. Thus the operational definitions were really those of the individual practitioner or agency, and they varied from agency to agency. It could not have been otherwise without forcing each agency to revamp its reports to fit a set of arbitrary definitions, an obviously impractical procedure.

TABLE 11-1

THE PREVALENCE RATES PER 1,000 OF HANDICAPPING CONDITIONS
FOR PERSONS UNDER 21 YEARS, AGENCY DATA ONLY BY RACE AND SEX

Conditions	Male	Female	White	Negro
Orthopedic	13.3	14.1	17.2	13.2
Epilepsy	2.6	1.3	2.0	1.9
Vision	14.8	13.5	15.4	9.4
Hearing	3.7	2.8	3.3	1.8
Cleft palate	1.9	0.9	1.6	0.7
Emotional	25.4	14.0	21.8	12.4
Speech	21.7	10.0	14.8	21.9
Mental (total)	37.8	18.1	27.3	31.4
Respiratory	8.9	7.3	8.2	7.8
Heart	4.6	5.5	4.8	5.8
Orthodontic	2.1	2.0	2.4	0.5
Cerebral palsy	2.0	2.0	2.2	1.1
Skin	1.6	1.3	0.8	4.1
Other	19.7	16.0	16.9	21.4
Numbers in population	18,600	17,900	29,100	7,400

Two major factors which serve to limit or bias the data collected from agency reports should be noted. The first is that agencies do not necessarily report every child known to them as handicapped. Children with handicaps may be known, but if the agency has no service, or has been called on for no service for the handicapping condition, they may be unreported. For example, an agency may be aware that a child is mentally retarded, but, since no service in this field is available from that agency, the fact of retardation may never appear in its files.

Again, it was recognized early in the study that the information in the files would vary in completeness and recency and that it would reflect the specific purposes, special interests, and historical accidents of the agencies studied. Moreover, its quality would vary with the training of those making the diagnoses. In many instances these had been medically determined, but many were based on the judgment, of nurses, teachers, or social workers.

In spite of these biases and limitations, the data from practitioners and agencies give a revealing picture of the problem as known to these sources of service to the handicapped children of the community. There was, surprisingly enough, very little overlap in these records: there was an average of 1.2 reports per child.

Table 11-1 gives the estimates of prevalence rates for the various conditions derived from the reports of agencies and practitioners. The most frequently reported condition was mental retardation, followed by emotional disturbance, orthopedic conditions, and speech defects. The mental retardation rate, nearly 3 per cent, agrees with previous estimates of mental retardation,[894] but from the limitations of these data enumerated above it was anticipated that this would be low. The degree of underestimation,

TABLE 11-2

THE PERCENTAGE DISTRIBUTIONS OF REPORTS BY SEX AND RACE FOR
THE LARGEST REPORTING AGENCIES OF THE COUNTY

Agency	% Male	% Negro	Total Numbers Reported
Health Department	53.8	16.0	999
Welfare Department	59.7	20.4	923
Schools	67.5	26.3	922
Hospitals	57.7	11.8	757
State Board of Health	55.2	17.9	565
All physicians in private practice	56.7	8.3	319
In the county population under 21	51.0	20.3	4,081

revealed by the clinical evaluations, suggested in Table 11-5 and reported elsewhere, was, however, a surprise.[921]

The breakdowns by sex and by color reveal results which were also unexpected. There is no physiologic reason why there should be a difference in the prevalence of handicapping conditions in boys and girls, yet these reports show a male excess for all conditions except orthopedic and heart. Of total conditions reported 61 per cent were in males although males are only 51 per cent of the population.

Since agency reports reflect in considerable measure those conditions for which assistance has been sought, the suggestion in this finding is that parents seek assistance more frequently for boys than for girls as a result of differential expectations for males in our society.

With respect to race, it was assumed that reported rates would be higher for Negroes than for whites because their socioeconomic conditions predispose to health needs. Yet, for the thirteen conditions, the Negro rates exceeded those in white children for only four: speech defects, mental retardation, heart conditions, and skin conditions.

Table 11-2 shows the percentages of male and Negro reports from the largest reporting sources in the county. Every agency reported a higher percentage of males than their proportion in the population, and all but two, the Welfare Department and the schools, reported a lower percentage of Negroes than their proportion in the population.

Table 11-3, showing the percentage distribution of conditions reported by the largest reporting agencies in the county, gives an interesting spectrum of their areas of specialization and interest. The highest percentages of reports from the Health Department are of orthopedic, visual, and emotional conditions. The Welfare Department's area of concentration is emotional problems and mental retardation. The high percentages of orthopedic and emotional problems in reports from the State Board of Health reflect the board's operation of orthopedic and mental health clinics around the state.

The fact that the schools report large numbers of children with mental retardation, emotional problems, speech defects, and orthopedic conditions is not so surprising as that they reported so few of some other conditions, as respiratory and heart disease, orthodontic defects, and cerebral palsy.[918] It was to be expected that private physicians would report larger numbers of the more clinically obvious conditions as orthopedic, heart, and respiratory conditions.

For comparison, the last column of this table gives the percentage distribution of handicapping conditions with moderate or severe disability as estimated from the clinical examinations. These figures are based on the assumptions that the distribution of morbidity for all health agencies should approximate the distribution of conditions estimated for the county. In other words, about 4 per cent of the handicapped children of the county are moderately or severely orthopedically handicapped.

From these data and from a comparison of agency rates with those derived from the clinical examinations, it is clear that agency reports give a biased and inadequate picture of handicapping conditions. For only five conditions, cleft palate, speech defects, mental retardation, orthopedic de-

TABLE 11-3

THE PERCENTAGE DISTRIBUTION OF DIAGNOSES REPORTED BY THE HEALTH
AGENCIES OF ALAMANCE COUNTY

Conditions	Health Department	Welfare Department	State Board of Health	County Schools	Physicians in Practice	Hospitals	Expected Distributions*
Orthopedic	20.5	2.2	31.8	11.7	19.0	16.2	4.0
Epilepsy	1.3	0.6	—	1.7	4.4	2.3	3.6
Vision	21.9	4.3	0.8	3.1	6.2	13.7	8.2
Hearing	2.0	1.1	2.2	2.5	2.0	1.7	2.8
Cleft palate	2.1	0.5	3.5	1.4	2.8	2.2	0.5
Emotional	10.4	21.9	27.3	12.0	4.0	23.1	17.8
Speech	3.8	1.3	1.2	28.5	3.2	0.9	3.5
Mental retardation	8.4	29.8	0.9	35.9	12.7	5.5	23.0
Chronic respiratory	2.2	1.0	2.8	0.6	17.1	10.0	8.6
Heart	6.5	1.4	6.2	0.2	17.1	9.9	1.2
Orthodontic	0.7	0.3	0.5	—	—	0.3	10.7
Cerebral palsy	3.6	0.4	2.5	0.5	6.7	1.1	1.9
Chronic skin	3.0	0.8	3.2	—	1.4	1.1	3.3
Other	13.6	34.4	17.1	1.9	3.4	12.0	—
Number of diagnoses	1,192	1,120	598	1,294	504	878	12,010
Number of children	999	923	565	922	319	757	7,071

* This distribution assumes the clinic estimates of moderate and severe cases are the best estimates as to the prevalence of medically significant conditions.

fects, and cerebral palsy, did agencies report as many as 25 per cent of the number of children estimated to have these conditions, and for six conditions, emotional disturbance, heart conditions, chronic respiratory disease, chronic skin disease, hearing defects, and orthodontic conditions, less than 10 per cent of the expected estimated number were reported.

It might be supposed that agency reports represent the more severe conditions, and there is doubtless a measure of validity to this, although the clinical evaluations revealed many exceptions. Comparing agency rates with the rates of moderately and severely handicapping conditions derived from the clinic examinations, we find that the number of agency reports of speech defects, heart conditions, and orthopedic defects exceed the estimated number by 24 to 41 per cent. At the other end of the scale, only 6.2 per cent as many orthodontic defects were reported as estimated, a probable indication of lack of recognition of this condition as a handicap. In other words, agencies underreport some conditions and overreport others.[918]

Of special interest is the low rate of reported epilepsy in comparison with the estimated rate. The tendency to try to conceal this condition probably accounts for only part of this discrepancy.

THE HOUSEHOLD SURVEY

The second phase of the study was a survey of a 5 per cent sample of the households in Alamance County to secure data for an estimate of the prevalence of handicapping conditions based on parental recognition or concern. These data were gathered using a questionnaire specially developed for this purpose, designed to measure the prevalence of conditions regardless of severity, prior treatment or professional diagnoses. The schedule of questions was simple and straightforward since it was to be administered by lay canvassers.[524]

Fifty-eight volunteer workers were recruited through the leading women's service organizations and given nine hours of instruction in three separate sessions. These volunteers did the greater part of the interviewing, but, as a partial control, some of the interviews were carried out by public health nurses, social workers, and professional interviewers secured through the Institute for Research in Social Science. Interviews were completed during the period March 1–17, 1962, on 1,032 households in randomly chosen areas of the county, and completed questionnaires were returned on 1,864 children, approximately 4.6 per cent of the population of the county under 21. Except for the necessity in some instances of repeated visits, the volunteers experienced no difficulty in completing the interviews, and their results were quite comparable to those of the professional workers.[524]

TABLE 11-4

PREVALENCE RATES OF PRESUMPTIVELY HANDICAPPING CONDITIONS PER 1,000 POPULATION BY SELECTED SOCIAL AND DEMOGRAPHIC CHARACTERISTICS (SURVEY DATA)

Presumptive Diagnosis	Total Sample	Age				Sex		Race		Social Class		
		0-4	5-9	10-14	15-20	Male	Female	White	Negro	Upper and Middle	Working	Lower
Any handicap	508	373	506	565	605	525	490	500	546	503	479	602
Orthopedic condition	63	39	42	70	109	68	59	64	60	64	58	83
Epilepsy	31	23	24	45	31	36	26	33	27	15	33	37
Vision	126	25	76	203	221	109	143	121	147	132	118	141
Hearing	30	2	38	50	25	40	20	26	48	22	28	43
Cleft palate	1	0	2	0	0	1	0	0	0	0	0	2
Emotional	30	16	42	35	23	32	27	24	54	11	22	63
Speech	64	32	99	85	40	85	42	55	87	60	43	123
Mental retardation	79	48	81	97	89	100	59	65	141	34	60	172
Chronic respiratory	163	126	162	158	213	181	145	148	225	170	148	207
Heart	27	6	31	22	54	23	32	27	30	11	31	31
Orthodontic	35	0	58	42	46	18	53	30	57	37	29	54
Cerebral palsy	5	0	9	5	8	9	1	6	3	3	5	5
Skin	148	131	126	160	178	141	156	133	213	128	143	175
Other physical handicap	105	112	113	90	109	101	109	108	84	136	105	86

Rates of presumptive handicapping conditions are given in Table 11-4, broken down by age, sex, race, and social class. As mentioned earlier, in this tabulation classification as presumptively handicapped was based on an affirmative answer to one or more of the questions on the questionnaire. The rates, therefore, are a measure of parental awareness of handicapping or potentially handicapping conditions, plus their concern over symptoms real or fancied.

Overall, the parents of slightly more than half of the children were concerned about possible handicapping conditions. The relative order of conditions differs from that of the agency data, the highest rates being for skin conditions, respiratory conditions, and visual difficulty. The rates increase with age and, as in the agency data, males have higher rates than females. Unlike the agency data, however, the reported rates for Negroes exceeded those for whites for the total with some presumptive handicap and for nine of the thirteen specific conditions. Finally, more families judged by the interviewers to be of the "lower class" reported their children to have possibly handicapping conditions than did families classified upper, middle, or working class.

A comment might be made regarding the higher rates in Negroes, a reversal of the situation shown in the agency data, where white rates were considerably higher. A possible explanation is that Negroes on the whole receive less medical care than do whites so appear less often in the records of practitioners and agencies. Not getting needed attention or reassurance, their level of continuing concern is higher. Available data did not permit classification of agency cases by social class, but the same differences between social classes probably exist and for similar reasons.

Thus, it appears clear that the various social factors are relevant to the reporting of medical conditions in a health survey and must be taken into account in interpreting the data secured. Some of the observed differences are probably due to real differences between age categories, the sexes, the races, and social classes, but some additional portion is due to factors other than real differences in health.

THE CLINICAL EXAMINATIONS

The purpose of the clinical examinations was not only to determine the validity, or lack of it, of the estimates from the agency and household surveys but to derive another estimate of the prevalence rates of the several handicapping conditions, the degree of disability present, and the facilities and services needed for optimum care and rehabilitation. The sample of children to be invited for examination was drawn from three sources: children reported by agencies as handicapped, children reported in the household survey as handicapped, and children from the household survey for whom no handicapping condition was reported, i.e., presumably normal children.

The proportion of children with each specific presumptive handicap who were included in the sample depended on the number of children reported as having that condition. It varied from 100 per cent of the reported cases of cerebral palsy to 14 per cent of the presumptive normals. There was no attempt to stratify the subsamples in terms of age, race, sex, or social class. The sample was stratified by source of information, i.e., agency or survey reported cases. There was no difference between the attendance rates for survey or agency reported children. There were 700 children invited to the clinic and 456 of these, or 65 per cent, attended. These included 87 presumptively normal children, 212 presumptively handicapped children from the household survey lists, and 157 presumptively handicapped children from the reports of agencies. The children reported only by a private hospital or practitioner were not included in the pool from which the samples were drawn.

The children were invited on the basis of random selection from the two lists (agency and household survey) classified by diagnoses. For sampling, each child was classified by primary diagnosis as reported by the reporting agency; for this purpose a more or less arbitrary list of children was prepared from the household survey reported cases by diagnoses.

The sampling ratio on which invitations to the clinic for each diagnostic category were based depended on three things: first, practical considerations, such as the number of children who could be examined in a single day of clinic operation; second, the number of children reported on the household survey to suffer from a particular condition; third, a sufficient number of cases had to be included to provide a statistically adequate sample of reported cases. Of course, the number of children examined differed from the number of children invited since attendance rates were shown to vary by diagnostic categories.[903]

The sampling of children examined varied from 9 per cent of the reported skin conditions to 83 per cent of the reported incidence of speech defects.

Invitation was by letter sent to each home one week before the child was expected at the clinic. A stamped, self-addressed postcard was to be returned by the parents if they planned to attend. It was necessary to follow up the letters with personal contact either by telephone or home visits. These contacts not only stimulated many of the doubtful but made it possible to determine the kinds of nonparticipation involved. Everything possible was done to motivate attendance: baby-sitting services, transportation, contacts with schools and employers, encouragement through health and welfare workers, and so forth.

Excellent space and facilities for the clinics were provided by the Alamance County Hospital which also performed, at cost, needed laboratory tests and x-rays.

The basic staff of each clinic was composed of a pediatrician, a psychologist, social workers, nurses, and five volunteer workers. Specialists in each area of disability were added to this staff as needed. The medical director of the study acted as supervisor for all clinic sessions.

A medical history, a social history, a screening of vision and hearing, a screening examination for mental retardation and emotional disturbance, and a pediatric examination were done on each child. For those children who had specific presumptive conditions, examinations were added which were relevant. For example, at sessions for children with cleft palate a plastic surgeon, an orthodontist, an otolaryngologist, and a speech therapist were added to the basic staff. The first four days were devoted to examination of presumptively normal children. This was done because it was felt that it would be easier to get the clinic routine established with normal children and because referrals could be made to later clinics if conditions were found needing further special examinations.

The sequence of interviews and examinations was not fixed. An effort was made to have the psychologist's examination precede that of the physician, although this was not always possible. The only absolute requirement was that the medical history be completed before the pediatrician examined the child. In all other stages of the clinic, patients were routed as an examiner was available. This necessitated the constant presence of a supervisor, but it reduced the time spent in the clinic by each child and made possible more efficient use of the examiners' time.

Following each clinic session a staff conference of all who had participated in the examinations was held. Here an attempt was made to arrive at a group judgment of the validity of the presumptive diagnosis, other significant conditions, severity of disabilities, the measure of correction or rehabilitation already achieved or possible with optimum care, and vocational prospects. A program of care was outlined for each child, taking into account the "whole child" and his family situation. These conferences were never dull and frequently involved facts not only of medicine but of sociology, law, ethics, and philosophy as well. On the other hand, they were not uniformly productive. Even this group of highly knowledgeable people were not always able to arrive at a definitive statement of the "ought to be" for every child. Moreover, there were problems growing out of limitations of presently available services and facilities, restrictions imposed by legal definitions, and agency or institutional policy.

Table 11-5 presents the clinically adjusted estimates of prevalence rates based on the clinical examinations together with the percentage distribution of severity of conditions as estimated in the staff conferences.

These rates are based only on the 299 children drawn from the household survey population. The adjustment procedure employed was quite simply a weighting of the survey rates to account for the overreporting and under-reporting of conditions. For example, the household survey data indicated that there were 804 normal children in the 5 per cent sample of the county. Of those, 87 were examined in the clinic and 59 were found to be normal. The estimate of the total number of normals in the household survey would be 59/87 times 804, further adjusted by addition of those children pre-sumptively handicapped who were found to be normal on examination. Similar adjustment was made for each diagnostic category. An assumption of this procedure is, of course, that the children who did attend the clinic sessions displayed the same distribution of conditions as those who for one reason or another were unable or unwilling to attend. The total rate for all handicapping conditions is 829 per 1,000 children, and 509 per 1,000 children, have some handicapping condition, an average of 1.63 conditions per handicapped child. The conditions with the highest rates, in order, are defects of vision, emotional disturbance, chronic respiratory conditions, mental retardation, and orthodontic defects. Three of these, mental re-tardation, emotional disturbance, and vision are also among the first five conditions in the agency data.

We were unprepared for the high total prevalence rates Table 11-5 re-

TABLE 11-5

RATES OF HANDICAPPING CONDITIONS IN CHILDREN PER 1,000 OF
POPULATION AND SEVERITY DISTRIBUTION BASED
ON CLINICAL EXAMINATIONS

Conditions	Adjusted Clinical Rates	None	Mild	Moderate	Severe	Rates with Moderate or Severe Disability
Orthopedic	60.0	17	61	17	6	13.2
Epilepsy	12.0	—	—	100	—	12.0
Vision	123.0	64	24	16	6	27.1
Hearing	49.0	24	57	19	—	9.3
Cleft palate	3.0	50	—	—	50	1.5
Emotional	106.0	—	51	38	11	51.9
Speech	46.0	3	71	19	6	11.5
Mental	90.0	—	15	55	30	76.5
Presumptive	(8.0)	—	(50)	(50)	—	—
Educable	(70.0)	—	(13)	(67)	(20)	—
Trainable	(9.0)	—	—	—	(100)	—
Custodial	(2.0)	—	—	—	(100)	—
Respiratory	103.0	4	65	21	7	28.8
Heart	63.0	77	17	3	3	3.8
Orthodontic	89.0	—	60	37	3	36.6
Cerebral palsy	8.0	—	20	60	20	6.4
Skin	77.0	14	71	14	—	10.8

Percentage Distributions of Severity of Disability span columns None, Mild, Moderate, Severe.

TABLE 11-6

THE AVERAGE NUMBER OF HANDICAPPING CONDITIONS
PER HANDICAPPED CHILD BY SEVERITY OF PRIMARY DIAGNOSIS

Severity of Primary Diagnosis	Average Number of Conditions
None	1.13
Mild	1.43
Moderate	2.04
Severe	2.61
Total group	1.60

Note: Number of children—456.

veals. The rates are far higher than any reported by other studies. That a considerable part of the difference may be due to more inclusive definition is suggested by the high percentage of conditions causing no disability or only mild disability. However, there is also reason to believe that, with the wholehearted interest and participation of the community, we may have succeeded in getting a more nearly complete picture of the existing handicapping problems than some of the previous studies. There is no apparent reason why Alamance County should have an exceptional prevalence of handicapping problems as compared to other counties in North Carolina or the southeast. It has a higher than average per capita income and better than average health facilities and services, and its draft rejection rate was one of the lowest in the state.[583]

From the standpoint of community planning, perhaps the prevalence rates of conditions causing moderate or severe disability, shown in the last column of Table 11-5, are more meaningful. Most of these figures are of the same order of magnitude as those reported by Wishik.[1127] In both studies mental retardation and personality disturbance are at the top of the list, though the Alamance rates for these conditions are double those he reported. His study did not include chronic respiratory or skin conditions.

It is interesting to note that the number of conditions found per child increased with the severity of the primary diagnosis, that is, the condition judged by the examining physician to be the most important. This is shown in Table 11-6. The conclusion is clear that the greater the medical significance of the primary condition the greater the likelihood of some other conditions being present. Of course, some of these other conditions are related to the primary condition, but interrelatedness was not specifically evaluated because it was not germane to the need for services.

Comment

Within the limitations of the definitions used and of methodological error, we have derived estimates of the prevalence rates for thirteen categories

of handicapping conditions in Alamance County. The small numbers involved in individual categories make for rather wide confidence limits, but
even so, it is believed that the figures give a measure of the order of magnitude and provide a sound basis for evaluating adequacy and needs with
respect to facilities, personnel, and services in this county. They are probably fairly representative of other counties in North Carolina and the southeast in which there is a well-established agricultural base and a significant
and rapidly expanding industrialization. It is obvious that much care must
be used in applying the data to other communities or in comparing them
with the results of other studies where methods and definitions may be different.

The most significant finding, of course, is the fact that the prevalence
rates of handicapping conditions, even when estimated on the basis of moderate or severe disability, are much higher than has generally been assumed.
This difference is particularly striking with respect to mental retardation
and emotional disturbance. The rate of mental retardation, 7.7 per cent, is
over twice the figure of 3 per cent usually quoted.[894] The only available
estimate with which the rate of 5.2 per cent emotional disturbance can be
compared is that of 2.9 per cent found by Wishik in his Georgia study.

It is evident that, even though these specific rates cannot be assumed to
apply to other communities, future planning of services, and facilities for
mentally retarded and emotionally disturbed children must take into account the probability that these problems have been significantly underestimated.

There is no comparable estimate of the prevalence of chronic respiratory disease among children, but its importance as a cause of childhood
handicapping, shown by the rate of 2.9 per cent moderate or severe disability, is borne out by the high number of disability days from this cause
in children as reported by the National Health Survey.[459]

The review of records of practitioners and agencies proved to be a very
difficult and time-consuming task, and it did not provide an adequate picture of prevalence. It did give an interesting profile of the specialized interests and limitations of the various agencies and served to point up the
fragmented nature of services to handicapped children, gaps which exist,
and the role which inadequate coordination and communication play in
the failure of these children to secure optimum care and maximum habilitation.

The household survey was conceived as the first step in a process of estimation, the second step of which was validation of presumptive conditions
by clinical examination. The measure of validation and the degree of correspondence of rates derived from the survey with the adjusted clinical
rates was gratifying. Some condition related to the positive answers on the

questionnaire was found by the examining physicians in more than 75 per cent of cases. There is, indeed, a remarkable measure of correspondence in the rates from the household survey and the clinical evaluations when allowance is made for the areas in which under- and overreporting could be anticipated: underreporting of mental retardation and emotional disturbance and overreporting of skin and respiratory conditions, where obvious presenting symptoms likely induce parental overconcern.

If a comparable measure of reliability can be demonstrated for similar surveys in different communities, this device may prove to be an effective and relatively inexpensive way of estimating a community's problems of childhood handicapping. Appropriate adjustment can be made for conditions shown to be especially liable to over- or underreporting and for the proportions of total cases of each condition found by the clinical examinations to cause moderate or severe disability.

The analysis of data regarding facilities, personnel, and services available and needed, and factors determining whether the child secures needed services or not, are the subject of another phase of the study. There are, however, a few observations which stand out and deserve comment here.

The community is already moving to correct three pressing deficiencies— the needs for more speech therapists and special education teachers, especially for the mentally retarded and for mental health services, including both testing and evaluation of children with mental retardation, and diagnosis and treatment of children with emotional and personality disorders. The problem with respect to speech therapists and special education teachers is compounded by the fact that personnel with the necessary special training are in very short supply.

The most striking shortcoming, and one which is doubtless shared in some measure by every community in the land, is the fragmentation of services for handicapped children. There are facilities and services, often of high excellence, for meeting various specific segments of the child's needs, but no effective coordination and no provision for any single agency or individual to have either the responsibility or the opportunity to see the child as a whole in the totality of his needs. Theoretically this coordination is a function of the parent and the family physician or pediatrician, but the limitations of knowledge and understanding of all too many parents are painfully evident, and physicians are given the opportunity to provide this kind of continuing total supervision to only a small proportion of children.

There needs to be experimentation with possible ways by which some agency can have available complete information on all that is known about each handicapped child and what is being done for him, so it can be in a position to evaluate needs that are not being met and bring about appropriate referrals.

Finally, mention should be made of one especially distressing deficiency, the one lack of services and facilities for children with multiple severe handicaps, such as those who are both blind and deaf, mentally retarded and blind and deaf, with progressive muscular dystrophy and severe emotional disturbance, and so on. Although the number of such children is not large, they are the most heartrending of the handicapped. Needed facilities are logically a state rather than a local responsibility. In North Carolina, and doubtless in many other states, the excellent facilities being provided for single specific conditions just do not have available the services needed by those with two or more serious handicaps. Here is a deficiency which urgently needs to be remedied.

In summary, although the present study has produced some estimates on the prevalence and seriousness of handicapping conditions in one community and is in the process of delineating some of the deficiencies and problems relative to needed services and facilities, it has raised more questions than it has answered. It has shown that a variety of social, economic, and educational factors play important roles in determining the recognition of handicapping conditions in children and the securing of needed care. It has shown how services in this field are limited and fragmented by shortcomings of interagency communication and limitations imposed by law and agency policy. These are among the aspects of the problem which are still under intensive investigation.

ACKNOWLEDGEMENTS

The population projections for June, 1962, used in determining rates were prepared by Mr. Josef Perry of the North Carolina Department of Conservation and Development. The study is indebted to Dr. Bradley Wells of the Department of Biostatistics, University of North Carolina School of Public Health for advice regarding statistical design and procedures, and to Dr. Samuel M. Wishik for making available forms and other materials from his 1954 study in Georgia and for helpful encouragement and advice. The authors wish also to express their appreciation to the many officials, professional people, lay volunteers and citizens of Alamance County without whose enthusiastic cooperation and participation the survey would not have been possible.

Chapter 12

The Onondaga Census—Fact or Artifact

Samuel A. Kirk and Bluma B. Weiner

ONE of the widely quoted recent studies of presumed prevalence of mental retardation is the *Census of Referred Suspected Mental Retardation*[822] conducted in 1953 in Onondaga County, New York, by the Mental Research Unit of the New York State Department of Mental Hygiene. This survey was "designed to measure the extent of socially recognized retardation in the community"[822(p.84)] in terms of "reported prevalence" according to criteria which were provided by the research team. Close examination of the most paradoxical findings in this study appear necessary in view of the frequent citation and the possible misconceptions it has produced.

In the Onondaga studies, a total of 3787 children were referred as mentally retarded or suspected of mental retardation, which corresponded to a prevalence rate of 35.2 per 1000 (3.5%) population under 18 years of age. Of the total 3787 cases, 2700 or 71 per cent were reported solely by the schools. Another 324 children or 9 per cent of the total were reported by the school and by one or more other agencies. An additional 327 or 9 per cent were referred by psychiatric, diagnostic, and treatment centers. The remaining 11 per cent were reported by miscellaneous sources. Because the overwhelming majority of referrals came from school sources, and because the schools have borne the brunt of criticism from many sources for "creating" mental retardation, it seems in order to look closely at certain of the findings.

Reported prevalence was lowest in the age group below five years; less than one-half of one per cent of the cases reported fell into this age range. However, at age five and thereafter sharp increases in reported prevalence were noted and were attributed to the introduction of a new major source of referral, the school system. Reported prevalence rose to about 22 per 1000 at age five and to nearly 40 per 1000 at age six. Thereafter, it rose as described below:

> After age six, the prevalence rate rises with increasing age reaching a maximum of approximately 80 per 1000 in the 10-13, 14, and 15 year age groups. In the 10 to 15 year age span, it may be noted that 2114 children were re-

Reprinted from *Exceptional Children*, 25:226-231, Jan., 1959.

ported under 18 years of age. Thereafter, a sharp decline in the rate—down to 28 per 1000—is noted for the 16 and 17 year age group. This later decrease may in part be associated with the partial disappearance from the scene of the school system as a reporting agency; since the legal age for quitting school in New York State is the sixteenth birthday.[822 (p. 90)]

The research team admittedly faced a monumental assignment. It appears to the present reviewers that, in an effort to reduce the problem to manageable propotions, a flaw in design was introduced which automatically affected the nature of the data that were obtained and materially reduced the usefulness of the total study. The original tactical error occurred in the formulation of the "definition of a case of mental retardation." In discussing their problems in this respect, the authors of the survey noted the following:

> The specific sign and symptoms included under the rubric "retardation" are heterogeneous, confused, and confusing because *retardation* is a word covering a variety of symptom manifestations which reflect many patterns of troublesome development. The reported children have in common the fact that they need special attention because they are having difficulty acquiring one or another of the skills of living which the responsible person regards as important.[822 (p. 86)]

They stated further,

> No one single criterion for mental retardation was suitable to this survey, since only a part of the overall social problem would have been uncovered.[822 (p. 87)]

The investigators finally arrived at the following solution to their dilemma of definition:

> Therefore, in order to be as inclusive as possible, *responsible child-care agencies were requested to report all children under 18 years of age, and and residents of Onondaga County on March 1, 1952 identified as definitely mentally retarded, or suspected of mental retardation on the basis of developmental history, poor academic performance, I.Q. score, or social adaptation when contrasted with their age peers.*[822 (p. 87)]

The critique of the results and generalization of this study is discussed below under the following points which indicate that the results are an artifact of the procedure because of (1) the overinclusive definition used, (2) failure to distinguish for teachers the differences between *educational retardation* and *mental retardation,* and (3), a demonstration that a different approach with school personnel does not obtain increases in age of referrals as shown in the Onondaga Study.

1. The overinclusive definition distorted the results.

In spite of the desire to avoid the use of a single criterion for mental retardation, or suspected mental retardation, it appears that the opposite effect was achieved. This definition clearly permitted the nomination of a child as suspected of mental retardation on the basis of any *one* of the accounts, namely: children with mental retardation, or poor academic performance regardless of the cause, or social adaptation. Furthermore, the survey team did not attempt to distinguish between clinically determined and "socially suspected" classification.

The reviewers suggest that the findings of the Onondaga studies were the inevitable outcome of the overinclusive definition which was furnished for the direction of the reporting agencies. In short, *they were artifacts of procedure.* By asking the cooperating agencies to report children who were suspected of mental retardation on the basis of an otherwise unqualified factor of "poor academic performance" or "social maladaptation," the Onondaga investigators increased the probabilities of spuriously elevated rates of reported prevalence in the school-age bracket. Under these circumstances, the reporting agencies were practically obligated to include children whom they might not otherwise have reported. As an example of such a possibility, attention is called to the fact that of the 2085 children of school age for whom I.Q. scores were available, 514 or 24.7 per cent were known to the reporting agency to have I.Q.s of 90 or above.[822(p.115)] Although the present reviewers deplore the use of the single I.Q. as the only criterion for making even a tentative diagnosis of mental retardation, it should be remembered that a significant degree of intellectual retardation is a necessary—although not always a sufficient—criterion for making such a judgment.

The use of a definition that did not define obviously affected the enumerations in the 10 to 15 year age range where inadequate school work and associated behavioral symptoms are more pronounced than in the lower age group.

2. The definition given resulted in referrals of educationally retarded children.

In this study, the investigators failed to take into consideration the concepts of retardation employed in school systems and by school personnel. Some teachers conceive of retardation as academic retardation but not necessarily as mental retardation. School children who are not achieving academically up-to-grade are considered retarded. But this educational retardation can be the result of any one of a combination of cultural factors, reading disabilities, emotional factors, and social factors as well as mental retardation.

What the investigators in effect asked teachers to do was to report to them children who were educationally retarded regardless of the cause, rather than those who were educationally retarded because of mental retardation *only.* The resulting gradual increase by age at the school age level is what is generally found for educationally retarded children. Unless some type of remediation is effective a child who is a half-year retarded at the end of the second grade will be one year retarded at the end of the fourth grade and two years retarded educationally at the end of the eighth grade. Hence, educational retardation becomes more noticeable as the child grows older because of the larger discrepancy between achievement and age. The suspected prevalence of mental retardation as reported by the investigators is probably the prevalence of educational retardation and the more noticeable adolescent behavior problems. The results thus become an artifact of the method since the data are contaminated with the prevalence of educationally retarded children.

3. A similar survey in Hawaii, which differentiated between mental retardation and educational retardation, did not obtain similar results.

In May, 1956, the Division of Special Services of the Department of Public Instruction and the Division of Mental Health of the Department of Public Health, Territory of Hawaii, conducted a joint survey of the special needs of children enrolled in the public schools of the Territory. The main purpose of the survey was to obtain information that would be helpful in estimating the extent of school psychological services needed to supplement the limited resources of the Division of Mental Health.

In designing the survey, it was decided to employ a procedure that would locate the children in the public schools who appeared to be classifiable according to four areas of special need: (a) the mentally retarded, (b) the gifted, (c) the socially or emotionally maladjusted, and (d) children with other special learning problems who were not primarily classifiable in any of the three preceding categories.

A guide sheet was prepared for the direction of teacher observers. The formulation of uncomplicated, yet technically acceptable guides for use by teacher observers posed a difficult problem for the category *Retarded*. It was considered extremely important to avoid misdirection. The following criteria were utilized for this category:

> *Retarded.* If group intelligence test scores are available, list all pupils who obtained Total Mental Factors I.Q.s of 65 and below. If group tests are not available, list children as follows:
>
> 1. Grade three and above: those whose achievement in reading *and* arithmetic computation is three or more years below grade.
> 2. Grades one and two: those who are unable to read a pre-primer *and cannot* do arithmetic computation with sums below 10.
> 3. Kindergarten: those who are unable to succeed in readiness activities in language *and* number.

Several considerations were taken into account in formulating these criteria. It was the joint opinion of the investigators that the observations should be directed toward objective evidence of school achievement rather than toward social and emotional behavior. The rationale for the distinction resided in the contingency that the teacher estimates of pupil capacity might be unduly influenced by estimations of pupil conduct. An effort was made to avoid this kind of contamination which apparently was very possible in the Onondaga Study by providing for primary or secondary classification in all the areas as well as in asking the teachers to report separately children who were disturbed, gifted, or had other learning problems.

The public school enrollment of June 15, 1956, was used as the basis of calculation. Figures reported by the Department of Public Instruction showed 116,314 children enrolled in grades kindergarten through 12. Of the total enrollment, 51 per cent were boys and 49 per cent were girls. Returns were received from 96.4 per cent of the public schools. There were 7312 record cards received from 167 schools throughout the Territory. The following table shows the number and per cent of children who were nominated for each category, according to both primary and secondary nominations.

Of the 2643 children nominated for the category *Retarded,* 70 per cent were boys and 30 per cent were girls. An excessive rate of male referrals was also reported in the Onondaga census. However, in strong contrast to the skyrocketing rates of referrals reported by the Onondaga investigators, the nominations for the *mentally retarded* category were quite evenly distributed from the first through the 11th grades, with no pronounced clustering. Table 12-2 shows the distribution by grade in the school districts of the 2377 children who were reported as primarily mentally retarded.

It was noted in the Hawaii study that the reported percentage of nominations approximated the two to three per cent limits ordinarily advised as a basis for planning special services for mentally retarded children in other American communities, and that the excessive boy-to-girl ratio reported in the Onondaga Study was obtained in Hawaii, also. However,

TABLE 12-1

NUMBER AND PERCENTAGE OF SCHOOL ENROLLMENT
NOMINATED IN EACH CATEGORY OF SPECIAL NEED

Category	Primary Deviation		Secondary Deviation		Total	
	N	%	N	%	N	%
Retarded	2,377	2.12	266	.24	2,643	2.36
Disturbed	1,725	1.54	329	.29	2,054	1.83
Gifted	2,474	2.21	17	.01	2,491	2.22
Other Learning Problems	736	.66	198	.17	934	.83
Grand Total	7,312	6.53	810	.71	8,122	7.24

TABLE 12-2

NUMBER OF CHILDREN NOMINATED AS RETARDED

Grade	N	Per Cent of Grade Enrollment
K	60	.6
1	231	2.0
2	174	1.6
3	273	2.4
4	255	2.5
5	301	3.1
6	260	2.7
7	197	2.3
8	198	2.7
9	157	2.5
10	132	2.3
11	114	2.2
12	25	.5
	N2,377	

the pattern of nominations in this survey, where the teacher observers were provided with more precisely formulated criteria for observations, was consistent with the overall prevalence of nominations. There were undoubtedly some children nominated who did not belong in that category and still others who were not identified but who should have been included. Errors of this type are a characteristic weakness of any survey technique that involves nomination, but the Hawaii investigators took measures to preclude the inclusion of children in the *Retarded* category who would be more appropriately classifiable elsewhere.

It was suggested by Weiner[1105 (p. 53)] that the low prevalence of nominations at the kindergarten level was, in part, a function of identification criteria that were not sufficiently discriminating, and that the similarly low rate reported for grade 12 was due to the fact that most of the significantly retarded children leave school when they reach the age of 16, the upper limit for compulsory school attendance in the Territory.

Although it is not possible to make a point-by-point comparison of the findings of the Hawaii Survey and Onondaga Census, some comments appear to be in order. The Hawaii investigators attempted to assist the Territory in the location of children in the public schools who appeared to be in need of additional special services because of marked limitations in capacity for school learning. Limited capacity was inferred by a significantly low total score on a group test of mental ability or by comparison of school achievement with criteria which had been formulated specifically for that particular purpose. On the other hand, the Onondaga investigators employed a very inclusive "definition" of *mental retardation* in order to determine the number of children who were "under social suspicion of 'mental retardation.' "[822] (p. 127) The present reviewers seriously question the defensibility of encouraging "suspicion" on circumstantial evidence of this character.

SUMMARY

Certain results of the widely cited Onondaga Census of Suspected Referred Mental Retardation are believed by the present reviewers to be an artifact of inappropriate procedure. The following reasons are given in support of this position.

1. The investigators used an all-inclusive definition which admitted unqualified academic retardation or social maladjustment as evidence of suspected mental retardation.
2. The Onondaga Study is essentially a study of "referred education retardation" rather than mental retardation.
3. A similar study which employed terminology and concepts used by school personnel did not find "reported suspected prevalence" increasing with age as did the Onondaga investigators.

PART THREE

The Multiply Handicapped Child in
Special Education

Introduction

A TEXTBOOK summary of the "state of the art" relative to the education of the multiply handicapped has notable limitations for it must try to clarify the complex principles and concepts from which pedogogical procedures are derived. The education of exceptional children is controversial and so are the positions taken by educators, psychologists, and others with respect to practical and theoretical issues. Special education programs have typically been based more upon expediency than upon sound pedagogical theory. Subsequent to more than a half century of public school programs for exceptional children, there is still no single source of comprehensive information providing a rationale, structure, and process for the administration of special education programs nor is there any evidence to show that the teaching techniques, materials, and content of special classes for the mentally retarded, to cite one area, differ significantly from those used in regular classes. It is not particularly surprising that educational services for multiply handicapped children have generally been less than adequate. The field of special education, however, is currently a recipient of popular support in proportions that would have staggered the imagination less than a decade ago.

Federal funding has made available large sums of money to support research and demonstration projects relative to the education of handicapped children. For example, the faculty of the Department of Special Education at Yeshiva University are currently engaged in the development of curriculum and methods of instruction for elementary-level educable mentally retarded children. Other federally supported projects are being conducted at the University of Southern California, the University of Oregon, the University of Maryland, and George Peabody College. Space does not permit a complete listing of all of the research and demonstration projects in progress throughout the country. In the near future, teacher training programs should begin to reap some of the benefits of the research and demonstration projects presently being sponsored by a variety of agencies.

Educators are optimistic that the next decade will be characterized by dramatic improvements in the quality of educational services for exceptional children. However, practitioners faced with the responsibilities of organizing and implementing educational programs for multiply handicapped children do not have the prerogative to wait for the development of a rationale for classifying and teaching these children. Parents and children must be served.

Some farsighted educators have attempted to meet the challenge presented by the growing numbers of children with multiple handicaps. The chapters in Part Three concern themselves with a variety of endeavors to develop better services for children with multiple handicaps.

The chapter by Doctor outlines the factors which are responsible for the increasing numbers of multiply handicapped children. Doctor stresses the notion that we must begin to think in terms of individuals who have several handicapping conditions rather than unitary disabilities. Data on the prevalence of multiply handicapped children in schools for the deaf are presented. Doctor concludes his paper with a plea for more definitive information about etiology, prevalence, and the training of teachers.

Henderson reviews incidence studies of multiply handicapped children and discusses the significant differences between multiple handicapped mentally retarded children and otherwise unafflicted mentally retarded children. Henderson concludes that the major problems in the diagnosis and education of the multiply handicapped are (1) lack of reliability and validity of diagnostic instruments when used with such children, (2) lack of specific clinical teaching methods and materials, and (3) disagreement concerning setting for the education of each group of multiply handicapped children.

Professors Steward and Coda recommend a multidisciplinary approach to the diagnostic and therapeutic procedures used with preschool multiply handicapped children at the Kennedy Child Study Center at Santa Monica, California. The initial evaluation routinely involves personnel from pediatrics, psychology, psychiatric social work, and in some cases, orthopedics, neurology, psychiatry, occupational therapy, physical therapy, and speech therapy. A description of the children and the content and organization of the program is presented. A concomitant parent group provides information, support, feedback, and observation of the child.

In Chapter 16, Dr. Cruickshank expresses his concern about the multiplicity of handicapping variants in the cerebral palsied child and suggests a classification of eight distinct types of multiply handicapped cerebral palsied children. The classification is based upon the type of physical and psychological problem which the child demonstrates. Research of an educational and psychological nature is necessary with each type to determine the most adequate procedures which can be used to facilitate learning, social adjustment, and physical growth and development.

Dr. Mattis concurs with the notion that a multidisciplinary approach is effective with visually impaired multiply handicapped children. At the Jewish Guild for the Blind in New York City, it is hypothesized that concept deficits are the primary disruptive factors in the development of many of the children evaluated in this particular patient population. In the training programs the goal is to facilitate the child's acquisition of organizing principles with which to comprehend and respond to his environment. Two outpatient treatment or training programs are described. The current project, jointly funded by N.I.M.H. and the Guild, has three major goals: (1) service, (2) research, and (3) demonstration of results.

Interim reports have been made in American Foundation for the Blind publications on the efforts in Michigan to change attitudes concerning multiply handicapped blind children and to provide improved services for them. Professor Elonen and Margaret Polzien present a résumé of these efforts and delineate the problems encounterd and proposals for the development of a program in the future for these children. The authors conclude that if special treatment and care were provided, a surprisingly large percentage of these children could be habilitated sufficiently so that they might enter either day school classes or residential schools.

Cruickshank indicates that the concept of the multiple handicapped child must go far beyond that of the deaf-blind child and observed that it is important to stress the individual needs of each child rather than the categories of handicapping conditions.

When educators consider the individual needs of each multiply handicapped child attention immediately focuses on the primary activity of the school learning. Many multiply handicapped children have learning disorders. Dr. Bateman surveys the field of learning disorders in terms of an integrative approach to the various disciplines which have been concerned with etiology, diagnosis, and treatment of children with communication problems, reading problems, and sensory-motor disturbance. Understanding of learning disorders is a prerequisite to understanding the multiply handicapped child in the school setting.

Chapter 13

Multiple Handicaps in the Field of Deafness

POWRIE V. DOCTOR

THE problem of rehabilitating persons handicapped with more than one disability is a growing one and a serious problem in the United States in the present century. Possibly, to an extent, it is being made more serious by the very advancements in science that would tend to alleviate the contributing conditions. A greater number of children and adults suffering from one or more handicaps are today confronting our teachers and our rehabilitation workers than in previous years, mainly, perhaps, because medicine has become so much more adequate that some patients who would have died twenty-five years ago are today being saved, but, in many cases, being saved at the price of living out their remaining years under the handicap of one or more major disabilities.

With a few exceptions, we have been oriented to thinking of people as being deaf, or as being blind, or as being crippled, but in this modern twentieth century we must adjust our thinking and our acceptance to include individuals who are both deaf and blind, deaf and aphasic, blind and crippled, and even those who suffer not only from a physical handicap but also from a mental handicap, and for these groups we need not only schooling, rehabilitation, and social service but a genuine acceptance of them into our present day scheme of life.

Many of us can recall at almost a moment's notice the founding of the first school for the blind or the first school for the mentally retarded in the United States, but aside from Helen Keller and Laura Bridgeman in the department for the deaf-blind in the Perkins School in Boston, few of us can name the first school or institution in the United States for the teaching of multiple handicapped children. No doubt the reason for this is that such schools and classes are of such comparatively recent origin, that very few have been established and also, possibly, because this is uniquely a twentieth century problem that has been accentuated by our great progress in science.

However, in discussing the broad field of multiple handicaps, we must

Reprinted from *Exceptional Children*, 26:156-158, 1959.

remember that any single physical handicap often drags with it many other social, educational, and emotional handicaps. In the field of deafness so many tend to think that communication is the one and only difficulty that requires attention. Because of the breakdown in communication in the field of deafness other problems arise, such as the inability to acquire language in the same manner as hearing people do, the difficulty to think in abstract terms, and the consequences on the personality of a deaf person brought about by a communication breakdown with his environment.

All of these by-products of deafness are being accentuated today as never before by the increased tempo of the times and, in some cases, by the advancement in medical science.

When communication breaks down between a mature deaf person and his environment, handicaps worse than his deafness may occur. Dr. Dohn of Denmark, in explaining the high percentage of deaf persons in mental institutions in Denmark, says it is mainly due to isolation. Thus we should remember that keeping active all forms of communication for the deaf: speech, speech reading, language, use of hearing aids, and manual methods such as the use of the manual alphabet and the language of signs, are of paramount importance in this respect.

Today science is helping in a great measure to diagnose properly those who have a single handicap and those who have an additional handicap. This is being pinpointed quite realistically by designating more accurately those who are deaf, those who are aphasic, and those who are both deaf and aphasic. It is fairly easy to label deafness and cerebral palsy or blindness and deafness, but it is extremely difficult and requires much more scientific technique to label such disorders as aphasia, especially when it involves another handicap.

PROGRESS IN UNDERSTANDING

We have come a long way in the past 150 years. In the early days most schools for the deaf were known as asylums. Calling an institution for the deaf a school for the deaf is a product of the present century. There are a few people even today who believe the deaf are mentally below normal people. It is interesting to note that in New York in 1887 a teacher of the deaf named Greenberg experimented quite successfully with tests for the deaf in an effort to differentiate between those who were deaf and normal and those who were deaf and subnormal, because, as we all know, a deaf person without language may easily be mistaken for a mentally retarded or a mentally deficient person.

For many years, the main double handicap brought to the attention of the layman was deafness with blindness. To an extent, this was because of the very great accomplishments of Laura Bridgeman and Helen Keller, both of whom received much publicity. Today we have the aphasic and deaf person, the aphasic and blind person, the mentally retarded deaf person, or the mentally retarded aphasic blind person, the emotionally disturbed deaf and the emotionally disturbed aphasic.

REPORTING THE HANDICAPPED

For the past three years the *American Annals of the Deaf* has been publishing the number of multiple handicapped pupils enrolled in schools for the deaf. We have asked for reports in six categories: the aphasic and deaf, the blind and deaf, the cerebral palsied and deaf, the orthopedic and deaf, the mentally retarded and deaf, and the brain injured and deaf. This does not imply by any means that our list is a complete census of all these categories. It merely means that the reports show the number of school age children so handicapped in all types of schools and classes for the deaf in the United States. In a few instances the classes for the deaf-blind as reported are in schools for the blind. How many more of these children there are of preschool age, I do not know. How many adults suffer from multiple handicaps is another question which I am unable to answer. In 1957 a total of 307 pupils were reported as being aphasic and deaf. This is an increase of 140 over the figure for 1955. In 1957 a total of 102 were reported as being deaf and blind, an increase of 58. Also in 1957 there were 483 reported as being cerebral palsied and deaf, an increase of 164. In 1957 there were 168 reported as being orthopedic and deaf, an increase of 43. In 1957 a total of 212 were reported as being brain injured and deaf, an increase of 105. And lastly, in 1957 there were 910 pupils reported as being mentally retarded and deaf, an increase of 487 in the three-year period.*

There is a distinct possibility that we are reporting cases more accurately than before, but essentially the same schools reported in 1957 as reported in 1955. There is a possibility that these figures may be attributed to increased enrollment. However, I doubt very much if the increased enrollments can account for all of them. Perhaps schools and classes are feeling their responsibility toward the multiple handicapped more keenly than before. Again, there is the very distinct possibility that more multiple handicapped children are being born than before. Is this problem of the multiple handicapped child a product of the great scientific advances made in this twentieth century, especially in the field of medicine? Are the new medi-

---

* *Editor's Note:* According to the author, the number of deaf pupils with additional handicaps in classes for the deaf and in special classes for children with multiple handicaps as reported in the January, 1959, *American Annals of the Deaf*, showed considerable increase over the figures given in this report. The figures for 1959 as reported were: aphasic and deaf, 509; blind and deaf, 122; cerebral palsied and deaf, 582; orthopedic and deaf, 202; mentally retarded and deaf, 1,125; and brain injured and deaf, 280.

cines keeping alive many children with multiple handicaps who, even a quarter of a century ago, would not have survived? If this is true we must see that adequate provision is made to have the professionally diagnostic services available with which to ascertain the various handicaps and to see that educational and rehabilitative services are available for these children. It is unwise to allow one field of service to outstrip all the others. If we give $1,000 to medical research, let us also give a similar amount to improving facilities for teaching the multiple handicapped and training them for positions where they may earn all or part of a livelihood.

But even this is not the complete answer. We must also see that society is oriented to the problem of accepting the multiple handicapped. In some ways this in itself is one of the major problems of this mid-twentieth century. We need sources of adequate information about this group of handicapped people. We need to know to an extent the number of persons with various multiple disabilities in the United States. We need to know if the number of trained teachers for the various groups is sufficient. This question, however, can be answered now. There is an alarmingly scarce supply of adequately trained teachers for all fields in special education and in rehabilitation. It may be that one of the frontiers in science in this country lies in what we will do with these handicapped people that in a measure science has bequeathed to us.

Chapter 14

Teaching the Multiply Handicapped Mentally Retarded Child

ROBERT A. HENDERSON

A LTHOUGH there has been, for many years, a recognition of the higher incidence of multiple handicapping conditions among mentally retarded school children as compared with "normal" or above average pupils, neither the accurate census of the number and kinds of additional handicaps nor the methodology for teaching such multiply handicapped children in public school or residential school facilities is available.

REVIEW OF INCIDENCE STUDIES

Ayres[56] found in 1909 that while the "normal" child averaged 1.30 physical defects, the bright had only 1.07, while the "dull pupil" averaged 1.65 defects.

Sandwick[958] found a positive correlation between health and intelligence in his 1920 study, and Dayton[241] substantiated this in 1928 by reporting a negative correlation between physical defects and intelligence.

A recent controlled study[348] of motor characteristics of mentally retarded children found that the retarded were significantly poorer in the performance of all motor tasks. The authors recommended a structured physical education program in the curriculum of the mentally retarded pupil to provide specific training to overcome these deficiencies. Using a larger population, the same authors[348] found the mentally retarded public school pupil was lower than children of the same chronological age in all of the 11 gross motor tests administered, averaging two to four years behind normal pupils.

Blatt[109] compared mentally retarded children in a special class with mentally retarded children in the same city who were enrolled in regular classes and found that the number of physical defects in the special class children averaged 1.55, while those still in regular classes averaged only 1.08.

Beck[79] studying the incidence of brain injury in public school special classes for the educable mentally retarded in Southern Illinois, found 60 to 70 per cent of the pupils had some neurological damage and that approximately 25 per cent were on anticonvulsive medication. Although there

Reprinted from *Exceptional Children*, 27:90-93, 1960.

is a wide discrepancy between authors, a 1955 book edited by Cruickshank and Raus[25] estimates that between 50 and 75 per cent of cerebral palsied children are also mentally retarded.

DiMichael[254] indicates that 10 to 14 per cent of blind children in the chronological age range 5 to 17 are retarded.

Myklebust[803] reports a study by Frisina showing 12 per cent of the pupils at a residential school for the deaf to be between 60 and 75 per cent I.Q. In two audiometric studies[928, 965] of school aged children in institutions for the mentally retarded, 19.8 per cent and 17 per cent respectively, were found to have a "significant hearing loss"—where that term is defined at 15 db loss or greater in two or more frequencies. Johnson and Farrell[549] report on a study of mentally retarded children at the Fernald State School in Massachusetts confirming the percentages above, and indicating that hearing loss is five times the incidence we would expect from a similar survey among public school children. Rittmanic[928] also reports on five other audiometric studies of mentally retarded children.

Many studies of speech handicaps among retarded children are available. Goertzen[399] reports two studies of institutionalized mentally retarded children which offered the following percentages of patients with speech defects (or no speech at all) in the three common subdivisions of the retarded level:

Intellectual Level	*(Kennedy) % Speech Def.*	*(Sirkin, Jacob & Lyons) % Speech Def.*
Educable M. R.	42.6	43
Severely M. R.	96.9	74
Total-Care M. R.	100.0	100

Lubman,[685] reporting on a speech program for severely retarded children enrolled in parent-operated classes in Cleveland, Ohio, found only 7 of 150 children did not need speech therapy. Wallin[1089] comparing mentally retarded and normal pupils in the public schools, found that 2.8 per cent of the average school population had speech defects, while 26.3 per cent of the mentally retarded special class children were afflicted. Kastein[567] discovered that of the 467 children accepted as patients at the Speech and Hearing Clinic of the Columbia Presbyterian Medical Center, New York, 267, or about 60 per cent seemed retarded.

This review makes no pretense at being comprehensive or even representative of the available studies. It should serve, however, to indicate that no matter from what direction the problem is studied, the mentally retarded as a group have a rather high incidence of physical defects of all kinds including sensory and speech handicaps. Another insight to be gained from the assortment of studies reported is that for the child with multiply handicapping conditions, a differential diagnosis of the major handicapping condition and the extent of the mental handicap is often a difficult and demanding task. As Norris, Spaulding and Brodie[824(p.41)] point out. "The use of numerical scores and concepts, such as mental age and intelligence quotient, or social age and social quotient, has been found of limited value in understanding the capacity of a blind child." How much more limited they must be if the child also appears to be mentally retarded with an undetermined hearing loss and perhaps mild cerebral palsy accompanied by distorted speech!

SIGNIFICANCE OF SECONDARY HANDICAPS ON A MENTALLY RETARDED CHILD

Let us consider for a moment what are the significant differences between multiply handicapped and otherwise unafflicted mentally retarded children.

First, I think, is the very pertinent question, is he really retarded? In the public school situation especially, the psychologist is under tremendous pressures to "test and certify" for special classes—usually on the basis of a single psychometric examination. Parents of multiply handicapped children are too often told their child is hopelessly retarded and should be committed to an institution forthwith, with even less evidence than that required for special class placement. Clinical diagnostic evidence seems to indicate that there is a wide variability in the functioning of individual children with multiple handicaps at different times, whether measured by intelligence or social maturity scales. This lack of reliability raises serious questions regarding the application of any single observation as an adequate basis for social or educational recommendations. Furthermore, I can find no instrument available which is designed for, and which has been standardized for the measurement of intelligence of children with multiple handicaps such as blind-retarded or deaf-retarded. Therefore we can and should expect that more extensive differential diagnostic studies be made in the case of mentally retarded children found to have additional handicapping conditions.

Secondly, I think we must consider the effect of multiple handicapping conditions upon the parents of the retarded child. Even with most retarded children, a bit of Emerson's Law of Compensation is possible: "He may not be able to go on to college, but he will be able to hold a job, pay his own way, and participate as an independent, tax paying citizen of his community." The larger the number, and the greater the degree of multiple handicaps, the less likely that these goals of independent self-sufficiency will be reached. Thus assisting the parents in attaining realistic educational, social, and vocational aspirations for their child becomes of increasing importance as additional handicaps are added to the diagnosis of mental retardation.

Thirdly, we must consider the question of the type of educational services needed by multiply handicapped mentally retarded children. Can we even talk of educating the "multiply handicapped mentally retarded" or must we break it down into the categories—blind-retarded, deaf-retarded, cerebral palsied retarded, etc.? Can we expect the teacher of the mentally retarded to be adequately equipped to educate any and all retarded children regardless of additional handicaps, such as blindness, deafness, or cerebral palsy? Are there sufficient numbers to justify and would it be desirable to encourage in our larger metropolitan areas the establishment of special centers for the multiply handicapped which would contain specialists in the various categories of handicapped children, working together as a team to provide educational services?

IMPLICATIONS

1. The lack of reliability and validity of current diagnostic instruments when used with multiply handicapped children requires more frequent re-evaluations and case conferences to assess the child's educational progress. These diagnostic shortcomings should not be viewed by psychologists or teachers as overpowering handicaps, but rather as more challenging areas with uneven and unique developmental patterns.
2. Coupled with the diagnostic problems is the lack of specific clinical teaching methods and materials for use with retarded children suffering with one or more physically handicapping conditions. Even now there are a few bright spots in this picture, and the future promises more. For instance, Ashcroft[43 (p.526)] reports that, "The passing of the wave of retrolental fibroplasia, use of improved optical and technical aids and expanded day school programs offer needed services. More attention can now be given to the visually-handicapped child who has additional problems or handicapping conditions. Facilities once crowded by RLF children and others can be made available to children previously not considered for services." Most of the latter are blind-retarded children, I am sure.
3. There is the more general problem of who should educate each category of the multiply handicapped retarded, and in what setting: special classes for the mentally retarded, special regional day centers for multiply handicapped, or residential school special facilities?

All of these problems indicate how lightly the surface has been scratched and how richly endowed this area is for research workers. We can be confident that increasing attention, stimulated by federal and private research monies, will provide answers soon to some of our problems of teaching multiply handicapped, mentally retarded children.

Chapter 15

An Integrative Multidiscipline Approach to the Multihandicapped Preschool Child

G. Kinsey Stewart and Evis J. Coda

D IAGNOSTIC procedures and therapeutic approaches encounter special challenges in the case of the preschool child with multiple handicaps. An integrative approach by various medical and paramedical disciplines has been utilized with such children and their families since 1962 in a special development program at the Kennedy Child Study Center in Santa Monica, California.

Approximately one hundred children have been evaluated each year. Thirty-five of these children were selected for a developmental group which provided opportunity for serial diagnosis as well as therapeutic experience.

Any child is eligible for the developmental program if he is under four years of age and demonstrating some deficit in his development in one or more of the following areas: motor, adaptive, language and personal-social. Initial evaluation typically involves pediatrics, psychology and psychiatric social work. Additionally, evaluations may be obtained from orthopedics, neurology, psychiatry, occupational therapy, physical therapy,. speech therapy, etc.

A staff conference is held about each of these children with the above disciplines present. Presentation and discussion of the separate findings and impressions result in an initial weighted multiple diagnosis which is more a mosaic than a pigeonhole. The case coordinator and one or more additional staff members discuss with both parents the findings and recommendations. If appropriate, the family is invited to enroll their child in the developmental group.

This preschool program is offered for six to eight children at any one time and is open-ended. The average length of time in the group varies from three to six months, but two children remained for nearly two years. The program is held from 9:00 to 11:00 on Tuesday and Thursday mornings. During one of the four hours each week when the child is in the nursery, the mothers participate in a psychotherapeutically oriented discussion group.

An occupational therapist is in charge of the children's group, with at least one adult assisting her. A special education consultant and a speech clinician are available during part of the time. A student in occupational therapy also assists during her placement at the Center. Volunteers with special training or skills may be selected as aides. The physical therapist coordinates appointments so that a child might be seen just prior to, during, or just after the group meeting.

The general purpose of the program is to promote the development of each child toward the realization of his own potential in all areas. Specifically, he is helped to improve gross and fine motor skills, to establish needed neuromuscular patterns, to experience creative and imaginative play activities, to be stimulated in both receptive and expressive language, to learn to initiate independent activities, to cooperate in interpersonal activities with peers or adults, and to gain in emotional control. Both regular developmental group staff members and other Center personnel are alert to the opportunity for observation in this setting for the purpose of ongoing diagnosis.

Many of the children who have been in this program have mental retardation as the problem of greatest degree in the initial total weighted multiple diagnosis. All types of cerebral palsied children have attended. Chronic brain syndrome is to be found in many of these children, with attendant problems of hyperactivity, short attention span, and perceptual motor deficits. Language problems have varied from unclear speech to total lack of language. Psychiatric disorders range from general immature behavior to separation anxiety to autism. However, the philosophical orientation held is that these are first and foremost children, just beginning to learn about the world and the people in it.

Five main factors must be considered in the group care of these youngsters: the physical setting, the program plans, the therapist-child relationship, the peer group and the personality of the individual child. The Kennedy Child Study Center nursery room is a large, well-ventilated room with windows along one entire side. A sliding door provides easy access to a fence-enclosed play yard with both grass and asphalt areas. Tables, chairs, toilet facilities, and counter with sink are all built at the proper height. A large one-way mirror in one wall permits observation by several individuals at once. Play materials and equipment are carefully chosen in the light of the special needs of these children.

The program is designed to provide for meeting the goals discussed above. The occupational therapist is concerned with the development of motor skills and self-care activities. She looks for the ways in which the child uses (or fails to use) his hands. Perhaps one hand is preferred or is kept tightly fisted, or he over-reaches or cannot grasp or release in a normal manner. Other children simply may not evince any interest in the objects provided. Another child becomes fascinated with colored shapes of circle, square, and triangle. However, instead of placing these on the flannelboard, he finds a small space in the outside fence through which he pokes these objects. The interest is there, but it is inappropriately directed. Considerable flexibility is permitted in the activities which the children are allowed to choose or in the selections made by staff members. Simple step-by-step directions are provided with limited goals that permit successful accomplishments. Puzzles of varying degrees of difficulty are provided. A chalkboard offers opportunity for free drawing or copying of graphic forms. The child may display an interest in the tricycle, the horse or the merry-go-round. Rather than lifting him in place, he is helped to feel the desired movements which will achieve his goal. Physical therapist and occupational therapist closely interrelate their efforts in such behavior as this.

The physical therapist uses the Rood Method of sensory stimulation which results in neuromuscular organization at the reflex level. Thus, the voluntary cooperation requested is minimal, an important factor with the mentally impaired. Coordinated efforts of the physical therapist and the speech clinician make progress possible at an accelerated rate. By stimulation of lips, tongue, and other oral mechanisms, the patient gains better control to be used in direct speech training. With one patient without speech, the physical therapist first brushed and iced the tongue. Then she placed a small amount of honey in various locations within the mouth, and the patient had to move his tongue in different directions to obtain it. In this manner, tongue control rapidly improved and the speech clinician's efforts became more successful.

The speech therapist is concerned with providing the proper environment for language growth. She uses the materials and the other children to assist in stimulating and motivating each child in need of speech help. In this situational speech therapy, the goals of physical therapy and occupational therapy can be incorporated in the speech work. Young children enjoy words and actions that go together. Ballthrowing, marching, and follow-the-leader all provide large muscle motor activity and also help the child learn to follow simple oral directions and use beginning language. Musical games and rhythms provide experience in listening and making appropriate responses to sounds as well as developing coordination and awareness of body image. Self-care activities are ideal for building associations between words and objects of practical value to the child. The attitude of the other children and adults permits practice of the newly acquired verbal skills in an accepting climate.

Educators experienced with mentally retarded or slow developing children, recognize that such preschool programs as this provide an opportunity for the most efficacious academic placement. This will serve to reduce the frustrations and possible emotional scarring of the child, to say nothing of the problems for teachers, parents, and others. Principles of learning are related to the developmental stages of the particular child. As the child is maturationally ready, those conditions which help in the acquisition of skills conducive to learning are introduced. Each therapist employs the motivating techniques of encouragement or discouragement, of supporting desired values by her behavior, or accepting the child as he is so that he gains self-assurance and a willingness to try.

The children in the group must be viewed both in terms of their chronological and their mental age. Parallel play may be appropriate, for example, in some of our children, even though chronologically we might expect more social interaction. This also involves the personality factor of the child and the distinct possibility of less than normal opportunity for personal interaction. The life experience he has had and his own unique personality characteristics as these have been revealed in the diagnostic study, largely determine the goals to be set for him in the developmental group.

The mothers' group provides an opportunity for interchange of ideas, concerns, and hopes with others sharing a similar problem, specific information to be gained, feedback relative to their own child and observation of the child. The psychologist who conducts this group attempts to create an atmosphere that encourages free discussion. Certain topics (most frequently toilet regulation techniques) are presented in an instructional manner. It is also possible to present information concerning the handicaps existing with these children in a general way, if the parent is not yet fully ready to cope with the acceptance of the problem on a more personal level. From the beginning, the mothers are prepared for the eventual "graduation" of their child into the most appropriate available program. In this regard, therapies, schools, and other possibilities are discussed.

The group provides support for individual members who suffer anxieties or depression whether the reaction is to the initial shock of discovery or the recognition of the extent of the problem they face. Great is the need to reveal to others who really can share their feelings, the cruel words of professionals, the blunders by well-intentioned friends and relatives, the doubts, the guilt, the feeling of helplessness and loneliness. Often the mothers have extended their relationship to visits at one another's home or social activities which include the husbands. One mother indicated recently that she still meets with mothers from the group that formerly met at our Center nearly two years ago. Fathers occasionally attend during the regular group meetings or are active along with their wives in the once a month night meeting of the parents' group.

From time to time the professionals who work directly with the children will meet with the mothers to report on progress and to answer questions. Each different professional, adding varied points of view which supplement or complement one another, provides greater evidence of the child's abilities or deficits. More formal conferences which include both parents are arranged during the year and at the end of the program for their child. This latter serves as an exit interview to evaluate what the Center has done as well as to assist the parents in the transition to the next phase of care for the child.

One of the most powerful techniques with many of the mothers has been the use of the observation room with its one-way mirror. In this manner, they can observe their own child in a room apart from the parent, in interaction with other children and adults, and in a different physical setting. This is done only when a staff member is present and usually with the whole group of mothers. The staff member must be aware of the dynamics in the case and sensitive to the impact on the mother. One mother, whose boy was severely handicapped both physically and mentally, had built strong defenses to make her adjustment to her son. When she saw him in comparison to other children, she was nearly overwhelmed. Another mother claimed that her little girl "could not tolerate being separated" from her and was "not sociable at all." When observing through the mirror, she saw her daughter happily engaged in play with another child and with the toys, and obviously getting along with no difficulty. This was the opening needed to help her look at her own role in the problem.

In order to deal in greater depth with individual problems, a psychiatric social worker may see a mother alone in addition to her group meeting. The personnel working with the children and those working with the mothers hold weekly conferences to discuss the program. Each child and his mother are discussed and this information can then be used in subsequent activities in the groups. Administrative details can be considered, such as timing of parent conferences and planning for the future.

In summary, a special developmental program has been designed to help children under four years of age who exhibit one or several mental or physical handicaps. Diagnostic procedures rely on multiple discipline impressions with varying degrees of weight given to elements within the total composite diagnosis. A group experience provides for serial diagnosis and integration of therapeutic approaches. A concomitant mothers' group provides information, support, ongoing feedback and observation of the child. Exit interviews serve to help in the graduation of the child to the next phase of his life and has provided significant evidence of the effectiveness of the developmental program.

Chapter 16

The Multiply Handicapped
Cerebral Palsied Child

WILLIAM M. CRUICKSHANK

SYSTEMS of classification do not solve problems. On the other hand, a classification system frequently makes a problem clearer so that one can see the essential elements of a complicated situation and thus take steps towards its partial or complete solution. There are few conditions found in human beings which are more complicated than that of cerebral palsy. The classification system developed in this paper attempts to give a fuller understanding of an already complicated problem, the implications of certain types of handicap in the multiply handicapped cerebral palsied child.

The staggering proportions of this problem for rehabilitation and education appear when one considers the multiplicity of variables which are possible in cerebral palsied children. This writer, realizing that there are other factors such as emotional development or maldevelopment, has considered three variables in the present classification. These are (1) the presence in the cerebral palsied child of other physical defects of whatsoever kind or degree, (2) the presence in the cerebral palsied child of retarded mental development, and (3) the presence in the cerebral palsied child of psychopathological characteristics of perception which are independent of mental retardation.

Before discussing each of these three variables, it must be pointed out that cerebral palsy itself, without the presence of any of the three, has many variables which complicate therapeutic and educational programs. These often make it difficult to work with cerebral palsied children in groups. Cerebral palsy itself, whether athetoid, ataxic, spastic, or other, produces problems and necessitates variation in method and procedure of both therapy and education. The extent of the lesion and the location of the lesion appear to complicate the broad adjustment and learning problems of the child. These are factors inherent in the condition of cerebral palsy as a clinical entity. The principle of individual differences in groups of cerebral palsied children is accentuated over that in normal children be-

Reprinted from *Exceptional Children*, 21:16-22, 1953.

cause of the extreme variations in the manifestations of the clinical characteristics themselves.

When secondary physical conditions are observed in a child with cerebral palsy, the problems of planning, care, and treatment are magnified. All types of physical disabilities are possible in cerebral palsied children just as they are in any child or in any group of children. That the incidence of such factors is greater in this group of children than in noncerebral palsied children has been recognized for some time.

Perlstein[877] found that, of 212 cerebral palsied children, 46 per cent had epileptic seizures. Spasticity, which indicates involvement of the cerebral hemispheres, was associated with convulsions in 60 per cent of the children in contrast to athetosis which showed an incidence of seizures in 17 per cent of the subjects. Blindness and impaired vision, impaired hearing, congenital defects of varying types, and physical defects due to accident, disease, or injury are to be found in many cerebral palsied children. Such conditions may be the result of the same factors which caused the cerebral palsy, or they may be the result of totally independent causative agents.

The second factor mentioned above was that of retarded mental development. This condition, as with physically normal children and with children who have other types of physical disorders, may also occur with cerebral palsy. The results of numerous studies differ insofar as the percentage of incidence of mental retardation in cerebral palsy is concerned. However, clinical observation and an increasing number of carefully developed research projects seem to point to a higher incidence of mental retardation than was formerly recognized in cerebral palsied children. It is accepted that, when lesions in the cortex of the brain or in other portions of the cranial structures are to be found, psychological problems frequently accompany neurological complications. The brain does not function as a segmented organ but in large measure as a totality whose parts are closely interrelated. Thus, when injuries take place, they often create multiple problems. Among such problems will be that of mental retardation. Early statements by Phelps[885] indicated that approximately 70 per cent of the total group of cerebral palsied children have intelligence quotients which are above 70. Studies by Heilman,[471] and by Asher[47] indicate that the percentage of mental retardation in cerebral palsied children is much higher than Phelps states. Asher, in a careful study of children with cerebral palsy, found that 72 per cent of the children have intelligence quotients below 89. In a normal population such should occur in approximately 22 per cent of the cases. These data have been independently corroborated in a study completed at the Children's Hospital, Buffalo, N. Y., with a group of 261 cerebral palsied children.[767] (See also a report on Bice's unpublished data which appeared in "Education of Children with Mental Retardation Accompanied by Cerebral Palsy," by M. H. Fouracre and E. A. Thiel, *American Journal of Mental Deficiency*, 57:402, Jan. 1953.) Taibl,[1051] using Raven's Progressive Matrices, has reported somewhat conflicting data which are of such importance as to indicate the need for further research in this area to determine the reason for the disparity between his results using the Matrices and those of other authors employing other instruments. The close relationship between the results of studies by Heilman, Bice, Miller, and Asher must be seriously considered pending further study of Raven's tests.

Studies such as these place in bold relief a significant problem for educators, therapists, and medical personnel. The course of therapy and education is in large measure a matter of the rapidity with which the child can form insights and cooperate with professional personnel who work with him in various capacities. Learning is also dependent on the ability of the child to generalize from one situation to another and thus facilitate achievement. The ability to abstract, the ability to generalize, and the ability to profit through transfer of training—all essential to the physical improvement and to the academic achievement of cerebral palsied children—are significantly restricted as the mental capacity of the child is reduced. The lower the innate capacity of the child, the more limited are the outcomes of the therapeutic and educational program.

The third variable frequently noted in cerebral palsied children, defects in perception, concerns aspects of the learning process about which we are not yet fully informed. Cotton,[208] Halstead,[433] Strauss and Werner,[1034] Dolphin and Cruickshank,[274] among others, have contributed to a further understanding of the perceptive problems of the cerebral palsied child.

TABLE 16-1

MAJOR VARIATIONS OF MULTIPLY HANDICAPPED CEREBRAL PALSIED CHILDREN

Type	Presence of Cerebral Palsy	Presence of Other Physical Defect	Presence of Retarded Mental Development	Presence of Perceptive Pathology
1	Yes	No	No	No
2	Yes	No	No	Yes
3	Yes	No	Yes	No
4	Yes	Yes	No	No
5	Yes	No	Yes	Yes
6	Yes	Yes	Yes	No
7	Yes	Yes	No	Yes
8	Yes	Yes	Yes	Yes

Dolphin and Cruickshank in a series of exploratory reports involving 30 cerebral palsied children[271-274] have demonstrated that such children have impairments in visuo-motor and tactual-motor perception. Further, these authors have demonstrated that numerous cerebral palsied children in their group are handicapped in their performance through an inability to differentiate between figure and background. Finally, it has been noted that many of these children show the same phenomena of dissociation, motor disinhibition, and perseveration characteristic of other groups of individuals with organic pathology which have long been recognized in psychology as important features of the behavior of such groups. While much further information is needed in this regard, there is no question but that these pathological features of perception retard learning and psychological growth in marked degree in those children wherein such are found if the learning situation does not take cognizance of them.*

In combination, these three variables produce seven distinct clinical problems. Arbitary groupings such as these always result in over simplification. This writer is fully cognizant that clinically "pure" cases are rare and that such matters as the degree of impairment, level of intelligence, extent of physical ability, auditory acuity, visual acuity, and so forth will each vary between individuals and complicate any classification including that outlined below. However, the following discussion may well point up a problem in a somewhat logical fashion and thus make it possible for professional workers to attack the many unsolved issues in a rational and profitable manner. Table 16-1 will serve to demonstrate the combinations of difficulties which may be observed in considering the three variables which we have mentioned.

Type 1

This type simply involves the basic form of the disability, i.e., cerebral palsy of whatsoever variety with no other physical or psychological deviations.

Type 2

This group of children includes those with cerebral palsy who also show defects of perception, but in whom there is no evidence of mental retardation or other type of physical disability. Type 2 in our classification of multiply handicapped cerebral palsied children constitutes a group about

---

* An extensive two-year study of this problem is now being undertaken in the Department of Education for Exceptional Children, Syracuse University, financed by a grant from the Assocation for the Aid of Crippled Children of New York City, Inc. The study is under the direction of William M. Cruickshank, Syracuse University, and Harry V. Bice, New Jersey Commission for Crippled Children.

which we admittedly know relatively little at the present time. The validity of this clinical type is assured, however, in the opinion of this writer. Strauss and Werner briefly report findings which are subjective but which were nevertheless gathered from the responses of a small group of children of normal intelligence and who demonstrated perceptive defects.[1034] In the group of children studied by Dolphin and Cruickshank there were fourteen children whose intelligence quotients were above 95. Within this group numerous children showed defects of perception which significantly differentiated them from their control subjects who were physically normal. Cotton similarly reports perceptive difficulties in a number of children whom she studied, some of whom were intellectually normal and without other physical handicap. The prognosis for this type of multiply handicapped child is good educationally and psychologically provided the child received his educational experiences in an environment which recognizes his basic learning problems,[218] and in the degree to which he can profit from a total program of physical reconstruction.

Type 3

This group includes those cerebral palsied children who show no physical handicap other than the basic one and who are free of perceptive disabilities but whose intelligence is retarded significantly. Psychologically these children appear like the endogenous mentally retarded children as defined by Strauss.[1034] Many of these children show the classical symptoms of primary mental retardation, indicating that mental retardation might have existed even had cerebral palsy not been present. Such children, in addition to the physical characteristics of cerebral palsy (which are assumed throughout the remaining discussion of each type), exhibit lack of ability to form insight, poor comprehension, restricted memory functions, poor judgment, faulty reasoning, and limited problem-solving ability. These factors are those, among others, which characterize all primary forms of mental retardation. In general, each of the above factors will, of course, be accentuated in direct proportion to the degree of mental impairment. Both the rate of growth and the ultimate level of achievement, physical as well as mental, will be governed primarily by the innate mental ability of the child. While no adjustments are required in the learning environment, such as are suggested in connection with Type 2, the same sort of adjustments in curriculum and teaching materials are necessary as for endogenous mentally retarded children. Prognosis—educationally, psychologically, and to a somewhat lesser degree, physically—depends directly upon the intelligence level and the adequacy of the educational program. At best, the level of achievement is significantly limited.

Type 4

This group of cerebral palsied children includes numerous problems of great seriousness. These are children who possess secondary physical disabilities other than cerebral palsy but whose intelligence is determined to be within normal limits and who do not show characteristics of perceptive difficulties. The frequency with which visual and auditory impairments accompany cerebral palsy is well known. Epilepsy, as we have stated, is common among children with cerebral palsy. As a matter of fact, there is no physical disability which might not also occur in conjunction with cerebral palsy. The degree of visual or auditory defect may, of course, vary from mild impairments to those of a profound nature. Epilepsy may take the form of petit mal or grand mal seizures.

Children who present this variety of multiple disorder constitute one of the most difficult educational and psychological problems of any to be mentioned. Teachers, psychologists, and medical personnel may well be confused with respect to the appropriate methods of education and physical training for these children. Secondary physical defects of mild degree may not constitute a serious block to the learning or to the adjustment of cerebral palsied patients. More involved physical defects, however, may seriously retard learning. Prognosis with Type 4 children is undetermined. Outcome is based primarily on the degree of severity of the secondary handicap and on the adequacy of the educational and therapeutic programs to cope with both primary and secondary disabilities. Educational methodology and therapy requisite to the secondary defect must, of course, be available to the child in order to insure even the most moderate psychological growth and educational achievement.

Type 5

With Types 5, 6, 7, and 8 the problem of multiple handicaps becomes more complicated. Cerebral palsied children in Type 5 category are those who have no secondary physical defects but who demonstrate both retarded mental development and psychopathological perceptive functions. This group insofar as psychological development is concerned corresponds to the mixed category in the classification of mental deficiency as described by Strauss.[1034] These children will demonstrate the psychological characteristics of both the exogenous and endogenous types of retarded children. Insofar as educational and therapeutic programs are concerned, this writer feels that the perceptive problems of exogeny will demand major consideration in program planning, in learning or therapy situations, and in teaching materials. On the other hand, the professional worker will also have to keep in mind those psychological characteristics briefly mentioned in connection with Type 3 which are typical endogeny. Prognosis—educationally and psychologically—will depend directly on the level of innate intellectual ability and the extent of the cranial damage which has caused both the manifestations of cerebral palsy and those of exogeny.

Type 6

These cerebral palsied children are those who are characterized by secondary physical defects of a nature described in Type 4 who also show retarded mental development but who do not have perceptive malfunction. It must be pointed out that to measure the intelligence of such children with accuracy is a most difficult operation since satisfactory instruments for the assessment of multiply handicapped children, and in particular those with cerebral palsy, are not yet available. Some important steps are being taken in this direction, notably the research of Blum, Burgemeister, and Lorge,[116] and the encouraging reports of studies wherein the Progressive Matrices have been used.[1051, 1066] But when cerebral palsy, secondary physical disturbances, and mental retardation are found in combination, extreme caution must be exercised and careful periodic re-assessments be made before a final decision is reached regarding the mental level of the child. Even then accuracy in establishing a mental age may be impossible. If mental retardation is a bona fide diagnosis, then the prognosis of the child will depend upon the level of mental ability. At best, the outcomes, educationally and psychologically, may be significantly restricted.

Type 7

Type 7 includes those cerebral palsied children who have secondary physical disabilities and who also demonstrate the peculiarities of perception which have been commented upon above but who are of normal intelligence. Prognosis here is better than in Type 6 because of the better intellectual ability of the child, although it, of course, depends upon the severity of the secondary physical disabilities. Experience has shown that some cerebral palsied children will superficially demonstrate auditory and visual impairments, but that in reality these may be manifestations of the perceptive difficulties and not actual sensory disorders. Such findings and observations would warrant careful and cautious psychological, audiological, and/or ophthalmological evaluations of cerebral palsied children to ascertain the exact etiology of the secondary physical manifestations.

Type 8

This final group of cerebral palsied children is one in whom are observed secondary physical disabilities, accurately diagnosed mental retardation, and the psychopathological perceptive characteristics. This group will constitute the most serious educational, social, and therapeutic problem. Prognosis will be exceedingly poor, and the possibility of any independent adult experiences will be significantly limited. Comments which have been made above in connection with other appropriate groups of children will, in combination, all apply in this instance.

A classification of eight distinct types of multiple handicapped cerebral palsied children has been made. This classification is based upon the type of physical and psychological problem which the child demonstrates. It is a functional classification. Research of an educational and psychological nature is necessary with each type to determine the most adequate procedures which can be used to facilitate learning, social adjustment, and physical growth and development.

Chapter 17

An Experimental Approach to Treatment of Visually Impaired, Multihandicapped Children

Steven Mattis

OUR mental health center for visually impaired, multihandicapped children was established at The Jewish Guild for the Blind in 1962. The center is jointly funded by N.I.M.H. and the Guild, and is composed of a demonstration research project directed by Walter Kass, Ph.D. and a psychiatric clinic directed by Arthur E. Gillman, M.D.

As a mental health facility, we, of course, see a biased or special sample of visually impaired children. Most of the children served have congenital visual impairment usually the result of RLF, and all except the very young had been previously known to other agencies and clinics. Parents have come to the mental health center because, in addition to the child's sensory problems, there is usually some disturbance in behavior and/or learning. Our patient population has previously reported diagnoses which range from "autism," "childhood schizophrenia," and "profound retardation" to the more usual diagnosis of "neurotic adjustment reaction." Most of the children, however, were viewed as neurotic or borderline with functional mild or moderate retardation.

While parents had been to many specialists, it was noted that, too often, the child's problems were segmented—that is, the parents went to an ophthalmologist for visual difficulties, to the school for learning disabilities, and to a psychologist or psychiatrist for behavior and management problems. The various specialists often did not have access to information of others or were not aware of difficulties which could affect assessment in their own area. In an effort to provide a comprehensive and integrated evaluation, a panel of specialists was obtained so that, as part of the routine clinic workup, the child is seen by an ophthalmologist, a pediatric–neurologist, an electroencephalographer, a psychiatrist, a psychologist, a speech and hearing consultant, and an educational consultant. A caseworker sees the child and, in addition, maintains contact with the parents during the diagnostic evaluation. A case conference is held in which a diagnostic

219

evaluation and treatment plan are evolved with all the data and most of the examining personnel present.

Since we served an unusual patient population, it was necessary in the beginning for all specialists to create new or adapt existing diagnostic procedures. While development of diagnostic tools was an important initial goal, it was subsequently observed that the knowledge generated by our evolving procedures necessitated development of new treatment modalities.

The clinic and research staff noted that most children evaluated at the clinic demonstrated either global or specific concept deficits. These deficiencies in perceptual–cognitive functioning did not appear to be consonant with or predicted by theoretical frameworks in which interpersonal or parent-child stress is the predominant factor. The children's adjustment and developmental difficulties appeared to be best understood if one postulated a C.N.S. disruption of integrative functioning. Thus, one could view the child as an aphasic or conceptually impaired child whose difficulties are compounded by lack of the primary information and corrective feedback modality, vision. This framework does not preclude the observation that such children are emotionally disturbed or manifest poor reality testing. The working hypothesis our evaluations suggest, however, is that for many of our children, reality testing and psychological defenses are poor because they are predicated on inadequate conceptual ability and that anxiety levels are high because the child is both unable to comprehend what is required of him and is limited cognitively to a narrow range of appropriate responses to his environment. Thus, the theoretical framework evolved in working with our particular patient population is not that psychological stress, the result of disruptive parent–child interaction, functionally retards the development of intellectual and adaptive processes but rather that conceptual deficits of probable organic etiology result in inappropriate behavior and high anxiety.

Stress in parent–child interaction is, of course, present not only because the child cannot integrate and interpret parental requests and motivation but also because the parents often misinterpret the child's behavior as negativism or perverse willfulness.

TWO EXPERIMENTAL OUTPATIENT PROGRAMS

With the hypothesis that concept deficits are the primary disruptive factors in the development of many of the children evaluated, two outpatient treatment or training programs were recently undertaken on an experimental basis. In each treatment program, the goal is to facilitate the child's acquisition of organizing principles with which to comprehend and respond to his environment. Both are highly dependent upon the clinic's diagnostic evaluation, particularly the psychological assessment. In the psychologist's examination, the patient is seen over a period of one to two weeks for a total of five to ten hours. Special emphasis is placed on determining the level and nature of the concepts available to the child and the mode of learning which the child has already developed. In practice, this often becomes a series of short learning experiments in which the specificity of information given, the complexity of response required, and the level of conceptual integration needed for solution are systematically varied.

The Concept Formation Program

In the first program, the Concept Formation Program, the goal is the development of concepts with children who are usually quite verbal but who demonstrate specific deficits and are often evaluated as aphasic and/or mildly or moderately retarded. This clinical research is being conducted by Lawrence Benjamin, Steven Mattis and Baylis Thomas, who are Project co-directors and clinic staff psychologists. The children are seen twice a week for one hour each session.

The initial problem for the worker in the Concept Formation Program is to analyze those concepts in which deficiencies were noted to determine their sensory–motor components. Problem-solving and discrimination tasks are then constructed so that this basic sensory–motor component is isolated and experienced by the child and the appropriate concomitant verbal label or verbalization is introduced. Gradually, tasks are presented in which the sensory–motor cues are diminished and the verbalization is accentuated until problems are solved using only the verbal components. For example, if the concept "shape" has not as yet developed, one might begin by presenting spherical objects differing in size, material, and weight and introduce the term *round*. After some practice, a new term *square* might be experienced in a similar manner. After two or three specific shapes have been learned, discrimination problems are presented. Up until this point, merely pointing to the correct object or labeling a specific shape is required. However, once discrimination between shapes has been demonstrated, one can then proceed to tasks requiring the child to verbalize similarities and differences in shape. Thus, when given several objects, all square but differing in size, texture, etc., the child is asked, "How are all these the same?" He gradually proceeds from statements like, "This is a square, and this is a square," etc. to "They're all the same 'shape.'"

A more difficult variation of the problem is to present several objects which differ along every other continuum, except that three are round and one is square. In this task, the question is asked, "Which one doesn't belong and why?" The child must then check to see that the abstraction or hypothesis holds for three of the items but not for a fourth. The solution of such a task requires not only deductive and inductive reasoning but also the processes of inclusive and eliminative thinking, that is, the formal testing of an hypothesis.

During this phase of the training, other concepts either previously learned or newly taught are worked into the problems so that the child must evoke the most appropriate concept from among several likely hypotheses and correctly discard this same concept as inappropriate in other tasks. As the child gains familiarity with the training stimuli and their names, it becomes possible to present items verbally without their being physically present. For example, one might ask, "How are a button, a penny, and a wheel alike?"

A good test of whether or not a verbalization is truly a concept or a symbol, as contrasted with a sign or sample association, is to introduce items verbally with which the child has had previous experience but which were not training objects. In the Concept Formation Program, we have developed such criteria tests, and they are given to the child before and after training. In addition, periodic interviews with the parents and the child are scheduled, and school reports are obtained. With these data, we plan to test our working hypothesis that the acquisition of specific concepts is transferable to other situations and allows the child to cope with previously disruptive events.

The Day Treatment Program

The second approach, the Day Treatment Program, is directed by Steven Mattis, Ph.D. This unit serves children who are often viewed as autistic, schizophrenic and/or profoundly retarded. The children demonstrate little or no receptive or expressive language and few self-care skills. They are referred to the program through the clinic after a diagnostic case conference. Structural facilities include a sound-deadened Group Treatment Area, which contains over five hundred square feet of free space, three individual treatment cubicles at the perimeter of the larger space, a boys' and girls' bathroom, both directly accessible to the Group Treatment Area, and an observation–conference room from which professional personnel and parents can view the activities and sound-film recordings can be made.

At present we plan to have a minimum of four and a maximum of eight children. Each child attends daily, Monday through Friday, from 9:30 A.M. to 2:30 P.M. There is one staff member for every two children and one assistant for the group. The workers are supervised by the clinic psychologists. At present we have appointed two members to the program, each of whom has an M.A. in psychology with a concentration in learning theory and child development.

Major Goals of the Project

This project has three major goals: (1) service, (2) research, and (3) demonstration of results. Although all professional personnel hold joint appointments in both the clinic and the project, the Day Treatment Program is viewed primarily as a service arm of the clinic. The children we will serve are rarely seen outside of a residential setting. However, we have interviewed a fairly large number of parents who, for many reasons, some quite reality-oriented and some quite pathological, have decided not to institutionalize their children at the present time. Therefore in addition to working with the children, an important aspect of the service is casework with parents.

The research goals cannot truly be separated from actual service, for, like all meaningful clinical research, the problems to be explored evolve from questions and contradictions observed in practice. If a satisfactory solution is found, it is re-introduced as soon as it is appropriate. What the researcher is in a position to do, however, is to maintain some distance so that the problems which arise are put into perspective in terms of past clinical experience and current theories of child, psychosexual, and cognitive development. The behavior of these children does not really conform adequately to any one theory; consequently, it provides an excellent opportunity to evolve new or amend existing frameworks.

We have found that sound-film recordings of our work are an effective method of demonstrating techniques we have developed and of disseminating information about such children. A room was therefore constructed which abuts both the Group Treatment Area and one of the individual treatment areas from which 16mm sound-film recordings can be made. These films will serve not only as clinical records, but also as a research tool for multiple observations. They can also be edited to serve as demonstration and training film for professional workers in the field.

While casework with parents, research, and demonstration procedures are being conducted intermittently during the course of the Day Treatment Program, the bulk of the work—that is, work with the children—will be in progress daily. The training and treatment programs are predicated, as in the Concept Formation Program, on a thorough diagnostic evaluation. In developing an individual treatment plan, it is important to determine those sensory and response modalities best developed by the child as well as those available to him. We have found, for example, that a given child may perform more adequately when presented with an auditory cue and asked for a vocal response, than when presented with a tactual cue and asked for a motor response. Another child, equally devastated intellectually, will perform in exactly the opposite manner.

The goal in this program is to develop organizing principles not at the level of concepts but rather more simply as reliable responses to a wide range of environmental and internal cues. Whereas in the Concept Formation Program training might begin with tasks which require the perception of similarities in identical objects, in the Day Treatment Program this same level is viewed as a long-term goal. That is, if we can facilitate the recognition of object constancy or similarities in situations, and the communicative verbal labeling of such events, we will consider our program a success.

I think it would be presumptuous and probably grossly inaccurate to speak of a specific treatment program at this time. In general, what we plan to do is to present the child first with tasks requiring the sensory–response mode best developed in order to broaden his experience with a variety of stimuli. Gradually tasks will be introduced which require inter-sensory integration and multiple modes of response. As is apparent from the terminology used in referring to the Day Treatment Program, while the cues and responses selected are dependent upon the literature in child and cognitive development, the manner of presentation and task situations are derived from learning theories, primarily classified, instrumental, and operant conditioning.

The ultimate usefulness of both the Concept Formation and Day Treatment Programs is still to be determined. There will probably be a great deal of trial-and-error in bridging the gap between the implications of our diagnostic findings and the development of effective treatment modalities. However, the theoretical approach to the problems of visually impaired, multihandicapped children presented today appears to be a promising alternative to existing frameworks.

Chapter 18

Experimental Program for
Deviant Blind Children

ANNA S. ELONEN and MARGARET POLZIEN

INTERIM reports have been made in American Foundation for the Blind publications[313, 421, 1157] on the efforts in Michigan to change attitudes and provide further services for the multiple-handicapped and deviant blind children. The present report gives a résumé of these efforts and delineates the problems encountered and proposals for the development of a program in the future for these children.

Although more recently a great deal of concern has been manifested in the needs of the blind child who possesses multiple handicaps, interest rather than actual resolution of the problem still persists. The child who has been designated as multiple-handicapped blind would probably be more accurately designated as the deviant blind child, for his development both intellectually and emotionally is retarded to such a degree that prognosis has been considered poor.

The various clinics and agencies to which these children have been referred have not, individually or collectively, been able to arrive at realistic diagnoses and/or recommendations. Too often the ophthalmologist, pediatrician, psychologist, and psychiatrist have worked independently without collaboration. As a consequence the same child may receive divergent and unrelated diagnoses.

Very often, clinics which use the team approach refuse to deal with severe cases, justifying their refusal on the basis that available resources are insufficient. Others who agree to assess these children arrive at completely erroneous conclusions. In cases in which parents are given adequate recommendations they often are unable to carry them through because of their own problems or because the contact is too brief to convince them of the necessity of working through the implications. Most parents need to be seen regularly over a long period of time in order that the recommendations can be realized.

In many states most of the education of deviant blind children has been relegated to the state schools, for the number of local classes depends on

Reprinted from *New Outlook for the Blind*, 61:1-5, 1967, by permission of the American Foundation for the Blind, New York.

the size of the locality and the degree of enlightenment of its school board to the educational needs of blind children. Entrance to these classes is usually limited to children who are able to demonstrate average or superior functioning level. Many administrators stoutly maintain that the chronological age of the child is the most important determinant in grade placement. A few are willing to consider mildly retarded blind children, but only on a trial basis. Unfortunately this trial period is unrealistically short and many of the necessary supportive services are not provided. There are, of course, variations in policy and practice in different areas of the country.

With the great increase in the number of blind children resulting from the advent of retrolental fibroplasia, school boards were persuaded to try different innovations. Some young blind children were accepted into nurseries and kindergartens with sighted children. This was ideal for those children whose development did not present gross problems, but for the great number of children whose development was delayed markedly it was obvious that if they were to attend school they could do so only if they were to receive therapy. Some could not be accepted for school until therapy had demonstrated sufficient change to indicate the child could be considered educable. Because of the reluctance of therapists to accept these children for treatment, only a few were able to benefit from such intensive support.

The pressures brought to bear by the parents of children for whom no treatment was available, and the insistence of schools themselves that they had been established for educable blind children, forced a reconsideration of the fate of this group of children for whom no appropriate facilities exist.

BEGINNING OF STUDY

In Michigan a new approach was initiated when schools finally recommended that a different program should be instituted. These recommendations were carried out by the establishment of summer sessions at the Michigan School for the Blind as has already been reported in detail.[313] To date, the numbers of children seen were twenty-eight in the first session, twenty-seven in the second, twenty-eight in the third, and twenty-four in the fourth. The age range was from two to thirteen years.

The only characteristic common to all these children was their visual handicap; some were totally blind and others partially seeing. The majority suffered from retrolental fibroplasia, with a smaller number of cataract, glaucoma, retinitis, central nerve disturbance, and macular degeneration cases. Although a small percentage was normally mobile, the majority demonstrated a very definite lag not only in mobility but also in general physical development. Some had been so overprotected that they had only been permitted to become proficient in a very few skills. Others had been so rejected and neglected that they had had no opportunity to develop either fine or gross motor skills. Achievement in such areas as eating, sleeping, speaking, and toilet training was extremely minimal. The degree of available sight did not determine the level of progress attained by any of the children in their physical, mental, or emotional development.

The physical conditions in the children varied from child to child, some being almost perfect specimens while others were unbelievably emaciated. One or two possessed peaks which approached their own chronological level in one or occasionally more developmental areas. Their mental development reflected the amount of encouragement given the children to begin the exploration of their world and thus achieve the first step in learning. Without exception all of these children had previously been judged to be mentally defective. In some cases this judgment was made at birth, while in others the parents had been forced to come to this conclusion since no discernible progress was noticed as the child grew older. They had been aided in reaching this decision after consulting numerous experts.

Emotionally, most of the children were so withdrawn as to be totally unaware of their environment, while a few were impulsive to the degree that they released their aggression so violently that they harmed themselves, their peers, and staff. One little boy's arms and legs were a mass of scar tissue because he persisted in biting himself until he drew blood, without any reason apparent to the observer. Another little girl would dart, lightning fast, to bite, only to be bitten in turn by another. The number of scratchers, pinchers, and kickers was many.

Socially, most of these children were at such an infantile stage that other children and their activities did not attract or concern them; they were content to remain aloof, lost in their autoerotic activity. The number of children who had begun to show any awareness of social interaction were few indeed. Like infants, they were most demanding of adult attention, being completely dependent on adult support.

The homes from which these children came varied from those of migrant workers to those of considerable wealth. The child's developmental stage in no way reflected the family's socioeconomic level. Parent reaction to blindness in these children ranged from rejection and ignorance to misguided efforts to overprotect. Some of the children had always been kept at home; others had been tried in various public and/or private institutions; a very few had been accepted by day or residential schools for the blind; and five actually had been committed as mentally defective.

DISCUSSION OF THE EXPERIENCES
GAINED FROM THE STUDY

Summarizing the four summer sessions from the viewpoint of learning opportunities for the staff, each session improved on the experiences of the previous summers by the staff knowing what to expect, knowing how to handle the children better, and being able to arrive at conclusions with greater confidence. In spite of the fact that the first summer program opened with a great deal of publicity, each summer, parents continued to appear declaring that they had only now heard of the program. Since this same lack of knowledge was manifested each successive year, undoubtedly there remain a great many parents who have not yet heard of the project.

The entire staff took part in making the final recommendations for each child. The categories into which the children were classified can be seen in Table 18-1, which indicates that only a very small percentage of the children seen each summer could be considered uneducable.

Tables 18-2 and 18-3 indicate what programs had been recommended for these children who, before these evaluations, had "no place to go."[421]

In reviewing what was recommended and what actually has been accomplished, the results can be considered from two different viewpoints:

First is the humanitarian aspect. Of the children who had been perceived as retarded and for whom little hope had been held for developing adequately, many have begun to function in school situations and even the very slowest are showing some improvement. At present most of the

TABLE 18-1

CLASSIFICATION OF THE CHILDREN'S PLACEMENT ACCORDING TO
THE OBSERVATIONS MADE AT EACH SUMMER SESSION

	1961	1962	1963	1964
Unquestionably educable	2	4	7	10
Educable with therapy for both child and parents	11	9	6	4
Severely disturbed, not educable until after therapy	8	6	4	4
Special, too young or with extreme physical handicaps (deaf, neurological, orthopedic)	3	6	5	3
Questionable (no definite conclusion reached)	4	2	1	0
Severely nonstimulated	—	—	3	1
Mentally retarded	—	—	2	2
	28	27	28	24

TABLE 18-2

PLACEMENTS RECOMMENDED FOR THE CHILDREN

	1961	1962	1963	1964
Local schools	3	7	7	7
Private schools	1	1	3	2
Michigan School for the Blind	11	9	10	6
Therapy	1	1	1	0
Not accepted at M.S.B. or local schools	7	4	3	1
Not of school age	4	3	2	5
Institutionalization	1	2	2	3

TABLE 18-3

THE EXTENT TO WHICH THE PARENTS AND LOCAL COMMUNITY RESOURCES
WERE ABLE TO CARRY THROUGH THE RECOMMENDATIONS

	*Present Placement of the Children**
Local schools (special classes)	18
M.S.B.	29
Private schools	8
Therapy	1
Not accepted by M.S.B. or local schools	9
Not of school age	14
Eventually institutionalized	12

* A number of children attended more than one session.

children are far happier than when first seen, and certainly most families are more hopeful concerning the future of their child.

These children and others like them, before the summer sessions existed, had had but one place to go—the community and the parents had concluded that since no facilities or personnel sufficiently interested to work with this type of child were available, commitment as defective was the only solution.

But over and above this first humanitarian consideration is the second, cold, hard, economic factor. Since the outlook for these children could not be expected to change, the only remaining possibility was placement in state institutions for the retarded. To resolve the problem in this manner is extremely costly in both human and monetary terms. The expense to the state per child for the rest of his life would eventually add up to a much greater sum than that required for evaluation programs. (Based on the life span of thirty-five years, the cost to the state would be estimated to range between $80,000 to $90,000 per individual. When multiplied by the number of children observed during these summers, it can be seen that the number of children who need not be institutionalized for the greater part of their lives represents an enormous saving to the state.)

One fact which prevented a more hopeful prognosis for some of these children was that many were too old to achieve marked developmental changes. The age of the children referred has dropped constantly. This is fortunate because the breaking of established habits of many years presents a difficult task. It was demonstrated that most of the parents had not been able to obtain adequate help at a crucial age. An obvious way to prevent such instances is to provide permanent facilities which would offer longer periods for training or treatment. The establishment of therapeutic centers would prevent distortion in development and permit the children to approximate their true potential earlier, thus diminishing the heartache felt by parents and family.

PROPOSAL FOR FUTURE CARE

One choice for such a center might logically be in conjunction with the state school for the blind. It has been demonstrated that the number of multiple handicapped children has continued to increase in spite of medical advancement. On the whole, local special classes have not been able to absorb these children because of the various specialized services required. The present integrated day school classes are not prepared to deal with the difficulties these children present. Such summary dismissal of the problems is not the solution. A separate unit devised to fit the program necessary to meet the treatment needs of this group can be envisioned within the existing residential state school structure. The personnel of these schools have long been faced with this problem and some have shown interest in considering such a possibility. In addition, the location of this unit in close proximity to existing services would permit the gradual interchange of children as they show indication of being able to benefit from more formal stimulation.

It has been demonstrated that the simple exposure of these children to educational stimulation, even in small groups, is not sufficient to permit a change in developmental growth. Rather, as the Michigan summer program demonstrated, these children require individual therapy in order to achieve growth by establishing an interest in and contact with their environment. We would envision such a proposed unit to serve about thirty children, requiring the following personnel:

A *director* to coordinate the staff and services, possessing a great deal of experience as well as interest in the atypical blind child. The success or failure of such a unit would depend to a marked extent on the ability as well as the enthusiasm of this individual. It would be desirable to have a full-time *psychiatrist*, but in view of the existing shortage of child psychiatrists the unit would probably have to rely on a consultant. *Pediatric* care could be provided through existing health services. A consulting *physiotherapist* would also be a desirable addition. At least two full-time *psychologists* are almost mandatory to such a program to provide the day-to-day therapy. Also, the interpretation of these children's potential abilities would fall to a great extent on the two psychologists and the consulting psychiatrist. A *social worker* is required to work with the family, for the experience to date has demonstrated that children whose parents are seen in casework concurrent with the therapy of the child make much greater progress than if they are treated alone. *Nursery school teachers* whose qualifications include work in the area of child development as well as experience with blind children should number at least six in order to provide concentrated constructive stimulation, individually and in groups. Since these children are so disturbed it would be difficult for a teacher to handle them alone, therefore an *aide* should be available to each teacher. On occasions when a particular child's reaction reaches such a point that it must be worked through then and there, the aide would be able to handle the remaining group until the teacher had been able to handle the crisis or obtain help. The aide could also attend to the minor needs of an individual child so that the teacher would be free to continue with the activity underway. Attendance being on a twenty-four hour basis, a staff of competent *houseparents* would be necessary. Because of the strenuous nature of such a service, houseparents should not be too old. Their qualifications must, of necessity, be quite high, with provision for inservice training. *Secretarial and janitorial* services should be included for the unit.

The needs of these children call for dormitory facilities separated from other dormitories. Ideally, the unit should open directly into an enclosed, equipped and shaded outside play area.

The suggested operational period would be twelve months, with the children's visits home and the parents' visits to the unit taking place at the discretion of the staff, since it has been demonstrated that parents' visits may prove to be disrupting. Experience gained from the summer session suggests that a minimal period of two years' work with the children should be set before exclusion from the unit is considered. This would apply to the children who have not progressed sufficiently well to have been advanced to some unit of the school program. If the child has not demonstrated observable growth in intellectual, physiological, and emotional areas within an experimental period of four years, further retainment probably would not be beneficial.

The environment usually found in a unit utilizing milieu therapy should guide the philosophy of the entire endeavor.

Case histories might best illustrate how intervention as a result of the diagnostic sessions helped to change the direction of development in two of the participants.

Two sisters, aged two and four, had been confined to cribs. As a result the amount of stimulation they had received had been minimal. When first seen neither child was able to walk. The older child achieved locomotion by scooting on her bottom, and Peggy, the younger, apparently had not moved about at all. Peggy possessed no speech, while Liza, the older, had a few echolalic words and phrases, not, however, used for communication. Neither was toilet trained. Liza ate only in the most primitive fashion and Peggy had to be fed. Both children received intensive care during their stay. After this period the older child was accepted in school; Peggy, too young for school, was returned home and the parents, under the supervision of a caseworker, were assisted in following through on the recommendations made to them.

Peggy, after one year, is beginning to speak, is able to walk, and partial toilet training has been achieved. In contrast, the older sister who has received much more concentrated training in school has made only minimal progress. She still is not able to communicate, although her use of words and phrases is greater. Walking is stiff and clumsy and eating is still by hand. Emotionally, she is very poorly adjusted. Both children now are able to show love for and dependence on the parents. These characteristics had been completely missing when the children were first observed. There is no doubt that had the younger child been permitted to continue unstimulated as long as her sister had been, development would be equally retarded. Without stimulation both children would eventually have been committed to an institution for the retarded.

SUMMARY AND CONCLUSION

The extended study of multiple handicapped and deviant blind children has shown that if special treatment and care were provided, a surprisingly large percentage of these children could be habilitated sufficiently so that they might enter either day school classes or residential schools. Since the problem of these blind children is still urgent and gives every evidence of continuing to remain so, suggestions for adequately staffed special treatment units as adjuncts to existing state schools have been submitted.

The importance of training and stimulation early, in the crucial stage, has been demonstrated in the dramatic changes possible in the developmental growth of deviant blind children as a result of the experimental summer sessions held at the Michigan School for the Blind.

Chapter 19

The Multiply Handicapped Child and Courageous Action

WILLIAM M. CRUICKSHANK

ONE by one the various clinical groups of physically and mentally handicapped children in the United States have come to the attention of professional personnel and attempts to meet their unusual needs have been undertaken. Beginning in 1817, Gallaudet drew the attention of his society to the needs of deaf children. A few years later Horace Mann, Samuel Gridley Howe, Dorothea Dix, and others who were their contemporaries focused attention on the mentally retarded, directed thoughtful people to the needs of children and adolescents who were housed with adult delinquents, made an issue of the lack of care for those with epilepsy and in general were effective in creating a wholesome feeling of disquiet and unrest regarding social problems of their day. In the early thirties of the nineteenth century, the blind child was included within the humanitarian purview, and institutions were begun whose goal was to meet educational and social needs of still another segment of the child population. In later years the crippled child, the severely retarded child, and in the immediate past and present the emotionally disturbed child and the brain-injured child have each in their turn gained needed attention.

In present day scientific society, practically every aspect of child growth and development which is amenable to defect is under study. Prematurity, congenital malformations, birth injuries, neurological disturbances, and a multitude of other clinical problems are being studied from the points of view of genetics, chemistry, physics, mathematics, agronomy, nutrition, psychology, pathology, obstetrics, and indeed from the point of view in every science which has a remote bearing on mankind. Furthermore, progress is being made. With increasing frequency science announces an inroad on a wide variety of human liabilities: retrolental fibroplasia, poliomyelitis, phenylpyruvic oligophrenia, kernicterus. True these represent small fractions of the total problem, a problem which will not be solved within our lifetime, but nevertheless progress in prevention is being demonstrated.

Reprinted from *The International Journal for the Education of the Blind*, 13:65-74, March, 1964.

Each of these developments has important implications for the social sciences: education, psychology, and sociology. Modern education, to be alert to its role, must not only have a long-term goal but must be flexible in its operation in order to respond to the scientific developments in its sister professions. This is especially true of the fields of special education and rehabilitation.

While significant gains socially and scientifically have been observed and are being experienced in a wide variety of clinical problems, the complex issue of the child with multiple disorders is still not a matter of concerted study or serious professional effort. It is true that some courageous efforts have been made, but these have been isolated and for the most part have lacked those things which make for strong professional programs. Many have been short-lived. Exceptions to this are the educational programs for deaf-blind children which have been important factors in the lives of many for a long time. These programs, kept in public attention primarily by the outstanding example of Hellen Keller, have served a small group of children, and oftentimes have served them well.

DEFINITION

The concept of the multiply handicapped child, however, must go far beyond that of the deaf-blind child, although this latter group can never be omitted from the definition or from professional thought. The definition of the *multiply handicapped child* is both simple and complex. It is simple in its very title: any child with more than one physical or mental disability which requires special services or which makes his adjustment impossible in the home or in the regular class of his neighborhood school is a multiply handicapped child. This only partially tells the story, for the possible combinations of disabilities are immense, and it is in these combinations that educators, psychologists, and medical personnel become confused and oftentimes discouraged—discouraged to the point of professional immobility. The emotionally disturbed blind child, the mentally retarded blind child, the brain-injured blind child, the epileptic blind child, the deaf-blind child, the hard-of-hearing blind child—these are multiple disabilities traveling in twos. The emotionally disturbed, brain-injured blind child; the mentally retarded epileptic blind child; the emotionally disturbed, brain-injured, epileptic blind child with endocrine disturbances—these are facets of the problem which add the note of complexity to the definition which once appeared so simple.

In this discussion the emphasis is being placed on multiple disabilities which include blindness as a facet. The problem goes beyond blindness, however, and the total issue must be considered by thoughtful professional people. The mentally retarded, epileptic, cerebral palsied child who has a speech disability is a significant issue in another phase of special education and child development. Studies indicate nearly 90 per cent of athetoid cerebral palsied children have speech disabilities, while approximately 70 per cent of the entire population of individuals with cerebral palsy have retarded mental development in various degrees. It has long been recognized that speech disabilities, language problems, and hearing losses go together. The brain-injured child with auditory perceptual problems and with speech or language problems but whose hearing acuity is normal is a new problem to the professions. The hyperactive emotionally disturbed child with or without diagnosis of neurological disability, but who has severe learning problems involving a variety of psychopathological characteristics, presents an educational challenge which most of the time causes educators to admit defeat. Significant inroads in understanding and in teaching methodology, however, are being made currently with this type of multiply handicapped child. Cardiac disturbances in combination with other disabilities, endocrine disturbances associated with other impairments, mental retardation in relation to the total gamut of physical disorders add further dimensions to the already complex problem.

It is easy to see that the very scope, depth, and magnitude of the problem has caused confusion in the professions. At times one does not know which handle to grasp first, or in grasping the first handle one does not know the impact of this thrust on other disabilities which may be present in a child. Confusion regarding the starting point for educational planning is exemplified in a child recently seen in the clinic who was characterized by total nerve deafness, congenital cataract of the right eye, autism, and mental retardation.

ROLE OF RESIDENTIAL CENTERS

In general, although public schools and community clinics will undoubtedly play an increasingly important role in the care, treatment, and education of the multiply handicapped child, it is this writer's considered opinion that the problem can be better handled in the residential setting. In stating this, it must not be assumed that this writer is attempting thoughtlessly to discharge a responsibility from one setting to another. The motivation is entirely different. Rather, looking at the complex issues involved, which agency is better geared to serve the needs of the multiply handicapped child? A decision will not be reached here regarding which residential school or institution is the best equipped to serve the multiply handicapped child, although the implication will be strong before a conclusion is reached. In one locality the residential school for mentally retarded children may serve some groups; the residential school for the blind, others. In still others, institutes for the emotionally disturbed may assist certain groups;

at times, new centers may be conceived and built. The matter of public school and community agency versus residential center is relatively clear, however. The long-term nature of the problems, the complexities regarding diagnosis, the small numbers of children with common problems, the detailed, patient, consistent, clinical approach which must be taken to education and to vocational or life preparation usually go beyond the abilities and reasonable expectancy of a public school program. For the best in diagnosis, treatment, education, and life planning of the multiply handicapped child, the residential center can play a significant and unique role. The problem is one not of acceptance of a problem which no one else wants but the acceptance of challenge involving the greatest complexities in human life, the gearing of a program to meet the needs of this challenge, and the development of an experimental clinical point of view which will tax the best professional people to their utmost in seeking solutions. The contributions which can be made to the individual, to his family, and to his social group are unlimited and are indeed heroic in nature. Let us hope, however, that residential superintendents who enter into this sphere of education and psychology do so with their eyes open and with the challenge in full view. Some residential educators are going to accept the challenge, thoughtfully study its implications, and carefully develop extensive programs. They will produce results over a period of time which will bring them the deserved gratitude of the Nation.

ESSENTIAL CONSIDERATIONS

In the remaining paragraphs of this paper, the discussion will be restricted to multiplicity in relationship to blindness and certain aspects of the multiply handicapped blind child will be highlighted for consideration. Some generalizations can be made which apply to all types of combinations of disabilities.

The Superintendent

First, the attitude of superintendents of institutions and of members of boards of trustees must be positive in approaching this problem. The acceptance of the multiply handicapped child into a residential program cannot be based on a motivation of keeping all institutional beds filled. True there has been a tremendous temporary increase in the number of blind children in the last two decades. This number is now declining to more nearly that of prewar figures. While the gross number may be greater, the percentage is declining in comparison to 1945 or 1955. This fact, however, cannot be the motivation for now accepting multiply handicapped children or, worse still, for accepting partially sighted children into an institution or residential program. This latter group is unequivocally the responsibility of the public day schools. The motivation for accepting the multiply handicapped child in the residential setting must be premised on the facts that a need is unmet in the community and that the nature of this need can better be served in a setting which can bring resources to bear consistently twenty-four hours a day for the duration of the need. Superintendents of schools for the blind have long looked upon their agencies as educational institutions. There is no criticism in this attitude. Education for life and preparation for higher education are laudatory objectives. When sound programs, rich curricula, and skilled teachers support these objectives, no criticism can be extended. The assumption of collateral educational programs for the multiply handicapped does not imply the abandonment of the earlier programs of the residential school, however. A custodial-and-care program, in contrast to an educational program, is not herein being suggested, implied, nor advocated. We are envisioning only a program of education which is clinically oriented. Indeed, the expansion of a residential educational program to include the multiply handicapped child will mean that other professional personnel may be present within the residential school program whose skills simultaneously can be used to strengthen the basic program of the school. The keystone in the success of the program, initially at least, is the point of view of the superintendent. He can raise his institution to new heights of social responsibility and community contribution if he desires. If he is not committed to a challenge which will require the best of himself and of his staff, better the job be done by someone else. This latter is a tragedy, however, for in many ways the present residential schools for the blind, through the expansion of their services, are the best locations for the development of the program for multiply handicapped blind children.

The Staff

It, of course, goes without saying that, in addition to a well-oriented superintendent, the professional and nonprofessional staff of the residential school must be oriented to the new challenge also. However, for the sake of completeness this important element must be included and mentioned. Staff members can become threatened and insecure through the addition of programs in the residential setting, or in any other setting for that matter, when they as individuals do not understand fully the relationship of the new program to the basic program or to their own positions.

Fiscal Considerations

This writer has spoken with numerous residential superintendents and staff members regarding the multiple handicapped child. Frequently the comment is made that the establishment of such a program is impossible because of the budget limitations of the current operation. The clinical diagnostic and educational program for multiply handicapped blind children is costly and will continue to be costly. Superintendents, members of boards of trustees, commissioners of state departments of education, and members of state legislatures must recognize that costs are great and are legitimate. They must recognize that this is a new program which is being added to an on-going operation. It is not a program which can be developed appropriately within the framework of a current legislative appropriation. They must recognize also that this problem is one which is greater emotionally and financially than the family base, is greater than the community base, and therefore must be shared by the state or region as a whole. In certain phases of the problem, numbers of children are small and regional planning is certainly warranted and appropriate. The leadership of such agencies as the Southern Region Education Board should be studied by all as the type of instrument which can effectively meet regional problems. Although this Board has not specifically concerned itself with multiply handicapped children, the nature of this agency is such as to make regional planning for the sixteen southeastern states a real possibility in the solution of this problem. Suffice to say, however, that significant increases in institutional budgets will be needed, for many additions will be required to current institutional programs in order to serve the needs of multiply handicapped blind children.

New buildings, geared to the special needs of these children, may have to be constructed. Small group, and often individualized, teaching will be required. This has bearing on the size of the educational staff. Cottage life personnel will have to be added in terms of the amount of individualization required by some children. The adult-pupil ratio will oftentimes be less than one to one, i.e., more than one adult to one child. Residential schools could not possibly add this type of a program to their present notion of the appropriate adult-pupil ratio. It can really be seen that this factor alone dictates an increased appropriation. What we are doing herein is not only to present a challenge to residential superintendents to enlarge the scope of their activities but to throw the gauntlet to members of State legislatures and to State commissioners of education to provide to residential superintendents the means whereby a realistic program (both experimental and service oriented) can be established to serve the needs of a group of children which is currently being almost completely overlooked.

Diagnostic Personnel

It is not being suggested that every residential school for the blind become a center for multiply handicapped children. Mention has already been made of the appropriateness of regional planning in certain portions of the United States. It is suggested that those residential schools which do establish these programs be geographically situated near medical centers. It is not implied that programs for the multiply handicapped are medical programs to be directed by medical personnel. These programs are educational in the strictest sense of the term. However, among the many needs which are required for an optimum program is that of adequate diagnosis. Diagnosticians representing many disciplines will be required, in addition to ophthalmology which is usually represented in the table of organization of a residential school. Pediatric psychiatrists, clinical psychologists with a specialty in the childhood years, pediatricians, pediatric neurologists, otologists and audiologists, endocrinologists, and educators with broad special education experience will all be needed at some phase of the program. Too many residential schools have been subject to local politics within their state governments and are unfortunately situated in localities to which it is difficult to attract outstanding professional personnel. These persons are essential not only to a good program for blind children in general but are mandatory for programs for multiply handicapped children. Not all of these professional persons are required full time, however. To be situated near a large and diverse medical center, or near or in a large metropolitan center, will mean that diagnostic and assessment personnel can be readily available as needs arise, both for direct examination and observation of a given child, and also for the very necessary interdisciplinary staff conferences required at frequent intervals for each child.

Team diagnosis and assessment, a term which has been indiscriminately used in the professions for years and worse administered, is an operational necessity in considering any good program for multiply handicapped children. To function in a team requires practice. The availability of the same personnel from the medical center is important. Too few ophthalmologists have seen enough brain-injured blind children to understand these children. Too few neurologists have seen blindness in relation to central nervous system disorders to understand the impact of one disability on the other. Too few psychologists have evaluated sufficient blind children with auditory or tactual perceptual problems to make realistic appraisals of the actual problem which exists for education. If a few skilled diagnosticians in a medical center can be given the opportunity of seeing a continuous stream of multiply handicapped children, i.e., blindness in relation to something else, their professional level of sophistication raises to a high peak of performance and their contribution to the residential school educational program can become unique.

The discussion of ancillary personnel to this point has assumed part-time diagnosticians attached to a medical center. In considering budget development, a table of organization for a center for multiply handicapped blind children must incorporate certain positions as full-time, i.e., psychologists and social caseworkers in addition, of course, to educators. Psychological and social casework personnel will be used not only in diagnosis but in obtaining information from parents, in counseling children and teachers, and in working with parents as the latter make frequent scheduled visits to the residential center. These two categories of professional persons, within the scope of their preparation and professional obligation, will have diagnostic, therapeutic, and consultative roles of a major magnitude.

It can be seen that the basis of the program being advocated is not a mere appendage to or inclusion within a present on-going educational program for blind children. To do the job adequately a vast enterprise must be envisioned, understood, and established. To do less is to do a disservice and to be professionally negligent.

Research Role

One of the important considerations in urging residential schools to assume the problem of the multiply handicapped blind child is that of the research potential in such a center. The professions literally know less about the problem than they know about the problem. Multiply handicapped children with common problems are seen in a day school system, in a hospital, clinic, or other facility with such rarity that there is little basis for generalization on the parts of those diagnosticians and educators who are employed in these agencies. To contemplate a research program which would logically deal with any aspect of the growth and development of the multiply handicapped child under present community programs is to be faced with the impossible, or certainly with the unrealistic. In a residential center sufficient numbers of children could be gathered together under stable environmental conditions so as to make possible growth studies, clinically oriented research, and experiment with methodologies. The hope for this type of information, based on our community programs as they are now operated or envisioned, is meager indeed. Once again, not all centers for multiply handicapped blind children need to be research centers. There should be, however, throughout the United States several excellent research developments. Other residential and community centers for the education of the multiply handicapped blind child should be affiliated with the major regional research centers in order that populations of children on which generalizations may be made will be as large as possible. The research potential in this phase of human growth and development is unlimited, or, to put it another way, is limited only by the perspective of the professional people of our day.

FIVE MAJOR GROUPS

Four major clinical groups of multiply handicapped blind children need consideration in addition to the fifth group of *the deaf-blind*. This latter group will not be discussed in this paper, since there is much already in the literature regarding the problem, and this writer could add nothing significantly new in this regard. All of what has been said regarding need for broadly based interdisciplinary diagnostic teams and research, of course, applies to the deaf-blind child. Other combinations of disabilities, however, are not so frequently identified and have not had the long history of attention by educators as has the deaf-blind. These groups warrant some special consideration here.

Blind Mentally Retarded Children

The first of these groups of children are those with a combination of blindness and mental retardation. This is a phase of the problem of multiple disability which can certainly be shared by the residential school and the public day schools of large communities.

The Study of Services to Blind Children completed in 1959 in New York State, the latest and most extensive survey of blind children reported in the literature, was based on 2,773 blind children in the state under the age of twenty-one as of October 1, 1956. Of this group, 856 or 30.9 per cent had intelligence quotients below 90. The intelligence levels of an additional 715 children, or 28.8 per cent, were unknown. In certain of the categories of mental retardation, the percentages in this population are higher than that reported and generally considered to be present in the normal population. Of the more than 2,700 blind children in the state, 583 were registered in local school systems and of his number 23.6 per cent were known to be of retarded mental development. Four hundred and sixty-nine blind children were enrolled in the state's three residential schools of which 37.8 per cent were retarded. While the residential schools were serving a smaller number of blind children, the percentage of those being served who were retarded was significantly greater than in the local school systems. This was particularly true of the group of educable mentally retarded children which comprised 4.6 per cent of the public school group and 14.3 per cent of the residential school population. These figures are probably actually higher for both groups, for in each there were large numbers of blind children whose intellectual levels were unknown.

These figures are interesting, particularly those relating to the residential schools. Frequently the residential school superintendents disclaim an interest or willingness to accept children of retarded mental development in their schools on the premise that their institutions are educational centers whose goals are college preparation or vocational preparation. The fact of the matter is, however, that in New York State, at least, the residential schools are already serving a higher percentage of educable retarded blind than any other state agency, including the state schools for the retarded. Here is an area where local day schools must increase their services and where they legitimately can serve more children. The situation is likely to be the same in most states if a careful study were undertaken to assess these facts.

In New York State 220 blind children were being cared for in state institutions for the retarded. Of this group, 10 children (4.5%) were educable; 35 children (15.9%) were mentally deficient with intelligence quotients between 25 and 50; and 149 children (67.7% of this population) had intelligence quotients below 25. It can be observed that the predominant function of the institutions is custodial care and treatment. However, 37 children were placed in institutions who were either trainable or educable (two with I.Q.s above 75) and not one of the five reporting institutions had a single person on the staff who was prepared professionally to work with the blind. It is the opinion of this writer that residential schools for the blind can do a far superior job in the education and training of blind retarded children than can the state institutions for the mentally retarded. However, regardless of the locus of responsibility, whichever institution is selected to perform the function, that agency must have qualified personnel. In the absence of such qualified personnel the program should not exist. Certainly today the professions are sufficiently mature to be able to insist on maximum personnel for maximum programs.

The situation as it existed in 1956 in New York State and as it remains today, essentially unchanged, is not an asset socially, economically, or professionally. Some growth has been made since 1956 in several centers, but this growth is indeed modest in terms of the need. In a forward-looking program the State Residential School for the Blind will have a well-developed program for these children, including a curriculum different in terms of the different developmental needs of retarded blind children, a staff of teachers fully oriented to both blindness and retardation, and those other important elements which have been previously described. If the program in any degree falls within the scope of operation of the institution for retarded children, then an advisory role should be established whereby the personnel of the residential school for the blind or those of nearby local day school programs should be available on a planned basis for advice, consultation, and information to the personnel of the institution. In the latter situation professionally prepared personnel in the area of the blind must be on the staff and be responsible for the institutional program for retarded blind children. The initiative for the upgrading of these programs lies in the hands of educators of the blind whether they be residential-school oriented or day-school oriented. Educators of the blind wherever they may be must assume a leadership role for blind children whatever and wherever they may be.

Blind Emotionally Disturbed Children

A second group of blind children sufficiently large and homogeneous to be considered as a unity is the group of emotionally disturbed children. Although the collection of accurate data regarding the emotional status of children is very difficult, an attempt was made to collect whatever information was available as a part of the New York State study. In the total group of 2,773 blind children in the State in 1956, 1,028 emotional problems of different categories were reported in 790 children (28.5%). The emotional characteristics of an additional 537 children (19.4%) was unknown, and 1,446 blind children were reported to be within normal limits for their chronological age insofar as emotional factors were concerned. Residential schools for the blind reported 112 emotionally disturbed children (23.9% of their populations). Day schools reported 152 emotionally disturbed blind children or 26.1 per cent of their populations. Interestingly the emotional status of residential children was unknown in 2.6 per cent of the cases and in 14.4 per cent of the day school children. Twenty-nine blind mentally retarded emotionally disturbed children were reported by the residential institutions for the mentally retarded, comprising 13.2 per cent of their population. Of significance is the fact that more than half of the emotionally disturbed blind children in residential schools were receiving no treatment whatsoever and an additional 19.6 per cent were receiving treatment by other than psychiatric, psychological, or social casework personnel. In total, 77.7 per cent of these children were receiving no or subprofessional treatment services. The situation as reported for the local day schools was nearly identical, i.e., 79.0 per cent of the reported emotionally disturbed blind children were receiving less than minimal treatment services.

It is in the area of the emotionally disturbed child that residential schools for the blind can perform a particularly important professional work. Admittedly, separate facilities may need to be constructed for these children. However, the availability of a larger educational institution in juxtaposition to a program for the emotionally disturbed has unique advantages when the child progresses to the point where trial integration into the academic program can be considered. A state department of mental hygiene has recently opened two special facilities, separate and apart from any other educational agency, established to serve a small number of emotionally disturbed blind children. The psychiatric leadership of these agencies is outstanding, but only one person on either staff including the psychiatric personnel has ever worked with blind children. A blind emotionally disturbed child does present a different clinical and therapeutic problem than does a similar child with sight. It is imperative that specialists in the education of blind children be appointed to play an appropriate role in the therapeutic team of these and similar institutions.

The long-term nature of the problem, the importance of being able to accurately evaluate the impact of blindness on the therapeutic milieu, the necessity for ultimate integration into an educational program as therapy and education are gradually effective—these among other factors indicate the wisdom of considering this development as an appropriate extension of the services of residential schools for the blind. Once again it should be stated that programs of this nature should be established in those schools adjacent to or nearby pediatric, psychiatric, and psychological services of sufficient diversity and interest as to make personnel constantly available for research and direct service.

Obviously local day-school programs serving blind children can also serve emotionally disturbed blind children. Concepts of treatment and therapy are foreign to most day-school administrators, however, and oftentimes unfortunate conflicts of interests develop when a psychiatrically oriented program is superimposed on a day-school educational program. Insufficient numbers of children exist in most day-school systems to make feasible a long-term therapeutic program for blind children except in the largest metropolitan centers. Here is a frontier of psycho-education where residential schools for the blind could produce outstanding results—results based on outstanding professional programs. Less cannot be condoned. Less is to perpetuate mediocrity and disservice to children.

Blind Brain-injured Children

A third group of multiply handicapped children is not so well known as those which have been discussed to this point. There are blind children with minimal central nervous system damage which produces serious psychopathological characteristics, and these in turn produce serious learning problems. Just how many of these children there are is not accurately known either in the general population or in programs for blind children. In the New York State study, 2.1 per cent were reported as having brain injury, i.e., 60 children. It is certain that additional such children are included in the 4.5 per cent noted as hyperactive and aggressive. This writer is particularly anxious that residential schools assume this specialized educational responsibility. This is not to say that day schools are unable to cope with this issue but that the residential schools can do it more effectively in terms of the relatively small numbers of children which exist. Research on the education of hyperactive and brain-injured children is generally limited; it is completely lacking in the area of the blind. Many teachers of the blind have brought to our attention certain blind children of normal intelligence who have been unable after much good effort to learn to read braille or to otherwise succeed in school activities. Oftentimes these children appear to have a tactual-motor perceptual impairment seemingly based on a minimal neurological disorder. These children present some of the most fascinating clinical problems, yet they remain almost completely ignored because insufficient numbers exist in a single agency either to bring the problem forcibly to the attention of professional personnel or to permit professional personnel to become sophisticated regarding its nature. Not a single piece of psychological or educational research exists which is carefully and accurately developed dealing with the tactual-motor behavior of the fingertips in brain-injured intellectually normal blind children in elementary school. Again, the relatively long-term nature of this significant educational problem and the relatively small populations of children point to the wisdom of establishing such programs within a residential school center. Exciting careers of research and education are possible in this single facet of the issue of multiple disability.

Blind Children with Physical Disabilities

A final group of multiply handicapped blind children exists which might be termed children with a variety of medico-clinical problems. These children present a great diversity of problems and they represent a great variety of clinical types. In the New York State study 859 blind children were reported to have more than two dozen physical problems, including poliomyelitis, cerebral palsy, epilepsy, cosmetic defect, club feet, congenital amputations, glandular disfunction, cleft palate, dental malocclusions, heart disease, and many other similar problems. More than a thousand defects were reported in the eight hundred children indicating that many had serious compound problems in addition to blindness. This group constituted 31 per cent of the total number of blind children in the State of New York. In addition, 778 children or 28.0 per cent were reported to have various types of speech disabilities, many children with more than one type of speech problems.

Cerebral palsy accounted for the largest single group of these clinical problems. Two hundred and five children (7.4%) of the total group had cerebral palsy. Epilepsy contributed the second largest group of 126 children (4.5%).

Residential schools in 1956 were playing a much greater role than the local day-school centers for these multiple handicapped children. Local schools reported 23.3 per cent of their blind children as having medico-clinical problems; residential schools, 35.8 per cent. An indication of the extent of the custodial problem in residential institutions for the mentally retarded is indicated by the fact that 75.0 per cent of the blind mentally retarded children in these latter institutions had other complicating physical problems. In large measure these data and others previously noted indicate the nature of the role of the residential unit for mentally retarded patients in the multiple-disability problem.

While this evidence indicates that some residential schools are playing a significant role in attempting educational programs for these children, a further suggestion is warranted. In keeping with the earlier discussion of research and small clinical groups, it is urged that some residential schools for the blind, again those located near large medical centers, establish residential diagnostic centers of a relatively short-term duration wherein the complete skills of many diagnosticians can be brought to bear on the complicated physical, psychological, and educational problems of these children. In a sense we are advocating the establishment in this area of what has apparently been a successful model in California, namely, the diagnostic residential centers of that state for cerebral palsy. A thirty- to ninety-day diagnostic residential center would make possible unique information for professional workers who would later, either in the residential academic school or in local day-school systems, assume responsibility for the education and growth of these children. Highly skilled diagnosticians would soon become fully conversant with the impact of blindness on other aspects of development and, when blindness is in combination with other disabilities, would become skilled in understanding the multiply handicapped blind child.

The multiply handicapped child is a problem of great diversity, nuance, and magnitude. While one can speak of the multiply handicapped child as such, the term does a disservice to the problems and to the profession, for it is incomplete in itself. To understand the multiply handicapped child one must see the total spectrum of possibilities for combinations of problems. One must keep in mind the subtle nuances resulting from differing degrees of one disability against another and as these degrees of disabilities differ also from one child to another. To speak of multiply handicapped children is convenient, but to use this term in a generic sense, simultaneously restricts solutions and understanding. Far better to think in terms of the clinical problems of childhood and to operate from a clinical base in the solutions of these problems. When one is dealing with children who fall in the fourth or fifth standard deviation from the "normal" child or mean, it is no longer possible to think of groups. One must think in terms of the child himself and the magnitude of his individualization. In this manner only can solutions to apparently insurmountable problems be perceived after careful and oftentimes exhaustively long study periods.

Chapter 20

Learning Disabilities:
Yesterday, Today and Tomorrow

Barbara Bateman

T HE child with special learning disabilities has recently become the
subject of numerous conferences and conventions, books, and articles.
Interest in his problems is shared by the fields of general medicine, psy-
cology, special education, neurology, psychiatry, and education. And above
all, his problems concern his teachers, parents, and himself. Who is the
child with special learning disabilities? He belongs to a category of exceptional children which, like many other categories, is easier to describe
than to define. Unlike other types of exceptional children, however, he is
often described in terms of characteristics he does not possess; e.g., his
learning problems are not due to mental retardation, deafness, motor impairment, blindness, faulty instruction, etc. The children who do have
special learning disabilities might be described by some clinicians as educationally retarded, autistic, dyslexic, perceptually handicapped, minimally
brain injured, emotionally disturbed, neurologically disorganized, dys-
graphic, aphasic, interjacent, or word-blind, etc.

Remedial procedures currently recommended by some learning disability
specialists include such diverse activities as psychotherapy, drugs, phonic
drills, speech correction, tracing, crawling, bead stringing, trampoline exercises, orthoptic training, auditory discrimination drills, and controlled
diet.

Regardless of the lack of agreement about etiology, definition, incidence,
and treatment of special learning disabilities which is implicit in the various terms given above, the child with learning disabilities is perhaps best
described as one who manifests an educationally significant discrepancy
between his apparent capacity for language behavior and his actual level
of language functioning.

Within this broad concept of learning disabilities, at least three major
subcategories can be delineated, although there is certainly much overlap among them.

Dyslexia, or reading disability, is perhaps the most frequent of all types

Reprinted from *Exceptional Children*, 31:167-177, 1964.

of learning disabilities or language disorders. Estimates of the incidence of dyslexia vary greatly, primarily as a function of the definition used. Those who distinguish "primary" dyslexia as a specific congenital syndrome find fewer cases than do those whose definition is based on a simple discrepancy between apparent capacity for reading and actual level of reading, regardless of etiological or correlated factors. A conservative estimate is that perhaps 5 per cent to 10 per cent of the school population has severe enough reading problems to require special educational concern and provisions. Disabilities in other academic subject areas such as arithmetic do occur, but much less frequently.

Verbal communication disorders, or difficulties with the comprehension or expression of spoken language, have been labeled aphasic disorders in the past. But the term *aphasia* is now felt by many to be inappropriate. The term *verbal communication disorders* is used here to designate those children whose comprehension or expressive language problems involve the spoken word.

Visual-motor integration problems have been widely noted, often in conjunction with reading problems. But there are also children who manifest severe spatial orientation, body image, perceptual, coordination, etc., problems and who are not dyslexic.

The appearance of the medical terms *dyslexia* and *aphasia* in the categorization is more than coincidence, as physicians were the first professional group to interest themselves in problems of this nature. A parallel development occurred in mental retardation, where the pioneer educators (e.g., Itard, Seguin, Montessori, and DeCroly) were also physicians. However, as Kirk[586(p.30)] has stated, "special education as viewed today, begins where medicine stops." Until the time of Orton and his followers, medical interest in learning disabilities had focused almost exclusively on the diagnosis and classification of these problems. Little progress was made in remedial techniques until the focus shifted away from the hereditary and cerebral-pathology correlates of learning problems. The very fact that we cannot exchange parents or repair damaged brains has led to the present-day concern of many with behavioral symptomatic rather than pathological or etiological factors. Kleffner[596] suggests that

> Those who have chosen to concern themselves with the *pathology* underlying language problems have rarely been able to go beyond speculation. From this group come guesses about brain damage, cortical inhibition, hemispheric dominance, cerebral plasticity, synaptic connections. . . . There is no practical value in guessing and speculating about the anatomic-physiologic bases. . . .
> *Etiologic* investigations . . . have told us little more than that such problems can occur with various etiologic backgrounds or without any significant etiologic factors being apparent. . . .

The *behavioral* approach . . . has been more fruitful in a practical sense than approaches through pathology and etiology.[596](pp. 106-107)

Cohn[191] points out that the basic reason for the present lack of success in following the neurological pathology or etiological approach is the "lack of definite correlations of brain pathology with inability to learn readily, to retain the meaning of what has been learned, and to recall that which is stored."[191](p. 34)

From a practical viewpoint one might ask how the remedial specialist would proceed even if there were definite correlations between brain pathology and learning disabilities. If it were known that Johnny could not read because (etiology) of a lesion in the angular gyrus (pathology), the remedial reading specialist would still have to plan remediation on the basis of behavioral observations.

This is by no means suggesting that learning disability personnel can ignore the medical–neurological contributions presently offered. Drugs, for example, can sometimes facilitate the learning processes of some hyperactive children by the indirect routes of increasing attention span or decreasing distractibility. Rather than ignoring medical–neurological ad-

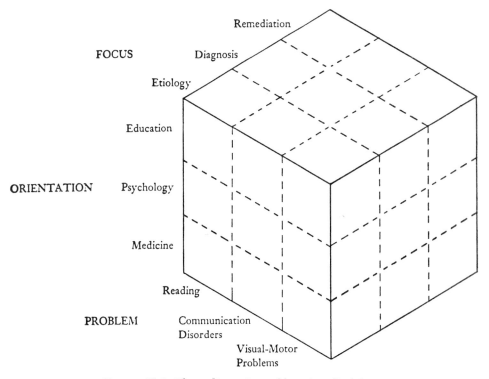

FIGURE 20-1. Three dimensions of learning disabilities.

vances, the field of learning disabilities will do well to utilize all the help presently available and to alertly watch for future developments that promise application. In the meantime, it appears that remediation must still be planned on the basis of observed behavior.

A reasonably thorough overview of work to date in the area of learning disabilities would have to include, as an absolute minimum, a discussion of (a) etiology or correlated factors; (b) diagnostic procedures, and (c) remedial practices in each of the areas of reading, communication disorders, and visual-motor problems. Each of these topics would be further subdivided by professional orientation—medical, psychological, and educational. Figure 20-1 suggests the dimensions that would be involved in such an undertaking. The omnipresent fourth dimension of time (past, present, and future) would also have to be superimposed on this model.

Since a complete overview as shown in Figure 20-1 would require a large volume, some of the terrain of the field today is summarized in the paragraphs that follow.

ETIOLOGY OR CORRELATED FACTORS OF LEARNING DISABILITIES

In all of education it would be difficult to find more voluminous literature than that on causes of reading disability. A large body of literature explores single factors that are believed to cause reading problems. The author wishes to acknowledge reliance on the discussion of single factor etiological theories presented by Corinne Kass.[566] These factors are often physiological and include (1) damage to or dysfunction of certain localized areas of the brain such as the angular gyrus,[484] second frontal gyrus (Wernicke, 1874) as reported by Penfield and Roberts,[876] connection between the cortical speech mechanism and the brain stem centrencephalic system,[876] and the parietal and parietal-occipital areas;[900] (2) hereditary or developmental lag factors such as inherited underdevelopment of directional function,[480] hereditary delayed development of parietal lobes,[283] slow tempo of the neuromuscular maturation,[318, 442] general development;[828] and (3) other factors such as lack of cerebral dominance,[829, 245] minimal brain injury,[1037] endocrine disturbance and chemical imbalance,[1006] and primary emotional factors.[110, 319, 373, 1085]

A very different approach to the causes of learning disabilities, reading in particular, is the multiple-factor view which emphasizes the characteristics frequently found in groups of children with learning problems. The multiple-factor symptomatology view is well represented by Malmquist,[727] Monroe,[779] Robinson,[931] and Traxler and Townsend.[1068] Prominent among the characteristics mentioned in this literature are visual and auditory defects, inadequate readiness, physical factors such as low vitality, speech problems, personality factors, and social adjustment difficulties.

A third approach to causation of learning disabilities is that referred to earlier as the behavioral or symptomatic view in which correlated (rather than causal) disabilities are assessed. This approach is perhaps the newest and is espoused primarily by those whose basic interest is in remediation of disabilities. Deficits in these areas are among the correlates frequently found in cases of learning disability: visual and auditory perception, perceptual speech, strength of closure against distraction, visual and auditory discrimination, phonics skills such as sound blending and visual–auditory association, visual and auditory memory span, kinesthetic recognition, visualization, laterality, verbal opposites, eye–hand coordination, and body image.[722]

Literature on the etiology of communication disorders has been somewhat limited in extent and scope, when contrasted to that in reading problems. Much of the older work has focused on cerebral pathology and language deprivation with a relatively recent upsurge of interest in the processes of language learning.[72]

Visual-motor disturbances are quite generally agreed to be a manifestation of organic dysfunction and as such the etiology is primarily a medical concern. However, the recent work of Frostig and Horne[362] and Witkin *et al.*[1128] suggests intriguing relationships between personality and visual-motor functioning.

DIAGNOSIS

General principles of diagnostic procedures for learning disabilities of all types are presented by Gallagher,[370] Haeussermann,[428] Kleffner,[596] Bateman,[73] Wood,[1141] and many others. Recent work emphasizing the diagnosis of reading disability includes Kolson and Kaluger,[617] Roswell and Natchez,[942] and Strang.[1031] In general, authorities agree that diagnosis must include assessment of both the level of performance and the manner of performance and that it must seek precise formulation of specific disability. Development of specific diagnostic tests has enabled diagnosticians to move from global classifications and labels such as reading retardation or delayed language or poor motor development based only on level of performance to more precise diagnostic hypotheses such as body image, spatial orientation, and directionality disturbances underlying reversals in reading or inability to integrate simultaneous visual and kinesthetic stimuli.

The specific tests used in the diagnostic process must vary from child to child, but frequently broad coverage tests such as the Binet, WISC, ITPA, or Kephart Perceptual Rating Scale are given first and followed by

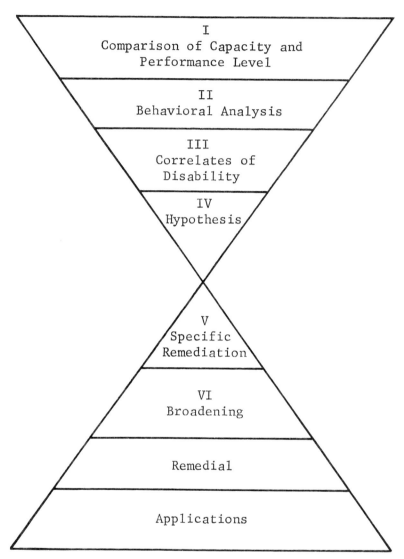

I Determination that a problem exists
II Behavioral analysis of problem area
III Diagnostic testing of possible correlated or underlying disability areas
IV Formulation of a diagnostic hypothesis which leads directly to remediation
 V Specific remediation directed to primary disability area as formulated in the diagnostic hypothesis
VI Broadening scope of remediation to include related disability areas and general application to broad problem area as outlined in I.

FIGURE 20-2. A schematic representation of the diagnostic-remedial process.

more specific tests in those areas of difficulty revealed by the comprehensive tests. Among the specific tests frequently used are visual and auditory acuity measures, articulation tests, tests of visual and auditory memory, discrimination and closure, spatial orientation, laterality and directionality, and visual-motor coordination.

A minor cleavage in philosophies of diagnosis is seen in the "standard battery" versus "individually chosen" test approaches. The former is perhaps more useful in screening and in some research, while the latter (discussed below) is most appropriate for clinical purposes.

One view of the relationship between clinical diagnostic and remedial procedures is diagrammed in Figure 20-2. The diagnostic process is conceived here as a successive narrowing of the disability area examined until the exact problem can be pinpointed and a diagnostic-remedial hypothesis formulated which is internally consistent and well supported by objective data. An hypothesis, so stated, leads directly to remedial planning. The remedial process is the inverse of the diagnostic process in that the initial focus is narrowed to the primary area of disability and then gradually broadens.

The first diagnostic step is a comparison of the expected level of functioning with the actual performance of the child. In almost all areas of possible disability, e.g., speech, reading, motor coordination, etc., our estimate of the expected level of functioning is based on some normative combination of mental age, chronological age, and certain experimental factors. Both standardized and informal tests are used in the assessment of the actual level of performance. When a significant discrepancy is found between expected and actual performance (e.g., in reading, a discrepancy between CA and/or MA and the level of difficulty of the misarticulated sounds), a disability exists.

The second step is obtaining as comprehensive and detailed behavioral description of the disability as is possible. If the disability is in reading, for example, the diagnostician would obtain from a standard diagnostic reading examination (in contrast to a reading achievement test) and behavioral description of how the child reads. He might find an absence of phonic skills, inconsistent word attack, lack of sight vocabulary, hurried and inaccurate oral reading, reversal problems, and so forth. If the disability involved spoken language rather than reading, this step would involve an exact and full description of the speech problem. An articulation inventory or vocabulary analysis, for example, might be part of this aspect of diagnosis.

The third step, a most crucial one for planning remedial action, is determining relevant correlates of the disability. The child who is found to have no phonic skills whatsoever, in spite of several years of reading instruction, will probably show deficiencies in auditory discrimination, auditory closure, or a closely related area. The youngster with a limited sight vocabulary will often show visualization and/or visual memory problems. The child who shows the perseverative, perceptual-spatial and hyperactive disturbances often called "Strauss Syndrome" characteristics frequently has weaknesses in interpreting visual information and in expressing ideas motorically. The child with so-called delayed language development may show basic deficiencies in incidental verbal learning, i.e., he fails to pick up "automatically" the intricacies of speech.

The number and scope of available standardized and informal diagnostic tests, useful in exploring these factors which underlie and/or accompany language disorders, is already large and growing rapidly. It is at this stage in the diagnostic process that a thorough familiarity with the correlates of learning problems and the available means of testing these functions becomes most important.

On the basis of the information gathered in the preceding three steps an hypothesis is formulated which must be both precise and comprehensive. It must take into account all the relevant factors and yet be so precise that it leads directly to remedial planning. An example of such an hypothesis is quoted from the following case report:

> A thorough review of Casee's test performances, general behavior, classroom functioning, and prior remediation led to formulating a new diagnostic hypothesis: the normal sensory integration processes, by which vision becomes dominant by about age five, had been interrupted. At this time Casee preferred to operate with her intact auditory-vocal skills, and when she was required to use visual–motor skills she was hindered by "interference" or lack of integration between the visual and tactile stimuli. . . .
>
> In summary, Casee showed primary motor encoding and visual decoding disabilities, manifested in these ways:
>
> 1. Visual-motor-spatial disturbances . . . (specifically) (a) gross interferences in response attempts to simultaneous visual and tactile stimuli, and (b) lack of body image and accompanying laterality and spatial orientation confusion.
>
> 2. Overly developed mechanical verbal skills, which were without full comprehension, seen as an overall discrepancy of about four years between the auditory–vocal and the visual-motor subtests of the ITPA.
>
> 3. Difficulty in everyday tasks such as buttoning, putting a lid on a box, getting into cars—disabilities presumably related to all of the above specific deficits and which involve substantial motor encoding functions.

Remediation was planned to correspond point-for-point to this diagnostic hypothesis. When the precise disability areas have been remediated, treatment can be broadened to include a more general focus. In the case described, more daily activities were later used in the further development and refinement of motor skills.

Further illustration of broadening remedial focus could be found in a case of reading disability related, for example, to a deficit in auditory closure. After this weakness had been strengthened, remediation could progress to an application of phonics, other word attack skills, and finally perhaps even to speed and comprehension.

REMEDIATION

In order to meaningfully relate the great diversity of remedial techniques abroad in the area of learning disabilities, it is essential to have a schema which shows all the possible areas of behavior in which a disability might occur and shows the relationships among those areas.

Figure 20-3 attempts to schematize language behavior in such a way that all possible remedial foci are included. Language is divided into receptive, intermediate, and expressive processes. Receptive language is further subdivided by the sense modality used in receiving the stimulus; expressive is subdivided into vocal and motor responses; and the intermediate processes are quite arbitrarily called assimilation, storage, and retrieval.

A further dimension is implicit vertically in that the activities at the top of each column involve a high degree of obtaining or conveying the meaning of language symbols, while those near the bottom involve only the perception or manipulation of the symbol, with little regard for meaning.

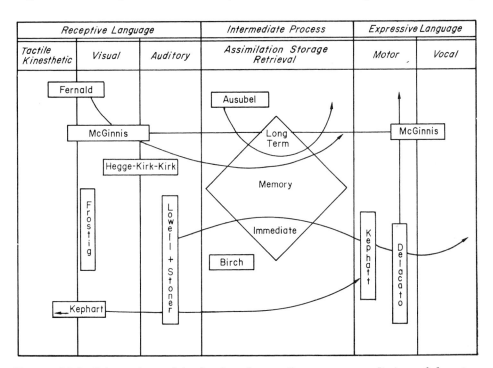

FIGURE 20-3. Schematic model of selected contributors to remediation of learning disabilities.

Memory is divided into immediate (rote), intermediate, and long-term storage.

Figure 20-3 indicates only sketchily the areas of primary focus in the work of certain remedial specialists in learning disabilities. Many others could have been chosen—these were selected only to illustrate the diversity of foci which can be encompassed by a schema of this sort. Each of the contributors whose work is represented could quickly and correctly point out that, in fact, he deals with more aspects of language behavior than are shown here.

Some work, such as that of Frostig and Horne, can readily be seen as focusing on remediation of visual perception and assimilation with some attention to certain motor responses. Lowell and Stoner's[680] work in auditory training, with some focus on certain vocal response characteristics, is somewhat parallel to Frostig's contribution but on the other primary receptive channel.

In the field of assimilation of stimuli, Birch[101] has contributed significantly to our knowledge of the integration of nonsymbolic material received on one receptive channel with that received simultaneously on another receptive channel. Ausubel[52] on the other hand, has done extensive investigations of certain relationships among assimilation, storage, and retrieval of highly complex, meaningful (symbolic) language information.

Fernald's[331] system of remedial reading can be conceptualized as employing the assimilation of simultaneous visual and kinesthetic symbolic stimuli as an aid to retrieval. The emphases in Fernald's approach are on the meaningfulness of the symbols presented to the child and the facilitation of visual storage and retrieval thereof.

In contrast, the Hegge-Kirk-Kirk[469] remedial reading system initially emphasizes auditory fusion or sound blending (assimilation with little regard for meaning) and vocal expression in response to the visual stimulus.

And finally, the currently controversial work of Delacato[245] can be schematized as being centered in neurological (dis)organization and moving through the entire developmental or sequential hierarchy of motor expression. Kephart's[578] well-established program appears to focus simultaneously on visual, receptive, assimilative (integrative) and motor expressive behaviors at the lower levels, with a gradual ascendance to more symbolic behaviors. Although the remedial programs of both Delacato and Kephart contain a large motor expression or motor activity component, this superficial resemblance reflects quite different theoretical formulations and rationale.

Remedial reading systems per se are legion and still multiplying rapidly. Two of the most helpful ways to categorize them as an aid in selecting the best program for a given youngster are (1) single versus multisensory approach and, (2) specific, eclectic suggestions for special problems such as improving rate of reading versus tightly integrated, comprehensive programs which are sequentially presented. Fernald's system is primarily visual-kinesthetic and is tightly and systematically organized. Gillingham and Stillman's[390] program is just as comprehensive and systematic, but is thoroughly multisensory, Monroe[779] and Harris[442] offer many specific suggestions for particular problems and are not as concerned with channel or sequence.

Remedial offerings in communication disorders have again been limited, in comparison to those in reading. One of the more comprehensive approaches to communication disorders (aphasia) is presented by McGinnis.[703] Interestingly, this system also provides an approach to remedial reading. Further remedial suggestions for children with communication disorders can be found in Agranowitz and McKeown,[10] Myklebust,[802] and Lowell and Stoner.[680] Treatment suggestions for some expressive problems can be found in standard speech correction and pathology texts.

Remedial reading spills over into remediation of visual-motor problems just as it does into communication disorders. Kephart[578] and Delacato[245] both offer programs which have an initial primary focus on motor and visual-motor activities followed by a somewhat eclectic reading approach. Teaching methods for children with perceptual disorders are also given by Cruickshank *et al.*,[226] Strauss and Lehtinen,[1037] Gallagher,[372] and Frostig and Horne.[362]

LEARNING DISABILITIES AND THE FUTURE

Within the field of learning disabilities, there is already evident a healthy trend toward early identification of potential cases of learning disabilities. Much, of course, remains to be done in the refinement of both diagnostic and remedial techniques, but it is not too soon to begin intensive work on prevention through appropriate educational experiences. The day may come when such preventive educational treatment at age five or six will be outmoded by medical prevention at a much earlier age. But that day is not as imminent as the day of educational prevention. This focus on early identification and selection of educational remediation is currently being paralleled by at least one pilot effort in the broader field of elementary education (Highland Park, Illinois) to identify the psychological-cognitive learning pattern of normal first-graders and to differentially gear instructional techniques to those patterns.

Another trend which is apparent in special education is that of more and finer categories. In one school system, for example, there is already a special program for culturally deprived gifted which differs from the culturally deprived nongifted program and from the nonculturally deprived gifted program! A glimpse into a rose tinted crystal ball might suggest some trends not yet so apparent. For example, in the future, this proliferation of programs will perhaps reverse itself and be replaced by an integrating and unifying application of certain concepts which are now being explored and applied in learning disabilities.

Some of these concepts which the field of learning disabilities will hopefully promulgate are offered here not as the sole property of this field by any means but as ideas evolved from many disciplines and belonging to all of education.

The concept of analyzing or evaluating specific cognitive patterns has been furthered by the recent work of Guilford[426] on the structure of intellect. In the same vein, Gallagher and Lucito[371] have demonstrated with the cognitive abilities measured by WISC subtests that retarded children are relatively stronger in tasks requiring perceptual organization than in those demanding verbal comprehension; the gifted show just the reverse or mirror pattern, being relatively stronger in verbal comprehension abilities than in perceptual organization, and that the average group showed patterns of abilities different from both the retarded and the gifted.

Recent work with the ITPA, which yields a profile of nine separate language abilities, has demonstrated identifiable patterns of language strengths and weaknesses among certain groups of children, e.g., retarded, culturally deprived, athetoid and spastic cerebral palsied, receptive and expressive aphasics, partially seeing, etc. But even more importantly, the individual ITPA profile of psycholinguistic strengths and weaknesses points the way for specific planning of educational techniques appropriate for that child. Similarly, Valett[1075] has recently suggested a clinical profile to be used in showing patterns of cognitive strengths and weaknesses as revealed by items passed and failed on the Stanford-Binet L-M.

Educators have long discussed the need for recognizing individual differences among children within a group. The application of these new developments in analyzing patterns of cognitive differences within an individual child is a logical and necessary extension of this interest in interindividual difference. In spite of this widespread acceptance of educational planning for interindividual and intraindividual differences, there has been an equally broad dissatisfaction with many of the traditional grouping techniques. Whether one favors homogeneity or heterogeneity of grouping, a crucial consideration is that such grouping be based on relevant variables. Neither chronological nor mental age has proven entirely satisfactory, since each is a highly global measure. Is it too idealistic to suggest that grouping by shape and level of those cognitive patterns most relevant to the subject or content area to be studied is both possible and worthy of exploration?

The field of learning disabilities may become a leader in demonstrating the feasibility of such an approach.

Educators have traditionally been concerned with promoting and developing achievement in specific academic areas. There are, however, certain cognitive abilities upon which academic achievement depends. Through a series of historical accidents American psychologists and educators have belonged to and been primarily influenced by the school of thought which held that intelligence (basic cognitive structures) was innate, hereditary and unchanged by experience. Only in fairly recent years has the concept of the "educability of educability" become even a little popular or respectable. The field of learning disabilities, and perhaps that of reading readiness, stand as primary contributors at the present time to the area of educating cognitive abilities directly. This type of ability training (focused, for example, on spatial orientation, visualization, retention, or auditory discrimination) is usually employed in a remedial setting after a youngster has evidenced an inability to achieve in an academic area which requires those underlying cognitive skills in which he is weak. If, in this case, an ounce of prevention is worth a pound of cure, it would follow that a broadening of curriculum to include ability as well as achievement training is in order. The work in early identification of children with potential learning disabilities[244, 390] mentioned earlier, is closely related to this concept of ability training.

"Meet the child where he is" is oft heard in educational circles—so oft, in fact, one might suspect that if we were better able to do it we might be less compelled to talk about it. A basic premise of remediation in cases of learning disabilities is that one must determine exactly where the child is functioning and begin instruction at or slightly below that point. Diagnostic teaching is a valuable aid in this determination. Recognition of the fact that a child's presence at a desk in the third grade room does not necessarily insure he is ready for a third grade book is widespread, but the actual doing something about it is not so prevalent. Too often we judge performance level by grade placement or mental age rather than by actual examination of functioning.

When the teacher and child meet, a major part of the teacher's armament must be a knowledge of principles of learning. Many normal children learn readily in spite of repeated violations of learning principles. However, children with learning disabilities cannot do this. By sharpening our awareness of some of these principles, as applied in teaching children with learning disabilities, we can anticipate broader adherence to them.

Some of these major principles of learning include overlearning, ordering and sizing (programing) of new material, rewarding only desired re-

sponses, frequent review, and avoidance of interference and negative transfer. (See Bryant, N. D., in press, for an excellent discussion of the principles of remediation.)

Analyses of patterns of cognitive abilities, grouping by these patterns,
curriculum planning to include the education of underlying abilities as
well as achievements, meeting the child where he really is, and teaching him
in accord with known principles of learning—all seem worthy of further
exploration.

If the promise of maturity now visible in the gawky, uncoordinated,
sprawling adolescence of the field of learning disabilities is fulfilled, we
will see one more example of special education's contribution to the education of all children, exceptional and not-so-exceptional.

PART FOUR

Evaluating the Multiply
Handicapped Child

Introduction

THE past decade has seen notable advances in psychological testing and assessment. The information supplied by test publishers continues to be increasingly more sophisticated and comprehensive both qualitatively and quantitatively. Psychologists have attained a high degree of skill in gaining rapport with the subject, applying the stimuli, recording the responses, and evaluating those responses. In spite of the competency of the examiner and the validity of the assessment instrument, it is difficult to avoid errors in measurement. This is particularly true with respect to the evaluation of exceptional children. Perhaps a statement by Dr. T. E. Newland, University of Illinois, best expresses the feelings of practitioners engaged in the psychological assessment of handicapped children:[1]

> The examination of exceptional children and youth is, by the very nature of their being exceptional, an exacting and difficult task requiring the services of highly skilled and qualified persons. The presence of motor and sensory handicaps and of major emotional involvements, singly or in combination, materially complicates the process. The psychological assessment of these children and youth, the necessary synthesizing of the results of physical, intellectual, socioemotional, achievement, and aptitude measurements, is even more difficult. While sound research is badly needed to show us how to make these processes more scientific and less a matter of art, their results can still play a significant part in educational and social planning for, and in our understanding of, exceptional children.

Many of the major problems facing the psychologist in the evaluation of multiply handicapped children are similar to those which confront him in diagnostic work with any exceptional child. When a child is orthopedically handicapped with no other concomitant handicapping conditions, the diagnostic procedures may be relatively simple and the recommendations for educational treatment may be rather clear-cut. However, one cannot assume that the various disability categories traditionally used to classify exceptional children are, in fact, "pure" groupings. A child with a hearing loss, for example, may have diverse concomitant physical, intellectual, and emotional handicapping conditions which interact in complex ways. The psychological assessment of multiply handicapped children em-

---

[1] Newland, T. E.: Psychological assessment of exceptional children and youth. In Cruickshank, W. M.: *Psychology of Exceptional Children and Youth,* Englewood Cliffs, Prentice-Hall, 1963, p. 112.

braces a compounding of the problems peculiar to each of the disability categories involved.

The five articles included in this section of the book include in their contents a wealth of experience, both theoretical and practical, in various approaches to the problem of assessing multiply handicapped children.

Haeussermann, in her paper on children with cerebral palsy, uses a practical and clinically oriented approach to the problems of testing multiply handicapped children. While advocates of a theoretical and mathematical analytic approach to testing might question the validity and reliability of her techniques when judged by stringent psychometric standards, there can be no question regarding the outstanding contributions which Else Haeuessermann has made to the development of practical methods and innovative materials to assess developmental potential in handicapped children. She describes in detail the items which she uses to evaluate preschool cerebral palsy children and discusses the specific problems which she encounters in testing such children. The specific problems are enumerated in detail and the approaches used in dealing with them are described. Congruent with her emphasis on a practical orientation, Dr. Haeussermann's primary objective is not to obtain a precise quantitative measurement of the child's level of functioning but rather to assess the child's development potential and the "intactness or lack of intactness" of his pattern of functioning.

Dr. Francis-Williams article, "Assessment of Cerebral Palsied Children," is a review of the general surveys and research findings relevant to cerebral palsied children published between 1958 and 1964 and a discussion of ways in which such findings should influence approaches to the intellectual assessment of such children. In addition, recommendations for educational provisions are made on the basis of the assessments. Again, the emphasis is upon "assessment," rather than on "testing," per se. Implicit in the use of the term *cerebral palsy*, is the assumption that it is rare to find a cerebral palsied child with only a motor disability and that the combination of handicapping conditions and their varying severity makes each cerebral palsied child a distinct entity. Various instruments for formally testing cerebral palsied children are described and the strengths and limitations of such tests are noted. In discussing a clinical approach to assessment, Francis-Williams recommends two books, one of which is Haeussermann's book, *Developmental Potential of Preschool Children*.

Professor Bateman outlines some of the issues confronting the psychologist in her article, "Psychological Evaluation of Blind Children." She identifies and discusses several questions relative to the feasibility of heavy reliance on *either* clinical judgement alone *or* mechanical applications of standardized tests in assessing blind children. As she describes the inadequacies of testing instruments and human judgements, her statement concerning the variables which confound a diagnosis—sensory deprivation, inadequate or unusual opportunities for learning, and emotional smothering or deprivation—seems to imply that even in the "pure" blind child, there are additional disabilities. In her schematic presentation of the process of evaluating a blind child, she has suggested that measures of functioning in the areas of language, mobility, and tactile sensitivity be obtained. Indeed, when the mobility problems of the blind are considered, just to mention one concomitant handicap, would it be inappropriate to say that all blind children are multiply handicapped?

Dr. Robert Frisina proposes a Hypothetical Profile System to determine the proper educational placement of hearing impaired children. He feels that, in addition to an evaluation of hearing ability, knowledge of the status of the child's environment and the involvement of the central nervous system would result in a more effective diagnosis and placement. Frisina suggests that these three aspects of the child's condition, if evaluated on a ranking system of 4 (i.e. ranging from mild through moderate, severe, and profound for the hearing loss) will give a truer picture of the child's ability to adjust to and profit from a specific educational program. Using this criteria for placement, a child with a mild hearing loss (Rank 1) but having an impoverished background (Rank 4) would be placed in a different program than would a child having a mild hearing loss (Rank 1) and a moderately satisfactory home background (Rank 2). Frisina refers to the recent history of maternal rubella and predicts that the resulting increased numbers of multiply handicapped children with hearing impairment will further diminish the already inadequate educational opportunities for relatively intact deaf and hard-of-hearing children. To meet the needs of all deaf children, Frisina suggests that the diagnostician must have eight program alternatives. Significantly, four of the necessary programs are for multiply handicapped deaf children.

The last article in this section describes a remedial program in which methods and techniques are geared to a precise symptomatic diagnosis. Dr. Marianne Frostig, with the assistance of Wilma Hart, discuss the diagnostic procedures and remedial program at the Marianne Frostig Center of Educational Therapy, Los Angeles, California. The program is predicated upon the assumption that a wide spectrum of testing and evaluation is necessary to diagnose the specific assets and disabilities of each child regardless of the suspected or apparent etiological category. A careful assessment of each child's strengths and weaknesses is made in each of six developmental areas. Certain tests are recommended as being especially valuable for providing information on which to base remedial programs. Suggestions are made for the diagnosis of sensory motor functions, visual perceptual abilities, auditory perceptual abilities, language functions, and higher thought processes. A case history is presented to illustrate how a specific remedial program involving the six developmental areas previously mentioned was devised for a nine-year-old boy.

Frostig's approach to the diagnosis and remediation of specific learning disabilities appears to have relevance for the education of multiply handicapped children inasmuch as the emphasis is shifted away from the disability categories to the handicaps, regardless of a label of "mentally retarded" or "brain damaged," or whatever it might be.

Chapter 21

Evaluating the Developmental Level of Cerebral Palsy Preschool Children

ELSE HAEUSSERMANN

THE GENERAL PROBLEM

THERE are several reasons why it is necessary to appraise the level of mental development of children handicapped by cerebral palsy. There are also several reasons, some general and some specific, why such an appraisal presents problems.

Twenty years spent in observing and teaching cerebral palsied children have resulted in some findings and approaches which might be of value to other workers in this field. Out of practical need and experience some items have been developed, which were first used only to serve as a basis for planning individual teaching programs; after several years data had accumulated which indicated a suitability for a more systematic and more generalized utilization.

Some of the reasons why tests for children handicapped by cerebral palsy are needed are (1) the percentage of retarded children is larger among the cerebral palsied than among the average population; (2) the exploration of possibly existing gaps and deviations in the mental development prior to planning individual training programs results in more effective planning and more complete correction of uneven development; (3) the scarcity of existing training centers calls for careful screening of the available candidates; (4) long-term planning for retarded and defective cerebral palsied children can be undertaken by parents, if reliable tests can be depended upon to give valid results; (5) premature discouragement of parents and others concerned with the child can be dispelled when it is possible to probe existing abilities in even the most severely involved child by suitable tests.

The most obvious reason why the evaluation of a cerebral palsied child's

Reprinted from the *Journal of Genetic Psychology, 80:3-23,* 1952.

(For more details on the Haeussermann evaluation, procedures, and techniques see: Haeussermann Else: *Developmental Potential of Preschool Children.* New York, Grune and Stratton, Inc., 1958. The following film shows Else Haeussermann evaluating multiply handicapped children: *Testing the Multiple Handicapped Child.* 16 mm film, United Cerebral Palsy, Inc., New York.)

mental development presents problems is the fact of the physical involvement. This involvement may range from the very mild degree of a slight difficulty in the motor ability of one hand to a degree so severe that a child can express himself neither by the spoken word nor by any voluntary motion of his hands, arms, or even his head.

Standard tests require a response from the person tested either by word or by action. Test items for children handicapped by cerebral palsy have to be constructed in such a way that the child's ability to comprehend an increasing difficulty or abstractness can be observed by the person testing him. If a child's only means of response is as minimal as an upward glance of his eyes for an affirmative answer and a sideward glance for a negative answer, then the test items have to be constructed so that an answer of this simple level of affirmation and negation can serve throughout the whole scale. The response remains always the same, the abstractness of the item increases in difficulty. The burden of the proof is placed from the child, who is being tested, to the item which tests the child's level of comprehension.

To make this very simple principle clearer, a look at the "Developmental Schedule" of Dr. Arnold Gesell will show how in the one case the burden of the proof rests with the child while in the other case it is placed on the item. By the most careful observation, Dr. Gesell and his Associates have established the sequence in the normal stages of manipulation. The behavior of the infant with cubes has been traced; from picking up one cube in the palm of the hand to picking it up with forefinger and thumb, from placing several cubes in a row to building a tower of increasing heights, or a bridge on imitation the increasing maturity of the infant and child is observed. The material remains the same: cubes. The child's increasing comprehension and motor ability is changing from stage to stage. It is this changing behavior which is measurable in terms of maturity. The burden of the proof rests with the child. This example naturally does not describe the complete schedules, but it gives an indication of the unsurmountable difficulties a cerebral palsied child might experience, if he were to provide proof of his comprehension and development by performances for which maturing motor ability is an essential prerequisite.

The items used by the writer in her attempts to evaluate the developmental level of preschool children handicapped by cerebral palsy have been collected in actual daily contact with a severely handicapped cerebral palsied child, who had additional difficulty in association and adaptation. The series of recognitions and of concepts formed progressively, as manifested by objects recognized and by colors, forms, symbols, and amounts perceived, by orientation and comprehension demonstrated, serve as the basis for a scale of items. Since in this child development was extremely delayed, it afforded the writer an opportunity to trace the gradual transition from noncomprehension to beginning partial comprehension to reliable comprehension in the form of something resembling a slow motion study. By taking daily notes for a period of fourteen years the gradual emergence of reactions and responses to situations and items of the daily routine and environment became clear. Continued contact with normal and handicapped children of normal intelligence and normal development rate afforded a comparison not only to the degree of delay but to the fact of the essential stages of development. The very fact of the delay of development and the very gradual change in increasing degrees of maturity of reactions and responses has trained the writer in the necessary sensitivity to anticipate the minute differences visible in the reaction of children at different stages of their development. The items used and this receptive sensitivity developed over a period of fourteen years constitute the scale and the range of possible approaches to explore the developmental level of cerebral palsied children of preschool age.

The items used are concrete life-size objects; large clear pictures of objects; pictures of children in different activities; pictures of landscapes at different seasons; large pegs of wood in matched pairs of different colors; a set of six wooden toy milk bottles; a set of three pairs of matched soundblocks; a sandpaper block and a zwieback; wooden blocks of matched shapes; several sets of cardboard cards with symbols, configurations, etc.; large cardboard circles and squares, cut in halves and in quarters; a set of eight miniature toys, half of which depict characters and objects of a story.

This list does not comprise the complete set, but it gives representative examples of the core of the scale. Auxiliary materials are used whenever a child is physically able to execute additional motions and when a further investigation of his mental equipment is desirable to the fact and extent of deviations from the norm. The scale at its present range is useful for children from two years to six years of age. It can be modified to test children below this level or those retarded and therefore below the two-year-old level. Some experimental items have been used for testing older children but not enough data have been collected on older children.

The presentation of the items is arranged so that there is always a choice of at least two objects, pictures or cards. The child is then able to indicate his choice of an answer by any response at his disposal: grasping, pushing, hitting, or pointing to the selected answer, or fixing the regard of his eyes upon it, or giving his sign of affirmation or negation, as the examiner points to each choice in turn.

The position of the choices is arranged far enough apart so that even a very flailing arm can indicate reliably which choice the child has selected, or so that the regard of the eyes can indicate the choice without doubt. In order to facilitate this technique of manual or visual indication, a stand has been improvised, which can hold·up to twelve 4-inch cards, or three and more large pictures, etc. It is a three-tiered wooden stand, 16 inches long, 8 inches deep, with deep grooves running the length of each tier for inserting the cards. This stand makes it possible to present the material even to a child who has been placed on his back because sitting is impossible or too tiring. A cot, a floor mat, if necessary an improvisation of newspapers, coats, rugs, etc., can be used for such a child, to place him in the only safe position to enable him to concentrate on the test items and his responses. For children who cannot look upwards or downwards or who have only partial vision, this stand can be brought into their line of vision, even where material placed on a table before them would be only partly visible to them.

The request is formulated to correspond with each child's possible means of response: "show me," "give me," "look at," or, for the child who can only indicate his answer by the shifting of the glance of his eyes, or perhaps a smile for Yes and a frown for No," "is this the . . . ?"

The concrete objects are asked for by name; then they are asked for by describing their function. This is repeated with the pictures of objects.

The contrasting activity of children in pictures is used for two different levels. On the lower level the request is to "show the children" doing the one or the other activity. On the higher level the child is requested to point out the picture which makes him think or which tells him that it is "nighttime." (Pictures used are of children eating at a table and of children sleeping in their beds.)

On the test for color matching only two contrasting pegs, red and yellow, are used at first, and the placement again is far enough apart to make the answer clearly definable. The second one of the pair of red pegs is held up for the child's inspection and he is asked to "find," "look at," "give," "touch" one like it, or for the child who can do none of these things the examiner asks, "Does it look like this one?" and then repeats it with the contrasting color, observing the child for his sign of affirmation or negation. The remaining colors are inserted one by one, blue, green, orange, purple, and the matching is continued until it is clear whether the child can perceive and discern the similarity and difference of the colors presented. The higher level then proceeds to name the colors, again starting with a choice of red and yellow, and have the child indicate his choice until all colors have been presented.

The technique of matching is then used in an item of 4-inch red symbols, except that here a set of three cards, representing a choice of three possibilities is used. The higher level of this item consists in finding from memory. The cards inserted in the stand are screened from view and one symbol is held up, after his attention has been secured, for the child's inspection. The card is then removed and the stand exposed to view. The child is requested to indicate his choice of an answer in the usual manner. Small black outline symbols are used in a similar way, again starting with matching and then finding from memory.

The hollow sound blocks are demonstrated by shaking them, slowly and distinctly, one after the other. The child is requested to indicate his choice of matching degrees of loudness. Several trials are necessary, the examiner shaking one block with one hand and then trying one after another the remaining blocks demonstrating three degrees of noise with the other hand to let the child find the one which sounds just like the first one. This process is then repeated with the second block and with the third one until all three pairs have been matched or until the child is satisfied with his choice. The higher level here consists in having the child indicate his choice in grading the three degrees of loudness from loudest to softest noise.

A gross evaluation of the sensory equipment is a natural outcome of such an evaluation interview. Tactile sensitivity is tested by having the child feel with his hands, screened from his view, after first familiarizing him with the materials visually and by rubbing his fingers over them, a piece of toast and a sandpaper block. His answer is secured in the usual manner. The good hand is tested first, the involved one last. Various materials are used to evaluate the amount concept of a child. Contrasting sizes in concrete objects, spoons, are used at first, then in a more abstract form in three pairs of circles, small, medium, and large. Matching again comes first, finding after the examiner names the size comes after that. The toy milk-bottle set is used to let a child indicate his ability to separate a requested number of things from a larger amount of them. The concreteness of the item makes it appealing even to young children. For a child who is physically unable either to touch or look at in turn the requested number of bottles, the examiner can slowly place one bottle after the other in a row until the child gives his sign for affirmation when the correct number is reached or when the child indicates that this is his choice, whether the answer is correct or incorrect. The cards with the configurations are inserted in the stand, depending on the child's age, in a choice of two or more. Matching comes first. Finding by memory after short exposure is the higher level. Finding the correct card, after the amount of dots is named, is the third level. The response again is possible by the usual means of grasping, pointing, regarding, or by giving the sign for affirmation or negation while the examiner indicates each card in turn.

The two contrasting seasonal scenes are used to test orientation in time. The request is to point out which one reminds him of Christmas or wintertime. For use in California and Florida this item would have to be modified.

The item in which the eight toys are used tests language comprehension in a form which is acceptable even to young children, because it has appeal and concreteness. A fair indication of language comprehension becomes gradually recognizable during the administration of all the items. This last item consists of the telling of the story of "The Three Bears." After completing this telling, the objects are lined up in alternating order and the request is to indicate which of the toys "go with the story" or "belong to the story?" The four-year-old child usually includes the wooden man in his selection without hesitation, while at four years and six months the child hesitates and indicates that the man could serve to be "Papa Bear." At five the child of probably normal mental development usually is able to exclude the wooden man without qualms.

The test items are now in the process of being standardized. They have been used experimentally for the last four years at the Cerebral Palsy Project of the New York Service for Orthopedically Handicapped which started a class for cerebral palsied preschool children, in coöperation with the Board of Education of the City of New York and other public and private community agencies, in 1946.

The test items used enabled the writer to distinguish between those children who were retarded and those who were able to learn at an approximately normal rate.

In addition to this value as a predictive and screening tool in the selection of the children to be enrolled, it has been useful as a diagnostic tool. Possible areas of specific disability, those directly due to the brain injury as well as those due to other developmental or environmental conditions resulting from the fact of the handicap can be detected and explored by judicious use of the items.

The areas explored are mainly perception, concept formation, comprehension of language, orientation in time and space on a simple level, visual memory, and a gross check of visual intactness, auditory intactness, tactile sensitivity.

The present practice at the cerebral palsy classes of the New York Service for Orthopedically Handicapped is to make an inventory of the child's mental development as revealed by his responses to the items. The educational program for the child is based on his readiness and his general and specific needs as indicated by the inventory. It is felt that such a description of the child's potentialities and achievement levels gives more information for future training purposes than a numerical score, which might only serve to disguise the actual potentialities in the areas tested.

Personality factors other than intelligence are observed during the test interview, and described in the inventory. The degree of stability, the absence or presence of resourcefulness, cheerfulness, perseverance, outgoingness of a child is noted. The degree of awareness of the handicap and the reaction to the handicapping condition is often revealed in the child's behavior during an interview. The child who is found to deal with his handicap without utilizing it, who has security, self-acceptance, and a willingness to come to terms with reality may respond better to educational opportunities, even though his intelligence may be lower than that of another child who is found to utilize his handicap, to rationalize his failures, or to indulge in dream fulfillment to the extent of escaping from reality.

Test items as described and their administration as explained in this paper are useful for a large group of cerebral palsied preschool children who have one thing in common: a direct contact with the environment, no matter how severely involved their physical response mechanism may be. Where comprehension is present and coöperation can be secured, the difficulty of the physical limitations in responding can be solved by the ways described in the foregoing.

SPECIFIC PROBLEMS

The second half of this article will attempt to describe specific problems in testing cerebral palsied children. Some of these problems are found frequently on testing young children and are mentioned only because their solution may be even more difficult in testing young cerebral palsied children. Other problems are found more frequently or exclusively in testing cerebral palsied individuals. It is important in any case, where the examiner recognizes that here is a child where direct contact is not established, that the previous developmental history, his behavior in the home situation, and other relevant factors be studied prior to attempting any testing.

Specific problems may be as follows: (1) immaturity; (2) infantilization; (3) negativism; (4) extreme deprivation of experiences; (5) extreme concretization; (6) retardation; (7) visual difficulties, such as visuo-motor, reduced visual acuity, peripheral vision, ataxic visual difficulty, involvement of eye muscles; (8) inaccessibility to human speech, such as deafness, pitch deafness, intermittent deafness, diphasia in any form and degree, inaccessible to English because of foreign language in home; (9) delayed response; (10) behavior deviations, such as perseveration, drivenness, flight of ideas, extreme distractibility.

Interference with the function of the sensory equipment is found in a large percentage of cerebral palsied individuals. In young cerebral palsied children impairment of vision or of hearing is sometimes overlooked even by the parents; this is because the range of action of the child is limited or his speech apparatus is involved. If a child cannot yet walk due to physical causes, if he does not reach for objects for the same reason, it is sometimes not suspected that he may have little vision or even be completely blind.

If a child does not speak, due to paralysis of the speech muscles or other causes stemming from his original brain involvement, it is sometimes not suspected that he may be hard of hearing or even deaf as well. Medical investigation of the sensory equipment, which should normally precede any attempt to test a child, is frequently inconclusive in the case of a young child, especially when his response mechanism is involved, as it may be in cerebral palsy. The test items used by the author give an opportunity for at least a gross evaluation of the vision and hearing. It has sometimes been possible to discover unsuspected and undetected difficulties during the administration of a test. The child, who responds satisfactorily to the visual items but fails to discriminate the difference in the sound blocks, or the child who fails the recognition of objects and pictures and then is found to be able to cooperate intelligently when the sound blocks are presented, are both examples of this kind. No conclusive results can be reached by testing such a child until the sensory involvement has been determined and, if possible, corrected, or at least is then taken into account in a retesting of the child. The impairment of the tactile sensitivity equally is detected as described in the foregoing. A knowledge of any impairment in this area is useful for both the teacher and the therapist, because such a child will need a little special consideration when he is taught how to manipulate crayon and pencil or pen as well as when the therapist teaches him self-dressing activities like buttoning or shoe lacing.

In order to discuss the specific problems in a semblance of continuity, it is perhaps best to start chronologically with the immature child. It must be emphasized, however, that the problems may overlap and that there may be present two or more in any given case. The task of the examiner becomes a constant sensitive observation of the child's reactions to any stimuli provided by the test situation. Based on intimate knowledge of child developmental stages, the approach to testing a cerebral palsied child, who appears immature, consists in a gradual tentative retreating to the level on which the child can begin to function. If such a child is not ready to identify the four objects used, when they are named, the choice can be limited to three or two objects. If this modification still does not meet the child's level, one object at a time can be presented in relation to a doll or possibly to the child's mother. In this way it is possible to determine the child's level of comprehension, even if he is not ready, able, or willing to respond directly. If, when the examiner presents the spoon, and places a doll across the child's lap, the child glances at the doll's mouth and back to the spoon, the child indicates that he probably comprehends the function of a spoon. To check this response, the shoe can be presented next, and it can be observed whether the child looks now towards the doll's foot, or even his own foot.

In a similar way the rest of the objects can be presented. The immature child will often respond to a request, which calls for an emotional function rather than an intellectual one; instead of asking him to "look at" the picture where the children are sleeping, he can be asked to "kiss" or "pat" the children in bed. His ability to recognize the difference in the pictures of this item becomes clear, even though his response is on an immature level. One utilizes the child's own inclination to play in testing such a child and adapts the tasks to his level of comprehension. In testing his ability to differentiate between colors, instead of matching peg to peg, the examiner plays a game with him: pegs and disks of the same color can be used. Each "peg child" wishes to sit only on a "chair" of the same color as his own dress or suit and begins to cry if it is placed on the "wrong" chair. After a while the child catches the idea and one is then able to observe if he can accurately match and differentiate the colors presented. Experience will give the examiner practice in inventing devices to meet a child's interest and fancy. All that is needed then is to observe closely how the child uses the material at hand and to probe his ability to perceive, discriminate, categorize while he is busy "playing." Discrimination of forms, for example, can be tested by presenting him with three square and three triangular blocks; the examiner selects a square block and hands it to the doll or the mother and encourages the child to give the doll the other blocks, but the doll "likes only this kind of a block." If he skips the triangular ones and selects the square ones, one checks by asking for the other kind on a second trial.

The infantilized child presents a problem which is related to the immature one but frequently more difficult to tackle. The child, who has never had to make a decision in his whole young life, the child who sees no reason for the need to respond, who does not want to be bothered, who has been fed and tended and coddled without any opportunity to assert himself until he has lost the impulse to do so comes to the testing interview woefully ill prepared to respond to any person other than his mother. Once the examiner has sized up the situation and the mother-child relationship, she has to improvise. One child may be coaxed into responding, while the mother, under direction and supervision, presents the material. Another one may be amenable to large doses of praise and even a little well-applied flattery, until some rapport is established with the examiner, and the child begins to think of himself as a being apart from the mother. Some badly infantilized children cannot be reached the first time and have to be retested after some time has elapsed, during which it can be attempted to instruct the mother how to help her child to mature a little. It is necessary to observe young children very shrewdly; infantilism can take the form of agreeing too readily with anything the examiner says. The child, who has earned praise and love by being angelic and compliant all the time, may continue this pattern during a test and appear to be completely without judgment. An investigation in the child's domestic behavior gives sometimes a clue to existing patterns of the type.

The negativism of the three-year-old is a well-known problem to any examiner. It is the rare three-year-old, however, who does not yield, in the end, to the examiner who remains calmly in command of the situation, does not allow any contest of wills by wise avoidance of opportunity, uses tons of patience but all the time assumes coöperation eventually. At this age the omnipotence of the adult and the belief in a routine to be followed usually is accepted by the child if one does not make the mistake to show doubt or annoyance; even premature praise could arouse suspicion in a contrary three-year-old and is best postponed until a working relationship has been established.

Sometimes a child is met who, having been considered hopeless by the parents or because the pressure of work with other children or duties have occupied all of the mother's time, has spent the first few years of his life almost completely isolated, except for the most necessary tending to his physical needs. The parents have long ago given up talking to him, since no response has been forthcoming, perhaps he has been spending his days in his carriage, on his back, with nothing but a ceiling to stare at until he was three, four, or even older. Or the deprivation need not be so complete. A child may have no speech and be difficult to handle physically, so that he is kept in the house, never being taken outdoors, and if he has tried to ask for information by looking at people and at objects, but unable to make these questions seen or heard by the environment, he may not have gathered much information even about the most familiar things, situations, and goings on. Even when the sensory equipment of such a deprived child is intact, his experiential learning may be seriously limited. Sometimes the flat shape of the back of the head as a result of years of lying on his back or an upturning stare of the eyes may be the first clue to make the examiner suspect this type of history, which then can be confirmed by careful inquiry of the parents. No generalized approach can be used in these cases. Several problems may play their part in such a situation. The child may have given up trying to follow conversations, which were too hard for him to comprehend, or he may have been kept out of the way and have had little opportunity to hear people speak. He may be frightened by being spoken to and looked at. He may not comprehend even the most simple words. Instead of a test in such an extreme case, exposure to carefully graded opportunities may be needed. It is then sometimes possible to bring such a child within a relatively short time through the stages of development he has missed up to the level he is ready for. While the content of his experiential range will be meager, his capacity to comprehend at potentially his level of readiness may be intact. If deprivation has been constant and extreme and if it has been continued for a considerable period of time, permanent damage will usually result. The periods of psychological readiness have been allowed to pass unutilized and the curiosity of the child has grown weaker or vanished altogether. Many children of this group will never function on the level on which they could have functioned if treated intelligently from the start, but they may be able to function satisfactorily on a lower level, if training is not detained any longer. The milder cases of this group may be able to demonstrate their capacity to perceive, discriminate, classify, and comprehend, at a potentially normal level but may show such gaps in their orientation that individual programs will have to be planned for them to compensate for the years of deprivation, until they are brought up to par. In testing such children, the examiner has to provide opportunities to demonstrate ability to learn even during one test interview. Instead of asking for a stated number of milk bottles the examiner lines up a certain number and has the child match this row of bottles. This can be repeated and enlarged with blocks, pennies, or pencils. His ability to imitate correctly can be probed by having him repeat a stated number of taps with his hand or foot or nods of the head, whichever way he can respond. His memory can be probed by hiding something while he watches and having him look for it after some other tasks have been given. In such a way one can arrive at an estimate of his potential functional level at this time. Frequent retesting after intensive training is necessary in these cases.

The child, who lives in an extremely concrete world, is frequently considered a behavior problem by the environment. He also may be too readily classed with the retarded group. While there exists of necessity a certain restriction of ability to comprehend when a child has lost or never developed the ability to categorize, to classify, to abstract, there exists a difference in the orientation of such children and of the ones whose retardation is of a more general kind. The extremely concretely functioning child may be the one who is punished for his "stubbornness," when he in reality cannot understand that a chair is just a chair, while for him it becomes connected with the person using it. Such a child will refuse to sit on any other chair but "his." He is unable to think in abstract terms. Once his restriction in his mental functioning is understood, the examiner can adapt the presentation of the items to this functioning. Amount concepts of such a child, for instance, can be probed by using concrete objects and situations, such as spoons and familiar persons. He can thus be requested to "set the table for Daddy, Mommy, Baby and Big Sister." This can be continued until it becomes clear that his amount concept has been established. It has been found that comprehension of isolated concepts may be high, while association may be completely absent. In a similar way his ability to perceive, discriminate, etc., must be tested by utilizing his own way of functioning. Instead of letting him match symbols, it may be necessary to show him how to sort them and having him repeat this task, while the examiner observes whether he does perceive the similarity of symbols. It may be necessary to name the symbols for him or to allow him to name them, as ball for circle, boat for triangle, window for square. His difficulty will be found to be in comprehension while the perception may be no difficulty for him at all, in contrast to the retarded child who understands the task but fails to discriminate between different symbols.

The retarded child may not present a specific problem in itself; many of them can be tested in the same way other cerebral palsied children are tested, with no other problem expected than the one caused by the motor handicap. The examiner has to be alert in order to discover the child who would try to camouflage lack of comprehension by mumbling his response or by indicating it purposely in an ambiguous way to cover his failures. On the other hand the examiner needs to observe very closely, where a severe motor handicap does exist, so that a correct first response is not missed and ignored and then substituted with an incorrect one by a timid or insecure child.

There are many degrees of retardation, and the range met by one who would try to test cerebral palsied children goes from the child who is almost of normal intelligence to the one who is low normal, to borderline and then feeble-minded and then all the way down the scale to children who have almost no manifestation of mental activity.

Where the retardation of mild degree exists in a severely handicapped child, whose response may be misread, the answer is to give several trials and compare the number of correct and incorrect responses. Parallel items may be invented as one goes along to make certain an apparently correct response was reliably correct. When failure happens, the item can be adapted to a lower level; if it is passed on the lower level and failed on the higher level, the reason for the failure is probably that the child functions on a lower level of development. The degrees in simplification, as described in the paragraph about immature children, can be used in a comparable manner with children of suspected retardation. In this way one can usually grossly rule out that the failure to respond correctly could be due to sensory impairment. If the same problem is comprehensible when there is only a choice of two answers, for instance, but seems incomprehensible to a child when there is a choice of four answers, the reason for the failure is obviously not likely to be an impairment of vision or hearing.

The child with a severe retardation in mental development presents one of the most challenging tasks for the examiner. Usually such a child will function on a level below two years of age and the test items used for children from two to six years offer little usefulness. The author uses a collection of materials such as: flashlight, bell, noisemaker frog, music box, doll, red celluloid ring on a string, dolls, mirror, cracker, ball, blocks, spoon and cup, small cars, doll carriage, paper, pictures, and anything which seems to offer any hope of eliciting a response. It would take a paper in itself to describe the ways used to get responses and to evaluate the maturity level of the highest response a given child is capable of. A long acquaintance with children, normal and handicapped, intelligent and retarded, is essential to undertake the testing of such a child. Sensory involvement is investigated first, because these children are usually so low in intelligence that a medical evaluation is not or not yet possible to determine their sensory intactness. The child's reaction to the sound of a bell is observed, then to the noisemaker, then to the music box. Crackling paper, dropped blocks, the sound blocks, are used. If it is made reasonably certain that the child can hear, his eyes are observed in their reaction to the flashlight. The light is brought slowly from behind his head towards the side, and the length of time it takes for his pupils to react is noted for each eye. Then he is given opportunity to follow the light with his eyes. Each direction is tried, each eye singly if possible. If he appears to see the flashlight, the red ball is slowly moved across his field of vision or the red ring is dangled before his eyes. If he follows this object with his eyes, it is attempted to find out if he can also follow the mirror image of the same moving object with his eyes or if his eyes glide over the mirror surface without recognition. A plain piece of paper is moved before his eyes, then one with a pattern on it. Both are then brought in his field of vision and moved slowly apart, and it is observed if he follows one or the other with his eyes. This is repeated several times in alternating directions to arrive at a definite conclusion. If he has seemed to listen to the music box, it is played for him a few times while he can see it. After a few minutes it is brought within his field of vision again, without playing it. His expression is observed. When it is played again, it is noted whether he looks in the direction of the box, possibly connecting cause and effect. A spoon is brought near his mouth and his reaction observed. Then this is repeated with a shoe or brush. Obviously the child, who opens his mouth on the approach of the spoon but turns his head, or closes his mouth, or smiles, or tries to withdraw on the approach of the shoe, is developed a little farther than the one who opens his mouth for any approaching object. In similar ways the child's reactions are studied, until by elimination and accumulation the examiner can arrive at an approximate level of functioning, namely: his responses may be more mature than those of a two-month-old but less mature than those of a six-month-old. He probably may have reached the developmental level of a four-month-old child.

This is an example only of the range at which one may arrive. This description of approaches is only a sampling of those which have been found helpful in evaluating defective cerebral palsied children.

Among the visual difficulties most frequently found in cerebral palsied children, the visuo-motor are perhaps most discussed. These are actually not due to visual impairment. It is not a perceptual difficulty primarily or at all in some cases but an inability to correctly execute a motion with his hand which his mind and his eyes are able to anticipate. It must be emphasized that this is not due to the motor handicap. A child with this visuo-motor difficulty may have one or two uninvolved hands and yet he cannot copy a square or a diamond. He experiences a difficulty similar to the one we would find if we tried to draw by observing our writing hand only in a mirror. He will try several times, immediately recognizing his failure as such. Some children will finally use devices to solve their difficulty such as using the shape of the paper as a guide or as drawing each line separately. If this difficulty is suspected, experimental use of other material can confirm the finding. Design blocks or mosaic blocks may be used and it can be observed whether the child has the same difficulty in the attempt to line up these blocks in a requested order. Teaching such a child practice with blocks of this type helps him to learn to circumvent his specific difficulty. Reduced visual acuity can be recognized by the child's behavior all through an interview. If he brings his eyes very close to the material or the material close to the eyes, if he squints frequently, if he fails to spot material when it is not directly in midline, or, as described earlier, if he fails visual items while seemingly able to succeed on the sound blocks, his vision must be questioned and a medical investigation should be suggested before any conclusive results can be obtained. In a similar way the child whose optic nerve has been affected by the original cause of his condition, and who has only peripheral vision left, can be observed by his behavior during the test. He may be able to find material placed to far left or right while ignoring the material in midline; he may turn his head to the side and look out of the corner of his eyes; he may move his head up and down or from left to right in an effort to catch a glimpse of the offered material; he may spot a detail within the whole picture and not even see the picture as a whole. Any response of the type makes the examiner suspect the child's difficulty and again a medical investigation of the vision is indicated.

It is different with a child whose difficulty may be ataxic vision. Here the acuity may be normal, but the effort of concentrating on visual material at a certain distance may bring on dizziness and nausea or result in blurred vision. The author prefers to test such a child by placing the material around the room at his eye level on chairs, window-sills, tables or other suitable spots and then to help the child to walk around, familiarizing him with the material of any given item. Only after this has been done is the child requested to proceed with the test, and his way of indicating his choice will be to draw the supporting adult towards the selected choice of his answer. With some children of this type it has been found necessary to carry on the whole test interview while examiner and child crept on a floor mat toward the material placed around it, leaning against blocks or the legs of chairs.

The child who has an involvement of the eye muscles is usually discovered while the first large concrete objects are presented. Since the examiner sits opposite him, he can observe the child's eye motion and he can spot the child who cannot raise his eyes or drop them, or who can only move his eyes a limited distance horizontally. The child who has a strabismus, the child whose eyes flutter constantly all have their specific difficulties. It becomes the task of the examiner to adjust the placing of the materials to the need of the child, to alternate between visual and auditory items, or to intersperse the test with periods of rest. Experimental verbal items may have to be substituted in the most severe cases. The child whose head cannot be still long enough to focus on the material may have to be helped physically by cradling his head against a pillow or against the adult's shoulder. The experienced examiner, who conveys to the child his casual and comradely acceptance of his predicament, can usually put such a child at his ease and so help him to accept necessary assistance.

The child who comes to an interview and is discovered to be inaccessible to human speech sounds presents perhaps one of the most difficult propositions. Here it becomes a process of elimination and experimentation to determine what may be the reason. Frequently the developmental history has to be investigated and the child's behavior with the family has to be observed. A prolonged warming-up period is often helpful in giving clues to the nature of the difficulty, toys being placed before the child and his reaction and use of them being observed. The author usually tries to eliminate first the possibility of deafness. A bell is sounded while the child is not looking and his reaction noted. Any loud noise, the dropping of blocks, knocking on the table while the child does not look, clapping of hands behind his back are devices to discover whether real deafness may be present. Stamping on the floor to test whether he can feel the vibration is tried next. If deafness is present and no other complications are detected, the items are presented and their presentation is adapted to the deaf child. He can be handed the concrete objects and encouraged to put them to their proper uses either on himself, the doll, or the examiner. The same is done with the pictures of objects. Once rapport is established and the child comprehends the reaction expected of him the rest of the items can be given by signs and examples. The author has given such children a spoon when showing the two pictures of contrasting activities and the child who comprehends holds the spoon against the picture of the eating children. To check the validity of this the child can be given a little piece of colored (not white) material. Again the child who understands the picture will place the material over the children in their beds. White material might be mistakenly used as a tablecloth in the other picture. The matching of material can be demonstrated nonverbally and the testing can then proceed until the child's level is established. With the two landscape scenes the author uses a toy Santa Claus and leaves it to the child to place him on the winter scene. If he can do so, he shows fairly conclusively that he recognizes the season.

Pitch deafness and intermittent deafness are sometimes revealed by the description of the parents, who in such cases frequently state that, "Sometimes he minds and sometimes he ignores us completely." Sometimes, but by no means always, these children have developed a beginning of reading of lips and the gestures most of us unconsciously use to emphasize our speech. Sometimes one suspects pitch deafness by the child's own omission of certain consonants in his speech. The use of the various means of making noise will reveal the nature of the deafness to a degree sufficient for beginning the test. One proceeds as with a deaf child. The teaching of such a child will then present problems other than those met in teaching deaf children and auditory testing should be undertaken before any program is planned.

The child who is "living in a world of his own," who ignores the conversation of his parents, of the examiner but who appears to hear music, noises, the sound blocks, the bell, and who on being given the opportunity uses toys quite constructively and meaningfully may be suffering from any of the forms of aphasia or diphasia, partial or complete, sensory or motor. Again a process of experimentation and elimination is necessary to find the nature of the difficulty. Very likely an overlapping of causes can be found here, where parents may not have suspected the nature of the difficulty and where the child's learning may have been a haphazard catching of such orientation in the environment as any one of us would be capable of in a foreign country, where no one spoke his language. Since in these children the involvement exists from birth, no previous normal orientation can have taken place. The examiner must take into account these considerations in trying to find the developmental level of such a child. Many of the approaches described for deaf children and for the very concrete child and for retarded children can be used here. Once rapport is found the testing can often proceed quite well by using gestures to indicate requests, by showing the process necessary, by using parallel items, and by other means which the examiner develops in contact with any given child. The author has on occasion found such a child overjoyed when he discovered that here was an adult who tried to penetrate into his shut-off world. Special care must be used where only a partial aphasia exists. Such a child may be found to be slow or even incapable of responding when asked for the objects or pictures by name, while he quickly responds when they are described in terms of use. This response should make one alert to the possibility of the involvement. For the teaching of these children the help of speech pathologists must be sought. A neurological examination should precede the attempt to teach these children. The child who does not understand or speak English is another problem. Where the mother cannot be used or trusted as an interpreter, the author proceeds as in testing deaf children. Overlooking nonfamiliarity with English in a child who cannot speak anyhow, due to the motor involvement, should be eliminated by the experienced examiner in all cases. Even where an English-speaking mother brings the child to the interview, it is sometimes revealed that the child spends much of his time with a non-English-speaking grandparent or other person. Even defensive incorrect statements about this by frightened, anxious parents must be anticipated and evaluated correctly before the test is begun.

Closely related to these problems but of a different nature is the problem of the child with a delay in responding. The author has found these children the most tantalizing problems of all. The most extreme case was that of a child whose response was delayed as much as fifteen to twenty or more minutes, but whose every response was correct. Infinite time, patience, and faith is required to test such a child and practical reasons make it often necessary to break up the interview into several sessions. It is the experience of the author that this problem is met most likely in the child with the type of cerebral palsy described as rigidity, with an etiology of encephalitis. Frequent retests will disclose whether with maturing development the delay becomes shorter. Ultimate limitations or ultimate potentialities are probably not yet observed and described extensively enough to allow for reliable prediction of the development in such extreme cases. For that reason exposure to a maximum of opportunities over a prolonged period of time seems at present to offer the best way to explore the potentialities or limitations. Careful observation of the child's reaction to situations and stimuli as well as an inquiry into his domestic behavior and previous history will give some further information about his probable developmental level.

Various types of behavior deviations are among the most distracting problems met with in testing children, and in brain-injured children such deviations are not infrequent. Knowledge of the possibility of such deviations is necessary if one would test cerebral palsy children, in order to recognize and take into account the difficulties resulting from them. A tendency to perseveration may make it impossible for the child to switch from one type of response to the next or from one type of material to the next. Here an interruption may help such a child to discard one set of expectations and be ready for another one. Giving fair advance warning that now something different will be shown may help another one, alternating motor activities, however incompletely executable, with the usual kind of response, may give a child the pause needed to be ready for another set of response. The truly driven child is recognized fairly easily, even if unable to walk. Drivenness is usually connected with retardation but is not present in every retarded child. It is a quality in addition to the retardation. The experiential learning of such children is handicapped by the quality of drivenness, so that their actual initial potentialities may be higher than their achieved level indicates. Frequently these children are destructive, and often their very drivenness prevents them from responding completely even where comprehension may exist. The behavior is not accessible to psychiatric treatment; it appears that the personality has been damaged in such a child, by the same cause that has damaged the motor areas of the brain. Since it is inconclusive to judge how much of an item the child can perceive in his driven state and since his spontaneous play is characterized by the same quality of drivenness, a combination of probing in his developmental history, his domestic behavior, his observable behavior during the interview are all called upon to make the level of the child's development recognizable. When applying the actual test items, the author proceeds cautiously, placing the material without his reach, using a reserve set of cards where a child has the tendency to throw, tear, chew, or bite the material. A quick presentation is utilized to keep the child's interest so captivated that his driven behavior subsides for short periods. Wherever possible physical restraint can be used, if it can be applied without antagonizing the child or his mother, such as locking him in a standing table for some items, or even tying him in his chair, or backing him between some large pieces of furniture for short periods of activity. In some cases a pretended ignoring of the child and a skillful placing of material in his way of wanderings can be used and the very drivenness sometimes makes it impossible for the child to pass the material without using it. All that is necessary then is to observe what he does with it. Many experimental items have to be kept on hand and used for the testing of such a child, such as form boards, nest of cubes, paper and crayon, blocks, cars, etc. The fact that such children are driven to activity constantly by some inner impulse makes it possible to employ a large range of material which in turn gives information about a good number of sections of behavior. In this way a tentative estimate of his level can be reached. This type of child is most exhausting for the examiner, and usually the difficulty of the child can be spotted by an experienced examiner by the first look at an exhausted mother, who has his care all day long. Flight of ideas and distractibility are not necessarily always present in the same child. It may be possible that what appears as a flight of ideas or a compulsion to talk incessantly and at random may be due to neurological impairment, but the author has not had enough experience with this type of difficulty to be able to do more than recognize it as pathological rather than a behavior problem. Presenting stimuli sharply with a distinct noise, as the sound of a bell or the rapping of the table preceding each new item, quickly turning to the child after ignoring him for a time and simultaneously presenting material, gentle pressure on the child to comply for a minute or even offering him a large wad of chewing gum has sometimes been successful for short periods of cooperation. It is perhaps the problem of drivenness, but limited to one area.

The distractible child can be helped to respond to his best ability if stimuli are cut down to a minimum. The child can be placed so that he faces away from the room perhaps toward a wall. The examiner can sit in back of him or beside him to leave the child completely free to concentrate on nothing but the presented material. Gentle pressure, calm firmness, quiet encouragement often are helpful. The presence of the parent is best avoided in these cases. Sometimes it is necessary to limit the choice of selections for such a child, at least at the beginning of a test, since too many choices distract him and lower his potential response level. Praise and exclamations are best kept to a minimum with such children, since this again distracts them from the tasks. Frequent retesting should be done in these cases. A trial period of teaching in an adjusted environment should be considered a better criterion to estimate potentialities in such children than their response in an initial test interview.

SUMMARY

The reasons for trying to find special tests for cerebral palsied children are described. The requirements these special tests should fulfill are described. Some test items used experimentally are described and their origin explained. The presentation of the items is described. The pragmatical use of the items is described and the fact that they are not yet standardized.

The areas explored by the use of the items are enumerated. The specific problems found in testing cerebral palsied children, independent of those caused by the motor handicap, are enumerated. The problems in detecting unsuspected sensory involvement in motor handicapped children are described.

Ten specific problems met with in testing cerebral palsy children and the approaches used in dealing with them are described.

CONCLUSION

A series of simple items used experimentally and a number of approaches used to reach children who have specific problems in addition to cerebral palsy have served to evaluate the developmental level in mental organization of preschool children handicapped by cerebral palsy.

Chapter 22

Assessment of Cerebral Palsied Children: A Survey of Advances Since 1958

JESSIE FRANCIS-WILLIAMS

F ROM this summary of recent studies, it is clear that children with cerebral palsy differ so much in the range and severity of their handicaps, in the kind of care and management they have experienced, and in their own personal attitude to their handicaps that those who make decisions regarding their future educational treatment must be aware of the many factors that are likely to affect the educability of the child. For this reason it is important to approach the assessment with as much information as possible regarding the range and degree of involvement of each individual child.

The purpose in making an assessment is to evaluate the child's assets and handicaps in order to advise on suitable educational provision.

At the core of our diagnostic procedure, and around which we construct our appraisal of what is possible and most suitable for any particular child, is a formal intellectual assessment insofar as that can be arrived at despite the handicaps to communication which the child may suffer.

TESTING

In order to select suitable tests it is important to be aware with regard to each child of the possibility of hearing loss, visual loss, speech disability and its causes as well as the severity and kind of motor disablement and whether there is any history of epilepsy. If the child is being treated with anticonvulsant drugs, this may be a distorting factor in his test performance. It is important also to remember that perceptual and spatial disabilities occur very frequently in certain kinds of cerebral palsy and that these are not necessarily in keeping with overall intellectual level.

In assessing the child's level of intellectual functioning it is well to

Reprinted by permission, National Association for Mental Health, London. Only Part Two of this article is reproduced. Part One emphasizes the "wide variation and extensiveness of the handicaps suffered by cerebral palsy children" and also reviews the general surveys and the research findings relevant to cerebral palsied children published between 1955 and 1964. On the basis of the review, the second part, reprinted here, is concerned with the influence of the recent findings on the approach to (a) formal intellectual assessment and (b) to advice and guidance regarding educational provision for the child.

have some awareness also of the limitations in life experience that the child may have suffered, partly because of the limitations of movement caused by his motor disability, partly through the intermittent periods of hospitalization, and partly due to limits on normal social learning through association and play with unhandicapped children.

Suitable Tests

The Stanford-Binet Intelligence Scale for Children

Despite the fact that many cerebral palsied children suffer motor handicaps and the deprivation caused by sensory defects and limited opportunities for normal "learning" as well as for social experiences, the Stanford-Binet intelligence scale is still accepted as the most satisfactory overall test for assessing the intelligence level of those cerebral palsied children whose speech can be understood or who can make clear, even though in a most limited way, what their response to questions and tasks is.

Since there are a number of test items in the Stanford-Binet Scale to which the severely handicapped child cannot respond, there has been much controversy regarding the justification for making modifications in the test procedure. Schonell[976] has listed the test items which she felt could justifiably be modified. Katz[569] is also working on a "pointing modification" of Forms L and M of the Stanford-Binet Scales. This is based on an earlier work in which each item of these two forms for Years II to VI inclusive was classified according to the physical ability each required for carrying out the task, i.e., vision, hearing, speech, arm-hand use, sitting, balance, and walking. Allen and Jefferson[20] have made a similar survey of all the items in the 1960 form L-M revision and have published this in the form of a table showing physical abilities necessary and adaptable for each item of the Scale.

In this country the view expressed by the Spastics Society's Subcommittee on Intellectual Assessment[1045] would seem to be the most generally accepted one. "If intelligence test scores are to continue to mean anything, the tests must be given and scored strictly in accordance with the rubric. Should the examiner feel that he would get some additional and helpful data by doing something other than strict administration this should be done apart from the normal test situation . . . and such 'results' should be recorded in a separate comment."

Any modifications should only be made out of a very clear understanding of the underlying purpose of the test. Dunsdon's[288] section on Assessing the Intelligence of C.P. Children in her book on *The Educability of Cerebral Palsied Children* still remains one of the most useful accounts of modifications valid in using the Binet.

The Wechsler Intelligence Scale for Children

This is of more limited usefulness as an overall test of general intelligence for cerebral palsied children since the Performance Scale has so many timed tests in which a child with a motor handicap and poor motor co-ordination inevitably scores badly. The Block Designs and Object Assembly Subtests present serious difficulties to children with spatial and perceptual problems such as are experienced by many hemiplegic spastics. While this test gives much useful additional information regarding a child's functioning, it is not as suitable an all-round tool of assessment as is the Stanford-Binet.

Since the aim in testing a cerebral palsied child is to assess those of his assets and disabilities that will be a guide to the best educational provision for the child, the real value of testing is not to produce an I.Q. figure but to chart, as it were, the child's intellectual abilities in order to get some guide to the child's level of functioning at the period when the assessment is made. For this reason, it is often helpful to supplement the standardized test chosen, with tests that give the child an opportunity to demonstrate his abilities through other media.

When a child is so heavily handicapped that he clearly cannot do himself justice in the Stanford-Binet test, tests to which the child can respond by eye-pointing or yes-no cues can be used. It should be remembered that this is a very limited type of testing and the results on a single test interview should not be relied on to decide the long-term educational provision for any child.

Supplementary Tests

TESTS OF VOCABULARY and verbal concept formation in which the child's comprehension of the meaning of a word or phrase can be demonstrated by pointing or otherwise indicating his choice of a picture. These are mostly American tests, the best known being the Ammons Full Range Picture Vocabulary Test (1948), the Peabody Picture Vocabulary Test by Dunn[291, 293] and the California Picture Information Test.[616] Of these the Peabody Picture Vocabulary Test has so far proved to be the most useful, particularly as it was designed specifically to be used with the cerebral palsied in which if an oral or pointing response is not possible the examiner may point to each of the four alternatives on each plate and elicit a Yes or No response by a head shake or even a pre-arranged coded message for Yes and No. Because this is an American test, a number of American words are not familiar to English children. An English version has now been prepared and standardized in collaboration with the original author.

The California Picture Information Test is still in the experimental stages and there is little research on its usefulness reported to date. The test, however, holds promise as a tool for assessment of young children. It is based on the principle of picture-word association. Four pictures are pasted on the right half of each page and a key picture is in the center of the left half of each page. The child has to identify one of the four pictures as belonging with the key picture. For example, the first page depicts a clock, a tire, a shirt, and a pair of shoes. The key picture on the left half of the page is a car. The child should choose the tire as belonging with the car. The pictures are brightly colored and of interest to young children. As a picture-verbal test for children between two and six years it would seem to be useful.

COLUMBIA MENTAL MATURITY SCALE. When a child is heavily handicapped and gesture and eye pointing are the only means available to him of indicating responses, this test can provide a valuable supplementary test for children ranging in mental age between 3 years 5 months to 13 years 11 months. This is a test of reasoning ability in which the child is presented with a series of cards on each of which are pictures of objects or variously colored shapes and forms, all but one of which are tied together by a principle of grouping. The task is to select the one picture on each card that "does not belong" with the others. The task becomes progressively more difficult requiring a higher level of abstraction for the solution of the problem.

There are one hundred cards in all and many examiners find that the test tends to become tiring and tedious particularly to children with cerebral damage many of whom have a short attention span and are quickly fatiguable.

Untestable Children

The tests described above assume that it is possible to make some assessment of the child's level of functioning even though the result must be regarded as a provisional or first estimate. Psychologists experienced in assessing children with cerebral palsy find that 10 per cent to 15 per cent of them cannot be assessed with any degree of certainty, even using the additional information that can be gained from scales that require neither articulate speech nor motor manipulation.

The value of re-assessment has become greatly recognized during recent years. Very frequently it has been found that much can be learned about the child's possible educability by observation of his progressive development from the time of one careful assessment to the next. In the early years, an assessment at six-month intervals is desirable.

Assessment Centers

For those children whose level of educability or training is uncertain, the Spastics Society has set up Assessment Centers where a child can live for some six months having requisite therapies and teaching under conditions where it is possible to make a more leisurely and consequently more reliable assessment of the child's educational potential. Unfortunately it is only possible as yet to offer this kind of assessment in a residential center. There is much need for day centers such as are described by Sheridan[989] and Williams.[1120] Many voluntary Spastic Day Centers have nursery groups which offer something of the quality of a constructive and useful assessment period in which their response to therapy and the stimulation of nursery play in a group under a good teacher throws light on the children's condition and makes possible sensible short-term planning for further education and treatment. In these conditions a great deal about the child's developmental progress can be learned from regular periodic reassessments.

Special Difficulties in the Assessment of Young Cerebral Palsied Children

Preschool scales for normal children now give a reasonable indication of a child's present level of functioning but the predictive value of tests given to young children is by no means established. Various reasons have been advanced to explain their poor predictiveness. Tests of young children measure different groups of functions at successive age levels. Various aspects of developmental behaviour are all facets of total mental growth but although these functions all contribute to what we understand as intelligent behaviour, they are really a series of developing functions each growing out of a previously matured behaviour pattern. During the early years even normal infants and young children vary widely in their rates of growth in different areas of development.

Most scales for the assessment of young children depend heavily on motor skills and there is evidence from long-term follow-up studies that while such tests provide a useful indication of a young child's level of functioning at the time of testing, they are not necessarily predictive of mental capacity later.[483] Illingworth,[507, 510] however, claims that it is possible to pick out the severely mentally subnormal child with considerable predictive accuracy in the first year. We do not know with certainty how the kinds of skills measurable in a young child relate to the skills needed later for formal learning in a normal school situation. Nor do we know how widely a normally functioning young child can deviate in specific areas of development.

Griffiths Scale

In clinical assessment of the development of infants up to 24 months of age, it is unwise to give a global developmental quotient. In the Griffiths Scale, at present the only infant scale standardized on English children, the items are divided into five subscales: locomotion, personal-social, hearing and speech, eye and hand, and performance. The results can be presented in the form of a profile and the total as a global developmental score or "general quotient." The presentation of a profile of areas of development is useful but where there is wide variability in a young child's areas of development an overall general developmental quotient can be virtually meaningless and in general it is better in presenting the results of an assessment to follow Illingworth's[509] advice that it is unwise to attempt to give an accurate developmental quotient but more meaningful to give a qualitative assessment of the child's various areas of development in relation to the average.

However well constructed the test, the accuracy of its measurement depends on the experience and skill of the person using it. This is particularly true of testing young children who have not yet made the big break with home into the world of school. When an infant is being assessed, the mother or person caring for the child as mother substitute should always be present. The examiner has to depend to some extent on the mother's report but apart from what the mother actually tells, a great deal can be learned from observing the mother and baby together.

Even some older preschool children cannot bear to be separated from their mother for an interview period with a comparative stranger. When this is so the mother should always be allowed to remain. Provided that the mother can understand that she should not actively help the child or interfere in the actual test procedure, the presence of the mother can be a positive asset not only in giving the child emotional support but in the picture that she presents of her attitude to the child, her way of handling him, and her capacity to accept him as he is. Young children are much more at the mercy of their inner fantasies and their emotional mood than are school-age children. They are also much more totally affected by their state of well-being at the time of testing.

All the difficulties inherent in testing infants and young children are exaggerated in the testing of handicapped babies and young children. These children frequently present a wide scatter in their level of abilities. They are generally more anxious, more quickly fatiguable, and their attention span is often much shorter than is that of an unhandicapped young child. For these reasons we must be prepared to discontinue a test if necessary and complete it at another time.

Over and above these difficulties, it is not easy to assess the full extent

of the damage these children have suffered and how much what remains
to them can be used to develop new patterns of learning. This is made
more difficult by the fact that in young children there has been little time
to assess the effects of environment and of physical and emotional nurture.
In choice and use of tests with these children, therefore, as much as possible should be known about the developmental history, the health record, results of medical and neurological examinations and the attitude of
the parents to the child, the emotional climate of his home, and the opportunities for intellectual stimulation. In the case of handicapped young
children the presence of the mother during the test can be a wholly positive asset. By observing the mother and child together a great deal can be
learned about the emotional quality of the mother-child relationship, about
the mother's capacity to accept the child's handicap and the ways in which
she is able and willing to bring to the child the experiences through which,
by his own exploration, an unhandicapped child learns and grows.

It is frequently the case that the mother provides a bridge of communication between the examiner and the child when the child's speech is
poor or when the child is too afraid at first to take instruction from a
stranger. Because, even from early infancy, the grossly handicapped child
shows such widely deviant rates of development, an overall developmental
quotient can be extremely misleading. Illingworth's comments[509] on the
assessment of intellectual potential in a child with physical or sensory
handicaps are relevant here. It is most useful, therefore, to make a careful assessment of all the significant aspects of development and follow this
up with regular testing at fairly frequent intervals over a period of time in
which careful comparisons of achievement from one test to the next can
be made.

No decision regarding placement or school provision should be made
on the basis of the results of a single test especially where the child has
severe and special kinds of handicaps. Over and above the qualitative
assessments of actual functioning the overall estimate of the child's potential can be increased in value if account is taken of all the aspects of behavior that can be observed in an interview situation where the child and
mother have been seen together. Such factors as the child's dependence
on the mother, his positive attempts to overcome or seek to find a way round
his handicaps, his courage in tolerance of frustration are all important
guides to our judgment regarding the kind of educational provision or
placement that would be best for a particular child.

Clinical Approach to Assessment

For those who are concerned to evaluate the intellectual potential of
cerebrally handicapped children, these two books would merit careful

study. In *Development Potential of Preschool Children* Haeussermann[428] published an account of some twenty-five years' experience in daily work with children handicapped by cerebral palsy. She describes her own assessment procedure as an "educational evaluation" on the results of which she constructs an inventory of developmental levels. For those who are concerned to assess the educational potential of young cerebral palsy children this book makes rewarding reading. *Psychological Appraisal of Children with Cerebral Defects* by Meyer Taylor[1055] presents also a clinical approach to assessment which is based on a long period of work in the Children's Hospital, Boston, in close association with Dr. Bronson Crothers and Dr. Richmond Paine. This book is an adjunct to the follow-up study presented in *The Natural History of Cerebral Palsy* by Bronson Crothers and Richmond Paine. In it the author makes a very outstanding contribution to the understanding of the behaviour and mental development of children with various cerebral defects. Dr. Taylor has worked in the neurological division of the Children's Hospital in Boston since 1943, when she succeeded Elizabeth Lord who up to her death had worked closely with Dr. Bronson Crothers. Together they established a pattern for the "appraisal" of cerebral palsied children, a pattern which Dr. Taylor has continued to follow while at the same time enriching it with her own extensive experience.

In this book she shows how a meaningful and reliable "appraisal" of a child by an experienced clinician can result from combining information obtained from many sources. The author demonstrates the great skill with which she combines test items that lend themselves to objective and quantifiable treatment with others that depend on psychological experience and intuition.

In Part I of this book she describes among others, seven case portraits of children suffering from fairly representative cerebral conditions dating from birth or before. "Appraisals" of these children are based on psychological interviews at 15 months, 4, 7, and 12 years. The portraits of these children are vivid and illuminating. They show how limited and indeed often misleading global I.Q. ratings in their rigid sense can be.

In Part II of the book the author describes very clearly the techniques of assessment she herself has found useful. She describes in detail the varied test materials that she uses and how she presents them, and she points out the significance of the various responses. Out of the wideness of her knowledge and years of experience of child development, Dr. Taylor brings to the task of appraisal a flexibilty in her approach to each individual child that makes possible a reasonably accurate assessment of the ability even of the so-called untestable child. Those who are concerned to make as accurate an assessment as possible of a cerebral palsied child can learn much from this book, particularly in the insights into the course of development of these very deviant children.

APPRAISAL

The purpose of formal testing is to make as accurately as is possible an assessment of the child's level of intellectual functioning at the time of testing in order to advise on suitable educational placement for the child. There are no tests standardized on a population of physically handicapped children. Indeed it would be virtually impossible to construct a test for cerebral palsied children since the range and severity of their handicaps is so varied. Although there are tests standardized on deaf children and on children with educationally defective vision, testing a cerebral palsied deaf child or child with severe visual impairment is complicated by the fact that he has also motor disabilities of varying kind and severity. It is important, therefore, in testing a cerebral palsied child to choose a test which is most suited to giving him an opportunity to demonstrate his potential intellectual ability. Having done this it is important not to take liberties with the standard procedure nor to present a result based on modifications of the test. Nevertheless in making a final appraisal of the child's situation there are many considerations which should be borne in mind in arriving at decisions regarding educational guidance.

It is important to remember that when a child is prevented by physical handicaps such as difficulties in articulation, in motor manipulation, and control as well as possible impairment of vision and hearing, from demonstrating what he can understand and do, the intelligence measurable by tests may well contrast considerably with his true potential. In this respect the value of regular periodic reassessments is inestimable. A great deal can be learned from a child's response to treatment and to suitable teaching as well as to opportunities for extended experience.

It is not uncommon for a child who is at first unassessible in view of the severity of his handicaps to be able to respond better to a formal test situation as he becomes more physically controlled and more articulate as a result of treatment. Regarding the value of periodic reassessments, Dr. Sheridan[989] says "At least so far as severely handicapped children under eight years are concerned, experience has taught me that it is unwise to assume that a child's capacity, let alone his potentiality, can be reliably measured in terms of I.Q. although it is feasible to assess and even predict in broad terms. I have also learned that in planning treatment and training for these young children we should resist the temptation to look too far ahead but rather concentrate on accurately determining their present levels of functioning and then work steadily towards achieving the next developmental stepping-stone."

In making an appraisal of the child's condition we need to have some awareness of the nature of his physical handicap because the different subtypes of cerebral palsy—athetosis, spasticity, etc.—present differing problems of effective movement for the child and also differ from one another in their effects on problems of learning. We need to be aware also of the specific disabilities such as difficulties in visuo-spatial perception not necessarily in keeping with general intelligence but which can distort early learning patterns and make it difficult for the child to learn to read and understand numbers. It is also useful to know to what extent the child's opportunities to learn have been limited by lack of normal experience of the world around him or by breaks in schooling by time off for speech and physio-therapy or long or frequent periods in hospital.

By observing a child's response to a standardized test situation, much can be learned that will add to the value of a total appraisal of the child and his situation. Children vary greatly in their ways of dealing with the problems created for them by their handicaps. It is generally the case that the more intelligent the child, the more readily can he respond to and cooperate in treatment. An intelligent child is usually also more able to compensate for and circumvent his sensory and motor disabilities.

Finally it is important to observe the child's assets and defects in the context of a total appraisal of the personality and emotional stability of the particular child in order to judge what can be reasonably expected of him at that particular stage of his growth and development.

Chapter 23

Psychological Evaluation
of Blind Children

BARBARA BATEMAN

MANY of the major issues confronting the psychologist in the evaluation of blind children are essentially the same as those he faces in
diagnostic work with any and all exceptional children. One of the first
issues he must deal with concerns the use he wishes to make of normative
data; or, in other words, from what frame of reference or vantage point
is he assessing the blind child? Is he concerned with how well the blind
child functions compared to sighted children? If so, in what areas of behavior is this question meaningful? Is he concerned with how the child
compares with other blind children? If so, how does he weigh age at onset of blindness, degree of remaining vision, previous educational experiences, home environment, etc.? Is he interested in estimating how well
the child might be functioning if he weren't blind? Is he concerned with
some assessment of manifest intelligence in contrast to potential intelligence?

There are no easy answers, no global answers, to these questions. But
the examining psychologist must be aware of these and other possible
approaches to his diagnostic procedures. The meaningfulness of the data
he obtains will depend on the extent to which he makes clear the frame
of reference he is using. He may, of course, use several simultaneously.
This problem in psychological diagnosis is one which always confronts
us with children who are, as a given, substantially different from the sample on which our normative data are obtained. But the obvious answer of
obtaining norms for each group of exceptional children falls short of adequacy for several reasons. A primary consideration is that many times the
psychologist's purpose in diagnosis is to examine the possibility of the exceptional child being able to operate among nonhandicapped children. A
further problem in using separate norms, especially for blind children, is
that it implies a homogeneity of handicapped groups which does not in
fact exist.

Once the frame of reference, or the purpose of testing, has been clearly

---

Reprinted from the *New Outlook for the Blind*, 59:193-196, June, 1965.

established, the examiner is then bound to be confronted with problems in test administration. He must address himself to two more somewhat difficult questions. He must ask "How meaningful is it to administer, in unmodified form, an item which isn't entirely suitable or relevant for a blind child?" On the other hand, "How appropriate is it to modify an item without such modification being explicitly in line with standardized procedure?"

The problems posed so far suggest that total reliance on standardized procedures is perhaps impossible and/or foolhardy. But the alternative of clinical interpretation and informal testing and observational techniques should be based on "built-in" standards for blind children's behavior.

And, if we are to be quite frank and realistic, how many school psychologists have had the extensive experience with blind children necessary for the development of such an internalized comparator? Worse yet, such a comparator must be continually revised and sharpened by feedback on the accuracy of our hunches and predictions. Seldom do we get adequate feedback on our reports of routine diagnoses and prognoses, let alone on a large sample of blind children.

In short, heavy reliance on clinical judgment alone does not seem much more feasible than does mechanical applications of standardized measures. Regardless of what diagnostic approaches and procedures we adopt and the success with which we answer the questions posed so far, we are still faced with one more difficulty.

The assessment of cognitive processes and products is a challenging task under the best of conditions. Many of our instruments and judgments are simultaneously relatively insensitive to variables we wish to tap and too sensitive to extraneous variables. Now, when we add not just one, but two or three confounding variables—sensory deprivation, inadequate or unusual opportunities for learning, and emotional smothering or deprivation—our job seems almost overwhelming.

In short, the problems in psychological evaluation of blind children are many and complex. Final answers have we none. However, the following tentative guidelines are suggested as possible means of approaching and minimizing, if not solving, some of the problems raised.

Standardized tests which have been designed or modified for use with the blind are much more abundant than is often realized. Lende's *Books About the Blind*[641] lists over 120 articles dealing with such standardized tests. If the compilation were brought up to date it would perhaps double. The tests which have been used with the blind include projective techniques, achievement tests, and interest inventories in addition to intelligence and aptitude tests. Most of the literature, however, deals with the use of these tests with groups of blind subjects rather than in individual diagnosis. The criticism of this group research is also voluminous and points out the problems of norms, item appropriateness, etc.

But the fact remains that there are many standardized tests which can be used with blind persons, especially beyond the early school ages. Among the tests currently widely used and recommended for blind children are the Interim Hayes-Binet Intelligence Test, WISC Verbal Scale, Merrill Palmer Scale of Mental Tests, the Maxfield-Buchholz Scale of Social Competence (preschool blind), the Guess Who Game, Vineland Social Maturity Scale, and the Emotional Factors Inventory (age thirteen and up).

A possible addition to this list in future years will be the auditory–vocal channel subtests of the Illinois Test of Psycholinguistic Abilities (ITPA). The norms extend from age 2-6 through 9-10 years. Language development of blind children is frequently an area which the psychologist must examine. The ITPA appears to be a promising instrument in determining both level of language behavior and patterns of strengths and weaknesses.

However useful some standardized tests may be for certain purposes with some children, it would seem desirable to view such tests only as launching pads from which the diagnostic flight may begin. One guideline in the use of standardized uses is derived from the concept of diagnosis *for* the purposes of decision-making, recommending remedial or educational procedures, or answering specific questions. This concept of diagnosis is actually very different from the notion of diagnosis as classification or naming. It is easy enough to conclude a report of formal or informal testing with a label such as "educationally blind," or "low average intelligence," or "eligible for placement as multiply handicapped." More sophisticated clinical powers are required to make such recommendations and prognoses as "readiness training for braille should include work on tactile spatial orientation, for which a raised version of Frostig's spatial relations materials is suggested," or "performance on the Hayes-Binet and the ITPA auditory–vocal association indicate that auditory closure is inadequate and exercises in riddles, rhyming, and categorization are recommended," or "while subject is technically eligible for multiply handicapped, the problems in auditory comprehension (resembling receptive aphasia) are probably remediable and therefore intensive work in noise recognition, sound localization, noise comparisons, following simple two-word commands, etc., is recommended. After such work is successfully completed, placement in a program for visually handicapped will probably be appropriate."

If the psychologist, in cooperation with parents, school personnel, or other professionals can obtain clear questions to be answered rather than the typically general and broad referrals, his job will be clarified and the selection of evaluative procedures simplified. For example, instead of seeing a six-year-old blind child to make an "educational prognosis," a series of specific diagnostic questions are posed, e.g., "Are his attention span, his auditory comprehension, etc., adequate to enable him to function in a first grade classroom?" "Is his tactual discrimination adequate for beginning braille?" "Does he use his hands adequately in exploring new objects?" "Does he localize and remember sounds and objects?" "Are his self-help skills in toileting, dressing and eating sufficient to handle first grade demands?" "Is his neighborhood school or local district able to provide the necessary special education services?"

Responsiveness to teaching is often more important than a blind child's present level of functioning. This is especially true in the area of mobility, where the youngster may have been grossly restricted and overprotected. Some children will not walk without tangible support or hand-holding. Occasionally, in a few minutes, the psychologist can shape this behavior substantially by using a taut rope (for support) which is gradually slackened.

Auditory receptive language can sometimes be assessed, even in the absence of expressive vocal language, by asking the child simple questions of high interest to him. Candy bars or soda pop, while not found in Hoyle's rules of testing, may be useful not only in checking auditory comprehension but also sound localization.

To sum up so far, standardized as well as informal assessment techniques form the launching pad from which the diagnostic-treatment flight begins. If we keep in mind that evaluation must go beyond a mere classifying or labelling and answer questions with specific recommendations, then the formulation of these specific questions will lead almost automatically to a proper selection of testing procedures. The information obtained from these measures can then be translated into educational procedures recommended for maximum development.

This concept of evaluation for the purpose of recommending procedures to maximize development is based on the underlying notion of the educability of the exceptional child. More and more evidence is accumulating which underscores the importance of recognizing that cognitive development is inextricably dependent upon and related to experience. If we err, and err we must occasionally, we must do so on the side of being willing to explore the possible beneficial effects of a stimulating environment in overcoming earlier deprivation.

In the context of environmental and sensory deprivation, it is well to briefly examine the continuum of the sighted world's perceptions of the limitations inherent in blindness. The extremes are perhaps exemplified by blindness seen as a minor annoyance and hindrance to unencumbered mobility versus blindness seen as the greatest deprivation, sensory and emotional, that can befall man. While psychiatric and psychoanalytic literature has had a heyday with speculations about blindness perceived as punishment for sin or as castration, etc., most educators prefer to emphasize that we are dealing with a *child* who does not see. It is very possible to impose limitations beyond those of loss of vision. The story is told of the young boy who wanted his blind father to go horseback riding. When the father protested that he couldn't because he was blind, the child countered "But, Daddy, the *horse* isn't!" All psychologists who evaluate blind children should examine their own attitudes toward expectations for the blind. Extreme positions of either denying the real limitations or of imposing unreal and unnecessary restrictions can bias the interpretation of a child's behavior.

One of the particular problems with which psychologists might be asked to deal is that of whether a visually handicapped child should be educationally classed as blind or partially seeing. In an ideal situation, the ophthalmologist and optometrist can help translate the child's visual functioning into an educational recommendation. But occasionally the data given to the school is limited to a Snellen notation of 20/200 in each eye, or "counts fingers at five feet," etc. One eye specialist's report was seen recently which indicated that the child's visual acuity could not be determined and therefore he should "be put in the front row or in the blind school." This kind of information is not too helpful in deciding whether a child should be taught braille or print reading. How should the psychologist proceed? Every effort, of course, should be made to obtain all pertinent medical information.

But the correlation between functional vision and visual acuity is far from perfect and these are cases where the child must be given an opportunity to answer the question for us by a trial period with print. He can also be a valuable guide in selecting type size, lighting conditions, and reading posture. Barraga[68] provides convincing evidence that specific training significantly increased the level of visual functioning of blind children, although acuity was unchanged. This study should perhaps become required reading for those professionally concerned with the legally blind child who is "borderline" educationally blind.

Whatever else blindness may or may not limit, it does hinder mobility. Thus willingness and ability to explore the environment often become of special interest. A few years ago a psychologist who specializes in the diagnosis of language disorders was observed evaluating a nonspeaking four-year-old blind child. The child was not the least interested in the red plastic cars offered to him but was highly intrigued by the radiator gurglings which he located immediately. Several times he left the too-large chair in which he had been placed in front of the pegboard and went swiftly and surely to his mother who was on the far side of the unfamiliar room. He thoroughly and systematically explored (orally, manually, and auditorily) several objects which he encountered in his unauthorized roamings around the room. However, the combination of his lack of language and his refusal to play the planned games (actually he appeared very undisciplined) totally outweighed his mobility and explorative skills in the psychologists' judgment and he was classified as severely mentally retarded.

Language problems are not infrequent in young blind children. Sometimes speech has not developed by the age of three or four. Occasionally excessive echolalia or other deviant verbal patterns (e.g., improper pronoun usage) associated with autistic behavior are reported. The fact that these language disorders perhaps occur more frequently in blind than in seeing youngsters suggests interesting etiological speculations. The implications of this greater incidence of language disorders (if thoroughly substantiated) could conceivably point either toward parental attitudes or toward physical factors as the etiological culprits. But neither line would be of immediate use to the psychologist who is attempting, hopefully, to recommend procedures for developing language rather than settling for a diagnosis of "delayed language development" or "inadequate language with some autistic-like characteristics." Some evidence[303] suggests that presence of speech by the age of five is a fairly good prognostication of future language development. Comprehension of the spoken word and the presence of any consistent, meaningful use of vocalization should certainly suggest that a trial period of specific language training is in order before a definite prognosis is attempted. The blind child's need and opportunity for expressive language in the home must be considered relevant.

Questions of where a blind child should be educated are often heard, perhaps even more frequently now that public schools are providing local programs for half the blind children of school age in this country. Years ago, in its *Pinebrook Report,* the American Foundation for the Blind outlined its position: namely, that residential schools, resource rooms, and itinerant teacher services all have necessary roles to play and that none will completely replace another. This position is as valid as ever and suggests to the psychologist that the problem is not one of residential school versus public school but rather one of which facility can best serve the individual blind child. Often the desirability of living at home or of being away from home will be a major consideration. In cases of borderline vision, the tendency found by Jones[559] for such children in residential schools to be braille readers and those in public schools to be print readers should be weighed.

Perhaps the process of evaluating a blind child can be schematically presented as shown in Table 23-1.

TABLE 23-1

EVALUATION OF BLIND CHILD

1 Test and Observation Data	2 Psychological Evaluation	3 Decision-Making or Recommendations

Language
  Speech present
  Speech echolalic
  Auditory comprehension
  Auditory memory
  Grammar and syntax
  And others
Mobility
  Motor coordination
  Strength
  Attitude toward mobility
  Sound localization
  And others
Tactile Sensitivity
  Discrimination
  Recognition
  Memory
  Attitude toward exploration
	1. Determination of area concern (Column 3). Exactly *what* is to be evaluated and for what purpose?
	2. Choosing best instruments and techniques available (Column 1) in order to check the *relevant* areas of function.
	3. Properly interpreting the data obtained in step 2, in order to make appropriate recommendations.
		Type of nursery school
		School readiness
		Speech correction
		Braille vs print
		Continuance in public school
		Placement as multiply handicapped
		Removal from home
		Parent counseling
		Need for travel training
		[*Note:* These are illustrative only.]

The reader will notice an absence of emphasis on global measures such as I.Q. and, instead, a concentration on specific abilities. This represents a bias, but one which is advocated on the grounds that it is practical. The bias is seen to extend to the concept that, above all, psychological evaluation of blind children "ought" to be practical, i.e., ought to lead to more definite action and procedures than mere classification or determination of eligibility for program *x* or *y*. The teacher, parent, speech correctionist, or whoever else might be concerned should know more about *what to do* with or for the child after the psychological evaluation than they knew before.

Chapter 24

Diagnostic Evaluation and
Recommendations for Placement

ROBERT FRISINA

THE organizers of this conference recognized the fundamental issue before us as conferees when they concluded that "Hearing impaired children will continue to be placed in public school programs with or without the development of guidelines and superior programs for these children."

The message emanating from the results of any comprehensive analysis of existing programs on a national scale will come as no surprise to those of us present. Unanimity regarding a general dissatisfaction with program organization and implementation on a nationwide basis probably exists among us. Most of us would agree, too, that exemplary programs exist in various spots around the country. But most important for us is that we would probably be unanimous in our recognition that much needs to be done if all hearing impaired youngsters are to be assured maximum educational opportunities.

DIAGNOSTIC EVALUATIONS

Diagnostic evaluations must lead somewhere if they are to be useful to an individual, and in order to lead somewhere, varietal systems of treatment must be available. Although much can be said regarding medical and psychologic treatment programs, my focus here is on the educational alternatives needed for hearing impaired children. The diagnostic evaluation phase, as might be expressed in the jargon of the electronic world in which we are immersed, requires consideration of at least three human functions: The Code for Input, The Code for Storage, and The Code for Retrieval.

Code for Input

The term, *Code for Input*, refers to information *available* for input. More specifically, it refers to information available *outside* the individual. The amount and kind of stimulation provided the individual, together with his personal abilities to deal with these sensory stimulations, will determine in large measure the forms in which his overall behavior will be shaped. Kids

Reprinted from *The Volta Review*, 69:436-442, September, 1967.

from slums are shaped differently from children growing up on farms or children reared in suburbia. The characteristics of the verbal world in which these youngsters are reared are not the same; the value systems generated within these different communities are not the same; information, as to content and form, available among these groups is not the same. In short, environmental opportunities differ among individuals. The results and effects of hearing impairment superimposed upon these differences will demand, therefore, multiple educational approaches.

Evaluation of the family and home, the understanding of the socioeconomic conditions of the family, the appraisal of values and goals established within the family, and an understanding of the amount and kinds of exposure the hearing impaired child has within and outside the family— these are among the significant variables with which we must deal but often glibly subsume under the term, *the whole child*.

Knowledge, skills, and measurement techniques derived from efforts in the behavioral sciences are required for the assessment of the facet of the hearing impaired child I have chosen to call "information available for input." The labels most frequently attached to the professional members of the evaluation team who contribute to an understanding of this important area include psychiatrist, clinical psychologist, linguist, sociologist, educator, educator of the deaf, social worker, audiologist, and speech pathologist. Others will become more prevalent as information in the behavioral sciences is reorganized as a result of new information which is growing at an exponential rate.

In this aspect of Code for Input, dealing with environmental influences, one could rank on a 1-to-4 scale, for example, the relative integrity and healthiness of a hearing impaired child's family life. In the case of a low socioeconomic, hearing impaired child whose parents are separated, whose mother is on relief and must care for five other children, whose mother is illiterate and not particularly interested nor capable of doing anything extra for him, the Code for Input-Environmental would be ranked as a 4. With a reasonable degree of certainty one could conjecture that marked limitations in practice effect in the use of the English language might result, that consistent use of a wearable hearing aid would not occur, that the child could not regularly attend infancy and early childhood education programs, and that few opportunities would be available for interaction with children outside that restricted environment.

At the other end of the scale one would find the child from the upper-middle socioeconomic level, with parents who are educated beyond high school, with parents who relate well with their hearing impaired child and his two siblings, with parents who actively play with him and afford him opportunities to practice the English language, with parents who take him on auto trips to see the airport, his grandparents, his cousins, etc. This case might well rank 1 in the environmental area of Code for Input. More will be said of this in a moment.

The Code for Input also includes the status and integrity of the sense organs. Of critical importance in diagnostic evaluations leading to placement of hearing impaired children is the end organ of hearing. Functionally, this is sometimes referred to as the inner ear or the "hearing" part, as opposed to the "listening" part, of the auditory system.

The physical, biologic, and behavioral sciences have provided fundamental knowledge related to the structure and function of the inner ear and the eighth nerve. On the diagnostic side, the primary evaluation team members required for the clarification of status of the hearing portion of the auditory mechanism, in the case of hearing impaired children, are the otolaryngologist and the clinical audiologist.

On the basis of a comprehensive auditory test battery, it is possible to rank the general integrity of the auditory system, particularly with respect to the inner ear and eighth nerve, on a 1-to-4 scale. The role hearing is likely to play in receiving speech from others, alone or in concert with lip-reading, and the extent to which hearing allows the monitoring of his own voice, might determine where, on the scale from 1 to 4, hearing status falls.

The Code for Input, then, is seen to consist of two very important components. The first relates to the quantity and quality of environmental stimulation available to the individual; the second involves the anatomical and resultant physiologic status of the input transducer we know as the end organ of hearing.

The respective rankings in each of these two components begins to say a great deal about the immediate needs of a given child. A "2-hearer" with a ranking of "1" in the environmental area requires quite different consideration from the child who might be classed as a "2-hearer" and a "4-environmental." I shall return to this hypothetical profile system shortly.

The Code for Storage

Information storage, and particularly verbal information storage, is made possible by the presence of the central nervous system (CNS). It is well known, however, that inner ear breakdown can preclude adequate perception of auditory verbal stimuli. Measurement of end organ function by the otolaryngologist and the audiologist is infinitely more precise and understood at present than how information is stored. Fundamental information concerning CNS function has emerged from widespread efforts in the physical, behavioral, and biologic sciences. Understanding CNS function for educational purposes in hearing impaired children has been performed most often by pediatricians, neurologists, educators, audiologists, psychiatrists, linguists, psychologists, and speech pathologists.

The Code for Retrieval

Analogs for the central nervous system have been proposed in the form of computers and other models. Yet the Code for Storage and Retrieval has not been broken. Again, in the case of Retrieval, as in the case of Storage, we must depend upon the physical, biologic, and behavioral sciences to provide working hypotheses in understanding the retrieval function of the brain. Short-term and long-term memory and abstraction of high level verbal and mathematical systems are aspects of brain function that elude other than indirect descriptions at this time. The professional examiners intimately concerned with the retrieval and output functions of hearing impaired children include such specialists as pediatricians, neurologists, psychologists, teachers of the deaf, speech pathologists, and audiologists.

At this point in time we are weak in our understanding of the interaction among these three major areas, arbitrarily classed as the Code for Input, the Code for Storage, and the Code for Retrieval. To admit our weakness in understanding the full impact of the interaction among these is not to say we are without a sense of direction. Nonetheless the state of the art does vary within and between types of practitioners dealing directly with hearing impaired children. What each attempts to do is assess the status of the individual in somewhat specific areas of function and then predict needs and outcomes.

Unfortunately, in too few instances are his findings actively interrelated with his fellow examiners. The manner in which different examiners in various sections of the country cooperate on a day-to-day basis on behalf of a given patient leaves something to be desired.

There are many reasons for this lack of comprehensive and integrated professional service to hearing impaired children. It is not my purpose to spend time telling you what you already know. Rather it is my function to set us about thinking and hopefully creating ways of improving existing conditions which most of us feel are less than optimal.

MANPOWER NEEDS

In order to increase the effectiveness of diagnostic evaluation services which lead to recommendations for placement, we must recognize that a fundamental problem is that of manpower. The recurrent references to clinical specialties evidenced in diagnostic evaluation of hearing impaired children include the pediatrician, the otolaryngologist, the ophthalmologist, the audiologist, the neurologist, the teacher of the deaf, the psychologist, the social worker, and the psychiatrist. Those interested and actively working with hearing impaired persons constitute a number much too small for the national need.

It is unrealistic at this time, because of the manpower shortage, for each school system to have its own comprehensive diagnostic center. Some kinds of pooling of resources are needed until such time as adequate numbers of qualified personnel become available. A question to which this group might address itself relates to various means by which diagnostic services can be strengthened through sharing, pooling, or reorganizing efforts at the local, state, and interstate levels.

Is it possible and/or feasible to establish regional diagnostic centers attached to or directly affiliated with universities which have professional preparation programs in the medical and allied fields enumerated above?

Is it possible that such regional centers might concentrate the limited number of professional specialists around the United States in such a manner as to develop professional teams that truly work together?

Is it possible that given teams within a common geographic area could better concentrate on specific age groups, such as birth to 5 years, 6 to 16 years, and 16 and above?

Could it be that there are too many one-man generalists around the country, and as a result arbitrary decisions are being made without adequate professional cross-fertilization and feedback covering one's hypothesis and the results of one's clinical experiment?

In addition, the question of special training, if any, which specialists should have before working in the area of hearing impairment could benefit from some discussion by your group.

HYPOTHETICAL PROFILE SYSTEM

In order to place children in programs that make sense, the diagnostic group might best consider communicating about assessment of at least the three areas of function suggested earlier in this paper. For purposes of communication now, let us view each area as one extending on a continuum; and further, let us arbitrarily rank each area from least involvement to most involvement.

For example, the area previously referred to as Code for Input begins with a careful assessment of the auditory system. Let us assume further that the children with whom we are dealing have a hearing problem which is not medically reversible and is neurosensory in kind. Through a series of auditory tests utilizing among others, speech, pure tones, and noise stimuli, it is possible to state that an Input Code of the inner ear has a mild problem, a moderate problem, a severe problem, or a profound problem.

TABLE 24-1

HYPOTHETICAL PROFILE SYSTEM*

| | Input Code | | Storage and Retrieval |
Rankings	Auditory	Environment	CNS Function
	1	1	1
	2	2	2
	3	3	3
	4	4	4

* A profile for each child consists of a single rank in each of the three columns; examples, 1-3-4, 2-4-1, 4-3-4, etc.

As suggested earlier, we could assign each of these a rank from 1 through 4. Four, therefore, would represent the least contribution audition is likely to provide that individual for the purpose of receiving the speech of others and monitoring his own production. And from the standpoint of traditional classroom structure and organization for nonhearing impaired children this would place him at a serious disadvantage.

Likewise, a rank of 1, 2, 3, or 4 could be assigned the relative status of the environment; and, lastly, the integrity of the storage and retrieval (CNS) as determined by the neurologist, psychologist, and others, could be ranked along the 1 through 4 continuum. Thus a profile could be determined for each child provided adequate diagnostic services were available. The various specialists could then communicate from a relatively standard frame of reference, and begin to fashion appropriate education programs for the numerous types of hearing impaired children.

According to the concept of the profile system, the child with 2 hearing, 4 environment, and 4 storage and retrieval would need immediate programming quite different from the individual with a 1-1-1 profile, or a 2-2-2 profile. It is interesting to speculate, for example, how a program for six- and seven-year-olds with 2 hearing, 4 environment, and 1 storage and retrieval, without early childhood educational experience would differ from the child who had early childhood experience. Some discussion of what kind of programs should be sought for the 4 hearing, 1 environment, and 4 storage and retrieval could be useful. What kind of programs should be planned for the 4-4-4 profile? What should be appropriate for the 1-4-1 profile? A summary of the various possibilities is presented in Table 24-1. Discussions by your subgroups regarding these might be helpful as guidelines are written for day programs.

PROGRAM ALTERNATIVES

When the diagnostician looks for program alternatives for hearing impaired children, he frequently is required to make compromises and arbitrary decisions. A frequent reason for this is the wide quality variations in programs he has available; more often, however, it is likely to be due to the absence of existing programs in the child's locale.

Too frequently the diagnostician discovers that a major weakness in many local programs is the virtual absence of qualified supervisory personnel. If one is charged with providing public education for the full spectrum of hearing impaired children within a given public school system, he can be certain to have a wide spectrum of needs as suggested in the hypothetical profile system.

The groups involved in assessment must realize that diagnostic needs and program needs do not remain static even in a given child. Without detailed program supervision the odds that optimum programs will be provided as the child proceeds from year to year drop to zero. We have witnessed too many 11- and 12-year-old "educational cripples" around this country during the past decade. Better that we reorganize our efforts on a local, state, and interstate basis to provide more optimal educational programs than proliferate mediocrity indefinitely.

All involved in assessment and placement must realize that a diagnostic work-up is not an end in itself; children change, techniques change, hearing aids change, teachers change. Reassessment at least on an annual basis, and even more frequently in the early years, should be considered a *routine* function of the educational program. Certainly this should be so in the areas of communication, intellectual function, personal and social development, educational attainments, and language development.

We must all consider the proposition that the reason for diagnostic evaluations varies on the basis of age and developmental status of an individual. Reasons for evaluating young hearing impaired children differ from the purposes of assessment of those approaching the secondary school years. Young adults leaving secondary schools require assistance different from elementary school children and it is well known that adequate educational, vocational, and personal guidance do not occur by chance. These important service functions need to be built into the system of education. In the planning of an educational program, these should be considered as important as any other component within the system and should be planned for accordingly.

When the diagnostician looks for programs in education, he sees the need for at least the following alternatives:

1. Full-time educational programs for profoundly deaf children.
2. Full-time special classes for hard-of-hearing children.
3. Part-time special help for selected profoundly deaf children.
4. Part-time special help for hard-of-hearing children.

5. Full-time educational programs for multiply handicapped deaf children.
6. Part- and full-time opportunities for hard-of-hearing multiply handicapped children.
7. Special programs for mentally retarded deaf and hard-of-hearing children.
8. Special programs for emotionally disturbed deaf and hard-of-hearing children.

With the recent history of maternal rubella, the multiply handicapped with hearing impairment is likely to cause a convulsion in the already inadequate educational opportunities for relatively intact deaf and hard-of-hearing children.

When the diagnostician looks for alternatives in educational programs for hearing impaired children, he looks for systems with adequately prepared teachers. He looks for those supervisors and teachers who are willing and able to translate his findings into useful pedagogical maneuvers for the benefit of the child. He looks for those who understand the value of constancy and consistency in the early use of amplification with all hearing impaired children in need of special education.

When the hearing-impaired child among us today looks around, he seeks diagnosticians, teachers, and administrators who communicate with one another about his special problems. He seeks diagnosticians, teachers, and administrators who are willing to try new and better ways of doing things even though change may be painful. He seeks a team that pays more than lip service to individual differences.

The hearing-impaired child seeks diagnosticians, teachers, and administrators who are aware of the fact that business and industry have reorganized their practices as a result of new technology and he hopes that he soon will see some of this new technology reflected in his educational program. He seeks a cooperating team that understands the vagaries of hearing impairment so that unnecessary limits are not set too soon. And, finally, he seeks a team that realizes that nearly 55 to 60 per cent of all high school graduates in the United States today enter college, and that he soon will reach college age realizing that at present only 10 per cent of his hearing impaired peers enter college.

SUMMARY

In conclusion let me say that this group assembled might very well discuss ways and means for

1. Extending the effectiveness of diagnostic efforts which, on a nationwide scale, are something less than comprehensive.

2. Regrouping of specialists on local, state, and interstate bases for more effective coverage of existing unmet needs.
3. Pooling of educational facilities in the face of manpower shortages. Although some kind of compromise is likely, priority should be established on local, county, statewide, and interstate bases.
4. Using the concept of the hypothetical profile system to facilitate discussion among various groups responsible for the organization, administration of programs required to meet the multiple educational needs of hearing impaired children and begin to establish objective criteria for appropriate educational planning and placement.
5. Incorporating modern technology and other approaches into special schools and classes for hearing impaired children as means for alleviating some of the personnel needs.
6. Translating diagnostic findings into active pedagogical procedures aimed at improving instruction.
7. And finally, obtaining additional qualified supervisory and teaching personnel for the large number of children who are detected and diagnosed early but for whom appropriate programs are lacking.

Chapter 25

Developmental Evaluation and the Institution of Remedial Programs for Children with Learning Difficulties

Marianne Frostig

(with the cooperation of Wilma Hart)

INTRODUCTION

THE advent of many new approaches to the treatment of children with learning disorders has lately aroused intense interest amongst professional workers and lay people alike. For example, Kephart,[578] has introduced a perceptual–motor approach for the education of the slow learner; Delacato[245] has evolved a neurophysiological approach which he advocates for the brain-damaged child, the slow learner, the alexic, and even for use in regular classrooms; Cruickshank[226] has developed further the methods first introduced by Strauss and Lehtinen[1037] and suggested new ones for helping the brain-damaged child. In addition, methods specifically designed for teaching reading have appeared, such as the linguistic method,[115] the Initial Teaching Alphabet,[282] and techniques for teaching reading to very young children.[785] It is difficult for the teacher to decide which of these methods to apply and in what situations, especially as most of these innovations have been advanced as methods of teaching which should supersede any others.

More and more psychologists and educators, however, such as Barsch[69] and Kirk and Bateman[585] are interested in developing specific training programs based upon the broadest possible spectrum of testing and evaluation. The present authors, therefore, do not presume to introduce any universally applicable technique to be regarded as optimal for all children of a single diagnostic category, such as "brain damaged" or "neurologically handicapped." This paper agrees with the views of Kirk, Gallagher[369] and others, who maintain that no single, narrowly defined treatment approach is sufficient to correct the varied symptoms found in any specific diagnostic category. Some brain-damaged children, for instance, are hyperactive, while others move exceedingly slowly; some are very fearful; others are daring,

Reprinted from *Academic Therapy Quarterly*, 2:76-88, Winter 1967.

aggressive, sometimes unaware of danger; some show difficulty in disregarding irrelevant stimuli and work best behind a screen; others are threatened by isolation and respond better to the presence of a teacher and the stimulation of a group; some have unimpaired intelligence, others are retarded; some can become leaders in society and work as scientists, teachers, or physicians, others will never be able to live anything but a sheltered life. The solution to the problem lies not in producing a remedial technique which will help every child in a diagnostic category, but in selecting from the range of techniques those which are appropriate for each individual child, regardless of his label of *mentally retarded* or *brain damaged* or whatever it might be. This approach has as its goal the exact gearing of methods of treatment to a precise symptomatic diagnosis which is derived from tests and observation. The remedial program is then based on individual test results.

DIAGNOSIS

Etiological diagnosis is, of course, essential for outlining the initial treatment approaches for children with learning difficulties. If epilepsy plays a major role in a child's condition, he will need medication. If his deviate behavior can be traced to a cataclysmic emotional trauma, such as the death of his parents, for example, he may need both psychotherapy and environmental therapy. If he is known to have a brain tumor, surgery may be indicated. If he has difficulties in school as the result of overprotection at home, counseling for the parents may be adjudged to provide the best help for him.

But whenever a remedial educational program is required, it is necessary to go a step beyond exploration of etiology and undertake in addition a very careful evaluation of the symptoms which may be inhibiting the ability to learn. At the Frostig Center,* this is done by a careful assessment of each child's strengths and weaknesses in each of six developmental areas: sensory–motor development, perception, language, higher thought processes, social adjustment, and emotional development. The results of the initial evaluation are quantified whenever possible and can be used as the bases for remedial programs specifically adapted to each child's needs. A wide variety of tests is used to evaluate each child, and these are augmented by psychiatric interviews and careful observation. Certain tests have been found especially valuable for providing information on which to base remedial programs, and they are regarded as standard procedure for children in the three or four lower grades. These tests are the Illinois Test of Psy-

---

* The Marianne Frostig Center of Educational Therapy, a center providing psychiatric, psychological, and educational services for children with learning difficulties and/or behavior problems, in Los Angeles, California.

cholinguistic Abilities,[588] the Wepman Test of Auditory Discrimination,[1109] the Marianne Frostig Developmental Test of Visual Perception,[363] and the Wechsler Intelligence Scale for Children.[1100] These four tests are basic to the research which is reported here, but it should be emphasized that they in no way constitute the only method of evaluation, just as the remedial program which is described is not the sole manner of treatment. Many of the children receive psychotherapy and/or their parents receive counseling in addition. Other methods of treatment, such as medication, occupational therapy, and speech therapy, may also be used. This paper, however, is restricted to the discussion of those symptoms which require educational treatment and to the educational measures themselves.

Although a diagnosis of the specific assets and disabilities of each child is considered essential for the formation of all remedial programs at the Center, it is especially helpful in cases where an etiological diagnosis cannot be made. There is a large group of children for whom it is impossible to pinpoint precisely the cause or causes of their learning disabilities. These children show retarded development in one or more of the six areas of psychological functioning referred to above, but there is no known reason for the condition. Although a common conclusion in these cases is that a "developmental lag" has occurred, the reason for its occurrence is often obscure.

Even in those cases where etiology is established, a survey of the child's abilities and disabilities is necessary for the construction of the most efficient teaching program. The choice of curriculum and teaching methods depends upon the presence or absence of such symptoms as hyperactivity, defects in concept formation, articulation difficulties, disabilities in visual perception or auditory discrimination, difficulty in the association of auditory and visual stimuli, inadequate eye movements, or poor directionality. What is needed, therefore, is that the teacher should understand both the exact nature of the learning disabilities and also the psychological abilities involved in the tasks which she wishes to assign the child, so that she can apply specific remedial methods and design an educational program which is appropriate. Whenever possible, the teacher should cooperate with the school psychologist in the initial evaluation.

SENSORY–MOTOR FUNCTIONS

Testing of sensory–motor functions has not yet reached its final form at the Center. At the present time we are experimenting in finding the best methods of appraisal for the following functions: reaction time, speed, laterality, muscular coordination, muscular strength, and flexibility. We also try to explore tactile perception, using a test for finger agnosia, and we test the ability to remember a kinesthetic sequence. As the test results of these sensory-motor functions are not yet quantifiable, the evaluation of the psychologist who did the testing is used instead.

In the public school situation, where such complete testing is not available, the classroom teacher can be trained to observe and test the motor skills of her charges with the help of such measures as the Kephart Scale,[578] the Kraus–Weber Test,[621] Cureton's Motor Fitness Test,[228] or the Winterhaven exercises.[1047] The teacher should also check on the child's ability to remember a kinesthetic pattern before choosing a tracing method for the teaching of reading, such as the Fernald[331] method.

Suggestions for sensory–motor training, including a program of physical education, have been included in the Teacher's Guide for the Development of Visual Perception,[362] and another experimental program of physical education, already in use in public schools, is available from the Center.

VISUAL PERCEPTUAL ABILITIES

The development of materials for training visual perception was based on findings made with the help of the Developmental Test of Visual Perception, which was constructed at the Center. The author had observed that many of the children referred to the Center because of learning difficulties seemed to have disabilities in the area of visual perception. Unfortunately, it was impossible to apply specific remedial measures at that time (1957), as there was no test available to pinpoint the subareas of visual perceptual disability and to provide age norms by which an individual child's performance could be measured. It was therefore decided to construct a test which would sample and quantitatively assess those subareas which observation had indicated to be the most important for school performance. The Developmental Test which resulted is a pencil and paper test which can be administered either to individual children or to groups and which evaluates a child's abilities in five distinct areas of visual perception, eye-motor coordination, figure-ground perception, constancy of perception, perception of position in space, and perception of spatial relationships. Each of these areas of visual perception is significant for school learning. Norms are provided, now based on a standardization sample of over 2,100 nursery school and public school children between the ages of three and nine years.[740]

The test now provides information on which to base training programs for visual perception, but because the other developmental abilities are interrelated with perception and all are required for adequate functioning in and out of school, training programs must take into account not only perceptual abilities but also sensory-motor and language functions, higher thought processes, emotional development, and group adjustment.

Therefore the Frostig Program for the Development of Visual Perception,[362] which grew out of the test, includes not only suggestions and exercises for training each area of visual perception tapped by the test but also a short physical education program specifically designed to aid the development of body image, body concept and body schema, gross and fine muscle coordination, correct eye movements, and directionality, all of which are basic to adequate perceptual functioning.

This program has been in use in public schools for about two years and is now being amplified. It should also be pointed out that a variety of skills such as vocabulary development, the ability to tell a story or describe an object, the ability to follow oral directions or to classify, and so on, may and should be trained while using the perceptual exercises. It is one of the goals of test construction to separate and sample distinct abilities, but in training the contrary goal is sought—to integrate the child's psychological functioning, so that he perceives, acts, thinks and feels in a harmonious, coordinated, and balanced manner.

AUDITORY PERCEPTUAL ABILITIES

Auditory perception is explored by the Wepman Test of Auditory Discrimination and by subtests of the Wechsler Intelligence Scale for Children (WISC) and the Illinois Test of Psycholinguistic Abilities (ITPA). For instance, the repetition of numbers required in the WISC (digit span subtest) and in the ITPA (auditory-vocal sequential subtest) tests auditory perception and memory for auditory sequences. Another example is the auditory decoding subtests of the ITPA, which explores understanding of oral language. All the WISC verbal subtests involve auditory perception, and give clues to the child's ability in this area.

The Wepman Test of Auditory Discrimination is a test of sound discrimination. It is easy to give, although preparatory work is necessary whenever the child is not completely certain of the meaning of the concepts "same" and "different."

The training of auditory perception has to include the skills which have been discussed, and also others—for example, the discrimination of sounds other than speech sounds. Practice has also to be given in speech sounds both in isolation and in words (phonics). The understanding of phrases, sentences, and paragraphs, and memory for auditory sequences can be helped through practice.

Auditory perceptual skills may also be developed in the course of academic learning. Spelling, reading, oral language, learning foreign languages, and using the listening skills involved in other subjects, all provide practice in auditory perception. But academic work can only contribute in this way if the child is succeeding in it. If not, the child with disabilities in auditory perception will probably require patient training in basic skills in auditory discrimination, phonics, understanding words, vocabulary, memory for auditory sequences, listening to and understanding oral language, and so on, apart from the academic curriculum. A program to develop these skills is included in the language training program discussed below.

LANGUAGE

The previous discussion of auditory perception necessarily includes language, because the perception of language is the most important auditory task of the human being. But language includes more than perceptual abilities. It includes expressive language (encoding is the term used in the ITPA), the association of language with movement (as in following directions or in writing), and the association of language with visual symbols (as in reading and many other skills). Because the authors of the Illinois Test of Psycholinguistic Abilities were concerned with the broadest spectrum of behavior which could be measured, the ITPA gives clues concerning every developmental function—motor development, perceptual development, concept formation, and memory functions—in addition to language in the usual sense.

A language program based on the Illinois Test of Psycholinguistic Abilities has been developed at the Center and is in an intermediate stage of verification. It has been in use at the Center for about two years and has been supplied to more than fifty public schools, who will provide the feedback which will help shape the program's final form.

HIGHER THOUGHT PROCESSES

We are following Aurelia Levi[650] in basing a program for the development of higher thought processes upon the results of testing with the WISC. This program is still not unified but, as will be gleaned from the case history which follows, the training of such functions as visualization, sequential thinking, and so on, can be included in the total training program.

RICPA—A CASE HISTORY

The purpose of the following case history is to illustrate how a specific remedial program involving the six developmental areas—motor functioning, perception, language, higher thought processes, social adjustment, and emotional development—can be devised and applied in an integrated way on the basis of a careful evaluation of the child's abilities and disabilities in these areas.

RICPA was 9½ years old when he was referred to us by a university clinic in December, 1964. He had shown poor school adjustment since kindergarten; had been held back once in public school and was now attending the low third grade. His report card showed C's in all subjects, but these grades were generously designed to prevent discouraging further a child who was actually completely unable to keep up with his classmates. RICPA was shy, withdrawn, evidently in despair because of his failure. Too far behind to be held back again, he was referred to the Center for full-time schooling.

RICPA is an adopted child. He has a sister, also adopted, who was 6½ years of age at the time of referral, and a brother, the natural child of his parents, who was then 9 months of age. RICPA's adoptive mother is a rather anxious, fearful woman, very unsure of herself, and eager for help in coping with RICPA. She was an only child and describes her family life as a happy one. Both she and her husband are Caucasian, college graduates, who live in comfortable circumstances and seem well-adjusted. Little is known of RICPA's natural parents, but the boy is partly of Indian blood. Nothing is known of his prenatal history nor of his delivery, except that he weighed 6 pounds, 9 ounces at birth and the natural mother was reported to be in a healthy condition.

RICPA was a healthy looking baby. He had a slight ptosis of one eyelid, but this caused no problem in seeing. Except for severe colic as an infant, for which he required medication (Donnatol®) he had no illnesses except chicken pox at the age of 3, and mumps at the age of 9½. RICPA was hospitalized overnight at the age of 2, when a glass door fell and his chin was cut. The scars are still evident, although he had plastic surgery. At 7 years of age, he had a tonsillectomy, but was not hospitalized.

RICPA was completely weaned from the bottle at 3 years of age, but he began self-feeding at 9 months. He crawled very little and walked at 15 months. He cut his first tooth at 9 months. The mother could not remember when he said his first words. His first sentence was spoken between 2 and 2½ years of age. Toilet training was completed at 3 years of age. Onset of training was early; the exact time was not recalled by the mother although she reported the process as "difficult."

From the age of 2 through 5, RICPA had frequent nightmares from which he would wake up terrified. During this period, he had a fear of animals "getting" him at night. At times he refused to go to nursery school, although at this age he had no difficulty with peer relationships.

In kindergarten and in the first grade, he was somewhat hyperactive and showed a poor attention span. From the second grade on, he complained about going to school and developed nervous mannerisms.

In the fourth grade, RICPA began having difficulties with his peers and felt that the other children were picking on him. He was not friendly with any of his schoolmates.

The university clinic conducted tests in December, 1964, when RICPA was 9½ years old. The results on the Wide Range Achievement Test were as follows:

Reading (Vocabulary) 3.8
Arithmetic Fundamentals 2.5
Spelling 2.3

At the time of referral, RICPA's physician wrote that the child was in good health. There were no visual or hearing difficulties, or signs of neurological impairment, but we found a weakness in the trunk muscles, a very slight ptosis of one eyelid, and other difficulties in motor development (see below).

At the Frostig Center, RICPA was included in a group with four other youngsters, ranging in age from 7 to 10. They worked at grade levels ranging from the second to the fourth. The educational therapist who worked with RICPA (Wilma Hart) developed his program with the help of Table 25-1, which charts the basic test results and also with the aid of the qualitative information she received from the psychologist.

Sensory-Motor Development

The sensory-motor testing showed that the trunk muscles were weak, fine motor coordination was in general poor (as the quality of RICPA's performance on the Frostig Test implied), and directionality was also very poor. He was clumsy in all his movements.

RICPA participated in a physical education program, as do all the children at the Center, and was also referred for additional exercises. Exercises specifically designed to help his difficulties in visual-motor coordination and in directionality are discussed below.

Visual and Auditory Perception

RICPA showed difficulty with only one subtest, "position in space," in the Frostig Developmental Test of Visual Perception. This may not have reflected the severity of his difficulties because of the low ceiling of the Frostig Test. A qualitative analysis showed that "position in space" and "spatial relationships" were both difficult for him. He missed one item in each subtest and finished others in an indecisive and unsure manner.

In auditory perception, as measured by the Wepman Test, he had no difficulties. He could perceive well single sounds and words, but his repetition of numbers, phrases, and sentences was poor. He had a defective perception of, and memory for, auditory sequences, so that the acquisition of number facts was difficult for him. He could not associate auditory and visual stimuli, and spelling was therefore a very hard task.

TABLE 25-1

DATE GIVEN	TRAINING NEEDED	ADEQUATE OR ABOVE	SUBJECT CATEGORY	TEST	
			EYE MOTOR COORDINATION	I	VISUAL PERCEPTION
			FIGURE GROUND	II	
			FORM CONSTANCY	III	
a.e.			POSITION IN SPACE	IV	
s.s.			SPATIAL RELATIONS	V	
			WEPMAN	AUDITORY PERCEPTION	
			INFORMATION	I	WECHSLER INTELLIGENCE SCALE FOR CHILDREN
			COMPREHENSION	II	
			ARITHMETIC	III	
			SIMILARITIES	IV	
			VOCABULARY	V	
			DIGIT SPAN	VI	
			PICTURE COMPLETION	VII	
			PICTURE ARRANGEMENT	VIII	
			BLOCK DESIGN	IX	
			OBJECT ASSEMBLY	X	
			CODING	XI	
			AUDITORY-VOCAL AUTOMATIC	VII	I.T.P.A.
			VISUAL DECODING	II	
			MOTOR ENCODING	VI	
			AUDITORY-VOCAL ASSOCIATION	III	
			VISUAL-MOTOR SEQUENCING	IX	
s.s.			VOCAL ENCODING	V	
l.a.			AUDITORY-VOCAL SEQUENCING	VIII	
			VISUAL-MOTOR ASSOCIATION	IV	
			AUDITORY DECODING	I	

Perceptual Quotient ▪
Verbal I.Q. ▪
Performance I.Q. ▪
Full Scale I.Q. ▪

Actual Grade ▪
Arithmetic ▪
Spelling ▪
Reading ▪

Sensory Motor Development
ITPA Total Language Age ▪

NAME
BIRTH DATE
C.A. ▪
DATE

BASIC TEST RESULTS

In regard to RICPA's perceptual training the educational therapist decided to work with the workbooks for training perception of spatial relationships. Because these two abilities are dependent on each other, the training in each would reinforce the training in the other. The exercises for spatial relationships also give training for figure–ground perception, in which there was some weakness, and the workbook also included many exercises to help train directionality. Eye–hand coordination exercises were later included, because the more complicated exercises in the workbook for this area necessitate visual motor planning, which was most difficult for RICPA. (See WISC, object assembly.)

As auditory perception of sounds was adequate, no specific preliminary auditory training was necessary. However, training in phonics was emphasized because of his inability to perceive auditory as well as motor sequences and because of his difficulties in associating visual stimuli both with movement and with auditory stimuli. These difficulties were evident in the sequencing test and in the visual-motor association subtests of the ITPA. Spelling therefore had to be taught by a careful color-coding method which will be described later.

Higher Thought Processes

In the WISC, RICPA had a verbal I.Q. of 92, performance I.Q. of 90, and a full-scale I.Q. of 91. Scatter ranged from a scale score of 11 in picture completion and block design to a score of only 5 in coding. The low areas, scores below 9, were in information (7) (difficulties in auditory decoding?); arithmetic (8) (difficulties with perception of position in space, keeping an idea in mind, visual imagery?); object assembly (7) (difficulties in visuo-motor planning); and coding (5) (difficulties in keeping an idea in mind, symbol association, speed of reaction?). His performance in both picture arrangement and similarities, in which he had a near-average score of 9, reflected basic difficulties. His score in picture arrangement was probably lowered by his difficulty in sequential thinking and his score in similarities by his difficulty in forming concepts. His concept formation was poorer than the score of 9 indicated, and it posed problems for his teacher.

Language

In the Illinois Test for Psycholinguistic Abilities, two scores were minimally below the standard mean scores: auditory decoding (–0.02) and motor encoding (–0.16), both appropriate for an age level of 7 years, 11 months (RICPA was 9 years, 6 months old). Deficits in these two areas were evident in RICPA's functioning. Here again, one has to keep the low ceiling of the ITPA in mind. Auditory decoding was indeed difficult for this youngster. Longer sentences and paragraphs were very poorly understood. It may be that the primary cause was an inability to attend to sequences, causing auditory decoding of verbally presented material to be so difficult.

The motor encoding subtest score was paralleled by a general lag in sensory–motor development. (See Table 25-1.)

The two scores on the ITPA which were distinctly low were visual motor association (–0.44) and auditory vocal sequencing (–0.54). The difficulty in visual motor association seemed to be reflected in RICPA's inability to form letters and words and to learn spelling; the difficulty in auditory vocal sequencing was a further sign of his general difficulty in learning sequences.

In general, observation of this boy revealed a slow tempo of all movements and a delayed reaction time. In class he was always the last one to react to the teacher's signal and also the last to finish his work. Although he seemed depressed and worried, and often indicated by words and gestures that he felt inadequate, the educational therapist gained the impression that his slowness was partly independent of his mood, and this seemed to be confirmed when his tempo remained below the class average despite a growing satisfaction with himself and the world.

The underlying and most basic difficulty which hindered normal progress for this youngster was this general slowness. He seemed to be too slow in his thought processes to follow and grasp spoken sentences and to memorize sequences. His performance on the ITPA in the auditory vocal sequences subtest was lower than the digit span forwards of the WISC. Both subtests consist of repetition of a sequence of numbers, but grouping is possible in the WISC, which is given much more slowly, while in the ITPA, the numbers are given much faster and have to be repeated automatically as a unitary sequence. Difficulties in learning sequences and in keeping a particular fact in mind while solving a problem played a role, but RICPA's major handicap was apparently his slowness in following rapid or prolonged verbal stimuli, so that he lost track of them and became confused.

Remedial Methods

The educational therapist decided to use several approaches to help RICPA in overcoming his basic difficulties. First: visualization. Visualization can refer to verbal imagery, visual imagery, or auditory imagery. The low score in object assembly indicated RICPA's special difficulty with visual imagery. Visualization is necessary for any planning, and RICPA's problems in utilizing it must have affected his scores in solving word problems and arithmetic. Planning ability is also necessary for coding, which was so very low. Exercises in visualization were easily integrated with instruction in reading, spelling, and arithmetic. RICPA was required to visualize the units of his carefully graduated tasks.

The second approach was to provide exercises in which an idea had to be kept in mind while solving a problem. Arithmetic problems were again used for this purpose.

Thirdly, practice was given in listening to, memorizing, and repeating sequences. In fact, the educational therapist presented sequences auditorily, visually and kinesthetically,* and required RICPA to develop sequences himself in thought and written language. The auditory sequencing was especially emphasized, because his inability to listen to and to remember a sequence of words constituted a barrier to his gaining information, as was reflected by his score on the information subtest in the WISC.

The scores on the information subtest in the WISC probably also reflect the youngster's difficulty in attending to sequences. Information makes the best sense and can most easily be remembered if it is grasped sequentially: information concerning such varied items as dates, distances, natural phenomena, or human endeavor is less likely to be assimilated if it is received as a series of isolated facts rather than sequentially related.

The inability to master sequences is an immense barrier to learning. Even such a simple number fact as "4 plus 3 are 7" is a sequence. Similarly, the coding subtest, which is concerned with the ability to keep one fact in mind while looking for another, involves associating sequences of symbols. RICPA's inability to keep in mind the idea of the code reflected a total inability to organize thought. He tended always to forget what he was after, and if the tempo of the presentation was not very slow, he became lost entirely. The difficulty of keeping a fact in mind interacted with the difficulty in attending to and memorizing sequences, so that thought became disorganized and information garbled.

Fourthly, therefore, RICPA was given training specifically designed to help him organize information. This consisted of

1. A great variety of coding exercises to give him practice in the manipulation and organization of symbols.
2. Exercises in reasoning given in the form of word problems.
3. Verbal discussion, in which he was encouraged to explain and elaborate upon information just given and discuss what he had seen or heard.
4. Written expression of the verbal discussion just mentioned.

The fifth area of concentration was RICPA's writing. His poor formation of letters was due to three circumstances:

1. His general disorganization pervaded his movements as well as his thinking, though to a lesser degree.

---

* Kinesthetic sequences were practiced by means of the "Blind Writing Game." This is done by having the child write the sequence he is to learn such as letters in a word, with his eyes closed, while the teacher guides his hand. When the teacher feels that the child has mastered the movements, she loosens her touch and the child continues to write by himself, tracing over and over the same sequence on the board or paper with his eyes closed. When the movement is completely fixed, the child opens his eyes and looks at what he is writing, thus transferring the kinesthetic perception to the visual modality. He then repeats the movement with his eyes open.

2. He had difficulties in directionality. He was disoriented in his spatial world also.
3. He had difficulty in associating movements with visual input.

The scores of ITPA subtests in visual-motor association and in motor encoding were only very slightly below the standard mean scores, but the low ceiling of this test also has to be taken into account. (The ITPA and the Frostig often give only slight indications of basic disturbances when administered to older children.)

On the basis of these findings, RICPA was given

1. Much work in the motor planning of sequences of gross and fine movement.
2. Exercises in directionality.
3. Eye–hand coordination exercises.

All of these were taken from the Frostig Program for the Development of Visual Perception.

In the actual formation of letters, particular attention was paid to the basic movements from which letters are formed and to joining one letter to another. When RICPA came, he did not know how to join letters nor how to form many capital letters and some lower case letters. By the end of the semester, he could write legibly, though slowly.

So far as the other academic areas are concerned, RICPA's reading test initially showed a third grade level. He began work in reading, therefore, at a low third grade level and completed books at both low and high third grade level in the course of the semester, finishing with some fourth grade material in the last month.

In spelling, no lists were given at first because of RICPA's extreme difficulty in this subject. Spelling material was taken only from his reading, a very few words being added each week. Spelling lists at the third grade level were given later but with a maximum of fifteen new words a week.

Color-Coding

The use of color cues helped RICPA to analyze and to remember the sequence of letters in words. RICPA's spelling words were presented with each sound in a different color. (At first the teacher wrote the word in this manner; later RICPA did it for himself.) After RICPA visualized the word, he then wrote it without the color cues (synthesis).

In mathematics, RICPA knew only a few number facts and did not know how to regroup, add, or subtract. During the semester, he went through all four basic processes, including long division. Number facts were taught by a visualization-notation method, in the following manner:

He looked at a number fact, such as "4 plus 5 makes 9." Then he tried to picture it in his mind with his eyes closed and then tried to write it down from memory. The same fact was then repeated in a number of ways: e.g.,

$$4 + 5 = 9 \quad \begin{array}{r} 4 \\ +5 \\ \hline 9 \end{array} \quad 5 + 4 = 9 \quad \begin{array}{r} 5 \\ +4 \\ \hline 9 \end{array} \quad \begin{array}{r} 205 \\ +104 \\ \hline 309 \end{array} \quad \begin{array}{r} 43 \\ +51 \\ \hline 94 \end{array}$$

By these means he was able to learn number facts, slowly at first, but gradually more quickly.

In language, RICPA was given much work in following directions. Some were given in writing but most were oral, because of the initial difficulty in decoding auditory sequences.

Finally, the emotional attitudes of this seriously handicapped child had to be taken into account. In order to ameliorate his poor self-image, it was necessary to ensure that he was continually able to experience success. This was done by presenting his work in carefully graduated steps. The work presented always took the preceding work a small stage further. It always had to be completed but was given in small enough amounts for him to be able to complete it successfully. As RICPA experienced success and his self-image changed, he began to make friends with the other children. His social adjustment, as is so often the case, depended upon his ability to feel that he could be successful and worth something.

So far as RICPA's growth is concerned, as reflected by test scores, a retest with the Wide Range Achievement Test (May 25, 1965) showed the following:

> Reading Vocabulary
> 5.0 (December 1964: 3.8)
> Arithmetic Fundamentals
> 4.5 (December 1964: 2.5)
> Spelling
> 3.4 (December 1964: 2.3)

Intelligence, language, and perception has been tested again in November, 1966. He gained 8 points on his intelligence tests (7 in the verbal; 9 in the performance part).

PART FIVE

A Theoretical Framework for the Multiply Handicapped Child

Introduction

THROUGHOUT the literature the need is frequently expressed for a more adequate conceptual framework and theoretical basis for consideration of problems relative to the education of multiply handicapped children. Indeed, there is still lacking a widely accepted theoretical frame of reference for the special education of all exceptional children. The paucity of significant literature suggesting a framework for conceptualizing the multiply handicapped is confirmed by the fact that only four articles appear in this part of the book. A fifth theoretical construct is summarized in the final chapter.

Professor Reynolds in his article schematically presents a conceptual framework of the comprehensive range of services provided under special education. These services are summarized in the form of a hierarchy, ranging from regular classes through several intermediate levels of special services to hospitals and treatment centers. The levels of hierarchy are ordered according to increasing specialization. As children are placed in higher level programs, their separation from normal home and school life increases.

Dr. Levine proposes a conceptual framework from which hypothetical propositions can be deduced relative to the personal and social development of individuals with physical and/or mental deviations. Levine refers to the generalized attitudinal set by which society conceptualizes such deviations as *defining attributes*. The personal, self-evaluative aspects of the individual's disability are termed *criterial attributes*. A scheme for assessing the strength of these attributes is presented in terms of categories offering the possibility of determining the relationship between cultural biases and stereotypes and the disabled individual's self-perceptions and personal aspirations. The concept of psychological and social distance is suggested as a criterion measure of social interaction.

One approach to the formulation of a comprehensive conceptual system is to develop a taxonomic structure which provides the basis for the isolation of previously unidentified problems that can be subjected to research. Blackman in the 1966 issue of the *Review of Educational Research* [p. 29] stated that

> Clearly the next step in educational research with the mentally retarded would involve the development and evaluation of a taxonomy of the school relevant disabilities of retarded learners. Theoretically, therefore, knowledge of

the psychoeducational abilities and disabilities of mentally retarded individuals coupled with an analytical understanding of the psychoeducational demands of specific school tasks, stated in comparable terms, should lead to maximally efficient matching of learners and materials in terms of whether the former possess the necessary prerequisites for the latter.

This rationale should apply equally well to the educational problems of the multiply handicapped.

One taxonomic model has been provided by Dr. Jordan as outlined in his paper. Jordan has attempted to delineate the factors affecting vocational success in the period after special instruction. A second taxonomic approach, proposed by Dr. Godfrey Stevens, is summarized in the last chapter. Holt, in Chapter 29, proposes a classification scheme in which equal prominence is given to each disability and, thus, useful with multiply handicapped children. Holt's words are not only appropriate to his classification system but also to all of the articles in Part Five: "This classification is advanced as an attempt to unify the approach to the problems of handicapped children. It may be considered to be Utopian; it may be considered to be impracticable; but some purpose will have been served if it is considered."

Chapter 26

Development of a Taxonomy for
Special Education

Thomas E. Jordan

O NE of the trends of the last several years has been an increasing dissatisfaction with the naiveté of work in disciplines concerned with
the welfare of children.[995] This dissatisfaction is due to the lack of an
adequate rationale for methods of instruction and child study. In all
young disciplines there is a period when precedent and simple utilitarian-
ism suffice as explanations. This soon passes as people acquire enough experience to view their work in perspective and feel sufficiently secure to ask
if there is a better way. There generally is a better way, and it is found by
programmed refinement of existing knowledge rather than by the seren-
dipity which characterized the first defensible procedures.

This general observation applies to all fields of knowledge and is equally applicable to special education. It is no longer adequate to use precedent as a rationale for our practices. It is no longer defensible to ignore
advances in disciplines continuous with special education. Programmed
research in the behavioral sciences has much to tell us, much to show. Increasingly, experimental evidence demonstrates the relevance of conceptual thinking and research to current practice. For example, Rosenstein's[939]
studies of the deaf clearly dictate some changes in the thinking of educators. Beliefs hoary with age and hallowed by precedent do not always
stand the light of critical thinking, and "the best current thinking" may be
firmly grounded in error. What is needed is examination of our beliefs
about handicapped children in a systematic fashion, substituting detached
scholarship for the clichés. Two examples will illustrate the heart of the
matter. The first is from one of the disciplines dealing with children, the
other from the history of science.

1. Child study is approached by contemporary home economists in light
of some of the most advanced thinking of the 1920's. At a recent meeting
with some thirty to forty deans of schools of home economics the writer
was cautioned to remember "the whole child" (as if one could forget him)
and to "study him" (meaning naïve observation with no perception of the

Reprinted from *Exceptional Children*, 28:7-12, Sept., 1961.

methodological problems involved). At the same time a child development specialist from a major center of study attempted to transmit his ideas and found little basis for communication. It is submitted that home economists influence child care practices very greatly. What a tragedy if their leaders should be incapable of responding to new findings. Their lack of responsiveness may be an inability to think in an idiom now current and thirty years beyond their own. Their thinking was firmly grounded in the idiom of the 1920's isolating them from contemporary thought.

2. A historical example of refinement of thought by conceptualization may be considered. It is an example of a very serious medical problem yielding to better conceptualization:

> Over the centuries scurvy was the sailor's worst enemy. Neither storms nor battles incapacitated as many men as did this vitamin deficiency. The crucial work on this disease was performed by James Lind,[658] the Scottish physician. Consider "the best current thinking" just prior to Lind's publication of *A Treatise of the Scurvy* in 1753. Gideon Harvey, physician to Charles II, considered the disease as follows: "preliminary, liminary, recent, inveterate or terminative." He described "a mouth scurvy, leg scurvy, joint scurvy, an asthmatic scurvy, a rheumatic scurvy, a diarrheous scurvy, an emetic or vomiting scurvy, a flatulent hypochondriac scurvy, a cutaneous scurvy, an ulcerous scurvy . . ." and so on. Lind proceeded to reduce the number of entities to one, a single disease, and demonstrated the requisite cure, lime-juice.

PROGRESS BASED ON THINKING

Now what have these two examples to offer special education. The first example illustrates the danger of a discipline, indifferent to new ideas, finding itself unable to communicate with the mainstream of thought about child behavior and growth. The second illustrates that "the best current thinking" is never a protection against what is wrong and what is later shown to be patently so. A third comment is in order. Special educators need to realize that progress is based on thinking. Thinking which leads to progress in a discipline is usually a self-conscious attempt to analyze the form and structure of knowledge. Today we need to impose form and structure on what we know about handicapped children. Merely citing precedent and popular prejudice will not result in progress; it will merely result in a good deal of satisfaction.

Over the years much of the difficulty in educating handicapped children developed because we knew very little about them. We were not sure what was wrong with them, or we did not know how they felt, how they were motivated, or their limitations. Advances in education during the last decades have remedied this situation. In most cases we can find a medical opinion about a child and there are some handicapped students on whom we have rather bulky folders full of medical and psychological information.

It would be interesting to make a blind comparison of children, guessing which youngsters had been studied in detail by scientific personnel, using the manner of instruction and the technique of teaching as the clue. In all probability we could not distinguish between the children with elaborate histories and those without them, at least on the basis of how they were taught. Put another way, we may say that a mass of clinical data about handicapped children does not necessarily mean they will receive better instruction.

There are several ways to explain this. The least useful is to say that special teachers are indifferent to the welfare of their children and ignore much useful information. A more sensible comment is to ask if the information gathered by doctors, psychologists, social workers, and the like has any bearing on the enterprise of teaching. Current practices suggest that information may not say anything to teachers, that there is a breakdown in the communication of information from one discipline to another.

It would be naïve to think that communication problems consist of one party in a discussion not knowing all the big words that the other party uses. The matter is more complicated than that. What is at the heart of the difficulty is the lack of conventions about what matters should be raised. This is far more difficult than the matter of big words. We may ask the question, What needs to be known about a child by any professional person? What are the categories, if you please, that basically define the functioning child?

THE FUNCTIONING CHILD

Important aspects of children's functioning may be identified as follows:

Somatic. This term refers to those instructionally significant factors which reflect, for example, neuromotor problems, or the problems of accommodating an amputee to the instructional process. A problem which will illustrate an item not in this category would be a metabolic disease such as those receiving attention in the literature of mental retardation, Fölling's disease (sometimes referred to as phenylketonuria), maple sugar disease, or Oasthouse disease. This is because such physical considerations are the irrelevant substratum to educational functioning.

Intellectual. The diseases just mentioned probably produce intellectual behavior which is relevant to educational processes. Children with Fölling's disease are commonly mentally retarded. Certainly the intellectual behavior of children is relevant to instruction and should be handled in a taxonomy.

Behavioral. To use the metabolic diseases for a third time, Fölling's disease produces abnormal behavior. It really does not matter what the disease is, but the hyperirritability and motoric excitement which occur in this and other diseases do matter. The disease underlying the behavior is irrelevant, since we do not cope with a medical entity but with its behavioral consequences, and, also, several diseases may produce similar behavior.

Communicative disorders are the disturbed processes of expressive and receptive language. Aphasia is often considered a "symbolic" disorder, but operationally it is either a disruption of expressive or receptive communication.

These categories do not avoid all problems, but they may facilitate communication. People in various coteries may still consider stuttering a neurotic problem (behavioral), or a phenomenal problem (communicative), or the result of an irritable nervous system (somatic). Whatever their formulation, it would be clear by their choice of terms.

A further advantage is that we can state the functional precedence of handicaps. To speak of a mentally retarded, physically handicapped child is to use syntactic precedence to communicate children's problems. The use of four categories with the convention of functional precedence can eliminate much confusion.

A final observation is conceptual. Two decades ago the theoretician J. R. Kantor[564] pointed out the need to make sure that there is no hiatus between constructs and the events to which they relate. The four categories described seem to observe that stricture.

It is important to realize that a conceptual issue has just been introduced into the discussion. There are several reasons for this: first, a taxonomy is a conceptual model of a substantive area of a body of knowledge; second, a taxonomy cannot be developed on the basis of naïve realism; third, a taxonomy must permit manipulation of knowledge in such a fashion as to elucidate relationships not immediately apparent in the primary data; and fourth, a taxonomy must act as the formal language of an area, much as mathematics is the formal language of physics and the natural sciences.

To elucidate, a taxonomy is a conceptual model of a substantive area. It reflects in its categories either a broad or a narrow range of concerns. Being a classification system it rejects and accepts items for consideration. It is a model that either has or has not a place to incorporate certain salient factors. If the framework is insufficient it will exclude vital matters.

THE UTILITY OF THE SYSTEM

A taxonomy must be developed with great care. Perhaps the matter that gives the greatest procedural difficulty in the end is the utility of the system. One thing which militates against utility is an endless list of categories. We need to apply Occam's Razor, the principle of parsimony, to our taxonomy. It is appropriate to recall Lind's[658] work: "it was found necessary to expunge all such terms as were contrived to give an air of wisdom to the imperfections of knowledge." The easiest way to break that rule is to simply start listing items that should be recorded. This is seen in the studies of parent-child or teacher-child interaction when interminable lists of such descriptive terms as *hostility, cooperation, affection,* and the like are compiled. These are then used to record and evaluate behavior. Perhaps the best advice is to set up criteria for judging the inclusiveness, the consistency, the coherence, and the construct validity of the terms employed.

A taxonomy is helpful if it helps us do things that are otherwise impossible. One such value is the need to describe relationships that are not obvious to the simple observer. A taxonomy should be a research tool, a technique for describing and communicating the processes of instruction in special education. It should help us understand how and why learning takes place.[1152]

If we were to compare growth in the various branches of knowledge it would be clear that the natural sciences have advanced further than most others. In considering why this is so it is well to compare their present form with their historical form. Mathematics, for example, begin with the simple proposition that one needs to keep track of the number of one's progeny. It no doubt moved along to keeping track of arrows when man was a hunter and to the length of building materials when he became an artisan. Today simple mensuration has been replaced by a wholly conceptual mathematics which deals with nonrepresentational matters and probes relationships in a fashion quite impossible when we deal with the "practical." This is possible because the number two or the quantity X is not restricted to two children, or X paces. Number is used in a theoretical, or to choose a less invidious word, conceptual, sense. Number is used as a formal language, as a set of notations ultimately reducible to reality but used to escape the limitations of the here and now, used to permit the imagination to deal with things outside of the accident of a particular place and a particular moment.

A taxonomy of special education should have the value of allowing us to leave the problem of what to do about a given child's problems in favor of grasping the heart of similar children's problems. In this way a taxonomy can help us solve our difficulties much as a problem expressed as an algebraic problem can be solved for more than one factor. In this fashion a formal language allows us to grow beyond the stage that accumulated knowledge would indicate. It is no accident that we say it takes four years to train a teacher and five years to make one. What we are really saying is that we can transmit just so much knowledge to a would-be teacher—there are vital matters that simply cannot be communicated to the beginner. Put another way we can say that there are items of knowledge that cannot be codified or transmuted in such a fashion that we can phrase meaningful, communicable statements. In terms of this discussion we may say that we have not been able to handle the accumulated wisdom of a master-teacher's experience. The reason, one might argue, is that there is no formal language available to the teacher and the student, there is no set of terms that are adequate to codify, to express, to manipulate the information. To use Bruner's[144] expression, taxonomy of special education should permit us to go beyond the information given.

APPLIED CONSIDERATIONS

The assumption on which this presentation rests is that a taxonomy of special education is a practical tool. As an example we may consider the problem of educating emotionally disturbed children. This particular practical problem is chosen because of the attention currently being given to the matter. Also, it is a good example of how not to go about developing an educational schema. At the moment, the education of emotionally disturbed children consists of a series of acts which are justified by either the criterion of precedent or by the accident of the discipline under whose auspices the problem is placed by an omniscient state legislature. It can be either physically endorsed baby-sitting until the play therapist arrives, or it may be quasi-normal instruction under the care of a motherly, non-neurotic teacher.

Looking to the future, and asking the question, Where do we turn next?, we may see a little light if we try to use a taxonomic approach. One of the functions of a taxonomy is the reduction of data to basic, irreducible terms in data language. In this fashion the path for educating emotionally disturbed children may be laid out by converting psychiatric terms and data into educational terms and data. Since this is a preliminary analysis and is not intended to be the solution of this problem, let us take the least educationally responsive child, an autistic child. Our task here is to make statements in the same data language about an autistic child as a psychiatric problem and an instructional problem. For reasons best discussed elsewhere we will use contemporary behavioral theory as the data language.

The psychiatric feature of an autistic child is the "aloneness." The youngster has object rather than person relationships. Educationally, the child simply does not make progress. The hiatus which causes much of our difficulty is the lack of articulation between what the psychiatrist knows and what the teacher does.

Viewed taxonomically, and using a specific data language, we might say that the problem should be formulated as one of interaction. Very briefly, interactions are contingent when one person's behavior produces changes in that of the other. When there is no give and take we say there is asymmetric contingency or noncontingency. The autistic child's problems is that his chief attribute in either educational or psychiatric settings is a lack of contingent behavior. He does not learn when the teacher teaches, he does not communicate when the therapist attempts to understand him. At the risk of blunting Occam's Razor we might say there is no "initiation of structure," in his role behavior.

Now what has this discourse on the autistic child done? It has not given a pedagogy for the autistic child. That would be beyond the scope, though not the implications, of this article. What it has done is to describe a behavior pattern, or a segment of it, in a language which can be applied to two disciplines. It has provided a *lingua franca* for psychiatry and education; it has described a problem in a fashion which is common to two disciplines. Secondly, it has related the emotional disability of a child to the emotional handicap of a learner. It has put in psychiatric data and produced educational data. The fact that it was possible to do this demonstrates the care to be used in choosing a data language. If the idiom worked for some conditions, but not for others, we might have a way of distinguishing those conditions which are disabilities in the organic sense, from those which are handicaps in the functional sense. For example, it is probable that color-blindness, an obvious disability, does not produce any meaningful data in interbehavior. If it did, it would be a problem requiring our sustained attention as educators. Failing that, it would not be a handicapping condition.

Another applied consideration is the value of a simple taxonomy as an aid in communication. A practical problem in instruction is deciding what to do with children who have several handicaps. Which handicap is functionally most important? Where shall we start? A third matter arises when we ponder whether a child should be placed in a special class on the basis of his motor handicap or his sensory handicap, or his intellectual handicap. A taxonomy can help solve these problems.

Recently Willenberg[1117] discussed safety matters affecting handicapped children. His approach was to develop a taxonomic model of factors in the external environment—modifiers—and factors in the internal environment—things to be modified. By plotting these items two-dimensionally he indicated certain conclusions that applied to three sorts of handicaps.

I should like to offer a third area of taxonomic endeavor. This is the understanding of factors affecting vocational success in the period after special instruction. A taxonomy of instruction is not necessarily applicable to post-instructional matters. In some ways there are common elements, but there are some significant differences. It is much like using a checkerboard to play chess. The board is the same, by analogy the ecology of

			UNFAVORABLE	IRRELEVANT	FAVORABLE
INTELLECT	a. verbal b. non-verbal				
CONCEPTS	a. work b. world c. self				
SKILLS	a. motor b. perceptual c. intermodal				
MOTIVES	a. occupational level b. money c. affiliation d. advancement e. independence				
COMMUNI- CATION	Expressive Receptive	a. oral b. written a. oral b. written			

FIGURE 26-1.

home and community, but there are different strategies and some extra ploys.

Figure 26-1 shows some elements on which postschool life may depend. *Intellect* is the same as in the instructional period, but its relevance decreases. *Concepts* of self, the world, and work, emerge as salient matters. *Motives* vary: *achievement motivation* is probably still more important, and new motives, *affiliation, power, money, advancement,* and *level of occupation* emerge. *Skills* refers to motor and perceptual abilities. In the post-school success-and-failure of the cerebral palsied, discrete abilities are important. Of equal importance may be what is referred to as *intermodal skills,* the input through one system and output through another: hand-eye, ear-hand-eye, for example. *Communication* acquires a new significance when we consider that young people may have been taught by people who could grasp the intent of students with poor propositional speech. As barriers are dissolved by communication, they are erected by inability to give and receive ideas. The only occupation that is exempt from this consideration is probably that of lighthouse keeper. Were this choice, or a comparable one, available it might well represent flight from reality into minority status, a step contrary to the spirit of all previous special education endeavors.

It is unrealistic to relate all abilities to all occupations; such an attempt would vitiate a taxonomy. For this reason we may consider three terms that apply selectively. *Irrelevant* would describe the application of color-blindness (see *skills*) to many tasks. On the other hand, serious hearing loss (see *communication*) might be *favorable* in places where a high background of noise is disruptive, in fact where a disability is no handicap. *Unfavorable* would describe the everyday limitations imposed on the special education graduate choosing an occupation.

SUMMARY

A comprehensive taxonomy is needed. This article has discussed two miniature and overlapping structures and commented on a third, that of Willenberg.

The development of a comprehensive taxonomy will occur when special education has developed a comprehensive data language.

Curriculum can acquire construct validity, as opposed to the face validity of many current procedures when it employs taxonomic refinements.

A taxonomy is a device to solve practical problems; it is also a conceptual model and so emphasizes the comprehensive needs of special education theory.

A comprehensive taxonomy can restore what has been lost since the demise of Herbart, the unity of theory and practice. It can further lead to a sophisticated pedagogy. This in turn has implications for the increased professionalization of practitioners in special education.

Chapter 27

A Proposed Conceptual Framework for Special Education

SAMUEL LEVINE

THERE has been a paucity of investigations in regard to the personal and social development of the exceptional child,* in spite of the growing body of knowledge and increased research activities on nondisabled children. In part this is because special education, to a great degree, has remained at a highly pragmatic level; the major concerns relating to program organization, curriculum development, and therapeutic devices and procedures. The need for systematic theoretically oriented research in special education has been stressed recently by Block,[113] Kvaraceus,[625] and Meyerson.[762] This paper proposes a theoretical framework relating to physical and mental disability from which hypothetical propositions are deduced, offering some direction for future research.

The writer is aware that the basis of the differentiations for exceptional children may be a physical, emotional, or intellectual deviation or any combination of these. The fact that the group is heterogeneous in regard to disability does not deny the usefulness of the proposed framework. One might modify, amplify, or make more specific any particular hypothesis based on one of the exceptionalities. However, as an orienting frame of reference the theoretical propositions and their hypothetical derivations appear heuristic.

This paper will not be concerned with the resolution of the practical implications of the proposed framework. However, it would be profitable to stipulate some of the more salient theoretical questions and their practical counterparts in regard to physical and/or mental deviation. The pervasive concern among special educators has not been with the "a" set of questions

---

Reprinted from *Exceptional Children*, 28:83-90, October, 1961.

* Exceptional child refers to all categories of children with mental and physical deviations other than the "gifted." Much of what is proposed here is not applicable to that group and it would appear preferable to exclude them from the present discussion. For the purposes of the article, the exceptional child is defined after Barker *et al.*[66] as a person having a physical and/or mental handicap and who is generally perceived in his cultural group as deviating sufficiently in these respects to prevent him from participating in important activities on terms of equality with normal individuals of his own age.

but, rather, with the "b" set of questions. A list of these concerns follows.

1. (a) What is the effect of physical and/or mental deviations on group cohesion?
   (b) How can families who have such children be helped in order to reduce intrafamily conflict and increase family integration?
2. (a) What are the effects of a physical and/or mental handicap on personality development?
   (b) What kind of educational and vocational planning is necessary for these children in order to reduce maladjustment?
3. (a) What is the relationship between the learning of stereotypes toward deviants and concept formation?
   (b) How can we reduce stereotyping toward individuals with physical and/or mental handicaps so as to reduce certain restrictive barriers to their adjustment and to improve their social acceptance?
4. (a) How does physical and/or mental deviation affect the socialization of the child, particularly in relation to parent-child interaction?
   (b) How can we reduce parental overprotection of the handicapped child and increase the child's self-direction and psychological independence?
5. (a) In what way does a physical and/or mental handicap affect one's status, position, or role expectations in society?
   (b) How can we reduce the marginality or isolation of individuals with such deviations so as to maximize their contribution to self and society?

CONCEPTUAL FRAMEWORK

Social psychological research regarding the exceptional child has been oriented primarily toward the phenomenon of acceptance-rejection. The major sources of such information have been sociometric and attitude studies. The effect of rejection on personality development has been inferred from these studies, the basis for the rejection being posited in the disability. They have generally sought to confirm or deny the existence of rejection without specifying the conditions under which rejection (or acceptance) may be increased, lessened, or modified. In effect, the obtained relationships between disability and acceptance-rejection have been interpreted solely in terms of the deviation as the basis for the findings.

The single variate approach in studies of disability is due, the writer believes, to the assumption that physical and/or mental deviations are sufficient conditions for explaining the observed or measured relationships. The lack of theoretical propositions has minimized other sources of variation as explanatory variables. Berreman[95(p.347)] states that the problem is to determine how much the psychological and social maladjustment of the disabled child is "an inescapable consequence of physical or other impairment, and how much results from social factors—from the status accorded such individuals in our culture and the position accorded to them by 'normal' people."

The implication of the above is that the concern regarding physical and mental variation must extend beyond solely some objective assessment of the individual's disability. Meyerson[762(p.9)] points out that the effect of such variations "is strictly relative to the expectations of the culture in which the person lives, the tasks that are required of him and the meaning the person himself and others may assign to the variation." "Disability," Meyerson[762(p.12)] contends, "is not an objective *thing in a person*, but a social value judgment."

These values relate to society's perception of leadership, contributions toward improving society, being a good citizen, being a family head and other essential aspects for maintaining society. These values are criteria against which behavior is assessed in terms of deviation. All members of society, whether handicapped or not, are evaluated primarily by these values. Where an individual cannot meet these demands or where there are questions as to the adequacy of the individual in relation to these demands, there will be some devaluation of him on society's part.[65, 376, 705, 761, 762, 796, 1115]

Disabled individuals are treated as members of a category which communicates to society some statement of the individual's present and/or potential contribution. These categories—e.g., blind, deaf, mentally retarded, cerebral palsied, orthopedic, or the more general inclusive category, disabled, or exceptional—contain the stereotypes, biases, and sets toward individuals who are members of these groups. Vinacke[1083(p.239)] suggests that the distinctive element in stereotyping is the social significance of the behavior: "The fact is that traits represented in stereotypes depend solely upon properties which a group of people agree are typical of a class just as is the case in practice for classes of other objects. In this sense the properties of stereotypes have a social reality regardless of whether objective measurement would support them or not. Indeed, it is very likely that such measurement would support, at least to some degree, some traits but would not in the least substantiate others."

CATEGORICAL TERMS

Society "understands" or conceptualizes the disabled individual in categorical terms. Those attributes which society utilizes for categorizing the disabled we term the defining attributes of the category.* Each behavior in the category has a degree of defining value in respect to its predictability to the stereotype. Those behaviors that afford maximal prediction to the category have a high defining value and are crucial to the stability of the category. Although these categories may be modified in relation to a particular individual, to a great degree they represent categorization based on biological resemblances. In a sense, these exceptionalities have a common or shared stimulus function. This leads to certain social distinctions and culturally imposed differentiations.[32, 65, 470]

The disabled individual may not share society's frame of reference in regard to his disability. He will develop for himself a way of understanding and of differentiating those aspects of his disability that present difficulties for him and those that he feels are of no consequences to his general functioning. Those aspects of his behavior he defines as most differentiating relative to his deviation we call the criterial attributes of his disability. The criterial attributes are specific to the particular individual's assessment of his abilities, interest, and aspirations. Vinacke[1083] makes the point that, in his studies, there is a marked general similarity in the content of self-stereotyping as compared to those stereotypes held by others. Dembo, Ladieu and Wright[247] found that disabled individuals tend to place themselves in positions on a fortune–misfortune scale similar to nondisabled individuals; whereas nondisabled placed the disabled low on this scale. These findings suggest that a study of the perception of disabled individuals' criterial attributes (self-attributes) as compared to the defining attributes may be fruitful.

The disabled individual will at times come into conflict with the existing structure, whether it be in regard to educational, vocational, or social aspirations. Conflict will be evidenced by overt rejection of the individual's aspirations, denial of his competence, and/or a refusal to extend consideration to him equal to that of a nondisabled individual. It is hypothesized that the greater the difference between the individual's criterial attributes and society's defining attributes, the greater will be the conflict. The obvious question arises as to whether conflict is a necessary condition in such situations.

It should be remembered that the defining attributes of a category represent attitudinal or behavioral stereotypes toward particular groups or individuals (i.e., blind, deaf, etc.). Insofar as these stereotypes have restrictive or devaluating effects on the individual, the basis for conflict is always present. It could be asked if conflict might be reduced, or perhaps eliminated,

---

* The terms *defining attribute* and *criterial attribute* are borrowed from Bruner, Goodnow and Austin.[146]

by having the disabled accept all of, or most of, society's defining attributes in respect to his disability. Meyerson[762](p.56) says, in this respect, "It is easy to contend that the disabled person must 'accept' his disability, but this is only a meaningless and contradictory platitude if the underlying situation of disability is not understood. If 'acceptance' means that the person must be content with an inferior position that requires him to acknowledge his inferiority as a person and permits him to strive only for intrinsically less satisfying goals, 'acceptance' is difficult. If there is no assurance that society will 'accept' the disability also and not penalize the person for it, it is unrealistic to endow 'acceptance' with the qualities of a panacea."

Depending upon the frequency with which conflict occurs and the degree of difference between the criterial and defining attributes, there will be a greater or lesser sense of isolation or nonbelonging. To the degree that the individual feels this sense of isolation or nonbelonging, there will be psychological and social distance* between society and the disabled person.[65, 761, 762, 1021]

The individual who seeks participation and acceptance in areas where the stereotypes are firmly established will come into conflict situations. The more crucial the stereotypes are for the definition of that category the greater will be the resistance to the disabled individual's participation. Bruner[145](p.208) has pointed out that expectancies mold perceptual organizations in a self-sustaining fashion. That is, "most people come to depend upon a certain constancy in their environment and, save under special conditions, attempt to ward off variations from this state of affairs."

PSYCHOLOGICAL AND SOCIAL DISTANCE

The creation of psychological and social distance is a reciprocal process. The disabled individual may become sensitized to group feelings and non-membership, or if he has had membership, it may have been unrewarding, and he may withdraw from social contact. The individuals in the disabled person's environment may interpret the withdrawing behavior as a confirming instance of the defining attributes. The stereotype is in part confirmed and the group acts in such a way as to reinforce the disabled individual's feelings of difference and isolation. Thus, psychological and social distance is increased. The withdrawal of the disabled person from the en-

---

* The term *social distance* has had long and considerable usage in sociology. Von Wiese and Becker[1084](p.241) regard such distance "as a condition resulting from the inhibition of tendencies toward association by tendencies toward dissociation from personal and/or situational factors." Newland[821](p.150) speaks of *psychological distance* and sees this process as both a general, attitudinal reaction as well as a highly situational phenomenon. He states, "attitudes, tempered in forms of certain value systems, may be regarded as indicative of such distance." The term *psychological and social distance* is used here in order to convey the sense of the interaction of the pervasive, generalized attitudinal system with the personal situational factors.

vironment decreases the communication between him and those around him, lessening the possibility of understanding his interests, aspirations, and the ways of his dealing with society's perception of his deviancy. The lessening of communication, of course, will tend to increase the psychological and social distance and more firmly establish the existing stereotypes.

To a great degree this psychological and social distance is anticipatory in nature. As the individual's sense of difference and nonbelonging is reinforced, the greater will be the anticipation of nonacceptance in future situations. The effect will be for the individual to avoid general social contact, thus increasing psychological and social distance and leading to a personal sense of inadequacy. The anticipation of psychological and social distance is an anticipation of failure. The individual may rationalize his feeling of inadequacy by, in fact, attributing to himself the existing stereotypes and perhaps seek what might be termed a *deviant adjustment.* A relatively extreme form of this is removing oneself from general societal contact and seeking companionship solely within the disabled group.

Murphy[795][(p.767)] points out that the deviant has his own world, his own deviant group, in which membership is experienced. One can only speculate about the effect of such deviant groups (such as associations and clubs for the deaf, blind, etc.) on the individual. It is suggested that the greater the individual's dependency on such organizations, the greater the reinforcement of existing stereotypes and the greater the psychological and social distance. The implications of the above statements for the present system of segregated special training schools and institutions appear obvious. To a great degree the educational channels for exceptional children are comprised primarily of children who are themselves disabled.

Meyerson[761][(p.4)] contends that variations in physique lead to a highly negative value and for more extreme deviations, positive restrictions. It is hypothesized that the more obvious or visible the defect and the greater the apparent relevance of the exceptionality for the performance of a task, the greater will be the psychological and social distance. These predictions are given some credence by the findings of Schachter[961][(p.201)] in a study of nonconformity. His data indicate that people who strongly reject the deviate perceive a greater difference between themselves and the deviate than do people who do not reject them. Force[341][(p.107)] concludes, in discussing his findings, "It would seem that a factor of visibility was also operating in which acceptance is more of a task for the child with a disability which is readily discernible or obvious to the viewer."

Kvaraceus[624][(p.331)] measured the degree of acceptability of deviations in children among professional workers. He concludes, "apparently this group of professional workers feel most comfortable with the most respectable and perhaps the least offensive of the deviates." Johnson[554] found that as intellectual ability decreased, acceptance by other children decreased and rejection increased. Lewis[652](pp.32-33) found that teachers assign traits that have definite mental health value, as determined by mental hygienists, differentially based on the child's intelligence. The geniuses and high I.Q. group were assigned the high value traits more frequently than the normative group. Both the retarded and the "problem" groups were assigned these traits less frequently than the normative group.

The hypothesis concerning the obviousness of the defect and the creation of psychological and social distance needs qualification. Wright[1151](pp.53-54) cautions, "Doubtless there are other factors associated with degree of disability, some favoring and some hindering adjustment, the resultant effect being quite removed from the objective fact of severity." One factor offered here relates to the role of achievement in the modification of the defining attributes and the lessening of psychological and social distance. It is hypothesized that, holding degree of disability constant, there will be an inverse relationship between the child's achievement and the amount of psychological and social distance engendered by the disability. More than likely there will be an interaction between the degree of disability and the child's competence with the amount of psychological and social distance created.

Evidence supporting this proposition is not readily available but some suggested support for our thesis can be found. DeGroat and Thompson,[242] (p.74) found that children who show evidence of having acquired more subject matter receive a higher proportion of teacher approval as rated by the pupils. They conclude that "children who experience a high degree of teacher approval have a better opinion of themselves, are more "outgoing," and have more confidence in their ability to adjust to social situations." As expected, they also found that the more intelligent children receive a significantly greater amount of teacher approval, while the less intelligent pupils experience larger amounts of teacher disapproval. Wright[1151](p.153) conjectures that attributes such as "perseverence, independence, intelligence, moral stamina, etc. may give genuine support to an ego that may be undermined by the negatively evaluated attributes of the disability itself."

CRITERIA FOR INFERRING PSYCHOLOGICAL AND SOCIAL DISTANCE

Any proposed scheme from which psychological and social distance is to be inferred must assess the strength of existing stereotypes as well as the effect of nonconforming or nonexemplary behavior on the reduction of these stereotypes. The categories within this scheme indicate the strength of the behavioral stereotypes toward the general category of disability or exceptionality or toward any specific category, such as blind or deaf.

We would have a nonexemplar of a specific category where the group's expectations are not borne out in regard to the individual's abilities. For example, each time the statement is made, "I didn't know blind people could do that," there is a tendency to break down that category. For that individual, at least, there is less predictability to the category, "blindness," and therefore less validity to the defining attributes of that category. This suggests some fluidity in regard to the defining attributes.

The following categorical scheme permits the determination of the defining attributes and the criterial attributes from which the inference of psychological and social distance is made.

Category One. This category contains all the behavioral stereotypes shared by society, relevant to a particular disability. These stereotypes apply to all individuals having a particular disability. Category One is akin to "biological determinism" in regard to physical disability. That is, the stereotypes are taken as a statement regarding the human nature of the disabled individual.

Category Two. A particular disabled individual performs in such a way on a defining attribute so as to make his behavior indistinguishable from a nondisabled individual. The disabled individual will be seen as a nonexemplar relative to that particular behavior by all persons who come into contact with him. In this case, the disabled person is seen as the nonexemplar rather than the behavior. There are undoubtedly many disabled individuals who, relative to a specific behavior, are nonexemplars. The particular behavior in question may vary from individual to individual. It is possible to predict for these individuals in respect to all other defining attributes.

Category Three. A particular behavioral stereotype through nonexemplary confirmation gradually becomes less important or less differentiating in regard to the defining attributes. This may occur through mechanical or other modifications that permit the disabled individual to now meet certain expectations that were not before possible. When a sufficient number of disabled individuals do not confirm the expectation relative to a particular defining attribute, this behavior becomes nonexemplary for all individuals. In this instance the behavior is the nonexemplar rather than the individual. The behavior now becomes nondefining, as it does not contribute to the scheme of attributes that have predictive value.

Category Four. A particular disabled individual, although evidencing some structural limitation, may not be differentiated from the nondisabled on a functional basis. For this individual, most defining attributes are nonpredictive and for all intents and purposes he is a nonexemplar. For example, "It's hard to think of him as a blind person" would be appropriate for such an individual. The defining attributes will, however, be present for other individuals having these same physical limitations. The nonexemplar is, again, the individual, but here he is, in effect, not thought of as disabled; whereas in Category Two the individual is so considered. Category Four is a considerable step or movement toward breaking down the defining attributes. Despite the fact that a few individuals are involved, the inability to predict for these individuals to any or hardly any important defining attributes raises two fundamental questions:

1. What are the conditions in the life situation of these individuals that permitted the development of nondifferentiated behavior?
2. Could many, or most, or all such disabled individuals function in this way, given these or similar conditions?

Category Five. Here the defining attribute breakdown has been virtually accomplished. A sufficient number of meaningful behaviors have become non-differentiating for most (or all) members of a particular disability. The defining attributes have no functional utility, except in those areas dealing with specific structural limitations. Functional questions regarding any disabled individual will be determined at the empirical level. However, no prejudgments will be made, as no stereotypes exist.

SUMMARY

The study in special education of variation in physical and mental development has been concerned primarily with the solution of practical problems rather than with theoretically oriented research.

The author proposed a conceptual framework from which hypothetical propositions were deduced relative to the personal and social development of individuals with physical and/or mental deviations. It has been suggested that these disabilities have both objective and value dimensions associated with them.

The generalized attitudinal set by which society conceptualizes such deviations are referred to as defining attributes. The personal, self-evaluative aspects of the individual's disability are termed criterial attributes. A scheme for assessing the strength of these attributes was presented in terms of categories offering the possibility of determining the relationship between cultural biases and stereotypes and the disabled individual's self-perceptions and personal aspirations.

The concept of psychological and social distance was suggested as a criterion measure of social interaction. Various hypotheses have been set forth specifying the conditions under which psychological and social distance will vary.

Chapter 28

A Framework for Considering Some
Issues in Special Education

MAYNARD C. REYNOLDS

GROWING attention is being given to creating a conceptual framework for consideration of special education problems. Outlined below is one way of thinking about the broad range of services provided
under special education. The framework is presented schematically, along
with a brief discussion of its features, and then utilized to discuss some current issues. Consideration is given only to handicapped children, since programs for the gifted seem not to fit the structure as developed here.

THE HIERARCHY OF SPECIAL EDUCATION PROGRAMS

The variety of programs which comprise special education may be summarized in a chart which takes the form of a triangle (Fig. 28-1). At the
first level, across the broad base of the chart, is represented the large number of exceptional children, mainly those with minor deviations who are
enrolled in regular classes in the schools. Much of the effort to provide
needed services for these children must be directed through regular classroom teachers.

Many exceptional children will not receive all required services in regular classes and thus the chart includes a number of more specialized services, organized in a succession of levels. The gradual narrowing of the
chart indicates the smaller numbers of children involved as programs become more specialized.

The second level of service is referred to as "Regular Classroom with
Consultation." Some children may be retained in regular classes if consultation is available to teachers and parents to help in understanding children and in making minor modifications in the school program. The schools
are rapidly becoming employers of school psychologists, special education
consultants, school social workers, and other personnel who provide such
consultation.

Children presenting more complex problems will sometimes need spe-

Reprinted from *Exceptional Children,* 28:367-370, March, 1962.

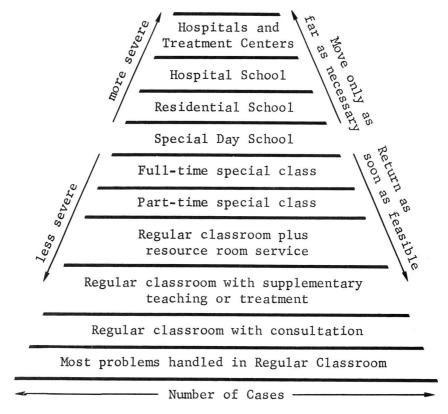

FIGURE 28-1. Special education programs.

cialized services in the form of "Supplementary Teaching or Treatment." This third level of service is illustrated by the work of itinerant speech correctionists who frequently work with individuals or small groups of children for brief periods each day or several times weekly. Similarly, some disturbed children may be given brief periods of counseling help on a regular schedule. Children with hearing or vision problems frequently receive needed supplementary help from specialists while basically enrolled in regular classes.

A next level in the chart is labeled "Regular Classroom plus Resource Room Service." This type of program has probably been most fully developed for visually-handicapped children and in the field of remedial reading, but illustrations may be found in other fields of special education as well. In such programs children are enrolled in regular classes, but special resource rooms are provided in their schools. The children spend a part of each day in the resource room, sometimes on a definite schedule and sometimes on an irregular schedule according to special needs as they arise through the school day. A blind child, for example, may take most instruction in regular classes with normal children but go to the resource room in his building for instruction in braille, mobility, or typing. The resource room includes all necessary special equipment and materials and is in the charge of a specially trained teacher who carefully coordinates her teaching with that of regular classroom teachers.

Succeeding levels, in order, are the "Part-time Special Class," the "Full-time Special Class," and the "Special Day School." Programs of these types are well known and need no description for present purposes. Each represents a further step or extension of program to a more specialized level.

Nearer the top of the chart is the "Residential School." Placement in such schools involves separation from the home environment as well as further specialization in the educational program.

Finally, two programs are listed in which the primary emphasis is on treatment, protection, or care, in contrast to the educational emphasis in programs of lower levels. The first of these is called the "Hospital-School" and the latter, "Hospitals and Treatment Centers." School departments in institutions of these types may have importance but usually referral of children to such institutions is based upon factors other than educational need. Overall program control is usually not in the hands of educators.

FEATURES OF THE FRAMEWORK

Several features of the organization of the above chart need to be indicated. In considering the several levels of program, proceeding from the bottom to the top of the chart, a number of changes may be observed:

1. the problems of children placed in programs tend to become more severe or more complex;
2. programs tend to become more expensive;
3. responsibility for administration of programs shifts from school authorities to health, welfare, or correction authorities;
4. children are more separated from ordinary school and home life;
5. demands for highly specialized personnel increase;
6. parent and general public understanding of programs decreases.

Perhaps the major feature of the scheme is that it presents the broad range in types of special education programs in an organized fashion. The descriptions of the various levels have been given with no thought that they represent the ultimate in types of programs. Indeed, many other types of programs exist and still others will be devised. Within this conceptual framework, several current issues in special education may now be considered.

ISSUES IN SPECIAL EDUCATION

Segregation

One of the continuing issues in special education is that of segregation—the separation of individuals or groups of children. It is correctly argued, for example, that removing a child from his home and neighborhood school for placement in a residential school is a serious matter. It may be convenient to make such placements routinely, but conflicting values emerge which in fact place extraordinary responsibility upon those who make such placement decisions. Similarly, it can be a disturbing experience for a child to be placed in a special class or any other type of special program. But it is also inexcusable to delay or deny special services when they are needed.

The framework outlined above may be useful in stating a general attitude or policy toward these continuing problems of separation or segregation. The prevailing view is that normal home and school life should be preserved if at all possible. When a special placement is necessary to provide suitable care or education, it should be no more "special" than necessary. In terms of the chart, this is to say that children should be moved upward only as far as necessary and be returned downward as soon as feasible. By stating such a principle within the structure of programs as proposed here, views about the segregation issue can be made quite explicit.

If programs are operated according to the above principle or attitude, we would find increasing numbers of blind and hearing handicapped children returning from residential to day schools after they have achieved special skills through intensive early training. Enrollments in special orthopedic schools at the junior high school level should be lower than at the elementary school level if elementary school programs are effective. Movement among the various levels will perhaps be less possible for the mentally retarded, but in most cases problems of transition would loom large and significant.

The strategy proposed here requires variety and range in programs for all handicapping areas, continuing assessment procedures to assure changes in placement at appropriate times, and coordinated planning and placement services covering all levels.

The Responsibility of the School to Severely Handicapped Children

Between the levels of responsibility well established in the schools, mainly for those with relatively mild handicaps, and programs operated by other public agencies, such as mental hospitals and training schools for delinquent children, there is a zone of indefiniteness in public responsibility. Trainable retarded children and many of the multiply handicapped fall in this "in-between" zone of responsibility. These children have more serious handicaps than the schools are prepared to consider and yet they often do not fit into programs of institutions geared to the very seriously handicapped. In recent years this "in-between" zone has become very active, with many voluntary groups goading public agencies to establish programs. Because programs for children in these categories have never been provided, agencies of all types can "beg off" on precedent.

An interpretation of problems of these "in-between" groups is suggested by the present conceptual framework. Historically, health, welfare, and correction authorities were given early responsibility in most states for the operation of institutions for the most severely deviant. In recent years, these programs have often been extended into the community in the form of outpatient mental health centers, growing numbers of social casework agencies, improved probationary services for delinquent youth, and in other ways. Schools, starting from the level of regular classrooms, have gradually extended their programs to more specialized levels and strengthened relationships with all varieties of community agencies. The separation of schools and other agencies has been lessened; levels of the "chart" have gradually merged.

Problems of the "in-between" children will need to be solved by even closer cooperation among agencies of many types. The trainable retarded, for example, often present life-long dependency problems. It is futile to think about responsibility for these children in terms of "education versus welfare." They need health, welfare, and educational services—not just one or another. The challenge in this field, as in many others, is to establish new and effective interagency community programs. One of the real and current dangers is that programs for such "in-between" children will develop in expedient forms without a clear formulation of public responsibility. Already, too many programs exist with only fragile support and token administrative services by public agencies. Such conditions bode ill for the quality and durability of these programs.

Other Problems Considered Briefly

Two additional problems will be examined briefly in the present framework. The first of these concerns the form of special aids as provided mainly by state governments. When the variety of programs is considered, it may be seen that financial aid programs tied to only one or a limited number of types of programs may introduce rigidities in programing. Aids on a per-classroom unit or per-pupil basis are probably less desirable than are aids tied to professional personnel, leaving some variety in the ways they may work with exceptional children.

Implications for terminology and classification may also be mentioned. First, the emphasis on "flow" of children among levels of program implies that categorization of children is always tentative and subject to revision. Second, it is suggested that more attention needs to be given to classification of programs rather than so exclusively to classification of children. The essential problem in educational placement is to allocate children to programs likely to be most valuable for them. Methods of classifying children now used in special education seem to have developed with all too little attention to subtle differentiations necessary to make the most effective placements. As more attention shifts to the program side of the classification and placement problem, it seems likely that approaches to individual child study and classification will be greatly revised. A child's potential is not independent of his situation, or of the methods used in his education, yet we so often proceed as if abstract study of the child himself is sufficient.

SUMMARY

A summary of special education programs has been presented in the form of a hierarchy, ranging from regular classes, through several intermediate levels of special services, to hospitals and treatment centers. The levels of the hierarchy were ordered according to increasing specialization. As children are placed in higher level programs, their separation from normal home and school life increases. Responsibility for programs at the highest levels of specialization has generally been placed with health, welfare, or corrections authorities. Schools have carried responsibility for programs serving the larger numbers of less severely handicapped children. Within this context, certain current issues in special education were discussed.

It was suggested that having a broad range of services is important and that children should be placed in programs of no more special character than absolutely necessary. There should be continuing assessment of children in special programs with a view toward returning them to more ordinary environments as soon as feasible. Problems of providing services to certain groups of children, such as the trainable retarded, have been interpreted as being partly historical in origin for reason of their "in-between" status in regard to school responsibility and functions of other agencies. To serve these "in-between" children, new patterns of interaction among a variety of agencies will be necessary. Finally, the importance of developing financial aid patterns which stimulate the development of a fuller range of services is stressed and a plea is made for more attention to program differentiation in developing systems of classification and terminology to be applied to handicapped children.

Chapter 29

A Suggested Classification of
Handicapped Children

R. S. HOLT

CONSIDERABLE attention is being given at the present time to the problems of handicapped children. A session at the Annual Meeting of the British Medical Association[136] and an entire issue of a medical journal (*Practitioner*, April, 1955) have been devoted to this problem. Every help possible should be given to these children for humanitarian reasons. By helping them to develop to the full such faculties as they possess, there should be a reduced demand upon the community when they reach adult life. A recent survey[161] showed that the provisions for handicapped children throughout the country were very patchy. A more extensive study of the problem is now being made under the auspices of the Carnegie Trust.

A *handicap* is a relative condition and its definition is difficult. Children may be considered to be handicapped, if, mentally or physically, they lag behind their contemporaries, or if they require special care, or if they have to make special adjustments in educational, emotional, or social spheres. Whatever definition is used there will always be a number of borderline cases.

Handicapped children are usually grouped according to the cause of the handicap. There are those with deficiencies of the special senses, the blind and the deaf; those with locomotor difficulties, the cerebral palsied and the paralysed; those with chronic illness, the cardiac invalids, the asthmatics and the diabetics; those who are emotionally disturbed, and those who are mentally retarded. This method of groupings gives no indication of the child's functional disability. For example, a child labelled "spastic" may have abnormal reflexes in one limb but no functional disability, while another "spastic" may be immobilized with quadriplegia. Quibell,[898] dealing with severely physically handicapped children, found that the anatomical diagnosis alone was inadequate and discussed a method of functional assessment suitable for this group. During a current study of the problems of the mentally retarded children a classification was devised

Reprinted from *Arch Diseases in Childhood*, 32:226-229, 1956.

TABLE 29-1

Section	Grade	Ability	Significance
P (Physique)	1	No deformity No reduction of exercise tolerance Medical supervision not required	This section indicates general physique, exercise tolerance and for children at school, attending centres, or in institutions, some indication is given of the need for medical supervision.
	2	Some deformity or reduced exercise tolerance, occasional medical care needed	
	3	Deformity or reduced exercise tolerance or both. Possibly frequent infections. Needs frequent medical care	
	4	Completely disabled. Possibly bed- or chair-ridden	
U (Upper limbs)	1	Able to feed, wash, dress self Can handle pencil and pen	This section indicates the possible need for physiotherapy and in a class the teachers will know the number of children needing help with dressing and feeding.
	2	Assists with feeding, dressing, and washing but needs help to complete task	
	3	Needs complete supervision for feeding, washing, and dressing	
	4	Arms are useless and cannot hold objects	
L (Locomotion)	1	Able to walk, run, go up and down stairs and climb	This section indicates possible needs for physiotherapy, orthopaedic appliances, special carriages. It may help when the family are advised about housing. It indicates the possible need for conveyance to school.
	2	Can walk and possibly run but needs help to go up and down stairs	
	3	With help can take a few steps or walk a short distance	
	4	Unable to walk even with help	
H (Hearing)	1	Normal hearing	These grades correspond closely to those already in use and recommended by the Board of Education (1938). Their Grade I would be included in 1, their IIa as 2, their IIb as 3 and their Grade III as 4.
	2	Partially deaf: with some help can make satisfactory progress in ordinary school	
	3	Partially deaf; unable to progress in ordinary school	
	4	Severely or totally deaf	

E (Eyes)	1	Normal vision. No strabismus	The grades used here correspond very closely with those formulated by the Ministry of Education (1945). They have similar significance with regard to training.
	2	Partially sighted but with help able to make progress in ordinary school	
	3	Partially sighted and even with help unable to progress in ordinary school	
	4	Blind	
S (Speech)	1	Speaks well; no speech defect, can relate a simple story	This section is closely linked with that of I (Intelligence). It is included to indicate those children who might be helped by speech therapy, those who may have difficulty conveying their wants and it may possibly indicate the need for investigation of hearing.
	2	Speech of short phrases, possibly with speech defect	
	3	Single words or sounds to indicate wants, possibly speech defect of such severity that understanding is difficult	
	4	No words, meaningless sounds	
T (Toilet)	1	Attends to self, dry at night	This section indicates to teachers the degree of attention to be given to the child. It also allows those children to be selected who cannot be handled at a centre because of defective toilet control. The parents of older children in Grades 3 and 4 may have a lot of expense replacing clothing and bed linen.
	2	Asks for attention, needs some help, may be wet at night	
	3	Accidents with wetting, but control of bowel	
	4	Doubly incontinent	
I (Intelligence)	1	Normal (average) intelligence	Grade 4 corresponds approximately with the classification of idiot at present in use, or of severe subnormality as recommended in the World Health Organization report (1954). In the other grades something can be achieved by training and from the profiles of the children the numbers for whom provision is necessary can be obtained.
	2	Educationally subnormal	
	3	Ineducable but trainable	
	4	Untrainable, complete ament	
B (Behavior)	1	Normal	Behavior problems are common in normal children and even more common in those who are handicapped. This section indicates those families where the child and the parents need special help and some indication is given by the grading as to whether this should be at home or elsewhere.
	2	Abnormal, but adjustment possible in home environment	
	3	Abnormal, adjustment not possible in home environment	
	4	Seriously abnormal; needs specialist care	

which indicated functional disability. This classification, somewhat expanded, is presented below as it is thought that its application to all handicapped children might be useful.

METHOD OF CLASSIFICATION

During the last war a comprehensive form of medical assessment known as the Pulheems System was introduced into H.M. Forces.[336] Using this system it was possible to construct a profile which indicated a person's abilities. Personnel were directed to posts to which they were best fitted, as shown by their profiles. The proposed classification of handicapped children is similar. It allows one to draw a profile of disabilities. The profiles will show the nature of the help needed by the handicapped children and will allow the selection, from a group, of those children who will benefit from any particular form of assistance.

The classification may be known by the initial letters of the sections, **P U L H E S T I B: P** relates to general physique, **U** relates to the upper limbs, especially to manipulative ability, **L** represents locomotion, **H** hearing and **E** eyes; **S** indicates speech, while **T** means toilet, **I** intelligence, and **B** behavior.

Each section is divided into four grades. Grade 1 is normal or full ability, and grade 4 complete absence of ability in each section. The addition of the suffix **A** to the grade indicates that that grade is achieved with the aid of special apparatus. The abilities covered by each grade together with comments upon their significance are shown in Table 29-1.

The classification in full would apply to children aged five years or over. It is important that younger handicapped children should be included. It would probably cause confusion if a young child were given a low grade simply because he was not yet old enough to have acquired those particular abilities. This applies to the sections, **U, L, T** and **S**. It is suggested that for the child under five years of age the sections **P, H, E,**

TABLE 29-2

ILLUSTRATIVE 'PROFILE'

JOHN S., Orchard Villas. Born July 6, 1951												
Date	*Age*	*P*	*U*	*L*	*H*	*E*	*S*	*T*	*I*	*B*	*Examiner*	*Comments*
July, 1955	4 yr.	2	X	X	1	1	2	2	3	2	A. Roe, G.P.	M.D. and hemi-
Sept., 1955	4¼ yr.								3	2	B. Shaw, psychia-	plegia
											trist	Walking appli-
Dec., 1955	4½ yr.			Xa							N. Ricks, orthopae-	ance
											dic surgeon	
July, 1956	5 yr.	2	2	2a	1	1	1	2	3	1	A. Roe, G.P.	
Nov. 1956	5½ yr.							2		1	B. Shaw, psychia-	
											trist	

TABLE 29-3

CASES CLASSIFIED BY 'PULHESTIB' SYSTEM

Name	Age	P	U	L	H	E	S	T	I	B	Comments
Lorraine	10	2	2	2	1	1	1	1	1	1	A girl with hemiplegia. She has physiotherapy. Her home has few steps and is very near her school to which she is able to walk. The teachers help her with dressing.
John	8	1	2	1	1	1	1	2	1	3	1	A boy classed as an imbecile. Whilst S2 may indicate the need for speech therapy, the therapist should realize from I3 that there may be little response. He attends an occupation centre.
Peter	8½	3	2	3	1	1	2	3	3	2	Another imbecile boy of similar age to John. He has a hemiplegia and epilepsy. He cannot walk far and has to be carried up and down stairs. His widowed mother is finding this a great strain. The house is on a hill so he is seldom taken out. He is aggressive. The Local Authority could help by considering rehousing to a flat area and by the provision of a power-driven invalid carriage. The Parents' Association might help by finding someone locally who would go in to take Peter to bed at night and bring him down again in the morning.
Christine	9	2	1	2	1	1	1	1	1	1	A girl with severe asthma and emphysema. The indications are for physiotherapy and either a school near home or a residential school. If the latter P2 indicates the need for occasional medical supervision.

I and **B** should be used as indicated. The sections **U, L, T** and **S** should be left open until the age of five unless the abilities of grade 1 are reached earlier. If there is evidence that retardation in these fields should be expected then a cross is entered in the section.

An alternative form of recording the emotional characteristics may be considered. The most typical feature of the child's behavior would be indicated: for example, **D**=destructive, **N**=noisy, **S**=sociable.

It is visualized that the parents or guardians of the child would have one copy of the assessment and that another copy would be kept in a central bureau. This central bureau might be organized and financed by the state, by voluntary organizations, or by some completely independent association. The assessment would be initiated by the family doctor.

A method of recording the classification is shown by illustrating the case history of a handicapped child (Table 29-2). The names and dates in this example have been altered deliberately.

John was examined by his family doctor when he was four-years-old. He was found to be mentally retarded and to have a hemiplegia. Because he had a very sheltered home life, he was quiet and timid and had to be placed in grade 2 for his behavior. Advice about his care was given to the parents. Physiotherapy and a walking appliance were arranged by the orthopedic specialist. When he was five-years-old, John was re-examined and the full classification was then entered. As a result of an improved parental attitude following advice and John's increased confidence as he became more mobile with his walking appliance, his behavior improved and he could be raised to B1. The second assessment of intelligence allowed him to be in grade I2 at least for a trial at an E.S.N. school. When he was ready to start at the E.S.N. school his profile indicated that he would probably require a con-veyance to school (L2A), and that the staff should be prepared to assist with feeding, washing, and dressing (U2), and with the toilet (T2).

A number of handicapped children seen recently have been classified by this system and the results are shown in Table 29-3.

DISCUSSION

Many different workers are interested in handicapped children—family doctors, school medical officers, social workers, almoners, physiotherapists, speech therapists, psychologists, teachers in both ordinary and special schools, and many others. Some of these, expert in their own spheres, would be helped to appreciate by the profiles of disabilities the other aspects and difficulties of the handicapped child. Because some of these professions are expanding and some employ a large proportion of women, there will always be a considerable number of young and relatively inexperienced workers. They should find the classification a useful guide.

It is seldom possible in rural areas to have groups of handicapped children such as are seen in cities. Those who work in country areas are likely to see children with a varied assortment of handicaps. Their work should be simplified by a uniform classification applied to all handicapped children.

Children often have multiple handicaps. In an unselected group of 100 ineducable children in Sheffield there were 29 children with other handi-caps. It is very easy for attention to be concentrated on one handicap with relative neglect of the other handicaps. In the proposed classification equal prominence is given to each disability. It is hoped that this will lead to the easier management of the child with multiple handicaps.

Ingram,[523] in a report on cerebral palsy, pointed out some of the fallacies of the surveys of handicapped children. The current survey of mentally defective children has confirmed these difficulties. A uniform system of re-cording handicaps should make surveys easier and more accurate.

The consideration of help for handicapped children requires a considera-tion of financial aid. It is sometimes said that money given to handicapped children would be better spent on healthy children. This is a hard view, but there never will be unlimited resources. It is necessary, therefore, that the best possible use is made of the funds available. The proposed classification should be helpful by making possible a reasonably accurate estimate of the needs of groups of children. Duplication of work would be avoided. Voluntary contributions should be used for the purpose for which they are given. Certain illnesses, however, have an emotional appeal greater than their relative needs so that their funds are over donated to the detriment of other, less "popular," illnesses. In an editor's column,[299] it was pointed out that the amounts raised by some of the "Funds" (in 1954) showed a total lack of relationship between the relative importance of the disease, as based on the number of victims, and the amounts raised. A classification of handicapped children according to their disabilities rather than their diseases might encourage a more even distribution of donations.

The parents of handicapped children often do not fully understand their child's difficulties and they may receive little guidance for the future. When they know their child's assessment, they should appreciate the directions in which their child might be helped. They should never feel that the case had been abandoned as hopeless. The parents of even the most derelict child can be helped by advice about feeding and nursing, by the provision of invalid carriages, by the occasional opportunity of a rest from their burden.

As the children grow older the pattern of their profiles should give a good indication of their capabilities in adult life. Rehabilitation to adult life would be made easier.

This classification is advanced as an attempt to unify the approach to the problems of handicapped children. It may be considered to be Utopian; it may be considered to be impracticable; but some purpose will have been served if it is considered.

SUMMARY

A system of classification of handicapped children is put forward which will give a profile of the children's disabilities. It is hoped that a system such as this will lead to a more uniform approach to handicapped children and will enable the various workers to appreciate all aspects of these children.

Acknowledgment

The current survey of mentally retarded children quoted in the text has been made possible by the encouragement of Professor R. S. Illingworth, the help of Dr. L. R. Roberts, Medical Officer of Health, and a research grant from the University of Sheffield.

Chapter 30

Compendium and Comments

JAMES M. WOLF and ROBERT M. ANDERSON

THE PROBLEM OF TERMINOLOGY AND CLASSIFICATION
Terminological Stability

A NUMBER of terms have been coined to describe children with two or more handicapping conditions. A review of the pertinent literature on this topic reveals that specific terms have come to have whatever meaning a writer wished to give them. The term *multiply handicapped* is used frequently, and since it has a degree of communicability, it has been embraced by a large segment of the professional and lay community. *Multi, multiple,* and *multiply* convey a consistent meaning to most readers. *Multi* is derived from a Latin word meaning "much" or "many"; *multiple,* the adjective form, means "having or involving many parts"; *multiply,* the adverb form, means "in the manner of multiple." Adjectives and adverbs are modifying words used to make the meaning of other words clearer or more exact.

It is hoped that the term *the multiply handicapped child* conveys an image to the reader of a child with multiplicity of variation. The word *child* is a noun and denotes "a person between birth and the time he or she reaches his or her majority." The word *handicapped* is used as an adjective and modifies the word *child.* The word *multiply* is used as an adverb and modifies the adjective *handicapped;* both the adverb and the adjective are used to convey the full meaning and exactness by which the writer wishes to describe a particular kind of child.

It is the word *handicapped* that causes difficulty and confusion in an attempt to provide terminological stability to the expression *the multiply handicapped child.* Some objections have developed to the use of the term *handicapped child* and over the years the descriptive term *exceptional* has received more common usage. Baker observed that "There is no single term which appropriately describes all types of exceptional children. The term 'exceptional' is probably the most suitable of several, although in the popular mind it means only the mentally gifted . . . 'exceptional' is a more inclusive term than 'handicapped,' since it includes children at both extremes of various scales."[60](pp. 11-12)

Barbe proposed the term *multiple exceptionality* in preference to *multiple handicapped.* He states,

. . . that attention needs to be given to those children who have more than one area of exceptionality in their make-up—to pay attention to obviously handicapping features, so commonly done today, is to approach the area of multiplicity in a negative manner. . . . If special education is to concern itself with the below and above average, and the author feels that it definitely must do so, a conceptual framework of "multiple exceptionality" must replace multiple handicapped.[64](p.69)

Barbe's objection is to the term *handicap* for he contends that a child who is only blind and gifted could not be considered multiply handicapped but could be considered in the framework of multiple exceptionality. The term *multiple exceptionality* illustrates an attempt to coin a term or develop a definition suited to one's area of interest. The term embodies both the below and above average under the same rubric. It reflects the attitude that special education is not concerned with children who have only a handicap.

The fact that most children with a handicap in one of the sensory areas are not handicapped in the mental area, and indeed may even be far above average, urges the need for a term which will not imply that a child handicapped in one area is incapacitated in all areas. . . . It must be recognized that all children may be classified as "multiply exceptional."[64](p.75)

When a term becomes all inclusive, it has more philosophical meaning than conceptual or theoretical implications. The term implies the author's philosophy that no child should be labeled for any purpose other than to aid better understanding of him; however, no implications can be deduced from the term for pedagogical procedures. This descriptive term, like many other synonyms for children with more than one deviation, offers little possibilities for the conceptualization of an educational *modus operandi*.

The objection to the term *handicapped* is readily eliminated when one includes only the underachieving gifted child under the domain of special education. The gifted child is frequently considered handicapped when the causes of his underachievement are isolated. Special programs and modifications needed for underachieving gifted children justify his inclusion under the province of special education.

The words *impairment, disability* and *handicap* are often used as synonyms and as a result confusion exists not only over the use of the term but also in determining what is a handicap and who is handicapped.

Stevens, in conceptualizing a taxonomy in special education for children with body disorders, presents an excellent discussion of the terminological problem confronting special educators and reviews attempts made to standardize the language of special education. He writes in reference to the terms *impairment, disability,* and *handicap*:[1021](pp.28-33)

Much of the basic professional language is in need of more specificity of meaning thus providing the basis for terminological stability. For reasons of this discussion, it will be useful to examine the meaning of certain key words dealing with human disorder.

Cruickshank tends to use the words *disabled* and *handicapped* as synonyms. For example he says,

> The physically disabled, being imperfect, were considered to be outside the pale of religion. As such, the handicapped were outside the thinking of not only the religious leaders but also the political leaders.[217(p.10)]

Wallin, noted for his strenuous effort to give precise definition to much of the terminology with which he deals, seems to make a distinction between *defect* and *handicap* when he says,

> Children are subject to many kinds of physical defects and anomalies and many kinds and degrees of psychological, educational, and social handicaps and maladjustments that interfere with their happy and successful adjustments to their physical environment and to the society in which they live.[1089(p.1)]

Somewhat later he uses the terms *defect* and *handicap* synonymously when he says,

> Just as the term *physically handicapped children* includes all children who are beneath par physically through disease, injury, or developmental defect, so the term *mentally handicapped* will be used to include all children falling short of intellectual normality through disease, accident, or limited native endowment as well as children who manifest specific mental limitations or aberrations.[1089(p.6)]

A governmental agency defined *disability* for the purposes of an interview survey.

> The term *disability* has several common usages. For example a *disability* often means a condition that interferes with ability to work. Also, conditions, are frequently classified as producing partial, temporary, total, permanent partial, or permanent total "disability."

This report goes on to say,

> . . . it was decided not to employ the term "disability" in this survey except in a very general sense where it is intended to cover the whole field of interference with activities caused by disease, injury, or impairment (in much the same way that the term 'morbidity' is used for a generic rather than specific concept).[458]

It is interesting to note that in another related report which attempts to define *impairments* there is some confusion when the term *impairment* seems to be used as a synonym for *disability* as previously defined. They report that

> . . . certain chronic or permanent defects are classified as *impairment* by the National Health Survey. These defects are, for the most part, conditions which cause a decrease in or a loss of the ability to perform certain functions and includes such conditions as blindness, deafness, paralysis, and missing or deformed limbs.[459(p.14)]

Hamilton, as early as 1950, made a clear-cut distinction between *handicap* and *disability.* He says, "the words 'handicap' and 'disability' are frequently used interchangeably, [and] the person who would understand rehabilitation must understand the distinction between them."[435]

Hamilton defines disability as "a condition of impairment, physical or mental, having an objective aspect that can usually be described by a physician." He defines *handicap* as, "the cumulative result of the obstacles which disability interposes between the individual and his maximum functional level."[435(p.17)]

For Barker, *handicap* refers particularly to the somatopsychological relationship which deals with "those variations in physique that affect the psychological situation of a person by influencing the effectiveness of his body as a tool for action, or by serving as a stimulus to himself or others."[65(p.1)]

Stevens points out how others have also emphasized that a handicap must be evaluated in terms of the demands of the situation in which a person finds himself.[1021(pp.33-35)]

Myerson makes a reference to the need for distinguishing between *impairment, disability,* and *handicap.* His views are summarized as follows:

1. The terms have been used interchangeably.
2. There is a measure of truth in the generalization that if a person is disabled he is handicapped.
3. Handicap may or may not follow from disability.
4. Disability is medical in character.
5. Handicap is a reduction of personal or social efficiency.[801]

The Association for the Aid of Crippled Children attempted to investigate the feasibility of developing a system of codes for use in rehabilitation. The purpose of the study was to determine the feasibility of developing a consistent vocabulary for rehabilitation which would have acceptance among the various disciplines (professions) who now utilize their own jargon and terms without a common understanding of their meanings.

The investigation attempted to standardize nomenclature in terms of the total psychosocial functioning of the individual. Attempts were studiously made to avoid the classification scheme that would be "medical" in character since studies of this sort were underway by appropriate medical agencies. The authors of the report make the observation that

Since the terms "impairment," "disability," and "handicap" are used loosely, most of the time interchangeably, by professional and lay personnel as well, they will be specifically differentiated for use in the codes and perhaps in time will influence usage and understanding.[48]

The Advisory Committee on Nomenclature and Classifications Relevant to Disability and Rehabilitation set forth definitions as follows, and their reports make some distinction between impairment, disability, and handicap.

Impairment was defined as
Any deviation from the normal which results in defective function, structure, organization, or development of the whole, or of any of its faculties, senses, systems, organs, members, or any part thereof.

They define *disability* as

    Any limitation experienced by the impaired individual, as compared with the activities of unimpaired individuals of similar age, sex, and culture.

Handicap is defined as

    The disadvantage imposed by impairment or disability upon a specific individual in his cultural pattern of mental, psychological, physical, social, economic, and vocational activities.

The report makes the additional point that

    An impaired individual is not necessarily disabled or handicapped by the impairment, but he may be either disabled or handicapped, or both.[748]

Stevens, in conceptualizing his taxonomy in special education, concludes that the strategic terms *impairment, disability,* and *handicap* have been unstable in their meaning. If the clear-cut meanings are assigned to these terms, it may be possible to evolve useful classification schema. Stevens defines *impairment* as defective (diseased or disordered) tissue; *disability* is the term intended to convey the meaning of general loss of body organ function—it is, in fact, a synonym for organ dysfunction; *handicap* is the term intended to convey the concept of the personal and social burden which is imposed on the person when confronted with a situation that cannot be resolved by reason of body dysfunction or impairment.[1021 (p.65,69,72)] Recently, more concern is being expressed in the literature for making a distinction between these terms.[76, 266, 1130, 1151]

Utilizing the evolving concept of handicapped as previously discussed, a definition of the *multiply handicapped child* is formulated as follows: a person between birth and the age of majority who has personal and social burdens imposed on him when confronted with a situation that cannot be resolved by reason of two or more body dysfunctions or impairments. The organization of special education classes presently leans heavily upon classification of pathomorphic and physioporthic phenomena and as a result the following addendum to the definition is required: and whose disabilities or impairments are so severe that it is impossible to profit from a program established for any one of the disabilities.

Primacy of Disabilities and Handicaps

Concurrent with the use of the terms *disability* and *handicap* is an implied hierarchy of these conditions. There are numerous references in the literature to the principal disability, the primary and secondary disability, and the major and minor disability. For example, Mackie and her co-workers, in reporting statistics on education for exceptional children, stated that many exceptional children have more than one disability, which creates a dilemma regarding how they should be classified:

    Many of them [children with multiple disabilities], furthermore, receive more than one kind of special education service, for example, speech correction and special teaching for the hard of hearing or cerebral palsied. The solution which has been used is to request that each child be counted once only according to his major disability.[715](p.5)

These authors do not suggest a rationale by which the primacy of one disability should be selected over another. Their position is illustrative of professional preoccupation with classification schemes that lean heavily on medical systems that categorize children by pathological descriptions. In such classifications a priority is assigned to the extant disabilities, and the professional worker tends to deal with each handicap in a unitary fashion, and in the case of two (or more) disorders a priority is established. Apparently, arbitrary decisions are made as to which disabilities are primary and which are secondary.

In the monumental study of handicapped children in Georgia, Wishik's task was not just a mere count of the various children with handicapping conditions. In addition to a tally, an attempt was made to classify children in terms of their functional disabilities. In this regard Wishik writes,

> In order to assess disabilities in terms of a single handicapping condition, it is necessary to try to avoid the composite and confusing effect of coexistent but independent multiple handicaps on any given child. For this purpose, there were selected from among the total group seen at clinic from all sources of referral those children who had only one primary diagnosis. Each diagnosis made at the clinics was classified as primary or else secondary to one of the other twelve conditions studied whenever sufficient basis seemed to exist for such labeling. A number of examples of the distinction made would help to describe the method and purpose. Cerebral palsy, cleft lip or palate, heart abnormalities and orthopedic impairment were always labeled primary. Mental retardation that existed with cerebral palsy was considered secondary, the cerebral palsy primary. If mental retardation coexisted with heart disease, both were called primary.[1126](p.35)

At an Institute on the Education of Blind Children, educators pointed up the lack of facilities to meet the complicated needs of the multiply disabled child who does not fit into any public education program. Development of educational methods appropriate to the child's greater disability were strongly endorsed. A committee recommended "That placement of multiply handicapped children be on the basis of the major handicap with continuous study and evaluation of each child for necessary changes in placement."[27](p.48) A rationale was not suggested for determining the greater handicap.

Barsch observed that mothers of handicapped children and professionals dealing with handicapped children each rank disabilities in an order of severity. An instrument called "A Handicapped Ranking Scale" was administered to parents of handicapped children, parents of nonhandicapped children, occupational therapists, physical therapists, speech correctionists, other professional persons, and college students. No attempt was made to obtain the reasons for the relative ranking. The sample of approximately 2400 were in close accord in defining the relative severity of ten handicapping conditions. The order, as judged by these individuals, is as follows:

1. cerebral palsy	6. epilepsy
2. mental retardation	7. deafness
3. mental illness	8. polio
4. brain injury	9. heart trouble
5. blindness	10. diabetes[70]

There was marked agreement that cerebral palsy, mental retardation, mental illness, and brain injury ranked as the most severe problems that could be inflicted upon a child.

Thomas, in making reference to this report writes, "If the author wanted evidence to show the confusion existing today in the minds of people with respect to the first four diagnoses, he succeeded beyond expectation because most of the parents thought cerebral palsy should be ranked ahead of brain injury, while most therapists and educators listed brain injury as more serious than cerebral palsy. Apparently none asked how to differentiate between these diagnoses."[1060(p.10)] Barsch's study illustrates that often there is no observable rationale for the ranking of disabilities.

The lack of an acceptable rationale for the determination of the primacy of disabilities is also a confusing problem in the discipline of medicine. Many studies have been reported in medical literature in which disabilities have been arbitrarily termed *major* or *minor*. The perplexities encountered in designating a major, primary, or principal disability is apparently a problem from birth to death. This is illustrated by the following statement appearing in the International Classification of Diseases:

> No specific rules are provided for selecting the primary or principal cause of an illness or injury involving two or more diseases or conditions. In many cases it is difficult to set down exactly what is the principal cause of an illness. . . .[734(p.x)]

In another volume of this manual, the following statement appears:

> The problem of classifying causes of death for vital statistics is relatively simple when only one cause of death is involved. However, in many cases, two or more morbid conditions contribute to the death. In such cases, it has been the traditional practice in vital statistics to select one of these causes for tabulation. This cause has been variously described in the past as "the cause of death," "primary cause of death," "principal cause of death," "fundamental cause of death," etc. In order to make uniform the terminology and procedure for selecting the cause of death for primary tabulations, it was agreed by the Sixth Decennial International Revision Conference that the cause to be tabulated should be designated the "underlying cause of death."

In the past this cause has been selected in various ways in different countries.[733](p.357)

Primary and secondary diagnoses also have presented a problem in the development of a standard nomenclature of diseases. Thomas and Hayden have written the following in their classic book:

> The determination of which of two or more diagnoses is primary and which is secondary is influenced by the interpretation of individual coders. No universal rule can be stated since a diagnosis which is primary in one situation may be secondary in another. *This fact invalidates the statistics of primary and secondary diagnoses.* [Editor's italics] Recognition of these facts has influenced many institutions to stop the cross-indexing of primary and secondary diagnosis and to record all conditions, whether primary, secondary, or associated on the appropriate disease-classification and without reference to their relationship.[1059](p.xi)

In the study of congenital anomalies (defects which are present at birth) repeated reference is made to major and minor anomalies. McIntosh[708] indicates that the problem of classification of congenital malformations presents certain difficulties, and after surveying systems of classification used by other investigators, he found that none seemed fully satisfactory. McIntosh and his associates formulated a classification based upon topographic systems which permitted several types of statistical analysis.

In an earlier study, Stevenson had also formulated a system for classifying congenital malformations. He cautions others who might use it by writing, "It should be obvious that such a procedure is arbitrary and that no two individuals are apt to follow it in the same way."[1024](p.38)

Stevenson further stated that "If an infant has more than one defect, and one third in this series did, there is a tendency to classify the infant according to his most severe defect and place him in the 'multiple' category only when he has several severe defects."[1024](p.42)

Marden stated that congenital abnormalities "are arbitrarily termed *major* or *minor.* . . ." However, he then provides one of the most specific definitions of a major and minor anomaly that appears in the literature:

> Our interpretation of a *major anomaly* is one which has an adverse effect on either function or social acceptability of the individual; a *minor defect* is one which is neither of medical nor cosmetic consequence to the patient.[736](p.363)

Whereas previous investigations of congenital abnormality had dealt with major defects, Marden's survey was principally concerned with those defects which were minor in character since a minor anomaly may be overlooked by a physician. The finding of several minor anomalies in a baby might alert the physician to the existence of other defects of a more serious nature. Smith and Bostian,[1007] in studying minor defects in children with selected major defects (i.e., cleft lip and palate, ventricular septal defect, mental retardation) and in a control group, found that the presence of two anomalies in an otherwise normal child is somewhat unusual, and three or more minor anomalies may suggest the possible presence of a major defect. Sometimes the major defect is immediately apparent, such as cleft lip, but if the major defect involved should prove to be mental retardation or cerebral palsy, the full spectrum of the disorder may not be apparent or recognized until the preschool or school years.

Classification Stability

It is not surprising that the multiply handicapped child is presenting special educators with a dilemma concerning an appropriate descriptive label and a suitable classification procedure. From its auspicious beginning in 1902 when the National Education Association adopted a definite program for the "Department of Special Education—Relating to Children Demanding Special Means of Instruction"[810] until the present time, terminology and classification schemes have been a critical issue in the field of special education.

Literature related to special education indicates a lack of stable classification. A review of the more prominent publications in the field will illustrate this point.

Heck, although engaged primarily in pupil-personnel work, became interested in exceptional children and produced one of the early general textbooks on this subject. His book presented a point of view as to what should be done for exceptional children and how it should be done. Heck organized his text into three broad classifications of exceptional children: (1) education of the socially handicapped child; (3) education of the physically handicapped child; and (3) education of mentally exceptional children.[468]

A committee of the National Society for the Study of Education dealing with the education of exceptional children stated that these children do not comprise a single homogeneous group. The following classification was used to include children with deviations in various ways:

1. Children with physical handicaps
   a. Crippled children—those with poliomyelitis, cerebral palsy, congenital deformities, and other orthopedic handicaps; also children with cardiac difficulties, sometimes called "crippled" hearts.
   b. Children with impaired hearing—the congenitally deaf, the adventitiously deaf, and the hard-of-hearing.
   c. Children with visual impairments—the blind and the partially seeing.
   d. Children with speech handicaps.

e. Children with other types of physical handicaps, such as tuberculosis, epilepsy, and endocrine disorders.
2. Children with mental deviations
    a. Children of low intelligence, including both the feeble-minded and those who are less seriously defective in intellectual development.
    b. Children with high intelligence, including both those with special talents and those who are superior in general intellectual abilities.
3. Children with emotional or social maladjustments, including those with serious behavior disorders or emotional disturbances.[811(p.7)]

Baker classified exceptional children under five main divisions according to the types of handicaps. He included (1) the physically handicapped, (2) mental growth and development, (3) neurological and psychogenic disease, (4) behavior adjustments, and (5) educational retardation. Baker writes "any such classification is somewhat unsatisfactory since it does not convey a completely true impression of the problem. There is much overlapping between and among types of handicaps, and many children are afflicted with two or more defects. However, some type of classification with its admitted imperfections is probably better than none at all. . . ."[60(p.12)]

After discussing four general classes of exceptional individuals, Goodenough summarizes by saying,

> . . . we shall consider here the following classes of exceptional children:
> 1. Those who stand at the extremes of some trait which all display to a greater extent or lesser degree.
> 2. Those who exhibit some outstanding peculiarity in which the majority do not share at all or, at most, only to a minimal degree. This group is made up chiefly of the physically handicapped.
> 3. Children who show very unusual combinations of mental traits.[403(p.6)]

Mackie and Dunn, in a United States Office of Education publication, refer to eight areas of exceptionality.[712] In a later publication by the same authors, reference is made to ten areas of exceptionality. These are (1) blind, (2) partially seeing, (3) crippled, (4) special health problems, (5) deaf, (6) hard-of-hearing, (7) speech correction, (8) socially maladjusted, (9) mentally retarded, and (10) gifted.[714(p.3)]

The *Review of Educational Research* reports the major research findings during a designated period, organized by specific areas. In a 1963 issue devoted to the education of exceptional children, seven categories of exceptionality were reviewed.[300] A similar review was completed in 1966 and eight categories were included.[301]

Cruickshank and Johnson classify exceptional children by (1) intellectual differences, (2) physical differences, and (3) emotional differences. These noted authorities state "The *exceptional child* is difficult to define, for the term represents many different medical and psychological groupings of children. . . . Terminology constitutes one of the unsolved problems in the field of special education. . . ."[217(pp.3-4)]

Kirk indicates that "the term *exceptional* means different things to different people. Some use it when referring to the particularly bright child or the child with unusual talent. Others use it when they refer to any atypical or deviant child. The term *exceptional child* has been generally accepted, however, to mean either the handicapped or the gifted child."[586(p.4)] Kirk classifies exceptional children into twelve categories for discussion purposes in his general text.

Dunn, in his publication, considers seven broad categories which include twelve types of exceptional children:

Pupils with intellectual limitations:
  1. the educable and
  2. the trainable mentally retarded.
Pupils with superior intellect:
  3. the gifted.
Pupils with behavior problems:
  4. the emotionally disturbed and
  5. the socially maladjusted.
Pupils with
  6. speech problems.
Pupils with impaired hearing:
  7. the deaf and
  8. the hard-of-hearing.
Pupils with impaired vision:
  9. the blind and
  10. the partially seeing.
Pupils with neurological and nonsensory physical impairments:
  11. the crippled and
  12. the chronic health cases.[290(p.7)]

It is apparent from this discussion that classifications used in professional textbooks have been based upon the classical quadrate of classifying human behavior: (1) physical, (2) mental, (3) emotional, and (4) social. The words of Frampton and Gall still appear to be appropriate:

Various authorities in the field of special education have established several different groupings of these groups for servicing purposes. No definitive classification has been accepted for the field as a whole. The current literature shows some overlapping of categories and treatment; in each instance, the reasons given seem logical for the specific purposes of those making the classifications. . . .

Time, strangely enough, does not always seem to clarify definitions, although it may crystallize and standardize the content of a discipline. Much too often some outstanding leader, whether individual or community, insists upon creating and defending the "only" suitable terminology or classification. Scholarship and the application of a more effective scientific method to the field of special education will in time create something more than inventiveness in augmenting the dictionary, for terminology does vitally affect the patient, his family, and his community.[347] (pp. 32-33)

TEACHER COMPETENCIES

Although in the past, general educators recognized the value of providing practical procedures to meet the needs of exceptional children in regular classrooms, it was believed that regular classroom teachers lacked the competencies needed to deal effectively with these children. Since children who deviated from the so-called normal sometimes interfered with the learning of others, it was thought that they could be taught more efficiently in small special classes with especially trained teachers.

Cruickshank indicates that perhaps the single most important essential to a program of education of exceptional children is the competency of special teachers.[217] (p. 126) Yet, general textbooks include very little information on the specific competencies needed by teachers of exceptional children.[60, 290, 586, 1067] The most significant study of competencies of special class teachers to date was completed by the United State Office of Education. In 1951, with financial assistance from the New York City Association for Aid of Crippled Children, the United States Office of Education undertook a comprehensive study of the qualification and preparation of teachers of exceptional children. This study dealt specifically with the distinctive skills and abilities needed by teachers in each category of special education.

A committee of experts prepared a list of competencies which they thought to be important and distinctive for teachers in the various areas of exceptionality. Inquiry forms were sent to from 100 to 150 superior teachers in each special area. Teachers were asked to rank each competency in terms of its significance for successful teaching. Teachers also rated their own proficiency on the competencies. Results of this study indicated that superior teachers of exceptional children did not place priority on knowledge of teaching methods in specialized areas other than the one in which they were working. For example, superior teachers of the deaf ranked "knowledge of methods of teaching children who are mentally retarded," 68th out of a possible 92. Mackie states,

It was found that a relatively small number of teachers rated their knowledge of teaching methods in areas other than their own as "good," and even more striking, many teachers reported that they had not even had opportunity for systematic observation of children with multiple handicaps. About two thirds of them said they had had "too little" or "none" of this type of observational experience as a systematic part of their own preparation.[714(p.57)]

Superior teachers of the mentally retarded ranked "the ability to teach mentally retarded having multiple handicaps, i.e., cerebral palsy, hearing or vision loss" as 89th out of a possible 100. The authors conclude that there was less interest in the total problem of exceptional children and in the multiply handicapped than might have been expected.[717]

A specific item relating to the ability to teach blind children with additional disabilities was not included in the list of 85 competencies directed to teachers of the blind. However, directors and supervisors of special education in state and local school systems considered their recently graduated teachers of the blind, in general, to be quite well prepared in specialized teaching methods and aids but less qualified in their knowledge of children with multiple disabilities.[716(p.24)]

The above mentioned competency studies reflect the special educators preoccupation with skills and abilities needed for teaching children with a unitary disability. These teacher competency studies were completed in a period of development of special education when extreme specialization was advocated and little recognition given to multiple disabilities. The words of Arthur H. Hill, a pioneer special educator, are applicable to that period of time. He said, "the walls between the various areas of exceptionality have often been higher than between general and special education."[290(p.vii)]

While the pattern in teacher training has been to develop course sequences to train teachers to work in one specific category of exceptionality, we know that children do not fall within such discrete boundaries. This pattern of training does not take into consideration the problems of the multiply handicapped child. As a solution to the problems of educating a child with two or more disabilities, the recommendation is frequently made that the teacher should be given a combination of course work in two categories of exceptionality, i.e., the education of the deaf and the education of the mentally retarded. The authors do not concur with this point of view. Classroom teachers with training in more than one area of exceptionality continue to express concern about their inadequacy to teach multiply handicapped children. In a recent study by Anderson, a number of teachers observed that a combination of course work in the education of the deaf and some course work in the education of the mentally retarded may not be the most effective solution to the training of teachers. An excerpt from one of the teacher responses is illustrative of this viewpoint:

> If I felt that courses for helping the deaf mentally retarded were available, I certainly would take them. In my mind, I cannot accept courses for the teaching of the mentally retarded child as being of value for the teaching of the mentally retarded deaf children. . . . In other words, I see a completely new field in special education, the education of the deaf mentally retarded child. This child requires special techniques, materials, and curriculum to do him justice.

Although this teacher reported fourteen years experience teaching mentally retarded deaf children and had more than thirty semester hours beyond a master's degree, she concluded,

> I am really pleading for help as a teacher of the mentally retarded deaf. My best is not good enough. The help I need will not come from taking courses on mental retardation or courses on deafness. It will come from courses on the mentally retarded deaf.[35]

In a recent study by Wolf, special class teachers in residential schools for the blind were asked to give their opinions about the five most important competencies needed by a teacher of mentally retarded blind children. Frequency of responses was the basis for the following rank order: (1) patience, (2) flexibility, (3) understanding of others, (4) imagination, (5) sense of humor, and (6) skills in subject matter. The first five are actually characteristics rather than competencies. Knowledge of retardation and knowledge of blindness were ranked 14th and 15th respectively.[1129(p.39)]

The comprehensive report of the Council for Exceptional Children Professional Standards Committee (1966) involved the efforts of approximately seven hundred leaders in special education in the development of standards for personnel in the education of exceptional children. The traditional categories of exceptionality served as the basis for organizing standards for the preparation of teachers, i.e., the mentally retarded, the physically handicapped. A specific category on multiply handicapped children was not included. Indeed, in only one traditional category, "the deaf and hard-of-hearing," was any attempt made to develop guidelines for teaching children with concomitant disabilities. The authors did state, however, that the standards for teachers of exceptional children would undoubtedly change in the years ahead. It was noted that throughout the process of the development of the standards "A need was often expressed for consideration of the common learning characteristics and problems of exceptional children and of the particular needs of multihandicapped children."[897(p.86)]

Schwartz proposes a teacher education curriculum for the preparation of teachers of exceptional children in which the traditional labels based on categories of disability are disregarded and emphasis is placed on the psychoeducational aspects of special education. Schwartz views the teacher as an educational diagnostician capable of providing for the variety of learning and behavior problems presented by exceptional children without regard to separate etiological categories.

The content of the proposed teacher training program includes (1) normal child growth and development; (2) deviations in physical, psychological, educational, and social development; (3) clinical child study practices and procedures for the diagnosis and remediation of learning disabilities; (4) remedial programs and services within the clinic, special classes, and regular classroom; (5) special class teacher as an educational diagnostician and tactician; and (6) interdisciplinary team approach.[978]

Special education appears to be rapidly maturing to a new stage of development in which there is an identifiable trend away from the traditional categories of exceptionality toward a broader based professional orientation around common learning and/or behavioral characteristics.

A concept concerning multiple disabilities may offer an approach to solving the complicated problems of competencies needed by teachers of children with more than one disability. A new classification scheme may have possibilities for providing a conceptual framework for formulating educational procedures to be used with multiply disabled children—educational procedures will in turn indicate the competencies needed for teaching such children as well as the pedagogical procedures to follow.

THE MULTIPLY HANDICAPPED: THE NEED FOR A CONCEPT

One of the principal assumptions underlying this book is the need for an educationally conceived concept and approach to a classification scheme relating to the education of children with multiple handicaps. There is need for a classification concept which may be more useful than current ones which lean heavily on medical systems which classify children with pathological labels. The purpose of a label not only helps us better understand a child but facilitates communicability and suggestiveness for formulating appropriate pedagogical procedures. The establishment of a hierarchy of disabilities has not facilitated educational planning since it is not always possible to convert such information into educationally meaningful concepts. For example, a child with a 70 decibel hearing loss and an I.Q. of 80 would probably be primarily considered a child with hearing impairment rather than a mentally retarded child. On the other hand, a child with a 35 decibel hearing loss and an I.Q. of 50 would probably be considered primarily mentally retarded. As the disabilities become more equal in severity, however, it becomes difficult to assign a weight to either disability.

Eventually a point is reached on the continuum between mental retardation and deafness at which it is virtually impossible to know where the handicapping consequences of hearing impairment end and the handicapping consequences of mental retardation begin. Consequently, professional workers tend to view the child who is deaf and mentally retarded in the light of their own particular professional frames of reference. The persons whose orientation is in mental retardation and who works in an institution or other facility for the mentally retarded, generally speaks of "the deaf mentally retarded." Conversely, the person whose professional experience is primarily in the education of the deaf and who works in a facility for the deaf, may refer to the "mentally retarded deaf." Each emphasizes that aspect of the mental retardation–deafness diad which is pertinent to his professional orientation.

Classification schemes built upon body impairment and disability are useful in only the most general terms. Such classification schemes require the application of logical inferences for education practices. When disability exists in a unitary fashion, it is reasonable to expect that logical inferences are likely to meet the demands of the situation.

In the case of a child who is blind, it is apparent that inferences drawn from the fact that the child is not able to see will provide the bases for certain kinds of educational planning. The same logic can be applied to all or most blind children. However, such is not the case when a child is described as being blind and mentally retarded. Here, the term mental retardation has only the most general bases for inferring appropriate educational procedures. One needs to know if the retardation is profound, severe, moderate, or mild. One also needs to know the etiological factors, i.e., birth injury, germinal defects, metabolic, and glandular disorders, or cultural cause of retardation. It is important to know the antecedent factor or factors without which the condition would not have occurred. This information sometimes determines whether or not the condition should be viewed as *irreversible*. All too often mental retardation is regarded as a unitary, pervasive deficit, i.e., lack of intelligence. Mental retardates are less deficient in some areas than they are in others. In certain learning situations, they perform as well as normal individuals.[392] Barbe states that "Even within intelligence itself there is such a wide range of abilities that it is quite possible for a child to be both mentally gifted and mentally handicapped."[64 (p. 70)]

Stevens' Concept

G. D. Stevens, professor of special education and rehabilitation at the University of Pittsburgh, examined the problem of classification and proposed a construct for a classification scheme and taxonomy for the concepts which interpose the processes of special education on children whose learning problems have their origin in body disorder. Stevens believes that the domain of special education lacks precise limitation and consequently, he has contrived a definition of special education on the assumption that the boundaries of the domain could be established by applying a comprehensive definition. For the purpose of constructing a taxonomy the following definition was proposed:

> *Special education* is that body of educational practice designed to accommodate children who vary from what is generally considered normal to the point where they (1) do not learn from usual educational practices in the ordinary setting of the school; (2) present unusual management problems to the school; and (3) whose variation is of such magnitude and complexity as to interfere with the learning of others.[1021 (p.40)]

Stevens then formulated the following three domains of special education from the definition:

1. Educationally Significant Somatopsychological Variants

This domain takes in the language and concepts that have significance for education. The concept of *impairment, disability,* and *handicap* which have been given precise definitions are considered strategic and represent operationally valid subdivisions of this domain. *Impairment* is the least modifiable variant and involves defective tissue at the cellular level. *Disability* represents the general loss or function and along with impairment may be seen as the etiological explanation of the handicap. The *handicap* is the most significant subdivision to educators and is always related to the learning process; the handicap must be evaluated in terms of the demands of the situation in which the person finds himself. The situation in this case is the school and the learning process. Since the handicap is the major concern of special educators this concept must be further refined by subclasses.

Four educationally relevant factors were isolated by Stevens. These include (1) *motility,* which is "intended to encompass the meaning of all modalities of human behavior which facilitate getting about in the environment."[1021 (p.66)] [It includes locomotion, walking, running, dancing, swimming, movement, turning, bending, etc.]; and (2) *communication,* which "is the term intended to convey the meaning of all modalities of semiotic."[1021 (p.66)] This subclass includes all behavior which is receptive or expressive of signs in the process of personal and social behavior. The remaining subclasses of handicap include (3) *self-concept* and (4) *social interaction*. Both convey some of the meaning of the previous language of personality. Defects in self-concept frequently have their origin in body disorder and also interfere with one's interaction with teachers, classmates, and others that one has contact with in the school setting.

2. Educationally Significant Attributes of Body Disorder

This domain concerns itself with the attributes of morbidity that have educational significance and consists of five subclasses. Of primary importance is (1) the nature of the condition, which includes a description of the disturbance. Educators have very little responsibility for or effect on the nature of the condition. However, the subclass has great significance to educators. It includes epidemiology data on incidence and prevalence rates, and contagion; temporal data on duration, chronicity, and recurrence; and symptomology data such as degree of severity, course, and sequelae. What is provided for the child through treatment to alleviate his condition has educational relevance. What is done for the child in the way of treatment has a bearing on the handicap and must be considered in determining what special education modifications are needed. These both represent (2) the nature of therapeutic procedure. Other subclasses in this domain include (3) psychological aspects of disorder; (4) social considerations; and (5) culture considerations.

3. Special Educational Procedures

Stevens indicates that over the past century a body of special education practice has developed that can be viewed as a domain. "Special education, by definition, is a modification of educational process."[1021(p. 76)] The major subclasses of this domain constitute the classification of educational process. These are (1) modifications of law; (2) modifications of finance; (3) modifications of instructional procedures; (4) noninstructional procedures; (5) administrative modifications; and (6) ancillary services.

Stevens contends that the nomenclature problem in special education can be attacked with a taxonomy since it is necessary to standardize and give precise definitions to terms and concepts used. The taxonomy also facilitates an educational diagnosis since subclasses can be used to assess the limitations of a child in terms of the subclasses that have educational relevance. An assessment of impairment and disability provide the etiological explanation of the handicap. "An analysis and statement of the educationally significant attributes of the condition will establish the basis for appropriate educational modifications."[1021(p. 82)] A diagram of Stevens' multidimensional matrix is shown in Figure 30-1.

It is Stevens' view that the dilemma involved in classifications of multiple disabilities can also be resolved by standardizing classification language, since it provides the rationale for shifting the emphasis to the handicapping consequence of two (or more) disabilities. For example, deafness and blindness is the partial basis for ensuing handicap:

> The educator will view the communication deficit as being of primary importance and translates the disability data language to mean he cannot build

THE DOMAINS OF
SPECIAL EDUCATION

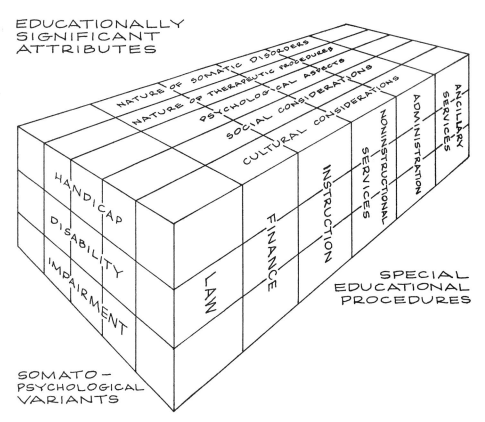

FIGURE 30-1. The domains of special education. Reprinted by permission from Stevens, G.D.: *Taxonomy in Special Education for Children with Body Disorder*. Pittsburgh, Department of Special Education, University Book Store, Copyright, 1962.

communication skills in visual or auditory modalities. The handicap is to be viewed as a description of the behavior phenomena and the description of the disability becomes the etiological explanation.[1021 (p.84)]

Little value is served by assigning weights to one particular disability since no educational purpose is achieved. If the educator needs to assign value he can best view H (handicap) as a higher value than D (disability). "The qualitative and quantitative description of the handicap cannot be viewed in terms of multiplicity but rather in terms of the value of the components which comprise handicap."[1021 (p.84)]

An example of the complexity of the problem can be found in a case of a visually impaired child in which the clinical picture may show blindness, mental retardation, and auditory deficit. The addition of $D_1 + D_2 + D_3$ will be of little educational value since the phenomena are not additive. Since $D_1 + D_2 + D_3$ cannot be reduced significantly, it is necessary to shift the emphases of services to the behavioral limitations described by H. This same logic applies equally well to other combinations of disability and provides a concept of multiple disability from which educational significance can be deduced which dictate the educational processes within predictable limits. Stevens' concept of multiple disability as a rationale for conceptualizing educational constructs related to the multiply disabled child may serve as a fruitful area for research.

A Similar Concept

L. J. Peter, after extensive personal communication with Stevens, borrowed the Stevens' construct and using a synonymous language proposed a similar theoretical rationale for a systematic approach for educating children who are having problems in the school setting. The Stevens' rationale employed by Peter in translating diagnostic findings into educational implementation includes the following ideas:

1. Learning impinges on factors which are broadly classified as mental, physical, social, and emotional. Therefore, diagnosis of learning problems should be interdisciplinary and include investigation into these areas.
2. Children with serious injuries and disabilities may not be handicapped significantly in terms of their educational goals, while others with relatively minor injury or disability may be seriously handicapped educationally.
3. The educational relevance of the handicap is determined by the injury and disability in interaction with a number of situational factors.
4. Educational modifications are made on the basis of educational relevance and cannot logically be made on the basis of medical, phychological, or social-work relevance.
5. The prime responsibility in education of the handicapped child is for modification of variables within the school program. The implementation of these ideas was accomplished through the development of a model which provided a structure for the translation of interdisciplinary diagnosis into a prescription for teaching.[880(pp.228-229)]

His model (Figure 30-2) has three main dimensions: (1) problem variables, which include injury, disability, and handicap; (2) the situational variable, which include four areas related to injury, disability, and

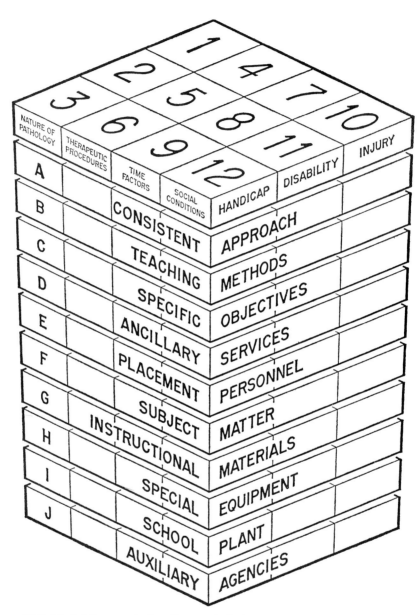

FIGURE 30-2. Model for translating diagnostic findings into a prescription for teaching. Reprinted by permission from Peter, L.J.: *Prescriptive Teaching*. New York, McGraw-Hill Book Company, Copyright, 1965.

handicap—the nature of the pathology, the therapeutic procedures, the time factors, and the social conditions (These variables are arranged in Peter's model from the most modifiable to least modifiable.); the last variable represents (3) the school variables. Peter writes in relation to this third set of variables: "The educational program is composed of elements which may be modified in relation to the pedagogically significant attributes of the handicap."[880][p. 72] The particular school variables are arranged from the top to the bottom of the model and again in order from the most modifiable to the least modifiable. The top section of the model consists of twelve cells and represents diagnosis. This model illustrates how a specific theoretical concept can be used to establish what is relevant in terms of the handicapping consequences of the impairment and/or disability into a remedial program to compensate for the child learning difficulties in a school setting.

THE MULTIPLY HANDICAPPED CHILD:
AN ISSUE IN SPECIAL EDUCATION

The multiply handicapped child has been a difficult, uncertain, puzzling, and perplexing problem to special educators; he represents a problem area begging for a solution. Although the solution is years away, the multiply handicapped child is about to become an issue as well as a problem in special education. The increased number of such children and increased demand for services are creating an issue on which special educators will soon be taking affirmative and negative positions. The issue over this group of children will intensify as more states enact legislation which gives permission to public school districts to establish and maintain special education facilities for children identified as multiply handicapped.

At the present time classes are being established in some residential and public schools for children with multiple disabilities. Unfortunately, some classes are started for reasons of administrative convenience rather than for instructional efficiency. The classes are established without a concept for viewing multiple handicaps. Unless caution is observed, these classes can become a "hodge-podge" of unidentified or partly diagnosed problems.[64][p. 70] Children with two or more disabilities who do not "fit into" special classes designed for any one of the disability categories are sometimes considered candidates for these classes. In some situations, motivation for establishing classes is done to provide relief to the special class teacher of children with so-called unitary disabilities. This is an interesting corollary to the original development of special classes for exceptional children—providing relief to regular class teachers. Historically, the function of special education has been to provide for those children who are outside of the range of acceptability for ordinary education. Special provisions were provided for children with visible disabilities. Segregation of the handicapped and modification of physical facilities were the principal tools of the special educator.

Attempts were also made to circumvent or compensate for the visible physical impairments of these handicapped children. Braille was taught to the blind, a manual system of communication was substituted for the deaf, and physical modifications and medical therapeutic services provided for the crippled. As the number of special classes increased for mentally retarded children so did the amount of discussion increase on the specific goals and curricular modifications needed for this group of handicapped children. It was believed that placing mentally retarded children in special classes was more helpful than leaving them in regular classes. There is, however, little evidence to demonstrate the value of special class placement for educable mentally handicapped children.

The addition of new categories in the organization of special education services has not taken place without controversy; trainable mentally handicapped children are an illustration of this point. In the 1950's an issue was raised over whether or not the trainable mentally handicapped were a public school responsibility. Goldberg and Cruickshank debated this issue in the literature. The question now is primarily an academic one since the number of day classes has become so extensive. However, many educators continue to question the presence of trainable children in a public school setting. The gifted child represented another issue in special education. Should special programs for the gifted be administered by general education or special education? Special educators who classified atypical children on the basis of medical disability could not accept the gifted in the domain of special education. The controversy over the gifted child has also subsided but in its wake, special educators began to question the traditional medical classification of exceptional children.

The prominent current issue confronting special educators involves children with learning disorders. This is one of the most rapidly expanding areas of special education. In the last several years, an avalanche of material has appeared in both professional and lay journals and a number of professional conferences have been devoted exclusively to this topic. New journals have appeared dedicated to the study of learning disabilities. Etiology, terminology, identification, and classification procedures are all subject to spirited discussion. The latest issue of the *Review of Educational Research* devoted to the education of exceptional children listed, for the first time, learning disorders as a category of special education. Barbara Bateman, author of this comprehensive review on learning disorders writes,

> Some of the factors instrumental in bringing about this newly crystallized interest in the child with a learning problem include (a) the increased growth

of all other areas of special education, which has served to highlight the problems of the "leftover" child with learning disorders who, after the treatment of the slow learners, the culturally deprived, and the emotionally disturbed, still fails to learn efficiently via regular educational procedures; (b) the post-Sputnik emphasis on achievement, which has focused attention on many low achievers, especially those who have average or higher intelligence as do many children with learning disorders; (c) increased meaningful communication among educators, psychologists, and medical specialists, which has opened up pertinent and significant research possibilities, e.g., exploring relationships between remedial techniques and psychological test findings, remedial techniques, neurological indices, and between psychological and neurological findings; (d) the development of a broad educational movement toward a more scentific approach to all learning situations—an approach, in which exact knowledge is sought of how each child learns and of the precise factors (teacher's verbal behavior, nature of reinforcement, etc.) which influences his learning; and (e) the emergence of new diagnostic philosophies and instruments which have direct educational implications for curriculum and remedial planning.[74(pp. 93-94)]

The last two factors (d) and (e) listed by Bateman also have significant implications for the multiply handicapped child. There are many children with two or more handicaps and when these children cannot make satisfactory educational progress in a special class for one of the handicaps they are considered under the classification of multiply handicapped. A severe or unusual learning problem is the principal reason for considering a child as multiply handicapped. He is not learning in the special class for children grouped by a unitary (primary) disability. A concept of learning disorders offers possibilities for more readily incorporating the multiply handicapped child under the domain of special education. This emerging concept of learning disorders with its new knowledge also offers possibilities for a new unified organizational structure for special education. As research studies are completed in specific disability categories, the implications for a unifying concept becomes more apparent. For example, Peabody and Birch report their findings in a study on over one thousand partially seeing children in over a dozen states and their results have certain implications; two stand out. First, curriculum materials for partially seeing children need not be limited to a particular type size for the majority of such children as formerly assumed. Second, the average partially seeing child, after receiving special instruction and materials in a special class for his total elementary school career, was two and one-half years retarded academically.[873] It seems reasonable to conclude that partially seeing children are also additionally handicapped by a learning disorder. It also seems obvious that teachers of the partially seeing need to become specialists in learning disorders if academic retardation of partially seeing children of at least average intelligence is to be overcome.

Of course, there is considerable opposition to a proposal that learning disorders become a unifying concept for the total field of special education and the dispute over learning disorders brings this opposition into focus. It is understandable that controversy must follow any suggestion that proposes to move special education so far off its present course. Clements writes,

With regard to the current discord surrounding the term "learning disabilities," two schools of thought are apparent and can be distinguished as follows:

1. First there are the numerous multidisciplinary oriented groups of child specialists from the fields of education, psychology, occupational therapy, medicine, and other health-related professions, who prefer to reserve the descriptive term "learning disabilities" as the educational counterpart to the more medically oriented diagnosis of minimal brain dysfunction. These contemporary groups of individualists tend to display three traits which seem to be much needed during this time of transition in child guidance and education, namely, great flexibility in thinking, an experimental attitude, and action-oriented concern for the thousands of affected children who sit or flit but do not achieve in thousands of classrooms throughout the country.

2. Secondly, there is a small, but stentorian group of ivory-tower educators who apparently wish to expand and retain the term "learning disabilities" for a yet-to-be-developed "unifying" concept throughout the field of special education. The term would then relate to the difficulties in learning experienced by most exceptional children and would thus enfold into the concept the mentally retarded, the cerebral palsied, the minimally brain dysfunctioning, the speech impaired, the culturally disadvantaged, the so-called (but undefined) "emotionally disturbed," etc. "We cannot teach to labels," they shout from their ivy-covered dormer windows to an unheeding audience. Since they seem to be the only ones preoccupied with such an obviously absurd notion, it seems to me they are verbally flogging themselves for their past failing at doing just that—teaching "labels" rather than children. I have always operated under the assumption that, indeed, educators did teach individual children regardless of the condition which makes them exceptional. Perhaps I have been wrong all these years. Although this viewpoint of a unifying concept of learning disabilities may represent the forerunner of needed philosophical reorientation within the field of special education, it seems to hold little practical promise for the near future, since it would require a phasing-out of the many specialty areas within special education, both in teacher preparation and certification; not to mention legislative funding for specific educational programs. I should think, also, it implies the lack of necessity for the many parent organizations dedicated to distinctive categories of children. The objective is apparently to produce a "super-educator–technician," well grounded in child growth and development, learning theory, individual differences, experimental design, etc., who must also be efficient with any and all of the teaching techniques and methodologies which an individual child might require. At the conversational level, the idea has some merit; but to my knowledge, no teacher training facility is willing totally to reorganize it various programs of specialization under this all-encompassing umbrella concept of learning disabilities.[183](pp.135–136)

The "super-educator–technician" is apparently what is needed for teaching children with learning disorders and also those classified as multiply handicapped. Tarnapol states that the answer is "super-teachers." He writes,

> During the past thirty years, diagnostic studies of children revealed that increasingly large groups have perceptual deficiencies which require special teaching methods.
>
> The solution to these and other contemporary educational problems requires an unusual flexibility on the part of school systems. American school systems are inherently inflexible. This inflexibility derives from several sources. The main dilemma of the school systems is that they need unusually creative, especially trained teachers for these children whereas historically, colleges of education have not trained such teachers and school systems have had no way of compensating for such skilled classroom teachers.
>
> In order to solve all of the different teaching problems of the perceptually handicapped, the culturally deprived, and those children with both problems, a new breed of teacher will have to be developed. These teachers should be recruited from among the very best classroom teachers with three years minimum experience with normal children.
>
> They should then receive several years training in the special education of perceptual deficiencies, including the visual, motor, oral, auditory, tactile, and kinesthetic sensory modes. They should become familiar with the latest behavior therapy and motivational-reward systems. They should be familiar with all of the diagnostic tests used, their interpretation, and the habilitation and remedial methods which differential diagnosis suggests.
>
> After this extensive training, how shall we pay these master teachers? There is no way to compensate them within the current educational structure, except to make them administrators and thus to lose the value of all of their special training which is so badly needed in the classroom. . . .[1053]

As the issue over learning disorders is resolved, new insights will be gained that have significance for the multiply handicapped child.

SUMMARY

There have been several systems, constructs, paradigms, conceptual frameworks, taxonomies, and models advanced in attempts to aid professional workers to better understand the problems of special education and to describe relationships which are not apparent through cursory observations. These educators have given serious attention to creating a conceptual framework of special education that might lead to a more sophisticated pedagogy that has educational significance for exceptional children. These models have not been offered for eternity but have been suggested by their respective authors as tentative proposals until better ones can be formulated; they have been effective in stimulating interest, discussion, and a readiness on the part of special educators to consider conceptual issues related to nomenclature and classification systems. However, it is not infrequent that a crown of thorns rather than an olive wreath is bestowed on the proposer of such models. Iscoe has observed that "new systems are not easy to introduce and changes in established procedures and rituals come slowly."[534(p.13)]

There are many avenues available for the solution of problems and several acceptable ways to formulate concepts and frameworks. One way, of course, is to constantly improve the system being used. A medical model is now in use. Concern in the past has been centered on multiple disabilities. There is ample evidence that an increasing number of exceptional children have more than one disability. Part Two in this book documents this fact. The emphasis now must shift to multiple handicaps. How is the child handicapped in the school setting? This is the important question to be answered. He may have more than one disability but his only handicap in the school setting may just involve a learning disorder. What are the handicapping consequences of the prevalent disabilities represented by exceptional children in special education programs? Current medical classifications do not provide this essential information nor tell us how to teach handicapped children. Educational relevance of the handicap is determined by the impairment and disability and how it interacts with a number of factors in the school setting. The handicap is the educationally significant factor. Research in this area will assist us to deal more effectively with the multiply handicapped child.

A shift from a primary and secondary concept of disabilities may be an effective prophylactic for the prevention of further "hardening of the categories" in special education. A functional classification similar to Holt's may have more relevance to educators and it may facilitate the translation of medical findings into educational modifications. A classification system is needed that more readily incorporates the multiply handicapped child into an appropriate educational program. Holt's proposed classification gives equal prominence to each disability and makes it possible to focus on the handicapping consequences of the disability.

In the future, new models may be proposed as solutions are sought for the problem posed by the multiply handicapped child. One way to formulate a new model is by combining those already at hand. This book represents a compendium on the multiply handicapped child. The time is ripe in special education for a systematizer to offer an eclectic model for translating psycho-educational data on the multiply handicapped child into education prescriptions. Stevens' model may serve as the archetype. There are certain advantages to eclectism; the eclectic seeks as much order and consistency as is possible at a particular level of development and at a particular time. Frequently, an eclectic model may serve as a compendium for the "state of the art" at a given time. The danger to be avoided is the uncritical combining of incompatible elements from several models. The objective is to find valid elements in principal models and combine them into a harmonious whole. It is our hope that the readers of this book will accept the challenge presented by the multiply handicapped child and utilize the reservoir of ideas presented by the contributing authors to formulate eclectic models which may enable special educators to better serve exceptional children. Of course, any model will constantly need revision as the frontiers of knowledge are ever expanded. The following generalizations about the multiply handicapped child may serve as points of departure:

1. There is a noticeable increase in the incidence of multiply handicapped children.
2. Special educators recognize that there is an increasing demand to provide more specialized services for multiply handicapped children.
3. There are conflicting viewpoints concerning the kinds of educational facilities that are most appropriate for children with multiple handicaps.
4. There is an apparent dilemma as to which concomitant or multiple disabilities have educational significance.
5. There is an absence of a specific theoretical concept concerning the the education of children with multiple handicaps.
6. Special classes for multiply handicapped children are being established based upon a specific diad of disabilities. The possible combinations of such diads is almost endless.
7. Curricula for the multiply handicapped are primarily eclectic; drawing from the content of two specific categories of exceptionality.
8. The addition of two specific disabilities is of little value for educational purposes since the phenomena does not appear to be additive.
9. There is a need to standardize the nomenclature and classification schemes used to describe and categorize children with more than one disabling condition. Such a step is a prerequisite for obtaining more precise epidemiological data.
10. There is a need for an educationally conceived classification scheme for multiply handicapped children.

References

1. ABERCROMBIE, M.L.: Eye movements, perception and learning. In *Visual Disorders and Cerebral Palsy*. Smith, V.H. (Ed.), Little Club Clinics in Developmental Medicine, 1963, No. 9.

2. ABERCROMBIE, M.L.: Perception and eye movements; some speculations on disorders in cerebral palsy. *Cereb Palsy Bull.* 2:142-148, 196.

3. ABERCROMBIE, M.L.: *Perceptual and Visuomotor Disorders in Cerebral Palsy*. Little Club Clinics in Developmental Medicine, 1964, No. 11.

4. ABERCROMBIE, M.L.; DAVIS, J.R., and SHACKEL, B.: Pilot study of vision movements of eyes in cerebral palsy and other children. In *Visual Research*. Long Island City, Pergamon, 1963, vol. 3, pp.135-153.

5. ABERCROMBIE, M.L., *et al.*: Visual, perceptual and visuomotor impairment in physically handicapped children. *Percept Motor Skills*, 18:561-625, 1964.

6. ABERNATHY, E.R.: The Auditory Acuity of Feebleminded Children. Unpublished doctoral dissertation, Ohio State University, 1938.

7. ABRUZZO, A., *et al.*: *The Identification and Vocational Training of the Institutionalized Retarded–Deaf Patient*. Washington, D.C., Office of Vocational Rehabilitation, RD 800, 1961.

8. ACHESON, E.D.: Oxford record linkage study. A central file of morbidity and mortality records for a pilot population. *Brit J Prev Soc Med*, 18:8-3, January 1964.

9. ADAIR, M.: Working with the slow-learning blind child. *Int J Educ Blind*, 1:37-39, 1951.

10. AGRANOWITZ, A., and McKEOWN, M.R.: *Aphasia Handbook for Adults and Children*. Springfield, Thomas, 1964.

11. AIRD, R.B., and COHEN, P.: Electroencephalography in cerebral palsy. *J Pediat*, 37:448-454, 1950.

12. Alabama Institute: Deaf-blind program in Alabama. *Volta R*, 58:1,10, January 1956.

13. ALBRECHT, M.: Curriculum for a class of mentally retarded blind children. *Int J Educ Blind*, 7(2):33-42, December 1952.

14. ALFORD, C.A.; NEVA, F.A., and WELLER, T.H.: Virologic and serologic studies on human products of conception after maternal rubella. *New Eng J Med*, 271:1275-281, December 17, 1964.

15. ALLEN, E.E.: *Education of Defectives*. Chicago, Lyon, 1904.

16. ALLEN, E.E.: The feeble-minded blind. *Outlook for the Blind*, 2:77-79, 1908.

17. ALLEN, E.E.: The feeble-minded blind. In *Proceedings of the National Conference of Charities and Correction*. Johnson, A. (Ed.), Philadelphia, Thirty-third Annual Session, 1906.

18. ALLEN, E.E.: An ideal matron for a school for the blind from the superintendent's point of view. *Proc Amer Assoc Instruct Blind*, 33:64, 1934.

19. ALLEN, F.H., and PEARSON, G.H.J.: The emotional problems of the physically handicapped child. *Brit J Med Psychol*, 8:212-235, 1938.

20. ALLEN, R.M., and JEFFERSON, T.W.: *Psychological Evaluation of the Cerebral Palsy Person.* Springfield, Thomas, 1962.

21. ALLEN, W.E.: Opportunity and adjustment rooms of the Texas School for the Blind. *Teachers Forum, 4*:25-27, 1931.

22. *Amer Ann Deaf, 109*:138-197, 1964.

23. American Association of Instructors of the Blind: The feeble-minded blind—what shall the schools do with them. *Proc Amer Assoc Instruct Blind, 24*:30-32, 1916.

24. American Association of Instructors of the Blind: Resolutions regarding the feeble-minded blind. *Proc Amer Assoc Instruct Blind, 26*:99-100, 1920.

25. American Association of Instructors of the Blind: What to do with the feeble-minded blind. *Proc Amer Assoc Instruct Blind, 25*:100, 1918.

26. *AAMD Educational Reporter.* (Theme of issue: The mentally retarded child with accompanying neurological handicaps.) 2:2, April 1962.

27. American Foundation for the Blind: The Multiply Handicapped. Report of Institutes on Education of Blind Children, San Francisco State College, July 14-25, 42-50, 1952.

28. American Foundation for the Blind: *Services for Blind Persons in the United States.* New York, The Foundation, November 1960.

29. American Foundation for the Blind: *A Teacher Education Program for Those Who Serve Blind Children and Youth.* New York, The Foundation, 1961.

30. American Printing House for the Blind: *Public Educational Institutions for the Blind and State Departments of Education Participating in the Federal Quota System.* Louisville, The House, November 20, 1964.

31. American Printing House for the Blind: *Report—The Survey of the Multiple-Handicapped, Visually Handicapped.* Louisville, The House, May 1955.

32. ANASTASI, A.: *Differential Psychology,* 3rd ed. New York, Macmillan, 1958.

33. ANDERSON, P.E.: Causative factors underlying congenital heart malformations; patent ductus arteriosus. *Pediatrics, 14*:143-151, August 1954.

34. ANDERSON, R.M.: Hearing impairment and mental retardation: a selected bibliography. *Volta R, 67*:425, June 1965.

35. ANDERSON, R.M., *et al.: Provisions for the Education of Mentally Retarded Deaf Children in Residential Schools for the Deaf.* U.S. Department of Health, Education, and Welfare, Office of Education, Cooperative Research Program, Pittsburgh, U. of Pittsburgh, 1966.

36. ANDERSON, R.M.: Provisions for the Education of Mentally Retarded Deaf Children in Residential Schools for the Deaf. Doctoral dissertation, University of Pittsburgh, 1965.

37. ANDERSON, R.M.: The visually impaired mentally retarded; a selected bibliography. *New Outlook for the Blind, 59*:357-360, December 1965.

38. ANDREWS, F.M.,JR.: The Educational Status of the Blind Mentally Retarded in the United States. Unpublished master's thesis, Boston University, 1938.

39. Annual Report: Bureau of Child Health, New York City Department of Health, 1961.

40. Anonymous: Slow learning deaf children can learn. *Volta R, 58*:3, 101, March 1956.

41. APGAR, V.: Drugs in pregnancy. *J Amer Med Assoc, 190*:840-841, November 30, 1964.

42. Ash, F.: The value of handicraft for the retarded blind. *Proc Amer Assoc Instruct Blind, 36:*123-126, 1940.

43. Ashcroft, S.C.: The blind and partially seeing children. In *Exceptional Children in the Schools.* Dunn, L.M. (Ed.), New York, Holt, 1963.

44. Ashcroft, S.C.: The blind and partially seeing. *R Educ Res, 29:*519-28, December 1959.

45. Ashcroft, S.C.: Delineating the possible for the multi-handicapped child with visual impairment. *Int J Educ Blind, 16:*2, December 1966.

46. Ashcroft, S.C.: Delineating the possible for the multi-handicapped child with visual impairment. *Sight Sav R, 36:*90-94, 1966.

47. Asher, P., and Schonnel, F.C.: A survey of 400 cases of cerebral palsy in childhood. *Arch Dis Child, 25:*360-79, 1950.

48. Association for the Aid of Crippled Children: *Development of a System of Codes and a Manual of Instructions for Use in Rehabilitation.* Progress Report for Office of Vocational Rehabilitation, Special Project 74-58. New York, Association for the Aid of Crippled Children, 1958, p. 3.

49. Athearn, C.R., *et al.:* General methods for the mentally retarded blind. In *Education of the Blind: A Study of Methods of Teaching the Blind.* Frampton, W.E. (Ed.), New York, World Book, 1940.

50. Atkinson, C.J.: *Perceptive and Responsive Abilities of Mentally Retarded Children as Measured by Several Auditory Threshold Tests.* U.S. Office of Education, Cooperative Research Project No. 176 (6471), Carbondale, So. Illinois Univ., 1960.

51. Attleweed, B.: Reading for the slow learner. In *Report of the Proceedings of the Fortieth Meeting of the Convention of American Instructors of the Deaf, Oregon School for the Deaf, Salem, June 1961.* Washington, D.C., U.S. Government Printing Office, 1962.

52. Ausubel, D.P.: The use of advance organizers in the learning and retention of meaningful verbal material. *J. Educ Psychol, 51:*267-272, 1960.

53. Avery, C.B.: The education of children with impaired hearing. In *Education of Exceptional Children and Youth.* Cruickshank, W.M., and Johnson, G.O. (Eds.), Englewood Cliffs, Prentice-Hall, 1958, pp. 339-385.

54. Ayres, A.: Interrelationships among perceptual–motor functions in children. *Amer J Occup Ther, 20:*68-71, 1966.

55. Ayres, A.: Tactile functions—their relationship to hyperactive and perceptual-motor behavior. *Amer J Occup Ther, 18:*6-11, 1964.

56. Ayres, L.P.: The effect of physical defect on school progress. *Psychol Clin, 3:*71-77, 1909.

57. Babbott, F.L., Jr.; Binns, W., and Ingalls, T.H.: Field studies of cyclopian malformations in sheep. *Arch Environ Health, 5:*109-113, August 1962.

58. Babbott, J.G., Jr., and Ingalls, T.H.: Field studies of selected congenital malformations occurring in Pennsylvania. *Amer J Public Health, 52:*2009-2017, December 1962.

59. Bailey, E.B.: Music's contribution to the growth and development of the blind child with an added handicap. *Proc Amer Assoc Instruct Blind, 40:*151-154, 1950.

60. Baker, H.J.: *Introduction to Exceptional Children.* New York, Macmillan, 1953, pp. 11-12.

61. Ballantyne, J.W.: *Manual on Antenatal Pathol Hyg.* Edinburgh, William Green & Sons, *The Foetus,* 1902; *The Embryo,* 1904.

62. BANGS, J.L.: A clinical analysis of the articulatory defects in the feebleminded. *J Speech Hearing Dis,* 7:343-356, 1942.

63. BANGS, J.L.: Preschool language education for the brain-damaged child. *Volta R,* 59:1, 17, January 1957.

64. BARBE, W.B.: *The Exceptional Child.* Washington, D.C., Center for Applied Research in Education, 1963.

65. BARKER, R.G., *et al.: Adjustment to Physical Handicap and Illness—A Survey of the Social Psychology of Physique and Disability.* New York, Social Science Research Council, Bull. 55, 1953.

66. BARKER, L.S.; SCHOGGEN, M.; SCHOGGEN, P., and BARKER, R.G.: The frequency of physical disability in children: a comparison of three sources of information. *Child Develop,* 23:215-226, 1952.

67. BARNES, J.F.L.: Emotional problems of children with speech defects. *Med Press,* 244(23):504-507, 1960.

68. BARRAGA, N.: Effects of experimental teaching on the visual behavior of children educated as though they had no vision. *New Outlook for the Blind,* December 1964. (Published under the title, Teaching Children with Low Vision.)

69. BARSCH, R.H.: Evaluating the organic child: the fundamental organizational scale. *J Gen Psychol,* 100:345-354, 1962.

70. BARSCH, R.H.: The handicapped ranking scale among parents of handicapped children. *Amer J Public Health,* 54:1560-567, September 1964.

71. BASSETT, D.M.: Our blind girls go to school. *Train Sch Bull,* 29:74-78, 1932.

72. BATEMAN, B.: *The Illinois Test of Psycholinguistic Abilities in Current Research.* Urbana, U. of Ill. 1964.

73. BATEMAN, B.: Learning Disabilities—an Overview. Paper read at CEC 42nd Annual Convention, Chicago, April 1964.

74. BATEMAN, B.: Learning disorders. *Rev Educ Res,* 36:93-94, February 1966.

75. BATEMAN, B.: Psychological evaluation of blind children. *New Outlook for the Blind,* 59:193-196, 1965.

76. BATES, R.E.: Meaning of "Disabled" and "Handicapped"—Their Relationship to Each Other and Specific Defects. Doctoral dissertation, University of Houston, 1964.

77. BAUMEISTER, A.: The usefulness of the I.Q. with severely retarded individuals—reply to MacAndres and Edgerton. *Amer J Ment Defic,* 69:881-882, May 1965.

78. BAX, M.C.O.: Terminology and classification of cerebral palsy. Report of group discussions. *Develop Med Child Neurol* 6:295-297, 1964.

79. BECK, H.S.: The incidence of brain injury in public school special classes for the educable mentally handicapped. *Amer J Ment Defic,* 60:818-882, April 1956.

80. BEKKER, B.V., and VAN DUYNE, W.M.J.: *Bull Ministry of Health.* Netherlands, The Hague, January 1963.

81. BENDA, C.E.: *Developmental Disorders of Mentation and Cerebral Palsies.* New York, Grune, 1952.

82. BENDA, C.E.: *Mongolism and Cretinism.* New York, Grune, 1946.

83. BENDER, L.: Autism in children with mental deficiency. *Amer J Ment Defic,* 64:81-86, 1959.

84. BENDER, L., and SILVER, A.: Body image problems of the brain injured child. *J Soc Issues,* 4:84-89, Fall 1948.

85. BENDER, L.: Brain damage in blind children with retrolental fibroplasia. *Trans Amer Neurol Assoc,* 1964, pp. 183-184.

86. BENDER, L.: *Psychopathology of Children with Organic Brain Disorders.* Springfield, Thomas, 1956.

87. BENOIT, E.P.: A functional theory of mental retardation. *AAMD Educ Reporter,* 2:4-6, April 1962.

88. BENTON, A.L.: Psychological evaluation and differential diagnosis. In *Mental Retardation.* Stevens, H., and Heber, R. (Eds.), Chicago, U. of Chicago, 1964.

89. BERGMAN, M.: Rehabilitating blind persons with impaired hearing. *New Outlook for the Blind,* 53(101):351-356, December 1959.

90. BERHOW, B.: Deaf-blind children—their educational outlook. *New Outlook for the Blind,* 57(10):399-401, December 1959.

91. BERKO, M.J.: A note on psychometric scatter as a fact in the differentiation of exogenous and enogenous mental deficiency. *Cereb Palsy Rev,* 16:20, January-February 1966.

92. BERKO, M.: Some factors in the perceptual deviations of cerebral palsied children. *Cereb Palsy Rev,* 15:3-4, 14, February 1954.

93. BERKSON, G., and DAVENPORT, R.K.: Stereotyped movements of mental defectives. I. Initial survey. *Amer J Ment Defic,* 66:849-852, 1962.

94. BERKSON, G., and MASON, W.: Stereotyped movements of mental defectives. IV. The effects of toys and the character of the acts. *Amer J Ment Defic,* 68:511-524, 1964.

95. BERREMAN, J.V.: Some implications of research in the social psychology of physical disability. *J Exceptional Child,* 20:347-350, 356-357, 1951.

96. BETTICA, L.J.: Attitudes influencing the interaction between professional workers and the deaf–blind clients. *New Outlook for the Blind,* 60(4):120-122, April 1966.

97. BEXTON, W.H., et al.: Effects of decreased variation in the sensory environment. *Canad J Psychol,* 8:70-76, 1954.

98. BIBEY, M.L.: A rationale of speech therapy for mentally deficient children. *Train Sch Bull,* 47:236-239, 1951.

99. BICE, H.V.: Psychological examination of the cerebral palsied. *Exceptional Child,* 14:163-168, 1948.

100. BINNS, W.; JAMES, L.F.; SHUPE, J.L., and THACKER, F.J.: Cyclopian-type malformation in lambs. *Arch Environ Health,* 5:106-108, August 1962.

101. BIRCH, G.H., and LEFFORD, A.: Intersensory development in children. *Monogr Soc Res Child Develop,* 1963, vol. 28, part 5.

102. BIRCH, J., and MATTHEW, J.: The hearing of mental defectives. *Amer J Ment Defic,* 55:384-393, 1951.

103. BIRCH, J.W., et al.: The non-professional worker in special education and rehabilitation—a review of the literature. *Rehab Lit,* 24:66-74,79, March 1963.

104. BIRCH-JENSEN, A.: *Congenital Deformities of the Upper Extremities.* Odense, Det Danske Forlag, 1949.

105. BISHOP, E.H.: Prematurity: etiology and management. *Postgrad Med,* 35:185-188, 1964.

106. BLACKHURST, R.T., and RADKE, E.: Testing retarded children for defects in vision. *Children,* 13:109-112, May-June 1966.

107. BLAKELEY, R.W.: Erythroblastosis and perceptive hearing loss—response of athetoids to tests of cochlear function. *J Speech Hearing Res,* 2:5-15, 1959.

108. BLAKELEY, R.W.: Speech defects and mental retardation. *Public Health Rep, 81* (4):343-347, April 1966.

109. BLATT, B.: The physical, personality and academic status of children who are mentally retarded attending special class as compared with retarded children attending regular class. *Amer J Men Defic, 62*:810-818, March 1958.

110. BLAU, A.: The master hand; a study of the origin and meaning of right and left sidedness and its relation to personality and language. New York, American Orthopsychiatric Assoc., 1946.

111. BLEIBERG, N.: Medical supervision in the child health conference. *New York J Med, 59*:438-444, February 1959.

112. BLEYER, A.: Role of advanced maternal age in causing mongolism; study of 2,822 cases. *Amer J Dis Child, 55*:79-92, January 1938.

113. BLOCK, W.E.: A study of somatopsychological relationships in cerebral palsied children. *Exceptional Child, 22*:53-59, 1955.

114. BLODGETT, H.: A keystone in rehabilitation. *Crippled Child,* April, June 1958, vol. 35, part 6; vol. 36, part 1.

115. BLOOMFIELD, L.: Linguistics and reading. *Elementary Eng Rev, 19*:125-130, 183-186, 1942.

116. BLUM, L.H.; BURGAMEISTER, B.B., and LORGE, I.: Trends in estimating the mental maturity of the cerebral palsied child. *J Exceptional Child, 17*:174-178, 1951.

117. Board of Education: Report of the Committee of Inquiry into Problems Relating to Children with Defective Hearing, H.M.S.O., London, 1938.

118. BOBRICK, G.: Speech—some factors in its nature and development with implications for the child who has cerebral palsy. *Cereb Palsy Rev, 17*:153-156, Nov., Dec., 1956.

119. BOLY, L.F., and DeLEO, G.M.: A survey of educational provisions for the institutionalized mentally sub-normal blind. *Amer J Ment Defic, 60*:744-749, April 1956.

120. BOLY, L.F., and DeLEO, G.M.: A survey of educational provisions for the institutionalized mentally sub-normal blind. *New Outlook for the Blind, 50*:232, 1956.

121. BOOK, J.A.: *Acta Genet, 2*:289, 1951.

122. BOOK, J.A., and RAYNER, S.: A clinical and genetical study of anencephaly. *Amer J Hum Genet, 2*:61-84, 1950.

123. BORDLEY, J.E.; HARDY, W.G., and HARDY, M.P.: *Pediatric Audiology.* Pediatric Clinics of North America, 1962, pp. 1147-1158.

124. BORIS, M.; BLUMBERG, R.; FELDMAN, D.E., and SELLERS, J.E.: Increased incidence of meningomyeloceles. *J Amer Med Assoc, 184*:768, June 6, 1963.

125. BOURGEAULT, S.E.: A continuum of excepional services for visual impaired children. *Minnesota Med, 43*:562-565, August 1960.

126. BOWLUS, D.E.: The organization of a training program for the cerebral palsied in an institution for mentally deficient. *Amer J Ment Defic, 58*:419-423, 1953.

127. BOWMAN, P.W., and JOBYNA, R.: The retarded deaf and hard of hearing. *Pineland Hosp Bull Ment Retardation, 1*:1-5, 1957.

128. BOYD, J.: Problems in the diagnosis of deafness in children. II. Deaf or severely mentally retarded. *Hearing Eye, 29*:6-9, 1961.

129. BRADDY, W.: *Anne Sullivan Macy, the Story Behind Helen Keller.* Garden City, Doubleday, 1933.

130. BRADLEY, E.; EVANS, W.E., and WORTHINGTON, A.M.: The relationship between

administration time for audiometric testing and the mental ability of mentally deficient children. *Amer J Ment Defic, 60*:345-353, 1955.

131. BREAKEY, A.S.: Ocular findings in cerebral palsy. *Arch Ophthal, 53*:852-856, 1955.

132. BRENNEMANN, J.: *Brennemann's Practice of Pediatrics.* Hagerstown, W.F. Prior, 1937.

133. BRIELAND, D.: Speech education for the visually handicapped child. *Int J Educ Blind, 1*:9-12, 1951.

134. BRILL, R.G.: The relationship of Wechsler I.Q.'s to academic achievement among deaf students. *Exceptional Child, 28*:315-321, 1962.

135. BRIMMER, M.A., and DUNN, L.M.: *English Picture Vocabulary Tests.* National Foundation for Educational Research in England and Wales, 1963.

136. British Medical Association: Report of Annual Meeting. *Brit Med J, 2*:222, 1956.

137. BROWN, G.C.; MAASSAB, H.F.; VERONELLI, J.A., and FRANCIS, T.J.: Rubella antibodies in human serum: detection by the indirect fluorescent antibody technic. *Science, 145*:943-945, August 28, 1961.

138. BROWN, M.S.C.: The multiple handicapped blind child. *Proc Amer Assoc Instruct Blind, 47*:21-28, 1964.

139. BROWN, S.F.: A note on speech retardation in mental deficiency. *Pediatrics, 16*: 272-273, 1955.

140. BROWN, W.M.: Training of the retarded child. *Proc Amer Assoc Instruct Blind, 33*:70, 1934.

141. BRUCKER, P.A.: HOYT, J., and TRUSLER, H.M.: Severe cleft lip with arrhinencephaly. *Plast Reconstr Surg, 32*:527-537, November 1963.

142. BRUNER, J.S.: The cognitive consequences of early sensory deprivation. In *Sensory Deprivation.* Solomon, P., *et al.* (Eds.), Cambridge, Harvard U. P., 1961.

143. BRUNER, J.S.: Education as social invention. *Saturday Review,* February 19, 1966, pp. 70-72, 102-104.

144. BRUNER, J.: Going beyond the information given. In *Contemporary Approaches to Cognition.* Cambridge, Harvard U. P., 1957.

145. BRUNER, J.S., and POSTMAN, J.: On the perception of incongruity: a paradigm. *J Personality, 18*:206-223, 1951.

146. BRUNER, J.S.; GOODNOW, J.J., and AUSTIN, G.A.: *A Study of Thinking.* New York, Wiley, 1956.

147. BRUTTEN, M.: Some problems relating to differential diagnosis of auditory disorders in children. In *Report of the Proceedings of the Thirty-ninth Meeting of the Convention of American Instructors of the Deaf, Colorado School for the Deaf, Colorado Springs, Colorado.* Washington, D.C., U.S. Government Printing Office, 1960, pp. 37-44.

148. BRYANT, N.D.: Some principles of remedial instruction for dyslexia. *Int Reading Assoc J* (in press).

149. BUCKMAN, F.G.: Multiple-handicapped blind children—an incidence survey. *Int J Educ Blind, 15*:46-49, December 1965.

150. BUDDS, F.C.: Some initial experiences with mentally handicapped children who are attending schools for the blind. *Int J Educ Blind, 10*:16-23, October 1960.

151. BUELL, C.: Motor performance of visually handicapped children. *Exceptional Child, 17*:69-72, 1950.

152. BURGEMEISTER, B.B.; BLUM, L.H., and LORGE, J.: *Columbia Mental Maturity Scale*, rev. ed. New York, World Book, 1959.

153. BURGEMEISTER, B.B., and BLUM, L.H.: Intellectual evaluation of a group of cerebral palsied children. *Nervous Child*, 8:177-180, 1949.

154. BURNS, D.J., and STENQUIST, G.H.: The deaf–blind in the United States—their care, education and guidance. *Rehab Lit*, 21:334-344, November 1960.

155. BURRITT, O.H.: The visually handicapped feeble-minded. *Teachers Forum*, 4: 9-12, 1931.

156. BYERS, R.K., and CROTHERS, B.: Extrapyramidal cerebral palsy with hearing loss following erythroblastosis. *Pediatrics*, 15:248-254, 1955.

157. CANDLAND, D.K., and CONKLYN, D.H.: Use of the oddity problem in teaching mentally retarded deaf-mutes to read—a pilot project. *Train Sch Bull*, 59:39, August 1962.

158. CANTOR, G.N.: A critique of Garfield and Wittson's reaction to the revised manual on terminology and classification. *Amer J Ment Defic*, 64:954-956, May 1960.

159. CANTOR, G.N.: Some issues involved in category VIII of the AAMD terminology and classification. *Amer J Ment Defic*, 65:561-566, March 1961.

160. CARDWELL, V.E.: *Cerebral Palsy—Advances in Understanding and Care*. New York, Association for the Aid of Crippled Children, 1956.

161. Carnegie Trust: Unpublished data, 1956.

162. CARNELL, C.M., JR.: Communication centered speech therapy in cerebral palsy. *Cereb Palsy Rev*, 24:3,4, March, April 1963.

163. CARRIKER, W.R.: Research related to physically handicapped and emotionally maladjusted children. *School Life*, 42:11-15, April 1960.

164. CARROLL, T.J.: *Blindness: What It Is, What It Does, and How to Live With It*. Boston, Little, 1961.

165. CARTER, C.H.: Emylcamate-hospitalized mentally retarded spastic patients. *Dis Nerv Syst*, 23:211-216, 1962.

166. CARTER, C.O.: A live table for mongols with causes of death. *J Ment Defic Res*, 2:64, 1958.

167. CARTER, V.R.: Where shall blind children be educated. *Int J Educ Blind*, 4: 21-23, December 1954.

168. CATTY, N.: The teaching of retarded blind children. *New Beacon*, 24:73-74, 98-99, 1940.

169. CAWLEY, J.F., and SPOTTS, J.V.: *Survey of Treatment and Educational Facilities and Programs for Retardates with Accompanying Sensory Defects—Auditory and Visual Impairments*. Storrs, Connecticut Univ., 1967.

170. CHAPPLE, B.P.: What is to be done with the feeble-minded blind? *Proc Amer Assoc Instruct Blind*, 26:31-34, 1920.

171. CHARNEY, L.: Minority group within two minority groups. *Int J Educ Blind*, 10: 37-43, December 1960.

172. CHASE, J.B.: The multiple handicapped blind child—implementation of programs. *Proc Amer Assoc Instruct Blind*, 47:18-21, 1964.

173. CHENOWETH, A.D.: The child with central nervous system deficit. *J Amer Phys Ther Assoc*, 45:283-289, April 1965.

174. The child from 0-6 years of age. *Bull Med Soc County of Kings*, 32:349-354, October 1953.

175. Child Health Services and Pediatric Education. Report of the American Academy of Pediatrics, New York Commonwealth Fund, 1949.

176. *Children Handicapped by Cerebral Palsy.* New York, Milford, 1937.

177. CHRISTENSEN, N.J., and SCHLANGER, B.B.: Auditory training with the mentally retarded. *Ment Retard, 2*:290-293, October 1964.

178. CHRISTMAN, D.: Problems of communication of individuals with cerebral palsy. *Cereb Palsy Rev, 17*:157,170, November, December 1956.

179. *Chronic Illness in the United States.* Chronic illness in a large city. Cambridge, Harvard U. P., 1937, Vol. IV.

180. CICENIA, E.F., *et al.*: The blind child with multiple handicaps—a challenge, part I. *Int J Educ Blind, 14*:65-71, March 1965.

181. CICENIA, E.F., *et al.*: The blind child wih multiple handicaps—a challenge, part II. *Int J Educ Blind, 14*:105-112, May 1965.

182. CLAUSEN, J., and ALLONARDE, H.: Bibliography of publications from the training school at Vineland, 1928-1958. *Train Sch Bull, 56*:15-28, May 1959, continued *56*:101-108, November 1959.

183. CLEMENTS, S.D.: Come to the wedding! *Acad Ther Quart, 11*:135-136, Spring 1967.

184. CLEMENTS, S., and PETERS, J.E.: Minimal brain dysfunction in the school age child. *Arch Gen Psychiat, 6*:186-97, 1960.

185. COBB, H.: Self-concept of the mentally retarded. *Rehab Rec., 2*:21-25, 1961.

186. COCKBURN, J.M.: Psychological and educational aspects. In *Cerebral Palsy in Childhood and Adolescence.* Henderson (Ed.), Baltimore, Williams & Wilkins, 1961.

187. COHE, P.: Rh child—deaf or aphasic? Aphasia in Kernicterus. *J Speech Hearing Dis, 21*:411-412, 1956.

188. COHEN, J., *et al.*: Clinical evaluation of school age children with retrolental fibroplasia. In *Research Bulletin, No. 7.* New York, American Foundation for the Blind, December 1964.

189. COHEN, J.: Development of a blind spastic child, a case study. *Exceptional Child, 32*:291-294, January 1966.

190. COHEN, J.: The effects of blindness on children's development. *Children, 13*: 23-27, January, February 1966.

191. COHN, R.: Neurological concepts pertaining to the brain-damaged child. In *Speech and Language Therapy with the Brain-Damaged Child.* Daley, W.T. (Ed.), Washington, D.C., Catholic U. of Amer., 1962.

192. College of Teachers of the Blind and the National Institute for the Blind: Doubly defective children. In *Education of the Blind: A Survey, Report of the Joint Committee.* London, Edward Arnold, 1936.

193. COLLMANN, R.D., and STOLLER, A.: A survey of mongoloid births in Victoria, Australia. *Amer J Public Health, 52*:813-829, May 1962.

194. Columbus State School for M.R.: *An Overview of the Education and Training Program.* Columbus, Ohio, 1963, pp. 20-74.

195. Commission on Chronic Illness. Chronic illness in a rural area. In *Chronic Illness in the United States.* Cambridge, Harvard U. P., 1956, Vol. III.

196. Committee on Child Health, American Public Health Association: *Services for Handicapped Children.* New York, The Association, 1961, p. 12.

197. Committee on Medical Care, Maryland State Planning Commission: Report on Diagnostic and Rehabilitation Centers for Handicapped Children. October 1957.

198. Conference of Educators of Deaf-Blind Children: Watertown, Mass., April 13 and 14, 1953, No. 16, Watertown, Perkins School for the Blind, 1954.

199. Conference of Executives of American Schools for the Deaf: Report of the conference committee on nomenclature. *Amer Ann Deaf, 83*:1-3, 1938.

200. CONNOR, F.: Safety for the crippled child and the child with special health problems. *Exceptional Child, 28*:237, January 1962.

201. CONNOR, F.P., and GOLDBERG, I.I.: Children with crippling conditions and special health problems. *R Educ Res, 29*:471-496, December 1959.

202. CONNOR, L.E.: Determining the prevalence of hearing impaired children. *Exceptional Child, 6*:337-344, 1961.

203. CONNOR, L.E.: Research in the education of the deaf in the United States. *Volta R, 65*:523-534, November 1963.

204. CONRAD, D., and SHIRLEY, J.H.: *Suggested Activities for Slow Learning and Retarded Blind Children.* St. Louis, Amer Assoc Instruct Blind, June 1960.

205. COOK, R.E., and ODELL, G.B.: Perinatal factors in the prevention of handicaps. *Pediat Clin N Amer*, 1957, pp. 595-609.

206. CORLISS, L.: Multiple handicapped children—their placement in the school education program. *J Sch Health, 37*:113-120, March 1967.

207. COSTELLO, P.: Where does Mike belong? *Volta R, 62*(2):66-67, February 1960.

208. COTTON, C.B.: A study of the reactions of spastic children to certain test situations. *J Genet Psychol, 58*:27-44, 1941.

209. Council for Exceptional Children: *Professional Standards for Personnel in the Education of Exceptional Children.* Washington, D.C., The Council, 1966.

210. COWGILL, A.G.: Our methods of handling the mentally handicapped or retarded child. *Proc Amer Assoc Instruct Blind, 34*:41, 1936.

211. CRABTREE, N., and GERRARD, J.: Perceptive deafness associated with severe neonatal jaundice, a report of sixteen cases. *J Laryng, 64*:482-502, 1950.

212. CRONBACH, L.J.: *Essentials of Psychological Testing.* New York, Harper, 1949.

213. CROTHERS, B.: *Disorders of the Nervous System in Childhood.* New York, Appleton, 1926.

214. CROTHERS, B., and PAINE, R.S.: *The Natural History of Cerebral Palsy.* New York, Oxford U. P., 1959.

215. CRUICKSHANK, and RAUS (Eds.): *Cerebral Palsy.* Syracuse, Syracuse, 1955.

216. CRUICKSHANK, W.M., and HARDING, N.C.: *A Demonstration-Assistants for Teachers of Exceptional Children.* Syracuse, Syracuse, 1957.

217. CRUICKSHANK, W.M., and JOHNSON, G.O. (Eds.): *Education of Exceptional Children and Youth.* Englewood Cliffs, Prentice-Hall, 1958.

218. CRUICKSHANK, W.M., and DOLPHIN, J.E.: The educational implications of psychological studies of cerebral palsied children. *Exceptional Child, 18*:1-8, 1951.

219. CRUICKSHANK, W.M.: The impact of physical disability on social adjustment. *J Soc Issues, 4*:78-83, Fall 1948.

220. CRUICKSHANK, W.M.: The multiple-handicapped child and courageous action. *Int J Educ Blind, 13*:65-74, March 1964.

221. CRUICKSHANK, W.M.: The multiply handicapped cerebral palsy child. *Exceptional Child, 20*:16-22, October 1953.

222. CRUICKSHANK, W.M.; BICE, H.V.; WALLEN, N.E., and LYNCH, K.S.: *Perception and Cerebral Palsy.* Syracuse, Syracuse, 1965.

223. CRUICKSHANK, W.M.: Psychological consideration with crippled children. In

Psychology of Exceptional Children and Youth. Cruickshank, W.M. (Ed.), Englewood Cliffs, Prentice-Hall, 1955.

224. CRUICKSHANK, W.M., and TRIPPE, M.J.: *Services to Blind Children in New York State.* Syracuse, Syracuse, 1957.

225. CRUICKSHANK, W.M. (Ed.): *The Teacher of Brain-Injured Children—A Discussion of the Bases for Competency.* Syracuse, Syracuse, 1966.

226. CRUICKSHANK, W.M.; BENTZEN, F.A.; RATZEBURG, R.H., and TANNHAUSER, M.T.: *A Teaching Method for Brain-injured and Hyperactive Children.* Syracuse, Syracuse, 1961.

227. CULBERT, R.W.; JACOBZINER, H., and OLLSTEIN, P.: Training program in school health service. *Amer J Public Health, 44*:228-234, February 1954.

228. CURETON, T.: 18-item motor fitness test. In *Physical Fitness Workbook.* Champaign, U. of Ill., 1942.

229. CURTIS, W.S.: The evaluation of verbal performance in multiply handicapped blind children. *Exceptional Child, 32*(6):367-374, 1966.

230. CUTSFORTH, M.G., and JACKSON, C.L.: Mental development of children with blindness due to retrolental fibroplasia. *J Dis Child, 96*:641-654, December 1958.

231. CUTSFORTH, T.D.: *The Blind in School and Society.* New York, American Foundation for the Blind, 1951.

232. CUTSFORTH, T.D.: A case of retarded development in the blind. In *Readings in Psychology.* Holder, R. (Ed.), New York, Wheeler Crowell, 1930.

233. DANBY. G.: Problems of mentally defective and inefficient blind. In *Proceedings of the World Conference on Work for the Blind.* Lende, Helga, *et al.* (Eds.), New York, April 1931.

234. DAUWALDER, D.D.: *Education, Training and Employment of the Blind.* Pittsburgh, The Western Pennsylvania School for Blind Children, June 1964.

235. DAVENPORT, R., and BERKSON, G.: Stereotyped movements of mental defectives. II. Effects of novel objects. *Amer J Ment Defic, 67*:879-882, 1963.

236. DAVEY, P.R.: Hearing loss in children of low birth weight. *J Laryng, 76*:274-277, 1962.

237. DAVIDOW, M.E.: A study of instructional techniques for the development of social skills of retarded blind children. *Int J Blind, 12*:61-62, December 1962.

238. DAVIDOW, M.E.: A study of special instructional techniques for the development of social skills of retarded blind children. *Dissertation Abstracts, 21*:1475, 1960.

239. DAVIS, C.J.: The assessment of intelligence of visually handicapped children. *Int J Educ Blind, 12*:48-51, December 1962.

240. DAVIS, M.D., and POTTER, E.L.: Congenital malformations and obstetrics. *Pediatrics, 19*:719-724, 1957.

241. DAYTON, N.A.: The relationship between physical defects and intelligence. *J Psycho-Asthenics, 34*:112-39, 1928-29.

242. DEGROAT, A.F., and THOMPSON, G.G.: A study of the distribution of teacher approval and disapproval among sixth-grade pupils. *J Exp Educ, 18*:57-75, 1949.

243. DEHIRSCH, K., *et al.*: Comparisons between prematurely and maturely born children at three age levels. *Amer J Orthopsychiat, 36*:616-628, 1966.

244. DEHIRSCH, K.: Test designed to discover potential reading difficulties at the six-year-old level. *Amer J Orthopsychiat, 27*:566-576, 1957.

245. DELACATO, C.H.: *The Diagnosis and Treatment of Speech and Reading Problems.* Springfield, Thomas, 1963.

246. DeLEO, G.M., and BOLY, L.F.: Program for the institutionalized blind and partially sighted mentally subnormal. *Amer J Ment Defic, 61*:134-140, July 1956.

247. DEMBO, T.; LADIEU, G., and WRIGHT, B.A.: *Adjustment to Misfortune.* A study in social-emotional relationships between injured and non-injured people. Final report to the Army Medical Research and Development Board. Office of the Surgeon General, War Department, 1948.

248. DENHOFF, E.: Cerebral palsy—medical aspects. In *Cerebral Palsy: Its Individual and Community Problems.* Cruickshank, W.M. (Ed.), Syracuse, Syracuse, 1966.

249. DENHOFF, E., and ROBINAULT, I.P.: *Cerebral Palsy and Related Disorders—A Developmental Approach to Dysfunction.* New York, McGraw, 1960.

250. DENHOFF, E., and HOLDEN, R.: Significance of delayed development in the diagnosis of cerebral palsied. *J Pediat, 38*:452-456, 1951.

251. DERSE, P.: The emotional problems of behavior in the spastic, athetoid, and ataxic type of cerebral palsied child. *Amer J Occup Ther, 4*:252-260, 1950.

252. DE SCHWEINITZ, L.; MILLER, C., and MILLER, J.B.: Delays in the diagnosis of deafness among pre-school children. *Pediatrics, 24*:482,1959.

253. DIEDRICH, W.M., *et al.*: Value of preschool treatment program for severely crippled children. *Exceptional Child, 27*:187-90, December 1960.

254. DiMICHAEL, S.G.: Meeting the needs of retarded blind children. *Proc Amer Assoc Instruct Blind, 43*:15, 1956.

255. DINSMORE, A.B.: National approach to the education of deaf-blind children. *Amer Ann Deaf, 98*:5:418-430, November 1953.

256. DINSMORE, A.: Services for blind-deaf adults and children. *New Outlook for the Blind, 60*(4):123-128, April 1966.

257. DINSMORE, A.: Unmet needs of deaf-blind children. *New Outlook for the Blind, 61*:262-265, October 1967.

258. DISHART, M.: Testing the blind for rehabilitation—using a psychological profile. *New Outlook for the Blind, 53*:1-4, January 1959.

259. DOCTOR, P.V.: Deafness in the twentieth century. *Amer Ann Deaf,* November 1959, p. 333.

260. DOCTOR, P.V.: Multiple handicaps in the field of deafness. In *Sixth Annual Conference on Problems of Hearing and Speech,* Syracuse, Syracuse, 1951.

261. DOCTOR, P.V.: Multiple handicaps in the field of deafness. *Exceptional Child, 26*:156-158, November 1959.

262. DOCTOR, P.V.: Multiple handicaps in the field of rehabilitation. *Amer Ann Deaf, 103*(2):409-413, March 1958.

263. DOCTOR, P.V.: A proposed study of the incidence of deafness structured geographically by school enrollments in states, 1948-1964. In *Proceedings, Conference on the Collection of Statistics of Severe Hearing Impairments and Deafness in the United States.* Public Health Service, Publication No. 1227, Washington, D.C., Superintendent of Documents, U.S. Government Printing Office, 1964, p. 24.

264. DOCTOR, P.V. (Ed.): Tabular statement of American Schools for the deaf. *Amer Ann Deaf,* October 31, 1960, Summary, 106:162, January 1961.

265. DODGE, P.R., and ADAMS, R.D.: Developmental abnormalities of the nervous

system. In *Principles of Internal Medicine.* Harrison, T.R., *et al.* (Eds.), New York, McGraw, 1958, vol. 2.

266. DOLBERG, M., and LENARD, H.M.: The concept of disability and handicap revisited. *Cereb Palsy J, 28*:3-9, March-April, 1967.

267. DOLL, E.A.: Essentials of an inclusive concept of mental deficiency. *Amer J Ment Defic, 46*:214-219, October 1941.

268. DOLL, E.A.: Is mental deficiency curable? *Amer J Ment Defic, 51*:420-428, January 1967.

269. DOLL; PHELPS, and MELCHER: *Mental Deficiency Due to Birth Injuries.* New York, Macmillan, 1932.

270. DOLL, E.A.: The mentally retarded. *Exceptional Child, 27*:487-493, May 1961.

271. DOLPHIN, J.E., and CRUICKSHANK, W.M.: The figure-background relationship in children with cerebral palsy. *J Clin Psychol, 7*:228-31, 1951.

272. DOLPHIN, J.E., and CRUICKSHANK, W.M.: Pathology of concept formation in children with cerebral palsy. *Amer J Ment Defic, 56*:386-392, 1951.

273. DOLPHIN, J.E., and CRUICKSHANK, W.M.: Tactuo-motor perception in children with cerebral palsy. *J Personality, 20*:466-471, 1952.

274. DOLPHIN, J.E., and CRUICKSHANK, W.M.: Visuo-motor perception in children with cerebral palsy. *Quart J Child Behav, 3*:198-209, 1951.

275. DONLON, E.T.: An evaluation center for the blind child with multiple handicaps. *Int J Educ Blind, 13*:75-78, March 1964.

276. DORWARD, B.: A comparison of the competencies for regular classroom teachers and teachers of emotionally disturbed children. *Exceptional Child, 30*:67-73, October 1963.

277. Doubly handicapped children. *Lancet, 226*:826, April 17, 1954.

278. DOUGLAS, A.A.: Ophthalmological aspects. Chapter in *Cerebral Palsy in Childhood and Adolescence.* Henderson, 1961.

279. DOUGLAS, J.W.B.: The age at which premature children walk. *Med Officer, 95*:33-35, 1956.

280. DOUGLAS, J.W.B.: Mental ability and school achievement of premature children of eight years of age. *Brit Med J, 1*:1210-1214, 1956.

281. Dow, J.J.: Borderline cases in special schools. *Outlook for the Blind, 6*:63-67, 1912.

282. DOWNING, J.: The prevention of communication disorders by the use of a simplified alphabet. *Develop Med Child Neurol, 6*:113-124, 1946.

283. DREW, A.L.: A neurological appraisal of familial congenital word blindness. *Brain, 79*:440-460, 1956.

284. DRILLIEN, C.M.: Physical and mental handicap in the prematurely born. *J Obstet Gynaec, 66*:721-728, 1959.

285. DRY, W.R., and COOPER, E.C.: The psychological study of blind children. *Psychol Clin, 20*:184-191, 1931.

286. DUBLIN, W.: Neurologic lesions of erythroblastosis fetalis in relation to nuclear deafness. *Amer J Clin Path, 21*:935-939, 1951.

287. DUNCAN, M.H.: Emotional aspects of the communication problem in cerebral palsy. *Cereb Palsy Rev, 16*:19-23, July, August 1955.

288. DUNSDON, M.I.: *The Educability of Cerebral Palsy Children.* London, National Foundation for Educational Research in England and Wales, 1952.

289. DUNN, L.M., and HARLEY, R.K.: Comparability of test scores with cerebral palsied children, 1959.

290. DUNN, L.M. (Ed.): *Exceptional Children in the Schools.* New York, Holt, 1964.

291. Dunn, L.M.: *Manual for the Peabody Picture Vocabulary Test*. Nashville, American Guidance Service, Inc., 1959.

292. Dunn, L.M., and Capobianco, R.J.: Mental retardation. *Rev Educ Res, XXIX*(5):151-170, December 1959.

293. Dunn, L. M., and Brooks, S.T.: Peabody picture vocabulary test performance of educable mentally retarded children. *Train Sch Bull,* 57:35-40, 1960.

294. Dustin, N.F.: What is adequate provision for the education of the backward (not feebleminded) blind child, and how can we meet this problem in our schools? *Proc Amer Assoc Instruct Blind,* 21:10-12, 1910.

295. Dybwad, G.: The role of community services. In *Survey Papers White House Conference on Children and Youth*. Washington, D.C., 1960, pp. 265-268.

296. Eames, T.H.: The relationship of birth weight, speed of object and word perception and visual acuity. *J Pediat,* 47:603-606, 1955.

297. Eblen, R.E., Jr.: Professional training for speech therapists in cerebral palsy. *Cereb Palsy Rev,* 16:12-15, July, August 1955.

298. Eckstein, H.B., and Macnab, G.H.: Myelomeningocele and Hydrocephalus: impact of modern treatment. *Lancet,* 1:842-845, April 16, 1966.

299. Editor's Column: The "Fund-for-a-disease" problem. *J Pediat,* 48:822-826, June 1956.

300. Education of exceptional children, *Rev Educ Res,* 33:1-138, 1963.

301. Education of exceptional children. *Rev Educ Res,* 36:1-202, 1966.

302. Egland, G.O.: Teaching speech to blind children with cerebral palsy. *Cereb Palsy Rev,* 16:12-15, July, August 1955.

303. Eisenberg, L.: The autistic child in adolescence. *Amer J Psychiat,* 112:607, 1956.

304. Eisenberg, L.: Behavioral manifestations of cerebral damage. In *Brain Damage in Children: The Biological and Social Aspects*. Birch, H.G. (Ed.), Baltimore, Williams & Wilkins, 1963.

305. Elkan, D.: Development of an aphasic child. *Volta R,* 57:2,71, February 1955.

306. Ellis, E.; Dershaw, J.D.; D'Avignon; Olow, M., and Saunders, R.V.: Papers on indications for residential treatment of cerebral palsy in the early years of life. *Develop Med Child Neurol,* 5(1):32-41, and (2):154-166, 1963.

307. Ellis, N.: Toilet training the severely defective patient—an s-r reinforcement analysis. *Amer J Ment Defic,* 68:98-103, 1963.

308. Elliott, M.: The association method for aphasics. *Volta R,* 57:1,13, January 1955.

309. Elliott, M.H., and Hall, F.H.: *Laura Bridgman, Dr. Howe's Famous Pupil and What He Taught Her*. Boston, Little, 1903.

310. Elonen, A.S., and Zwarensteyn, S.R.: Appraisal of developmental lag in certain blind children. *J Pediat,* 65:599-610, 1964.

311. Elonen, A., and Cain, A.C.: A diagnostic evaluation and treatment of deviant blind children. *Amer J Orthopsychiat,* 34:625-633, July 1964.

312. Elonen, A.S., and Polzien, M.: Experimental program for deviant blind children. *New Outlook for the Blind,* 59:122-126, April 1965.

313. Elonen, A., and Zwarensteyn, S.: Michigan's summer program for multiple-handicapped blind children. *New Outlook for the Blind,* 57(3):77-82, March 1963.

314. Erhardt, C.E.: Reported congenital malformations in New York City 1958-1959. *Amer J Public Health,* 54:1489-506, September 1964.

315. Erhart, C.B., *et al.*: Brain injury in the pre-school child. Comparison of brain

injured and normal children. *Psychol Monogr*, 1963, vol. 77, no. 11 (Amer. Psycho. Assoc., Inc.).

316. ERHART, C.B.; GRAHAM, F.K., and THURSTON, D.: Relationship of neonatal apnea to development at three years. *Arch Neurol*, 2:504-510, 1960.

317. ETHUN, C.A.: Physical management of the multihandicapped child. *Family Physician*, 11:38-44, August 1966.

318. EUSTIS, R.S.: The primary etiology of specific language disabilities. *J Pediat*, 31:448, 1947.

319. FABIAN, A.A.: Clinical and experimental studies of school children who are retarded in reading. *Quart J Child Behav*, 3:15-37, 1951.

320. FARNEY, W.R.; ROBINSON, S.J., and PASCOE, D.J.: Congenital heart disease, deafness, and skeletal malformations—a new syndrome? *J Pediat*, 68:14-26, January 1966.

321. FARRANT, R.H.: The intellectual abilities of deaf and hearing children compared by factor analysis. *Amer Ann Deaf*, 109:3, May 1964.

322. FARRELL, G.: The blind mentally retarded in America. *New Beacon*, 19:285-288, 1935.

323. FARRELL, G.: The feebleminded blind—what shall the school do with them. *Proc Amer Assoc Instruct Blind*, 24:30-32, 1916.

324. FARRELL, N.J.: A state facility for the blind retarded. *New Outlook for the Blind*, 49:166-168, May 1959.

325. FAY, T.: Cerebral palsy: medical considerations and classifications. *Amer J Psychiat*, 108:180-183, 1950.

326. FAY, T.: Observations on the rehabilitation of movement in cerebral palsy. *W Virginia Med J*, 42:77, 1946.

327. FAY, T., and DOLL, E.: Organic impairment stimulating mental deficiency. *Amer J Orthopsychiat*, 19:112-119, January 1949.

328. FAY, T.: Overall considerations of seizures in cerebral palsy. *Cereb Palsy Rev*, 15:4-12, August 1954.

329. FEATHERSTONE, W.B.: *Teaching the Slow Learner*. New York, Bureau of Publications, Teach. Coll., Columbia U. P., 1941.

330. FERNALD, G.G.: The relationship of visual defectiveness and mental inadequacy. *Outlook for the Blind*, 8:35-36, 1914.

331. FERNALD, G.: *Remedial Techniques in Basic School Subjects*. New York, McGraw, 1939.

332. FISCH, L.: Aetiology of congenital deafness and audiometric patterns. *J Laryng*, 69:479-493, July 1955.

333. FISCH, L.: Deafness in cerebral palsied school children. *Lancet*, 2:370-371, 1955.

334. FISCH, L.: *Speech*, 21:43, 1957.

335. FLETCHER, M.C., and THOMPSON, M.M.: Eye abnormalities of the mentally defective. *Amer J Ment Defic*, 66:242, September 1961.

336. FLETCHER, R.T.: Pulheems; new system of medical classification. *Brit Med J*, 1:83-88, January 15, 1949.

337. FLOTTORP, G.; MORLEY, D.E., and SKATVEDT, M.: The localization of hearing impairment in athetoids. *Acta Otolaryng*, 48:404-414, 1957.

338. FOALE, M., and PATTERSON, J.W.: The hearing of mental defectives. *Amer J Ment Defic*, 59:254-258, 1954.

339. FOGH-ANDERSEN, P.: Incidence of cleft lip and palate: constant or increasing? *Acta Chir Scand*, 122:106-11, September 1961.

340. FOGH-ANDERSEN, P.: *Inheritance of Harelip and Cleft Palate*. Copenhagen, Busek, 1942.

341. FORCE, D.G.: Social status of physically handicapped children. *J Exceptional Child, 23*:104-107,132-133, 1956.

342. FOURACRE, M.H.: Educational abilities and needs of orthopedically handicapped children. *Elem Sch J, 51*:331-338, February 1950.

343. FOURACRE, M.H., and THIEL, E.A.: Education of children with mental retardation accompanying cerebral palsy. *Amer J Ment Defic, 57*:401-414, 1953.

344. FRAENKEL, W.A.: Blind retarded—or retarded blind. *New Outlook for the Blind, 58*(6)165-169, June 1964.

345. FRAMPTON, M.E.: General methods for the mentally retarded blind. In *Education of the Blind*. New York, World Book, 1940.

346. FRAMPTON, M.E., and KERNEY, E.: *The Residential School: Its History, Contributions and Future*. New York, New York Institute Educ. Blind, 1953.

347. FRAMPTON, M., and GALL, E.D. (Eds.): *Special Education for the Exceptional*. Boston, Porter Sargent, 1955.

348. FRANCIS, R.J., and RARICK, G.I.: Motor characteristics of the M.R. *Amer J Ment Defic, 63*(5):792-811, March 1959.

349. FRANCIS-WILLIAMS, J.: Assessment of cerebral palsied children—a survey of advances since 1958. National Association for Mental Health, London, 1965.

350. FRANKLIN, A.W.: Physically handicapped babies—some thalidomide lessons. *Lancet, 1*:959-965, May 1963.

351. FRANTZ, C.H., and O'RAHILLY, R.: Congenital skeletal limb deficiencies. *J Bone Joint Surg, 43*:1202-24, December 1961.

352. FRASER, F.G.: Genetics and congenital malformations. In *Progress in Medical Genetics*. Steinberg, A.G. (Ed.), New York, Grune, 1961.

353. FRASER, G.R.: Cleft lip and palate: seasonal incidence, birth weight, birth rank, sex, site, associated malformations and parental age. A statistical survey. *Arch Dis Child, 36*:420-423, August 1961.

354. FREEDMAN, S.: Psychological implications of the multiply handicapped person. *New Outlook for the Blind, 61*:185-189,204, June 1967.

355. FREEDMAN, S.J.; GRUNEBAUM, H.W., and GREENBLATT, M.: Sensory deprivation and personality. *Amer J Psychiat, 116*:878, 1960.

356. FREEMAN, G.G., and LUKENS, J.: A speech and language program for educable mentally handicapped children. *J Speech Hearing Dis, 27*(3):285-287, August 1962.

357. FREZAL, J.; KELLEY, J.; GYILLEMOT, M.L., and LAMY, M.: Anencephaly in France. *Amer J Hum Genet, 16*:336-350, September 1964.

358. FRIEHL, M.: Personal communication, 1964.

359. FRISINA, D.R.: A psychological study of the mentally retarded deaf child. *Dissertation Abstracts, 15*:2287-2288, 1955.

360. FROSTIG, M., and HORNE, D.: An approach to the treatment of children with learning difficulties. In *Learning Disorders*. Helmuth, Jerome (Ed.), Seattle, Special Child Publications, 1965, vol. 1.

361. FROSTIG, M.; LEFEVER, D.W., and WHITTLESEY, J.R.B.: A developmental test of visual perception for evaluating normal and neurologically-handicapped children. *Percept Motor Skills, 12*:383-394, 1961.

362. FROSTIG, M., and HORNE, D.: *The Frostig Program for the Development of Visual Perception*. Chicago, Follett, 1964.

363. FROSTIG, M.; LEFEVER, D.W., and WHITTLESEY, J.R.B.: *The Marianne Frostig*

Developmental Test of Visual Perception. Palo Alto, Consulting Psychologists, 1964.

364. FUCHS, F.R.: What if you were deaf–blind. *Volta R, 53*:6,262, June 1951.

365. FULTON, R.T., and GRAHAM, J.T.: Puretone reliability with the mentally retarded. *Amer J Ment Defic, 69*:265-268, September 1964.

366. FURST, R.T.: An approach to multiply handicapped blind persons through physical education. *New Outlook for the Blind, 60*:218-221, 1966.

367. FURTH, H.G.: A psychologist's view on the slow learning deaf child. In *Report of the Proceedings of the Fortieth Meeting of the Convention of American Instructors of the Deaf, Oregon School for the Deaf, Salem, Oregon, June, 1961.* Wash., D.C., U.S. Government Printing Office, 1962, p. 189.

368. FURTH, H.G.: Scholastic ability of deaf children and their performance on nonverbal learning tasks. *J Clin Psychol, 17*(4):370-373, October 1961.

369. GALLAGHER, J.J.: A discussion of the bases for competency. In *The Teacher of Brain-Injured Children.* Cruickshank, W.M. (Ed.), Syracuse, Syracuse, 1966.

370. GALLAGHER, J.J.: Educational methods with brain-damaged children. In *Current Psychiatric Therapies.* Masserman, J. (Ed.), New York, Grune, 1962, Vol. ii, pp. 48-55.

371. GALLAGHER, J.J., and LUCITO, L.J.: Intellectual patterns of gifted compared with average and retarded. *Exceptional Child, 27*:479-483, 1961.

372. GALLAGHER, J.J.: *The Tutoring of Brain-Injured Mentally Retarded Children.* Springfield, Thomas, 1960.

373. GANN, E.: *Reading Difficulty and Personality Organization.* New York, King's Crown, 1945.

374. GARFIELD, S.L., and WITTSON, C.: Comments on Dr. Cantor's remarks. *Amer J Ment Defic, 64*:957-959, May 1960.

375. GARFIELD, S.L., and WITTSON, C.: Some reaction to the Revised Manual on Terminology and Classification in Mental Retardation. *Amer J Ment Defic, 64*:951-953, May 1960a.

376. GARRETT, J.F. (Ed.): *Psychological Aspects of Physical Disability.* Washington, D.C., Office of Voc. Rehab. Dept. of Health, Education and Welfare, Bulletin No. 210, 1953.

377. GATES, M.F.: A comparative study of some problems of social emotional adjustment of crippled and non-crippled girls and boys. *J Genet Psychol, 68*:219-244, 1946.

378. GAUGER, A.B.: Mental deficiency as it complicates physical rehabilitation. *Amer J Ment Defic, 58*:306-309, 1954.

379. GELLNER, L., M.D.: Various sources contributing to the clinical picture of abnormal behavior in a retarded child. *Rehab Lit, 21*:218-219, July 1960.

380. GENS, G.W.: The speech pathologist looks at the mentally deficient child. *Train Sch Bull, 58*:19-27, 1951.

381. GENS, G.W.: Speech retardation in the normal and subnormal child. *Train Sch Bull, 48*:32-36, 1950.

382. George Peabody College: *Potentialities and Problems of Severely Disturbed Blind Children, Workshop Report.* New York, American Foundation of the Blind, 1950.

383. GERBER, S.E.: Cerebral palsy and hearing loss. *Cereb Palsy J, 27*:6, November-December 1966.

384. GERRARD, J.: Nuclear jaundice and deafness. *J Laryng, 66*:39-46, 1952.

385. GERTRUDE, SISTER R.: Psychological and intellectual problems of the multiple handicapped. *Nat Cath Educ Assoc Bull*, 58:399, 1961.

386. GESELL, A., and ILG, F.L.: *The Child from Five to Ten*. New York, Harper, 1946.

387. GESELL, A., *et al.: The First Five Years of Life*. New York, Harper, 1940.

388. GHENT, L.: Form and its orientation: a child's-eye view. *Amer J Psychol*, 74(2): 177-190, 1961.

389. GILBERT, J.G., and RUBIN, E.J.: Evaluating the intellect of blind children. *New Outlook for the Blind*, 59:238-240, September 1965.

390. GILLINGHAM, A., and STILLMAN, B.: *Remedial Training for Children with Specific Disability in Reading, Spelling and Penmanship*. Cambridge, Educators Publishing Service, 1960.

391. GILLMAN, A.E.: The multiple handicapped blind child—diagnostic studies of emotionally disturbed blind and visually impaired children—verbal facility masking concept deficit. *Proc Amer Assoc Instruct Blind*, 47:18, 1964.

392. GINZBERG, E., and BRAY, D.W.: *The Uneducated*. New York, Columbia U. P., 1953.

393. GITTELSOHN, A., and MILHAM, S.: Statistical study of twins—methods. *Amer J Public Health*, 54:286-94, February 1964.

394. GLICK, S.J.: Emotional problems of 200 cerebral palsied adults. *Cereb Palsy Rev*, 14:3-5, December 1953.

395. GLOVSKY, L., and RIGRODSKY, S.: A classroom program for auditorally handicapped mentally deficient children. *Train Sch Bull*, 60:56-70, August 1963.

396. GLOVSKY, L., and RIGRODSKY, S.: Auditory training procedures for certain mentally retarded children. *Train Sch Bull*, 1961:76-94, August 1964.

397. GODA, S., and RIGRODSKY, S.: Auditory training procedures for certain mentally retarded children. *Train Sch Bull*, 59:81, November 1962.

398. GODA, S.: Vocal utterances of young moderately and severely retarded non-speaking children. *Amer J Ment Defic*, 65:269-273, 1961.

399. GOERTZEN, S.M.: Speech and the mentally retarded child. *Amer J Ment Defic*, 62:244-253, September 1957.

400. GOLDBERG, B.; FOSTER, D.B.: SEGERSON, J.A., and BAUMIESTER, J.: Congenital malformations in the mentally retarded. *Bull Menninger Clin*, 27:275-290, 1963.

401. GOLDBERGER, L., and HOLT, R.R.: Experimental interference with reality contact. In *Sensory Deprivation*. Solomon, P., *et al.* (Eds.), Cambridge, Harvard U. P., 1961.

402. GOLDWASSER, M.: Physical defects in mentally retarded school children. *Calif Western Med*, 47:312, 1937.

403. GOODENOUGH, F.: Multiple handicaps. In *Exceptional Children*. Goodenough, F. (Ed.), New York, Appleton, 1956, pp. 393-399.

404. GOODHILL, V.: The educational treatment of the pre-school deaf child. *Laryngoscope*, 57:555-563, 1947.

405. GOODHILL, V.: Nuclear deafness and the nerve deaf child—the importance of the Rh factor. *Trans Amer Acad Ophthal Otolaryng*, 54:671-687, 1950.

406. GOODHILL, V.: Rh child—deaf or aphasic? Clinical and pathologic aspects of kernicteric nuclear deafness. *J Speech Hearing Dis*, 21:407-417, 1956.

407. GOODSTEIN, L.D.: Intellectual impairment—children with cleft palates. *J Speech Hearing Res*, 4:287-294, 1961.

408. GOTTWALD, H.L.: A special program for educable emotionally disturbed retarded. *Ment Retard,* 2:353-359, 1964.

409. GRAHAM, F.K., *et al.:* Brain injury in the pre-school child. Performance of normal children. *Psych Monographs,* Amer. Psych. Assoc., Inc., 1963, vol. 77, no. 10.

410. GRAHAM, F.K.; BERMAN, P.W., and ERNHART, C.B.: Development in preschool children in the ability to copy forms. *Child Develop,* 31:330-359, 1960.

411. GRATKE, J.M.: Speech problems of the cerebral palsied. *J Speech Hearing Dis,* 12:129-134, 1947.

412. GRAUNKE, L.W., *et al.:* Counseling and vocational planning. In *Report of the Proceedings of the Fortieth Meeting of the Convention of American Instructors of the Deaf, Oregon School for the Deaf, Salem, Oregon, June, 1961.* Washington, D.C., U.S. Government Printing Office, 1962, p. 206.

413. GRAYSTON, J.T., *et al.:* Congenital abnormalities following gestational rubella in Chinese. *JAMA,* 202:1-6, October 2, 1967.

414. GREAVES, J.R.: Helping the retarded blind. *Int J Educ Blind,* 2:163, April 1953.

415. GREAVES, J.R.: What shall we do with our backward blind children? *Proc Amer Assoc Instruct Blind,* 29:306-309, 1926.

416. GREEN, M.R., and SCHECTER, D.C.: Autistic and symbiotic disorders in three blind children. *Psychiat Quart,* 31:628-646, October 1957.

417. GREEN, R.H.; BALSAMO, M.R.; GILES, J.P., and KRUGMAN, S.: Studies on the experimental transmission, clinical course, epidemiology, and prevention of rubella. *Trans Assoc Amer Physicians,* 77:118-125, 1964.

418. GREENE, J.C.: Epidemiology of congenital clefts of the lip and palate. *Public Health Rep,* 78:589-602, July 1963.

419. GREENBERG, L.H., and TANAKA, K.R.: Congenital anomalies probably induced by cyclophosphamide. *J Amer Med Assoc,* 188:423-426, May 4, 1964.

420. GREGG, N.M.: Congenital cataract following German measles in mother. *J Ophthal Soc Aust,* 3:35-46, 1942.

421. GRUBER, K.F., and MOOR, P.W.: *No Place to Go.* New York, American Foundation for the Blind, 1963.

422. GUESS, D.: Body Image Disturbances of Brain Damaged Persons. Unpublished master's thesis, University of Kansas, 1963.

423. GUESS, D.: The influence of visual and ambulation restrictions on stereotyped behaviors. *Amer J Ment Defic,* 70:542-547, 1966.

424. GUESS, D.: Mental retardation and blindness—a complex and relatively unexplored dyad. *Exceptional Child,* 33:471-479, 1967.

425. GUIBOR, G.P.: Some eye defects seen in cerebral palsy with some statistics. *Amer J Phys Med,* 32:342-345, 1953.

426. GUILFORD, J.P.: The structure of intellect. *Psychol Bull,* 53:293-297, 1956.

427. HADRA, R.: Occupational therapy in a diagnostic and evaluation center for children with multiple handicaps. In *Occupational Therapy for the Multiply Handicapped Child.* Proceedings of the Conference on Occupational Therapy for the Multiply Handicapped Child, April 28-May 2, 1965. Chicago, U. of Illinois, Dept. of Occupational Therapy, 1965, pp. 108-121.

428. HAEUSSERMANN, E.: *Developmental Potential of Preschool Children: An Evaluation of Intellectual, Sensory and Emotional Functioning.* New York, Grune, 1958.

429. HAEUSSERMANN, E.: Evaluating the developmental level of cerebral palsy preschool children. *J Genet Psychol,* 80:3-23, 1952.

430. HALL, C.B.; BROOKS, M.B., and DENNIS, J.E.: Congenital skeletal deficiencies of the extremities. Classification and fundamentals of treatment. *J Amer Med Assoc, 181*:590-599, August 18, 1962.

431. HALLENBECK, J.: Pseudo-retardation in retrolental fibroplasia. *New Outlook for the Blind, 48*:301-307, November 1954.

432. HALLENBECK, J.: Two essential factors in the development of young blind children. *New Outlook for the Blind, 48*:308-318, November 1954.

433. HALSTEAD, W.C.: Preliminary analysis of grouping behavior in patients with cerebral injury by the method of equivalent and non-equivalent stimuli. *Amer J Psychiat, 96*:1263, 1940.

434. HAMILTON, C.A.: Mental and standard tests in schools for the blind. *Proc Amer Assoc Instruct Blind, 28*:174, 1924.

435. HAMILTON, K.W.: *Counseling the Handicapped in the Rehabilitation Process.* New York, Ronald, 1950, p. 16.

436. HANHART, E.: Mongoloid idiocy in mother and two children from an incestuous relationship. *Acta Genet Med (Roma), 9*:112-130, January 1960.

437. HANNIGAN, H.: Rh child—deaf or aphasic? Language and behavior problems of the Rh aphasic child. *J Speech Hearing Dis, 21*:413-417, 1956.

438. HARDY, W.G., and PAULS, M.D.: Atypical children with communication disorders. *Children, 6*(1):13-16, 1959.

439. HARDY, W.: Auditory deficits of the kernicterus child. In *Kernicterus and Its Importance in Cerebral Palsy.* American Academy for Cerebral Palsy. Springfield, Thomas, 1961.

440. HARDY, W.G.: Hearing impairment in cerebral palsied children. *Cereb Palsy Rev, 14*:3-7, September 1953.

441. HARDY, W.G.: The relation between impaired hearing and pseudo-feeble-mindedness. *Nervous Child, 7*:432-445, October 1948.

442. HARRIS, A.J.: *How to Increase Reading Ability.* New York, Longmans, Green, 1956.

443. HARRIS, L.C.; HAGGARD, M.E., and TRAVIS, L.B.: The coexistence of sickle cell disease and congenital heart disease: a report of three cases, with repair under cardiopulmonary by-pass in two. *Pediatrics, 33*:562-570, April 1964.

444. HARRIS, Y.Y.: *Special Needs Survey Report.* Honolulu, Department of Public Instruction, Territory of Hawaii. Office of Research and Evaluation Report No. 25, October 1956.

445. HARTH, R.: The emotional problems of people who are blind. *Int J Educ Blind, 15*:52-58, December 1965.

446. HARTMAN, B.: Study of therapeutic and functional values of hearing aids for the mentally handicapped. *Amer J Ment Defic, 62*:803-809, March 1958.

447. HARTUNG, J.: The diagnosis and teaching of aphasic children. In *Report of the Proceedings of the Forty-second meeting of the Convention of American Instructors of the Deaf, Michigan School for the Deaf, Flint, Mich., June, 1965.* Washington, D.C., U.S. Government Printing Office, 1966, pp. 111-115.

448. HATFIELD, E.M.: Causes of blindness in school children. *Sight Sav Rev, 33*:218-233, Winter 1933.

449. HATHAWAY, W.: Administrative procedures for children with multiple disabilities. In *Education and Health of the Partially Seeing Child.* New York, Columbia U. P., 1954.

450. HAVIGHURST, R.J.: *Human Development and Education.* New York, Longmans, Green, 1953.

451. HAYDEN, R.R.: What to do for the mentally retarded pupil. *Teachers Forum, 13:* 82-90, 1941.

452. HAYES, C.S.: Audiological problems associated with cleft palate. Proceedings of the Conference Communicative Problems in Cleft Palate, ASHA Reports, Washington, D.C. *Amer Speech Hearing Assoc, 1:*168, April 1965.

453. HAYES, S.P.: First Regional Conference on Mental Measurements of the Blind. Watertown, Massachusetts, Perkins School for the Blind, February 1952.

454. HAYES, S.P.: How mental tests may help teachers and principals. *Proc Amer Assoc Instruct Blind, 42:*29, 1954.

455. HAYES, S.P.: Mental measurements of the blind—old and new. *Proc Amer Assoc Instruct Blind, 40:*202, 1950.

456. HAYES, S.P.: Mental tests—a general survey of the field. *Proc Amer Assoc Instruct Blind, 28:*133-142, 1924.

457. Health Statistics from the U.S. National Health Survey Reports, Series A2. *The Statistical Design of the Health Household—Interview Survey.* Washington, D.C.:, Public Health Service, 1958.

458. Health Statistics from the U.S. National Health Survey Reports. Series A3. *Concepts and Definitions in the Health Household—Interview Survey.* Washington, D.C., Public Health Service, 1958, p. 13.

459. Health Statistics from the U.S. National Health Survey Reports. Series C1. *Children and Youth: Selected Health Characteristics.* Washington, D.C., Public Health Service, 1959.

460. Health Statistics from the U.S. National Health Survey Reports, Series D5. *Health Interview Responses Compared with Medical Records.* Washington, D.C., Public Health Service, 1961.

461. Health services for the school age child. *JAMA, 165:*1669-1677, November 30, 1957.

462. *Health Supervision of Young Children.* New York, American Public Health Association, 1955.

463. HEBB, D.O.: *The Organization of Behavior; a Neuropsychological Theory.* New York, Wiley, 1949.

464. HEBER, R., et al.: *Bibliography of World Literature on Mental Retardation.* Washington, D.C., U.S. Department of Health, Education, and Welfare, 1963.

465. HEBER, R.: A manual on terminology and classification in mental retardation. *Amer J Ment Defic* (monograph supplement), 1961.

466. HEBER, R.: Modifications in the manual on terminology and classification in mental retardation. *Amer J Ment Defic, 65:*499-500, January 1961.

467. HECHT, F.; BRYANT, J.S.; GRUBER, D., and TOWNES, P.L.: The nonrandomness of chromosomal abnormalities. Association of trisomy 18 and Down's syndrome. *New Eng J Med, 271:*1081-1086, November 19, 1964.

468. HECK, A.O.: *The Education of Exceptional Children.* 2nd ed., New York, McGraw, 1953.

469. HEGGE, T.G.; KIRK, S.A., and KIRK, W.: *Remedial Reading Drills,* Ann Arbor Wahr, 1940.

470. HEIDER, F., and HEIDER, G.M.: Studies in the psychology of the deaf, No. 2: II. The adjustment of the adult deaf. *Psychol Monogr, 53:*57-158, 1941.

471. HEILMAN, A.E.: Appraisal of abilities of the cerebral palsied child. *Amer J Ment Defic, 53:*606-609, April 1949.

472. HEILMAN, A.: Intelligence in cerebral palsy. *Crippled Child, 30*:11-13, 1952.
473. HELSEL, E.D.: Avenues of action for long-term care of the multiply handicapped. *Rehab Lit, 26*(9):262-269,278, 1965.
474. HENDERSON, J.L.: *Cerebral Palsy in Childhood and Adolescence.* E.&S. Livingstone, 1961.
475. HENDERSON, R.A.: Teaching the multiply handicapped retarded child. *Exceptional Child, 27*:90-92, 1960.
476. HENNEY, N.B.: Annie Sullivan—a teacher's preparation. *New Outlook for the Blind, 60*(4):102-105, April 1966.
477. HENRIELLA, S.R.: The slow learning deaf child. *Volta R, 63*:380, October 1961, continued in 63:444, November 1961.
478. HEPFINGER, L.M.: Psychological evaluation of young blind children. *New Outlook for the Blind, 56*:309-315, November 1962.
479. HERD, H.: *The Mentally-Defective Blind.* Sheffield, Northern Counties Association for the Blind, 1930.
480. HERMANN, K.: *Reading Disability.* Springfield, Thomas, 1959.
481. HILL, A.S.: Cerebral palsy, mental deficiency, and terminology. *Amer J Ment Defic, 59*:587-594, 1955.
482. HILL, A.S.: The status of MR today with emphasis on services. *Exceptional Child, 25*:298-299, March 1959.
483. HINDLEY, C.H.: The Griffiths scale of infant development: scores and predictions from 3 to 18 months. *Child Psychol Psychiat, 1*:99-112, 1960.
484. HINSHELWOOD, J.: *Congenital Word-Blindness.* London, H.K. Lewis, 1917.
485. HISKEY, M.S.: A study of the intelligence of deaf and hearing children. *Amer Ann Deaf, 101*:329-339, 1956.
486. HOAKLEY, Z.P., and FRAZEUR, H.A.: Significance of psychological test results of exogenous and endogenous children. *Amer J Ment Defic, 50*:264-271, October 1945.
487. HOFF, J.R.: Education and the deaf-blind child. *New Outlook for the Blind, 60*(4):109-113, April 1966.
488. HOFFMEYER, B.E.: The multiple handicapped child—a product of improved medical care. *Med Times, 89*:807-810, August 1961.
489. HOHMAN, L.B., and FREEDHEIM, J.: Further studies in intelligence levels in cerebral palsied children. *Amer J Phys Med, 37*:90-97, 1958.
490. HOHMAN, L.B.: Intellectual levels of cerebral palsied children. *Amer J Phys Med, 32*:282-290, 1953.
491. HOHMAN, L., et al.: Sensory disturbances in children with infantile hemiplegia, triplegia, and quadriplegia. *Amer J Phys Med, 37*:1-6, 1958.
492. HOLDEN, R.H.: Improved methods in testing cerebral palsied children. *Amer J Ment Defic, 56*:349-353, 1951.
493. HOLLORAN, I.M.: The incidence and prognosis of cerebral palsy. *Brit Med J, 4751*:214-217, January 1952.
494. HOLT, K.S.: Mentally handicapped children with cerebral palsy—the problems of home care. *Spastics Quart, 9*:4-12, 1960.
495. HOLTERHOFF, L.: The feebleminded blind. *Sch Soc, 14*:174-179, 1921.
496. HOPKINS, T.W., et al.: *Evaluation and Education of the Cerebral Palsied Child—New Jersey Study.* Washington, D.C., International Council for Exceptional Children, 1954.
497. HORSTMANN, D.M., et al.: Maternal rubella and the rubella syndrome in infants. *Amer J Dis Child, 110*:408-415, 1965.

498. Huffman, M.B.: *Fun Comes First for Blind Slow Learners.* Springfield, Thomas, 1957.

499. Huffman, M.: Growth Through Interest and Experiences in Young Children Who Are Mentally Retarded and Emotionally Disturbed in a Residential School for the Blind. Unpublished master's thesis, San Francisco State College, 1957.

500. Huffman, M.: Teaching retarded disturbed blind children. *New Outlook for the Blind, 54:*237-239, September 1960.

501. Hungerford, R.H.: The schooling of the mentally retarded—a history and philosophy of occupational education. *J Educ, 417:*5-16, 1964.

502. Hunt, B., and Patterson, R.M.: Performance of brain-injured and familiar mental deficient children on visual and auditory sequences. *Amer J Ment Defic, 63:*72-80, 1958.

503. Hunt, E.P.: The occurrence and distribution of handicapping conditions in childhood. In *Proceedings of the Institute on Prevention and Management of Handicapping Condition in Infancy and Childhood.* Ann Arbor, U. of Mich, School of Public Health, 1959.

504. Hunt, J.M.: *Intelligence and Experience.* New York, Ronald, 1961, p. 7.

505. Hunt, J.T.: Children with crippling conditions and special health problems *R Educ Res, 33:*99-108, February 1963.

506. Illingworth, R.S.: The changing pattern of paediatrics in a children's hospital *Proc Roy Soc Med, 54:*1011, 1961.

507. Illingworth, R.S., and Birch, L.B.: Diagnosis of mental retardation in infancy: a follow-up study. *Arch Dis Child, 34:*269-273, 1959.

508. Illingworth, R.S.: The increasing challenge of handicapping children. *Clin Pediat, 3:*189-191, April, 1964.

509. Illingworth, R.S.: *An Introduction to Developmental Assessment in the First Year.* Little Club Clinics in Developmental Medicine, No. 3, 1962.

510. Illingworth, R.S.: The predictive value of developmental tests in the first year, with special reference to the diagnosis of mental subnormality. *J Child Psychol Psychiat, 2:*210-215, 1961.

511. Illingworth, R.: *Recent Advances in Cerebral Palsy.* Boston, Little, 1958.

512. Illingworth, W.H.: How to deal with the incompetent blind. *Int Conf Blind, 1914:*148-170,195-203.

513. Illinois Census of Exceptional Children: *The Prevalence of Exceptional Children in Illinois in 1958.* Report of the 1958 Illinois Census of Exceptional Children, Circular Census 1A, Springfield, Superintendent of Public Instruction, 1959.

514. Ingalls, T.H.; Taube, I.E., and Klingberg, M.: Cleft lip and cleft palate: epidemiologic considerations. *Plast Reconstr Surg, 34:*1-10, July 1964.

515. Ingalls, T.H., and Klingberg, M.A.: Congenital malformations, clinical and community considerations. *Amer J Med Sci, 249:*316-344, March 1965.

516. Ingalls, T.H., and Murakami, U.: Cyclopia, ectromelia, and other monstrosities in Zebra fish. *Arch Environ Health, 5:*114-121, August 1962.

517. Ingalls, T.H., and Cordon, J.E.: Epidemiologic implications of developmental arrests. *Amer J Med Sci, 214:*322-328, September 1947.

518. Ingalls, T.H., and Klingberg, M.A.: Implications of epidemic embryopathy for public health. *Amer J Public Health, 55:*200-208, February 1965.

519. Ingalls, T.H.; Babbott, J., and Philbrook, R.: The mothers of mongoloid

babies: a retrospective appraisal of their health during pregnancy. *Amer J Obstet Gynec,* 74:572-581, September 1957.

520. INGALLS, T.H.; BABBOTT, F.L.,JR.; HAMPSON, K.W., and CORDON, J.E.: Rubella: its epidemiology and teratology. *Amer J Med Sci,* 239:363-83, March 1960.

521. INGALLS, T.H., and KLINGBERG, M.A.: Unpublished data.

522. INGRAM, T.T.S.: *Paediatric Aspects of Cerebral Palsy.* E.&S. Livingstone, 1963.

523. INGRAM, T.T.S.: Study of cerebral palsy in childhood population of Edinburgh. *Arch Dis Child,* 30:85-98, April 1955.

524. Interviewing response bias in a survey of handicapping conditions among children. *Amer J Public Health,* 54:1092-1099, July 1964.

525. Iowa Braille and Sight Saving School: *Proceedings of the Regional Conference of the Slow Learning, Visually Handicapped Child.* Vinton, Iowa, The School, 1952.

526. IPSEN, J., and OKKELS, H.: Congenital esophageal atresia and esophagotracheal fistula; synchronism in origin of malformations. *Hospitalstid,* 75:1083-1091, September 8, 1932.

527. IRWIN, J.V.; HIND, J.E., and ARONSON, A.E.: Experience with conditioned GSR audiometry in a group of mentally deficient individuals. *Train Sch Bull,* 54:26-31, 1957.

528. IRWIN, O.C.: Correct status of a set of six consonants in the speech of children with cerebral palsy. *Cereb Palsy Rev,* 17:148-150, November, December 1956.

529. IRWIN, O.C.: Correct status of vowels in the speech of children with cerebral palsy. *Cereb Palsy Rev,* 21:6-7, 11-12, September, October 1960.

530. IRWIN, O.C.: Difficulties of consonant sounds in terms of manner and place of articulation and of voicing in the speech of cerebral palsied children. *Cereb Palsy Rev,* 24:13-16, May-June 1963.

531. IRWIN, O.C.: Substitution and omission errors in the speech of children who have cerebral palsy. *Cereb Palsy Rev,* 17:75, May, June 1956.

532. IRWIN, O.C., and JENSEN, P.J.: A test of sound discrimination for use with cerebral palsied children. *Cereb Palsy Rev,* 24:5-11, March, April 1963.

533. IRWIN, R.B.: The recognition and training of blind feeble-minded children. *Outlook for the Blind,* 9:29-32, 1915.

534. ISCOE, I.: The functional classification of exceptional children. In *Readings on The Exceptional Child.* Trapp, E.P., and Himmelstein, P. (Eds.), New York, Appleton, 1962, chapter 2, p. 13.

535. ITARD, J.: *The Wild Boy of Aveyron.* New York, Century, 1932.

536. IVY, R.H.: Congenital anomalies as recorded on birth certificates in the Division of Vital Statistics of the Pennsylvania Department of Health for the period 1951-1955 inclusive. *Plast Reconstr Surg,* 20:400-411, November 1957.

537. IVY, R.H.: The influence of race on the incidence of certain congenital anomalies, notably cleft lip and palate. *Plast Reconstr Surg,* 30:581-5, November 1962.

538. JACKSON, A.D.M., and FISCH, L.: Deafness following maternal rubella; results of a prospective investigation. *Lancet,* 2:1241-1244, December 13, 1958.

539. JACKSON, C.L.: Blind children. *Amer J Nurs,* 61:52-55, February 1961.

540. JACOB, W.: Servicing the multiple handicapped. *Train Sch Bull,* 54:13, 1957.

541. JACOBZINER, H., *et al.*: How well are well children? *Amer J Public Health,* 53:1937-1952, 1963.

542. JACOBZINER, H.: *Treatment of Upper Respiratory Infections.* Service Order No. 64, MCH 22, 1960. The City of New York, Department of Health, September 13, 1960.

543. JAMES, W.C.: American Association of Mental Deficiency presents panel on training the mentally retarded deaf. *Amer Ann Deaf, 112:*20-22, 1967.

544. JAMES, W.C.: Mentally retarded deaf children in a California state hospital. In *Report of the Proceedings of the Forty-first Meeting of the Convention of American Instructors of the Deaf, Gallaudet College, June 1963.* Washington, D.C., U.S. Government Printing Office, 1964, pp. 573-577.

545. JENKINS, R.L.: Etiology of mongolism. *Amer J Dis Child, 45:*506-519, March 1933.

546. JERSILD, A.T.: *Child Psychology.* New York, Prentice-Hall, 1941.

547. JEWELL, B.T., and WURSTEN, H.: Observations on the psychological testing of cerebral palsied children. *Amer J Ment Defic, 56:*630-637, 1952.

548. JOHNS, C., and BARNETT, C.: Relationship of physical stigmata to intellectual status in mongoloids. *Amer J Ment Defic, 66:*435-437, November 1961.

549. JOHNSON, and FARRELL: An experiment in improving medical and educational services for hard of hearing children at the Walter E. Fernald State School. *Amer J Ment Defic, 62(2):*230-237, September 1957.

550. JOHNSON, A.: The blind feeble-minded. *Train Sch Bull 11:*40-42, 1914.

551. JOHNSON, A.: Consultations—children who are doubly defective. *Train Sch Bull, 2:*40-42, 1914.

552. JOHNSON, A.: Where should blind feeble-minded children be taught. *Outlook for the Blind, 8:*90-91, 1914.

553. JOHNSON, E.W.; GOVE, R., and OSTERMEIRER, B.: The value of functional training in severely disabled institutionalized brain-damaged children. *Amer J Ment Defic, 67:*860-864, 1963.

554. JOHNSON, G.O.: A study of social position of mentally handicapped children in the regular grades. *Amer J Ment Defic, 55:*60-89, 1950.

555. JOHNSON, H.H.: The problem of the backward child. *Proc Amer Assoc Instruct Blind, 21:*12-14, 1910.

556. JOHNSON, R.K.: The institutionalized mentally retarded deaf. In *Report of the Proceedings of the Forty-first Meeting of the Convention of American Instructors of the Deaf, Gallaudet College, June 1963.* Washington, D.C., U.S. Government Printing Office, 1964, pp. 568-573.

557. JOHNSTON, P.W., and FARRELL, M.J.: Auditory impairments among resident school children at the Walter E. Fernald State School. *Amer J Ment Defic, 58:*640-644, 1954.

558. JOHNSTON, P.W., and FARRELL, M.J.: An experiment in improved medical and educational services for hard of hearing children at the Walter E. Fernald State School. *Amer J Ment Defic, 62:*230-237, 1957.

559. JONES, J.W.: *Blind Children, Degree of Vision Mode of Reading.* Bulletin No. 24, Washington, Section on Exceptional Children and Youth, U.S. Office of Education, 1961.

560. JONES, J.W., and COLLINS, A.P.: *Education Programs for Visually Handicapped.* U.S. Department of Health, Education and Welfare, Washington, D.C., Office of Education, 1966.

561. JONES, J.W.: Problems in defining and classifying blindness. *New Outlook for the Blind, 56:*115-121, April 1962.

562. JONES, J.W., and COLLINS, A.P.: Trends in program and pupil placement practices in the special education of visually handicapped children. *Int J Educ Blind, 14*:97-100, 1965.

563. JORDAN, R.V.: The slow learning child at the junior high and high school level. In *Report of the Proceedings of the Forty-second Meeting of the Convention of American Instructors of the Deaf, Michigan School for the Deaf, Flint, Mich., June, 1965.* Washington, D.C., U.S. Government Printing Office, 1966, pp. 123-127.

564. KANTOR, J.R.: A preface to interbehavioral psychology. *Psychol Rev, 5*:173-193, 1942.

565. KARLIN, I.W., and STRANZZULLA, M.: Speech and language problems of mentally deficient children. *J Speech Hearing Dis, 17*:286-294, 1952.

566. KASS, C.: Some Psychological Correlates of Severe Reading Disability (Dyslexia). Unpublished doctoral dissertation, University of Illinois, 1962.

567. KASTEIN, S.: The responsibility of the speech pathologist to the retarded child. *Amer J Ment Defic, 60*(4):750-54, April 1956.

568. KATZ, E.: Intelligence test performance of athetoid and spastic children with cerebral palsy. *Cereb Palsy Rev, 16*:2-9, 1955.

569. KATZ, E.: The pointing scale method—a modification of the Stanford-Binet procedure for use with cerebral palsied children. *Amer J Ment Defic, 60*:838-842, 1956 and 62:698-707, 1958.

570. KAUFMAN, M., and LEVITT, H.: A study of three stereotyped behaviors in institutionalized mental defectives. *Amer J Ment Defic, 69*:467-473, 1965.

571. KAWI, A., and PASAMANICK, B.: The association of factors of pregnancy with the development of reading disorders in childhood, *JAMA, 166*:1420-1423, 1958.

572. KAWI, A., and PASAMANICK, B.: Prenatal and paranatal factors in the development of childhood reading disorders. *Monogr Soc Res Child Develop, 24,* No. 4 (Serial No. 73), 1959.

573. KELEMEN, G.: Rubella and deafness. *Arch Otolaryng, 83*:520-532, June 1966.

574. KELLER, H.: Letter to Peter J. Salmon, dated April 3, 1959. In *World Council for Welfare of the Blind.* Report of Committee on services for the deaf–blind to the world assembly, Rome, Italy, July 1959. Brooklyn, The Industrial Home for the Blind, 1959, p. 152.

575. KELLEY, V.S. (Ed.): *Practice of Pediatrics.* Hagerstown, Prior, 1964.

576. KENNEDY, E.: Workshop II—curriculum for the slow learning deaf child. In *Report of the Proceedings of the Fortieth Meeting of the Convention of the American Instructors of the Deaf, Oregon School for the Deaf, Salem, Oregon, June, 1961.* Washington, D.C., U.S. Government Printing Office, 1962, pp. 203-205.

577. KENYON, E.L.: The multiple handicapped blind child. *Proc Amer Assoc Instruct Blind, 47*:17, 1964.

578. KEPHART, N.C.: *The Slow Learner in the Classroom.* Columbus, Merrill, 1960.

579. KERBY, C.C.: *Manual on the Use of the Standard Classification of Causes of Blindness.* New York, American Foundation for the Blind and National Society for the Prevention of Blindness for the Committee on Statistics of the Blind, 1940.

580. KERR, M., *et al.*: Chromosome studies on spontaneous abortions. *Amer J Obstet Gynec, 94*:322-339, February 1966.

581. KERSHAW, J.: *Handicapped Children.* Heineman's Medical Books, 1961.
582. KILLE, E.O.: Therapy and training program for middle grade, epileptic, physically handicapped, and emotionally disturbed older children. *Amer J Ment Defic,* 58:88-92, 1953.
583. KING, S.P., JR.: *Selection Service in North Carolina.* Chapel Hill, U. of N.C., 1949, pp. 426-427.
584. KINSEY, G., and CODA, E.J.: An integrative multi-discipline approach to the multihandicapped preschool child. *Amer J Orthopsychiat,* 36:315-316, March 1966.
585. KIRK, S.A., and BATEMAN, B.: Diagnosis and remediation of learning disabilities. *Exceptional Child,* 29(2):73-78, October 1962.
586. KIRK, S.A.: *Educating Exceptional Children.* Boston, Houghton, 1962.
587. KIRK, S., and JOHNSON, G.O.: *Educating the Retarded Child.* Cambridge, Riverside, 1951, p. 12.
588. KIRK, S.A., and McCARTHY, J.: *Illinois Test of Psycholinguistic Abilities.* Urbana, U. of Ill., 1961.
589. KIRK, S.A.: Needed projects and research in special education. In *The Education of Exceptional Children, II. The Forty-ninth Yearbook National Society for the Study of Education.* Chicago, U. of Chicago, 1950.
590. KIRMAN, B.H.: The treatment of children with dual defects. *Amer J Ment Defic,* 56:589-602, 1952.
591. KIRSCHEN, M.: A study of visual performance of mentally retarded children. *Amer J Optom,* 31:282-288, 1954.
592. KITE, E.S.: The feeble-minded blind. *Train Sch Bull,* 13:135-141, 1916.
593. KLAPPER, Z.S., and WERNER, H.: Developmental deviations in brain-injured (cerebral palsied) members of pairs of identical twins. *Quart J Child Behav,* 2:288-313, July 1950.
594. KLAPPER, Z.S., and BIRCH, H.G.: A fourteen-year follow-up study of cerebral palsy: implications for community planning and education. *Amer J Orthopsychiat,* 36:317, March 1966.
595. KLAPPER, Z.S., and BIRCH, H.G.: A fourteen-year follow-up of cerebral palsy: intellectual change and stability. *Amer J Orthopsychiat,* 37:540-547, 1967.
596. KLEFFNER, F.R.: Aphasia and other language deficiencies in children: research and teaching at Central Institute for the Deaf. In *Speech and Language Therapy with the Brain-Damaged Child.* Daley, W.T. (Ed.), Washington, D.C., Catholic University of America, 1962.
597. KLEFFNER, F.R.: Teaching speech and language to aphasic children. *Volta R,* 60:326, September 1958.
598. KLEINMAN, H.; PRINCE, J.T.; MATHEY, W.E.; ROSENFIELD, A.B.; BEARMAN, J. E., and SYVERTON, J.T.: ECHO 9 virus infection and congenital abnormalities: a negative report. *Pediatrics,* 29:261-269, February 1962.
599. KLOVOSKII, B.N.: *The Development of the Brain and Its Disturbance by Harmful Factors.* New York, Macmillan, 1963.
600. KNOBLOCH, H., and PASAMANICK, B.: Complications of pregnancy and mental deficiency. Ment. Retard., Proc. 1st Internat. Cong. Ment. Retard., 1960, pp. 182-193.
601. KNOBLOCH, H.; PASAMANICK, B.; HARPER, P.A., and RIDER, R.J.: The effect of prematurity on health and growth. *Amer J Public Health,* 49:1164-1173, 1959.

602. KNOBLOCH, H., and PASAMANICK, B.: Mental subnormality: medical progress. Part I. *New Eng J Med, 266*:1046-1051, 1962.

603. KNOBLOCH, H., and PASAMANICK, B.: Mental subnormality: medical progress. Part II. *New Eng J Med, 266*:1092-1097, 1962.

604. KNOBLOCH, H., and PASAMANICK, B.: Mental subnormality: medical progress. Part III. *New Eng J Med, 266*:1155-1161, 1962.

605. KNOBLOCH, H.; RIDER, R.; HARPER, P., and PASAMANICK, B.: Neuropsychiatric sequelae of prematurity: a longitudinal study. *JAMA, 161*:581-585, 1956.

606. KNOBLOCH, H., and PASAMANICK, B.: Seasonal variation in the births of the mentally deficient. *Amer J Public Health, 48*:1201-1208, 1958.

607. KNOBLOCH, H., and PASAMANICK, B.: Syndrome of minimal cerebral damage in infancy. *JAMA, 170*:1384-1387, 1959.

608. KODMAN, F.: The incidence of hearing loss in mentally retarded children. *Amer J Ment Defic, 62*:675-678, 1958.

609. KODMAN, F., *et al.:* An investigation of hearing loss in mentally retarded children and adults. *Amer J Ment Defic, 63*:460-463, 1958.

610. KODMAN, F.; POWERS, T.R.; PHILLIPS, T.P., and WELLER, G.M.: An investigation of hearing loss in mentally retarded children and adults. *Amer J Ment Defic, 58*:460-463, 1959.

611. KODMAN, F., *et al.:* Psychogalvanic skin response audiometry with severe mentally retarded children. *Amer J Ment Defic, 64*:131-136, 1959.

612. KODMAN, F., *et al.:* Pure tone audiometry with the mentally retarded. *Exceptional Child, 24*:303-305, 1958.

613. KODMAN, F.: Sensory processes and mental deficiency. In *Handbook of Mental Deficiency.* Ellis, N.R. (Ed.), New York, McGraw, 1963.

614. KODMAN, F., *et al.:* Some implications of hearing in defective juvenile delinquents. *Exceptional Child, 25*:54-56, 1958.

615. KOFFKA, K.: *Die Grundlagen der Psychischen Entwicklung.* Osterwieck am Harz, Zickfeld, 1925.

616. KOGAN, K.L., and RIPLEY, H.S.: *Standardization of the Children's Picture Information Test: Final Report.* Seattle, U. of Wash., School of Medicine, 1959.

617. KOLSON, C., and KALUGER, G.: *Clinical Aspects of Remedial Reading.* Springfield, Thomas, 1963.

618. KOMISAR, D., and MacDONNEL, M.: Gain in I.Q. for students attending a school for the blind. *Exceptional Child, 21*:127-129, 1955.

619. KOPATIC, N.J., *et al.:* An analysis of a speech therapy program carried out within an institution for the mentally retarded. *Welfare Reporter, 15*:93-97, October 1965.

620. KOPATIC, N.: The reliability of puretone audiometry with the mentally retarded: some practical and theoretical considerations. *Train Sch Bull, 60*:130-137, November 1963.

621. KRAUS, H.: Krauss-Weber tests for minimum muscular fitness. In *Therapeutic Exercises.* Springfield, Thomas, 1953, pp. 125-126.

622. KRUGMAN, S.: Personal communication, 1964.

623. KUHLMANN, F.: Definition of mental deficiency. *Amer J Ment Defic, 46*:206-213, May 1941.

624. KVARACEUS, W.C.: Acceptance-rejection and exceptionality. *J Exceptional Child, 22*:328-331, 1956.

625. KVARACEUS, W.C.: Research in special education: its status and function. *J Exceptional Child, 24*:249-254, 1958.

626. KVARACEUS, W.C.: Selected references from the literature on exceptional children. *Elem Sch J*, March 1960, p. 343.

627. LACROSSE, E.L., and BIDLAKE, H.: A method to test the hearing of the mentally retarded children. *Volta R, 66*(1):27-30, January 1964.

628. LADSON, M.R.: The education of emotionally handicapped deaf children. In *Report of the Proceedings of the Forty-second Meeting of the Convention of American Instructors of the Deaf, Michigan School for the Deaf, Flint, Mich., June, 1965.* Washington, D.C., U.S. Government Printing Office, 1966, pp. 115-119.

629. LANE, H.S.: The deaf and hard of hearing. *R Educ Res*, February 1963, pp. 48-61.

630. LANGAN, I.W.: The education of the blind mental defective. *Amer J Ment Defic, 52*:272-277, 1948.

631. LATIMER, H.R., *et al.*: Adequate provisions for the blind feeble-minded—report of the Committee of the Association of Executives of State Commissions and Associations for the Blind. *Outlook for the Blind, 22*:34-37, 1928.

632. LECK, I.: Examination of the incidence of malformations for evidence of drug teratogenesis. *Brit J Prev Soc Med, 18*:196-201, October 1964.

633. LECK, I., and MILLAR, E.L.M.: Incidence of malformations since the introduction of Thalidomide. *Brit Med J, 2*:16-20, July 7, 1962.

634. LECK, I., and MILLAR, E.L.M.: Short-term changes in the incidence of malformations. *Brit J Prev Soc Med, 17*:1-12, January 1963.

635. LEENHOUTS, M.A.: The mentally retarded deaf child. In *Report of the Proceedings of the Thirty-ninth Meeting of the Convention of American Instructors of the Deaf, Colorado School for the Deaf, Colorado Springs, Colorado, June, 1959.* Washington, D.C., U.S. Government Printing Office, 1960.

636. LEENHOUTS, M.A.: Problems Accompanying Children Who Are Deaf and Mentally Retarded. Paper presented at the Central Coastal Region III Meetng of the American Association on Mental Deficiency, April 4, 1964.

637. LEE, T.M.: The child of low intelligence—what can be done for him? *Proc Amer Assoc Instruct Blind, 37*:37-41, 1944.

638. LEJEUNE, J.; GAUTIER, M., and TURPIN, R.: Study of somatic chromosomes from 9 mongoloid children. *Comptes Rendus, 248*:1721-722, March 9, 1959.

639. LELAND, H., and SMITH, D.: Unstructured material in play therapy for emotionally disturbed, brain damaged mentally retarded children. *Amer J Ment Defic, 66*:621-628, 1962.

640. LELONG, M.; BORNICHE, P.; KREISLER, L., and BAUDY, R.: Mongolien issu de mere mongolienne. *Arch Franc Pediat, 6*:231-238, 1949.

641. LENDE, H.: *Books About the Blind.* New York, American Foundation for the Blind, 1953.

642. LENDE, H.: Education of the young blinds: the blind mentally retarded. In *Books About the Blind.* New York, American Foundation for the Blind, 1953.

643. LENZ, W., and KNAPP, K.: Thalidomide embryopathy. *Deutsch Med Wschr, 87*: 1232-42, June 15, 1962.

644. LERNER, H.A.: Spastic and cerebral palsy squint problems. *Rehab Lit, 22*, September 1961.

645. Leshin, G.J., and Stahlecker, L.V.: Academic expectancies of slow learning deaf children. *Volta R, 64*:599-602, December 1962.

646. Leshin, G., *et al.*: Slow learning deaf child—evaluation and research. In *Report of the Proceedings of the Fortieth Meeting of the Convention of American Instructors of the Deaf, Oregon School for the Deaf, Salem, Oregon, June, 1961*. Washington, D.C., U.S. Government Printing Office, 1962, pp. 202-203.

647. Leslie, M.: Services for the visually handicapped (including multiply disabled in the Portland school program). *Sight Sav R, 31*:1, Spring, 1961.

648. Letson, F.: Unpublished data. Children's Rehabilitation Unit, University of Kansas Medical Center.

649. LeVann, L.J.: A concept of schizophrenia in the lower grade mental defective. *Amer J Ment Defic, 54*:469-472, 1950.

650. Levi, A.: Treatment of a disorder of perception and concept formation in a case of school failure. *J Consult Psychol, 29*(4):269-295, 1965.

651. Levine, S.: A proposed conceptual framework for special education. *Exceptional Child, 28*:83-90, October 1961.

652. Lewis, W.D.: Some characteristics of children designated as mentally retarded, as problems, and as geniuses by teachers. *J Genet Psychol, 70*(29):51, 1947.

653. Lilienfeld, A.M., and Pasamanick, B.: Association of maternal and fetal factors with the development of epilepsy. I. Abnormalities in the prenatal and paranatal periods. *J Amer Med Assoc, 155*:719, 1954.

654. Lilienfeld, A.M., and Pasamanick, B.: The association of maternal and fetal factors with the development of mental deficiency. II. Relationship to maternal age, birth order, previous reproductive loss and degree of mental deficiency. *Amer J Ment Defic, 60*:557, 1956.

655. Lilienfeld, A.M., and Pasamanick, B.: The association of prenatal and paranatal factors with the development of cerebral palsy and epilepsy. *Amer J Obstet Gynecol, 70*:93, 1955.

656. Lilienfeld, A.M.; Pasamanick, B., and Rogers, M.E.: The relationship between pregnancy experience and the development of certain neuropsychiatric disorders in childhood. *Amer J Public Health, 45*:637, 1955.

657. Lilienfeld, A.M., and Pasamanick, B.: A study of variations in the frequency of twin births by race and socioeconomic status. *J Hum Genet, 7*:401, 1955.

658. Lind, J.: A Treatise on the Scurvy. Edinburgh, 1753.

659. Linde, T.: Unique neighborhood program aids severely retarded palsied. *J Rehab, 28*(1):10-12, January, February 1962.

660. Lipmann, O.: *Hanbuch Psychologischer Hilfsmittel Der Psychiatrischen Diagnostik*. Stuttgart and Berlin, Deutsche Verlags Anstalt, 1922.

661. Little Club: Memorandum on terminology and classification of cerebral palsy. *Cereb Palsy Bull, 1*:27-35, 1959.

662. Little, S.W.: Suspected hearing defects in phenylketonuria. *Arch Otolaryng, 75*:515-518, 1962.

663. Lloyd, L.L., and Frisina, D.R. (Eds.): The audiologic assessment of the mentally retarded. Proceedings of a National Conference, Parsons, Kansas, Speech and Hearing Dept. (PSH&TC), 1965.

664. Lloyd, L.L.: A Comparison of Selected Auditory Measures on Normal Hearing Mentally Retarded Children. Doctoral thesis, University of Iowa, 1965.

665. LLOYD, L.L.: The new audiology program at Parsons State Hospital and Training Center. *Hearing News*, 33:5-7,12, March 1965.
666. LLOYD, L.L.; SPRADLIN, J.E., and REID, M.J.: Operant conditioning audiometry with low-level retardates: a progress report. Parsons Demonstration Project Report 57, 1966.
667. LLOYD, L.L., and REID, M.J.: The percent of hearing impaired and difficult-to-test patients at Parsons State Hospital and Training Center (a special report presented to the March Audiology conference, 1965). In *The Audiologic Assessment of the Mentally Retarded: Proceedings of a National Conference*. Lloyd, L.L. and Frisina, D.R. (Eds.), Parsons, Kans, Speech and Hearing Dept. (PSH&TC), 1965.
668. LLOYD, L.L., and REID, M.J.: The reliability of pure tone audiometry with institutionalized MR children. Parsons Demonstration Project Report No. 51 (in preparation).
669. LLOYD, L.L., and MELROSE, J.: The reliability of selected auditory responses of normal hearing mentally retarded children. *Amer J Ment Defic*, 71:133-143, 1966.
670. LLOYD, L.L., and REID, M.J.: The reliability of speech audiometry and institutionalized retarded children. *J Speech Hearing Res*, 9:450-455, 1966.
671. LLOYD, L.L.: Use of the slide show audiometric technique with mentally retarded children. *Exceptional Child*, 32:93-98, October 1965.
672. LOCH, C.S.: Provisions for the defective blind children. Conference on Matters Relating to the Blind, Westminster, 1902, pp. 61-67.
673. LOCHHEAD, H.M.: Backward children in school and after school. *Teacher of the Blind*, 34:118-123, 1934.
674. LOGAN, W.P.D.: Incidence of congenital malformations and their relation to virus infections during pregnancy. *Brit Med J*, 2:641-645, September 15, 1951.
675. LONG, E.H.: *The Challenge of the Cerebral Palsied Blind Child*. New York, American Foundation for the Blind, 1952.
676. LONG, E., and PERRY, J.: Slow learner and retarded blind child. *Proc Amer Assoc Instruct Blind*, 43, 1956. (As cited in Fraenkel, W.A.: Blind retarded —or retarded blind? *New Outlook for the Blind*, 58:167, June 1964.)
677. LORBER, J.: Personal communication, 1964.
678. LORD, E.E.: *A Study of the Mental Development of Children with Lesions in the Central Nervous System*. New Haven, Psycho-Clinic, 1929.
679. LORETZ, W.; WESTMORELAND, W.W., and RICHARDS, L.T.: A study of cleft lip and cleft palate births in California, 1955. *Amer J Public Health*, 51:873-877, June 1961.
680. LOWELL, E.L., and STONER, M.: *Play It By Ear*. Los Angeles, John Tracey Clinic, 1960.
681. LOWENFELD, B., and SPAR, N.J.: The education of the mentally handicapped blind child. *Teachers Forum*, 13:62-66, 79-80, 1941.
682. LOWENFELD, B.: The role of the residential school in the education of blind children. In *Concerning the Education of Blind Children*. Abel, G.L. (Ed.), New York, American Foundation for the Blind, 1951.
683. LOWENFELD, B.: The visually handicapped. *R Educ Res*, 33:43, February 1963.
684. LUBCHENCO, L.O., *et al*.: Sequelae of premature birth. *Amer J Dis Child, 106*: 101, 1963.

685. Lubman, C.G.: Speech programs for severely retarded children. *Amer J Ment Defic*, 60:297-300, 1955.

686. Lucey, J.F.; Mann, R.W., and Friedman, E.: An increased incidence of spina bifida in Vermont in 1962. *Pediatrics*, 33:981-4, June 1964.

687. Lucito, L.J.: Multiple handicapped children: mental retardation. *Proc Amer Assoc Instruct Blind*, 45:20, 1960.

688. Luria, A. R.: *The Mentally Retarded Child.* New York, Macmillan, 1963.

689. Luszki, W.A.: Application of deprivation concepts to the deaf retarded. *Ment Retard* 2:164-170, 1964.

690. Luszki, W.A.: Hearing loss and intelligence among retardates. *Amer J Ment Defic*, 70:93-101, July 1965.

691. Luszki, W.A.: Intellectual functioning of spastic cerebral palsied. *Cereb Palsy J*, 27:7-9, March-April 1966.

692. Maberly, A.: Delinquency in handicapped children. *Brit J Delinquency*, 1: 128, 1950.

693. McBride, W.G.: Personal communication.

694. McBride, W.G.: Personality factors in the success of classroom teachers of the multihandicapped. *Cereb Palsy J*, 26:3-5, 1965.

695. McBride, W.G.: The teratogenic action of drugs. *Med J Aust*, 2:689-92, October 26, 1963.

696. McBride, W.G.: Thalidomide and congenital abnormalities. *Lancet*, 2:1358, December 16, 1961.

697. McCarthy, J.J.: A test for the identification of defects in language usage among young cerebral palsied children. *Cereb Palsy Rev*, 21:3-5, January, February 1960.

698. McCarthy, K.; Taylor-Robinson, C.H., and Pillinger, S.E.: Isolation of rubella virus from cases in Britain. *Lancet*, 2:593-598, September 21, 1963.

699. McDonald, A.D.: Deafness in children of very low birth weight. *Arch Dis Child*, 39:272-277, 1964.

700. McDonald, A.D.: Maternal health in early pregnancy and congenital defect. Final report on a prospective inquiry. *Brit J Prev Soc Med*, 15:154-166, October 1961.

701. McDonald, E.T., and Chance, B.: *Cerebral Palsy.* Englewood Cliffs, Prentice-Hall, 1964.

702. MacFarland, D.C.: Serving multiply disabled blind persons. *New Outlook for the Blind*, 58:206-209, September 1964.

703. McGinnis, M.A.: *Aphasic Children: Identification and Education by the Association Method.* Washington, D.C., Alexander Graham Bell Association for the Deaf, 1963.

704. McGinnis, M.A.; Kleffner, F.R., and Goldstein, R.: Teaching aphasic children. *Volta R*, 58:6,239, June 1956.

705. MacGregor, F.C.: Some psycho-social problems associated with facial deformities. *J Abnorm Soc Psychol*, 16:629-638, 1951.

706. McIntire, J.T.: The incidence of feeble-mindedness in the cerebral palsied. *Amer J Ment Defic*, 50:491-494, April 1946.

707. McIntire, J.T.: A study of the distribution of physical handicap and mental diagnosis in cerebral palsied children. *Amer J Ment Defic*, 51(4):624-626, 1947.

708. McIntosh, R., *et al.*: The incidence of congenital malformations—a study of 5,964 pregnancies. *Pediatrics, 14*:505-521, November 1954.
709. MacKensie, D.Y.: The handicapped child. *Nurs Times, 60*:1255-257, September 25, 1964.
710. McKeown, T., and Record, R.G.: Malformations in a population observed for five years after birth. In *Ciba Foundation Symposium.* London, Churchill, 1960, pp. 2-16.
711. McKeown, T., and Record, R.G.: Seasonal incidence of congenital malformations of central nervous system. *Lancet, 1*:192-196, January 27, 1951.
712. Mackie, R.P., and Dunn, L.M.: *College and University Programs for the Preparation of Teachers of Exceptional Children.* Bulletin 1954, No. 6, Washington, D.C., Office of Education, p. 12.
713. Mackie, R.: *Education of Visually Handicapped Children.* Bulletin 1951, No. 20, Washington, D.C., Office of Education, Federal Security Agency.
714. Mackie, R.: *Professional Preparation of Teachers of Exceptional Children; an Overview.* U.S. Department of Health, Education, and Welfare, Bulletin 1959, No. 6, Washington D.C., U.S. Government Printing Office, 1960, pp. 15, 57-58.
715. Mackie, R., *et al.*: *Statistics of Special Education for Exceptional Children and Youth, 1957-58* (final report). Washington, D.C., U.S. Department of Health, Education and Welfare, Office of Education, 1963.
716. Mackie, R.P., and Dunn, L.M.: *Teachers of Children Who Are Blind.* Bulletin No. 10, Washington, D.C., Office of Education, U.S. Government Printing Office.
717. Mackie, R.P., *et al.*: *Teachers of Children Who Are Mentally Retarded.* Bulletin No. 3, Washington, D.C., Office of Education, U.S. Government Printing Office, 1957.
718. McKusick, V.A.; Egeland, J.A.; Eldridge, R., and Krusen, D.E.: Dwarfism in the Amish I. The Ellis-Van Creveld syndrome. *Bull Hopkins Hosp, 115*: 306-336, October 1964.
719. Macmahon, B.; Pugh, T.F., and Ingalls, T.H.: Anencephalus, spina bifida, and hydrocephalus; incidence related to sex, race, and season of birth, and incidence in siblings. *Brit J Prev Soc Med, 7*:211-219, October 1953.
720. McMurray, J.G.: Visual perception in exogenous and endogenous mentally retarded children. *Amer J Ment Defic, 58*:659-663, 1954.
721. MacPherson, J.R.: The evaluation and development of techniques for testing the auditory acuity of trainable mentally retarded children. *Dissertation Abstracts, 20*:45-88, 1960.
722. MacPherson, J.R.: The status of the deaf and/or hard of hearing mentally defective in the United States, I. *Amer Ann Deaf, 97*:375-386, 1952.
723. MacPherson, J.R.: The status of the deaf and/or hard of hearing mentally defective in the United States, II. *Amer Ann Deaf, 97*:448-469, 1952.
724. MacQueen, J.C.: Services for children with multiple handicaps. *Children, 13*: 55-59, March-April 1966.
725. McQuie, B.: Severely disturbed blind children. *Int J Educ Blind, 9*:39-97, May 1960.
726. McWilliams, B.J.: The speech pathologist looks at the non-verbal child. *Exceptional Child, 25*:420, 1959.
727. Malmquist, E.: *Factors Related to Reading Disabilities in the First Grade of the Elementary School.* Stockholm, Amquist and Wiksell, 1958.

728. Malpas, P.: Incidence of human malformations and significance of changes in maternal environment in their causation. *J Obstet Gynaec Brit Comm, 44:* 434-454, June 1937.

729. Malzberg, B.: Statistical aspects of mental deficiency with congenital cerebral spastic infantile paralysis. *Amer J Ment Defic, 55:*99-104, 1950.

730. Mangan, K.R.: A state program of services for the mentally retarded deaf child. In *Report of the Proceedings of the Forty-first Meeting of the Convention of American Instructors of the Deaf, Gallaudet College, June 1963.* Washington, D.C., U.S. Government Printing Office, 1964, pp. 565-568.

731. Manshardt, C.: The role of the public school system in the education of blind and sighted children. In *Concerning the Education of Blind Children.* Abel, G.L. (Ed.), New York, American Foundation for the Blind, 1959.

732. Manson, M.M.; Logan, W.P.D., and Loy, R.M.: Reports on Public Health and Medical Subjects, No. 101. H.M.S.O., London, 1960.

733. *Manual of the International Statistical Classification of Diseases, Injuries, and Causes of Death.* Geneva, Switzerland, World Health Organization, 1957, Vol. I, p. 357.

734. *Manual of the International Statistical Classification of Diseases, Injuries, and Causes of Death.* Geneva, Switzerland, World Health Organization. 1957, Vol. II, p.x.

735. *Manual of Procedures for the Child Health Conference,* 2nd ed. New York, Bureau of Child Health and the Bureau of Public Health Nursing, Department of Health, City of New York.

736. Marden, P.N., *et al.:* Congenital anomalies of the newborn. *J Pediat, 64:*357, 1964.

737. Markle, D.M., and Miller, M.H.: Nature of deafness in athetoid cerebral palsy. *Arch Otolaryng, 78:*794-796, 1963.

738. Marticorena, E.: Personal communication, 1964.

739. Maslow, A.: Deficiency motivation and growth motivation. In *Nebraska Symposium on Motivation, 1955.* Jones, M.R. (Ed.), Lincoln, U. of Nebraska Press, 1955, pp. 1-39.

740. Maslow, P.; Frostig, M.; Lefever, D.W., and Whittlesey, J.R.B.: The Marianne Frostig developmental test of visual perception, 1963, standardization. *Percept Motor Skills, Mongr,* Supplement 2-V19, 1964.

741. *Massachusetts, Special Unpaid Commission Relative to Blind Feeble-minded, Blind Epileptic, and Blind Feeble-minded Epileptic Persons.* Report, Boston, Wright Potter, 1946.

742. Massachusetts, W.E. Fernald State School: Plans for the Walter E. Fernald State School unit for the blind retarded. *Ment Hosp, 6:*12-15, 1955.

743. Mathews, J.: Speech problems of the mentally retarded. In *Handbook of Speech Pathology.* Travis (Ed.), New York, Appleton, 1957.

744. Mattis, S.: An experimental approach to treatment of visually impaired multi-handicapped children. *New Outlook for the Blind, 61:*1-5, 1967.

745. Mautner, H.: Congenital heart diseases in the feeble minded. *Amer J Ment Defic, 55:*546-556, 1951.

746. Maxfield, K.E., and Kenyon, E.L.: *A Guide to the Use of the Maxfield Field Tentative Adaptations of the Vineland Social Maturity Scale for Use with Visually Handicapped Children.* New York, American Foundation for the Blind, 1953.

747. May, L.W., and Riviere, M.: *An Investigation Into the Feasibility of Develop-*

ing a System of Codes for Use in Rehabilitation. New York, Association for the Aid of Crippled Children, 1957.

748. Mayo, L.W., and Riviere, M.: *An Investigation Into the Feasibility of Developing a System of Codes for Use in Rehabilitation.* New York, Association for the Aid of Crippled Children, 1957, p. 3.

749. Mecham, M.J.: Complexities in communication of the cerebral palsied. *Cereb Palsy Rev, 15*:9-11, 14, February 1954.

750. Mecham, M.J.: The development and application of procedures for measuring speech improvement in mentally defective children. *Amer J Ment Defic, 60*:301-306, 1955.

751. Mecham, M.J.: A selected bibliography in cerebral palsy—communication. *Cereb Palsy Rev, 18*:13-17, July-August 1957.

752. Mellin, G.W.: *Birth Defects.* Philadelphia, Lippincott, 1963.

753. Mellin, G.W., and Katzenstein, M.: Increased incidence of malformations— chance or change? *JAMA, 187*:570-573, 1954.

754. Mellin, G.W., and Katzenstein, M.: Saga of thalidomide—neuropathy to embryopathy, with case reports of congenital anomalies. *New Eng J Med, 267*:1184-1193, 1238-1244, 1962.

755. Menninger, W.C.: Emotional adjustments for the handicapped. *Crippled Child, 27*:4-7,26-28, 1949.

756. Menolascino, F.J.: Emotional disturbance and mental retardation. *Amer J Ment Defic, 70*:248-256, 1965.

757. Menolascino, F.J.: Psychosis of childhood—experiences of a mental retardation pilot project. *Amer J Ment Defic, 70*:83-92, July 1965.

758. Mental health center for disturbed blind children. *New Outlook for the Blind, 57*:65, February 1963.

759. Meshcheriakov, A.I.: The main principles of the system for education and training of the blind and deaf and dumb. *Int J Educ Blind, 12*:43-47, December 1962.

760. Messer, A.: *Psychologie.* Stuttgart and Berlin, Deutsche Verlags Anstalt, 1922.

761. Meyerson, L.: Physical disability as a social psychological problem. *J Soc Issues, 4*:2-10, Fall 1948.

762. Meyerson, L.: Somatopsychology of physical disability. In *Psychology of Exceptional Children and Youth.* Cruickshank, W.M. (Ed.), New Jersey, Prentice-Hall, 1955, pp. 1-60.

763. Michal-Smith, H.: Problems encountered in the psychometric examination of the child with cerebral palsy. *Cereb Palsy Rev, 16*:15-16, 1955.

764. Mildenstein, F.; von Massenbach, W., and Ruther, K.: Extremitatenm inus-missbildungen 1950-1962. Ergebnisse einer Umfrage. *Geburtsh Frauenheilk, 24*:1-27, January 1964.

765. Milesky, S., et al.: Multiple handicapped workshop. *Proc Amer Assoc Instruct Blind, 47*:109-111, 1964.

766. Milham, S.: Congenital malformation surveillance system based on vital records. *Public Health Rep, 78*:448-452, May 1963.

767. Miller, E., and Rosenfeld, M.D.: The psychological evaluation of children with cerebral palsy and its implications in treatment. *J Pediat, 41*:613-621, November 1952.

768. Mills, M.A.: Facilities and programs for mentally retarded, severely involved cerebral palsied in the city and county of San Francisco. *Cereb Palsy Rev, 22*:5-9,14-16, July-August 1961.

769. MINEAR, W.L.: A classification of cerebral palsy. *Pediatrics, 18*:841-852, 1956.
770. MINER, L.E.: A study of the incidence of speech deviations among visually handicapped children. *New Outlook for the Blind, 57*:10-14, January 1963.
771. Ministry of Education: *Handicapped Pupils and School Health Service Regulations.* 1955, No. 1076.
772. MINNER, L.E.: A study of the incidence of speech deviations among visually handicapped children. *New Outlook for the Blind, 57*(1):10-14, January 1963.
773. MINSKI, L.: *Deafness, Mutism, and Mental Deficiency in Children.* New York, Philosophical Lib., 1957.
774. MINBACH, D.: Happy gracious living for the mentally retarded blind child. *New Outlook for the Blind, 47*:61-66, March 1953.
775. MITCHELL, P.: The education of the ungraded blind child. In *Special Education for the Exceptional.* Grampton, M., and Gall, E.D. (Eds.), Boston, Porter-Sargent, 1955, Vol. II.
776. MONAGHAN, A.: Educational placement for the multiply handicapped hearing impaired child. *Volta R, 66*(7):383-387, September 1964.
777. MONEY, J.: Intelligence quotient and school performance in 22 children with a history of thyrotoxicosis. *Bull Hopkins Hosp, 118*:275-281, April 1966.
778. MONEY, J. (Ed.): *Reading Disability: Progress in Research Needs in Dyslexia.* Baltimore, Johns Hopkins, 1962.
779. MONROE, M.: *Children Who Cannot Read.* Chicago, U. of Chicago, 1932.
780. MONSEES, E.K.: Aphasia in children—diagnosis and education. *Volta R, 59*: 11,392, November 1957.
781. MONSEES, E.K.: Aphasia and deafness in children. *Exceptional Child, 25*: 394-399, May 1959.
782. MONSEES, E.K.: Experiences with children who failed to learn to talk as deaf or hard of hearing. *Volta R, 60*:9,328, September 1958.
783. MONTAGU, M.F.A.: *Prenatal Influences.* Springfield, Thomas, 1962.
784. MOOR, P.: Blind children with developmental problems. *Children, 8*:9-13, January-February 1961.
785. MOORE, O.K.: *Autotolic Responsive Environments and Exceptional Children.* Hamden, Conn., Responsive Environments Foundations, Inc., 1963.
786. MORRIS, M.: What affects blind children's development. *New Outlook for the Blind, 50*:218-227, September 1956.
787. MORRIS, M.: Guide for Teacher-Aides. Unpublished paper, Harrisburg, Pennsylvania, Department of Public Instruction, 1960.
788. MOSHER, L.H.: The feeble-minded blind. *Sch Soc, 14*:174-179, 1921.
789. MOSS, J.W.; MOSS, M., and TIZARD, J.: Electrodermal response to audiometry with mentally defective children. *J Speech Hearing Res, 4*:41-47, March 1961.
790. MOWAT, J.: Ear, nose and throat disorders: deafness. In *Cerebral Palsy in Childhood and Adolescence.* Henderson (Ed.).
791. MUHL, A.M.: Psychometric and personality studies of blind children. *Proc Amer Assoc Instruct Blind, 31*:568-573, 1930.
792. MUNSON, S.E., and MAY, A.M.: Are cleft palate persons of subnormal intelligence? *J Educ Res, 48*:568-573, 1930.
793. MURCH, E.T.: *Chondrodystrophic Dwarfs in Denmark.* Copenhagen, Munksgaard, 1941.
794. MURPHY, D.P.: *Congenital Malformations.* 2nd ed., Philadelphia, Lippincott, 1947.

795. MURPHY, G.: *Personality.* New York, Harper, 1947.

796. MUSSEN, P.H., and BARKER, R.G.: Attitudes toward cripples. *Child Develop,* 39:351-355, 1944.

797. MUSTACCHI, P.; SHERINO, R.S., and MILLER, M.J.: Congenital malformations of the heart and the great vessels. Prevalence, incidence, and life expectancy in San Francisco. *J Amer Med Assoc, 183*:241-244, January 26, 1963.

798. MUTHARD, J.E.: MMPI findings for cerebral palsied students. *J Consult Psychol,* 29:599, December 1965.

799. MYERS, C.R.: Application of control group method to problem of etiology of mongolism. *Proc Amer Assoc Ment Defic, 62*:142-150, 1938.

800. MYERS, M.: Education of children with hearing disorders who are resident of Lincoln State School for the mentally retarded and brain injured. In *Report of the Proceedings of the Forty-second Meeting of the Convention of American Instructors of the Deaf, Michigan School for the Deaf, Flint, Mich., June 1965.* Washington, D.C., U.S. Government Printing Office, 1966, pp. 119-123.

801. MYERSON, L.: Somatopsychology of physical disability. In *Psychology of Exceptional Children and Youth.* Cruickshank, W.M. (Ed.), Englewood Cliffs, Prentice-Hall, 1955, pp. 8-9.

802. MYKLEBUST, H.R.: *Auditory Disorders in Children.* New York, Grune, 1954.

803. MYKLEBUST, H.: The deaf child with other handicaps. *Amer Ann Deaf, 103*(4):487-509, September 1958.

804. MYKLEBUST, H.: *The Psychology of Deafness: Sensory Deprivation, Learning, and Adjustment.* New York, Grune, 1960.

805. MYKLEBUST, H.R.: Rh child—deaf or aphasic, four variations in the auditory disorders of the Rh child. *J Speech Hearing Dis, 21*:418-422, 1956.

806. MYKLEBUST, H.R.: Rh child—deaf or aphasic? Some psychological considerations of the Rh child. *J Speech Hearing Dis, 21*:423-425, 1956.

807. MYKLEBUST, H., and BRUTTEN, M.A.: Study of the visual perception of deaf children. *Acta Otolaryng* (supplementum 105), 1953.

808. MYKLEBUST, H.R.: Training aphasic children. *Volta R, 57*:4,149, April 1955.

809. National Association for Retarded Children: *Survey on Blind Retarded Children.* The Association, 1960.

810. National Education Association Proceedings: 41st Annual Meeting, Minneapolis, 1902, pp. 828-829.

811. *National Society for the Study of Education. Forty-ninth Yearbook.* Part II. The education of exceptional children. Chicago, U. of Chicago, 1950.

812. National Study Committee on Education of Deaf–Blind Children: Report, meetings, Washington, D.C., July 12, 1953, and Council Bluffs, Iowa, January 25-26, 1954.

813. NEEL, J.V., and SCHULL, W.J.: *The Effect of Exposure to the Atomic Bombs on Pregnancy Termination in Hiroshima and Nagasaki.* Washington, Nat. Acad. Sci., Nat. Res. Counc. Pub., 161, 1956.

814. NEEL, J.V.: A study of major congenital defects in Japanese infants. *Amer J Hum Genet, 10*:398-445, December 1958.

815. NEELY, L.: A case report—tongue and mandible thrusting in an athetoid cerebral palsied child. *Cereb Palsy Rev, 24*:6-8, July-August 1963.

816. NELSON, M., and SIBILIO, J.P.: Audiologic aspects of a deaf retarded population. *Volta R, 64*:426-427, 1962.

817. NELSON, M.: Identification and training of institutionalized and retarded deaf patients. *J Speech Hearing Res, 4*:398, 1961.

818. NELSON, W.E.: *Textbook of Pediatrics.* Philadelphia, Saunders, 1959.

819. NESBITT, R.E.L., JR.: Perinatal casualties. *Children, 6*(4):123-128, 1959.

820. NEWLAND, T.E.: The blind learning aptitudes test. In *Report of the Proceedings of a Conference on Research Needs in Braille.* New York, American Foundation for the Blind, 1961.

821. NEWLAND, T.E.: Psycho-social aspects of the adjustment of the brain-injured. *J Exceptional Child, 23*:119-153, 1957.

822. New York State Department of Mental Hygiene: *Technical Report of the Mental Health Research Unit.* Syracuse, Syracuse, July 1, 1955.

823. New York State Department of Mental Hygiene, Mental Health Research: A Special Census of Suspected Referred Mental Retardation, Onondaga County, New York. In *Technical Report of the Mental Health Research Unit.* Syracuse, Syracuse, 1961.

824. NORRIS, M., et al.: *Blindness in Children.* Chicago, U. of Chicago, 1957.

825. NUDO, L.A.: Comparison by age of audiological and otological findings in a state residential institution for the mentally retarded: a preliminary report. In *The Audiologic Assessment of the Mentally Retarded: The Proceedings of a National Conference.* Lloyd, L.L., and Frisina, D.R. (Eds.), Parsons, Kansas, Speech and Hearing Department (PSH&TC), 1965.

826. Office of Vocational Rehabilitation, U.S. Department of Health, Education and Welfare and the Industrial Home for the Blind: *Rehabilitation of Deaf-Blind Persons.* Brooklyn, N.Y., Industrial Home for the Blind, 1959.

827. OLSON, W.: *Child Development.* Boston, Heath, 1949.

828. OLSON, W.C.: Reading as a function of the total growth of the child. In *Reading and Pupil Development.* Gray, W.S. (Ed.), Chicago, U. of Chicago, 1940, pp. 233-237.

829. ORTON, S.T.: Specific reading disability—strephosymbolia. *JAMA,* 1928, pp. 1094-1099.

830. OSLER, S.F.: The nature of intelligence. *Volta R, 67*:285-292, 1965.

831. OSTER, J.: *Mongolism.* Copenhagen, Munksgaard, 1953.

832. PALMER, M.: Managing overprotective tendencies with speech impaired children. *J Speech Hearing Dis, 25*:405-408, November 1960.

833. PANTELAKOS, C.G.: Audiometric and otolaryngologic survey of retarded students. *N Carolina Med J, 24*:238-242, 1963.

834. PARASKEVA, P.C.: A survey of the facilities for the mentally retarded blind in the United States. *Int J Educ Blind, 8*:139-149, May 1959.

835. PARKMAN, P.D.; BUESCHER, E.L., and ARTENSTEIN, M.S.: Recovery of Rubella virus from army recruits. *Proc Soc Exp Biol Med, 111*:225-230, October 1962.

836. PARMELEE, A.H.,JR.: Developmental studies of blind children, I. *New Outlook for the Blind, 60*(6):177-179, June 1966.

837. PASAMANICK, B.: Anticonvulsant drug therapy of behavior problem children with abnormal electroencephalograms. *Arch Neurol Psychiat, 59*:3, 1951.

838. PASAMANICK, B., and LILIENFELD, A.M.: Association of maternal and fetal factors with the development of mental deficiency. I. Abnormalities in the prenatal and paranatal periods. *JAMA, 159*:155, 1955.

839. PASAMANICK, B.; DINITZ, S., and KNOBLOCH, H.: The association of summer temperature and the birth of schizophrenics. (MS)

840. PASAMANICK, B., and KNOBLOCH, H.: Brain injury and reproductive casualty. *Amer J Orthopsychiat*, 30:298, 1960.

841. PASAMANICK, B.: Comments on the papers of Prof. James Walker and Prof. G. Gordon on obstetric viewpoints and features related to cerebral palsy. *Cereb Palsy Bull*, 2:78-81, 1960.

842. PASAMANICK, B., and KNOBLOCH, H.: Complications of pregnancy and neuropsychiatric disorder. *J Obstet Gynecol Brit Comm*, 66:753-755, 1959.

843. PASAMANICK, B., and KNOBLOCH, H.: The contribution of some organic factors to school retardation in Negro children. *J Negro Educ*, 27:4, 1958.

844. PASAMANICK, B.: Determinants of intelligence. In *Conflict and Creativity: Man and Civilization*. Farber, S.M., and Wilson, R.H.L. (Eds.), New York, McGraw, 1963, pp. 3-26.

845. PASAMANICK, B.: Discussion of the epidemiology of mental disorder associated with damage to the brain after birth. *Milbank Memorial Fund Quart*, 39:105-110, 1961.

846. PASAMANICK, B.: Discussion of physical damage to the fetus. *Milbank Memorial Fund Quart*, 39:80-82, 1961.

847. PASAMANICK, B., and KNOBLOCH, H.: Early feeding and birth difficulties in childhood schizophrenia: an explanatory note. *J Psychol*, 56:73-77, 1963.

848. PASAMANICK, B., and KNOBLOCH, H.: The effect of summer temperature upon spring birth rates.

849. PASAMANICK, B.: The epidemiologic investigations of some prenatal factors in the production of neuropsychiatric disorders. In *Field Studies in Mental Disorders*. New York, Grune, 1961.

850. PASAMANICK, B., and KNOBLOCH, H.: Epidemiologic studies on the complications of pregnancy and the birth process. In *Prevention of Mental Disorders in Childhood*. Caplan, G. (Ed.), New York, Basic Books, 1961, chap. 4.

851. PASAMANICK, B.: Discussion of Chapter XI. Epidemiologic studies of the prenatal environment in mental retardation. *Res Publ Assoc Nerv Ment Dis*, Baltimore, Williams & Wilkins, 1962, Vol. XXXIX.

852. PASAMANICK, B.: The epidemiology of behavior disorders of childhood. In *Neurol Psychiat Childh Res Publ Assoc Nerv Ment Dis*, Baltimore, Williams & Wilkins, 1956.

853. PASAMANICK, B., and KNOBLOCH, H.: The epidemiology of reproductive casualty. In *Child Psychiatry and Prevention*. VanKrevalen, D.A. (Ed.), Berne, Huber, 1964.

854. PASAMANICK, B.: Future explorations in mental health and disease. *Amer J Public Health*, 47:1242-1249, 1957.

855. PASAMANICK, B.; DINITZ, S., and KNOBLOCH, H.: Geographic and seasonal variation in birth rates. *Public Health Rep*, 74(4):285, 1959.

856. PASAMANICK, B.: The intelligence of American children of Mexican parentage: a discussion of uncontrolled variables. *J Abnorm Soc*, 46:598-602, 1951.

857. PASAMANICK, B., and LILIENFELD, A.M.: Maternal and fetal factors in the development of epilepsy. II. Relationship to some clinical factors of epilepsy. *Neurology*, 5:77, 1955.

858. PASAMANICK, B.; ROGERS, M.E., and LILIENFIELD, A.M.: Pregnancy experience and the development of childhood behavior disorder. *Amer J Psychiat*, 112:613, 1956.

859. PASAMANICK, B.; CONSTANTINOU, F.K., and LILIENFELD, A.M.: Pregnancy experience and the development of childhood speech disorders: an epidemiologic study of the association with maternal and fetal factors. *Amer J Dis Child,* 91:113, 1956.

860. PASAMANICK, B.: The prevention of juvenile delinquency. *NY Acad Med Symposium on Records,* 1954.

861. PASAMANICK, B., and KNOBLOCH, H.: Race, complications of pregnancy, and neuropsychiatric disorders. *Soc Probl,* 5:267-278, 1958.

862. PASAMANICK, B., and KNOBLOCH, H.: Retrospective studies on the epidemiology of reproductive casualty: old and new. *Merrill-Palmer Quart Behav Develop,* 12:7-26, 1966.

863. PASAMANICK, B.: The scope and limitations of psychiatry. In *Basic Problems of Psychiatry.* Wortis, J. (Ed.), New York, Grune, 1953.

864. PASAMANICK, B., and KNOBLOCH, H.: Seasonal variation in the births of the mentally deficient—a reply. *Amer J Public Health,* 50:1737-1742, 1960.

865. PASAMANICK, B., and KNOBLOCH, H.: Seasonal variation in complications of pregnancy. *Obstet and Gynecol,* 12:110-112, 1958.

866. PASAMANICK, B.; DINITZ, S., and KNOBLOCH, H.: Seasonal variation in neonatal death rates due to immaturity. (MS)

867. PASAMANICK, B.; KNOBLOCH, H., and LILIENFELD, A.M.: Socioeconomic status and some precursors of neuropsychiatric disorder. *Amer J Orthopsychiat,* 26:595-601, 1956.

868. PASAMANICK, B., and KNOBLOCH, H.: Some early organic precursors of racial behavioral differences. *J Nat Med. Assoc,* 49:372-375, 1957.

869. PASAMANICK, B., and KAWI, A.: A study of the association of prenatal and paranatal factors with the development of tics in children: a preliminary investigation. *J Pediat,* 48:596, 1956.

870. PASAMANICK, B.; DINITZ, S., and KNOBLOCH, H.: Variation in birth weight by season. (MS)

871. PAUL, M., SR.: Psychological and instructional problems of the orthopedically handicapped child. *Nat Cath Educ Assoc Bull,* 58:400, August 1961.

872. PAULINE, M., SR.: Invited papers II: the multiple handicapped deaf child. *Volta R,* 62:2:350-55, 1960.

873. PEABODY, R.L., and BIRCH, J.W.: Educational implications of partial vision: new findings of a national study. *Sight Sav Rev,* 37:92-96, Summer 1967.

874. PEARLMAN, H.B.: Sensory neural deafness. *Arch Otolaryng,* 77:226-239, 1963.

875. PEARSON, P.H.: The forgotten patient: medical management of the multiple handicapped retarded. *Public Health Rep,* Department of Health, Education and Welfare, 80(10):915-918, October 1965.

876. PENFIELD, W., and ROBERTS, L.: *Speech and Brain-Mechanisms.* New York, Princeton U. P., 1959.

877. PERLSTEIN, M.A.; GIBBS, E.L., and GIBBS, F.A.: *The Electroencephalogram in Infantile Cerebral Palsy, Epilepsy.* Baltimore, Williams & Wilkins, 1947, p. 377.

878. PERLSTEIN, M.A., et al.: The electroencephalography in infantile cerebral palsy. *Proc Assoc Res Nerv Ment Dis,* 24:378-384, 1946.

879. PERRY, N.: *Teaching the Mentally Retarded Child.* New York, Columbia U. P., 1960.

880. PETER, L.J.: *Prescriptive Teaching.* New York, McGraw-Hill, 1965, pp. 228-229.

881. PETERSON, B.H.: Congenital deaf mutism, pigmentary degeneration of retina and amentia. *Med J Aust, 2*:854-858, 1950.
882. PFEIFFER, R.A., and KOSENOW, W.: On the problem of exogenous causes of severe malformation of the extremities. *Muchen Med Wehnschr, 104*:68-74, January 12, 1962.
883. PHELPS, W.M.: Characteristic psychological variations in cerebral palsy. *Nerv Child, 7*:10-13, 1948.
884. PHELPS, W.: Evaluation of all handicaps. *Cereb Palsy Rev, 14*:9, March-April 1953.
885. PHELPS, W.M., and TURNER, T.A.: *The Farthest Corner.* Chicago, National Society for Crippled Children and Adults, Inc., 1944.
886. PHELPS, W.: The management of the cerebral palsies. *JAMA, 117*:1621-1625, 1941.
887. PHILBRICK, W.A.: Implications of state legislation for aphasic children. *Volta R, 60*:10,428, October 1958.
888. PHILLIPS, C.J., and WHITE, R.R.: The prediction of educational progress among cerebral palsied children. *Develop Med Child Neurol, 6*:167-174, 1964.
889. PITT, D.B.: *Aust New Zeal J Obstet Gynaec, 2*:231, 1962.
890. PLOTKINS, S.A.: Virologic assistance in the management of German measles in pregnancy. *JAMA, 190*:265-268, October 26, 1964.
891. PLOTKIN, W.H.: Situational speech therapy for retarded cerebral palsied children. *J Hearing Speech Dis, 24*(1):16-20, February 1959.
892. PORTER, V.: The cerebral palsied deaf pupil. *Amer Ann Deaf, 12*(4):359-363, September 1957.
893. POTTER, E.L.: and COVERSTONE, V.A.: Chondrodystrophy fetalis. *Amer J Obstet Gynec, 56*:790-793, October 1948.
894. The President's Panel on Mental Retardation: A Proposed Program for National Action to Combat Mental Retardation. Washington, D.C., 1962.
895. PREIZLER, J.: Vaccine effectiveness in prevention of poliomyelitis. *Wisconsin Med J, 58*:489-491, 1959.
896. PRINDLE, R.A.; INGALLS, T.H., and KIRKWOOD, S.B.: Maternal hydramnios and congenital anomalies of central nervous system. *New Eng J Med, 252*:555-561, April 7, 1955.
897. Professional Standards Project Report: *Professional Standards for Personnel in the Education of Exceptional Children: Report of the Committee on Professional Standards.* Washington, D.C., The Council for Exceptional Children, National Education Association, 1966, p. 86.
898. QUIBELL, E.P.: The physically handicapped child. Functional assessment of the disability as an aid to planning. *Brit Med J, 2*:991-993, October 27, 1956.
899. QUIBELL, E.P., *et al.*: A survey of a group of children with mental and physical handicaps treated in an orthopedic hospital. *Arch Dis Child, 36*:58-64, February 1961.
900. RABINOVITCH, R.D.: Reading and learning disabilities. In *American Handbook of Psychiatry.* Arieti, S. (Ed.), New York, Basic Books, 1959, vol. 1, chap. 43.
901. RAPAPORT, I.: Mental handicap—diagnosis and placement. *New Outlook for the Blind, 55*:291-293, November 1961.
902. RAPAPORT, S.R. (Ed.): *Childhood Aphasia and Brain Damage: A Definition.* Narberth, Livingston, 1964.
903. Rates of attendance and reasons for non-attendance at a clinic of handicapping conditions. *Amer J Public Health, 54*:1177-1183, August 1964.

904. RAY, J.E.: The problem of the backward child. *Proc Amer Assoc Instruct Blind,* 21:14-17, 1910.

905. RECORD, R.G.: Anencephalus in Scotland. *Brit J Prev Soc Med,* 15:93-105, July 1961.

906. RECORD, R.G., and McKEOWN, T.: Congenital malformations of central nervous systems; survey of 930 cases. *Brit J Prev Soc Med,* 3:183-219, October 1949.

907. RECORD, R.G., and EDWARDS, J.H.: Environmental influences related to the aetiology of congenital dislocation of the hip. *Brit J Prev Soc Med,* 12:8-22, 1958.

908. RECORD, R.G., and McKEOWN, T.: Observations relating to aetiology of patent ductus arteriosus. *Brit Heart J,* 15:376-386, October 1953.

909. REGLER, J.: An experimental program for slowly developing blind children. *Int J Educ Blind,* 9:89-93, May 1960.

910. REHN, A.T., and THOMAS, E.,JR.: Family history of a mongoloid girl who bore a mongoloid child. *Amer J Ment Defic,* 62:496-499, 1957.

911. RENFREW, C.E.: Speech problems of backward (mentally retarded) children (and their treatment). *Speech Path Ther,* 2(1):34-38, April 1, 1959.

912. Report of the Conference Committee on Defective Blind Children. *Blind,* 2:29-36, 1903.

913. REYNOLDS, M.C.: A framework for considering some issues in special education. *Exceptional Child,* 28:367-370, March 1961.

914. RICHARDS, B.W.: Congenital double athetosis, deaf mutism, and mental deficiency: 5 cases. *J Ment Sci,* 96:280-284, 1950.

915. RICHARDS, B.W., and RUNDLE, A.J.: A familial hormonal disorder associated with mental deficiency, deaf mutism and ataxia. *J Ment Defic Res,* 3:33-35, 1959.

916. RICHARDS, M.R.; MERRITT, K.K.; SAMUELS, M.H., and LANGMANN, A.G.: Congenital malformations of cardiovascular system in series of 6,053 infants. *Pediatrics,* 15:12-32, January 1955.

917. RICHARDSON, E.G., and KOBLER, R.H.: Testing the cerebral palsied. *Exceptional Child,* 21:101-103, 1954.

918. RICHARDSON, W.P.; HIGGINS, A.C., and AMES, R.G.: An Evaluation of the Reliability of School Teachers in Supplying Estimates of Handicapping Conditions in Children. (Forthcoming)

919. RICHARDSON, W.P., *et al.: The Handicapped Children of Alamance County, North Carolina.* Wilmington, Nemours Foundation, 1965.

920. RICHARDSON, W.P., and HIGGINS, A.C.: A survey of handicapping conditions and handicapped children in Alamance County, North Carolina. *Amer J Public Health,* 54:1817-1830, November 1964.

921. RICHARDSON, W.P., and HIGGINS, A.C.: The Usefulness of Public Health Records in Estimating Morbidity Prevalence in Children. (To be published)

922. RIDER, R.V.; TABACK, M., and KNOBLOCH, H.: Associations between premature births and socioeconomic status. *Amer J. Public Health,* 45:1022-1028, 1955.

923. RIGBY, M.E.: Some of the problems of the multiply handicapped. *Int J Educ Blind,* 12:97-103, May 1963.

924. RIGRODSKY, S., and GODA, S.: Language behavior of non-speaking brain-injured mentally retarded children. *Train Sch Bull,* 58:52-60, August 1961.

925. RIGRODSKY, S., and STEER, M.C.: Mowrere's theory applied to speech rehabilitation of the mentally retarded. *J Speech Hearing Dis,* 26:237, August 1961.

926. RIGRODSKY, S.; PRUNTY, F., and GLOVSKY, L.: A study of the incidence, types

and associated etiologies of hearing loss in an institutionalized mentally re-tarded population. *Train Sch Bull, 58*:30-44, 1961.

927. RILEY, B.: A new plan in Kansas (deaf-blind). *New Outlook for the Blind, 53*(5):161-165, May 1959.

928. RITTMANIC, P.A.: Hearing rehabilitation for the institutionalized mentally re-tarded. *Amer J Ment Defic, 63*:778-83, March 1959.

929. ROBBINS, N.: Educational beginnings with deaf-blind children: a developmental plan. *New Outlook for the Blind, 54*:206-210, June 1960.

930. ROBBINS, N.: *Educational Beginnings with Deaf-blind Children*. Watertown, Mass., Perkins School for the Blind.

931. ROBINSON, H.: *Why Pupils Fail in Reading*. Chicago, U. of Chicago, 1946.

932. RODDA, M.: Social adjustment of hearing impaired adolescents. *Volta R, 68*:279-283, April 1966.

933. ROGERS, M.E.; LILIENFELD, A.M., and PASAMANICK, B.: *Prenatal and Paranatal Factors in the Development of Childhood Behavior Disorders*. Copenhagen, Munksgaard, 1955.

934. ROOT, F.K.: Evaluation of services for multiple-handicapped blind children. *Int J Educ Blind, 35*:71, 1938.

935. ROOT, F.K., and RILEY, B.G.: Study of deaf-blind children: a developmental plan. *New Outlook for the Blind, 54*:206-210, June 1960.

936. ROSEN, J.: Rh child: deaf or aphasic? Variations in the auditory disorders of the Rh child. *J Speech Hearing Dis, 21*:418-422, 1956.

937. ROSENBAUM, B.B.: Neurotic tendencies in crippled girls. *J Abnorm Soc Psychol, 31*:423-429, 1937.

938. ROSENBAUM, S.Z.: Infantile paralysis as the source of emotional problems in children. *Welfare Bull, 34*:11-13, 1943.

939. ROSENSTEIN, J.R.: Cognitive abilities of deaf children. *J Speech Hearing Res, 3*:108-119, 1960.

940. ROSENTHAL, C.: Social adjustment of hearing handicapped children. *Volta R, 68*:293-301, April 1966.

941. ROSS, A.T., and DAVISON, V.A.: Psychological handicaps of cerebral palsied children. *Public Welfare in Indiana*, 1947, pp. 15-16.

942. ROSWELL, F., and NATCHEZ, G.: *Reading Disability: Diagnosis and Treatment*. New York, Basic Books, 1964.

943. ROWE, E.D.: *Speech Problems of Blind Children: A Survey of the North California Area*. New York, American Foundation for the Blind, 1958.

944. ROY, R.: Incidence and Severity of Hearing Loss of Institutionalized Mentally Retarded Adults of Various Intelligence Levels. Master's thesis, University of Nebraska, 1959.

945. ROYER-GREAVES SCHOOL FOR THE BLIND: Academic subjects for retarded blind children. *Int J Educ Blind, 1*:84-88, 1952.

946. ROYER-GREAVES, J.: Teaching the retarded blind child. *Proc Amer Assoc Instruct Blind, 35*:71, 1938.

947. RUBEN, R.J.: Anatomic diagnosis of non-conducive deafness by physiological tests. *Arch Otolaryng, 78*:47-51, 1963.

948. RUFF, G.E.; LEVY, E.Z., and THALER, V.H.: Factors influencing the reaction to reduced sensory input. In *Sensory Deprivation*. Solomon, P., *et al.* (Eds.), Cambridge, Harvard U. P., 1961.

949. RUSALEM, H.: Anne Sullivan: an analysis of her teaching techniques. *New Outlook for the Blind, 60*(4):106-108, April 1966.

950. RUSALEM, H.: Comparative values in a population of home bound individuals. *Exceptional Child, 29*:460, May 1963.

951. RUSALEM, H.: Deprivation and opportunity: major variables in the rehabilitation of deaf-blind adults. *New Outlook for the Blind, 60*(4):114-120, April 1966.

952. RUSALEM, H.: Homemaking without vision and hearing. *J Home Econ, 51*:861-863, December 1959.

953. RUSALEM, H.: Vocational status of deaf-blind adults. *Voc Guid Quart, 7*(2):124-126, Winter 1958.

954. SALMON, P.J.: Modern program for blind persons with other disabilities. *New Outlook for the Blind, 59*(1):15-17, January 1965.

955. SALMON, P.J.: Services for deaf-blind persons abroad. *New Outlook for the Blind, 60*(4):133-134, April 1966.

956. SALMON, P.: Vocational rehabilitation of deaf-blind persons. *New Outlook for the Blind, 53*(2):47-54, February 1959.

957. SALVIN, S.T., and LIGHT, B.: *Curricula, Practices, Instructional Supplies and Equipment for the Multiple-Handicapped Retarded.* Los Angeles, U. of Southern Calif., 1963.

958. SANDWICK, R.L.: Correlation of physical health and mental efficiency. *J Educ Res, 1*:199-203, 1920.

959. SAYRE, J.M.: Communication for the non-verbal cerebral palsied. *Cereb Palsy Rev, 24*:3-8, November-December 1963.

960. SCHACHT, W.S., *et al.*: Ophthalmologic findings in children with cerebral palsy. *Pediatrics, 19*:623-628, 1957.

961. SCHACHTER, S.: Deviation, rejection, and communication. *J Abnorm Soc Psychol, 46*:190-207, 1951.

962. SCHEIN, J.D.: Factors in the definition of deafness as they relate to incidence and prevalence. In *Proceedings of the Conference on the Collection of Statistics of Severe Hearing Impairments and Deafness in the United States.* Public Health Service, Publication No. 1227, Washington, D.C., Superintendent of Documents, U.S. Government Printing Office, 1964, pp. 28-32.

963. SCHLANGER, B.B.: Analysis of speech defects among the institutionalized mentally retarded. *Train Sch Bull, 54*:1,5-8, March 1957.

964. SCHLANGER, B.B., and GOTTSLEBEN, R.H.: Analysis of speech defects among the institutionalized mentally retarded. *J Speech Hearing Dis, 22*:98-103, March 1957.

965. SCHLANGER, B.B., and GOTTSLEBEN, R.H.: Clinical speech program at the training school at Vineland. *Amer J Ment Defic, 61*(3):516-54, January 1957.

966. SCHLANGER, B.B.: Environmental influences on the verbal output of mentally retarded children. *J Speech Hearing Dis, 19*(3):339-343, September 1954.

967. SCHLANGER, B.B.: A longitudinal study of speech and language development of brain damaged retarded children. *J Speech Hearing Dis, 24*(4):354-360, November 1959.

968. SCHLANGER, B.B.: Mentally retarded and/or aphasic. *Train Sch Bull, 54*:4,64-66, February 1958.

969. SCHLANGER, B.B.: Speech examination of a group of institutionalized mentally handicapped children. *J Speech Hearing Dis, 18*(4):339-349, December 1953.

970. SCHLANGER, B.B.: Speech measurements of institutionalized mentally handicapped children. *Amer J Ment Defic, 58*:114-122, 1953.

971. SCHLANGER, B.B.: Speech therapy with mentally retarded children. *J Speech Hearing Dis*, 23(3):298-301, August 1958.
972. SCHLANGER, B.B., and GOTTSLEBEN, R.H.: Testing the hearing of mentally retarded. *J Speech Hearing Dis*, 21:487-493, 1956.
973. SCHNEIDER, B., and VALLON, J.: A speech therapy program for mentally retarded children. *Amer J Ment Defic*, 1954, pp. 663-679.
974. SCHOLL, G.: Intelligence tests for visually handicapped children. *Exceptional Child*, 20:116-120,122-123, 1953.
975. SCHOLL, G.: What should be included in the curriculum for the slow learner. Proceedings of the American Association of Instructors of the Blind, St. Louis. *Amer Assoc Instruct Blind*, 40:53, 1950.
976. SCHONELL, F.E.: Intelligence testing. Chapter in *Recent Advances in Cerebral Palsy*. Illingworth, 1958.
977. SCHUNHOFF, H.F., and MacPHERSON, J.R.: What about the deaf or hard of hearing mentally defective? *Train Sch Bull*, 48:71-75, 1951.
978. SCHWARTZ, L.: An integrated teacher education program for special education— a new approach. *Exceptional Child*, 33:411-416, 1967.
979. SCOTT, C.W.: The evaluation of verbal performance in multiply handicapped blind children. *Exceptional Child*, 32:367-374, February 1966.
980. SEELYE, W., and THOMAS, J.E.: Is mobility feasible with: a blind girl with leg braces and crutches? a deaf-blind girl with a tested I.Q. of 50? a blind boy with an I.Q. of 51? *New Outlook for the Blind*, 60(6):187-190, June 1966.
981. SEELYE, W.S., and THOMAS, J.E.: Is mobility feasible with multiply handicapped blind children? *Exceptional Child*, 32:9, May 1966.
982. SELLIN, D.F.: The mentally retarded hearing-handicapped learner: implications for teacher education. *Volta R*, 66(5):258-261, May 1964.
983. SHAFER, S.A.: Speech reading as a remedial technique for the doubly handicapped. *Amer Teach Mag*, 48:11-12, December 1963.
984. SHAPIRO, R.N.; EDDY, W.; FITZGIBBON, I., and O'BRIEN, G.: The incidence of congenital anomalies discovered in the neonatal period. *Amer J Surg*, 96:396-400, September 1958.
985. SHELLEY, U.: Problem of the child with multiple handicaps. *Spastics Quart*, 6(4):10-15, December 1957.
986. SHEPHERD, J.: Intelligence testing of the multiple handicapped child with communication difficulties. *Spastics Quart*, 14:28, 1965.
987. SHERE, M.O.: The cerebral palsied with a hearing loss. *Volta R*, 62(8):438-441, October 1960.
988. SHERIDAN, M.D.: High tone deafness in school children simulating mental defect. *Brit Med J*, 2:272-274, 1944.
989. SHERIDAN, M.D.: Mentally handicapped children. *Develop Med Child Neurol*, 4:71-76, 1962.
990. SHERIDAN, M.D.: Simple clinical hearing tests for very young or mentally retarded children. *Brit Med J*, 5103:999-1004, 1958.
991. SHUTTLEWORTH, C.E.: Mongolian imbecility. *Brit Med J*, 2:661-665, September 11, 1909.
992. SIEGEL, M., and GREENBERG, M.: Fetal death malformation and prematurity after maternal rubella. *New Eng J Med*, 262:389-393, 1960.
993. SIEGENTHALER, B.M., and KRZYWICKI, W.F.: Incidence and patterns of hearing loss among an adult mentally retarded population. *Amer J Ment Defic*, 64:444-449, 1959.

994. SIEVERS, D.J., and NORMAN, R.D.: Some suggestive results in psychometric testing of the cerebral palsied with Gesell, Binet, and Wechsler Scales. *J Genet Psychol, 82*:69-90, 1953.

995. SIGEL, I.: *The Need for Conceptualization in Research on Child Development.* 1956, vol. 27, pp. 241-252.

996. SILVA, H.: Teaching the mentally retarded blind child. *Exceptional Child, 12*:137-140, 1946.

997. SILVERMAN, S.R.: Need for a standard classification of causes of severe hearing impairments and deafness. In *Proceedings: Conferences on the Collection of Statistics of Severe Hearing Impairments and Deafness in the United States, 1964.* Public Health Service, Publication No. 1227, Washington, D.C., Superintendent of Documents, U.S. Government Printing Office, 1964, pp. 48-50.

998. SILVERMAN, W.A.: *Dunham's Premature Infants.* 3rd ed., Springfield, Hoeber, 1961.

999. SIMON, A.B.: Clinical notes on speech from a deaf person. *Volta R, 52*:9,412, September 1950.

1000. SIMPSON, P.E.: The problems of the backward, deaf child. *Teacher of the Deaf, 59*:232, 1961.

1001. SIRKIN, J., and LYONS, W.F.: A study of speech defects in mental deficiency. *Amer J Ment Defic, 46*:74-80, 1941.

1002. SKALVEDT, C.P.: A clinical study of 370 cases. *Acta Paediatrica.* Oslo U. P., 1958, vol. 47, suppl. III.

1003. SLATER, B.C.S.; WATSON, G.I., and McDONALD, J.C.: Seasonal variation in congenital abnormalities. Preliminary report of a survey conducted by the Research Committee of Council of the College of General Practitioners. *Brit J Prev Soc Med, 18*:1-7, January 1964.

1004. SLOAN, W.: Motor proficiency and intelligence. *Amer J Ment Defic, 55*:394-406, 1951.

1005. SMITH, B.F.: The social educaton of deaf-blind children at the Perkins School for the Blind. *New Outlook for the Blind, 60*(6):183-186, June 1966.

1006. SMITH, D.E.P., and CARRIGAN, P.: *The Nature of Reading Disability.* New York, Harcourt, 1959.

1007. SMITH, D.W., and BOSTIAN, K.E.: Congenital anomalies associated with idiopathic mental retardation. *J Pediat, 65*:189, 1964.

1008. SMITH, J.O.: Speech and language of the retarded. *Train Sch Bull, 58*:111-123, February 1962.

1009. SMITH, V.H.: *Visual Disorders and Cerebral Palsy.* Little Club Clinics in Developmental Medicine, No. 9.

1010. SMITHELLS, R.W., and LECK, I.: The incidence of limb and ear defects since the withdrawal of thalidomide. *Lancet, 1*:1095-1097, May 18, 1963.

1011. SMITHELLS, R.W.: The Liverpool congenital abnormalities registry. *Develop Med Child Neurol, 4*:320-324, June 1962.

1012. SMITHELLS, R.W.: Thalidomide and after. *Develop Med Child Neurol, 4*:425-428, August 1962.

1013. SNYDER, J.R.; KNAPP, J.J., and WILLIAM, A.: Dental problems of noninstitutionalized mentally retarded children. *Rehab Lit, 21*:219, July 1960.

1014. SOLOMON, P. (Ed.): Sensory Deprivation. Cambridge, Harvard U. P., 1961.

1015. SPORGEN, C.E.: The training of the mentally retarded blind child. *Teacher of the Blind, 21*:55-66, 1932.

1016. Spragge, C.M.: Speech therapy for the mentally handicapped child. *Speech Path Ther*, 2:79-86, October 1962.
1017. Stein, V.: Living democracy—classroom experience with multiple handicaps. *Exceptional Child*, 8:107-108,122, 1942.
1018. Stephen, E.: C.P. and mental defect. Chapter in *Mental Deficiency, The Changing Outlook*. Clarke and Clarke, 1958.
1019. Stepp, R.E.: Using 8-millimeter films to teach the cerebral palsied deaf. In *Report of the Proceedings of the Forty-second Meeting of the Convention of American Instructors of the Deaf, Michigan School for the Deaf, Flint, Mich., June, 1965*. Washington, D.C., U.S. Government Printing Office, 1966, pp. 105-110.
1020. Stevens, G.D.: An analysis of the objectives for the education of children with retarded mental development. *Amer J Ment Defic*, 63:225-235, September 1958.
1021. Stevens, G.D.: *Taxonomy in Special Education for Children with Body Disorders*. Pittsburgh, U. of Pittsburgh, Department of Special Education and Rehabilitation, 1962.
1022. Stevenson, A.C.: The association of hydramnios with congenital malformations. In *Ciba Symposium on Congenital Malformations*. London, Churchill, 1960, pp. 241-263.
1023. Stevenson, R.E.; Patterson, R.B., and Goodman, H.O.: Possible autosomal isochromosome in a malformed child. *Amer J Dis Child*, 111:327-333, March 1966.
1024. Stevenson, S.S.; Worcester, J., and Rice, R.G.: Six hundred and seventy-seven congenitally malformed infants and associated gestational characteristics; general considerations. *Pediatrics*, 6:37-50, July 1950.
1025. Stewart, G.K., and Coda, E.J.: An integrative multi-discipline approach to the multihandicapped preschool child. *Amer J Orthopsychiat*, 36:315-316, 1966.
1026. Stifler, J.R., *et al.*: Follow-up of children seen in the diagnostic centers for handicapped children. *Amer J Public Health*, 53:1743-1750, November 1963.
1027. Stinchfield, S.H.: Motor-kinesthetic speech training applied to visually-handicapped children. *Outlook for the Blind*, 38:4-8, 1944.
1028. Stinchfield, S.M.: *Speech Pathology*. Magnodia, Expression, 1928.
1029. Stockwell, E.: Visual defects in the deaf child. *Arch Ophthal*, 48:428-432, 1952.
1030. Stonehewer, B.: Blind people with other handicaps. *Soc Serv*, 28(4):165-170, March-May 1955.
1031. Strang, R.: *Diagnostic Teaching of Reading*. New York, McGraw, 1964.
1032. Strauss, A.A., and Werner, H.: Comparative psychopathology of the brain-injured child and the traumatic brain-injured adult. *Amer J Psychiat*, 99:835, 1943.
1033. Strauss, A.A.: Diagnosis and education of the crippled brain deficient child. *Exceptional Child*, 9:163-168, March 1948.
1034. Strauss, A.A., and Werner, H.: Disorders of conceptual thinking in the brain-injured child. *J Nerv Ment Dis*, 96:153-172, August 1942.
1035. Strauss, A.A.: The incidence of central nervous system involvement in higher grade moron children. *Amer J Ment Defic*, 45:548-554, April 1941.
1036. Strauss, A.A.: Neurology in mental deficiency. *Amer J Ment Defic*, 46:192-194, May 1941.

1037. STRAUSS, A.A., and LEHTINEN, L.E.: *Psycho-Pathology and Education of the Brain-Injured Child.* New York, Grune, 1947.

1038. STRAUSS, A.A.: Typology in mental deficiency. *Proc Amer Assoc Ment Defic,* 44: 85-90, 1939.

1039. STRICKLAND, H.: Meeting the problems of social behavior of retarded blind children. *Proc Amer Assoc Instruct Blind,* 40:135-138, 1950.

1040. STROTHER, C.R.: Evaluating intelligence of the child handicapped by cerebral palsy. *Crippled Child,* 23:82-83, 1945.

1041. STROTHER, C.: *Discovering, Evaluating, Programming for the Neurologically Handicapped Child.* Chicago, National Society for Crippled Children and Adults, Inc., 1963.

1042. STUART, H.C.; REED, R.B., *et al.:* Description of project. Longitudinal studies of child health and development series II. *Pediatrics* (suppl.), 24:875, November 1959.

1043. STUART, I.R.: Objective scale rating the physically handicapped for educational purposes. *Personnel Guid J,* 38:211-216, November 1959.

1044. STUBBLEBINE, J.M.: Group psychotherapy with some epileptic mentally deficient adults. *Amer J Ment Defic,* 61:725-730, 1957.

1045. Subcommittee of Spastics Society Medical Advisory Committee: *Notes on the Assessment of Educational Needs of Children with Cerebral Palsy,* 1957.

1046. SUMMERS, M.D.: Placement of the subnormal blind child. *Teachers Forum,* 3: 13-16, 1930.

1047. SUTPHIN, F.E.: *A Perceptual Testing and Training Handbook for First Grade Teachers.* Winterhaven, Florida, Winterhaven Lions Research Foundation, Inc., 1964, pp. 15-16.

1048. SWAN, C.; TOSTEVIN, A.L.; MOORE, B.; MAYO, H., and BLACK, C.H.B.: Congenital defects in infants following infectious diseases during pregnancy, with special reference to relationship between German measles and cataract, deaf-mutism, heart disease and microcephaly, and to period of pregnancy in which occurrence of rubella is followed by congenital abnormalities. *Med J Aus,* 2: 201-210, September 11, 1943.

1049. Tabular statement of American schools for the deaf: Schools and classes for the multiple handicapped in the United States.

Amer Ann Deaf, 97:99, 1952.	*104*:152-153, 1959.
98:131, 1953.	*105*:156-157, 1960.
99:158, 1954.	*106*:160-161, 1961.
100:206, 1955.	*107*:156-157, 1962.
101:220-21, 1956.	*108*:158-159, 1963.
102:116-117, 1957.	*109*:177-178, 1964.
103:118-119, 1958.	

1050. Tabular statement of American schools for the deaf: Summary of school and classes for the deaf.

Amer Ann Deaf, 100:207, 1955.	*104*:154, 1959.
101:222, 1956.	*105*:158, 1960.
102:118, 1957.	*106*:162, 1961.
103:120, 1958.	

1051. TAIBL, R.M.: An Investigation of Raven's "Progressive Matrices" as a Tool for the Psychological Evaluation of Cerebral Palsied Children. Unpublished dissertation. University of Nebraska, July 1951.

1052. TARJAN, G.; DINGMAN, H.F., and MILLER, C.R.: Statistical expectations of selected handicaps in the mentally retarded. *Amer J Ment Defic, 65*:335, November 1960.

1053. TARNAPOL, L.: Dilemma of educaton. Newsletter, San Francisco Chapter CANHC, July 1967.

1054. TAYLOR, C.E.: Personal communication.

1055. TAYLOR, E.M.: *Psychological Appraisal of Children with Cerebral Defects.* Cambridge, Harvard U. P., 1959.

1056. TEMPLER, D., and HARTLANGE, L.: The reliability and utilization of the hand-face test with the retarded blind. *Amer J Ment Defic, 70*:139-141, July 1965.

1057. TENNY, J.: The minority status of the handicapped. *J Exceptional Child, 19*:260-264, 1953.

1058. Testing the Multiple Handicapped Child. 16 mm. film, United Cerebral Palsy, Inc.

1059. THOMAS, E.T., and HAYDEN, A.C.: *Standard Nomenclature of Diseases and Operations.* New York, McGraw, 1961, p. xi.

1060. THOMAS, E.W.: The validity of brain injury as a diagnosis. *Hum Potential, 1*: 9-16, 1967.

1061. THOMPSON, M.W.: Reproduction in two female mongols. *Canad J Genet Cytol, 3*:351-354, December 1961.

1062. THOMPSON, R.E.: Two boys with retardation. In *Report of the Proceedings of the Forty-first Meeting of the Convention of American Instructors of the Deaf, Gallaudet College, June 1963.* Washington, D.C., U.S. Government Printing Office, 1964, pp. 560-565.

1063. THURSTON, J.R.: Attitudes and emotional reactions of parents of institutionalized cerebral palsy retarded patients. *Amer J Ment Defic, 65*:227-235, 1960.

1064. TIZARD, J.P., *et al.*: Disturbances of sensation in children with hemiplegia. *JAMA, 155*:628-632, 1954.

1065. TOOMER, J.: Weaning the blind and additionally handicapped child. *J Nurs Times, 60*:955-956, July 1964.

1066. TRACHT, V.S.: Preliminary findings on testing the cerebral palsied with Raven's Progressive Matrices. *J Exceptional Child, 15*:77, December 1948.

1067. TRAPP, E.P., and HIMMELSTEIN, P. (Eds.): *Readings on the Exceptional Child.* New York, Appleton, 1962.

1068. TRAXLER, A., and TOWNSEND, A.: *Eight More Years of Research in Reading: Summary and Bibliography.* New York, Educational Records Bureau, 1955.

1069. TRETAKOFF, M.I., and FARRELL, M.J.: Developing a curriculum for the blind retarded. *Amer J Ment Defic, 62*:610-615, January 1958.

1070. TRETAKOFF, M.I., and FARRELL, M.J.: Two essential factors in the development of young blind children. *New Outlook for the Blind, 48*:308-315, November 1954.

1071. TUPPER, L.: A state program for multiply handicapped blind children. *New Outlook for the Blind, 54*:243-246, September 1962.

1072. TYNAN, M.E., *et al.*: Adequate provision for the blind feeble minded: Report of the Committee of the Association of Executives of State Commissions and Association for the Blind. *Outlook for the Blind, 22*:34-37, 1928.

1073. USDANE, W.: Employability of the multiple-handicapped. *Rehab Lit, 20*:3-9, January 1959.

1074. VALADIAN, I.; STUART, H.C., and REED, R.B.: Contribution of respiratory infections to the total illness experiences of healthy children from birth to 18 years. *Amer J Public Health*, 51:1320-1328, September 1961.

1075. VALETT, R.E.: A clinical profile for the Stanford-Binet. *J Sch Psychol*, 2(1): 49-54, 1964.

1076. VERNON, M.: The brain-injured (neurologically impaired) deaf child: a discussion of the significance of the problem, its symptoms and causes in deaf children. *Amer Ann Deaf*, 106(2):239-250, March 1961.

1077. VERNON, M.: Characteristics associated with post-rubella deaf children: psychological, educational and physical. *Volta R*, 69:176-185, 1967.

1078. VERNON, M., and BROWN, D.W.: A guide to psychological tests and testing procedures in the evaluation of deaf and hard-of-hearing children. *J Speech Hearing Dis*, 29:414-423, 1964.

1079. VERNON, M.: Measurement of the Intelligence and Personality of the Deaf by Drawings. Unpublished master's thesis. Florida State University, 1957.

1080. VERNON, M.: Multiply Handicapped Deaf Children: A Study of the Significance and Causes of the Problem. Unpublished doctoral dissertation, Claremont Graduate School and University Center, 1966.

1081. VERNON, M.: Prematurity and deafness: the magnitude and nature of the problem among deaf children. *Exceptional Child*, 33:289-298, 1967.

1082. VERNON, M., and FISHLER, T.: Vocational needs in educational programs for deaf youth. *Amer Ann Deaf*, 111:444-451, March 1966.

1083. VINACKE, E.W.: Stereotypes as social concepts. *J Soc Psychol*, 46:229-243, 1957.

1084. VON WIESE, L., and BECKER, H.: *Systematic Sociology*. New York, Wiley, 1932.

1085. VORHAUS, P.G.: Rorschach configurations associated with reading disability. *J Projective Techniques*, 16:3-19, 1952.

1086. WALLACE, H.M., *et al.*: Newborn infants with congenital malformations or birth injuries. *Amer J Dis Child*, 91:529-541, 1956.

1087. WALLACE, H.M., and FISHER, S.T.: Use of congenital malformation data reported on live birth certificates. *Public Health Rep*, 81:631-638, 1966.

1088. WALLEN, V.: A stutterer with a low I.Q. *J Speech Hearing Dis*, 26:89, 1961.

1089. WALLIN, J.W.: *Children with Mental and Physical Handicaps*. New York, Prentice-Hall, 1949.

1090. WALNUT, F.A.: A personality inventory item analysis of individuals who stutter and individuals who have other handicaps. *J Speech Hearing Dis*, 19:220-227, 1954.

1091. WALSH, F.B.: Blindness in an institution for the feeble-minded. *Arch Ophthal*, 69:1965, 1963.

1092. WARKANY, J., and KALTER, H.: Congenital malformations. *New Eng J Med*, 265: 1046-1052, November 23, 1961.

1093. WARREN, S.A., and KRAUSE, M.J.: Deaf children, mental retardation, and academic expectation. *Volta R*, 65:351-358,383, 1963.

1094. WATERHOUSE, E.J.: Helping the deaf-blind to face the future. *J Rehab*, 23(6): 6-7, November-December 1957.

1095. WATERHOUSE, E.J.: The multiple-handicapped blind child. *Proc Amer Assoc Instruct Blind*, 64:28-31, 1964.

1096. WATERHOUSE, E.J.: Status of the deaf-blind in the world. *New Outlook for the Blind*, 60(4):129-132, April 1966.

1097. WATSON, C.W.: *Survey to Identify Mentally Retarded-Deaf Children with Severe*

Handicaps Other than Mental Retardation. Sacramento, Bureau of Special Education, California Department of Education, May 1963.

1098. WEBB, C.; KINDE, S.; WEBER, B., and BEEDLE, R.: *Procedures for Evaluating the Hearing of the Mentally Retarded.* U.S. Office of Education, Cooperative Research Project No. 1731, Mt. Pleasant, Central Michigan University, 1964.

1099. WEBSTER, T.E.: Problems of emotional development in young retarded children. *Amer J Psychiat, 120*:34-41, 1963.

1100. *Wechsler Intelligence Scale for Children.* New York, The Psychological Corporation, Inc., 1949.

1101. WEDELL, K.: Follow-up study of perceptual ability in children with hemiplegia. Hemiplegic c.p. in children and adults, pp. 76-85, 1961.

1102. WEDELL, K.: Variations in perceptual ability among types of cerebral palsy. *Cereb Palsy Bull, 2*:149-157, 1960.

1103. WEDELL, K.: The visual perception of cerebral palsied children. *Child Psychol Psychiat, 1*:215-227, 1960.

1104. WEINBERG, B.: Stuttering among blind and partially sighted children. *J Speech Hearing Dis, 29*(3):322-36, August 1964.

1105. WEINER, B.B.: Hawaii's Public School Program for Mentally Retarded Children. Unpublished doctor's thesis, University of Illinois, 1958.

1106. WEINER, G.: Psychologic correlates of premature birth: a review. *J Nerv Ment Dis, 134*:129-144, 1962.

1107. WEINER, L.H.: Educating the emotionally disturbed blind child. *Int J Educ Blind, 11*:77-83, March 1962.

1108. WEIR, R.C.: Impact of the multiple handicapped deaf on special education. *Volta R, 65*:287-289, June 1963.

1109. WEPMAN, J.M.: *Wepman Test of Auditory Discrimination.* Chicago, Language Research Associates, 1958.

1110. WERNER, H., and BOWERS, M.: Auditory-motor organization in two clinical types of mentally deficient children. *J Genet Psychol, 59*:85-99, 1941.

1111. WERNER, H.: Perceptual behavior of brain-injured, mentally defective children: an experimental study by means of the Rorschach technique. *Genet Psychol Monogr, 31*:51-110, 1945.

1112. WERNER, H., and STRAUSS, A.: Types of visuo-motor activity in their relation to low and high performance ages. *Proc Amer Assoc Ment Defic, 44*(1):163, 1939.

1113. WEST, W.L. (Ed.): Occupational therapy for the multiply handicapped child. In *Proceedings of the Conference on Occupational Therapy for the Multiply Handicapped Child*, April 28, May 2, 1965. Chicago, U. of Ill., Department of Occupational Therapy, 1965.

1114. White House Conference on Child Health and Protection, Special Education: the handicapped and the gifted. In *Report of the Committee on Special Classes.* Section III, Education and Training, New York, Century, 1931, vol. 11-7.

1115. WIDENBAKER, R., et al.: Sensory discrimination of children with cerebral palsy: pressure pain thresholds on the foot. *Percept Motor Skills, 17*:603-610, 1963.

1116. WIEDEMANN, H.R.: Indications of a current increase of hypoplastic and aplastic deformities of the extremities. *Med Welt, 37*:1863-866, September 16, 1961.

1117. WILLENBERG, E.P.: A conceptual structure for safety education of the handicapped. *Exceptional Child, 27*:302-306, 1961.

1118. WILLIAMS, D.: Sunland's program for the blind. *Ment Retard, 2*:244-245, 1964.

1119. WILLIAMS, J.M.: Some special learning difficulties of cerebral palsied children. *Cereb Palsy Bull, 1*:9-20, 1958.

1120. WILLIAMS, J.M.: When is a child with cerebral palsy ineducable? *Cereb Palsy Bull, 3*(5):435-437, October 1961.

1121. WILSON, E.: Group therapy experience with eight physically disabled homebound students in a pre-vocational project. *Exceptional Child, 29*:164-169, December 1962.

1122. WILSON, H.J.: *The Feeble-minded Blind*. London, International Congress on School Hygiene, 1907, pp. 810-816.

1123. WILSON, H.J.: The problem of the defective blind and its best solution. International Conference on the Blind, 1905.

1124. WILSON, J.L.: Testing of drugs. Letter to the editor. *Pediatrics, 31*:154, 1963.

1125. WINSCHEL, J.F.: *Facilities for the Education and Care of Mentally Retarded Blind Children*. U. of Pittsburgh, March 1960.

1126. WISHIK, S.M.: *Georgia Study of Handicapped Children*. Georgia Department of Public Health, 1964.

1127. WISHIK, S.M.: Handicapped children in Georgia: a study of prevalence, disability, needs, and resources. *Amer J Public Health, 46*:195-203, 1956.

1128. WITKIN, H.A.; DYK, R.B.; PATERSON, H.F.; GOODENOUGH, D.R., and KAPP, S.A.: *Psychological Differentiation: Studies of Development*. New York, Wiley, 1962.

1129. WOLF, J.M.: *The Blind Child with Concomitant Disabilities*. New York, American Foundation for the Blind, 1967.

1130. WOLF, J.M.: Leprosy: an impairment, disability or handicap? *J Rehab, 32*:18-19, July-August 1966.

1131. WOLF, J.M.: *Mentally Retarded Blind Children in Residential Schools for the Visually Impaired: Epidemiology and Educational Modifications*. Doctoral dissertation, University of Pittsburgh, 1965.

1132. WOLF, J.M.: Multiple disabilities—an old problem with a new challenge. *New Outlook for the Blind, 59*:265-271, October 1965.

1133. WOLF, J.M: *Temple Fay, M.D.: Progenitor of the Doman-Delacato Treatment Procedures*. Springfield, Thomas, 1968.

1134. WOLFE, W.G.: A comprehensive evaluation of 50 cases of cerebral palsy. *J Speech Hearing Dis, 15*:234-251, 1950.

1135. WOLFE, W.G., and MACPHERSON, J.R.: Comparative investigation of methods of testing auditory and visual acuity of trainable mentally retarded children, part I. Washington, D.C., U.S. Office of Education, Cooperative Research Branch, SAE-6447, 1960.

1136. WOLFE, W.G., and HARVEY, J.E.: A comparative investigation of methods of testing auditory and visual acuity of trainable mentally retarded children, part II. Washington, D.C., U.S. Office of Education, Cooperative Research Branch, SAE-6447, 1960.

1137. WOLFENSBERGER, W.: Schizophrenia in mental retardates: three hypotheses. *Amer J Ment Defic, 64*:704-706, 1960.

1138. WOLFF, P.: Developmental studies of blind children, II. *New Outlook for the Blind, 60*(6):179-182, June 1966.

1139. WOLFF, W.: *The Personality of the Preschool Child*. New York, Grune, 1947.

1140. WOOD, G.E.: Some observations on 141 cases of infantile hemiplegia. *Cereb Palsy Rev, 24*:11-16, January-February 1963.

1141. WOOD, N.: Evaluation of language disorders in children of school age. *Speech and Language Therapy with the Brain-Damaged Child.* Daley, W.T. (Ed.), Washington, D.C., Catholic U. of America, 1962.

1142. WOODEN, H.Z.: Deaf and hard of hearing children. In *Exceptional Children in the Schools.* Dunn, L.M. (Ed.), New York, Holt, 1963, p. 344.

1143. WOODFORD, D.E.: An investigation into the problem of deaf and partially deaf children with additional handicaps. *Teacher of the Deaf, 60:*120, 1962.

1144. WOODS, G.E.: Epidemiology of Cerebral Palsy. Paper read to Spastics Society Study Group on the learning difficulties of the cerebrally palsied and the school curriculum. To be published in the *Spastics Quarterly.*

1145. WOODS, G.E.: A lowered incidence of infantile cerebral palsy. *Develop Med Child Neurol, 5(5):*449-450, 1963.

1146. WOODS, G.E.: Mentally subnormal spastics. *Rehab Lit, 22,* November 1961.

1147. WOODWARD, K.F.; JAFFE, N., and BROWN, B.: Psychiatric program for very young retarded children. *Amer J Dis Child, 108:*221-229, 1964.

1148. WORCESTER, J.; STEVENSON, S.S., and RICE, R.G.: Six hundred and seventy-seven congenitally malformed infants and associated gestational characteristics; parental factors. *Pediatrics, 6:*208-220, August 1950.

1149. World Health Organization: *The Mentally Subnormal Child.* WHO, *Techn Rep Ser,* No. 75, 1954.

1150. WORTIS, J.: Schizophrenic symptomatology in mentally retarded children. *Amer J Psychiat, 115:*429-431, 1958.

1151. WRIGHT, B.A.: Physical Disability—A psychological approach. New York, Harper, 1960.

1152. WRIGHT, E.M.J.: Development of an instrument for studying verbal behaviors in a secondary mathematics classroom. *J Exp Educ, 28:*103-122, 1950.

1153. YANNETT, H.: Multiple handicaps in the cerebral palsied. *J Pediat, 33(5):*639-644, November 1958.

1154. YEPSEN, L.N.: Defining mental deficiency. *Amer J Ment Defic, 46:*200-205, May 1941.

1155. YUM, L.G.: Adapting the nursery school for the multiply handicapped cerebral palsied child. *Exceptional Child, 22:*7-9,45, 1955.

1156. ZUBEK, J.P., and WILGOSH, L.: Prolonged immobilization: changes in performance and in the electroencephalogram. *Science, 140:*306-308, 1963.

1157. ZWARENSTEYN, S.B., and ZERBY, M.: A residential school program for multihandicapped blind children. *New Outlook for the Blind, 56(6):*191-199, June 1962.

CROSS-REFERENCES OF BIBLIOGRAPHICAL ENTRIES

The entries in the comprehensive bibliography have been listed alphabetically and numbered consecutively. To expedite the use of the bibliography, each entry has been cross-referenced by number under selected appropriate headings. For example the article entitled "The Incidence of Feeblemindedness in the Cerebral Palsied" would be cross-referenced under the headings *Incidence and Prevalence; The Educable and Trainable Mentally Handicapped; The Orthopedically and Neurologically Handicapped;* and *Noninstructional Services.*

Traditional categories of exceptionality have been used to aid the reader in locating books and periodicals on multiple disabilities associated with one particular handicapping condition. In addition, selected headings have been taken from Stevens' tentative *Taxonomy of Special Education.**

Etiology

85	187	265	333	412	508	662	805	936	1087
86	188	277	335	424	515	684	806	960	1133
107	206	284	337	430	541	688	836	1023	1140
131	211	286	350	437	548	729	862	1026	1150
139	230	298	384	439	558	736	881	1029	
156	243	320	400	448	573	752	895	1064	
160	248	325	405	491	580	753	914	1077	
165	249	326	406	497	599	754	915	1081	
184	250	327	407	503	613	769	926	1086	

Medical Services

11	156	249	326	437	662	758	895	1032	1140
67	165	277	350	439	684	867	911	1044	1147
81	187	284	384	497	701	878	936	1077	1150
85	211	286	405	503	709	881	1013	1086	1153
86	213	298	406	515	752	884	1023	1087	
88	243	317	407	541	753	886	1026	1121	
107	248	320	431	580	754	888	1029	1137	

Classification

64	91	199	266	325	447	561	661	769	1133
65	113	203	267	374	465	579	701	913	1142
76	158	209	268	375	466	623	736	1021	1152
77	159	249	270	413	481	651	747	1130	1154
87	160	265							

Incidence and Prevalence

28	62	202	264	503	610	723	919	1001	1127
30	79	217	284	508	661	752	920	1026	1129
31	102	224	290	513	667	753	926	1035	1131
34	109	234	338	541	684	772	943	1052	1132
35	119	243	342	544	706	809	944	1081	1134
36	120	249	343	557	707	823	962	1091	1153
38	149	260	475	579	708	834	963	1097	
47	160	261	488	608	715	862	969	1108	
56	169	262	493	609	722	899	993	1126	

---

* Stevens, G. D.: *Taxonomy of Special Education for Children with Body Disorders,* Pittsburgh, University of Pittsburgh, 1962.

Traditional Categories of Exceptionality

Auditorally Handicapped

6	129	259	405	557	664	781	928	982	1082
7	142	260	406	563	665	782	929	986	1093
12	147	261	412	573	666	789	930	987	1094
30	154	262	440	576	667	800	932	988	1095
34	156	264	441	608	668	803	934	990	1096
35	157	286	446	609	669	805	935	993	1097
36	169	309	447	610	670	806	936	999	1098
40	177	320	452	611	671	807	940	1000	1108
50	187	321	454	612	689	812	944	1005	1114
51	198	333	455	614	690	817	948	1014	1129
56	199	337	456	620	701	825	949	1019	1131
70	202	338	476	627	714	833	951	1021	1132
89	203	355	477	628	721	862	952	1026	1135
90	207	383	485	629	722	872	953	1029	1136
96	211	384	487	635	723	881	955	1049	1142
102	217	395	488	636	730	884	956	1050	1143
106	220	397	508	645	737	914	962	1062	
107	255	401	527	646	759	915	972	1072	
127	256	403	543	662	773	926	977	1077	
128	257	404	556	663	776	927	980	1081	

Educable and Trainable Mentally Handicapped

6	87	204	344	464	553	664	768	945	1033
7	88	207	345	465	555	665	773	946	1035
9	91	210	355	466	556	666	774	957	1036
13	93	217	356	472	557	667	778	963	1039
15	94	220	359	475	558	668	789	964	1044
16	98	221	364	477	565	669	792	966	1046
17	102	224	365	478	576	670	800	967	1052
23	106	230	366	479	578	671	809	968	1056
24	108	232	367	481	584	672	816	969	1062
25	109	233	368	482	590	673	817	970	1063
26	119	235	374	485	591	676	823	971	1069
28	120	237	375	486	592	681	824	972	1072
30	126	238	378	488	608	685	825	973	1088
31	127	239	379	489	609	687	833	975	1089
34	128	241	380	490	611	689	834	977	1091
35	130	246	381	493	612	690	862	980	1093
36	139	254	389	494	614	691	875	981	1097
37	140	267	395	495	618	701	879	982	1098
38	142	268	396	497	619	706	881	985	1099
40	149	270	397	498	620	707	883	986	1110
42	150	281	398	499	623	714	884	988	1111
43	155	284	399	500	627	717	891	990	1114
44	157	285	400	501	629	720	892	993	1122
45	158	294	401	502	630	721	899	996	1123
46	159	295	403	508	631	722	901	1000	1125
47	167	307	407	512	635	723	904	1001	1129
49	168	310	408	525	636	729	911	1004	1131
50	169	311	414	527	637	730	912	1008	1132
51	170	322	415	533	639	741	914	1013	1135
56	171	323	424	540	642	742	915	1014	1136
62	177	324	431	543	645	743	924	1015	1137
70	180	327	437	544	646	745	925	1016	1146
77	181	330	439	548	649	750	926	1020	1147
79	182	335	441	550	659	756	928	1021	1150
81	185	338	446	551	662	757	934	1025	1154
83	194	343	451	552	663	759	944	1026	

Orthopedically and Neurologically Handicapped

5	156	248	337	439	548	706	815	941	1064
11	160	249	342	447	553	707	816	950	1076
19	162	250	343	452	568	708	862	959	1077
26	163	251	349	472	569	714	871	960	1086
47	165	253	350	481	570	720	878	967	1087
56	173	265	355	486	582	729	883	968	1089
63	178	271	361	489	584	737	884	980	1103
65	184	274	377	490	593	741	886	985	1111
70	187	284	383	491	594	749	887	986	1112
79	189	287	394	492	595	751	888	987	1114
81	200	288	396	493	597	754	891	994	1115
84	201	297	400	494	610	755	892	1014	1119
85	213	298	401	496	629	761	895	1019	1121
86	217	302	403	502	639	763	899	1021	1129
91	219	304	406	505	644	767	902	1023	1131
92	220	305	411	508	659	768	914	1026	1132
99	221	308	412	511	661	769	915	1033	1133
107	222	317	422	515	675	780	917	1040	1134
113	223	320	423	528	691	781	924	1041	1140
118	225	325	425	529	694	798	934	1043	1146
126	226	326	427	530	697	805	936	1044	1151
131	241	327	428	531	701	806	937	1058	1153
142	243	328	429	532	704	808	938	1063	1155
153	245	333	437	547					

Perceptually Handicapped

5	97	220	271	401	578	639	948	1041	1114
50	99	221	304	403	582	701	986	1064	1115
54	107	222	305	422	591	714	1014	1086	1119
55	142	225	308	447	593	720	1021	1103	1129
56	184	243	328	491	597	807	1026	1110	1131
70	211	245	355	502	613	862	1032	1111	1132
84	217	249	361	508	629	884	1036	1112	1156
92									

Socially and Emotionally Handicapped

19	153	251	391	508	701	761	937	1025	1129
56	163	276	394	582	714	791	938	1026	1131
65	185	287	401	614	725	832	940	1039	1132
67	217	355	403	628	755	862	941	1063	1137
70	219	377	408	639	756	871	986	1099	1147
81	220	379	416	649	757	884	1014	1107	1150
83	223	382	445	692	758	932	1021	1114	1151
142	226	385	499						

Speech Handicapped

56	162	355	416	665	743	815	914	968	1026
62	178	356	437	666	749	825	915	969	1027
63	187	365	452	667	750	832	924	970	1028
67	217	380	508	668	751	833	925	971	1088
70	220	381	528	669	772	836	934	973	1090
83	229	396	529	670	773	862	936	986	1098
98	245	398	530	671	780	881	943	999	1104
108	260	399	531	685	781	884	959	1001	1114
118	287	401	565	697	782	887	963	1008	1129
130	297	403	597	701	792	891	964	1014	1131
133	302	406	619	704	806	902	966	1016	1132
139	305	407	663	714	808	911	967	1021	1134
142	308	411	664	726					

Visually Handicapped

9	71	172	257	368	495	647	778	949	1069
12	75	180	258	382	498	672	784	951	1070
13	85	181	274	389	500	673	786	952	1071
15	89	188	275	391	508	675	791	953	1072
16	90	189	281	401	512	676	807	954	1091
17	93	190	285	403	525	681	809	955	1094
18	94	192	294	414	533	682	812	956	1095
21	96	194	302	415	539	683	816	960	1096
23	119	198	309	416	544	687	824	974	1104
24	120	204	310	421	550	701	834	979	1107
25	125	210	311	423	552	702	836	980	1112
27	129	217	312	424	555	713	862	981	1114
28	131	220	313	425	558	714	881	986	1118
29	133	224	322	431	560	716	884	996	1122
30	138	229	323	432	561	720	904	1005	1123
31	140	230	324	434	562	725	909	1014	1125
37	142	232	330	445	570	731	912	1015	1129
38	149	233	335	448	577	741	923	1021	1131
42	150	234	344	451	579	742	927	1026	1132
43	151	235	345	453	591	744	928	1027	1135
44	154	237	346	454	592	746	930	1028	1136
45	155	238	354	455	618	758	934	1029	1138
46	167	239	355	456	630	759	935	1030	1143
49	168	246	359	476	631	765	943	1039	1157
56	169	254	364	478	637	772	945	1046	
59	170	255	366	479	642	774	946	1056	
70	171	256	367	487	644	775	948	1065	

Other Handicapping Conditions

26	103	220	313	482	562	702	950	1044	1095
27	138	234	320	488	577	714	954	1052	1114
28	142	259	328	503	584	715	981	1065	1121
31	172	260	347	505	589	724	983	1071	1129
43	173	261	355	508	590	744	985	1073	1131
44	180	262	385	515	629	745	986	1077	1132
45	181	275	401	539	647	765	1014	1081	1143
46	192	290	403	540	687	862	1017	1086	1153
56	200	295	429	551	692	883	1021	1087	1155
59	201	3!1	449	560	701	884	1026	1089	1157
70	217	312	475						

Instructional Modification

(Objectives, Curriculum, Methods, Materials, Equipment, Organization for Instruction, Evaluation Procedure, Teacher Competence, etc.)

12	56	169	294	408	584	681	776	946	1033
13	59	172	297	447	586	685	780	949	1041
15	63	194	307	475	590	689	787	954	1043
21	71	204	308	476	594	694	800	955	1046
23	75	209	309	487	597	702	808	956	1069
25	79	210	312	498	618	713	817	957	1077
29	90	216	343	499	619	714	824	959	1082
35	119	225	345	500	628	716	871	975	1107
36	120	226	346	501	630	717	886	979	1108
38	126	237	347	543	631	730	888	982	1114
42	129	238	356	553	635	731	909	983	1129
43	133	245	359	558	636	742	913	996	1131
44	140	246	361	560	639	744	929	1005	1132
45	147	249	366	562	645	746	930	1015	1155
46	154	253	368	563	647	759	934	1017	1157
49	157	276	395	576	659	768	935	1019	
51	168	288	404	582	675	775	945	1020	

Noninstructional Service

(Case-Finding, Transportation, Pupil Personnel Service, Speech Correction, Counseling and Guidance, Psychological Diagnosis, Certification, etc.)

6	103	241	379	455	582	675	816	954	1063
7	106	245	380	456	584	691	817	955	1077
12	109	249	382	472	590	697	820	956	1090
18	113	257	385	478	591	721	824	963	1098
21	128	258	389	485	595	726	825	969	1108
25	130	271	391	486	611	742	832	974	1111
35	147	274	396	489	612	746	833	986	1112
36	151	275	397	490	618	763	883	990	1113
38	153	276	406	492	620	767	884	994	1119
47	154	285	427	493	627	768	886	1004	1129
50	177	288	428	496	663	776	888	1016	1131
62	185	310	429	502	664	777	891	1026	1132
75	188	311	434	527	665	780	901	1027	1134
77	216	321	441	532	666	787	913	1033	1135
91	223	349	446	533	667	789	917	1040	1136
92	226	354	447	547	668	791	934	1041	1138
98	229	361	452	548	669	798	935	1043	1155
99	236	365	453	568	670	806	940	1056	1157
102	239	367	454	569	671	812	950	1058	

Administrative Modifications

(Organization, Personnel, Plant Facilities, etc.)

17	38	206	295	451	594	682	768	934	1125
18	79	226	313	473	631	702	824	935	1129
23	98	234	323	482	635	724	834	954	1131
24	125	249	324	515	647	730	886	955	1155
25	126	255	346	540	659	731	887	956	1157
35	167	256	421	552	672	742	904	1072	
36	172	294	449	584	675	744	913	1108	

Ancillary Services

(Medical Diagnosis, Classification and Treatment, Casework Service, Rehabilitation Services)

7	169	250	412	659	792	886	952	1025	1129
38	206	258	427	724	824	911	953	1032	1131
89	226	262	473	726	833	913	954	1073	1133
96	234	298	494	746	862	934	955	1082	1146
103	248	378	540	758	875	935	956	1113	1155
154	249	394	558	765	884	951	1013	1121	1157

Bibliographies

34	38	231	464	642	751	806	1129	1131	1132
37	182	302	626						

Author Index

For additional references, the reader is referred to the Bibliography, pp. 390-442.

A

Adams, 10, 401
Agranowitz, 257, 390
Aird, 15, 390
Alford, 61, 62, 390
Allen, 288, 391
American Academy of Pediatrics, 146, 398
Amer Ann Deaf, 24, 391
American Association of Instructors of the Blind, 27, 391
American Foundation for the Blind, 30, 367 391
Amer J Public Health, 176, 179, 413, 430
American Printing House for the Blind, 28, 29, 30, 391
American Public Health Association, 131, 410
Anastasi, 343, 391
Anderson, P. E., 75, 391
Anderson, R. M., 18, 24, 375, 391
Annual Report: New York Bureau of Child Health, 131, 391
Apgar, 55, 391
Artenstein, 61, 427
Ashcroft, 205, 392
Asher, 13, 212, 392
Association for the Aid of Crippled Children, 365, 392
Austin, 343, 396
Ausubel, 256, 392
Avery, 19, 392
Ayres, A., 16, 392
Ayres, L. P., 202, 392

B

Babbott, F. L., Jr., 61, 413
Babbott, J., 73, 412
Babbott, J. G., Jr., 50, 59, 392
Baker, 362, 371, 373, 392
Ballantyne, 103, 392
Balsamo, 61, 62, 408
Barbe, 363, 377, 383, 393
Barker, L. S., 340, 393
Barker, R. G., 340, 342, 343, 344, 365, 393

Barraga, 301, 393
Barsch, 313, 368, 393
Bateman, 251, 313, 385, 393, 416
Bates, 366, 393
Baudy, 73, 418
Bearman, 51, 75, 416
Beck, 39, 202, 393
Becker, 344, 439
Bekker, 53, 55, 393
Benda, 8, 42, 73, 393
Bentzen, 257, 313, 400
Berkson, 30, 394, 400
Berreman, 342, 394
Bexton, 16, 394
Bice, 13, 212, 394
Binns, 71, 394
Birch, G. H., 256, 394
Birch, H. G., 14, 416
Birch, J. W., 18, 385, 394, 429
Birch, L. B., 291, 412
Birch-Jensen, 50, 394
Bishop, 90, 91, 394
Black, 45, 53, 61, 437
Blatt, 39, 202, 395
Blau, 250, 395
Bleiberg, 145, 395
Bleyer, 73, 395
Block, 340, 395
Bloomfield, 313, 395
Blum, 13, 217, 395, 397
Blumberg, 68, 395
Boly, 30, 395
Böök, 50, 55, 57, 66, 67, 395
Bordley, 90, 395
Boris, 68, 395
Borniche, 73, 418
Bostian, 369, 435
Braddy, 26, 395
Breakey, 15, 396
Brennemann, 94, 396
Brill, 92, 396
British Medical Association, 355, 396
Brooks, M. B., 48, 409
Brooks, S. T., 289, 403

449

Subject Index

E

Ear, 306
    rubella defects of, 83 ff.
Ectromelia, 62 ff.
Education, 5, 6, 9
    for blind, 28, 30, 241 ff., 299 ff.
        deviant, 225 f., 228 (T), 230 ff.
        mentally retarded, 28, 30, 31
    for cerebral palsied, 12 f., 272, 287 ff.
        multiply handicapped, 211 ff.
    classification for, 376 ff.
    conceptual framework for, 329
    coordination of services in, 123
    for deaf, 16 ff., 24, 92, 93 f., 121, 265, 310
        ff.
        intelligence quotient and, 21, 22
        mentally retarded, 16 ff., 22 ff.
            curriculum for, 22, 23, 24, 26
        premature, 93 f.
    diagnosis in, 379
    of emotionally disturbed, 336 f.
    of exceptional children, 195, 349 ff.
    of handicapped, 332 f.
        in medical center, 125
    of mentally retarded, 23, 38, 42
        multiply handicapped, 202 ff., 205
    of multiply handicapped, 39, 195 ff.,
        200 n., 236, 239, 329 ff.
    multiply handicapped issue in, 383 ff.
    placement in, 367
    program classification in, 354
    responsiveness to, 300
    for rubella handicapped, 86, 87 (T)
    segregated, 345, 352
    for service to handicapped, 119 ff.
    of slow learner, 20
    vocational success and, 337 ff.
    See also Residential schools; Schools; Special education; Teachers.
Educational retardation, 187 ff.
Emotional adjustment, 100, 140 (T), 142,
    326, 371
    birth weight and, 95, 96 (T)
    classification of, 359
    of premature deaf, 95, 96 (T)
    teacher rating of, 96 (T)
Emotionally disturbed
    blind, 243 f.
    education of, 336 f.
England, 53, 54, 65, 78 ff.
Environmental factors, 67, 71, 73, 305
    See also Perception.
Enzyme systems, 103

Epidemiology, 45, 57, 73, 74, 75
    naturalistic investigations in, 106
    of reproductive casualty, 102 ff.
Epilepsy, 6, 107 (T), 108, 109, 176
Exceptional children, 9, 195, 340 n., 372
    classification of, 366 f., 370 ff.
    clinic for, 122
    conceptual framework for, 341 ff.
    definition of, 362
    education for, 195, 349 ff.
    evaluation of, 253
    services for, 129 f.
    See also Disability; Handicapped; Handicaps; Multiply handicapped.
Eye. *See* Blind; Vision entries.

F

Familial defect
    achondroplasia, 69
    cleft palate, 73
Family adjustment, 156
Family counseling, 158 f.
Family evaluation, 305
Family health plans, 119 f.
Fatigue, 118
Fertility in mongolism, 71, 73
Fetus
    infections of, 104
    See also Rubella.
Films, 223
Financing, 162, 195, 229, 237 f., 353 f.,
    360 f.
Flight of ideas, 285
Fluorescent antibody test, 61
Fölling's disease, 333
Functional status, 333 f.

G

Gamma globulin, 62
Gastrointestinal conditions, 140 (T), 142
    See also specific conditions.
Genitourinary conditions, 136, 140 (T), 141
Geographic factors, 42, 116 f.
Georgia, 9, 129, 146 ff., 148 (T), 149 (T),
    367
German measles. *See* Rubella.
Gesell Developmental Schedule, 268
Gifted
    underachieving, 363
    See also Exceptional children.
Griffiths scale, 292
Group treatment, 207, 222